Born on the outskirts of Manchester, Northern England, in 1946, Geoff Olton attended St Peter's College, Oxford, majoring in mathematics. After failing his final examinations, he spent a year teaching English to Saudi Arabian Air Force cadets before moving to Kobe, Japan, where he has since lived for 50 years, working in teaching, interpretation, and translation.

His writings include a 5,000-page analysis of the spoken English language in its relationship to Japanese and similarly grouped languages, and a novel, *The Anemone Bowl*, (both as yet to be published).

To all who have (in even the smallest of manners) contributed to my progress through life – and subsequently to the contents of this book, with sincere gratitude.

Geoff Olton

The Way We Are

Notes on the Realities of
Negotiating (a) Life

AUSTIN MACAULEY PUBLISHERS™
LONDON • CAMBRIDGE • NEW YORK • SHARJAH

Copyright © Geoff Olton 2022

The right of Geoff Olton to be identified as author of this work has been asserted by the author in accordance with section 77 and 78 of the Copyright, Designs and Patents Act 1988.

All rights reserved. No part of this publication may be reproduced, stored in a retrieval system, or transmitted in any form or by any means, electronic, mechanical, photocopying, recording, or otherwise, without the prior permission of the publishers.

Any person who commits any unauthorised act in relation to this publication may be liable to criminal prosecution and civil claims for damages.

A CIP catalogue record for this title is available from the British Library.

ISBN 9781528993746 (Paperback)
ISBN 9781528993753 (Hardback)
ISBN 9781528993760 (ePub e-book)

www.austinmacauley.com

First Published 2022
Austin Macauley Publishers Ltd®
1 Canada Square
Canary Wharf
London
E14 5AA

With many thanks to all who have made this publication possible.

The book cover was assembled (with many thanks to the publisher's creative department) from a photograph taken by the author of shadows on a few hundreds of years old temple wall in Arashiyama, Kyoto.

The inner section of this type of wall is created from brushwood and clay, held together by stakes and horizontal strips of bamboo – one section of which can be seen on the cover front – now exposed as the outer layer of cream-coloured plaster has been worn away over the years. The greenish effect is caused by the sunlight passing through the maple trees and bamboo plants adjacent to the wall.

Table of Contents

An Introduction	11
Chapter 1	22
A Recall of Days Gone By	
Chapter 2	44
Life's Lessons Delivered Early	
Chapter 3	71
Saudi Arabia (and a Visit to Iran)	
Chapter 4	86
Young at Heart (Lives Intertwined)	
Chapter 5	114
Coming to Accept What Cannot Be	
Chapter 6	147
A New Perspective	
Chapter 7	171
Finding a Way Out	
Chapter 8	228
"You Only Live Twice"	
Chapter 9	250
Tales from the Mountains (Japan)	
Chapter 10	270
Tales from the Mountains (Korea)	
Chapter 11	296
The Way We Are Identity	

Chapter 12   303

The Way We Are Venturing out Into the World and Coming up Against Different Cultures

Chapter 13   324

The Way We Are Understanding Formative Influences: Religion and Religious Principles

Chapter 14   345

The Way We Are Understanding Formative Influences: The Fine Line Between Influencing and Controlling Others' Thoughts and/or Actions Philosophies and Religions as Power Centres

Chapter 15   360

The Way We Are Understanding Formative Influences: Social Constructs and the Internal and External Promotion of Authority

Chapter 16   415

The Peculiarities of Confucianism in the Modern Age

(1) Personal Relationship

Chapter 17   443

The Peculiarities of Confucianism in the Modern Age

(2) The Workings of an Economy

Chapter 18   466

Family Affairs

Chapter 19   500

Coming to Terms with Myself

Chapter 20   517

In Conclusion

An Introduction

***

Now look the stranger in the eye and see within a spark
of that which you could not before:
That echo of your own heart and mind –
of what you are, or at least were
before the world got its hands on you
A life no more than a shadow cast on the edge of time.

***

My objectives in writing this book:

A mere 60 or 70 years ago when I was young, it was perfectly natural that one grew up with one's beliefs and in the large part stayed with them throughout a lifetime. However, today, with the average person's far greater exposure to alternative cultures through both travel and the Internet, there is a very serious need for all people around the globe to understand that whatever they might choose to believe as a result of their personal upbringing, there are other approaches to life which do need to be taken into consideration.

While everything included in the book is, of necessity, personal, I fully respect that everyone is entitled to their own beliefs. (And if you are not open to acceptance, at least to some extent, of this latter point, this book is probably not for you.) The text is not in any way an attempt to try to prove that one system or way of thought is superior or inferior – all political systems, religions and philosophies have points to be admired and those that can, from certain perspectives, be criticised – but rather comes from a belief that, prior to any attempt to reach some accommodation with other societies or individuals, some awareness of the real differences involved has got to be of some benefit. The starting point here would have to be a recognition of the fact that you, as an individual, are as much under the influences of your society as the other person is under theirs. [15.4]

(It is possible here that the reader will find certain countries, religions or philosophies brought up repeatedly in the text while others are seemingly ignored. The reason for this is that I have, as much as possible, limited my comments to intake from areas in which I am more fully informed.)

Although certain strong criticisms are included, nothing has been written with the intention of being deliberately offensive. Or perhaps to be more honest, statements that on second reading I recognised as presenting an obvious bias have very commonly been rephrased, hopefully to make them more acceptable. That said, any reader is fully entitled to disagree with any and every opinion stated within, in that that is what opinions are there for. (There would have been no point writing the book without the assumption of a degree of dissent.) At the same time, if the reader does find any points that go as far as personally angering them, perhaps before taking the matter any further, they might consider why. I have had a lot in life that has angered me, but, particularly as I have got older, I have learned not to automatically put the blame for that elsewhere. And if you do find a point that is excessively annoying, perhaps as a suggestion, you could mark the section concerned for some future reference (that or rip the page out, if you will), take a deep breath (as is required in most similar situations in life) and move on. Covering a full life as it does, the book is not intended to revolve around (or be judged by) any one single action or comment.

The fact that I am gay is noted (in the main, in the first three chapters when I was growing up) as one (relatively minor) part of a total life experience, and I would appreciate it if it could be accepted as just that.

The book references 50 years of teaching experience (together with a certain amount of translation and interpretation); worldwide travels, a considerable amount of walking in the mountains (in Japan and Korea), the studying of Japanese ink-painting (sold semi-professionally), 'ikebana' flower arrangement and calligraphy; photography, vegetable and flower gardening, Japanese pottery, singing (karaoke in Japanese, English and Korean), Kobe's 1995 earthquake (detailing the local government's frighteningly ineffectual response), and the occasional dance for fun.

Although not in any manner intended as a self-improvement book, if read carefully (this being the Japanese way [7.3]), there is much to be garnered if only in the most casual of manners.

The storyline:

In retrospect, I have spent a good two thirds of my life on the outside looking in; first off as a gay person growing up in England and then in Saudi Arabia, viewing myself as reflected in the eyes of heterosexual society, then in Japan for coming on close to fifty years observing both my own nature and life in general as an expatriate and 'gaikokujin' (foreigner/outsider). And then (Cpts 6–10), in my early forties, having been inducted (/inveigled) through no will of my own into a 'secret society', and when suddenly becoming fully aware of every thought that passed through my head (every thought voiced in my brain as it occurs), together with a world of dreams and visions; this in turn followed by 'other voices' (/telepathy) and including the odd 'ghost' and 'poltergeist', etc., I had no alternative other than to turn my consciousness inwards and, in the process, discover that I wasn't quite the nice person that I had up to that time considered myself to be. For the record: Although, being English, I do drink beer, no other drugs of any nature were involved here.

In that I had a number of associated experiences coming much earlier in my life, I do know that my mental state at this point was not directly related to the existence of the 'society'. However, this event very much did become a turning point, in the sense that I was at this time reduced to a state of complete exhaustion, which did take me a considerable time to recover from, most of my efforts here being involved in trying to restore some elements of structure (/understanding) into the utterly unexplainable chaos that my life had become.

During this period, I did, in a moment of inadvertency, learn how to project an inner image first onto the surface of my eye and then on to other more distant objects, which I then came to understand as the origin of (at least a considerable number of) my visual apparitions. And from this point on, I found myself able to, if not explain, at least approach each new experience as it occurred in a far more positive manner, allowing me in time to reach a full acceptance of my condition. [8.11]

Spiritual development:

Living within a culture where the concepts of Zen and enlightenment are taken as nothing exceptional, I did quite quickly develop an interest in these areas, this including ten years of the serious practice of Hatha (physical) yoga in my thirties and early forties, and much of my 'progress' in this area is included in the text. Regardless of anything that I might have achieved here, the effort did make me extremely conscious of my considerable inadequacies. (With regards to my interactions with the 'society's' members, I quickly came to understand that, beyond the need for careful thought and analysis, a strong awareness of my emotional reactions to a whole range of events – some of which were not entirely pleasant – did lead to considerable efforts at self-reappraisal.)

Everything described throughout was (inasmuch as the word can be understood to have meaning) 'experienced' and is recorded as and how it happened. (Referring to accuracy of memory, I can only say that certain scenes, good and bad alike, become embedded; burned into the brain and remain with you, presumably until you feel free to let them go.) And ultimately, regardless of the reality of the situation, of far greater relevance is how these events affected my development into the person I now am.

Presentation:

Although early chapters can on the whole be recognised as roughly following the order of events as they happened, even here, when I am trying to clarify some particular point or detail a certain type of experience – for easier readability and taking advantage of the fact that I am looking back on everything from the vantage point of old age – I have found it practical to group quite separate occurrences together under the one headline. (In Chapter 4, describing my early life in Japan, where there is considerable overlapping in the stories and the actual sequence of events becomes of relative unimportance, the presentation has been manipulated to a certain extent for dramatic effect.)

Chapter 5 is a serious attempt to explain the reasons for the love-hate relationship, including at times a sense of utter frustration and bursts of anger, that I know, even today, a considerable number of foreigners who live in Japan find themselves subject to, and I would consider this essential (start here) reading for anyone in this position.

Note: Particularly in the sections on Japanese society, those who have had no previous connection with the country could perhaps view the account primarily as an opportunity to recognise the very human foibles of a completely atypical society. (Viewed from the Western perspective, life in Japan is based on a guiding principle, Confucianism, that has distinctly contrasting expectations as to how an individual in that society should act/react.) Although not intended as a guidebook for travellers, I am sure that there is much included that would be of interest to anyone who is considering visiting the country, this most certainly being true for those who plan to spend a certain amount of time here.

Chapters 11 through 15 ("The Way We Are") cover the constraining elements of an individual's identity and how that affects relationships with others, an overview of religions and the spiritual, and finally a consideration of political/social controlling forces together with the contrasting concept of 'freedom'. Chapters 16 and 17 are detailing the real problems with Confucianism in the modern world. And then in the final two chapters, I have included what might be referred to as a self-reckoning; a coming to terms with myself, together with all those who have played more significant roles in my life.

Being of its nature, and with a considerable amount of cross-referencing, the book's chapters do not have to be read in any particular order, although certain groupings, as can be judged from the initial listing of contents and the above explanation, are perhaps recommended.

Allowing myself to be a cipher:

"If you wish to truly take a man's measure, give him the opportunity to treat you badly." Mito Kohmon. (Tokugawa Mitsukuni: prominent feudal lord in Tokugawa period.)

I have what almost certainly will appear to the reader as an overly passive side, times when I don't react – not 'don't react as you would expect' or 'as one should', but rather just 'don't react, period'. However, as I have learned to understand more about myself (and subsequently strengthened my interest in how others are liable to act/react in any particular situation), I have, rightly or wrongly, come to accept this as simply myself in observation mode, and in cases where people have been openly offensive or antagonistic – a remarkably common occurrence here, Japan not quite being the excessively polite society it is often made out to be – it has always intrigued me to see how far they might go in the process.

Although I have included suggestions for reference, these are not in any manner intended as solutions: Every individual has to find his or her own way. However, in all countries today, there is clearly the need for some serious reconsideration of how both individuals and societies approach relationships, and if this book in any sense can help in this manner, it will have served its purpose.

Notes:

- As a matter of protecting the privacy of the individuals concerned, pseudonyms are used throughout.
- Statements placed in double quotation marks without any particular reference are simply points which I have, for one reason or the other, wished to emphasise.
- In certain segments, I have used the third person pronoun, 'he', rather than 'I'. This has been done more on instinct than with any particular design. However, other than the benefit of setting myself aside for short periods, this does allow a scene to be presented in a more descriptive manner.
- The usage of 'them', 'their' and 'themselves' to avoid over-usage of 'he or she', etc. is (as I was educated to understand) Standard British English and has no connection with the present gender-neutral selections under consideration in the US.
- The poem, "Child." Initially written for inclusion in the novel "The Anemone Bowl", this covers as much as possible all aspects of what we are as human beings – with comments on learning processes, character development, attitudes/beliefs, discrimination, war, ageing, etc. Short excerpts are included as relevant in the text, and the full poem can be found at the end of the final chapter.

Abbreviations:

FF: (For Fun.) Short stories originally collected as a means of providing my memory with a certain relief when I was tackling the less pleasant of my experiences, they have been inserted in the final text to hopefully provide a similar balance for the reader.

WGFTG!: "What's good for the goose is good for the gander."

(AI): Noting statements or concepts that I feel might present a serious challenge to anyone who actually believes they can create a computer system that can in any sense replicate the 'human experience' – certainly not as we exist today (or unless you are truly out to create a world of zombies).

JT: The Japan Times. NYT: The New York Times (International Edition) – articles from both of which are referenced considerably in the text. (Comments not paraphrased are noted as such.)

References:

A list of names – "The cast (in order of appearance)" – together with a brief description of how they fit into the overall narrative is given immediately following this introduction.

Newspaper articles, books, films etc. referenced, together with Japanese and other foreign language references, are listed at the end of the book.

The cast (in order of appearance)

Chapter 1

[1.1] Carl: Studied together at Oxford. Together with his wife, Susan, we have remained lifelong friends. / [8.5]

[1.1] Kensuke: My present partner of seven years...

[1.1] Rodney (public school): Another student belonging to the same group. Paired with Carl for tutorials. He and his wife have stayed in close contact with Carl and Susan right the way through.

[1.1] Ben (Christian): Another student belonging to the same group. Visited my home. / [18.3]

[1.1] Koji: My Japanese partner of 40 years, now deceased. / [4.5] ...

[1.5] Postgraduate students at Oxford including Hiroaki, from Japan, and others from South Africa, Canada, America, India, and Peru, etc.

[1.7] Jack: Older gay friend at Oxford.

[1.7] Adrian: Lifelong friend from my time in Oxford. (Town)

[1.11] Andy: Eldest son in the Maltese family who looked after me in New York. / [7.25]

[1.13] Wanda: A young black woman of about my age who worked with me in a pancake house in New York.

[1.15] Julio: Met in summer in New York. Introduced me to Paris, et al.

Chapter 2

[2.4] Christine: My childhood (not-to-be) sweetheart. / [2.14]

[2.5] William (/Will): My middle brother. / [2.13] / [18.3]

[2.9] Auntie Beth: Worked in my father's shop and helped to look after us through a large part of our childhood.

[2.11] Ray: Friend at grammar school, broken off with in unfortunate circumstances. / [2.13] / [19.4]

[2.14] Helen: First (and last) serious girlfriend before I left home for college.

[2.16] Martin: Head boy at grammar school.

[2.17] Satu: Swedish blonde bombshell. Worked with on the Isle of Wight (IOW), subsequently visiting her home in Stockholm.

[2.18] Paul and Brian: Owners of hotel on IOW. Became lifelong friends.

Chapter 3.

[3.8] Peter: Teacher in Saudi Arabia. Arrested for being in possession of a bottle of whiskey.

[3.11] Bob and Terry: Teachers in SA Joined on a trip to Iran.

Chapter 4

[4.1] Gail: Teacher at language school in Kobe. Have remained lifelong friends. / [4.8]

[4.1] Aki: Receptionist at Osaka school. / [4.15]

[4.1] Derek: Teacher at Osaka school. Aki's boyfriend. / [4.15]

[4.2] Gordon: Head of Kobe school.

[4.2] Matt: Teacher at Kobe school. Gail's husband. / [4.8]/ [11.2]

[4.2] Neil: Teacher at Kobe school. Married Keiko. Have remained lifelong friends with them and their children. / [4.8]

[4.2] Mr and Mrs Oka: Owners of the school building. Mrs Oka became my legal guardian. / [7.19]

[4.2] Minoru: Mr and Mrs Oka's son.

[4.2] Yoko: Original receptionist at school.

[4.2] Yukiko: Receptionist at school. Remained lifelong friend. / [7.24]/ [11.3]

[4.2] Yoshimi: Receptionist at school. Remained lifelong friend. / [18.16]

[4.3] Greg: Resident singer/guitarist at The Nook, where Matt played the piano in the evening.

[4.6] Robert: Foreign gay friend. Graduated from Oxford and then from one of the better Tokyo Universities, only to die in his early thirties from some combination of a spinal disorder and drugs. / [7.14]

[4.7] Janet (/Jan): One of a group of Americans (Pauline, Brenda, and Kerry) plus one Canadian (Sally), who were all teachers at one of the local international schools. Have remained lifelong friends. / [7.25]/ [15.7]

[4.7] Hiroshi: Japanese gay businessman. / [6.8]/ [6.22]/ [7.35] … /[18.6]/ [19.9]

[4.8] Keiko: Neil's wife. Have remained lifelong friends.

[4.8] Mr Hamada (Receptionist Yukiko's father). Helped me obtain my original visa after the school closed. Together with his wife, have remained lifelong friends. / [15.31]/ [18.15]

[4.10] Sono Mise: Koji's bar.

[4.11] Isamu and Carl: Japanese-foreigner couple. Close friends until Carl died of cancer in his early fifties. Isamu opened a bar close to Koji's Sono. / [8.9]

[4.12] Mr and Mrs Honjo: Koji's woodcarving teacher and wife. Remained lifelong friends. / [18.1]

[4.14] Takako: Koji's second eldest sister. / [18.14]

[4.14] Mr Hosoda: Owner of the land neighbouring our plot in the countryside. Ran his own small construction company and helped us considerably with the development of the land.

[4.14] Mr Hosoda: (unrelated) From the other side of the stream. Helped us with practical gardening hints, and we became lifelong friends with both him and his family. / [18.7]

Chapter 5

[5.7] Jim: Transferred to the head office to work with me following the expansion of the teaching programme at the multinational company I was working with at the time.

[5.14] Makiko and Dr Sugiyama: Professor of Spanish and her doctor husband, who remained lifelong friends.

Chapter 6

[6.12] John and Mark: An American in his sixties and his Japanese partner of more than twenty years in his late forties. Mark died of cancer shortly after the exhibition described in this chapter.

[6.13] Mr and Mrs Ohta: Brought me roses at the exhibition. Became lifelong friends with their whole family.

[6.22] Mr Shimizu: The man who purchased the Chinese peony painting on the night before the opening. / [7.22]

[6.22] The Tani family: Mr and Mrs Tani, and children Yuta and Aiko: Taught both children and the mother privately over quite a long period of time. / [15.8]

Chapter 7

[7.8] Jeff: A lifelong Australian friend who we originally met on a ferry boat returning to Kobe from Kyushu. Much later, visited his home in Sydney. / [8.6]

[7.22] Mrs Kawano: The owner of a residential hotel along the coast and also one of my first students in Japan. / [8.9]

[7.27] Adam: Australian teacher. Worked with for two years or so at the head office. Visited in Australia.

[7.31] Tomonobu: Paraplegic friend in Kyushu.

[7.31] Sachiko: Koji's eldest sister. / [18.2]

[7.33] Shino: The daughter of one of our close friends, who up to the present day has been unable to fully come to terms with her membership in the 'society.' / [18.20]

[7.36] Mr Kondo: Worked under Hiroshi [4.7] in his office.

Chapter 8

[8.5] Kazu: Initially a customer at Sono and a 'drinking companion' until his death, I have remained friends with his wife and son throughout.

[8.13] Mr Kuromaru: Artist friend.

Chapter 9

[9.2] Mrs Osaka from Osaka: Purchased a painting at the exhibition.

[9.8] Mr Morino: Met walking in the mountains before the exhibition. A (relatively rare) Japanese Christian, who became a good friend.

Chapter 10

[10.4] Mr Lee: Owner of first Korean bar I encountered in Osaka. Suggested I go walking in the Korean mountains.

[10.4] Mr Kan: Mr Lee's partner. Worked in the same bar.

[10.4] Shinji: Met in Mr Lee's bar. "James Bond."

[10.12] Big Boy (BB) and Chib: Koreans who waylaid me at the top of Seoraksan mountain.

[10.15] Mr Koh: The man who had been walking across the street towards me in my dream before I collapsed.

[10.15] Mr Kang: The second man from the dream, who I actually got to meet.

[10.19] Mr Cho: Close friend of Mr Lee. / [10.23]

[10.22] Mr Kim: University professor. Friend of Mr Lee.

Chapter 12

[12.4] Henry: From northern New Zealand, lived in Japan for some six years.

Close friend until he died.

[12.4] Saburo: Henry's partner. Still friends.

[12.5] Donald: Scottish university teacher and artist. My example of, at least for me, a 'difficult man'.

[12.13] Kaori: Koji's niece. / [18.17]

Chapter 18

[18.4] Ted: My eldest brother.

[18.4] Barry: Older English teacher in Saudi Arabia. Only attracted to boys in a certain age range.

[18,9] Akane: The owner of what originally was a seaman's bar in Kobe's port area. A lifelong friend. / [20.4]

[18.14] Narumi: Koji's third eldest sister. Married into a 'burakumin' (lowest caste) family.

[18.14] Ryuta: Koji's younger brother.

[18.14] Shinichi: Sachiko's husband.

[18.14] Kayo: Ryuta's wife.

Chapter 1
A Recall of Days Gone By

[1.1] A chat over dinner:

Carl: "You would like some more wine?"

Me: "I don't think so. Neither of us drink so much wine. Particularly now I'm getting older. I tend to stick to beer. And on the whole Kensuke stays with me. But if you and Susan would like to open another bottle, certainly."

C: "Shall I?"

Susan: "You don't have to right now."

C: "OK. You were about to say?"

Me: "Yeah. About the e-mails and having lunch with Rodney. I'm sorry, but I couldn't let it happen. And as I said, I would explain, if you don't mind?"

C: "Of course not."

Me: "When I came out at university, there were six of us, or rather five of you. And, um, the five of you each had a rather different reaction, quite naturally, but… At any rate, it was in its own way 'educational'. The two Christians – Evangelists? I don't know, but at least the one of them was. At any rate, he never spoke to me again for the full three years."

C: "You are kidding?"

Me: "No. Not once. The second one – I can't remember his name – I think it was Ben. We became friends, and he even came up home the one time."

C: "I didn't know that."

Me: "No. I know. And the guy who spent all his time in the theatre; the name has gone – the guy who was paired with me for tutorials – he didn't need to say anything, because he was quite familiar, naturally, with that sort of thing. Whether he himself was or not I wouldn't have a clue, but…

"And then there was you. And you, perfectly in character, asked me if I'd had any girlfriends. I said I had, and your suggestion then was that 'if I could be attracted to both women and men, then why not choose women?'"

C: "I said that?"

Me: "Yes. And I said that, in that case, I would choose men. That was done for two reasons. One, I was already heavily bent in that direction, and also, I know that if I had married, I would've hurt whoever had become my wife.

"And" looking across at Susan, "I don't like hurting people.

"And then there was Rodney. One afternoon, sometime after I told you all, he just walked into my room in college, plonked himself down at my desk, his back to the window, and proceeded to put me through a Nazi routine, I mean the type you get in the movies; leaning back in the chair – my study chair; his feet – boots and all, legs stretched out, up on the top of the desk; the study-light in my face; supercilious in the extreme. I was low on the couch facing him, and it was evening, and him being seated against the window I couldn't see his face or anything. And he just let me know how disgustingly filthy I was. And it wasn't just me being gay. He let me have the 'I-am-public-school,' 'elite,' 'everything-that-you-are-not,' 'far-superior-in-all-ways,' bit as well. Which wasn't very nice. I reckon it must have taken him about 10 to 15 minutes. And then he just stood up and left. And that was that. So what do you say?

"At any rate, I just left it as something that had happened, and I went on with my life. I had other things to do. However, it made me wonder. And you understand why I didn't want to have Kensuke here meet him. With Koji, I could've put up with anything that might have been said: It wouldn't have touched him. But with Kensuke here; we have only been together for a relatively short period, and this is his first trip abroad, and if Rodney had made even the slightest comment in that area, I would've been up with my fists – and I wouldn't want either you or Susan, and particularly Kensuke, to have that ruining our time here with you. Actually, with the present condition of my heart, I would probably have killed myself into the bargain."[1]

C: "It never occurred to me that you were, you know. Not before you told us."

Me: "No, I guess not."

Susan: "We never really got on with them, you know." (This drawing a quick glance from Carl.)

Me: "No, that's OK. At any rate, that was that. And you will understand. I

---

[1] A statement that is, unfortunately, a little too close to the truth.

told Kensuke here the whole story a while back, and so he knows. We try to tell each other everything. We had to get to know each other fast. What was our tutor's nickname? Fat Jack?"

C: "I don't remember now."

Me: "You know he only ever gave us three tutorials in three years."

C: "No!"

Me: "Yes. We went there three times and then that was it. Nothing given to work on. No 'See you next week.' And after that, nothing – right the way through all our sherry parties and everything; not a hint that something might be wrong somewhere. Actually, I rather envied you with Rodney. I saw you once going off to the Bodleian. I never went in. I wouldn't've known where to start.

"And then right at the end, the lessons – six weeks we all had with that group from another college."

C: "I don't remember that."

Me: "No. Well that was the sum total of my education at Oxford. So, you follow why I didn't get though my finals. All a bit of a joke, really. However, that was that, and here we are. And thank you for cancelling the lunch. It would not have helped."

The above conversation took place in the autumn of 2014 when I was visiting England with Kensuke (my present partner). I met Susan for the first time at college when she came up to attend a ball at, if I remember correctly, Christ Church college. And it happening that Carl was the one college friend that I kept in touch with after I failed to graduate, after they married and I had settled with Koji (my original partner), with visits to London on our side and a period when Carl (having worked his way up through his bank) was based in Tokyo, we have remained good friends right the way through – a friend to my mind (being of my age) being someone who you can pick up on a conversation with six weeks or even six years on as if you had met them two days ago, which, when in need, can be a very reassuring concept.

University was my 'time-out', my 'I've-had-enough-of-this' moment, which lasted for three years. At some point, it occurred to me to remember the time after I first got into grammar school when I was told that; "It was good that I had done that, but having done it, it 'no longer mattered.' Now the thing to aim for was my O-levels." And once passed, of course, they were of no importance, and it was A-levels. And then university. And now that also was gone, and it was "passing my finals." And then of course there would be that job, and so on, and on and on for the rest of my life. And I just turned off. Either that or I got turned off, with the results to be played out as they have been, for better or worse, throughout the rest of my life.

[1.2] Coming out:

This was my big trial balloon, and unfortunately it got fully deflated before it could even take to the air. My first reaction at the time to the 'Nazi interrogation' described above was one of mild incredulity – something of a 'Excuse me, are we on the same page?' moment. (Much later in life, it occurred to me to wonder whether I had, in a previous life, been a member of the SS, and this was some form of retribution. Or, possibly, that this was a straight repeat on his side.) I could more easily understand the reaction of the Christian who just walked away, but here also, this was Oxford, and these were the 'crème de la crème', supposedly intelligent people, and it did make me wonder. However, not having anyone in particular to discuss the matter with, and still very much being in the learning mode – too occupied with life to really question what was going on around me – it became just another of those things that you let pass by, at least until I got into my late fifties and early sixties, particularly after my first partner, Koji, died and I began the recap that resulted in this book. Recalled now, it was beyond nasty. It was totally vicious.

I never again came out as gay, and even now the word will only reluctantly come out of my mouth. And beyond that, the whole thing left me with a very bad impression of our so-called public-school elite, and I still find it difficult in my mind not to automatically classify persons with a moneyed or upper-class background in the light of this experience. I understand that this is almost certainly unfair but, Rodney not being the only one who sniggered at me around the college grounds, the matter got deeply embedded.

(May, 2018) Thinking now about the above, by coming out in front of the whole group as I did, I was in fact presenting myself as an equal; putting myself at his level, and possibly, by indicating my degree of self-confidence – the whole thing was (/had to be) done in the most natural of manners – above him, which to him, being both public school elite and presumably non-gay (although public schools do have a certain reputation in this area, I do know that he married), would likely be highly challenging, offensive even, to his sense of identity on two fronts, with the resulting frustration building up to that particular outburst.

In reality, we were all just beginning to take our first steps out into the world, and it was certainly a possibility that he was taking out the worst of his insecurities – to have it instilled in you that you are 'elite' as a child must present its own set of quandaries – on what must have been for him the closest convenient target, that being me. At least, on a personal level, this is perhaps the most generous of explanations I can come up with.

[1.3] Trauma controls:

A recent report noted a trend among modern psychiatrists in the US as putting less emphasis on treatment of traumas from the past and concentrating more on what can be done with a patient's future life. I fully understood the argument but having been subject to two or three very bad personal experiences, the effects of at least two that still remain with me even today at 70+, I would suggest some caution. At a minimum, the person affected should be fully aware that they are, in certain areas, going to be living with a possibly very severe mental handicap – this essentially being what a trauma is – and that if they are to be able to handle that, a whole relearning (/a resetting) of their concept of what is possible in life – what life is, even – becomes essential.

When something merely 'bad' (a rap across the knuckles) happens to you, you remain in control: You retreat, as necessary, put yourself in order, nurse the wounds, and then move out and try again. However, when the bad amounts to more than 'merely' and reaches the level of a traumatic experience, regardless of your level of awareness of the matter, it becomes a compelling, controlling force that, being in no manner approachable or negotiable, cannot simply be ignored. When I was first introduced to the word, psychological trauma was invariably linked to 'the hidden', something that happened in early childhood that the brain had deliberately put aside, but I consider both the above interrogation and the following, although strictly 'out in the open' and simply passed over at the time, to be of the same nature. At least both affected me very strongly right through my life, far more than I would have expected at the time.

The second incident referred to, occurring when I was aged 20 in New York, was the result of a pick-up in the park on the East Side taking me to his apartment for what was lukewarm sex, this until his partner returned (he had called him in?) and they got it on together totally at my expense. Neither of them demonstrated any wish to have me leave. Rather they kept me close, an arm stretched out to hold me within reach – at a distance, but close enough to ensure my involvement.

And that was the sum of interest shown: I was there as nothing more than a prop, a torn fragment of the staging – significant only to the extent that I was insignificant, required only to the degree that I ignited some spark. Physically, I was left flaccid, extinguished. But far beyond that, I was empty; my whole existence negated and totally drained of all meaning. I once used part of what I felt at this time to try to describe an attempted rape in a novel, but that didn't come near it. That would have been acceptable. In a rape, they would at least have been utilising, taking some pleasure from my body, my physical being. But here I was just useless, slabbed meat, and extremely conscious of my nakedness.

At the time, this also was let by; New York is not a city that allows for reflection. But again, it stayed with me, and throughout my life I could never again accept a threesome or it's like – not in any combination. And I invariably required a certain warmth in a relationship. This right up to the present.

Fifty years ago, we had one hotel for gays, well hidden in the narrow backstreets of the lowest class area of Osaka; huge rooms spread from wall to wall with mattresses, an open bath area and steam-room, and blankets to spread if you were staying the night, which I did quite regularly at one stage. And here, also, I would totally reject anything other than a one-on-one pairing, repeated as many times as you liked in the one night, but each relationship remaining exclusive. Finding and holding onto the person you were with at the time and rejecting the advances of any outsider who tried to join you was for many a game, but psychologically – my brain at all times requiring the assurance that I was not in any manner being (or in a situation where I might be) used or abused – it was the only game in which I could participate.

And then I was in my late forties, and Koji invited two friends home for a drink; a couple – an American and a Japanese who were going out together. I knew both of them, but not closely, and found neither of them particularly attractive, but it was an afternoon spent. And then things progressed, as they are likely to do in this kind of situation – when the alcohol kicks in just that tiny amount – and although I sensed I could recognise Koji's intent in the matter, I was led to follow his suggestion and we ended up in our bedroom in a split foursome. I took the foreigner as far away as I possibly could from the other two (our sleeping mattresses were out on the floor) and kept him satisfied for as long as I could, until he just stood up and crossed over the room to join the other two for what had clearly been intended from the start. And without any to-do, Koji was on his back – his legs in the air – with the Japanese guy kneeling to his left and fondling his chest and the American about to penetrate him, clearly something they were all quite accustomed to. And I was again left naked. And a scream arose in my throat – a primal, uncontainable shriek issued at full volume, that went on and on; not caring who in the neighbourhood might hear me, until they were all out of the house and gone.

[1.4] Trauma erodes (/diminishes/destroys):

A young female student was told by her father at the age of twelve that she had to study hard to become a doctor, the reason given being that it would provide the income she needed to live her life alone, as she was too ugly for anyone to ever consider asking her to marry him. As to how this situation came about, I do not know, but she certainly wasn't/isn't ugly in any sense of the word. However, this was the explanation that she gave to her class, all students of thirteen or fourteen, in the most natural manner, as the reason for her 'dreams for the future', which was that lesson's theme. Presumably, she trusted her father's word. After teaching her for a total of over ten years, the only way I could attempt to explain her would be to say that she was trapped in some odd form of warp, which affected her whole way of viewing the world.

Some years later, with a different group of older students, talking about (in the most cases, friendly) relationships with classmates in their respective schools, she described her whole class (every one of them) as 'herikutsu' (argumentative, self-opinionated to the point that they couldn't be talked to), which brought the rest of the class up sharp.

"That couldn't be all of them?"

"Yes, it was all of them."

And no way could she be persuaded otherwise.

They did, as a group, actually do very well together. She had one big blow-up with a Korean student who was in the group when she joined, but then they became fast friends, which helped the overall atmosphere. And then, in her final group of (far senior) adult students, they very quickly cottoned on to the fact that there was some problem – as she had grown older, she had developed a very strange, weird even, no-way-can-be-laughed-at sense of humour – and they very kindly did their best to try to nudge her towards a more standard view of reality. But even when I met her in town a couple of years after she had started work (she did become a doctor), whatever it was was still with her – the same 'tic' beneath the surface – and I can only hope that, at some point, she gets through it all. All the consequence of one short, and very unneeded, comment.

[1.5] Postgraduate students:

A child at least one of whose parents has had the experience of attending a higher-level university has a considerable advantage in that they can be drilled, at least to a certain extent, as to what to expect once they enter that world. The only knowledge that I seem to have gleaned in this regard from my more distant relatives was that I would require a set of cups, saucers and plates, suitable for serving morning coffee or afternoon tea in my room. Much effort was put into the selection of the same, and I was actually able to put to them to use very shortly after my arrival with my next room neighbour, who happened to be a Japanese in his early thirties named Hiroaki, the first of a number of postgraduate students who, over time, I became loosely acquainted with, and all of whom, in their own ways at one point or another chose to help me move forward with my life, and to all even now I am extremely grateful. Coming from a range of different countries; Japan (2), South Africa, Canada, America, India, and Peru, each one of them had reached an age and position of responsibility in their respective societies and were mature in the very best sense of the word; totally self-sufficient and far past the floundering around stage of the (including myself) average undergraduate. And, more than anything, although I was still young, every one of them chose to communicate with me at their own level.

Although I did not in the end become a member, Hiroaki invited me to the first gathering of the British-Japanese Friendship Society, where I distinctly remember the 'yorokonbu' (twisted strands of salted seaweed, considered lucky and – at least used to be – commonly consumed at the New Year) and 'ebi senbei' (small, circular, white rice crackers including the tiniest of shrimps). And then – it would be in my third year – he arranged for a sukiyaki party at his lodgings house; a very beautiful cottage out in the countryside, with huge cans of shoyu sauce specifically imported from Japan for the purpose. And when I did finally arrive in Japan, he was the first person I visited.

Academic progress:

I purchased (even read an odd chapter of) all the books initially listed by my tutor, attended half a dozen lectures – actually at one point being subject to a brief flash of understanding that vanished as quickly as it had come (this probably amounting to my one true academic achievement during the whole period of my stay), and I also managed to scrape through my first-year examinations. Other than that, the last six weeks of group lessons were a doddle: I was being taught in a way that I was fully accustomed to, and I was quite capable of progress. Unfortunately, this was one more case of 'too little, too late'.

Regarding the above 'flash of understanding', (which actually gave me a similar kick – the lecturer being considered one of the top mathematical minds in the university at the time), two or three years ago, walking around in Osaka, my mind registered a group of voices behind me speaking in Korean, which I had been studying by myself over a number of years, and I was able to follow every word that they were saying, only to realise a moment later when relating the matter to Kensuke, that my memory had not recorded even one small detail of what had actually been said.

[1.6] On being gay:

FF: A 'not-to-be' moment: I fell for three of my teachers at school (and also for the leader of my Boy Scout pack), all of whom had a certain 'overt physicality', but it was to the gym instructor (an ape of a man who liked to terrify the younger boys with his deep-throated, "Youuu… Boii…!") that I came closest to confessing my feelings. One evening, walking back to the changing rooms from the playing field, he put down his guard and I sensed a warmth that had been lacking – circumstances never having allowed us this kind of quiet moment before. However, perhaps fortunately, the moment was left to be, and some three weeks later he was discharged from the school, the rumour being that he had been having an affair with the headmaster's (female) secretary.

"Getting to know you".

In the 'straight' world as it existed at the time (the American hippie/ flower-power movement was still literally a whole world away), dating was in the main a trial-and-error process to determine compatibility with some possible future marriage partner. Naturally this included sexual elements; kissing, (heavy) petting, and for some the inevitable slip-ups and a father-of-the-bride-steps-in wedding, but in the main, the process would start with getting-to-know-you socialising at dances or parties, followed by a somewhat standard, carefully choreographed and socially approved procedure, finalised by that walk up the aisle, all of which (it also being a socially obligated procedure) I did get the opportunity to experience. [2.14]

And in roughly the same period (I would be 16 or 17), as I became at first aware of and then susceptible to other influences, a world where marriage was in no way in the cards and socialising in any normal sense out of the question, the above process was inevitably reversed; starting with the (initially, extremely rare – very few people were interested in anyone of my age) search for a sexual encounter; this invariably involving some mild sense of attraction (where necessary, fabricated in pursuit of the moment) inevitably followed by a quick release, after which – only after, and circumstances permitting – some consideration of the 'social niceties' – a word passed, nod of recognition, attempted smile – became possible. I do not claim this in any manner to be a pleasant form of introduction. Toilets themselves not being the cleanest of places, the idea of two men eyeing each other up in such locations is naturally not going to appeal to those accustomed to more gentile circumstances, but in consideration of the fact that (1) we did have to meet somewhere and (2) the necessity that we remain out of the public eye, the matter was certainly not one of personal choice. Right from the start, particularly in my hometown, I was inordinately conscious of the need to avoid unnecessary attention, to remain hidden – always 'walking with purpose' (it would not do to loiter) and never along the same street twice. But none one of us involved were in effect doing anything more than concede to the realities of our situation, and others, in all honesty, may consider themselves lucky.

[1.7] University. Town and Gown:

Oxford has two quite distinct societies: "Town" (the well-developed industrial sector, including motor manufacturing, and everything that supports it) and "Gown" (university life), both of which could actually exist quite happily apart, but due to historical reasons find themselves lumped together in a somewhat ungainly embrace. For the average student, who is only in the city for roughly half a year at most, college life will of necessity be central to their existence, but with far more time on my hands than I actually required, I found myself straddled between the two, and particularly in my final year when I was living in lodgings and college had lost any relevance in my life, most of my time was spent with friends made in the town – all coming from or connected in some manner to my chosen world.

Jack (in his mid-forties) liked treating people somewhat roughly, literally knocking them around, and as a first experience it was something I found to be mildly erotic, but after this one time, he refused to have anything to do with me again in that area. (I sense now that he actually did not want me to move in that direction.[2]) Whatever, our relationship quickly progressed, slipping into one of casual friendship, with us regularly meeting up with an assorted group of his friends, inevitably ending up in one of the central pubs in town. This was not strictly a gay pub, every evening involving a very much 'mixed crowd', including a number from the local theatre, but we were well enough represented to feel free to let loose as we wished, and on two or three occasions at least I do remember helping out behind the bar – particularly one evening when my should-have-been-tutorial-partner walked in with his Playhouse theatre mates and we shared a grin.

"Just an old-fashioned girl."
Adrian (mid-thirties) This was from the start a totally platonic relationship, and also one that lasted. He was just someone who was there for me, for whatever reason, I cannot conceive; letting me have a key to his house so that I could walk in at any time of the day and start talking to him about anything that had been happening, either in college or in the town – something that I had never been able to do with anyone before in my life. And he would put on one of his older (Eartha Kitt) records and listen to me prattling on; never criticising, just letting me be, acting as a sounding board for all my (at that point, seemingly stifled) dreams. He also knitted me an Irish sweater, used for a number of years until (as we all do at one point) I allowed my figure to slip that extra few inches and it could no longer be worn. And later, working through several permutations of his own, he moved on into a very different life, becoming a very happily married father with his own son.

Two professors:
The ultimately handsome Spaniard (think matador), who very quickly made it clear that he regarded me as 'the ultimate pain', but was someone I could not give up on, and in the end, my persistence playing out, I actually got to spend

---

[2] Much later in Japan, Koji, presumably for similar reasons – habits, even those started for fun, do tend to stick – put his foot down when I started playing about with openly gay expressions in Japanese. And thinking over the arc of my life here in Japan, where even today worlds are strictly delineated, I have to admit that he was completely correct in doing so.

one night with me, only later to learn that he had a Spanish partner who had crossed the Channel with him working at one of the local restaurants in town. Where he was that night, I do not know, but I remain forever grateful. And, although I in reality met very few, he turned me onto Spanish men for life.

There was also a relatively brief relationship with a senior professor (in his fifties?) at one of the older colleges. Here, from the very start, there was a strong element of the abnormal involved. Everything about the association constrained. Even at the initial encounter, he showed nothing other than a minimal sexual interest in me, but taken to his room, I was presented with a necktie taken from his wardrobe that had to be worn immediately (he tied it for me – single knotted, not my preference), and it very quickly became apparent that I was in some way a figment of his imagination, a 'youth' whom he sought to mentor. Neither he nor his position could be questioned. Every encounter was staged: I was expected to speak, act, and more importantly react, in a certain manner, and when expectations were not met, he would give me a certain odd look of disapproval, with the implication being that (naturally he could not stoop to that level but) a scolding would have been in order.

Clearly, he occupied a very precisely demarcated world, that later I could only surmise as related in some manner to a traditional public-school upbringing connecting seamlessly into the highly cloistered (and equally traditional public-school) world of academia. And this not being anything that I was at all accustomed to (or truthfully interested in), the attraction quickly waned – although I must admit to keeping (and wearing) the tie for a certain length of time.

Why it is so, I do not know, although I clearly must be creating some form of expectations on the other side, on a number of occasions throughout my life, I have found myself in essentially what is a repeat of this type of relationship. In each case, what has appeared to be a mutual attraction has developed into a situation where I find myself assigned to a certain 'role' that in some manner constricts or reduces – under the other's 'guidance', but at all times at the other's convenience and inevitably directed to some elevation of *their* status in *their* eyes, which eventually I cannot keep up with. I do understand that the reason must to some degree reside in what the other side sees in me, and possibly it is that my overall upbringing has led me to assume a level of independence that is not immediately apparent in my demeanour: I have always looked younger than my age, and I tend to 'take a quiet approach', letting small slights pass by without any particular consideration until I am pushed badly, at which point I am very capable of pushing back myself.

[1.8] FF: Piccadilly Circus's 'Midnight Cowboy':

To anyone who knows the movie; basically, we are talking a youngish John Voight – six-foot-something stud with a buffed-up muscular physique – here without the cowboy hat, which would have been a little too much in central London at that time, giving me a come-on in a far too obvious manner in the Men's circle at Piccadilly, and leaving me with something of a dilemma.

I have always been attracted to those who train themselves physically and or mentally, muscularity naturally included here, although I do dislike the preening that commonly goes with the bodybuilder's psyche. (I am similarly hesitant about the perfected looks associated with models, which are far more about lighting and angle than reality.) And in terms of character, men who have kept something of the child in themselves, some natural warmth, particularly if it is contrasted with a certain element of (self-perceived) 'toughness' have always intrigued.

And this man in all respects fit the bill (in the vernacular, the description would be 'butch cute'); excepting for the fact that the look in his eye clearly indicated that he had me set up in his mind as an easy mark – almost certainly under the circumstances correctly, as I was having great difficulty keeping my eyes off him. However, with his general appearance (including an overall state of dishevelment), creating an element of unreliability/unpredictability that both attracted and served as a warning in equal measure, I wavered.

Also, considering myself at least sufficiently attractive in my own right, I had never considered the possibility of paying for sex before. So quite what was to be done? However, in the end not able to resist – these chances not coming up too often in life – I walked him to the closest cheap hotel in the area and, understanding that as even here appearances might be important, sat him down in the centre of the lobby while I booked a room, where we went about a satisfactory conclusion of our business (as in the film, who should be paying for what services was not entirely clear here, but…), upon the completion of which, he promptly fell fast asleep. And now finding myself thoroughly relaxed and having nothing else to do – I couldn't check out without taking him with me, and he clearly needed the sleep – I took a walk around outside the hotel, until, thinking I might have a cup of coffee, I found that I had left my wallet, with quite a considerable amount of money in it, back in the room, resulting in some very fast (and highly panicked) backtracking.

Fortunately, he had remained fast asleep, and with the wallet safely retrieved, I got him out onto the street as quickly as I could, where following a certain amount of haggling, I handed him a ten-shilling piece – then at 20 shillings to a pound – and we parted without too much ill will on either side. And as to whether it was worth the money; coming out unscathed and to a certain degree on my terms, and more importantly (which also happens to be the case in the movie), him turning out underneath (or at least under the sheets) to have a somewhat gentle and loving personality, the answer has to be yes. And this being so, I was left to ponder on how some people get to follow their so-called 'paths in life'.

[1.9] A note on roles:

As a younger person, I commonly came up against the idea, invariably put forward by members of the heterosexual community, that the active role in a homosexual relationship implied 'masculine', as against the 'feminine' passive role. Knowing that as a matter of practicality (that is if I like the person enough), I can take on either role without any particular problem, and equally that I can be just as strong (expressing my dominant side) when taking on a passive role as I can be as gentle as needs require when I am assuming the active role, the above does come across as a somewhat simplistic concept. I would also, without taking the matter too far into unknown waters, imagine that much of the above is equally relevant to relationships in the heterosexual world. At least, from everyday observation, I do know that they are as many highly domineering women out there as there are softer mannered men, and presumably this will affect their relationships in all walks of life, including when they, too, 'get under the sheets'.

[1.10] Sex education (and the dean):

Sex education sixty years ago was non-existent, and although, being at a boy's grammar school, odd terms and references were banded about freely, it was inevitably up to the individual to piece them together, which presumably the large majority of us one way or another learned to do. However, sixty years on, I can only say that some clearer understanding of what I was about to get into, particularly in terms of knowledge and prevention of disease, would have been very much appreciated. In particular, in relationship to the usage of condoms, initially input as yet one more 'dirty word' not to be mentioned in public (at the time, finding a discarded condom and trying it on was something of an event in a teenager's life) some indication of where and at what age they could be respectably purchased would have in the long run helped.

You don't need any sex education. "Just say no!"

Much as I can understand this historically as a religiously based injunction, and fully understanding that some people are not particularly strongly sexually orientated, in terms of present-day reality, I can only interpret it as a highly convenient and, in the end, ultimately cheap 'cop-out' – a total evasion (to the point of abandonment) of any responsibility towards by far the greatest majority of young people, who at some point are going to find out that (1) sexual urges do exist and (2) they can hit you with a strength and immediacy that pre-empts any pullback, particularly if the other person is to any degree insistent, as a lot of people – both male and female – are. Equally, every onus here is being put upon the individual: "If you do not follow this advice, you are a bad, you are wrong. And you alone must face the consequences!" And presumably the adult 'adviser', high on their perch in life, and having with that one simple phrase fulfilled what they consider to be their 'responsibilities to society', is then assuming that all subsequent matters (prevention of pregnancy – and the subsequently related matter of abortions – or the spreading of disease) can, with full peace of mind, be dismissed as irrelevant. All very pleasant sounding and refreshingly simple, but from someone who has been on the receiving end, not ultimately very practical and certainly not very generous (or Christian, at least as I was taught to understand it) in concept. Even to have been informed that what I was doing was, at the time, strictly against the law, would have made some sense.

The dean:

My mathematics tutor also happened to be the dean of our college, which meant that he was in charge of our well-being, and in this capacity, strangely, we had a very different relationship to the one of total exclusion described above. Put simply, he was very generous towards me both in my actions (climbing over the wall into the college compound after midnight, for which I got a simple warning), and more particularly at the time I contracted an extremely bad, fully developed, case of syphilis, when he was exceptionally kind with me, arranging for a private room in hospital and generally covering for me in the college so that other students would not know what had happened. (Until informed after the fact, I had no idea what was happening to me, and all I really remember of the treatment, other than the high temperatures, was the endless layers of dead skin being washed away from the top my skull.) And he never once took a 'moral stance' or censured me as to what had happened, even though I would have understood this as quite normal: He must have known, or at least strongly suspected, what I was about.[3]

One of the easiest criticisms to throw at a younger person is that they always believe that "nothing bad will ever happen to them" – the point here being that; "Things not only can, but do!" – and particularly to those who repeatedly choose to thrust themselves into harm's way. That said, throughout my life, I have ceaselessly amazed myself with my ability to immediately throw myself back into the fray the moment I have been cured of any sexually related disease. Looking back, at the time HIV/AIDS appeared, I was extremely fortunate as a foreigner here to be declared a persona non grata by all the gay hotels/saunas in the area. At the time, it was generally believed that excluding foreigners was the key to keeping the disease at bay, which initially rather annoyed, but in the end, I came to accept the restriction as almost certainly having been to my advantage.

And as a practical suggestion to sexually active younger men (regardless of whether you do or do not use a condom, but particularly if you don't), I would strongly recommend urination as quickly as possible after an ejaculation in that it does help clean out the remains of any semen and at the same time 'anything else unwanted' that may remain in the urinal tract after intercourse. (As a matter of record, I do know that every time I didn't, I ended up at a specialist clinic having to explain how I came to be in that particular condition, which as I got older did become embarrassing.)

[1.11] New York. Living in the Imperative:

Towards the end of my second year, I was standing in the entrance hall at college when the American man from my postgraduate group walked in and suggested that I take advantage of a cheap student's flight to the US that was

---

[3] As a footnote here, a year or so later and at home, when my teeth begun to 'fall away', I could only presume the worst – I had been informed in the hospital that rotting teeth also was a possibility in very bad cases. Fortunately, at my parent's advice, I visited our local dentist and, to my great relief, was introduced to the concepts of plaque and scaling.

being advertised on the notice board there. He knew a family who I could stay with until I found a job, and he would contact them for me. And after a brief checking of the announcement, I said "Yes! Thank you, yes!" And I flew to New York.

The family's home was in Flushing in the borough of Queens, the parents originally coming from Malta. They had a son of my age (Andy) and two younger daughters, and I was welcomed as another son. The daughter's names don't come to me just now, but I remember being entrusted to take them on a first trip into the city (the eldest would be sixteen or seventeen at the time). It would be my first trip onto Manhattan also, but for some reason their mother reckoned they would be safe with me, and the three of us spent a full day 'doing the sights'.

At the time, it seemed a little odd that they had never been there as a family and I never asked them, but in the end, I sensed that the parents either didn't like and/or were rather frightened of the place.

Finding work didn't come easy. We worked faithfully through the newspaper ads and made enquiries every day, but the only ones that seemed at all promising were with agencies in the city, and Andy's parents were adamant that I should not go that route: "City agencies had a bad reputation in terms of both treatment and not paying what they promised." "I would have to find somewhere to live on Manhattan," and etc. And it took three weeks before they would give in. But, in the end, I had no choice – I had to have some kind of work. And following a brief telephone call and interview, and with no further ado, I had a job as a waiter in a pancake house on the corner of 42nd and 9th, just off Times Square, together with a one-room apartment two subway stops up from my workplace (with resident, supersized, 'everything in New York is a cut above' cockroach to welcome me home in the evening), and I was set to go.

Work: Once ordering was mastered; triple pancakes with one scoop each of vanilla and chocolate ice-cream and blueberry topping, two eggs over light and a double side of bacon – this for breakfast (a revelation to a young man just out of England), work was easy enough and the staff were all friendly. Only one, as there always is, constantly grumbled because he wasn't getting the tips he felt he was due, invariably blaming it (not strictly correctly) on whatever run he had been given for the week. Working the counter involved a high, fast, turnover – mainly just coffees, and subsequently small (ten-cent) tips. The window table seats got filled easily, but turnover was relatively high, so tips came in at the average. However, it was working the back tables, where people came to spend time, that, with the right approach (and a perfect English accent) you could earn a decent return. Even so, regardless of the run, on average I received essentially the same amount, which was double my basic salary, every week, and understanding this, when eating out, I myself I learned to tip (not done in England at the time), this psychologically tackled by adding a requisite amount onto the price shown in the window menu and establishing a total payment in my brain before I actually walked into the restaurant.

[1.12] 'A Day in the life…'

New York was a whole city on Speed, with no time to even register the passing reality; every action a matter of moment (/moments); every moment accentuated, punctuated; a matter of consequence – or none; gone.

It would be late morning, and as I turned up into one of the central avenues leading up to Central Park, she came down against me, totally preoccupied, with a forward, almost aggressive stride; face set, lost in her own world, with clearly no interest in or sympathies for whatever else might be out there – the other faces in the crowd. (At that moment, the time of day being as it was, we were completely by ourselves, but the street could have been overflowing and I doubt it would have made the slightest bit of difference.) And hardly stopping, she crossed the lights over to the next block and was gone. And, in some manner – I still have a clear image of how she looked in my mind – she epitomised what the city was, and presumably still is today. And I was left to face the empty well of the street on my own. But then again, a short walk of my own and there was the park, bustling with its own approximations (/impersonations) of life, or whatever it might to be to live.

***

A scuffle and shouts, and then a crowd gathering outside the restaurant window. (Serving the back tables at the time, I could only really notice the action after the fact.)

"What is it?" (This from a passing waitress to a customer at a window table.)

"Someone just knifed someone." (Judged from tone of voice alone, this could just as easily have been, "A child sneezed.")

"Oh." (The waitress walking on. She had an order to serve.)

And only a short moment later, the police arrived, the crowd was dispersed, and our customers were back at their lunch. And I was left to wonder whether there was any blood on the pavement. (At least, I hadn't noticed anyone wiping it up.)

***

Casual encounters were the easiest thing to search out in the city, with everyone (yet again) offering that magical illusion (it could never be more than an illusion) of brushing up against another's life: "Hello, goodbye. And here we go again!" – each new face overriding the last even as it overlapped into the next; garbled fragments of time and space. The young have seemingly unlimited energy, and all New Yorkers at that time were apparently young.

All pants down in Central Park. Then gunshots (too close) in the darkness, followed by a single cry of (yet again!!!) "Police!" and the whole patch of scrub and bushes suddenly coming alive with bodies scrambling to flee anywhere but in the direction of the headlights. Everyone always warned everyone about the police, and nobody ever listened.

But it was fun – one morning-to-night-to-morning, exhilarating blowout – with me losing as much weight in ten weeks as I did later in ten months in the heat and humidity of Saudi Arabia. But here it was the urgency of the city; the tension that came with forever being on the move: museums, musicals, art galleries, the Rockefeller Centre, Radio City Music Hall, performances in the park, Greenwich Village, Wall Street and the Battery. And walking, walking and walking – legs seemingly endlessly thrusting their way up a downward moving escalator, on to nowhere I could ever really know. But the effort was (/had to be) made.

***

[1.13] Learning to believe in oneself:

"Hallelujah Baby" was an off-Broadway musical picking up events in the life of a young black woman as she strives to become a professional singer, with the twist being that as the play progresses, the period in which the play is set also moves forward, so that in the opening scenes the audience is in the very early 20th century and, by the time of the finale, in present time at the end of the 1960s

– so apart from the very basic success story, you got a sense of how circumstances for black people had changed over that period. And it being a 90% black musical, the audience (in a totally celebratory mood) was also roughly in that ratio, making the atmosphere in the auditorium wildly over the top. There was also the token white 'love interest', who naturally lost out to his black counterpart, and then the truly huge, "has-to-be-seen-to-be-believed, red-hot mama" bringing the house down right at the end as she belted out her own showstopper (referring to her now successful daughter's singing ability), the totally ironic and self-parodying: "She sure didn't get it from me!"

And being completely bowled over by its energy, I had to see it again, in the end roping in Wanda, a young black woman of about my age who worked with me in the restaurant, as an excuse. We actually got on very well together, making it unavoidable that, walking back after the show, I had to explain to her that it could only be a one-time outing, which (this not being Oxford) she took very well.

***

[1.14] An introduction to a very foreign culture:

And at some point along the way, I met a young Jewish man of roughly my own age. Tellingly, particularly as I spent a certain amount of time with him, I cannot remember his name, but I do remember travelling to the Catskills (of Patrick Swayze of "Dirty Dancing" fame) with him to watch a weekend performance he gave on the stage at a hotel there. However, more than his singing (he could manage the basics well enough, but I don't think he ever became the next Sinatra), it was the impression that the Jewish community there left on me that has remained. We stayed there two nights, but right the way through, whether I was walking around the hotel with him or sitting alone at a table in the concert hall, nobody at all, not one person, acknowledged our existence – not even with a nod. And someone must have been aware of who he was (he was on the stage more than twice each night). Or perhaps he was really bad.

Later, I was told by someone quite separately that this was how things were, simply that it was a highly closed community and that they wouldn't notice me because that is not what they do. And if so, so be it. However, it has stayed with me right to the present as a truly unique experience; I have never felt so coldly isolated in a social setting in my life. (I also saw "Fiddler on the Roof" and "Hello Dolly" at this time, and although I enjoyed the shows themselves, I found it very difficult to make any personal connections.) Totally, this was very much evidence of a cultural 'gap-too-wide', and for me, viewed over the long term, a point of education, but at the time it was certainly not a good introduction to Jewish life or the Jewish mind.

However, he in his own way was fun, and he provided a window. And thanks to his efforts, I got to see Judy Garland live at Carnegie Hall – in one of her last performances before she took her life. I had seen her in films before, without being particularly attracted, but this was something different: You couldn't take your eyes away from her; she compelled (/riveted), making the live recording of the exact same performance that he had me listen to three days later somehow dead – just a singer, just music. And we were in the best seats in the house. He had purchased the cheapest seats right at the back of the theatre (either that or we were standing), but, in the interval, he wheedled an usherette into letting us have two unoccupied seats in the front row of the Dress Circle so that we could watch the second half (when she was on stage by herself) in style. Apparently, he did this regularly. Essentially, the patter went:

"A friend has flown all the way from (wherever) especially to see Judy. He is a great fan, and I somehow stupidly managed to lose the tickets just two hours before the performance started."

That plus lots of carefully shed tears.

That said, whatever kind of relationship it was (I can't remember anything of a sexual nature), it ended with a round of cheap bickering wandering along some narrow back street running between one avenue and another.

And then:

There was a man who was introduced to me along the side of Central Park and essentially conned me into overpaying for a what upon closer examination I later found (it being summer, I had no cause to wear it at the time) to be a somewhat over-worn, double-breasted, navy blue jacket that was really too small for me. (When I met him two or three years later in the gay bars in London, I know I kept my distance.) I can't now remember with compete accuracy, but I sense that the two men – this one and the young Jewish man described above – were one and the same. At least, in style and manner of approach, they would most certainly fit.

***

[1.15] Julio:

Julio was the big affair of the summer, with us spending a full weekend together (this probably being the best one could do in the time available), for the large part in bed.

And during this (what in normal terms would be regarded as) briefest of periods, he also insisted on introducing me to a friend in Paris; at whose home I later stayed, but who showed no personal interest in me; this leading me to meeting a man who informed me that he was related to the deposed Czar of Russia (a second or third cousin in the Romanov family exiled to Paris at the time of the Russian Revolution), and who gave me two eighteenth-century Russian coins, the better one of which I had mounted in silver and strung on a long necklace (again silver) in Saudi Arabia, which subsequently was carelessly lost (and is presumably still deep down there) in the watery depths of the Persian Gulf, and the second of which I still have. (I had it evaluated on a recent trip to England, but apparently it is of little value due to its condition, and I was recommended to keep it as a memory – which it is, and I have.) And life goes on.

And how did it come to pass that such an intense affair should end so abruptly? This I do clearly remember: Having been out for the first time on my own (a ten-minute walk to buy something to eat) and making my way back up to his apartment along the side of Central Park, I was distracted (/waylaid) by a group of young men, one of whom sold me a blue, double-breasted jacket for a very (at least as he claimed it) moderate price.

***

[1.16] The Montreal World Exposition:

This was a day-trip taken with Andy shortly before the end of my stay, notable for the fact that we managed to go around some twenty-three or -four pavilions in the one-day (it being very close to the end of its run, the place was almost empty), and that I got to see the Japanese pavilion with its immense ikebana (Japanese flower) arrangement over the entrance, resulting in a promise that we would go to see the Japanese Expo that was to be held three years later in Osaka, Japan. (I made it. Andy didn't.)

Chapter 2
Life's Lessons Delivered Early

(Taken from "Child": On learning.)

Child.

What child would not trust the teachings of his parents? And that is right. Or else how would he grow?

What child would not question the teachings of her parents? And that is right. Or else how would she grow?

And if parents, why not teachers?

Not less the words of passing strangers.

***

[2.1] Schooling at a young age:

A walk downhill. Expanding my universe at my own speed:

(At seven or eight?) My bus was late, that or I had taken longer than usual to get to the bus-stop and missed it, and standing waiting there by myself, I decided that before the next one came, I might be able to get down to the stop lower down the road. At first moving slowly and giving repeated quick looks back over my shoulder so that I could run back if I had got things wrong, I worked my way down to the bend, where I lost my view of the road behind me completely, and from where I could only hurry as quickly as my (still short) legs would allow me. And with beginner's luck – not always so in later cases – I very proudly made it with time to spare. And from that simple start, as the weeks and then months went by, I worked out how to cut down the backstreets to the second stop directly from my school. And then to make it down as far as the bridge, from where I learned I could walk up the course of the river to the asbestos factory – where I had known the slope up to my father's shop since I was a really small child. (This in total would be a mile and a half?) And then all the paths and short cuts in-between. I avoided the full bus route until much later, presumably because it involved a much steeper climb, and probably more to the point that the course by the river, even though it still at this time stank from effluent from the local factories, allowed for a fuller experience – the plop of a fat rat dropping back into the thick bluish water – and the freedom of mind to be as I wished. And then as we moved from above the shop to our first real home, and then on to grammar school, which was on the far side of town, I learned to take other paths and other routes, one section at a time, creating a physical map of my hometown in my brain, until I was free to walk just about anywhere I needed as and when necessary.

One of the key determinants to my life as it has would have to be the fact that I was born right at the start of the post-war baby-boom, this leading me to being sent to a primary school quite separate from my two older brothers and also at quite some distance from my home. One result, as described above, was the development of a good sense of direction, something I have kept with me right through to the present. Also, throughout this initial period (until the age of twelve), a large part of my life was being spent in a world quite separate from my siblings, and I had no way of knowing who their friends were, what they were doing or how they were developing. And equally, other than for the odd birthday party, when I brought my friends home, they can have had no idea as to what that area of my life involved. Thus this one simple happen-chance gave me the opportunity to become truly independent from a very young age – to create my own way of doing things, question my surroundings and, in the end, learn how to approach life. That is, I was into the process of creating myself before I had ever really been moulded, and I guess this habit of making my own decisions became, for better or worse, the guiding principle of my life.

[2.2] Music and musicals:

From a very young age, before there was ever a radio or record player in the house, we sang: climbing up or down mountains, as my father always put it, "to keep our legs moving" ("I had a good home and I left! I left! I left!") or walking back along the valley from "Waters Meet" in the Yorkshire Dales – a favourite family picnic spot where, as suggested by the name, two rivers meet, and where in spring the bluebells create their own special carpet – with enough to be spared for a small bunch to be taken home. If Japan has its plum and cherry blossoms in spring, we had our snowdrops, crocuses, bluebells, and daffodils. I am not actually sure whether I ever saw the daffodils as they are described in Wordsworth's poem – I know we did visit the Lake District once as a child, and I have a vague memory of a hillside covered in yellow – but I loved both the flower and the poem so much as a child that I always have imagined that I did, and as such it is recognised as an official part of my personal spring.

And then returning home in the car, with my father zigzagging us back and forth from one side of the road to the other or sending us round and around roundabouts as if he would never let up: "Show me the way to go home…" – which, when we were a little older, we transliterated into our own, rather more 'posh' family version: "Indicate the route to my abode…"

(In my fifties in New Zealand, returning from a "Maori Village Experience", our Maori driver set us off on a singalong including the above song (standard version), at which point, with perfect timing, we entered a roundabout which, to the delight of the whole bus, he refused to exit – proving, if nothing else, that much is the same the world over.)

Then, at Christmas, there would always be singing around the piano (my uncle playing his heart out) and the family's rowdy rendering of "On Ilkley Moor bah'tat" in the Lancashire dialect. For readers who might not know the song, the story in brief would be: "If you go out on the moors in winter without a hat (bah'tat), you will catch your death of cold (caud), we will have to bury you (thee), the worms (t'werms) will eat you up, the ducks will come and eat the worms, we will eat the ducks, and then we will all have eaten you ('etten thee)!" which seemed a quite reasonable portrayal of life, certainly as it was at the time.

We also had regular musicals (and pantomimes at Christmas) put on by a local operatic society, and these – a number of which are referenced in other sections – in many ways, gave me my dreams. I still know a number of the songs, learned by heart and kept to be sung as I feel the need.

[2.3] "Money doesn't grow on trees."

The concept of work – and the understanding of money as something that is received in return for work done – was instilled very early on in life, and this is something that, as an adult, I have remained ever grateful for.

From as far back as I can remember, I worked with my mother and both my brothers in my father's shops; initially a grocer's shop, then a butcher's next door – which my middle brother eventually took over – and finally a foreign imports 'speciality' shop in the centre of town (chocolate-covered ants and bees sold in cans and a 'Rotissimat' that roasted full chickens on rotating spits – they still exist today, but were a brand-new concept back then). Initially, we 'helped'; counting spaces and filling shelves, then carrying boxes up from/down into the cellar or the storage rooms above or at the back of the shop, and serving customers with simple requests. Then, with everything – butter, cheese, lard, bacon, dried fruits – having to be cut, sliced, weighed, packed, etc. by hand, one by one we moved through and mastered each job, together with the requisite tricks of the trade: that extra dab of butter for the regular customer (and be sure you let them see you giving it to them), neatly layered bacon slices, displayed before wrapping (with those few scrappy end bits to make up the full weight tucked way under out of sight), until we could fill any customer's order for just about anything. And for the above, I got my weekly allowance, my 'spence', with occasional bonuses for Christmas or for special jobs – cleaning out and putting in order the storerooms – which became the foundation for all my organisational skills in life. (See 'kaizen' [17.1].) And in time 'spence' became an allowance, and 'help' became understood on both sides as work for which I was being paid.

Among all this, I do not even now understand why, but I intensely disliked being called on to sell – that is, touch – packets of cigarettes, and if I noticed any of our regular customers hanging around by the till, where the different brands were lined up on the shelves, I would make myself busy in some other corner of the shop, or preferably somewhere out back in the store rooms, so that I couldn't be called upon to "serve Mr So and so." Also, right through my life, I have had an aversion to (again, finding them very difficult to touch) matches and cigarette lighters, so I guess there must have been something in there from very young. This was not (and still isn't) connected with the act of smoking itself: I was not yet anywhere near that age. My father (and later, both my life partners) smoked, something which "men did" and (at least, respectable) "women didn't," but, from my perspective, it was easy enough for me to recognise that a number of my uncles and older male cousins, all of whom I felt close to, didn't, so there was never any particular attraction there, and when my eldest brother started (and tried to get both myself and my middle brother interested – I would be around 12 or 13 the time), neither of us reacted well, both of us coming close to puking on our first drag, and that was it, with alcohol (or rather, being English, beer) becoming my ticket to adulthood.

Related to the above, and as an indication of how my mind works (left on my own, I have always had a very bad tendency to imagine the worst outcome possible), I remember being sent out by my father, at the age of five or six, on my first errand to purchase a packet of cigarettes that was needed to complete an order from another grocer's shop some two or three hundred metres up the road. I'm not sure whether this was done deliberately with knowledge of my aversion, but I do remember repeatedly holding back, partly due to the fact that, in obtaining such 'goods' in this seemingly underhand fashion from what I understood to be our competitors, I had the sense that I was doing something very wrong, something akin to stealing. And by extension, I was extremely conscious of the possibility that if they chose to, that is in the event that they recognised me as the son of their competitor, they could have me arrested for being legally underage. And where might that lead? (I had what was essentially a repeat of this at 15 or 16 when I was sent – again, my father – to buy a bottle of wine from an off-licence liquor store, quite some distance away, at a time when even entering such a place under the age of eighteen was illegal.)

Then, at one point in my early teens, I started to help my father with weekly deliveries, mainly to our local municipal housing estate, with one time that I particularly remember when he had me come with him collecting debts. Most customers paid on delivery, but this particular woman, a regular customer in her early forties, was commonly out by the time we reached her house, meaning that she was considerably in arrears. Coming to the door, it appeared that she was very much in a hurry to leave, and claiming that she didn't have time to search out even a few pounds to help lower the rather large amount she owed, she disappeared back into the house, only to return in a rather plush fur coat and high heels, pushing past my father along the path to the garden gate where, once outside, she was quickly lost into the darkness. But what remained with me more than the clothes, was the fact that the front living room of the house was totally empty – nothing but bare floorboards, with presumably the rest of the house in a similar condition. And my father was faced with the dilemma of stopping deliveries and then probably having to write off everything she owed or continuing and potentially having the amount grow even further.

And then there was Christmas, when he would, particularly at the 'better' houses, insist that I go up front with the heaviest-looking box, knowing that the owner, who almost certainly would not consider giving him a tip personally, would not be able to resist the son. And I got to keep the proceeds.

[2.4] A first brush with Church hierarchy:

The following conversation with my mother was referring to my childhood sweetheart, Christine, at my elementary school. (I would be 10 or 11 at the time.) The talk had arisen due to a mislabelling of Christmas gifts; a glass diamond brooch intended for my grandmother and a similarly glass-diamond 'engagement ring', both purchased at our local Woolworth's store in town – resulting in a slightly embarrassing recall of the ring from my grandmother, together with the necessity of then explaining who the ring was originally intended for.

"You can't marry her."

"Why not?"

"She's Catholic. We're Methodist."

"I wouldn't have to be Catholic."

"No, but your children would."

"I don't see why."

"If they weren't brought up Catholic, they would go to hell."

"And why would that be?"

"That's what the Church says."

(Pause for thought)

"What gives anyone the right to tell me that my children are bound for hell?"

This last line remained unspoken, but it does give a very clear indication of how my mind at the time (and subsequently) related to what I would define as 'outside interference' in my life.

The ring was given (and kept, at least for a number of years that I know of) in good faith, and even today, I still wonder if (and at times, truly wish that) things could have been otherwise.

[2.5] Pastimes:

At a time when we had no TV or radio to provide distractions, as small children we were left with the natural world.

The first animals I knew were our dog and cat. They were not kept as pets. The dog was there to warn off anyone who might try to break into the shop when the family was asleep, which did occasionally happen, and the cat to stalk and catch rats: Every so often, when it seemed it hadn't been around a while, it would lay them on the back step just to let us know that it was still on the job, and as kids, it was left to us to flush these down the outside toilet.

Up the valley from the shop, we found our own 'hidden spot' along the side of the river, with a small pond where we could net water beetles, gather frogspawn or catch newts, or just go to break the ice on a winter morning. And even higher up, where the valley broke out onto the moorland, in season you could collect bilberries, and there was an old slate quarry, where I once found a sizeable ammonite fossil, which, at my parent's suggestion, got donated to my elementary school.

And after we moved to our new home and the section above the shop where we had previously lived became vacant, my middle brother (Will) started breeding budgerigars and I, for whatever reason, chose to keep two grass-snakes in the same room – fed on live frogs in our old bathtub – one of which very quickly managed to escape its box and slip down the stairs and presumably out of the house (terrifying my mother in the process), but the other of which turned out to be overly broody. Its own eggs not hatching, it took to climbing up into the stack of budgerigar cages and curling up on top of a freshly laid batch of eggs, invariably in the same nesting box, sending the mother bird frantic; this being repeated so often that my brother, normally the quietest and most pliant of the three of us, started insisting that it had to go. And although I did protest that it hadn't actually eaten any of the eggs (a point which I actually found rather fascinating) in the end I had no choice. (As to the baby snakes which never were, though as a child I would have loved to see them, now I can only imagine twenty plus of the tiny things slithering around my father's grocery shelves, so maybe it was better that things ended up as they did.)

Agricultural fairs, with their fully-dressed shire horses, bulls in pens, sheepdog trials, and the huge, heavy-smelling marquees packed full with sections for every type of vegetable, fruit and flower; pickled cauliflowers and homemade almond tarts, were held once a year on an open stretch of grassland 'somewhere on the outskirts of town' (which many years later, as I filled out my surroundings, I worked out to be the open playing fields directly behind my elementary school). And for small children, we had "Best arrangement of wildflowers in a jam-jar," – two first prizes and a second in my three years of entries – after which, apparently having become too much of a financial burden on the municipality, they no longer were.

The three of us being members of the local Cub and then Boy Scout troupe led to attendances at our church (followed by once-a-month parades), whist drives to raise money for and then assisting with the building of a brand-new clubhouse, this followed by monthly dances to which parents and friends were all invited, and (with the scouts), summer camps around the country.

And then each summer holidays, we decamped to Llandudno on the north coast of Wales, to a world of sand dunes, Welsh porridge, Knickerbocker Glories (fruit and ice-cream sundaes in a super-tall glass and attacked with a superlong spoon – both growing shorter every year) and a ride on "The Rack," a somewhat rickety (planks on wheels) open car that ran on rails as far as Colwyn Bay (both treats allowed only once throughout each whole long summer), walks around the Orme (free), with its small blue butterflies invariably clustered around the same outcrop of rocks searched for eagerly every year, and the "Happy Valley," with its bandstand, "Most beautiful grandmother!" (All in their early forties at that time) and fashion (matching handbags and hats) contests, and three little boys (Pip, Bubble and Squeak – the last being me) each in identical short-sleeved sweaters dragged up on the stage to receive small bags of sweets, or whatever they handed out in those days as compensation prizes. (I don't think we actually ever did anything to deserve more.) My father always appeared during the last weeks, when we had the van to travel around in rather more widely.

And then there was always that very special fish-and-chip shop to be searched out on the way home.

***

Reading: This being the main form of entertainment available, I read just about every child's book to be had at the time, the three below only noted because I found them, in some sense, special.

- "Winnie the Pooh": This was received very young and re-read faithfully once a year, every year, up until the time I went to university, each time with me finding some new point to laugh at – subtleties that at a younger age I had not appreciated.

In my mid-forties, walking up in the mountains behind my home here in Kobe, I actually found something very close to Christopher Robin's 'Magic Circle' clearing in the woods, where he says goodbye to Pooh, and, at the time, it crossed my mind that it might be nice towards the end to walk up there and just rest myself against the trunk of the tree and let the world go. And, if not that, at least to use it as a place I could associate with my youth – somewhere you can return to but then, in the end, never do. (True to form, I also didn't, although if my legs would carry me that far now, I'm still fairly sure that could find it.)

- "The Water Babies", with the somewhat severe, but then far more practical Mrs Bedonebyasyoudid, also struck a chord. (As a note from the present: Much as people regularly quote Mrs Doasyouwouldbedoneby as the key to a morally/ethically correct life, this is actually only going to work to the extent that expectations match – that is in societies (/relationships) with the same (or at least similar) cultural backgrounds.)
- "Rory": I cannot remember the name of this book but I do remember the name of the protagonist, a young boy named Rory, who, when he is by himself on one of his walks, meets an older man who lives in the woods near his home and who is initially a little frightening: In the town he is considered to be a rather 'odd' person (something of a recluse) and to be avoided. However, after a certain hesitation on both sides, they become friends, and one chapter at a time, he teaches Rory to recognise the ways the woods, and of the trees, flowers and animals that live there. And being very fond of nature from the start, I naturally took to it. And then, much later, I did wonder if the presence of the older man had also been an attraction.
- Christmas was marked by the receipt of our annual book of 'political cartoons' to be shared between us. Beautifully drawn and highly detailed, it was perfect to be poured over lying on the floor in front of the fire and was probably the present that all three of us looked forward to receiving the most each year.

And then there were the boys' adventure books, (my mother's) women's magazines, (college) newspapers, Sherlock Holmes, Agatha Christie, and all the classics and modern novels – English, French, Russian, American… – and on and on until my mid-forties when, deciding that I would try a book of my own and wanting it to be 'me', I put everything aside, and somehow, to date, never got back to the habit.

[2.6] Just because you can't see something doesn't mean it doesn't exist:

Having been placed at the front of the class from the time I first attended school, it was only when I was 13 or 14 that it was discovered that my eyesight was not quite up to the mark. Fortunately, my uncle being an optician, the matter was solved fairly quickly and efficiently, but I do remember sitting on the upper deck of the bus on the way home and being totally taken aback to find myself able to see the branches on the trees, something I had never been able to recognise previously other than as a blur.

[2.7] 'Advice for a lifetime':

At the time of our 11+ examinations to determine which school we would attend for our further education, I was encouraged to try for a much larger, regional grammar school, which naturally would be that much more difficult to get into. I didn't get in, but my mother's advice prior to taking the tests, namely: "If you pass, well and good. But if you don't, don't cry. It won't worry either of us and trying for it won't harm you," served me well both at the time (I didn't cry) and has stood me in good stead every time I haven't quite got the answer from life that I would've liked.

There is also the, perhaps more common, advice; "You can do anything you want if you work hard at it," almost invariably quoted by those who have succeeded in their field. However, taking into consideration all those others who don't get there (and most never do), it is perhaps limited in its portrayal of the truth.

Instilling the same attitude would be; "If people ever tell you that you can't, tell them to go to Hartford, Hereford and Hampshire." People (and I have come across a number) who tell you that you can't, either want to use that 'fact' to put themselves above you and/or (almost invariably) aren't really very clever themselves.

And finally, also taken very much from personal experience, I could suggest; "If you can't get over it, get round it. That, or just get over it!"

If you choose to put your mind to the matter, there is always another path.

[2.8] The power of a lie:

I have a stamp – taken from a book of stamps for sale that a friend at the time (we would be about thirteen) lent me to see if I might be interested in any. All were priced and, being relatively rare, this one was the most expensive (and therefore for a child the most attractive) of the bunch, and it became the star event of my collection – the one that I later always opened the page to admire. And I took it without paying. I swore repeatedly that I hadn't, and nothing could be proven, but I took it. And the friend disappeared from my life. And at some point, when I was much older with an adult's understanding, I was no longer able to look at that stamp or my collection, and today they remain locked away at the back of an overfilled closet, presumably until the time I die.

The other time I deliberately lied was when I was out on a walk with a school friend (I remember the spot exactly) who, without any warning, asked me if I was gay, and not being yet ready to give him an honest reply, I said no. And we completed our walk, and he went home, and again that was the end of the relationship.

[2.9] "Don't tell your child what they don't need to know."

(Aged thirteen) "I don't know whether I should tell you this…" is how she (my mother) started. And then without any further ado, she went straight into the story of how my father, on their wedding night, had told her that he hated her; He had never wanted to marry her in the first place and he really "didn't want anything to do with her." Also, apparently, he had been having an affair with the woman I had known all my life as my Auntie Beth, the woman who had always been with us working in the shop and helped to look after us through a large part of our childhood. This latter fact I found really hard to believe, as she was the last person I could imagine anyone having an affair with ('mousey' or 'insipid' are the words that come most easily to mind), but my mother told my middle brother the same story and he immediately cut off all relations with her, so presumably there was something to it. However, either way, these are not facts that children of any age should be made privy to, and even now, I wonder what caused her to come out with the story – what benefits she imagined it might provide for her or our relationship?

[2.10] "You can't always have what you want." (Or, at least, not at the time you want it.)

At one point in grammar school, I had to decide how I wanted to progress with my studies up to and beyond O-levels, and as a personal choice, I would've liked to group mathematics (which right up to university, I never had in any sense to study – I could just do it), French (which, even with three visits to our twin-town in France from when I was 13 and a private tutor who my father found for me, I was pretty hopeless at, but did like) and art (which I also enjoyed). However, schools at the time divided studies into arts or sciences, which, to study French and art, would have meant me eliminating mathematics. And more importantly here, my art teacher refused point blank to teach me – "I didn't have any artistic abilities whatsoever!" And so, for my A-level exams, I was left with mathematics, advanced mathematics, and physics (which, together with chemistry, I didn't really enjoy at all), and my course into university was set. Considering how I have ended up; with my Japanese, Korean and Japanese ink-painting, etc., the whole thing seems rather ironic, but I guess much in life is a matter of timing.

[2.11] "Just whistle a happy tune."

"The killer stalks his (now third) victim, but she can only hear the taunting echo of his tightly pursed lips forever whistling the same plaintive refrain as she attempts to make her way through the ever-thickening layers of fog. And as she vanishes into the murk, yet another strangulated scream. And once again the audience, held in the same vicelike grip, as of one mind recoil into their seats." ("Jack the Ripper." Early 1960s.)

***

He decided he would walk through the cemetery. It wasn't really much of a shortcut – the path from the side gate to the main entrance wound somewhat – but it would cut off a corner and he wasn't in any particular hurry. Ray wouldn't expect him to be at his home too early. Inside the small entrance in the wall, the world fell quiet. Noting that the grass between the gravestones, as always, was neatly cut, he wondered idly who actually kept it all in order. The cemetery itself was of a considerable size. He knew this because his grandmother was buried in a bare plot of land way out in the rear section close to the outer wall, where the paths narrowed into tight loops, roping off the clusters of bare headstones into small islands. Just once, on the first anniversary of her death, he had revisited her grave with his parents and brothers, but this had been, as far as he knew, the last time that any of them had been there. Some time later, he had tried, unsuccessfully, to search out the place on his own, but had merely ended up walking in circles. At the time, it had seemed to him to be a lonely place to be put to rest, and thinking now he couldn't recall there being anything like a lawn or trace of anything green there at all. Maybe it had been the season. He still missed her.

The sky had been dull all day, and now the afternoon was approaching its close, with a dampness gathering along the low lines of trees that marked the course of the main pathways. Someone was walking up the slope ahead of him; a young woman – he guessed she couldn't have been that much older than he was – a solitary figure, half-shadow cast against the grey-green of the path, which was now entering the long, final stretch up to the main gates. The scene from the movie he had been to the previous weekend slipped into his mind, and for no other reason than to see what effect it might have (and possibly something of a sly urge to torment), he tightened his lips and expelled a soft stream of warm air in her direction – a fine reed of sound hollowed out by the mist, but still, he reckoned, capable of carrying far enough to reach her ears.

For the briefest of moments, the shadow paused. She had heard him. Then, apparently shaking off what might have been a pass in her imagination, she continued onwards seemingly lost in her own thoughts. He would try again.

And this time the sound cut straight through the haze, truly as if it had been a knife. And she turned, and he could see that she both recognised the melody and could see him. Except that the image in her brain wasn't one of him, but rather the shapeless form of the killer in the movie, as the victim had beheld him in her final moments. He upped the volume one more level, and it was as if he could now read her every thought. She could not run, as that would be admitting her fear for him to see. But again, she could not ignore the fact that whoever was following her might not be of sound mind. (The whole scenario was scripted too close.) Or again, there was the possibility that she had stepped into some form of alternative reality?

At the point where she was now walking, the path suddenly rose into the final stretch up to the main gates. Neither of them could see the gates, but both of them knew they were there. And making a final push forward, she left him and was gone.

And left alone in the mist, he too (if only mildly) succumbed to the fear.

***

And it is in such a manner that discoveries (of who you are, or what you might become) are made.

[2.12] The Art of the Deal:

(At fifteen or sixteen.) I had set my heart on a certain shirt set back in the window of a recently opened, and to me, at the time, rather elegant, men's wear shop on our high street (we had a couple of shopping streets in town and this was the wider of the two) but it being somewhat fancy – a deep mauve, felt-like material – it was not anything I could ask my parents to buy for me, and so I bided my time and waited around for the winter sales, at which time, without any hesitation, I strode in and (with the money I had made working for my father) made the purchase for the price of £4.10s, which, though expensive at the time, I found very satisfying, and the trophy, neatly packed, was proudly carried home. Then unwrapping the parcel on my bed, I noticed that there were two price labels, one stuck on top of the other, and peeling off the top layer, I revealed to myself the original pre-sale price of £3.00. Caveat emptor.

[2.13] 'Breaking up is hard to do.' (1) Ray:

Ray was initially one of my 'television friends'. That is, not having a television to watch at home (this right up to the time I went to university), at any time I was invited to visit a schoolfriend's house and they did have a television, the visits tended to be repeated. And his parents, as I would guess most parents at the time did, were very kind and put up with the extra body in the house. Left at this level, I think the relationship would have gone very well. He was a quieter person by nature, and I also do have a quieter side. However, when we started to go around together outside the house, things started to go wrong: Somehow, we never managed to be able to do things, to complete whatever plan had been made, with something inevitably coming up or getting in our way. And as time progressed, this (not being the type of situation that I was familiar with – I was used to doing things) came to be highly frustrating.

One example I clearly remember was when we set out on our bicycles to ride to the coast (this was at his suggestion, his ideas invariably being wide-reaching in scale), only to have him become unsure as to "whether he had turned the gas off before leaving the house" – this when we had completed some 30-odd of the 50 miles intended. Naturally, we went back (he was fast approaching a state of panic), and, equally naturally, he had turned the gas off; but we never got to the coast, something which would have been nice to be able to say we had done.

And then we had our trip to the Norfolk Broads, the original plan being to "spend a week on a houseboat on the canals there" (roping in my middle brother, Will, who was old enough to sign off for the boat), which after an inordinate amount of dithering (and/or parental influence?) got reduced to five days on a caravan site, which, being something that I had done repeatedly as a small boy, did not appeal. (In my defence, at this point I had been to France three times and also camping up and down the country with the Boy Scouts at least four or five times, and to travel that distance and to what at that time was quite an exotic location, merely to stay on a rundown caravan site, was too much of a downgrade.)

However, we did go, and up to a point we managed, until on the third or fourth morning, I woke up with my mind set (I had had enough!), and when the two of them set out to walk to the camp store to purchase our daily provisions, which as far as I remember had become the event of the day, I refused to go with them. (I have no memory of actually doing anything on that trip other than go to that store.) Then hearing their voices as they returned, without any thought, I deliberately turned my eyes inwards, holding them out of focus. And by the time they had climbed up the steps into the caravan, they were met with nothing more than two dead orbs staring out into space. And that is how I held them until they left, and then subsequently returned with the local police officer, who held a penlight close up to my pupils – at which point, understanding that I had perhaps gone a little too far, I returned them to normal. How we returned home, I am not sure, but I do remember being taken by my father to apologise to his parents (Ray didn't come out at the time), after which it was a matter of simply avoiding each other at school. There was no personal dislike here. It was simply the fact that I felt excessively tied down by the whole relationship and sensing I would be incapable of presenting my feelings in a satisfactory manner, this was my way out – a means of escaping all the messiness involved with explanations, not just to Ray but also to his parents. (They had been very kind to me.)

What I did on that morning is not something that I have ever done since – simply because I would not know how to. It was not anything that I had in any way planned. But that I was capable of manipulating my eyes in that way at that age, that I knew how to 'turn myself off' / 'withdraw' (and subsequently 'turn them on again'/'return to normal' at will) without a moment's consideration or any guidance – has invariably disquieted. From my mid-twenties onwards, I have had a wide range of experiences which, taken one by one, I have had no choice other than to bow to the reality of, but this was blatantly out of the range of what might be considered a reasonable action (in any sense 'normal') for a 15-year-old boy. Regardless of the degree to which it was an indicator or a foreshadowing of things to come (questioning the matter of 'normality' and 'self' seemingly having been a recurring theme in my life), it came far too early, and became a memory that was not revisited for a considerable number of years.

[2.14] 'Breaking up is hard to do.' (2) Helen:

"I can't see you again. I'm sorry. Goodbye!"

The "Goodbye!" was added here to clinch the matter, to present enough sense of determination (/resolution) so that she would know not to call me, although before I spoke them, I had had no idea what words I was actually going to come out with. And four seconds later, before she had any chance to reply (I doubt the words had had time to fully register), I was down the steps, the doors closed, and I was waving at her passing image in the coach window. And it was done. It had been said, and the weight was lifted.

***

Knowing that in a few more months I would be gone to another life at university, two weeks or so previously, when Helen had to come out with, "My dad said he wanted you to meet the family. My grandparents, too," it had been in equal parts a message that needed no elaboration and an alert that something had to be done. In the RRMP (Rituals Related to the Matrimonial Process) of the time, we were now closing in on Stage 5: "The Relatives" – this irrespective of whatever my personal wishes in the matter might be; that is, things were getting rather too much out of hand.

Rather oddly, right through the full period we were dating, the only member of her family that I actually met was her father, and that only a brief glance when, on one extremely cold winter's night, he had been thoughtful enough to let us into the house (normally we were left to work through our goodnight routine out on the street doorstep), and then an hour or so later, when the two of us were getting far too aroused for our own good, again another glance when he had had the good sense to come halfway back down the stairwell to suggest that I leave.

And then shortly after the above invitation, there had been a totally unplanned meeting with Christine. Closing the gate to her back garden, she had called across the road to where I was standing waiting for Helen to come out of her house.

"Helen says I have to give her your ring."

This was the diamond ring that had originally being given to my grandmother, and in asking for it, although totally in character (I can imagine her outstretched hand), as far as I was concerned Helen had gone one step too far.

As a general note, it has been my experience throughout life to note that when a situation is in any manner related to a matter that they consider important, very few women come even close to being the "highly subdued young ladies" that they imagine their social upbringing has conditioned them to be, and Helen, also, was as fully capable of being as self-assertive as the occasion required.

"No way!" (This from me.)

That Christine had told Helen about (shown her?) the ring – presumably some six or seven years earlier when we had all been in the same class at elementary school together – and more so that Helen apparently set such store by the matter that some six or seven years later she had demanded it from Christine, now brings a smile, but in my mind at the time, the two of them were positioned in such totally different orbits that the idea of her possessing that ring was not anything I could even begin to consider.

However, the above being quite enough of an answer for her, Christine simply gave me a cheery smile and bounced her way off down the street towards the centre of town, this being the last time I ever saw her and the only time that I ever saw her as she would have been as an adult (other than in a very recent dream, where she appeared, I sense, to let me know that things could not have been otherwise – at least, it cleared my mind).

And now we were on the coach coming back from a Cliff Richards concert (two hours of incessant screeching and screaming female teenager's voices – an experience I fortunately have never had to repeat), and we were approaching the point where something had to be said. Except that I didn't know where to start – or rather if I started, where it would end. The coach being packed full, I had no desire for an argument or streams of tears, both of which I knew she was very capable of. And at no point able to find the right moment, I could do nothing but sit there for a full two and a half hours until, now being no more than 200 yards from my stop and still nothing said, I could only stand and reach for my bag from the overhead net, and then as the driver pulled in, let the half-mumbled words tumble out. Not the most elegant of exits, but it worked.

[2.15] A glimpse at how the media works. (And a sniff of politics.)

(Age 16–17.) At the time I became a senior student, the school organised a fifty-mile, overnight walk for charity, with all participating students receiving a card upon which to register sponsors, who would donate a small amount of money for each mile completed. (This type of event was quite popular at the time.) Already knowing the last section of the walk quite well (it passed our homes) a friend and I decided to make a serious effort with the whole thing and started our own 'training programme,' which involved taking a bus up into the hills and walking back, and then the next weekend taking the same bus considerably further along the route and again walking back; and again, until we had actually completed (and more important were familiar with) a good half of the course which we knew was to be tackled. And it was at this time I had the clever (at least it seemed so at the time) idea of telephoning up the local newspaper to ask if they would sponsor me, leading to a full frontpage article about the event and our training, and a photograph of self, peering through a pair of up-close and well-blistered feet, naturally plus a 'sponsorship' (ten shillings a mile?), which was all very nice.

And the walk took place, and three of us came in way out in front of the pack, the headmaster having to be woken up to come to the centre of town to greet us – flash photos and applause and all. (The addition was a younger student who wouldn't let us throw him off at the start, and who eventually we accepted as part of our 'team'.) And again all was well, until I decided to telephone into the newspaper offices and ask when it would be all right to come in and collect the money, at which point, they started asking me for details of the walk and how it had all felt, etc. etc., which I answered in full.

And then on the Monday, at school, as all the students were filing into the hall for morning assembly, my classroom teacher came hurrying past me with the information that "I should 'look out' because I was going to be 'had.'" Not having a clue what he was talking about, I walked into the hall myself and found my seat as I always did. And after the usual hymn and prayers, the headmaster stood up and, without any of his usual preamble, laid into: "That arrogant student (I was not named) who, for his own personal benefit (/advancement), had taken all the glory from what had been a magnificent effort by so many students, and particularly from the organiser (another senior student)," and so on, and so on. And I still did not know what was happening.

Back in the classroom, my teacher showed me a copy of the problem paper, in which again I was frontpage news, with a half-page photo of us crossing the finishing line and a long article with every other sentence starting: "And Olton said…" or "And Olton agreed…" And it finally clicked. And I was a little angry. Not with the newspaper: Newspapers (or any media organisation) need an angle, a selling point, and in this case I was 'the story that sells'. I hadn't particularly put myself out to be so. I merely had wanted to make more money for the charity, which I had. And when I called them after the event, it had not been to promote myself. I had merely wanted to be paid. And things had taken their natural course. They could have chosen to call the chief organiser for further information, but they didn't, and that was their choice. However, I could not understand (and still don't) why, rather than being called out in public, I could not have been called into the headmaster's office and asked to explain my side of the story before any judgement was made.

And the matter was left there – never referred to again – right the way through to the end of my schooling. In other words, I got zero credit for what I had actually done, including promoting the walk. And as a separate point that grated (and also never got mentioned): Including the payment I received from the newspaper, the three of us at the head of the walk together made more than a third of the total amount raised by all the walkers together, which I don't think was a bad effort.

***

The following year, I was chosen to be deputy head boy. This wouldn't have caught anyone's attention at all, except that the head boy, who again was a good friend, was the son of a local politician. He also was the least popular prefect in the school and became one of the most unpopular head boys we had had in quite a while. However, understanding that political hierarchies do exist in all types of societies or organisations, and that people do get promoted for a variety of reasons, this, being part of the world as it is, was accepted.

And then two things happened after this that made me wonder whether there wasn't something really personal involved.

Prefects were in charge of milk-break – the distribution of bottles of milk to all students during the morning break, and one day, being a little late after tidying up the empty crates, I was hurrying to get to the stairs so that I wouldn't be late for class, just as the headmaster came out of his office; for which I was called inside for "running in the corridors" and summarily strapped. (Again, I was not allowed to offer any excuses for my actions.) However, this also was accepted. He was headmaster.

He also happened to be the head Latin teacher in school, and when two of us (both mathematics students) got into Oxford and neither of us had the required classic language (Greek or Latin O-levels) qualification required for entry (neither of us had been considered possibilities for Oxford or Cambridge at the time we took our O-levels), he gave us private lessons for six months, resulting in the both of us getting top grades (As) in the subject. Calling us to the classroom to inform us of the results, he gave the other boy a 'Good job! Well done!' speech, and then looking me up and down (and in front of the other boy) came out with an unnecessarily curt: "You didn't deserve an A," and, leaving it at that, walked straight out. I don't know how he came to that particular conclusion: As far as I was concerned, I had studied as seriously as the other guy, and much more importantly, I had got an A. So what exactly was the problem?

Right the way though my life, and even now, I have struggled to understand why the above sequence of events occurred as they did. The strapping I can, in one sense, understand – the need for someone in my position to 'follow rules' and 'set an example' – but that said, a strapping being the highest form of punishment that could be administered apart from suspension or expulsion, a quick admonishment and apology on my side would surely have been sufficient, my offense being no more than to cross the corridor (a total of ten paces) at an angle to reach the foot of the staircase (we were supposed to walk straight and then turn at a right angle), and no other students being present at the time.

However, in the end, for me this series of events became an example of the type of actions/attitude that I chose not to copy, and hopefully I became a little better teacher into the bargain.

"Shaming or demeaning do not automatically equate with the acceptance of authority. Neither does a forced application of pedantry."

[2.16] Learning to respect people rather than their titles.
Martin:

"Circumstances (/the social construct) can at times draw you in far more rapidly than might be expected, and not always in a manner that you might choose."

Lacking confidence, the head boy didn't know how to relate to junior students and/or express his authority other than by leveraging his official title, using his position as a form of self-protection, a wall or barrier, and the younger students recognised that and read it as arrogance. This is a reality that runs right through to the topmost echelons of society, where the most casual of observations will bring you to people who are lacking the required breadth of experience and/or are in some manner not fully rounded, and thus have to rely on their ranks or titles to command attention, as against others who, regardless of their position in society, have long outgrown the need to impress. I wouldn't in any sense blame Martin himself. He was, as I said, a good friend and wasn't in any way arrogant, and he could certainly not be held in any manner responsible for his father's occupation. It was simply a matter of the job requiring a certain 'character' or 'attitude' which he had not at the time had the opportunity to cultivate (that, or it was not in his nature), and he was managing the best he could. That said, I do wonder now how it would have affected him to occupy that position for say three or four years rather than the just one? – how long it might've taken him to actually become hardened into the role of the (extremely unattractive) person he appeared to be?

[2.17] Hotel work:

Just short of seventeen, my parents took me down to the Isle of Wight (IOW) on the south coast, where, through an agency, I was introduced to a job washing-up in the kitchen of a rather large and very pleasant residential hotel on the south side of the island. (My mother's cousin lived in the centre of the island at the time, which presumably was the reason the place was chosen.) The work itself was not in any sense hard, except perhaps that I had to be up early in the morning to clear away any dishes that had built up after I had finished my work the previous evening; that and keeping the glasses and silver cutlery clean. The (mainly young Spanish and Italian) staff all got on well together, except for one occasion when the other washer-up blamed me for a set of glasses that he hadn't cleaned properly, and I had to stand up for myself. However, having handled the dishes and cooking utensils for fifty to sixty meals three times a day for a full summer, washing-up never ever again posed a problem for me, and rather, as I got older, I found it a very good, simple way to release tension – always different but always the same: producing some sense of order in a chaotic universe.

The next three years (this was before New York), I worked as a waiter; two seasons in a small boarding house (M), just off the seafront, run by two sisters (with occasional help from their husbands), and the final year in a very beautifully situated three-star residential hotel that was on the verge of collapsing (at one point the service got so bad that the guests went on strike). This was not the staff's fault – the reality only coming out little by little throughout the summer – but rather that the owner had died recently and his wife had taken to drink (late one night, I found her in the kitchen making a desperate attempt to climb over the barred-up counter to get at a bottle of whiskey that her daughter had hidden there to keep it out of her way), leaving the daughter (who had no real interest in the place – she was off all day horse-riding) to fill in as and how she could. The daughter could create the most beautiful desserts (with each creation being whipped up to order), but as the summer went on, the dining-room staff learned to dread the nights she was on duty, as she invariably came in late (in one case, over an hour, resulting in the above-mentioned strike) and we invariably had to calm the guests down each time it happened.

(Working first in my father's shops, and then in hotels and restaurants, my whole upbringing required me to present an 'agreeable' face to the world. Later, in Japan, I did fairly quickly find that in the wrong circumstances, this can be misunderstood as a sign of pliability or even weakness.)

Satu:

Satu, who I worked with in the dining room in my second summer on the island, was the ultimate Swedish blonde bombshell; tall, beautifully proportioned, and with long, straight blonde hair falling down close to her waist, and drawing eyes wherever she went. She also had a lovely character to match, and the next spring I visited her in Stockholm where, in a short week, she taught me how a proper diet (lots of raw – I specifically remember the cauliflower – and par-cooked vegetables) could lead to a neat bowel movement three times a day, and her (newlywed) husband taught me how to fish through holes in the ice.

Festivals:

Every community on the island held a summer festival with a parade, and the two summers I was at the M, the staff got together with our guests to see if we could produce something for fun. Essentially, both years, we produced a set of (rather terrible) visual puns. The first year the theme was tires, with Satu very arrestingly resting on one tire that had been attached to the hood of the owner's jeep (our main 'float', no other decorations required) – naturally holding the placard "Satired" – and with myself dressed in pyjamas and top hat and tire suspended around the waist ("Well-attired"), etc., etc., and the second year, we all became beans: I was a (thickly made-up) "Bile-Bean" (personally, a favourite role) – taking swills of dirty green water from a bottle carried at my side, which I then, after sufficient rolling of the eyes, wild wanderings and vague graspings at the stomach, spewed up into the gutter in front of whichever group of onlookers seemed closest to panicking. This is one area that I was good at, and actually improved on as I got older. (Zombies hadn't yet been invented, but the principle is the same.) The first year, the judges didn't have a clue about what we were at, but then spread out along the parade route, we proved very popular, and the second year we very proudly carried off the top prize.

Crabs:

When you are young and desperate to meet someone (/anyone), you get very little choice as to who you get to link up with, and in my hometown when I was 14 and 15, the only man who would come near me wasn't anyone I would have normally gone for, but on the few occasions we met, he would at least approach and let me touch him. He also had a habit, each time accompanied with a knowing smile, of very strongly rubbing his crotch against mine, which at the time (/my age), although it seemed a little odd, I had no means of fathoming: It was certainly nothing that I enjoyed, but presumably he was getting something from it. And then the itching began, and I discovered that those small darkish marks around the base of my longer hairs could be peeled away, and, with some shock, that they had the tiniest of legs that wriggled on one's fingertip and were in fact alive. However, with a certain persistence, to the best of my ability they were picked off and cleared. Until their eggs hatched, and I had to repeat the process. (Or I had met the same man. At this time, I hadn't made the connection.) And this went on repeatedly until, in my third year on the island, I went swimming in mid-September on a very cold and windy day – it was the thrill of breaking through the high waves that kept me in the water – and I came out with my whole torso literally blue. And they were gone.

(Much later, in Japan, having being obliged to cheek-dance with the owner of a lesbian bar in town [14.3], I found myself with the same problem of lice burrowing in behind my ears (she had very thick matted hair, making me seriously later wonder if it ever got washed), but fortunately I was now of an age where I knew to go to the local pharmacy, and with a medicated powder recommended and quickly purchased, they were gone with one shake.)

[2.18] A summer affair:

Shortly up from the entrance to the three-star hotel where I was working in my final year, there was small, roadside public convenience, normally much too close to my work for me to even consider going in there, but the one time I did (I was on my day off and was actually walking up to the bus stop), I met Paul (mid-forties), the joint owner together with his Australian partner, Brian, of a very smart and successful residential hotel along the coast, who immediately took me there to be introduced (they were open about having other relationships), and where I was shortly 'wined and dined' along with the regular guests. After the meal, I was then driven out way along the coastal road to a short promontory, where he parked his car and we followed a path down the slope to his 'spot' – presumably where he took all his assignments. A picnic rug was spread, and we again drank wine. It was suitably – the intention being highly 'romantic' – a moonlit night (my memory? – at least on one of the occasions we were there), and I do remember lying with my head in his lap singing love songs. However, beyond that, I do know that there was very little that actually happened between us, and although I didn't make the connection at the time, there was in fact a strong similarity between the relationship here and the one with the professor in Oxford. I was there (/existed?) to suitably impress and simultaneously to be suitably impressed, quite who or to whose benefit I am not sure even now. At one point, he asked me whether the owner at the first hotel where I had worked on the island had slept with me: Apparently, he was well known for his appreciation of young men (I remember Dino, the young Italian waiter who I shared a caravan with there that year as classically beautiful), and with me being just sixteen at the time, it had been generally assumed that I had also been hired for the purpose. He hadn't. To my mind he was merely a married man with a lovely wife and the sweetest of five-year-old daughters. However, with Paul being the only gay person I had actually made any contact with on the island right through the four years, to find that I had been 'news' on the island circuit from that far back was, all things considered, a little disturbing.

And then, in the autumn, both of us being in London at the same time one weekend and having agreed to meet him for the short time our schedules overlapped, for no reason that I can understand even now, I withdrew (/recoiled): I simply could not bear the idea of him touching me. I could not even take his hand to shake it when he approached me at the station. The illusion (/fantasy/ make-believe/ idealisation) – whatever it was that had been there, had gone and been replaced by this rather short, puffy, puffed-up older man with a line moustache and overly fashioned goatee – the latter something that has, in projecting that certain type of personality (/artifice/ artificiality), served as a warning signal to me ever since – and suddenly he physically revolted. And having nothing more to do, we could only say goodbye.

Even today, any projection of myself in that situation; the attention paid to the simple laying of a car rug ("The Grass is Greener"), the plying of the wine ("Cleopatra"), and more than anything my own rather bathetic attempt at emotional presentation (the minstrel to the cause in any movie worthy of the name) tends to draw shudders to my imagination. But in that it did help me to determine what I wasn't (and now being far more conscious of the fact that a considerably large proportion of life's experience is in this vein), it has been given its due.

And as one final twist, quite how we negotiated the above situation I am not sure, but we did in fact over the years all become friends, and I ended up visiting and exchanging letters with them until the both of them died, this now being some years ago.

[2.19] Finding something to do with my life:

Circumstances prescribed early on in life will naturally, depending upon what you are aiming for, result in accepting certain limitations. My mother (with my teacher's support) would've liked me to become a pianist, which, turning out as I did (a high proportion of pianists – for heaven knows why – being gay, as I was informed at one point), would probably have been a perfect match. I actually got as far as coming in middling-well in a regional contest when I was 13–14, but after seven or eight years of study, still not having any full confidence in my ability to read the music fluently, and no one informing me at the time that a lot of the world's top pianists actually get there by putting more trust in their hearing than their eyes, I decided that I would put my future elsewhere, and there not seeming much point in continuing lessons, I chose to quit.

Job hunting at university: The only company that stood out for me in the job manual we received was Cathy Pacific in Hong Kong, in large part because I had the Far East in mind as a destination. Also, being put in charge of two hundred employees as initial training appealed: Dealing with people was something I had confidence that I could handle, but naturally that was not enough. Also, from quite a young age, I had had the idea that I should become a teacher – mathematics, naturally, being the initial choice, and actually, with the help of the Peruvian member of the postgraduate group at college (on the condition that I passed my finals) obtained the offer of a job in Peru. And for the record, for whatever reason (but indicating that there was something on that side pushing to get out), I wrote to one of the larger producers of crystal glass in the Midlands (they even interviewed me) to let them know that I was interested in design work for engraved glass. It was only many years later, watching a series of interviews of young men (still eighteen) being interviewed for Oxford in a documentary on Japanese television, with every one of them expressing very clear objectives about their future life plans, that it really hit me as to quite how deficient my approach had been at the time.

Ending up in Japan involved a certain degree of serendipity – a summer job extended into a ten-month sojourn teaching English to Air Force cadets in Saudi Arabia, a short stint as a hotel-manager trainee in London, with the rhythm (/the desire to make a go of it) fortunately broken by a two-week stay in hospital to drain and heal an extremely painful cyst that appeared at the base of the groin – apparently caused by the excessive heat and humidity in SA – followed by a desperate jump out of the frying pan into the fire to attempt a seven-day training course to become an encyclopaedia salesman, of which, quickly understanding that foot-in-the-door sales were not for me, I managed three days. And then, luckily spotting an ad put out by a language school looking for teachers to send to Japan, after a short spell of teaching in London, I arrived here just in time for the opening of the World Fair in Osaka. And on and on… until seventy.

In retrospect, I'm sure that I could have made it either as a mathematics teacher or hotel manager, but in either case I almost certainly would not have had the independence that I have managed here, and particularly not getting into school teaching, which (understanding my own weaknesses during my time at grammar school) could have involved certain embarrassments, in the end made a lot of sense.

Chapter 3
Saudi Arabia (and a Visit to Iran)

[3.1]

Saudi Arabia was originally intended as a final, 12-week summer job, before graduating and hopefully starting a career teaching mathematics in Peru. However, failing my finals and unable to see any future going back to another year of nothing, at the end of the summer, I extended my contract and stayed on for close to a full year.

About 40 of us – part of an American, British, and Saudi government effort to develop the Saudi Arabian Air Force – were there to teach English (from six in the morning to noon, six days a week) to some 350 young Saudi recruits literally taken out of the desert, with no apparent knowledge of anything. They would later be trained by British Air Force personnel to become ground forces, engineers, etc. (Upper-level trainees; future officers and pilots, were sent to the US.)

Life for the teachers was not in any sense difficult (we actually only taught four hours each morning), and after lunch at the mess each day, those of us who wished to go were bussed out to a local bay with crates of Coca-Cola – immediately immersed in the sea in an attempt to preserve what remained of the chill – and then picked up again in the evening to return to the base for dinner and table tennis, or an evening walk to the airport building (there being little else to do). In contrast, the cadets had six hours of lessons every morning, and afternoons and most Sundays were taken up with military training.

Although the bay (essentially a bottlenecked inlet) was of a considerable size, neither it nor the surrounding area had anything that would lead you to recommend it: there were no trees or buildings or other signs of life; no road – only the tire tracks of our transport vehicle where it ran up and turned each day, and a flat expanse of sand spreading out in all directions as far as the eye could see. And the water; ever still, with never even the slightest of waves, and – other than along a narrow ledge that was no more than a metre and a half at its widest running around its edge – dark and murky deep, did not seem in any way availing. None of us swam far out: More than anything it was the excessive heat which prevented any overly strenuous activity, but also we had been warned about poisonous sea snakes, and on my third or fourth day out, after finding a small but intensely vigorous member of what I assumed to be the species winding along at my side, other than for the occasional but essential cooling-off dips, which at a push could be managed on the ledge, for the most part, I stayed out. Still, determined to enjoy life as we could, we faithfully went out every day and spread our towels, talked as we would about nothing in particular, and sipped at our warm bottles of Coca-Cola until the last one was gone and we could then respectfully retreat to the evening cool.

Perhaps the only true event of record here throughout the whole summer occurred in the late August, when we arrived to find the ledge alive with a dark, silvery ribbon of motion; a thick, unbroken column of small fish fry (each roughly 15–18 cm) all headed west around the perimeter of the bay, presumably as yet too young and afraid to enter the deeper waters. I reckoned that if they had chosen to cross the neck of the inlet, they could have cut at least a day off their journey. (But then again, I couldn't have vouched for how many of them would've made it, so perhaps they had made the right choice.) Any attempt to block their movement was inevitably met with a brief hesitation – a stir of confusion – before, with a nervous switch of their tails, they would venture out just far enough to enable them to relocate and dart back to the shelf beyond our position. And we played with them through the early afternoon – until they tired of us and we let them be. But they were still there in the evening when we left. And the next day when we arrived. And the next; crowding the ledge, with no sign of a break, for at least 10 to 12 days; hundreds of thousands of restless migrants – until, just as suddenly as they had arrived, they were gone. And the summer was over.

[3.2] Base life:

The base was an expanse of low, drab barrack buildings, and teaching was initially done in prefabricated blocks of single rooms. (They were still building what was to become the administrative centre.) The only exception here was the very small but elegant airport terminal building [4] itself, which had been completed only a few years earlier and presumably was an indication of what the country was to become. All meals were taken in the mess, and curry nights (the kitchen crew all being Indian), when they went overboard with the huge trays of 'extras' to be sprinkled on the main dish (crushed boiled eggs, coconut flakes, dried fruits of every variety, and a whole range of pickles) were events not to be missed.

The only tension on the base, if you could call it that, came from the military/civilian divide. All English teaching staff were initially expected to wear a formal tie and jacket provided by the Air Force administration. This was in midsummer with temperatures of well over 40 degrees Centigrade and, as we were very close to the coast, extremely high humidity, meaning that the moment we stepped out of our (still most rudimentary of) classrooms, we were instantaneously drenched in sweat. Who we were there to impress, I am not sure, but thankfully the older teachers – not being of a military mindset – were not having it, and it took them no more than a quick run-around to get us into short sleeves with open necks. And later on, when the administration office threatened to refuse to renew my initial summer contract unless I promised never to again wear my thobe and rhutra (Arab robe and headdress) that I had purchased for fun and taken to wearing in the evening (shades of "Lawrence of Arabia" and/or "A Passage to India" – "'going native' and all that"), without saying anything, they stepped in again and, though apparently it required the threat of a strike, won the day. Shortly after, a number of us moved off the base into the local town to make way for the next batch of newcomers, so in the end it was not that much of a victory, but just once I had the pleasure of wearing it (to cheers!) in the mess. I would note here that the Arab officials had no objection to my dress, but they did note, quite correctly, that they would appreciate it if I put a little more energy into learning the language. Unfortunately, other than for the very basics, this is not something I got into, and all serious studies had to wait until I got to Japan.

---

[4] The Dhahran Air Terminal: Designed by a Japanese architect (Minoru Yamasaki) combining traditional Islamic forms with modern technology, its primary purpose was to serve international traffic, particularly for Arabian American Oil Company (Aramco) personnel based in the Dhahran area traveling to and from Europe and the United States. It still exists and is now known as the Royal Saudi Air Force; King Abdulaziz Air Base.

[3.3] Developing a new relationship with time:

Time in Saudi was extremely slow moving and at the same time a highly passive construct – something to be submitted to rather than manipulated to one's advantage. In reality, that is in terms of its (what I had been brought up to assume normal) relationship with the hands of a clock or watch, one could perhaps describe it as non-existent. Best indicating this concept would be the word "Inshallah" ("If God so wills it.") – one of the first Arabic expressions I learned upon my arrival in the country – which I quickly found inserted into just about any sentence involving future activities. Similar in concept to the Italian "Que sera, sera," and even more so the Japanese "Naru mono wa naru sa," ("Whatever is going to happen is going to happen,") in terms of actual usage, it perhaps came closest to "If things turn out that way," which I could actually understand if one was planning to meet out in the middle of the desert, but not referring to a 300-yard walk to a coffee shop in the airport lounge, which happened to be the first occasion on which I came up against its nuances.

Receiving an invitation from a group of my students to meet them in the afternoon of the following day, and having hung around for so long and with nobody arriving, I had simply left it at that, until three weeks later, happening to be in the same area, the three of them walked up and, in the most natural of manners, came out with a, "Oh, good. You are here," whereupon we all sat down for a coffee. And regardless of an original questioning of the situation – just quite what was going on here? – I did find myself pulling in (/slowing down), particularly in regard to any question of immediate expectations. And as the weeks and months moved on, certainly to a degree I would not have expected, I found myself (if not strictly acknowledging) at least adjusting to the reality: "It didn't really matter." "If it was meant to happen, it would."

[3.4] Further encounters with nature:

As a child, watching "The Living Desert", which, with its staged battle between tarantula spider and wasp (the wasp in this case winning and getting to lay its eggs on the dead carcass) and the final scenes when the rains came and the whole desert bloomed in slow-motion, all set to classical music, was in many senses a revelation. The film being set in quite another (South African) desert, naturally I was in a separate world (and there was no music), but it was a desert, and it did have its own points of fascination.

A short scare:

Walking into the terminal building late one evening to get myself a taxi into town, I found myself face-to-face with what I quickly realised was an oversized scorpion – a good 30 cm in length, this with its extra-large sting fully raised – moving back and forth at full speed. The area outside the building was completely dark, and presumably the creature had been drawn in (and possibly trapped) by the contrasting brilliance of the outdoor spotlighting in the area of the taxi stand – whatever, it was moving in a highly erratic manner. (In one of the "Indiana Jones" movies, he notes that it is only the small scorpions that are truly poisonous, and this I saw confirmed in a TV programme where a naturalist is digging out a nest of the tiniest, and apparently highly dangerous, of creatures from between the cracks in a stone wall in the English countryside – up to this point, it had never occurred to me that we might even have scorpions in England.) However, at this moment, not in a position to sit back and take stock of the situation (this was my first brush with a scorpion of any kind, and even out in the desert, I would have expected nothing of this size), I swerved back and across into the alternative entrance on the darkened side of the traffic island, where I was able to calm myself a little. It would take me that little bit longer to get around to the stand, but with a bit of luck it would have left by then, or a taxi would have pulled in and scared it out of the way. And naturally (and here we could have been in an Indiana movie), halfway in, I found it coming at me from the opposite direction, zigzagging across the road and up onto the pavement, and then back again, seemingly countering every move I tried to make to avoid it. And again I retreated, back around to the lit entrance (it had returned), until it finally got to me that my best move might be not to – which in fact worked – and apparently without any further do, it scuttled its way out into the darkness.

[3.5] A trip to Riyadh:

Taken in a rented taxi with two or three of the other recent graduates, other than the road itself, which provided a single, straight, and dusty connection between the two cities (it was as if the two points had been connected by a ruler on the map), I have only two memories from this trip, and of the two, the first was most definitely of more interest.

Hot springs exist in many countries, but a short walk off the main road between Dhahran and Riyadh, there was what must be a considerably rare combination of cold-spring and hot-spring rising literally side-by-side out of the desert sand. Divided into two separate pools, they had become a weekend attraction for the locals, with the cold pool occupied by the children and younger members of the family while the older women used the heated water, which was far too hot for bathing, to wash the family's clothes and other articles in. We were only there long enough to test the reality with our own hands, but the scene has stayed with me very clearly right up to this time.

Riyadh: Our entrance to the capital was made in the early evening, with my only recollections being of the tall, dark, sandstone walls of the houses – their enclosing height blocking our view in every direction; that and the unpaved streets completely devoid of any life other than the packs of feral dogs ferreting in the corner grime (we did not see one human being in the place). But then, with even them ignoring our presence – presumably determining us to be the strangers we were, they showed no interest in our car at all – we returned the sentiment and settled on a fast retreat to Dhahran.

In hindsight, all I can really say here is that we were very young and other than to express a sense of 'adventure', we did not really have any idea why we had set off in the first place. Even before we left, we were fully aware that, as non-Muslims, the religious sights would be totally off-limits, and thinking now I doubt that there would have been much else of any particular attraction in the area. I don't in any sense regret going there (and I did enjoy the pools), but at the same time one side of me wonders why.

[3.6] Winter:

Winter, if it could be called that, brought temperatures down into the early thirties, which, together with a slight drop in the humidity, became a welcome source of relief.

The entrance to my apartment in town had a fairly high (40 cm) concrete 'step', which one had to lift one's leg over to get into what would be understood as the entrance hall, which was on exactly the same level as the stairs' landing outside. This was standard in all buildings, and although it initially did seem a little odd, it was very quickly accepted as part of the 'local ambience'. Being on the third floor, a short walk would get me up onto the open rooftop, which was shared by the building community as an open space for drying clothes or for small children to play safely (there was more than one staircase). Also, it being easy to cross over from one building to the next, it could as necessary be used by the upper-level residents as a convenient (and perhaps more private) alternative to the street below.

And then, in mid-December, with no warning whatsoever, the rains came; one long, unrelenting downpour that lasted for days (/weeks?) on end, and as the building staircase became a conduit for all the excess water that was accumulating on the roof, with it came a somewhat fuller appreciation of 'local ambience'. (During this whole period, my door opened out on to a heavily cascading waterfall, which without those 'steps' would have left my own and every other apartment in the building flooded for the duration.) And then just as suddenly, it was gone, leaving nothing but wide areas of standing water – unfortunately, no desert flowers, just thick, muddy pockets to be navigated seemingly endlessly, until nature took its course, and they were cleared by the once-again rising heat.

[3.7] A 'man's world':

The idea of Arab men being promiscuous was instilled very early on in my brain. Morocco was the country always referred to, but it turned out that Saudi was no exception in this regard. Very few appeared gay in the sense that we understand it in the West[5] – sex was for the most just that, with no or very little emotional involvement – but a large number of them were clearly opportunists in the field: women were not available, and we were providing an alternative outlet for their urges. Taken from the viewpoint of an outsider, it might be considered that we were in some sense 'objects of disdain' – but this was, certainly not in the large part, actually so. It was a convenience on both sides, a pastime – presumably one that had been going on long before any of us arrived and would continue long after we were gone. And in many senses (certainly in terms of numbers available), we were the ones in control: On the whole, we could pick and choose as we wished, which, each according to our preferences, is exactly what we did.

---

[5] For the record, there was one younger man, just one, who very urgently wanted me to use him (presumably, he had been trained into the role), but unable to react to him, I could do nothing but turn him down. At the time, I assumed that it was because I had, since arriving in the country, established myself into a passive role, but thinking since, it is much more likely that it was the pleading, almost begging, look in his eyes, even as I left him, that made any physical reaction to him impossible.

[3.8] Dealing with the authorities:

A record:

The following is (I would hope) very much 'the world as it was,' but may be of interest to those who have trouble dealing with officialdom even today, wherever they might be around the world.

Considering the outcome, I am still not sure why, but I wrote asking Andy to send me a recording of "Hallelujah Baby", the black musical I had seen in New York, the arrival of which was heralded with a notification that I should apply at the base authority to arrange for customs clearance, which I duly did. Directed to a small office, I identified the package and explained the contents. Papers were completed and signed, a stamp affixed and validated, a small payment was made, and then I was told to take the package and document down the corridor to a second office, where essentially the above process was repeated (except that I do remember not having to pay anything at this particular stop). And then onto a third and then fourth office, where with a final payment and a flourish of the pen, it seemed that we were through, until I was again handed the package together with what was now a small pile of documents to be taken to the central customs office in Dammam, a one-hour trip away by taxi. Again, a series of repeat performances in yet another five or six offices before I was instructed to return to the base, where with three or four more approvals, I finally officially received my package. Irrespective of the time wasted, totalling up the different payments made in the separate offices together with the cost of the taxi rides, I worked out that just getting the package into the country had cost me far more than the price I had paid for the record itself. And if I remember correctly, I don't think I had a record player to play it on at this time, making it not the best of moves.

"The case of the attempted rape":

I was on my way up to the mess in the evening – the sky heavily overcast, so I am guessing this must have been at some point in the rainy season. There were three of them, one an officer, a short man who I had known very well from the beginning (he was everywhere on the base), and two others, one of whom was very tall and who I had never seen before. And the officer indicated that I should join them, and then, having done so, turn around. Knowing that it was not in anyone's best interests for me to do anything other than obey (the police had absolute power on the base), I did as I was told. (I would note here that this whole thing happened in a very good-natured manner, and, in the end, it amounted to a very amusing incident.) However, seemingly two of them wanted to watch, and I guess the tall man, who was supposed to perpetrate the act, had been dragged into the matter more on the spur of the moment than by design. At the same time, they, rather than myself, were putting themselves on the line, as we were just off one of the main streets on the base, fully in the open, and anyone could have walked up on us. And personally, I was determined that nothing they wanted to happen was going to, and I simply tightened myself up and bided my time. And not too much later, realising that they were not going to get the show they wanted, they gave up, and following a general round of apologetic laughter, I continued on up to the mess for my evening meal.

There was actually a sequel to this, when the tall man turned up at my apartment door a week or so later with a full erection under his thobe. And now understanding why they had wanted to watch, I let him in.

Drink:

Consumption of alcohol was another "No, no" that actually was, under the right circumstances, permitted. It hadn't to be done in public, and also not to the degree that it couldn't be overlooked. Right from the start, we were advised off the local Arab-produced 'hooch' – rumoured capable of sending you blind – and even the better-quality liquor distilled in Aramco (the then American-controlled oil drilling company) wasn't drinkable unless heavily diluted with Coke, and other than the odd session in the barracks right at the beginning, it not seeming worth the effort or the subsequent, inevitable, rotten hangover, for the most part I kept away.

I do remember, rather later, an Officers Club for the base administration's senior personnel being set up in town and, by all accounts, all the town's top officials (naturally including the chief of police) being invited to partake of the liberally served whiskey and other alcoholic drinks at the opening party, and presumably there were the requisite nods and winks, and everyone enjoyed the evening. And they could still arrest you when it suited their purpose.

Peter:

Particularly if you are tanned and slim, and this being one of the few times in my life when I was both, there is nothing that can make you feel more attractive on a cool evening walking up to the mess than a light, long-sleeved cashmere sweater worn directly to the skin. And Peter (recruited the previous summer from Cambridge), who I was with that evening, presumably picked up on this, coming out with a (very shocked): "Geoff, you are sexy!" This was not the beginning of any type of relationship – nothing more than a recognition of who we were – but given the right circumstances, we could have become good friends. Unfortunately, shortly afterwards, he crashed his motorbike on his way into town and was subsequently arrested – not for the crash itself, but rather for the bottle of whiskey found strapped behind his seat, and three or four months later, at the time I left the country, the personnel on the base were still trying to get him released from prison so that he could be sent home. It wasn't that I envied him, but even so, I couldn't get over the idea that he (or, at any rate, the police) might be enjoying his extended stay.

[3.9] Learning how to teach. "To Sir with Love."

To anyone who has seen the Sidney Poitier movie, or any of the many similar 'teacher-steps-in-to-turn-a-bad-class-around' movies, the following will be an automatic – the teacher providing an opening; unclogging the pipe to restore the natural flow. However, the experience here did manage to instil a strong dose of self-confidence as to my own capabilities as a teacher, and also in time made me far more aware of the potential of those who, for various reasons, have difficulty finding their path during their youth (many do get left behind), and as such, in terms of my overall teaching career, it was an invaluable experience. Also, from the students' viewpoint, it can be read as one more example of the luck of the draw.

Around five to six months before the end of the year-and-a-half course that all students were enrolled in, I found myself rotated to a position as assistant teacher to the bottom class in a group of a total of 350 students. I would guess that their class teacher, who taught them four lessons each morning as against my two, was a retired professional teacher of English. He himself was a very pleasant person, but I quickly recognised that there were clearly problems in the way he was handling the class, the main point being that, with his personal manner of teaching and testing, he had managed to elevate the one student who was in fact the weakest in the whole group to the position of top of the class, thus turning off the other ten or so students, none of whom were making any effort whatsoever, and at least a couple of whom were immediately obvious to me as having very good minds. After a certain amount of observation and having no problems at all with teaching the students myself, I took the matter to the central office, and after pointing out the problems, got them to allow me to take over the class.

It then took a couple of fast lessons to bring them over to my side; one to dethrone the top student – the others had to be shown very clearly that he wasn't (which was naturally hard on him, but very necessary) – and one to get them under my personal control, the latter being done by giving a quick clip over the back of the head to the class leader, who was fooling around with another student when he should have been listening. This actually did momentarily stop him until, clearly giving the matter a second thought, he came out with a: "You can't do that to me. I am a Muslim!" and "I am going to report you to our commanding officer," which I fully agreed with, and also told him that I would tell his commander exactly what he been doing (i.e., grabbing in at another student's crotch) to provoke my action, whereupon, point made, we all got along very well. And some months later in the final English examinations, the class leader, who was also the really clever one, ended up in the top fifteen, with one more student in the top fifty, followed by a third, who turned out to be middling in English but a natural learner at mathematics (which I also taught them during the last three months).

[3.10] Tears:

"Desert Song" was one of the more romantic musicals that I saw as a child and the following is my own personal (grown-up) Saudi version.

One night early on, on the base, I was taken to an area of barracks quite apart from the ones I had visited previously and there led to a rather more senior officer's room, considerably larger than the ones I had been in previously. Nothing was said. The younger man who had taken me, simply nodded to his superior and then left. (Presumably, this had been done before.) And, understanding that this was what was intended, we went to bed and had sex and I left. I don't remember that any words were said at all, but he was both facially and physically attractive and I do remember that he very much treated me with a careful respect, and in any another situation (he clearly had his position to consider), I would have asked to see him again without any hesitation.

And life went on. I passed the man who had initiated the introduction regularly on the base and we would exchange greetings and nothing more. (I'm fairly certainly that he was into a more serious relationship with one of the other teachers who I saw him with quite often.) And again, with too much living to do, particularly after I left the base and moved into town, the event was forgotten.

And then the time came for me to leave, and I am not quite sure how it came about, but it must have been only very shortly (in the last week?) before my flight out, the young man found me on the base and took me once again to the same room. And he was there, and we went to his bed, and I lay under him.

I have encountered only a few, truly warm, generous (/loving) moments of this type in my life, but this was one of them. And knowing that this was it – that with almost 100% certainty I would never see him again in my life – I, too, cried.

[3.11] "The closest thing to heaven." A side trip to Iran:

This was a very short (two and a half day) trip – starting at Shiraz airport in the south and then moving straight up north through Esfahan to the capital, Tehran – made at the suggestion of Bob and Terry (Bob was the man who was chiefly responsible for getting us out of ties and jackets when we first arrived, and also getting me rehired when I had had the problem with my thobe. And with all of us living in town, by this time we had become good friends.)

Coming from the desert of Saudi, with its religion's strict prohibition of the representation of all living things, be it flora, fauna or in human form (Saudi stamps at the time substituted with pictures of oilwells), Iran, with its abundance of art forms, was for me a deep and soothing, crystal-clear pool. From the start, I understood that what I was actually observing was Persian, but that this could also be an Islamic country (Saudi was my first experience of a Muslim country and I had no understanding of Sunni-Shiite differences at this time), I found something close to astounding.

I had already found (and been fascinated by) a small-sized, fine-silk Iranian carpet that I had seen in the window of one store along our shopping street in Dhahran – a pure work of art – which if I had in the end bought (I seriously considered the matter) would have cost me close on my full earnings for the period I was working there, and now I discovered miniature paintings on brooches and bracelets that (particularly in the high price range) were beyond belief. (Japan also has a tradition of miniature paintings on the inner side of shells, but this is one area where they do not even begin to come close in beauty or detail.) And then there were the mosques, which were a riot of colour. Over the course of my life, I have learned to celebrate beauty in all its forms – both natural and manmade, and in Iran the creative forces of the human mind were on shockingly full display.

On the road (we hired a car and driver at the airport), there was glass after glass of ice-cold, freshly squeezed lime juice, which I very quickly learned to drink without any added sugar, and stands selling mutton kebab, sliced to order from the spit, and the colourfully dressed and exceptionally beautiful women in the villages. The men, in contrast, for whatever reason, did not particularly attract, but I allowed this to pass as a matter of unfamiliarity.

Tehran: The high range of snow-covered mountains rising behind the city give Tehran its point of focus and, other than that, all I can really remember is the countless streams running beside every path in the city, every one of them glittering in the strong sunshine, which did not cease to fascinate even after Terry pointed out that they were in fact nothing other than open sewers, indicating a blob of brown excrement bobbing along with the current to make his point. (This, as with everything, was a matter of contrasts: I had never seen a flowing stream in SA, never mind one where the water sparkled, and regardless of any other reality, to me this is what they were, and how they stayed with me.)

And then there were the Shah's jewels.

At the time of our visit, the Shah Reza Pahlavi was still in power, and for whatever reason (how Bob obtained the information here I do not know), the three of us got into what amounted to a private viewing of the Crown Jewels. All I do recall is entering an oversized elevator in a rather drab building, which from its appearance I assumed was a bank, and following a very smooth descent, exiting into what was clearly a vault; an extremely large open room, all four walls enclosed in floor-to-ceiling glass sheets, with the upper sections subdivided to enable the creation of a series of showcases encircling the room. And occupying the centre, there must have been five or six rows of similar individual units.

Rising from the centre of the floor of each case, which would be at around waist height, there was an upright column of some 35 to 40 cm in height, on top of each of which was a padded display stand with its own crown, tiara, brooches, earrings and/or necklace combinations – every single one an example of brilliant craftsmanship. (In particular, I clearly remember a pair of elongated, emerald drop earrings with a matching pendant necklace, for which 'absolutely exquisite' would be an understatement. The emeralds were of such a size that I found it difficult to believe that a woman's ear would support their weight, but being on display as they were, presumably they had been worn at some point.) And then, just to make a point of the obvious, the bottom sections of every single case had been packed full of uncut stones – diamonds, sapphires, rubies, emeralds or whatever – presumably all somewhat casually poured in as an afterthought.

Having the whole floor to ourselves for well over an hour did make me wonder whether any of the Iranian populace actually got in there at any time but, either way, this apparently being nothing more than a minor example of the Shah's predilection for ostentation, it does not surprise me at all that there was a revolution some ten years later.

Equally, I will say that the experience left my brain sated to the extent that it spoilt me for the rest of my life with similar exhibitions, excessively crafted jewellery and large jewels (size not automatically equating with beauty) in particular no longer impressing.

The remains of Persepolis, the ceremonial capital of ancient Persia situated 60 km northeast of the city of Shiraz, which was actually our first stop, also affected me in a rather similar manner, but here it was the pristine condition of the bas-relief carvings – this well over 2,000 years after the work was originally completed (the lack of erosion apparently due to the peculiarities of the meteorological conditions in that area) – that pre-empted any desire to visit the ancient temples or pyramids in Egypt (every photograph of which I have seen seemingly promoting an image of deterioration) and in the end, rightly or wrongly, this is something I have never done.

"All learning invariably involves a certain element of loss – an inability to return to that previous state of 'unknowing innocence' – but exposure to a truly high level of perfection, where the mind subsequently rejects similar experiences as 'of lesser value' can, if not suitably tempered, eliminate what otherwise would be the simpler pleasures of everyday living."

Kochi Prefecture on the island of Shikoku has a particularly distinctive dish known as 'tataki' – thick segments of bonito fish with the outer layer repeatedly flame-roasted and then basted in a traditional sauce, imbuing it with a highly distinctive flavour (the inner section remains uncooked), prior to each segment being sliced and served with yet another sauce – and I was extremely fortunate (/unfortunate) to be exposed to the dish for the first time sometime in my thirties in a small 'minshuku' (B&B) in the very south of the prefecture. We were circling the island in the car and had arrived late in the area (it was already dark) without any booking and simply taken potluck with the closest place we could find. However, the lady was very welcoming and made us a delicious meal (we were the only guests) including the above tataki very proudly served with a homemade sauce including "thirteen different herbs and spices" (we were told five or six would be normal) which proved to be overwhelmingly delicious. And, although it is now available seemingly just about everywhere, I have not been able to really enjoy the dish since. I travelled with Kensuke on a similar route recently, and we ate in a local restaurant where we watched the owner roasting the fish in front of our eyes, which had him totally hooked, but although the dish was delicious, it still lost out to the memory, and now when he brings a portion home from the local supermarket and devours it, I leave it to him for his enjoyment.

In contrast, I have found similar experiences with natural beauty that much easier to handle. I have two (possibly three) photographs of sunsets selected from hundreds taken locally that still move me, but when I find an evening sky on a beach lacking interest (which would be the norm these days), in order to obtain pleasure from the scene, I do know to turn my eyes to the sand or, as needed, reference my other senses, which in the end is one way to keep moving forward. And occasionally, even now, I do find some new facet in the landscape that has the power to shock me anew.

And on the short flight back to Dhahran, I made up my mind: I was out. Life in Saudi was slow and easy, with an extremely limited workweek, food and lodgings provided and/or generously covered and – having nothing to spend it on – money piling up in the bank, but I had seen another world and understood what I was missing. I would hand in my notice, take a break back in England, and then see if I could find another job on the other side of the Gulf. The latter never happened (I sense Japan was in there all the time), but Iran and everything I had seen there had played its part: Without it, I could very likely still have been in Saudi even today.

The trip home: The above was followed by a six week wait for an exit visa, some fond goodbyes, and then a brief panic in the airport lobby when I had to throw out a third of my luggage (including, unfortunately, my thobe) to get my bag weight down to an acceptable level. And then we were in the air, and with a brief glance behind, it was all gone.

Finding myself with a short evening stopover in Lebanon, I came out of the airport with the intent of walking briefly into the town, but very quickly the oncoming darkness and the total lack of any apparent life along the dusty road – an echo of Riyadh without the dogs – frightened, and I turned back. It is a truth that (even today) I am not at my bravest on my own in unfamiliar territory.

Chapter 4
Young at Heart (Lives Intertwined)

[4.1]

Gail: "Aki says she wants to have a talk with you."

    Me: "Why would Aki want to have a talk with me?"

Gail: "She says it's about her and Derek."

    Me: "They had another fight?"

Gail: "No. Apparently he's proposed, and she's not quite sure what to do about it."

    Me: "But why would she want to talk to me? I hardly know her."

Gail: "She's worried about his family."

    Me: "Oh, OK. She's in today?"

Gail: "No. She's going to be in Osaka most of the week."

    Me: "OK. Whenever."

[4.2]

The language school that sent me over from England had three schools in Japan at the time; one in Tokyo, one in Osaka and the third, to which I had been assigned, just opened six months previously and rather smaller in scale, in Kobe, and I was replacing a teacher who had recently resigned. (Some months later, I found that he had been privately active in the gay community here, so it could be said to have been a fair swap.)

Myself included, the school had five core teachers; the somewhat older head teacher, Gordon, who shortly moved on to take a local university position, which he then kept for the rest of his life; Matt, a graduate of Cambridge, who eventually, after returning to England, became a behind-the-scenes coordinator for wide range of Japanese international television productions, and Gail, his half-Malaysian-Chinese, half-American wife (adopted and brought up in England), both of them around my own age; and finally Neil, who would be some ten years older than we were.

Neil was rapid thinker, so much so that with the workings of his mind vastly outpacing his verbal output, filling in the gaps to get a grasp of any point he was trying to make became something of an art form. He also was the real linguist in the group. Having lived in China for a number of years before coming to Japan, he had kanji (the Chinese ideographs, also used in written Japanese) at his fingertips before he even started here, and in time he became a professional translator working between French, Chinese, Japanese, Korean and English.

Based in a rather old building, owned by a Mr and Mrs Oka, which amazingly some 50 years later still exists, the atmosphere from the start was very friendly and open, with originally one receptionist (Yoko), later replaced by two younger women, Yukiko, and Yoshimi, both of whom, as is the case with the majority of the characters introduced in this section in one context or another, became lifelong friends. Mrs Oka was at heart an extremely independent woman: Taking it upon herself to join one of my first classes – "I needed students" – when the school closed, she became my official 'sponsor' (legal guardian), and also much later she had me teach English to her eldest son, Minoru, who would in time visit England with myself and my partner Koji. And from the start, when she had been listed as the joint president of her husband's company, she had decided to permit herself the privileges associated with the position, including the standard golf, travel and regular (four nights a week minimum) late-night drinking sessions, which in the end resulted in an overly early demise. However, shortly before this, in her early sixties, she was sighted in full Brazilian carnival dress, sambaing in a highly vigorous manner down Kobe's main festival route right behind the standard quota of Rio Carnival Queens who are brought over every year to head-up the final entry in the parade, so she in no way lost out on living.

Teaching (other than having to travel in and out to Osaka twice a week to take company classes), did not require any particular effort, except for the fact that the textbook we were obliged to use was exceptionally bad; so bad in fact that it was at this time that I determined to write my own material (which some 40 years later resulted in a full series of texts plus a – unfortunately, in the end, unpublished – 5,000-page comparative analysis of the English and Japanese spoken languages.) Regardless of the final outcome, this did provide me with enough interest in my work to allow me to continue right through to my retirement.

There was also a problem that quickly developed of us not (officially) being allowed to use Japanese in class. Matt, Neil and I were all studying the language, and we all very quickly came to understand that the easiest testing ground for the latest piece of vocabulary or structure we had picked up was with our students – in or out of the classroom. (Matt's wife, Gail, left the matter to him, until much later when she picked up the language by ear.) Our (proffered) excuse here was that it made teaching easier, and in fact, over time as we improved, this became a truth, but the school policy/key sales point being English-only lessons, when the situation leaked out, which over time it naturally did, it was not looked on kindly. The head of the school in Osaka (which, being based in a smart office building in the centre of the city, was a far more formal outfit altogether), was senior in position to our head teacher, and this in the end did cause a certain amount of friction. However, as a group, being that much more carefree in our approach to life, we did persevere – to the point that at the time the school was (for no immediately apparent reason) closed, this discretion was cited (/mumbled privately) as one of the reasons for the decision; our conclusion being that, regarded as a rather too independent bunch (which was in reality what we were), they wanted us out.

[4.3] The Nook:

The Nook was (by Japanese standards) a fairish-sized bar where Matt played the piano three or four evenings a week together with Greg, the resident singer/guitarist, a tall, slim (and until you got around to knowing him, seemingly cool) man with an Afro-cut that referenced his background, and from early on, it became a habit to walk around from the school after work and take up a position with Gail on one of the stools around the piano to have a couple of drinks before I made my way home. Greg was fluent in English, and he and Matt would sing a whole range of pop songs from Elvis and The Beatles onwards, and customers could make requests and on occasion sing along.

[4.4] 'Breaking up is hard to do.' (3) A necessary brawl:

Walking in, I found him seated at one end talking somewhat intensely with the man at his side, and there being no other seats in his vicinity, I walked along to the far end of the counter and ordered a beer. Having been in the place a number of times by now, the barman was very friendly, and we exchanged a few words in the best Japanese I could produce (this being still very early on in my stay), and in normal circumstances it could have been a pleasant evening. However, even before I had come in, I had recognised that the situation could not continue as it was and ordering a second and then third beer (for courage), and looking down along the bar only to see a back firmly turned against me (right the way through, he had made no attempt at all to acknowledge my existence), I decided that it was time for a reset in the relationship.

"I'd like my key back."

This was met by a rather stubborn silence, necessitating a further, "My key back!" stated in a very loud and unmistakable manner, at which point (with me having gained the attention of the whole bar) he had no choice other than to pass it to me. This was the spare key to my apartment, which I had rather foolishly given to him after asking him (the first gay man I had met in Japan, and this while walking along a darkened back street and totally without any consideration as to the realities of the situation – we had yet to even go to bed together) to come and live with me. And naturally it had not worked out; with him appearing and disappearing at will and me totally at a loss as to how to proceed. (At this point I had started to worry seriously about the possibility of money or other valuables disappearing while I was not at home.) However, the job was now done and, matter settled, I was free to go back to my seat.

The thrust of a large-sized (750 ml.) beer bottle breaking across the back of your skull is not easily describable as other than perhaps a 'muted thud', but the blood I found on my hand after carefully wiping it across the affected area was sufficient to indicate a fairly heavy blow. I had barely sensed him approaching, but now a quick look indicated that he was back in his seat and again fully immersed in his conversation with his neighbour, and with nothing else to be done (the cut clearly needing to be seen to), I paid my tab, took up my own bottle, walked along the short distance to where he was sitting and, with my best right-hand swing, returned the favour – following this up with a pleasant and equally polite "Goodnight" to all before I walked out. And that was it. Fortunately, it appeared he was not particularly liked in in town, and I never saw him again.

On the plus side here, he did introduce me to the local gay bars, and (in the first moments of elation) he also induced me to write a coming-out letter to my parents ("I have fallen in love and intend to be with him for the rest of my life!"), which my mother, correctly or otherwise, chose not to show to my father. Opportunities to come out with your parents being somewhat limited, and the letter being addressed to both of them, this did actually annoy me at the time. Exactly when or how my father became (/was made) aware of the reality of my existence was never really clear, but in the end, as was the case with just about everyone I knew, I left the matter to be assumed or otherwise. Also, as I had to get Gail away from her seat at the piano to help me out with the cut (it was running badly), it also involved a coming-out to both her and Matt. Even now, I do not remember the man's name, but (indicating the sometimes-strange workings of the world), when Matt came to visit Kobe a couple of years ago, he told me that he had met him on a number of occasions in the UK, where he has apparently been working as an interpreter for a considerable period of time now. He also noted that he was still something of an "odd fellow."

[4.5] Koji:

Very much after the fact, I was told that (as in the above case) I had invited just about everyone I slept with during this early period to come and live with me, but it seems the large majority had had the good sense not to take the invitation too seriously. However, there was – had to be – one who did.

(This was in all likelihood, a both quite distinct and contrasting consequence of my elementary school experience; the strong need for a certain level of stability in my life – someone to be with – that even today remains upward in my mind.)

Koji was based in Yokohama (near Tokyo), but on the night I met him, he was in Kobe to visit an American seaman friend who had suddenly had to be hospitalised here in the city. He himself at this time was working as a cook on cargo ships going between Japan and the US (he was a very good cook, originally trained in a Chinese restaurant), and as he told the story, he had spent three months in Montana with this friend and was seriously considering going to live with him in America. However, he came and stayed the night, and some two or three weeks later, when he came down again (the friend was hospitalised for quite some time), the process was repeated. And then there was a break of some three or four months, during which time I essentially forgot him, until late one night when he arrived on the doorstep, with no warning, carrying a small bag of clothes and a rather battered-looking lampstand, which he never explained but must have had some value for him. At least, we kept it safely for a considerable number of years until we found a suitable replacement in Thailand, and even then, I don't think it was thrown for quite some time.

There was, at the time, the inconvenience of having another (half-undressed) man in the apartment, and the fact that he had come up the coast taking well over an hour by train to be with me for the weekend, but this was dealt with a swift motion of the hand indicating the door, together with the admonition (direct translation); "This is not a place for a person like you (/of your level?) to be." And being rather smaller in stature than Koji was, he took the hint and left. (Koji was not particularly tall himself, but he had practiced judo when he was younger and his nickname from that time, as he proudly liked to tell me, was "mini tank", which is probably a fair description. And, as indicated by the below cases also, size is of importance in matters like these.)

The weekend over, I took him into the school in the morning and introduced him all round, and in the evening, we were at The Nook and seated around the piano as if it was the most normal place in the world to be. And, like it or not, I had got what I asked for.

[4.6] Acting out a part. Tears, laughter, and making your point:

Given encouragement, I have (possibly more than) a little of the closet exhibitionist in me that is clearly encouraged with the intake of alcohol – singing too loudly, stripping in public, and generally hamming things up; and on more than one occasion reacting to groups of entertainers begging for members of the audience to come up on the stage, and then when I have, getting a kind of 'Who asked you?' reaction.

One of Matt and Greg's favourite songs in the bar was an old folk/pop song, "I went to your wedding", describing a wedding ceremony attended by an ex-lover of the bride, who obviously still cares too much for her – ending up crying with her parents as she is given away. It was not a song I had ever heard before but, it being the parody version, it ended up with both parents and the ex-lover laughing, and it was invariably very funny. And occasionally, when we had people I knew at the piano, I would cover my eyes and pretend to cry and then at the end break into laughter, which was my, intended if not always appreciated, way of contributing to the entertainment. (Neither Matt nor Greg really liked customers joining in.)

And then, one evening, for whatever reason, I let myself be fully drawn into the part; my body slumping over onto the piano top, tears forming, until suddenly, without account, they were flooding down across my cheeks and totally unstoppable – this getting Gail worried enough to call over the barman to try and do something to help me, which he naturally couldn't, right until the last line ("Your mother was laughing…") when I, too, burst out into a raucous laughter. (Game over.)

Fifty years ago, women were not generally welcomed into gay bars, but this particular evening (this would be before Koji arrived), one woman did come in and sat up at the other end of the bar. The owner clearly knew her, and I was talking privately with a foreign friend, Robert, and naturally it did not occur to us to say anything, at least until she suddenly and for no apparent reason (we had given her no more than a quick glance as she came in) started spurting out obscenities in English, with us as the clearly intended targets. Not wanting to make any particular fuss, we initially ignored her, but then when she did not stop and neither the manager nor the younger barman were showing any signs of reacting (I don't actually think they knew what she was about), I stood and walked around the bar to try to speak with her, this only resulting in further obscenities and a very nasty leer, at which point I snapped, and wrapping the hair at the nape of her neck firmly around my hand, I dragged her head down to a point where it was touching the floor, and whispering into her ear, informed her that if I heard one more word of that nature directed at us, I would break her neck. And presumably she understood me. (Ditto.)

Two or three years later, in a separate (and far larger) bar, a much older, somewhat scruffily dressed man who had asked me for a dance suddenly started slandering Koji, who I was with that evening, in the nastiest of manners. ("He was a dirty, filthy, lowest of the low, scum-like form of existence, not to be trusted," and on and on until the music stopped, and I could walk away.) What initiated this outburst, I do not know? Koji claimed to have never met him before, and I hadn't, at least that I could recollect, but somehow, in the final analysis, I sensed the whole diatribe had in fact been more directed at me than Koji himself. And if the intent had been to cause me discomfort, he fully succeeded, and walking back to Koji, who was seated at a side-table right in the back corner of the bar, I suggested we leave, which we shortly did.

Walking back across the 'dance floor' – a rather awkwardly shaped space just large enough to allow a tight shuffle but not much more – we found the same man, legs casually crossed and seated at the corner table with a very self-satisfied smirk on his face. And smiling politely back (I am nothing less than a gentleman in these cases), and simultaneously letting my inner nature take its hold, I allowed my right foot to swing up against his lower shin, just enough to encourage his body to pivot forward and bring his face directly up against a conveniently placed fist. I then placed my hands carefully on his shoulders and returned him to his original position, where he sat in a rather dazed manner, the whole thing having happened so quickly that I doubt it had really registered. To any onlooker, it could have been that, momentarily dizzied – he was of that age – I had just saved him from a nasty fall. And that done, I joined Koji along the bar section where he was paying our tab, and then looking back, suggested to the bar owner that he might want to go and check on one of his older customers who appeared to be having a nosebleed. (There is no pleasure in having an evening spoiled.)

***

The fine line: And here we have what I later came to refer to as 'the fine line.' (Also, [6.16])

In the first case described above, I was acting fully consciously and simply 'expressing an intent'. That is, I wanted to cry. That the results were quite so spectacular (Gail was totally convinced that something was seriously wrong), in retrospect, surprised me also, but in reality, all I was doing was acting a part, much as I had done when taking on the role of a bile-bean on the IOW. [2.17]

However, in the second[6] and third cases, up to the point my body reacted, there had been no conscious intent at all to act in that particular manner. And in particular, in the third case, where the whole incident was over in no more than two (or possibly a maximum of three) seconds, the total precision involved left me questioning the reality of what had actually happened (Who or what had been in control at that moment?); the 'just-so' strength applied in the kick to the shins, enough to carry his head forwards onto a stilled fist, precisely at the right speed to cause a delayed nose bleed (and nothing more – I checked later). I had made no attempt to hit him (which I could have understood): My elbow had remained

---

[6] Some 20 years later, when I tried the above move on yet another Japanese woman, who in this case was deliberately blowing smoke directly into my face – this when I was in the middle of consuming a bowl of ramen noodles – she being rather taller and the stool much higher, I didn't come close to pulling things off and got thrown out of the restaurant for my troubles. I do, on this occasion, also admit to being very drunk, which was not the case in any of the above incidents.

fully relaxed at my side right the way through, and I had merely raised my forearm to the (preordained?) point of impact; it was almost as if, in the time it took to cross that two-step dancefloor, my brain had calculated all the speeds and angles; his positioning, body weight, etc. instantaneously in my head just to achieve that result. With the foot or fist applied even slightly more aggressively, I almost certainly could have got him into hospital with a serious injury (and no doubt myself in the police station for assault), but this is not what happened.

So how had I slipped so easily from my conscious (be a gentleman) reaction into that ever-so-precisely calibrated series of motions that were, in the final analysis, moves of a level that I suspect would normally require years of structured training? However, as with the 'turning in of the eyes' described in [2.13], this also could only be put aside and left for some future reckoning.

For the record, the above are the only three times in my life when I have (successfully) taken other people down deliberately. When at all drunk (on the understanding that it is a far safer proposition), I have invariably moved to take any irritants out on the closest object available rather than people. There is also the fact that during this period I had the advantage of being relatively tall. In England, I was an average 172 cm. in height. However, whenever I found myself having to stand in crowded trains here, which was very common, I initially had the pleasure of an open view way across a sea of dark heads, with only the odd other person – a stray island – here and there with whom I could exchange a knowing nod.

[4.7] "What the lady wants…"

Janet (/Jan) was the perfect person to hug; big and bouncy, with a joy expressed in life and living that was infectious in the extreme. At the same time, she was also a good five years older than me and quite tall and seeing her coming around the corner on that particular day in her pale-blue summer frock and with her long gingerbread-blonde hair coiffed upwards to even greater heights (this especially done for the occasion), all I could do was blush intensely. I did note that she also reddened slightly, so it seems that the reality of the situation had come home to the both of us very much at the same time.

Love hotels, where a room decorated with an emphasis on the exotic/erotic can still be rented for anything from one hour to a full night as required (privacy guaranteed), had at the time a mildly unsavoury reputation, but three nights earlier, when we had all been gathered at The Nook and Jan had expressed a certain regret that, shortly due to leave Japan, she would never get to see inside one, something she had had on her mind the full two years she had been here, with no one else suitably unmarried in the immediate vicinity, and with the convenience of my apartment being situated on what was then referred to as 'Kokusai-doro' (International Street), famous for a full row of this type of hotel (they are commonly grouped together), it had been left to a somewhat beer-mellowed me to volunteer, leading to our (or, at least, my) present state of acute embarrassment. However, the promise had been made, and having come this far, we couldn't exactly backtrack.

Love hotels are generally designed to be slipped into; under the cover of darkness, from an underground carpark or through a rear (unlit and generally carefully concealed) entrance/exit, where with one quick step to the right or left a couple can literally vanish from the sight of any other passer-by. However, here in the daytime, and with all the hotels aligned along the open street, we had no other choice than to make bold and assume that not too many of my neighbours (we were a hundred yards or so from my apartment building) were taking note of our presence.

And once inside the lobby and alone apart from the room panel display, from which we obtained our key, we took the elevator up to our floor and finally were in. Where again, reality taking hold, all we could do now was look at each other and laugh.

Both Jan and I still have the photographs taken that day; her beckoning (seductively?) through pink-lace curtains; demurely pouring green tea – which we drank (we had to fill up the time, somehow); her stretched out in the (very uncomfortable-looking Western-style) bathtub; me in the bed proffering a ¥5,000 note for "services to be rendered," etc. and then finally outside the hotel (presumably having overdone things) grasping vainly at my back. But, for me personally, the real pleasure of the afternoon came when, having paid our account at the small window in the lobby, the very small, elderly lady seated at her desk came out with a totally formal, "Mata Irrashaimase!" ("Please do come again"), accompanied by an extremely charming (and ever-so cheeky) smile.

***

Janet was one of a group of Americans (Pauline, Brenda, and Kerry) plus one Canadian (Sally), who were all teachers at one of the local international schools

– all of whom became friends who Koji and I stayed in contact with one way or another for a long time after they had left Japan. Most of our initial contact came in the evening at the Nook, but also involved dance parties and the occasional trip outside town. And they were all fun. Jan was here for the shortest period, just two years, after which she went off to Nepal, where she adopted a baby girl, who she then took back to bring up in America. And even today, she is still totally open to new experiences – her most recent (close on eighty and now dependent on a scooter to get around), a two-week tour into the Ecuadorian rainforests and then the Galapagos islands, which seemingly she fully enjoyed. And if you can love a lady for being what she is, I do.

Also loosely attached to this group, there was a young Japanese man, Hiroshi, who weaves his way in and out of this story, sometimes perhaps not in the most pleasant of ways. At this time, he barely registered on a personal level, but it would seem now that when I first met him, Koji had already made his acquaintance. (A detailed background is given in [7.35], but prior to this the reader will find the name appearing in two or three key sequences in [6.8] and [6.22].)

[4.8] Out of work:

Quite what the intention of management had been in closing the school was never made clear, but from the Immigration Office's viewpoint, our visas having been approved on the understanding that each one of us was required in Kobe, to simply have us transferred to Osaka or Tokyo was not in the works. At the same time, the company being considered in the wrong made them considerably sympathetic towards our position. Even so, we were all now left in the position of having to determine how we should proceed with our futures.

Matt and Gail:

Matt and Gail used the opportunity to go down to Australia, where Matt had a brother, but within a very short time, they returned to Kobe where they opened their own school and Matt returned to the Nook. In both countries, being half Chinese, Gail was viewed as 'Asian' – one problem initially here in Japan being the number of times Matt had ended up having fights when Gail had been misidentified as a local bargirl. Gail not being able to speak in Japanese had made the situation worse, as it gave the (totally incorrect) impression of her being deliberately stuck-up into the bargain. And beyond this, in Australia, women were not yet being allowed into public drinking spaces, which would have left her very much by herself, presumably in the end making Japan the preferred choice.

A matter of confidence:

Matt, in effect, was a model extrovert, with a public-school confidence and general indifference to the world that would carry him through two (and possibly a third coming up) marriages and three kids, although it was Gail who got to bring them up. Although we have stayed in contact right the way through, I do not feel at any time to have been particularly close to him, this to a large extent being the fact that we have both been extremely busy in our own worlds. However, in this early period, we did have one brief interlude when we would go climbing up in the mountains together, deliberately getting off the main tracks into what we described as 'Gaijin (Foreigner's) Country'. There were still relatively few Japanese climbing in the mountains at this time, and most of these stuck to the main paths, and therefore this made for a perfect means of getting away from all the pressures of everyday living: Knowing that there was no one there to hear us, we could shout our heads off as much as we cared to.

And then, suddenly, for no apparent reason, he could no longer speak Japanese, or at least not in front of me, which for quite some while baffled. Initially, with him having arrived in Japan some six months before me, the boot had strictly been on the other foot (I was forever, the junior, the learner; and regardless of where we happened to be, in front of him my brain would simply blank), and even returning from Australia (where clearly there had been a gap on his side) there had been no problem, but now if I walked into a room where he was talking with someone in Japanese, it was his brain that suddenly blocked and he would immediately switch into English.

And the reason? It turned out that at some point he had learned that (in his absence) I had mastered the initial 2,000 Chinese characters essential for basic reading, and not having any of that knowledge at his fingertips, psychologically it had knocked him: He was no longer the exemplar in the relationship. And although the effect of this naturally wore away with time, even today I have found he defers to my (not strictly brilliant, but still presumably higher) knowledge in this area, which is something that – not being public-school bred – I naturally do not flaunt. (Or, at least, not too obviously.)

Gail, in contrast, was from the start totally uncomplicated; very easy-going

– and for Koji and myself very easy to relate to. Back in Japan, together they did well with the school, but then after the first two girl babies arrived, with Gail not prepared to accept the traditional Japanese divisions of labour – where the children become the responsibility of the mother and the father concentrates on life outside the home (which Matt, on his part, apparently took overly full advantage of) there was the natural resulting divorce and a return to England, the third (boy) child apparently being conceived as a result of some last minute back-sliding.

Neil:

Prior to the school closing, Neil had got married to a nurse, Keiko, who had looked after him during a brief stay in hospital, and with her continuing with her job, he was able to use this switch-over period to get himself established in the translation business. However, after ten years or so, with two boys to be educated (he was not at all a fan of the Japanese education system) and a workload that was in many ways getting out of control (he was at the mercy of every translation agency that would give him work, with ridiculously unnecessary overnight deadlines, which still had to be met or you were out), he decided to take his whole family back to England, where they established themselves on the south coast. And we kept up our relationship from there, his eldest son now married and working in Tokyo.

And myself. "Knowing people does help":

From early on in my stay, I had been teaching one class at the head office of a multinational company in the city, and hearing of our situation, the Japanese manager who had originally requested the class talked with his superiors, resulting in the offer of an initial two-year contract for teaching and editing of company documents and letters, which I was very happy to accept. Mrs Oka volunteered to be my guarantor (essential for any furthering of my position), and Mr Hamada (our receptionist, Yukiko's father) who was the head of the Prefectural Offices at the time, facilitated the matter of a visa by writing a short accompanying letter to the head of the Tokyo Immigration Bureau, who he knew personally. In consequence, the visa was received within a week. (This in comparison with a full five months plus for Neil, who, as noted, had a Japanese wife, which should have made his position reasonably secure.) Also, at this time, I did make friends with a young officer from the immigration bureau who had been charged with investigating the matter of the closure, which for a number of years did ease my visits to that office. (At this time, visas had to be updated every year, which meant regular visits.) From the outset, he totally got a kick out of the fact that I had a Japanese 'hanko' seal (actually created for my ink-paintings), and every time I had a need to visit him, he insisted that I bring it to be used on all official documents where a signature would be the norm, and I was always greeted with a cheery smile.

[4.9] Two visits:

"They invited us all the way to their house just to give us cold tempura!"

It had been my father who had insisted that we take him out for a drink, and this being the smallest and thus least obvious of the gay bars that we frequented, Koji had made a call and everyone (we knew most of the customers) had been on their best behaviour, my father's only comment being that it seemed a little odd that there were no women drinking with us, to which I could only answer that women didn't go out drinking so frequently in Japan, which was at the time a truth. And then, quite out of the blue, we had been invited to the owner's home for a meal (he was married with two children), resulting in the above reaction from my mother. What really surprised me at the time, more than the somewhat arrogant tone in which this was expressed, was that this being close to 50 years ago, my mother knew what tempura was, and also that it should be served hot. Additionally, as we had we been treated with a fully spread table (far more than just tempura) and also, she and my father had been given a number of expensive gifts including (for her) a very attractive Japanese kimono, the comment did come over at the time as not particularly polite.

Taken from the present timeline, I can understand that my mother, having been only recently thrust into this new world (she would only have received my coming-out letter a few months earlier), would not be particularly comfortable in this situation, but even so this outburst, which came after we had returned to our apartment, has always stayed with me as somehow totally unnecessary and out of character. (Children think they know their parents.)

***

My parents visited us twice in Japan, the first time being while I was still working at the school, for one tightly packed month – a whirlwind of meeting people and sightseeing, and then a long sea trip back on the Canberra liner via Australia and South Africa, the money I had earned in Saudi Arabia covering the whole trip. This was not intended as such, but it became my 'oyakoukou' (acting as a good son should) moment, an essential part of the parent-centred culture here, and as such thoroughly approved of by all of my – at least, more senior – Japanese acquaintances. The second came in the early spring of 1974, when they stayed for a full three months and, with much more time and subsequently a much more relaxed attitude, they got to the point where they could make their way around by themselves, actually managing to fit in a number of places and traditional events that I have even now not covered.

Benefits:

The greatest benefit incurred from these two visits had to be my mother's peace of mind. Prior to my coming here, for whatever reason she had convinced herself that she might never actually see me again. The world at this time was still a very large place which few got to explore. And it was not strictly the distances involved – I imagine if I had been going to Australia or New Zealand, she would have had no qualms at all about the matter – it was rather me going off into vast unknown labelled "The Far East," a world that she was incapable of imagining. However now, everything she needed to picture my existence was at her fingertips; the names, the places, the people, the faces (including Koji's immediate family) – everything. And from this time on, with us visiting them regularly and them receiving visits from a number of the people they had met here, including a six-months-plus stay by Yukiko (our school receptionist) all adding to the familiarity, in terms of ease of mind, I could just as well have been living in the south of England.

Also, quite separately, on their cruise home after their first visit, apparently for the first time in their lives, they had the time (and the lack of the presence of others) to be together enough to finally get to know each other (as my mother noted, all they could do for large parts of the journey was sit out on the deck and talk), and subsequently a great part of the tension that had existed between them cleared. And from this time on, they did actually become as happy as any elderly couple you might imagine, which must be considered an achievement.

[4.10] 'Sono Mise':

'Sono Mise' (That Place/Garden Place) was the name that Koji gave to his bar, opened in the Chinatown area of town, and named so because he wanted it to be a 'place of calm'.

The bar was not promoted in any manner as gay, and by far the largest proportion of customers were not so, but it was natural that certain sympathies leaked out, and it came to attract a certain number people who were on the edge – people who due to their position at their company or for whatever other reason would (/could) not normally be seen in a place associated with gay people but liked a place where they could feel comfortable enough to talk quietly when the atmosphere was right. And far more importantly, it became yet another source of lifelong friendships; students from the company; couples who came in on their first dates and stayed, and a variety of local characters (restaurant and bar owners) – together with their now fully grown children and grandchildren – all of whom provided the sense of community and continuity essential for what for us became the closest we could approach to a normal life.

Positioned towards the back in a rather old building, it initially required a certain amount of redecorating (DIY, with wallpaper brought over from England), but with a dozen or so seats, it was a perfect size to be run by one person. (Unlike the UK, where to large extent customers are quite happy talking among themselves, visitors to bars and clubs in Japan to a large extent expect to be entertained, requiring a bar of any size to employ additional help, but here Koji could essentially be on his own.) That said, in the early stages, to help attract custom (the term in Japanese here being 'sakura' – unrelated to the word's far more commonly known meaning of cherry blossom), most evenings I had to take my position on the opposite side of the bar, where new or regular customers would on occasion be polite enough to buy me a drink (one for the till), or far more commonly my students would come knowing that they could have a general gripe about work at the company. This, at times, did cause problems in that I was initially obliged to accept whatever drink was offered, and certain drinks should not be mixed imprudently. However, once custom became established, I became able to say that I would stick with my beer. Also, from this time, not wanting to have to sit in the same position every night after my own full day's work, my legs began to wander. This, for the most part, even though I did commonly go to the gay bars, was not at all serious. (They all knew who I was, and they all knew Koji.) However, much later, when I had expanded my territory considerably and in fact did find one other person with whom I could have settled down easily (Koji also, by this time, had learned to find his way around the local bars where foreign seamen were still at the time congregating), sensing that this time it could be serious, he made a decision to stay with me and sold. And from then on then we remained together for a total of 40 years.

[4.11] Three concerts and a funeral:

Hibari Misora:

Isamu and Carl were one of the first Japanese-foreigner couples that we knew. Isamu's age fell somewhere in between Koji's and my own, while Carl was a considerably older Australian businessman, but with his easy-going ways, we found being together extremely relaxing, and together we started going to concerts, the first one being that of Hibari Misora, a Japanese 'enka' singer, even today recognised as unrivalled in both her stage presence and range: Beyond enka, she had what to me was an astounding ability to carry over whatever she chose to sing as *her* song, be it pop, classic or jazz (and this in Japanese or English). In same manner as Judy Garland, she started as a child actor in films, and as with Judy, being in part tragic in her own right (she was, as were a large number of her contemporary singers and film stars, Korean in origin, a point which could not at the time be overly promoted, and even today is rarely mentioned), she had developed a strong gay following, of whom Isamu was one. Although this was only the one time I saw her live, I remained a proud fan for life, and at the end of the concert, Isamu having insisted, I got to present her in person with a bouquet of flowers I had taken for the purpose, something which even today I still bring out in the gay community as a 'badge of honour' that not so many have!

Fubiki Koshiji:

"And I've got this really handsome guy gazing at me here in the front row."

This from Fubiki Koshiji, a Takarazuka Revue star who, upon retiring from the troupe, became a star in her own right singing Japanese versions of chanson. At this performance, the four of us were seated on the front row, and when she looked into my eyes as she pronounced the above, even understanding that it was (with almost all certainty? Was it really?) a touch of show business, I could not help feeling a sharp thrill run down through to the pit of my stomach.

And then walking back up the central aisle after the final curtain had fallen, and just before I could come out with my 'news', I was outmanoeuvred by Isamu.

"You heard what she said about me."

"That was me!" (This from Carl)

"No, that was me!" (Koji)

But then couldn't have been any of them. I knew she had been looking directly at me as the words came from her mouth. And for the rest of the evening, out in the bars, each time the subject came up, there was a brief but very direct run of antagonism (recognisable to all) that cut between us, and even the occasional stir of anger. And from that time on, the subject of the concert itself remained off limits to all.

Chikuzan Takahashi (blind "tsugaru shamisen" player):

(Claude Debussy, composer (died 1918): "With a chord struck on the piano, more is heard than those notes alone. The other strings vibrate with sympathetic overtones, forming a halo over every note.")

The shamisen is a long-necked, three-stringed instrument which, when plucked, produces a very hard and distinctive twanging sound. The body of the instrument, traditionally covered with animal skin, when struck sharply with the fingertips can also serve as a drum, and Chikuzan, who was from a northern rural part of the main island and who for the first half of his life was what in the England of some centuries ago would have been described as 'wandering minstrel', was considered a master of his craft. And in the concert we attended, again from the front row, he was joined by a second player, a 'deshi' (student) who also doubled as singer. And now with Chikuzan playing both around and across the edges of her high-pitched voice, the three became a single, indivisible entity – an elemental contrasting and blending of reverberations that with its final upsurge came to penetrate the most innermost of landscapes, at which point I found that I had physically become a part of the performance, my whole-body quivering from tip to toe.

***

And then, when I was in my early thirties, Carl was hospitalised with cancer. Called in to help certify the translation of his will (which actually involved a certain amount of deception, as my written Japanese was nowhere up to that level at the time), and then after the funeral, with him not having any family members here in Japan and Isamu only having close friends, we also attended his cremation, following the hearse and one solitary black mourner's car back up a narrow valley into the mountains to a seemingly insignificant, low building, where the coffin was wheeled into a small room, and after a final viewing, slid into a square metal gap in the wall and was gone. And now thinking that that would be it, I got ready to leave, but Koji indicated that we needed to wait a little longer, and this we did, until eventually we were led back into the same room, where the metal doors once again slid apart and the tray, with what had been Carl's oversized body was returned to us, the main skeleton still roughly in place, but otherwise with no more than a thickish spreading of grey ash for us to recognise what had been a human being. And it was at this point that Isamu blacked out and collapsed.

(Much later, when I started walking in the mountains more seriously, this same valley became my entrance point into the foothills, but with the discrete positioning of the building, one level up from the side of the road among the trees, and the only sign that it was in use being a faint haze rising from a single chimney, it was some time before I realised that it was the same place, and that only because occasionally I would be passed by long parades of black cars winding up or down the same road, and all to that same lone destination.)

[4.12] Koji: Finding his artistic focus (and expanding mine):

From the time of his arrival, Koji had informed me that he wanted to study woodcarving, something which, having only come across very mediocre examples in local culture centres, I was not initially in favour of. However, in time, he was able to locate a man, Mr Honjo, a professional in his field, who for the large part of his life specialised in traditional Western-style furniture. And later, upon semiretirement, when he moved over to more Japanese themes centred on the creation of Buddhist sculptures, Koji was also able to study with him in this area. (Some of his teacher's better work can be seen at the Akasaka Palace State Guesthouse (Geihinkan) in Tokyo, used today to accommodate visiting state dignitaries, and also on the side of one of the large floats used in the Kyoto Gion Festival.) And once found, Koji remained with him right the way through, eventually creating his own designs – these including a large cabinet fronted with two male and two female nudes (all four reworked from modern erotica), which was one of a number of pieces kept at home until after he died. And travelling together both in Japan and abroad as we did most of the time, it was natural that we both start searching out sculpted forms – whether they be in wood, metal or stone (/marble) – leading to my own discovery that a very large number of small temples remaining in the countryside here still do have quite exquisite carvings incorporated into their structures, these in turn becoming a source for my own painting.

[4.13] Partying:

Two or three years after moving into our new apartment, this only amounting to three small rooms but far larger than the school apartment, which had consisted of no more than a single room with a kitchen unit, toilet and bathroom (we were still in the age of living in 'rabbit hutches', as the foreign media cared to label Japanese housing at the time), we started to organise occasional parties, inviting just about anyone we knew and/or felt comfortable with, and this continued right the way through for some thirty-odd years. Koji would be in charge of the cooking, while I set up the apartment, and the guests would bring additional alcohol and sweetmeats/desserts. Essentially open houses, guests would start to arrive around 10:00 or 10:30 in the morning, and then there would be a natural turnover throughout the afternoon until, as evening-time came around, we would be left with our friends, both foreign and Japanese, from the gay community ('The Boys in the Band') who would stay around anything up to midnight. This was not in any sense planned (people were free to come and go as they wished) but in the end it became a very pleasant means of enabling a certain intermingling of the different communities – friends from the original school, the company (mainly students), Sono and the Nook, etc. together with a number of gay couples – that made up our lives. It was also at one of these parties that I found Koji, with tears in his eyes (having taken in far too much of his share of alcohol), confessing to one of my students how he and I were "much more than friends." And from this point, the secret, if there ever had been one, was out. The matter was never ever taken beyond this, but rather simply accepted as the way things were, and this has been so with all the friends we kept throughout our lives, which did make for a very pleasant way of living.

Japanese people will seemingly take any excuse to gather together for a party, restaurants in the greater parts of December and January being fully booked with Year-End, Christmas and then New Year parties, and more recently, we have Halloween as yet another reason to let loose. And then there is naturally the cherry blossom, together with a whole range of local festivals, all of which provide an excuse to prepare special food dishes (and yet that one more bottle to be opened). And (as long as the energy lasted) they were fun.

Daytime classes at the company were reserved for those who had already achieved a certain level in the language and were being groomed for higher positions and/or training abroad. In contrast, evening classes were open to anyone who chose to attend (a number came to both), and it was with these classes that Year End parties were held. (These were not the only parties that I had to attend, and with each of these events involving eating and drinking at a minimum of three locations, I could not possibly have handled more. Invariably starting off well in my role as 'entertainer in chief', by the time we reached the last of these evenings, my energy was close to spent and I would just have to hope that there was someone in the group who could take over the lead. And when there wasn't, particularly with the lower-level groups, time stretched.) There was, however, one advantage here, which I eventually learned to take full use of. Japanese male office workers who (it not being socially permitted) would never think to criticise anyone during the daytime, do tend to open up after a few drinks, and in time I did learn to use these sessions as opportunities that allowed me to make certain points (in some cases, quite strong criticisms) that would not have been acceptable (or accepted) during regular working hours.

New Year parties, in contrast, tended to be more culturally associated events, particularly with my ink-painting group, where every year well over a hundred of his students would gather in our teacher's home in the countryside (not a 'rabbit hutch'), to sample a fully traditional New Year, this naturally including me in my kimono. At the time, kimono being considered standard wear for both men and women (particularly during the New Year period) even as a foreigner, there was no sense of being out of place. The summer (yukata) kimono, which being light and casual, is easy to wear, has been re-gaining its popularity recently, but unfortunately the heavier winter kimono is now very rarely seen other than in museums or rented out to tourists. Fashion hint: To look effective in a kimono and emanate 'kanroku' – a 'sense of presence' or 'an air that befits one's position' – a man requires a certain natural bulk (or padding around the waist).[7]

---

[7] Kanroku: I would be approaching my mid-thirties when one of my students noted that I had developed "that certain air" required as a teacher. However, his inference seemingly more directed towards the developing expanse around my waist, I did not at the time take it particularly as a compliment, and not requiring any 'airs' of that description, shortly afterwards I did start with my yoga routines.

[4.14] Planning a future:

More than anything, coming to Japan gave me a chance to restructure my life. This not only involved planning finances, but also touched on the style of life I felt I would like and included the choice of what interests to pursue, with the intention that I should have at least a couple of things I could continue with as I got older. And understanding that I had nothing and no one to really fall back on, I became extremely (possibly overly) conscious as to what might go wrong with my future, and as is commonly the case in these matters, working from my very limited understanding of what life (particularly living in a foreign country) involved, nothing that my mind came up with at the time actually came to pass, while much else of a far worse nature did. But at least a minimum effort was applied.

At the time, foreigners were not allowed to join the social security system: It was only much later, as the government here came to realise that they were running out of money to pay out to their aging population that they started suggesting that foreigners possibly could, and then had to contribute (on the understanding that no pension payment would be made without a full 25 – now apparently 10 – years of input to the system, but for me this came too late. Falling ill in my early thirties, I did have the good fortune (this, again, with the aid of Mr Hamada [4.8]) to be able to join the health insurance system, "on the understanding that I stay with the system throughout my life," which I have.

'Win some, lose some':
In my very early teens, for whatever reason, my brain picked up an association between the buying of shares/bonds (/making money gratuitously from the system) and gambling, only to be quickly hushed by my mother. (At the time, we were at the house of one of her aunts, who with her husband had profited considerably in this manner, so perhaps my timing was a little off.) However, not knowing what to do otherwise, I initially placed the money I had made in Saudi Arabia in an investment fund, and then after watching its value do nothing but drop over six months, abruptly withdrew it. (I have never had the nerve, time, or money to consider going into shares since, though I do understand that if you do, to have any chance of success will require a certain serious studying of the market.)

Buying a home. Two pieces of luck:

Our present apartment – bought when I was in my mid-thirties – was purchased at a very reasonable price, mainly as a result of the original buyer's misjudgement. Initially purchased strictly as an investment when the place was newly built and then left to be (the interior was filthy, with dead pigeons in the veranda storage space), and presumably followed by the need for a quick sale, and with each potential Japanese buyer rejecting the prospect (when making a purchase of this type, the average Japanese will not accept even the smallest scratch on the paintwork), at the time we came to take a look, the initial asking price had been reduced by a good third, and advised by the agent not to push too hard, we accepted it as the bargain it was. Also, around this time, the price of gold was hitting an all-time high, and having purchased a small amount a few years earlier, with a little careful observation of buying and selling prices, which at the time appeared in the newspaper every day (an understanding of certain basic mathematical principles can on occasion serve a purpose), I managed to hit the sweet-spot: the day after I sold, the price went into a dive and didn't recover for a long time. So all we needed now was a very small loan to clear the full payment at one go.

And then, to bring us to our senses, there were the banks. At my British bank in town, I got, without a second of consideration, a straight-out "No," and so I told them that they could close my account – which did cause a bit of a disturbance, but I was angry. I had been with them for fifteen years and the amount I was requesting was less than my monthly salary at the time (a fact which they must have been fully aware of), and it could have been cleared very easily, but for some reason, it could not be contemplated. And then, there was my Japanese bank, where I got a double "No!" Not unless I already had the equivalent amount of money in my account. The Japanese system is, essentially, either you provide property as collateral or, if you already have money in the bank, they will lend it to you. That is, if you deposit a million, they will lend you (up to and not more than) that exact same amount. (In England, around this same time, my middle brother, who had invested the little money he had in a local building society, but with essentially nothing in collateral or in the bank, received a loan to purchase his home without any problem. However, there are systems and systems.) Fortunately, one of Koji's sisters, Takako, was in the money-lending business, and she was prepared to consider our request (at a rather higher interest rate than the banks, but that at the time seemed fair). So we got our loan and paid it back – rather faster than his sister would have liked (she would have preferred to make a bit more out of us, but I insisted). And we got our home.

And that many years later, a plot of land:

The moment we saw it, we both knew it was what we wanted. Positioned among a small cluster of houses hidden from the main valley behind a deep screen of bamboo plants (and at the same time ten minutes from the centre of town and the expressway home), it felt 'right'. And as we broke into open smiles (we had been carefully guarded in our reactions to everything else that he had shown us), the agent, knowing he had us, for whatever reason given, put the price up 10%. And still we bought it. It was 'right'. And then even after the payment had been made and we were breaking the soil for the first time only to discover that we had purchased a fill-in, which did actually result in jolting us back to earth for one moment, it remained right the way through, with its surrounding bamboo groves, fireflies, fruit trees, misted mountains and limpid moons, a beautiful place to be.

Basically a long, narrow strip of land at the side of a narrow mountain stream, which had been built up by the local authorities to prevent further erosion of the original bank (above which our closest neighbours had their land), it took five years of hard work to clear completely, but once that was done, we could grow just about anything. The larger rocks that we extracted were used to build up banks around the neighbourhood to help prevent soil erosion, and in time the really bad waste that we had removed (two full truckloads of it) was carted away gratis by our next-door neighbour, Mr Hosoda, who ran his own small construction company.

Mr Hosoda helped us in many ways, including running a fence along the deep concrete channel that now carried the stream, and when we finally brought in a small prefab building (previously used to house those who had lost their homes in the Kobe earthquake of 1995), I worked with him to build a concrete base to place it on (Koji added a porch) and finally we laid a pipe from the upper section of the stream so that we could have running water (perfect for drinking) on hand. Up to then, water for the plants had had to be hauled up by bucket. He also, when the opportunity presented itself, brought back truckloads of good soil for us to spread. Another Mr Hosoda, from the other side of the stream (it being an old community, 80% of the families had the same name, which could make life confusing when you were trying to give directions for deliveries), took on the role of 'gardening consultant'. A farmer in his own right, he helped us at every point along the way and we became very good friends with both him and his family.

Practicalities:

And to cut away a little at the idyllic, we also had to deal with the ever-present crows, who knew just when a watermelon was ripe for consumption; overly persistent deer, that would take on up to three layers of fencing to get at any fresh shoot available; and a visiting snake that somehow got itself into the front section of the car, terrifying me enough to have Koji swing us deep into a ditch alongside the road. This occurring directly in front of the local police station, the policeman in charge did kindly inform me that if I wished to press charges against Koji for endangering my life, I could. However, it not really being his fault – I was the one who had screamed – and still needing him to drive, I declined.

Koji had his own running battle with a family of moles (the sign of a healthy plot in that it indicated a surplus of worms) that had made their home among the roots of the privet hedge planted at the far end of the strip, and I also had the pleasure of unearthing the same fat toad from its hibernation every spring, each year it amazing me that it had somehow managed to evade the rotating blades of our tilling machine. And close to the end of our stay, we had the pleasure of a family of raccoons (originally from the US, they have now almost replaced the local badger species) that appeared on the scene to devour just about anything in their way (most notably a full crop of perfectly ripened sweetcorn Kensuke had worked hard on – this after Koji's death), and also the odd human intruder, who took to selecting the best of our produce at will. Being absent at most times during the week, there was little we could do to control this, but it was not appreciated. (In recent years, this has become a serious problem for professional farmers who are waking up to find their orchards and greenhouses plundered, the offenders apparently coming in in trucks.)

And insects:

Mosquitoes, on the whole, could be dealt with by using spray, and more practically by ensuring that there were no patches of still rainwater left for the larvae to develop in.

However, fill-ins with their jagged rocks and metal waste providing a perfect breeding ground, centipedes (with their nasty bites) were ever-present, and in one particular case I did have one which took the liberty of traveling home with me. Presumably having been thrown up together with the soil on my pickaxe, it had curled up on the crown of my head, only to be discovered when I washed it out onto the floor of the shower, quickly to be flushed down the drain. (Not in the countryside, but possibly the worst encounter I had of this kind was during a heavy burst of rain as I was returning home from a swim at the local pool, when quite another variety of centipede/millipede – roughly 25 cm in length, with a finger-thick, green, yellow and brown-striped body – fell directly onto my head from the tree branches above me before scrambling down my body onto the pavement and into the bushes.)

Anthills were dealt with one at a time with the requisite pack of pesticide, only to reappear at will in some fresh location. In reality, they weren't of any particular harm, and they did help with the occasional spread of green or blackflies, but they could aggravate when you were working close to the soil – in the early planting stages, or the seemingly eternal weeding process. (Left for three weeks in summer, the whole plot would literally become a meadow.) They did finally have their revenge by infiltrating a bowl of noodles that I was eating for my lunch, not noticed until I already had one or two stinging at the inner sides of my cheeks before they were swallowed. This was actually not totally unpleasant – live ants in a bowl of noodles are apparently an Asian delicacy – but it is not an experience that I would deliberately search out.

And then (yellow being nature's most to-be-trusted warning sign) knowing that I shouldn't, but still reaching out to touch a brilliantly coloured yellow caterpillar, and the ensuing intense pain lasting over a month.

Financially, the place was a total loss: Shortly after we made the purchase (paid for by my share of our inheritance after my parents' death), the financial bubble burst [17.1], and living in the countryside, at least for most, lost all its attractions. And after Koji's death, when I could no longer handle the work and (construction company) Mr Hosoda's son was kind enough to take it off our hands, we found that it was valued in the city office at no more than a few thousand yen. (Today, in numerous areas in the countryside, you can buy or rent a large piece of property and/or house for virtually nothing – or in some cases even be paid to take a place on.) However, not strictly intended as an investment, we did get a full thirty years of pleasure (fresh flowers, vegetables and fruit, plus regular physical workouts and all the kindness of our neighbours) out of it, certainly nothing that I would regret. We could have gone around the world another half dozen times with the money we spent on it, but in our somewhat lackadaisical manner, we actually managed a different (and possibly more satisfying) route.

[4.15] Life is fragile:

Gail: "Aki is dead. After she went back with him to England, they got married. And it didn't work out and she committed suicide."

When Aki had to come to see me so much time ago, I hadn't really understood why she was asking me, why she would trust me to help her make a decision about something which I clearly knew nothing about, but she had been serious, and I had given her the best advice I could under the circumstances.

One of the receptionists at the Osaka school, she had been dating Derek, a teacher at the same school, and I knew both of them from very casual acquaintance. (I had possibly met her three or four times at the time, but I had never had a close conversation with either of them.) However, she had come, and we had talked. It had previously been mentioned that Derek came from a 'good family', but it now appeared that his father was an established member of the aristocracy, with all that that entails, including a large country estate where, if she chose to marry him, it was assumed that she would live, and coming from a very average background herself, this was a point that she was rather concerned about.

So what was there for me to say? They were both very nice (we were all in the same age range), and they clearly cared about each other. How much my experiences at Oxford (the part that should have come out with an immediate "No") influenced my comments here, I'm not sure, but I also have a side of me that likes to think the best of people and Derek had never struck me as 'aristocratic' in any way, which at the time seemed to say something about his family also. However, after an hour-or-so of discussion, my conclusion was that "I wasn't in any position to say marry him, but I couldn't see any reason not to go and see how she might or might not fit in." I do not know quite how much weight she gave to this particular opinion (or anything else I might have said) in her final decision, but to have to feel even a slight responsibility for someone's suicide is not a pleasant experience, and from this point onwards I became very much more cautious about how I addressed people's requests for advice.

At the small gym that we started going to shortly after Koji and I got settled, there was one man in his early thirties who had clearly been training for a number of years. We were not at all friends, but training together we got to know each other well enough to exchange greetings and pass the time of day, until one day when he came in to report that he wasn't feeling well enough to do a workout, and then a few days later (by this time his facial features considerably haggard) to say that he was having to go into hospital. And within two weeks, he was gone. Apparently, if he had been in his late sixties or seventies, he could have lived with whatever the disease was for another 10 or 20 years (the medical term for the disease here was beyond me, but this was long before HIV), but with him being in his prime, the activity of his cells had, more than just speeding up the process, actually invited the spread.

And then there were two women in their early twenties who were regular customers at Sono and who had determined that they would be partners for life. However, coming up strongly against their parents' wishes and being young and seeing no other way out, they had travelled up to the north of Japan, where they had taken their lives by jumping from a bridge onto a local railway line. This Koji only told me after the fact: I had noticed that they hadn't been in for a few nights, but that had been the extent of my interest.

Life is fragile.

Chapter 5
Coming to Accept What Cannot Be

[5.1] Why Japan:
As a child of eight or nine, I remember paying sixpence (at 240 pennies to the pound) to strain my eyes watching Godzilla (a remarkably stiff, lumbering, monster-like creature rising up out of the sea to destroy a lot of tall buildings) from the front row of our local theatre – nothing that stirred my imagination then or even now, but it was a first recognition. A quick jump to 1963 and the Sukiyaki song, which together with "Non ho l'eta", the Italian winner of the European Song Contest in 1964, are the two foreign songs that I learned fully by heart in my early teens. And then nothing until university and Hiroaki [1.5], and where otherwise I was completely blown away by an exhibition of Japanese swords, assembled by an Englishman collector travelling around the Japanese countryside shortly after the war and billed (truthfully or not, I would not know, but) as the "finest collection in the world." Either way, even with the very little understanding I had of the subject at hand, the workmanship – on the blades themselves, and even more so for me at the time, the carving and inlay work on the sheathes and guards, was something close to unimaginable. And that they drew me is, in retrospect, a matter of course.

And then probably, most importantly (and this a point that Japanese people, particularly younger people today, find very difficult to believe), the ultimate attraction was that it was a place that *I knew absolutely nothing about*. Nothing I had covered at school either historically or geographically had touched upon the country, and working on the IOW, the 1964 Olympics had passed me by. Also, at the time, Japan had not yet begun to develop as an economic giant – if anything (other than, perhaps, cameras), it was a country that was known for producing cheap imitations of quality European goods. I had never even heard of Mt Fuji, cherry blossom or geisha, and I can recall nothing about it in the newspapers, even at college, where we were reading everything available. (Shortly after I arrived, my mother sent me a one-paragraph article she had cut from the newspaper detailing the problem with discarded waste on Mt Fuji and this was the first time I ever saw any detail about Japan in print.) In other words, in my mind, it was a total blank, and for that very reason the place fascinated.

[5.2] "They are human beings":

(Shortly after my arrival.) Positioned at the head of the station stairs looking down in the direction of the main thoroughfare and the sea – I still can point to the exact place I was standing – it occurred to me that the people I was watching weren't. That is, they weren't the inscrutable (and totally clichéd) "Oriental" – not-to-be-trusted eyes narrowed to the finest of slits, the unreadable countenance – that I had somehow been led to expect upon my arrival in this most distant of distant lands. (Admittedly, this particular image was of the Chinese – but how would one be expected to know the difference? They were the same Asian.) On the contrary, they were people; with immediately recognisable facial expressions, clearly manifesting their own individual range of sensitivity, inner conflict, generosity, composure, arrogance – anything you could name that I might have seen in any of the countries that I had visited up to that time.

Kensuke, then in his mid-fifties and after a five week visit to the UK (he had never been abroad before), noted that although he had expected to be entering a different or somehow special world, everything was remarkably the same. As there are in Japan, there were well-off and not-so-well-off people, happy and sad, nice and not-so-nice people, people living on the streets. And "Everyone has the same worries – about their children, about old age, their health, life in general." And, inasmuch as he could be expected to take in the situation in such a short period, he was completely correct.

And from that common line, of necessity the learning process steps in.

When a society is as different from one's own as Japan's is from that of England, the differences themselves – the potential for discovery – can keep you buoyed for a considerable period. For myself, I had the challenges of learning the language, teaching, the traditional arts (ink-painting, calligraphy, and ikebana) together with all the people (literally hundreds) you meet in these areas and the (in many cases, very different) social customs they entail, and in addition I had to discover and settle into my own private world.

And then, at some point, one by one, you come up head on against the reality that certain values that you have assumed universal are not in fact so, and even very small incidents (inexplicable reactions to an offhand question) can knock you off balance. And from this point, for a number of years, life became a love-you-hate-you relationship; a series of ups and downs, now-you-see-it, now-you-don't peaks and troughs; a roiling tsunami of emotions that took years to settle into the ripples of every-day living. (This is a reality that, even today, all young people who have chosen to settle for any length of time in Japan face.)

And for the simple reason that the average Japanese at that time (and, to a great extent, even now) really had no understanding of Western culture, acceptance had to be on the other society's/culture's terms, and it took a considerable number of years (in reality, the large part of my life) for me to understand that my own upbringing would not allow this.

Note (AI): Direct translations and dictionary definitions: Particularly, for any word that is in any manner connected with feelings or emotions, one can assume that there will be no direct equivalence – that is, there is no one word in either language that will equate with a single word in the other. It is not that any feelings here are unique, but rather that, according to the expectations of our separate cultures, we express (/gather) them in different ways. And in this sense, unfortunately, dictionary definitions can only ever be of limited help (and in many cases considerably add to the confusion) in terms of true understanding of what is being expressed.

[5.3] 'Joushiki' (the socially accepted norm):

(To aid the explanation, a number of Japanese words and phrases have been introduced into the below text. However, of these, 'joushiki', 'sunao', and 'mujun' are central to the overall theme and will also be found in later sections of the text. All others, although of relevance, may be noted more in passing.)

Japan is as well-organised a nation and Japanese people in general are as nice as you will find in any other country around the world. At the same time, as with all other nationalities, they do have their blind spots, one of which, joushiki, is examined in detail below. In terms of practical applications, the following is not a matter that any casual visitor needs to consider but may be of some use for those intending to study the language or stay for any particular length of time in the country, and for the reader, the concept has been introduced chiefly as a means to illustrate quite how different societies can be.

There is a (originally Chinese?) saying in Japanese that a frog in a well knows nothing of (/can have no way of knowing anything of) the world outside. This can be compared in a sense to the English saying about an ostrich with its head in the sand, but while the English tends to refer to an individual person's obstinacy (/determination not to observe reality), with the Japanese quote, the individual (or, commonly, group) involved, living deep in a well, is merely ignorant of what is beyond their very limited surroundings, that is they are unaware of what they do not know. However, perhaps somewhat ironically, Japan represents what might be considered the ultimate example of both expressions. At one level, they are incapable of seeing anything other than through their very limited view of the world (living in the well). And at the same time, in many respects, in their desire to be special (/ 'unique'), they are not prepared to admit what they do not want to see – i.e. countless similarities to other cultures.

Note: As is the case with the English language, the Japanese language contains a very large number of words (including the above 'unique' and the below 'frank') that have been taken in directly, commonly from English or other European languages. And as is the case with the English language, together with the intake, both pronunciation and nuances of meaning invariably change, commonly to the point of being incomprehensible to a speaker of the original language.

Not 'just another culture (/language)':

The following is one of many basic differences between the English and Japanese cultures and subsequent usage of their respective languages, but right from the beginning, this is the one that has been the major stumbling block to my enjoyment of my life here, and even now, on occasion, I still find myself brought up against certain situations which, in terms of my basic upbringing, take a considerable effort (and yet one more deep breath) to bring myself to comprehend.

In the West, it is assumed that all people will develop their own individual ideas. And, therefore, when we engage in a conversation with another person for the first time, it is both very natural to anticipate disagreement and to work to handle that situation with a reasonable sense of composure, and our training from childhood aims to teach us the techniques – suitable choice of words, tonal expression, body language, the usage of (self-deprecating) humour, etc. – to allow us, to the best of our ability, to do this. Beyond this, scientific/business training involves both reasoning and logic, and also the ability to listen carefully and analyse in an overall manner the other party's intention, but again requires the linguistic ability to offer different (/opposing) viewpoints without causing offense. We also, in time, learn to agree to differ.

In contrast, in Japan, everyone starts with the same (generally accepted) opinion and in a polite conversation, care is taken to keep the discussion within a certain central range. The group as a whole may shift the initial opinion to an appropriate degree, but in the end, it is necessary that (at least superficially) "We all agree." This agreement ('tatemae', speaking as one is expected to by society) naturally need not automatically be indicating the speaker's real feelings ('honne'), and socially, in the West, we have a similar concept. But the important difference is that in Japan the group is very much expected to <u>stay within the consensus</u>, and in a public forum there is little room for the concept of agreeing to disagree. Naturally, within their own circle, Japanese will offer their opinions about a whole range of matters, but even so, certain constraints (joushiki – as detailed below) still apply.

The Japanese in general are taught to look down on the above expression of 'individuality' in the West as something that is socially harmful, and to stress the 'harmony' (social cohesion) created through their system, but provided (as described above) that you start with the fact that, as a group, each one of us is entitled to our own opinion, there seems no reason why any Western society should be less harmonious in our relationships. And as a basic tenet, without some sense of agreement on social principles, any society is bound at some point to show signs of collapse.

[5.4] So what do we agree upon?

The dictionary translation of the Japanese joushiki will likely give you "common sense," but "common understanding" or "socially accepted realities" might come closer, and, in fact, when examined from the Western perspective, in many cases what it amounts to is "an imposed social consensus." The population is in fact being very carefully and (this being Japan, in the most gracious of manners) manipulated. There is nothing particularly of note about this, in the sense that we are all subject to manipulation through our own education systems, the media, advertising, etc. (See [15.4]), but what is important here is the all-enveloping nature of the system.

In the sense that the highly convenient myth of the English Gentleman is intended strictly for the trained elite, or at least those prepared to join the club, your average Englishman (presumably, provided they accept the guidance of those said elites) is left to be, free to get on with their lives and develop their own respective (middle- or lower-class) cultures as they wish; that is, those who are not gentlemen at least have the pleasure of being ignored.

In contrast, it is assumed that all Japanese without exception will, as a matter of course, be aware of themselves as 'representatives of their nation', with all that that entails, this resulting in what can be an exceptionally overbearing culture. This is something quite beyond the concept of 'controlled' that Westerners commonly associate with dictators or Communism. Japanese citizens are not in any way being forced to accept the system: They are, in the most benign manner possible, and from their very early youth onwards, being guided towards their inherent place in the wholly natural scheme of 'things as understood to be', that is the (self-perceived) 'unique' cultural entity of the Japanese race. And each time that, as a foreigner, I have found myself coming up against this particular fact too directly, I have invariably found myself in trouble. The reaction here, at its most intense, is as close as you are going to get – without actually identifying it as such – to what we understand as 'religious fervour'. (To get a sense of the strength involved, the reader could imagine the kind of reaction they might receive having been invited into a strongly religious stranger's home, if they directly questioned that person's belief in the existence of God and/or the Devil.)

[5.5] 'Sunao':

This is a word that I initially had thrust on me repeatedly, commonly introduced as an untranslatable word that both defined the essence of being Japanese, and a word that, as a foreigner, I could never be expected to understand. (I have not heard the word at all recently and suspect that it may have gone out of fashion. However, I do know that it does still exist.) This did not at the time particularly concern me – the English language also can have a degree of complexity – but later looked up in the dictionary, I found the translations of "gentle" or "kind," which I could easily relate to. At the same time, neither seemed to resonate as what might be considered a national trait. (I could count on two hands the number of people I have met here who I would choose to include within the meaning of those words, at least as they are used in English.) And then there were the concepts of "being submissive, docile or tractable" – all of which at the time I took within a religious context, and assuming the word had some connection with Buddhism or possibly Shinto, things were left at that. And then, today, re-reading the entry with rather more care, I find "accepting another person's advice without question," and this is, in effect, the answer: "the requirement to act at the other's bidding, to be pliant, malleable (in the extreme), to allow oneself to be put to use 'for the common good,'" (this final phrase still used by certain older politicians today to exhort the populace to do as bidden).

If you are an adult moving around in what is recognised as Western society – including transitioning to other Western countries – when entering a new group or set of relationships, there is a natural (conscious or otherwise) adjustment in the sense of determining to what extent you make an effort to fit in, or to what degree you choose to openly exert your 'individuality' (/personal preferences) within that new framework. However, in Japan, to gain entrance to the society (or any subgroup within the whole), there is far more emphasis on that need to fit in.

And now returning in my mind to those initial years, I can only sense that I was being walked through my paces. The challenge to understand that one-word sunao was in fact a baited hook, with the implication that if I wished to be accepted, it would be on *their* terms. Or perhaps more directly, to be of any practical use, it was essential that I be suitably house broken. And with no particular reason not to (very early on, I had made the decision to stay here), that is what I chose to do.

[5.6] 'Ishin, denshin':

This is one more comment (still commonly paraded today) to the effect that: "Japanese people do not have to talk to each other because they understand each other intrinsically." However, if you take this from the standpoint of joushiki (i.e. parroting the same set of 'facts'); that a society that has been conditioned to think in the same way should 'understand each other' is not especially remarkable – particularly (if we wish to go around in circles), when one of those deeply instilled facts (/beliefs) is "We do not have to talk to each other because we understand each other intrinsically."

And then, living here, in time you do come to understand that the statement is not really any truer than it would be for people with a similar background in England having common understandings, which naturally do not need to be paraded to be understood. And, as I would imagine to be the case in any other country around the world, when Japanese people do not understand each other, *they do not understand.*

[5.7] Joushiki as it affects the reality of daily living:

Within Japanese society itself, one of the clear benefits of joushiki is that it allows a common ground for two or more people who are meeting for the first time and/or provides a means to ease into another group's conversation without any embarrassment. However, if a foreigner is present and presents them with an opinion that conflicts with their (essentially highly parochial) understanding of the world, they will tend to become flummoxed (/panic) and find themselves with no way of responding, and this is a problem.

At an international gathering in Canada, an official welcoming party for a group of artists and musicians centred on a local shrine here in the Kansai area (I had been taken along to help with interpreting for the group), a Malaysian gentleman, speaking to the leader of our group (a higher-level priest from the shrine), simply in the way of making conversation, asked him whether the Japanese Shinto religion [13.9] was at all similar to the nature-worshipping religions that exist in his own country, at which point the Japanese man's features totally blanked and, without even attempting to reply, he turned his head and (very rudely) stalked away. And I was left not knowing quite what I should say: He was, after all, the official head of a 'cultural mission', all the Canadian guests were of a certain social level and well-educated, and it was a situation where, at a minimum, basic politeness would be expected. (I was about 30 at this time, and to me this would have been a perfect opportunity for self-education; to learn about another society and compare it with my own.) Fortunately, however, no strong offense was taken, and matters were left to be. (There had been some form of miscommunication!)

At the time, I took this in large part as resulting from the man's character – he had a certain, rather prickly, innate pride, which he was not afraid of showing. The conversation was also touching on religious beliefs, which in any circumstances can be tricky, and it is highly likely in his position that he felt his beliefs were being slighted. But viewed with my present knowledge, in the final analysis, he had no choice. Both psychologically (to envisage the possibility of two realities in the one conversation – in this case, the fact that his 'unique' religion and one that existed in another Asian country might have similar roots) and equally importantly, linguistically (natural usage of the Japanese spoken language is essentially premised on the existence of the one 'reality') he was not equipped in any manner with the means to engage. (Quite possibly, the best he could have come up with in the circumstances is a polite murmur of demurral, but that was not to be.)

There is also a quite separate problem that can occur when you as a foreigner are actually accepted as a member of a Japanese circle/group.

Jim was the second teacher to be transferred to the head office here to work with me following the expansion of the teaching programme at the company. Although a number of years younger than myself, at the time of his arrival, he had already lived in Tokyo for a certain length of time and therefore was able to speak quite reasonable basic Japanese, and shortly after his arrival, he was very happy to be invited to the home of one of the members of the Personnel Dept., where a few of the younger members had gathered for a drink – presumably this was intended as a welcome party. (Never having received this type of treatment, I was in fact initially a little jealous here.) However, coming into our room at the company on the following Monday, the first thing that he did was to break down into tears, the reason being that for the large part of the evening he had been subject to whole range of insulting comments about the insufficiencies of foreigners in general, together with quite a number of direct comments about the foreign management in our own company, to which, with his limited Japanese, he had not been able to sufficiently respond.

At first glance, this might seem to be a case of "familiarity breeding contempt." However, listening more carefully, (I knew all the members of the group personally, and equally that they were all very nice people, not the type at all to be deliberately rude), my own reading had to be that they had presumably, with the aid of a certain quantity of spirits, gone far beyond the polite stage and accepted him as a part of their group – to the extent that it had slipped their minds that he actually was a foreigner in their midst. He was 'one of them'. And this being the case, it would not occur to them that he might be interpreting their statements from a foreigner's viewpoint, and thus be offended. However, to him, they had been talking in front of him as if he didn't exist and he had reacted accordingly.

I have had similar experiences on a number of occasions, one of particular note in my late forties, when one of my best classes, a group that I taught for roughly 16 years, all fluent in English and all of whom remain good friends, suddenly started coming out repeatedly with the phrase 'igirisubyou' ('English sickness'), referring, if my memory is correct, to the period when Mrs Thatcher was in conflict with the unions, and which was also the period when Japan was approaching the peak of its bubble economy), which was popular in the media at the time and invariably presented in a very derogatory manner, and this naturally over time came to rather annoy. But here again, they had placed me in their camp (at this time, I was fluent in Japanese) and clearly, they were not in any manner intending offense. And not having the energy to argue the point, I chose to let it be.

[5.8] The shoe on the other foot:

One common joushiki that I encountered from very early on in my stay here was that all Americans – and by extension all Westerners (all Westerners at the time being assumed to be Americans) – are 'frank'; that is, very direct in their speech and always indicate their wishes by clearly stating "Yes" or "No." Naturally, all Westerners can, as the situation requires, speak directly, but at the same time are also capable of being markedly subtle in their approach, but this was not at the time (and even now) understood by the average Japanese person, this being the main reason why the nation as a whole cannot, and at this rate never ever will be able to, speak English fluently.

Speaking in Japanese, a request for help or an invitation, particularly made by a senior or a person in a socially superior position, or in a more formal relationship, can be very difficult to turn down. However, one means of doing this that I learned through a somewhat prolonged observation was the repeated usage of a carefully presented "Yes", while all along meaning "No." (This is made acceptable by the fact that 'Hai' in Japanese can be understood as both "Yes" and the much more neutral, "I hear you.") The other person has to very persistent and/or a bit slow on the uptake for it to be necessary to actually use the technique, but I do remember once taking a rather perverse pleasure in being able to come out with: "Sure." "Yes, certainly." "By all means, of course." ("Hai." "Hai." "Hai.") again and again over a period of a number of weeks, until the lady finally gave in.

However, there was also one occasion when I had to turn down a request speaking in English (from Mr Hamada [4.8], the man who had expedited the arrival of my visa and who invariably insisted in speaking in his rather stilted version of the language), and at this point I found that I was incapable of using the word "No." That is, speaking in English as we were, to respond with a very direct "No!" to a polite request for help; "Can you help me?" was, psychologically, an impossibility. Actually, I was fully aware that it wouldn't have worried him if I had used the word. To his mind, I would've been speaking in the direct manner expected of me as a foreigner. However, from my side, it would have been overly rude to even consider using the word to a man of his age and in his position, and the workings of my brain would not in any way allow it. At the same time, he was not capable of understanding my more carefully phrased rejections, which would have been obvious to a native speaker, and in the end, I had to force him into Japanese – also not polite as he was quite proud of his ability to speak in English, but I had no alternative.

(There was also the point here that, as a teacher, I was not prepared to compromise my English. If I had at that point allowed him to dictate (or even influence mildly) the terms of our engagement by adapting my language to meet his expectations, any value or meaning I might have had as a teacher would have been totally lost.)

[5.9] The real problem with joushiki:

For a Japanese person who has the concept that English speakers are 'frank' and/or that the English language lacks subtlety firmly installed in their minds, or at a somewhat milder level simply believes that what they have been taught as English in school is 'not to be argued with' (this to the extent that they will not believe a native speaker when he or she tells them that a large proportion of what they have been taught is incorrect), the chance of appreciating the reality of the other language is close to zero. And this can amount to a very serious bind.

Three or four times, in my early fifties, I was involved in interviews for the National Professional Guide Examinations in Kyoto. Applicants have first to pass an extremely high-level written test related to their knowledge of Japanese history and geography, etc., and written papers in the language of their choice, and in the final stage are interviewed by a native speaker (in this case, me) and a senior professional guide, who are charged with evaluating the level of the interviewee's spoken English, and a third person who gives a thumbs-up/down on "overall suitability," related to the applicant's general appearance or perceived character. (The only person turned down strictly related to the latter over the four years I was involved, was a (to me) very pleasant middle-aged man with quite suitably sufficient English, who chose not to wear a suit, and was penalised for such. He also had a beard – a case of the proverbial nail that sticks up still being hammered down.)

Most of the applicants were young women sent from language schools specialising in this area. Most had clearly been drilled on what they were supposed to say and a number of these passed, 3.0 out of a maximum of 5.0 being the pass mark. However, we also had one young lady in her early twenties who had been educated in England (from the age of 12 or13), and she spoke English – real English (as opposed to a regurgitation of Book 4, Lesson 23). In this situation, it was both shocking and a delight to hear my own language spoken as it should be – a complete breath of fresh air – and naturally, without any question, I gave her a 5.0. And the Japanese professional guide (a very pleasant man whose English ability was superficially perfect – I never heard him make even one grammatical mistake with his speech), not even beginning to understand what he was hearing, gave her a 3.0 + a (just) pass mark. And he had no means of understanding why I had chosen to give her a 5.0. Basically, trained not to expect subtleties in the language, naturally he could not appreciate them even when placed directly under his eye.

Around this same period, I was told by the Japanese owner of a bar, in a highly disparaging manner, that one of his Japanese customers who had spent (all of! – my insertion) two years in Canada spoke better English that I did – although how he reckoned, he might be able to judge that, I still do not know. In the end, I could only presume that he no longer wanted my custom, and I obliged.

The present prime minister, Abe, has at least a couple of times floated the (dead-on-the-ground) idea that the whole country should take up English as an (/the) official language. Presumably, he has absolutely no idea of what that might entail.

[5.10] Joushiki as applied to the world; the loaded meaning:

The Japanese dependency on joushiki would not particularly be of any concern if they restricted their 'facts' to their own society, but unfortunately, they also have created a whole system of (assumed) realities about other societies around the world, much of this information picked up from whatever casual input they have found available. And additionally, in this type of case, there will commonly be an implied comparison with the home team. The comment "Americans/Westerners are 'frank,'" noted above, viewed from the Japanese side could perhaps be better understood as "incapable of subtlety in the way we

Japanese are." And, in fact, the statement was (still is) often coupled with a: "The Japanese language is very nuanced in its approach," or some equivalent statement. And at this level, we are talking a matter of one-upmanship.

Food: Food, presumably because it is relatively easy to classify, has always been a favourite defining topic. However, here again you have a limiting factor in that, to avoid any possible misunderstandings, overlapping is not allowed: The Germans eat potatoes and sausages. The English eat bread, but not potatoes or sausages – because that is what Germans eat. (I have actually had this quoted at me in full seriousness.) "French food is delicious," commonly presented together with the deliberately contrasting "English food is bad." (Not appreciated, and perhaps should be noted here as an opinion rather than a fact.) "The Swiss eat fondue. The French are famous for their cheeses," (which is perfectly true, and to be recognised). However, that the UK has over 400 varieties of cheeses is far, far beyond their comprehension, and when I, very rarely, have attempted to point out this or similar facts to people I have met, all I have ever received is a rather blank 'Why would you be telling me that?' reaction.

What you actually have here is the 'preconceived notion', which exists throughout the world, and again would not matter if the Japanese version were not so set in stone.

Every country around the world, down to the smallest of regions within that country or even the individual home, has its own range of tastes and flavours, herbs and spices that define its cuisine, and when you visit another country, or even a separate area within the one country, the chances of you enjoying that food are very much going to depend on (1) the tastes you are familiar with (inevitably the baseline for any judgement) (2) your sense of adventure, this together with the size of your purse, and (3) the luck of the draw. Having eaten in restaurants all over the world, I do know that there are certain strong herbs that I find it hard to take in, and equally that every country, including Japan (where I have eaten out widely), has restaurants that serve good, bad, indifferent and, on occasion, quite disgusting food. Also, living in the Kansai area, I find the far stronger-tasting sauces and soups served in the Tokyo (/Kanto) area very difficult to enjoy. (People from the Kanto area naturally complain about the lack of flavour found in Kansai – particularly Kyoto – food, and on and on.)

For a tourist, if you go to a country assuming that the food is good, the chances are you will give the benefit of doubt if you meet anything which does not meet your tastes. Alternatively, if you go to a country assuming that the food is bad, the chances of having your opinion reversed during the short period of your stay are going to be pretty limited. But far more important here is the fact that if a Japanese person who has been to England and actually enjoyed the food (I do know some who have), after returning to Japan, if they choose to share that information publicly, they are (as I, also, am in a similar situation) likely to be laughed out of the room. That or totally ignored. And this is where frustrations can arise.

(This is not a matter limited to food. A Japanese friend who has spent much of her life coming and going between Japan and the UK recently remarked that, although she gets on very well with her (quite well-off, and thus presumably reasonably educated) neighbours, any discussion that touches on that area of her life is virtually impossible. They are in no way mentally equipped to handle the whole range of possibilities that that fact involves. Also, from a Japanese woman who has lived in Africa for more than ten years in a not un-rare comment in the newspaper regarding struggling to blend in on visits back to Japan: "Japanese in Japan are not very accommodating to Japanese-looking people with a different outlook on life. It would be much easier if I was a foreigner.")

There is, also, the enormous difference between living in a country and visiting it as a tourist. A woman student who had lived in Germany for a considerable period noted that it took her over ten years living there before she could even begin to appreciate German cuisine. (German food also does not have a particularly good reputation in Japan in the sense that nobody here seems to understand – other than perhaps sausages and potatoes – what it is really about.) For the record, (starting from the totally repulsive concept of actually putting raw fish in my mouth – this being long before sushi or sashimi had been promoted overseas), ten years was also about the time it took me to reach a certain level of discernment as to what good-quality sushi was. There is a vast difference in quality, and on the whole, as is true around the world, you will be paying for what you get.

[5.11] 'Mujun' (incompatibility/impossibility):

This is another word that was introduced to me very early on in my stay and that has the meaning of "a contradiction in terms" or "clash of realities." Used in a legal context, it amounts to conflicting accounts of an incident; if the suspect says that he left his home at 3:00 while a witness claims seeing him in his home at 4:20, then clearly you have a mujun. However, related to the concept of joushiki, and in particular assumptions about a foreign society, mujun results in the inability of an individual to accept whatever (real, but to their mind impossible) situation they are facing.

From television:

A Japanese reporter was introducing a large English Country Home that had been, at least in part, developed into a hotel, and at the point I picked up the programme, he was in the restaurant, where he had just been served an example of a (to me, somewhat plain-looking, but perfectly reasonable) main steak dish.

Reporter: "This is French cuisine?" (It actually did look like a steak dish as it would be presented in a French restaurant in Japan.)

The hotel manager: "No, no, no! It is English cooking."

Reporter: "It is not French?"

The hotel manager: "No. It is English."

And here (literally visible in the disbelieving expression on his face), the interviewer was presented with the true power of mujun: "The manager of the restaurant has just told me that this is English food," BUT "The food looks delicious and is perfectly presented, and therefore it cannot be English," (which, by the Japanese definition of the time was neither delicious nor well presented).

And as to what can be done in this type of situation (it was live coverage): Naturally, the scene (the media equivalent of a quick turn of the heels), with no attempt at any further explanation, was cut!

Ever since the Michelin guide started awarding stars to restaurants in foreign countries, and a number of restaurants in both Tokyo and London received recognition, of necessity (it could not be easily argued that Michelin was right in Tokyo but wrong in London), there has had to a certain acceptance of the reality of the existence of 'English cuisine'. However, this has yet to filter through in any degree to the public at large. (See [5.15])

FF: In my early thirties at a group exhibition.

Seated at the reception table next to my teacher, which was part of our duties at such gatherings, I watched as one of our visitors (a lady possibly in her seventies and dressed in a kimono as was common at the time) carefully worked through a tableful of 'shikishi' paintings (small square card paintings done by the students to help cover the cost of the exhibition and also to give them the satisfaction of a 'sale', if only a minor one), and was very pleased to see that she had selected five or six of mine, all of which she apparently liked, and now she was deciding which one she would presumably purchase. Only having started painting relatively recently, for me this was quite a thrill – the number of paintings you actually sell on these occasions contributing to your overall prestige in the group. And then having made her final selection, which I assumed she was going to buy, she paused, and I realised that she couldn't read my hanko (seal). (This was the same seal that the immigration department official had found fascinating at the time the school closed. The Chinese characters on the seal had been chosen for me by my teacher, but as phonetic equivalents they would not be easily readable for a Japanese person.) However, after a certain amount of careful consideration and musing, she walked across the lobby to where we were sitting and asked my teacher (who she clearly knew well – both treated each other very politely) which of his students was responsible for the painting. My teacher proudly indicated my position next to him. I smiled my nicest smile. And presumably at this point the unlikeliness of the situation must have registered. (She had spent a considerable amount of time and care selecting, from hundreds of pictures, a traditional Japanese painting that, it turned out, had been painted by foreigner.) However, there was no frown here or any other sense of a reaction: Her face did not change for one moment. And without looking again in my direction, and politely thanking my teacher for the information, she walked back across the lobby, returned the card carefully to the pile, turned, bowed deeply in our general direction, and exited down the staircase. My teacher, also following her with his eyes, said nothing. And I was left to wonder.

This is one of the events that I have kept in my mind right the way through my life here as somehow very special in that the apparent rejection did not in any way anger me. The lady herself was in her own way very sweet, and at the same time totally, formally – down to her carefully wrapped kimono – polite, and, upon consideration, there was nothing she could have been expected to do any differently.

In present day Japan, with the fall off in interest in the traditional among the majority of young Japanese, it has become quite common for foreigners who have become deeply involved in such traditional arts as bonsai, Japanese gardening techniques, shoyu and sake production, etc. to be featured in television documentaries, and I imagine that the chances of a similar situation to the above happening today would be relatively low, but the concept itself still has considerable relevance.

[5.12] 'Chestnuts':

"Japan has four seasons."

In reality, if you choose to count the rainy and typhoon seasons, the country has six, and all the southern island areas are semi-tropical, but that apart, in many Japanese minds this pre-empts (or at least used to) the possibility that other countries around the globe might also have four seasons that they call spring, summer, autumn and winter. (The recent twist on this, very recently heard on television: "Japan has four clearly defined seasons" – which presumably other countries don't, whatever "clearly defined" might mean.) To any outsider, this may sound stupid (even asinine), but in Japan, this is a fact; it being a primary definition of Japan in their minds, one of the first they learn when they are starting the English language, that they also connect with laying claim to their uniqueness as Japanese.

"The Japanese love (/have a special relationship with) nature."

Originating in Shinto teachings, this is perfectly acceptable until, yet again, it becomes a means of defining the (we have it, you haven't) 'Japanese spirit'. At the same time, however true it may have been in the distant past, it is certainly not so in modern Japan, whereby far the greatest proportion of the population reside in the ever-expanding metropolitan areas and have no real knowledge of and/or interest in nature at all. As an extreme here, you have the latest commercial for upscale housing promoting the concept that: "You no longer have to suffer the crowding (or those nasty mosquitoes) at a regulated campsite. You can now experience the full joy of camping by simply putting a tent up on your own personally designed roof veranda (fully illustrated)."

FF: In my early thirties.

In Japanese art and poetry, the plum blossom is invariably paired with the 'uguisu' (Japanese nightingale) and its very attractive and easily identifiable birdsong (a harbinger of spring), and there are countless paintings of this somewhat petite olive-feathered bird resting on its branches. Today, far more commonly, and seen pecking rather aggressively at the heart of the blossoms, is the very similar in size 'mejiro' (Japanese white-eye), and in this situation the two birds are commonly misidentified. (At this point, although I had not yet seen an uguisu, I was very familiar with the white-eye.) And on this particular day, when I was making sketches of the blossom in a small and relatively quiet plum-tree garden attached to a local shrine, I noticed two middle-aged ladies climbing the hillside towards me, but concentrating on my work at hand, I was too busy to follow their movements until one came out with, "Oh, look! An uguisu!" This naturally captured my interest enough for me to turn, only to find that the bird being referred to (although suitably pale in its colouring) was far too large for the species (I suspect it might have been a woodpigeon). In terms of proportionality this would be like seeing an elephant and calling it a goat. The lady's friend did express certain doubts, but these were not accepted and, quite naturally, I did not intervene.

And here you have the power of ill-placed logic. She knew that the uguisu (a bird) was renowned for perching on the branches of the plum tree, and that there was a bird (in her favour, only the one) here in front of her eyes perched on the branches of a plum tree. And her mind made the required association: The bird was an uguisu. And nothing could change the fact. And they wandered a little further around the garden until finally, fully satisfied, they made their way back down the slope. And, again, I was left to wonder.

And as a similar case:

Certain varieties of the Japanese maple, as does the sycamore tree in England and presumably the Canadian maple (all of them being related), have winged seeds that spin in the wind as they fall. There are actually relatively few of them, but they do exist quite commonly. However, for my own pleasure (I had played 'helicopters' with the sycamore seeds on the trees near my home when I was a child), I made a sketch and then a painting of a short spray, which I then took for sale at our annual group exhibition, resulting in the following conversation with another of my teacher's students (again an older lady).

"What is this?"

"It's a picture of maple leaves."

(Pointing at the seeds.) "What are these?"

"They are the seeds."

"Maples don't have seeds."

(Again, the maple leaf is a very common motif in Japanese art, and I personally have never seen any representations where the seeds are included – which is in fact why made the painting. But to her, the fact that she had never seen seeds represented in any painting almost certainly going back hundreds of years would automatically preclude the possibility of their existence. Even so, I persevered.)

"It's a sketch." (This being as close as I could come to trying to prove my point.)

"Maples don't have seeds."

This expressed with an air of absolute finality. And as we do in cases of this nature, she turned abruptly and walked away.

***

And in a more serious vein:

The Grand Shrine at Ise is central to Shinto beliefs in Japan and the main shrine buildings are rebuilt every 20 years as a part of the Shinto belief in the death and renewal of nature and the impermanence of all things. (Ref: Wikipedia.) An American political journalist, Elizabeth Drew, who was in Japan at the time of the 2013 rebuilding, wrote a column in our local newspaper based on an interview with the chief priest at the shrine emphasising how Shinto beliefs (and subsequently Japanese people) were unique in their closeness to and consideration of nature, a tale that I was told in exactly the same manner some 40 years ago at our local shrine, and which I am not prepared to argue here. However:

Around the time of the rebuilding, I happened to watch a one-hour documentary on television regarding the manner in which the wood for the new shrine had been obtained. The whole structure being built with Japanese Cypress (with an emphasis on 'Japanese' here, imported wood not being considered acceptable for religious reasons), and with the main pillars requiring logs from trees that are in the hundreds-of-years-old category, naturally, with each rebuilding, the number of trees available has dwindled considerably, which became the central theme of the programme. From some time previously, there had been reports of a number of temples in Shikoku finding large cypress trees in their grounds dying off without any warning and for no apparent reason, and it was in investigating this problem that the documentary team came to find that brokers contracted to provide wood for the shrine had been approaching temples in the area in order to procure logs of a suitable size, and when turned down, had, on a number of occasions, returned at night to drill holes in the base of the trunks of the larger trees and insert poison (at least one of holes was photographed as evidence), then returning a few weeks later to make a second offer, which naturally the temple priest would not refuse, with the sacrificed tree (in the form of a carefully trimmed and planed log) delivered as requested, presumably with the intermediaries taking their share of any monetary gains. Ignoring the fact that it was Buddhist temples that were suffering the damage here, (the island of Shikoku is famous for its pilgrimage of 88 temples associated with the Buddhist monk, Kobo Daishi), as to quite how this reality can be considered in any manner consistent with the above-proclaimed 'caring/respect for nature', I find extremely difficult to comprehend.

The Ise peninsula, which I visited many years ago, is a very pleasant area to visit, and the shrine itself quite unique in the fact that the surface of the wood, rather than being painted in the standard vermilion, is left in its natural state, the only disappointment that I had at the time being the fact that the central shrine is not open to the general public and, in fact, being placed behind locked gates, not visible.

[5.13] The origins of modern joushiki:

(The following is based on a series of reports read over time in the local newspaper.)

At the time the Europeans were moving out into the world, trading, and creating colonies in their name, Japan chose to pull inwards, with the resulting period of isolation ('Sakoku') lasting from 1633 to 1854, at which time the 'Black Ships' with Americans on board arrived in Shimoda, resulting in a forced opening of the country, first to the US and subsequently to the other Western powers. Up until this time, the ruling Tokugawa Shogunate, in order to consolidate their power, had only really needed to be concerned about how they were viewed by the other regional 'daimyo' (provincial lords). Beyond this, the caste system, which divided the populace into the four groups of samurai, farmers, merchants, and the 'burakumin' outcasts – those with occupations considered impure or tainted by death, including slaughterhouse workers and tanners – was fully sufficient to maintain control. However, it would now be understood that in order to promulgate their power, they required a firmly established identity that would promote them as both unique and worthy of respect on the international stage. Also, if foreigners were to be free to wander at will throughout the land, there would be a need for an overarching ideology for the general populace that would allow them to present an undivided face to the world (and at the same time prevent any inner disturbances or revolts). And from this point on, regardless of the reality, you came to see the elevation of the Shinto religion with its (apparently up to then not emphasised) promotion of the Emperor as a 'kami' ('god' [13.9]) – this presumably to match up against the royal houses and religious organisations that they recognised as part of the trappings of colonial power – together with a promulgation of the samurai warrior spirit as something quite distinct from the militaries of the West. And equally, within, as society expanded and the caste system weakened, it would be vital to have the overall populace, in what up until that time had essentially remained separate fiefdoms, unified under the semblance of a preferably uniquely 'Japanese' insignia.

***

And as it is promoted today:
(The following is limited to Japan as I have seen it presented on television here over a long number of years, but presumably the other media have their own equivalents.)

Most Japanese will understand Prime Minister Abe's stated desire to work towards a 'utsukushii' (beautiful) Japan as precisely the political propaganda that it is (here with utsukushii perhaps best translated as "shining" / "Japan as it was in the days of yore" / "at its most brilliant.") However, there are also the following, on the face of it much more benign statements, that I have found to be repeated incessantly in the news, on talk shows, in interviews with the general public, and at times (where you actually might expect to find statements of this nature) in commercial promotions.

"How lucky I am (/we are) to have been born in Japan." // "Every time I slip into a hot spring (/catch a glimpse of Mount Fuji /taste fresh sushi), it makes me so happy that I was born Japanese."

"Japan is 'sugoi'." / "The Japanese are 'subarashii'." – fantastic, wonderful, unbelievable – any description that may be read as self-congratulatory.

This is not a matter of simply expressing pleasure or joy, which naturally exists around the world. Rather it is the direct verbally expressed connection between that strong emotion and their identity as Japanese. And simultaneously, the statement is precluding the fact that a foreigner could experience a hot spring, Mt Fuji, or sushi in that same manner.

When I have noted the above to my students, none of them have been aware of the existence of such statements, i.e., they exist as such a natural part of the dialogue that (entering the realm of the subliminal) they pass unnoticed. To me, they have stood out simply because I could not possibly imagine similar sentences (with 'Japan/the Japanese' replaced with 'England/English people') used in similar television programmes in the UK.

***

And then, from the experts:

"No doubt that this is something unique to Japan" (Casually slipped into an exposition on Buddhist statues.) The reality apart, it is this invariable emphasis on uniqueness that comes through in programmes of this nature.

"Japanese people do…"/ "Japanese people are…" – all of which are used to distinguish or emphasise perceived differences.

Note: In presentations of this nature you are extremely unlikely to hear, "Japanese people don't do…" or "Japanese people aren't…", this for the reason that a negative statement (in that it admits the possibility of some other, possibly preferable, option), would leave the speaker open to the presentation of alternatives, and, in effect, out of control of the conversation. Equally, unless you are extremely well prepared and have a considerable amount of time available, it is extremely difficult to criticise statements of what people are or claim to be.

"Nihonjin dakara koso…da." This is an extremely strong statement, which in direct translation would amount to something like: "It is only because we are (/were born) Japanese that… we can feel like this /we have the sensitivity to appreciate…etc., etc." // That or: "It is only Japanese who can feel… / have the sensitivity to appreciate…" – either way, the ultimate 'frog in the well' view of the world.

And today we have 'shin (new) joushiki'. Truly the 'plat du jour': "This is what we are telling you to believe until we tell you to believe something different. That may be tomorrow or a couple of weeks from now, but just hang around!"

[5.14] Matters of formality:

Note: Although the basic premise is the same, I have used the word 'gatherings' (rather than parties) here to cover the somewhat more formal get-togethers with Japanese friends, acquaintances and numerous strangers that I have attended over the years.

Makiko was a young Japanese woman, roughly of the same age as Koji, who we met on our first trip back to England, when we also visited France, Spain, Italy, and Switzerland. Highly gregarious and confident in the extreme (she had already been to Europe a number of times), although we spent only a limited amount of time together, by the end of trip we had become friends enough to exchange phone numbers and addresses and subsequently meet up occasionally. A professor of the Spanish language at one of the larger universities in the Kansai area, shortly after our return (as was common at the time) it was arranged that she marry a doctor (Sugiyama) some ten years older than herself and, once settled, she began what became a whole series of gatherings to which personal friends and university colleagues were invited. Get-togethers would take place in the afternoon, with a dozen or so guests seated around a long low table, and conversations tending to be limited to the persons in your immediate vicinity. However, with Makiko having a wide range of acquaintance, each time the group would include some new face or faces (commonly foreign), which allowed for a wide range of topics to be introduced and thus making for a very pleasant experience.

And it was here, for the first time, that I was introduced to 'the introduction'.

The strictly hierarchical nature of Japanese society has resulted in the need for certain forms of address (including specific verb endings) that indicate the (superior or inferior) social standing of the person being spoken to, and therefore in a more formal situation, when addressing someone for the first time, it naturally becomes important to know who you are talking to – their 'status' – and this, preferably, before any personal interaction takes place. In the business world, this has resulted in the well-known exchanging of 'meishi' (business cards), while at more formal parties or gatherings, social custom commonly requires a (pinned-on) nameplate and/or a 'personal introduction', the latter commonly requiring every guest to give a brief speech including name and general background before the party actually begins. (Beyond indicating a person's social position, this also does allow for an easy introduction of subject matter that can be used to initiate a conversation, something which many Japanese people are not overly comfortable with, this doubly so with foreigners.)

Some time later, we also did experiment with forming a new group outside the home, where at our first meeting (in a bar that had been rented for our usage only) I insisted that, in order to create some sense of cohesion, the group circulate and that every member spend some time introducing themselves to people they had not met before – something not normally done. And it worked (Also, [7.15]).

Subsequently, we met two or three times a year until, for reasons unknown, someone decided that we join forces with another similar (but unfortunately considerably larger) group operating on a strictly Japanese-style basis – speeches, self-introductions followed by yet more speeches, attempts at karaoke (led by a close to manic Russian professor from Makiko's university, who kept insisting that other members should sing, and when they wouldn't, kept at it himself) and otherwise small groups of middle-aged ladies sitting around at tables speaking with the one or two friends they had come with, which was not something I saw as having any real meaning.

The Russian professor actually appeared again on a couple of other occasions, and I did get quite to like him. He was exceptionally intelligent, with good Japanese and a strong sense of wit, which unfortunately went completely over the heads of his audience, resulting in a total mismatch. And he understood the problem in exactly the same manner that I did, but coaxing not being his style, he was determined to use whatever means he had at his disposal to poke them out of their holes, and naturally each time he tried this, they simply dug their heads in deeper. Almost certainly, his attitude must have come from a deep sense of frustration (he took an almost perverse delight in provoking), which at one level I could fully understand. (In the name of 'international communication and friendship', he was setting himself up – or had been set up – against exactly the same deeply entrenched system that I was having to deal with.) And then, he drank (he was a Japanese sake fan) – at a pace which I could not come close to matching – and at some point, he would leave them (and occasionally me) far behind. I do remember at one party where I was thanked by Doctor Sugiyama for helping to "keep him under control." While this was not strictly so, I could understand why they might find him difficult going. However, the situation was not anything he or they could have prevented. He would have been perfect in any other country, certainly any Western country. And presumably shortly after this, he went back to Russia, where I know he had a family.

[5.15] Responses (essentially only two) to hearing that I am English:

Very occasionally, the more sophisticated will come out with, "Oh, you are a gentleman!" to which my standard reply is, presented in as light a tone as possible: "Yes, of course. I usually wear my necktie, but (unfortunately) today (for some reason) it has been mislaid." (Or something to that effect.) How much of this gets through, I am still uncertain, but it does tend to suffice in a pinch.

And the ubiquitous (essentially parroting the television channels): "English food isn't very nice, is it?" / "English food doesn't taste good, does it?"

Even today, I get this very commonly in gay bars when someone I have not met before is attempting to communicate with me, and it has got to the point that I am not quite sure whether it is merely a matter of (1) it is the only thing they have been educated to know about the country, which is for most Japanese true (2) it is intended as a put-down – that is, to put me in my place in the (Japanese first) order of things (this can normally be easily picked up in the tone of voice), or (3) being 'tough' by nature, they actually want to attract me by putting me in my place. I actually had a case that approached (3) very recently, when having walked around the bar to try a serious explanation, which I occasionally do, the man would not let me return to my seat, repeatedly pulling my hand against his tightened biceps. Fortunately, I was with Kensuke, and had a good reason to return.

I also have one very clear recollection of this particular sentence being used as an opener at a friend's party, where the man was speaking perfectly seriously and in an extremely studious tone. All things said, I don't care what other people may think about English food. I was brought up on it and – my mother being a good cook – to me there is nothing wrong with (/quite a lot of good about) it. However, you do not walk into a party and start off with the equivalent of, "I hear your wife is ugly." Not unless you are asking for a fight. However, as they say, you keep calm; although in this case I do admit to turning on *my* heel and searching out someone who I might have a more pleasant exchange with.

As an excuse, I can say to myself a million times, as they often do, that "They are not used to foreigners," or "They don't know how to converse in English," but this does not make it any less frustrating. If it was the one person, it wouldn't matter, but this has been going on since I arrived here, and it can get a little hard on the ears.

(To Japanese speakers of English, or anyone involved with the teaching of the same, learn (/first teach students) to use the softer, indirect question forms. When approaching a person for the first time, you do not ask, "Where do you live?" which for politeness' sake requires a clear answer. (I do not wish to point out my house or give my address to every Tom, Dick or Harry I meet in the park.) The indirect question, "You live near here?" indicates that you wish to speak to the person and can be answered with a nod and a smile without offending anyone.

Equally, "Do you like sushi?" to someone who is eating sushi sounds stupid ("If I didn't like it, I wouldn't be eating it."), while "You like sushi?" is merely a confirmation of the situation, and again simply indicating that you would like to start a conversation. And if you wish to know someone's nationality, the open question, "You are from?" will not offend anyone.)

[5.16] Promoting change: Minor skirmishes in an unwinnable war:

Shortly after arriving, I read a letter in the newspaper written by a teacher of the English language who was leaving Japan after a period of some thirty years, noting that he had not been able to make even the slightest dent in the manner in which the language was taught here. And fifty years on, unless I can work up the energy for one more effort, I am afraid I am going to have to say the same thing. I have taught a considerable number of students who have managed to acquit themselves quite reasonably (some extremely well) in their stays (many working) abroad, but the system as promoted through the national education system, despite minor improvements, remains as it always has been. (Foreign teachers – normally young and in the main part hired on a temporary basis – have been introduced into the system, but in that they are totally subservient to the Japanese teacher as to what areas of and how the language is taught, they can in reality only be very limited in their effectiveness.) This is not a problem limited to just the English language, but rather the attitude of the authorities (both national and local) towards outsiders' opinions, even when they are debating matters where you would normally expect an outsider opinion to make sense.

Over the years, Osaka City Hall has repeatedly held discussions on a variety of schemes (few of which have been particularly successful) as to how they could manage to increase foreign investment or attract foreigners in general to the city. Official committees formed to debate such issues have regularly included one or more foreigners to proffer their advice, but – the presumption being that a foreigner cannot possibly know more than what they as Japanese experts 'know' about foreigners – with amazing regularity, almost invariably this has been ignored. In effect, the foreigners were being placed to add a certain gravitas or prestige to proceedings – a presence co-opted as a signature of the nation's international outlook ("globalisation" was a government slogan around this period) – this before they came to understand that they were getting nowhere and started pondering whether they might not truly turn inwards and become a

"Galapagos nation." It is only in the past couple of years or so, with the sudden increase in tourism, and the government's apparent support for development in this area, that certain members of the media have actually picked up on the fact that foreigners are fascinated by a whole range of experiences that they had never even begun to consider as possibilities. How this will develop is for the future, but perhaps, after all this time, this latest influx may lead to some real reconsiderations as to how they can learn to relate to 'people from other parts of the world'.

[5.17] Offering the other a way out. Saving face:

Nothing presented in this chapter has anything to do with a particular individual's intelligence or character. Everything comes (as with my inability to say "No" in the above example in [5.8]), as the result of a highly ingrained social conditioning. But the results can, on occasion, appear to an outsider who is not aware of the problem as something close to ignorance. Basically, Japanese people are barred by their upbringing from the possibility of anything that, in the West would be understood as 'intellectual engagement', and when they are confronted, even in a very light manner, with facts that do not match their understanding of 'what is', we reach an un-negotiable wall, where they react very strongly with some combination of outright rejection, turning inwards (/blanking out on the conversation entirely) and/or exploding in frustration: "We are Japanese."/ "You are not Japanese (and therefore you can never be expected to understand)." Describing a similar situation in England here, I would be tempted to say anger, but it is not that. They just do not understand what is happening – why the conversation should have taken such an unruly course.

***

I know how to sing badly:

When I got to a certain level with singing karaoke in Japanese (initially there were no English songs), I very quickly came up against two problems which remain even today. In a bar where, even if I knew the bar staff well, I had not met a number of the customers before, invariably someone who disliked being upstaged by a foreigner (even at the time, I could sing reasonably well), would come out with something to the effect that, the song had been "learned by heart," that is, I couldn't possibly be reading the Japanese on the screen (this or, "I didn't really understand the meaning," which in many cases was a fair criticism). And when I started singing in Korean, this naturally became, "He isn't reading (Korean) Hangul characters." Therefore, to counteract this, whenever I sensed a certain antagonism in a group of new faces, I learned to misread a certain phrase or to falter with the melody at key points, which would, in most cases, pre-empt any unwanted discussion on the matter, and this actually became something close to a habit, even a signature – my own 'version' of whatever song was being rendered, although, these days, it tends to be kept for situations when I really need to keep my head down.

And then there are those who take their sense of national pride seriously (this not restricted to right-wingers), and where you are commonly dealing with an underlying strain of arrogance. And here, without a certain amount of care, you are very likely to get strong (socially, highly disruptive) anger. In one recent encounter of this type, it clearly intensely frustrated the man that I, as a foreigner, could take everything he threw at me and give back as good as I got – not really the fact that I could do it, but that I could do it fluently and in his language. I have been around a long time now, and I do know how to hold my own (sing, dance, joke, strike Kabuki poses, whatever) and in a case like this, it would be very likely that he felt that I had in some manner usurped his identity. (The equivalent would be an Indian with more of the gentleman in him than his British overseers.) And in the end – actually, as I am very familiar with the type, right from the beginning – to keep the peace, I was obliged as always to butter him up (/allow him his say). However, at my age, that I have to keep doing this eventually tires.

There are also two other factors here that can contribute to the problem, one being the fact that when I am drinking I tend to move into the local dialect, which works against me in both ways: Local people of this nature tend not to like the fact that I am fully in tune with what they are saying, and people from other areas – particularly the Kanto (/Tokyo) area – feel that I should be speaking in a more 'gentile' (i.e., as they do) manner. The second point, which can be even more problematic, is that now that I am not working and no longer carry a business card, if I don't particularly wish to spend time talking with the other person, I normally limit my introduction to the fact that I am (/was) an English teacher. And with English teachers now ranking very low in the foreigners-you-look-up-to category, this gives the other person yet that one more opportunity to feel or act superior.

"You like intelligent games!": This was presented as a criticism of me as a teacher. We were at a farewell party for my students, and the speaker actually meant games that required a certain amount of thought (and which he was not personally able to solve), e.g., a simple set of four-line riddles that I had posted up around the room for the fun of it (prizes given): "I have eyes, but I cannot see…etc. What am I? Answer: a potato." Presumably, I had offended him by not keeping to my 'inferior position' (think, movies of educated blacks coming up against prejudices in the Southern States) as perceived in his brain. (At the time, he was officially my boss, but I was very happy to see him go.)

[5.18] When words no longer suffice:

Our present apartment block has 24 units, with each occupant owning a proportion of the land directly related to the size of apartment purchased. Larger 'mansions', as such blocks are known, will normally hire an outside company to handle repairs and assume responsibility for the general upkeep of the building, but being relatively small in size, it was decided from the beginning that we would work together and make our own decisions as to when and how repairs should be made. The system itself was totally democratic, with the roles of committee head and treasurer rotated systematically among all apartment owners, and initially, although there was a clear division between certain groups of residents, in terms of practicalities, everything worked extremely well. Backroom consultations ('nemawashi'), essential to determine each group's position, were held every year prior to the annual meeting, and at the meeting itself, opinions were exchanged, and plans put to the vote and suitably executed. It took up a certain amount of time, but it worked.

And then as time passed and ownership changed hands, the original groups, which had initially formed the backbone of the system, at some point lost their sense of cohesion, and the long-term occupants, who had initially depended upon the strength of their group to present a unified face to the proceedings, were now left to fight for their respective positions on their own. And people began to scream.

The first time I faced this problem, I would be in my early sixties. Koji was not in good health, and I took on the job of committee head, which, buildings as they get older requiring that much more care, involved a considerable amount of work the year round. However, everything went reasonably smoothly until the very end, when we had all the fencing around the lower side of the property replaced, except in one small section where there already was a very high wall in place. (The construction company, who had done a lot of good work for us throughout the year, had made the suggestion, and I had gone along with it without thinking too seriously about the matter.) And the family in the one apartment that was affected, having understood that the old fence was to be replaced "exactly as it had been," took umbrage and hit the roof. In retrospect, the whole situation was approaching the ludicrous. They were in the right, and the problem could have been solved extremely easily: A simple explanation and I would have apologised, and everything could have been settled on the spot. However, for a full month, every time I went around to their apartment to discuss the matter with them, they stood there and screamed at me – first the wife, then together with her husband, and finally the daughter standing behind them, all three screaming at the top of their voices. At this point, I set in and told them that I would listen to the mother and father, but that I would not have a 15-year-old girl acting in that manner with me, and I insisted that she come out and apologise, which she did have the good sense to do. And finally, it now having become a problem which could only be settled by the whole community, I argued my position back and forth in a series of letters (everything having to be done in Japanese, this became quite an effort, but more than anything I needed a record) and the community made their decision, which, although not quite as I would have preferred it, was respected by all.

However, from this time on, not knowing who was going to start screeching next (the level of frustration correlating directly with the degree of stridency), annual meetings became something of a trial. Almost inevitably, it was the older members (including myself on one occasion) who, caught up in the heat of the moment, let loose. The younger owners, quite sensibly not wishing to get involved more than they needed to, tended to take a heads-down approach in these cases. However, again we still managed until:

(Spring, 2018) "I always knew you were a gaijin!" This thrown at me in the nastiest manner possible by yet another apartment owner who I had chosen to disagree with at our annual meeting. In return, he had been exceptionally (and very deliberately) rude to me; lecturing me in front of the whole group – something that I had had no choice but to accept from my headmaster when I was 17 but was not prepared to do so from someone who was essentially a stranger when I was 71. And not wishing to let it go at that, (I had been too tired to react fully at the time), two or three days later, I had told him a couple of truths about his attitude, which he did not know how to respond to – he was clearly trying to wriggle his way out the situation, which, in the mood that I was in, I would not let him do. And yet again, we had arrived at that impasse, that wall that can never be breached. And other than yet another letter that I circulated, the matter has been left at that, and I am beyond caring.

[5.19] An alternative viewpoint:

Japanese people love to be agreed with. They love to be praised, and there is an overwhelming desire throughout the society to be approved of in every respect. Common questions running right the way through into my fifties were, "What is your favourite Japanese food?" or "What do you like best about living in Japan?" Even the more open, "You like living in Japan?" when you got down to it, essentially meant, "Please tell us what you like about living in Japan? No bad comments, please!"

(At one point with a group of my better students, it occurred to me to answer: "I don't live in Japan." That is, viewing Japan from the perspective of someone who was brought up in a different culture, I am incapable of experiencing the society as someone born and brought up here naturally will, and for that reason the Japan as it exists for them is not the same Japan that I live in. They did understand me, but this is not an argument that you can normally bring up in any casual conversation.)

And, in equal part, while they are very quick to point out others' faults, they are not, themselves, very open to criticism. For a foreigner to indicate disagreement is inappropriate. To openly criticise is yet another level. (This does present real difficulties for anyone living here in that, as a foreigner, you are never truly in a position to know exactly what is going to offend until whatever the situation is evolves.)

(Early summer, 2018) From a local news programme: Asked to comment on the latest innovation of Japanese truck companies; introducing trackers on the vehicles so that they could work towards maximum efficiency and reduce the number of trucks running without loads – the Englishman who had been invited to comment on the matter cared to tell them the truth. Basically, "So what's new? This kind of system was introduced in the West some 20 years ago. And essentially this kind of situation is why Japan is falling behind the rest of the world!" The tone of the programme up to that point being very upbeat, the only response the announcer could come up with was a rather hurt, "Kitsui desu ne."

("That's a bit hard on us, don't you think?") And coming from an honest Englishman, the answer was, "No, not at all!" (What actually made matters worse was that the above explanation had been inserted to balance the fact that the trucking companies would be putting up prices sharply from the following day, "so get off anything you need to send urgently today" – this at six in the evening.)

The above can also be understood as another example of a foreigner 'going off script', which is very much not approved of, particularly during live broadcasts when any editing is virtually impossible without shutting down the programme. And presumably 'staying on script', that is, keeping comments interesting enough to entertain and bland enough not to offend local sensibilities (and in particular not introducing any subject matter that has not been approved prior to the broadcast) will be the first lesson that any foreigner who wishes to last any length of time on any of the major channels here will quickly learn. (A limited few have. Others with more independent attitudes have gone their ways.) As a result, those who do appear do not in the main say anything that might be considered original or add any fresh input, and even today to a large degree they are there to provide nothing more than a touch of the exotic.

In the above, less common, case, the Englishman concerned has lived in Japan for a considerable period and clearly fully understands the system as it exists. Originally invited in as an expert in his field, and being that much older than the norm, he cannot be drawn into the system quite so easily. At the same time, he makes his points both carefully and politely and thus is respected enough to be asked back when he is available. In actuality, he is doing them a service, and I sense this is understood on both sides.

So exactly who is the egoist here?

As noted earlier in this chapter, Western societies are commonly presented in the media here as individualistic to the point of being egocentric. Dictionary-defined egotism will give you "systematic selfishness," "being self-opinionated," or the more direct "too frequent usage of 'I' and 'me'."

However, what you have in reality in Japan is a very large proportion of the population who like to (and knowing nothing else, can in fact only) talk about the way they are. Totally self-centred, and devoted entirely to their own interests, fascinated with how special they are, how they feel, and with a complete lack of interest in anything other than what they have been taught to value, if you take away the above requirement of using 'I' and 'me' and replace it with "an excessive use of 'we,' 'Japanese people,' 'we Japanese,' etc.," you will be as close to the definition of an egoist as you are likely to find anywhere.

The same usage of 'we' or any similar sentence subject also allows a sense of speaking authoritatively (as to whether the speaker is correct or not being quite a separate matter), and when it comes to a real difference of opinion, they are effectively leaning on their identity as Japanese to present what are in fact nothing more than personal beliefs. If this was simply a cry "For the Emperor! For the nation!" it would not be of any particular note (extreme views exist in all societies), but the concept has permeated the whole system to the point that, in the end, you are left with a people who are willing to interact with you (and eventually, inevitably, among themselves) only within their own set limits and on their own terms, resulting in a very closed world.

And finally coming back to the personal (this addressed to any Japanese person who might happen to be reading the book), considering the countless number of times I have been obliged to comment on the beauty of the cherry blossoms in spring, I have never in close on fifty years had anyone ask me what spring in England might be like, although (See 'Chestnuts', above) presumably this would be akin to admitting that there might be such a season outside Japan. Perhaps as a suggestion to anyone anywhere who likes to promote the exclusivity of their country and society, if nothing else, it could perhaps be considered a matter of politeness to offer the person you are engaged with a chance to talk a little about theirs.

Chapter 6

A New Perspective

[6.1]

Up to this point, I have been noting everyday events (and my reactions to them) as they might happen to any person living in a foreign land. However, from this point onwards, the story, if it is to retain any real meaning, requires the taking on of a whole additional area related to the inner workings of the human brain, including both telepathy and what I have chosen to call 'dreams': the brain's ability (asleep or awake, and with or without the influence of any chemical influences) to dictate (/overrule) our basic senses, creating images – 'visions', 'ghosts,' 'poltergeists,' as you wish – smells, sounds and tastes that a person (singly or as a group) recognises as 'there', even when one is fully aware that they are not, or – in the everyday experience of a person who accepts washing his face in the morning or cleaning her teeth at night as normal – cannot be. (Any relationship here to what are normally referred to as 'paranormal activities' or the 'spirits' of those who have passed on, I will, for the moment, leave open.) There is also the question of control – as it exists in hypnotism and the usage of what is referred to in this part of Asia as Ki – to directly or indirectly control another person's physical movements. For those with some knowledge of Aikido, no explanation is required here. Otherwise, for fans of "Star Wars", Ki is probably most easily understood as something similar to the Force without any fancy light swords, and reflecting Yoda's advice, something I would most certainly advise as not to be applied indiscriminately. And, perhaps more importantly, in terms of telepathic 'messaging' and the mind, there are the questions of the degree to which any individual can be controlled and/or the degree to which it is possible for an individual himself or herself to control those somewhat random inner musings. For any reader who has not had similar experiences in any of the areas described above, the whole of the following may easiest be taken in initially as some rather odd form of fiction, but regardless of however real or unreal it may appear, it is intended as a faithful representation of a full 35+ years of my life – a world that I experienced and continue to experience, that to me is very real, including all attendant consequences from which my present 'self' derives. It is also a tale of how I came through a whole range of experiences without losing my soundness of mind (although, at certain points, I admit to coming very close), and as such – that is, if taken overall as a positive experience – may be of help to anyone who might be faced with similar circumstances.

[6.2] Ordering and details:

With so much that happened during this very long period (half of my life), and with so many of those occurrences (at least, in terms of experience) coming close to repetitions of earlier events, I have had to be very selective in terms of what details are presented, and equally, in terms of 'what happened when', the reader should expect a considerable amount of movement back and forth throughout the text. I have tried to select situations that to me were definitive in the sense that they should, without too much effort, be understandable to any average reader. Also, to aid the initial explanation, I have deliberately grouped similar types of events together somewhat at random, and then in Chapters 9 and 10, with rather more filled-out stories, I have tried to give some sense of how all the various parts fit into a whole.

[6.3] An exhibition:

Traditionally, young Japanese up to the age of 40 have been referred to as 'seinen', and therefore quite possibly, this occasion could have been, at least from the Japanese side, understood as a coming-of-age initiation ceremony.

I had become familiar with (and had had no particular trouble accepting) a considerable number of the above type of happenings (to the point that I had already attempted to use what I understood as 'the power of my mind' to cure a friend of cancer) some time before the events described in this chapter occurred – relating them in my mind without any particular problem to eight to ten years plus of serious practice of Hatha yoga [13.13]. However, it was not until the below-described exhibition, when I was inveigled into joining a 'secret society' and a very large spanner got thrown into the works, that I found myself involved with a far larger and more incomprehensible world than I could possibly have imagined. And perhaps most importantly, it was here for the first time that I was actually obliged to think about what was happening to me: Before this, all my life, I had simply taken at face value whatever life had thrown up at me and reacted accordingly, but from this time on I discovered that I was no longer to be allowed the luxury.

[6.4] The lead up:

My first large exhibition, held in my early thirties, might best be described as a 'happyoukai' – a display of a student's progress in their respective field, with much of the work displayed derivative to one's studies. However, at this point in my mid-forties, I had been painting independently for a number of years, and everything displayed, in terms of both subject and technique, was intended as very much my own, that is, it was in every respect what in the West we would refer to as 'an exhibition'.

The whole thing was decided upon at very short notice, a gallery that had recently opened suddenly receiving a cancellation, allowing me about six-months preparation time. I already had a certain number of completed paintings from which I could select, but I did need one centrepiece, and also had to paint a sufficient number (in the end, 200) of shikishi (square cards with simple paintings [5.11]). A recognised artist will, as in the West, be sought out by galleries, who will then take their profit in terms of a (considerable) percentage, but otherwise you pay a fixed (essentially, rental) fee up front, and any 'profits' become the artists to pocket. Thus the shikishi were painted so that friends or casual visitors could take a 'souvenir' home, with the relatively small amount of money paid intended to help cover basic (framing, etc.) costs.

[6.5] Two paintings and a 'shi' (Chinese guardian lion)

Bamboo:

Bamboo is traditionally taught to all beginners of ink painting as one of the 'shikunshi' (The four gentlemen: the orchid, chrysanthemum, plum/peach blossom and bamboo), before students then move on to mountain scenery. However, probably because I couldn't catch the essence of the Chinese mountains, and also presumably because my little 'stick-men' Chinese sages invariably, as my teacher put it, looked like 'gaijin' (he was quite correct – you can't paint what you don't know), somewhere midway through my studies, he had me spend a full three years painting bamboo and nothing but. (I also did spend a certain amount of time sketching the branches and leaves.) However, once done, that was it, and we moved on to other styles. And then much later, in my early forties, growing very frustrated about a rather fiddly painting that I was attempting, I took a separate blank sheet of paper, and just 'let it all out'. And it came, just like that, with no thought or planning at all – one of the few times when I have had the full confidence to really allow everything accumulated up to that point to flow freely. (Photo 1.) The total painting took no more than possibly ten loadings of the brush (which is repeatedly applied until dry), and possibly four (maximum five) minutes to complete. (The brush has to be manipulated at a certain speed to bring the painting alive.) And in every respect it was perfect – so much so that the last few strokes were painful to apply; even as my arm moved, my brain was finding it almost impossible to accept what was happening, and I was terrified of messing the whole thing up, which can be done, even on a last stroke. And I have never been able to really approach the subject again: Whenever I used my mind to plan some different composition, I found it impossible to get that touch, and in the end, not being able to accept something less, I just gave up and moved on.

Chinese peonies:

This was the aforementioned centrepiece, the largest painting in the exhibition – a full plant as you might see it in a garden with two fully opened flowers and one bud – done on a thicker-than-normal, full-sized sheet of 'washi' (Japanese handmade) paper that I had found in the countryside on the island of Shikoku, which allowed for a very lush rendering of the petals and also removed the need for any colouring.

In the 'Nanga' Southern Style school of Chinese painting, to which my teacher belonged, it is very common to add a soft wash of colour over the whole scene, or in certain cases at a single point, and the latter I had come to understand as a technique in larger paintings to 'draw the eye', and in particular (during the learning process) equally as a technique to draw the eye away from any particular weakness in a painting. (That is, if you got it correctly, the application of a small amount of colour would allow for a somewhat mediocre painting to become a 'masterpiece', or at least make it suitably presentable to the more amateur eye.) In the case of the Chinese peony, my teacher commonly (and quite respectably) added a certain amount of colour to the central cluster of black stamens in order to deepen the effect and bring out the strong curves of the inner petals. However, as a challenge, I had decided that I wanted to do the whole painting in black and white only, which is considerably more difficult, and in the end, through repeated efforts, I did get it right. (Photo 2.) (Actually, in this case, it being central to the whole exhibition and thus very important, Koji would not it let me stop working at it until I had completed it to his satisfaction. And in terms of actual outcome, he was correct.)

Pairs of Chinese guardian lions carved in stone or bronze are a common sight throughout Asia in front of temples, shrines, or the homes of important people. In Japan, such statues are referred to as 'komainu' or 'shishi'. (See: "A-Un." [13.12]) Considered mythical creatures with protective benefits, the lions themselves can also be found portrayed in wood carvings or paintings frolicking among Chinese peony flowers, the young one's half hidden beneath the enfolding leaves. And one or two nights before the exhibition was due to start, a live 'shi' appeared, walking slowly towards me, in my dreams – a totally elegant creature with a deep cream coat (and, incidentally, nothing like a lion). It only stayed with me a few moments and then it was gone, but considering subsequent events, it would seem it appeared there as it should have. (As to how I knew it to be a guardian lion, see 'Dreams': [8.18]) Also, shortly after the exhibition, I had the Chinese sound 'shi' transmitted into my conscious brain, one time only but very clearly. At the time, (I was not aware of any meaning of the word at this point), I took it to be an indication that I could be taught languages through my brain system, but it would now seem much more likely that it was an attempt to teach me that particular word.

Chinese peonies (60cm. X 90cm.)

Bamboo (35cm. X 90cm.)

[6.6] The media:

After sending a selection of my paintings and general introduction to the media, I was lucky enough to be given a half-page introduction (interview and photographs) in the Mainichi Newspaper, considered the top newspaper here as far as art is concerned as it regularly sponsors full-scale exhibitions of both top-level Japanese and foreign artists. Also I was covered in three other local newspapers/magazines, and perhaps most importantly in the JR (National Railways) magazine, which is offered free at stations throughout the Kansai area, resulting in visitors coming from considerable distances, many from outside the prefecture.

After the event itself, I was offered the chance to go professional by the president of the Mainichi, but I had already developed a strong aversion to being used by the system, and at the time I was asked, I had seen more than enough examples where the distributing arm; department stores, strings of wholesalers and interim nobodies, had all combined to take far more than the lion's share – a minimum of 70% of the final selling price – on works produced by the artist. (I also had gained inklings as to how the system was actually worked around, but even so it was not something I wanted to get involved in.) And more importantly, I had my work to do and a book to be written. Even understanding that, it being so far away from mainstream English teaching, it had relatively little chance of actually being published, it was my life work, and I couldn't just give it up.

[6.7] The event:

The night before the exhibition actually started (we were still hanging frames), a man I had never met before walked in, asked me which was my best painting and how much I wanted for it and made the purchase on the spot. And it, in the end, being a good painting (the Chinese peonies – one that I still count, with the above bamboo, as very special), I had the confidence to ask what I wanted for it, and in large part, the exhibition was paid for.

And it didn't stop. From the following morning, we had a flow of visitors that kept the gallery close to packed from the moment the door was opened each day right through to lock-up time, every day for a total of six days. Every painting in the gallery (including the 200 shikishi) was sold, quite a number to people I had never met before (some of whom became lasting friends), which, at my level at the time, was extremely satisfying, and I received 10 or 12 orders for "the same painting," which was of course, using sumi ink, impossible, but I did manage to complete all in one way or another satisfactorily. And therefore, at one level, I had a success on my hands.

[6.8] An introduction:

At some point in my early teens, I learned that my favourite uncle belonged to the Freemasons, explained to me at the time as a 'secret society', and for the short time that I thought about the matter, it cheapened him in my eyes. I don't know why but, even with the understanding that they were there to help each other in need, which is about as much as I was told at the time, I could not see the point. Why would you need a secret society just for that? And more than anything, the concept itself of a 'secret society' seemed incredibly childish. However, reading a little about it on the Internet just now for the first time, I understand that it is a group that you can apply for, which was not the case with the following, where I was simply informed that I was a member of such a group, that everyone I would meet in the gallery during the exhibition was also a member, and more importantly that no one who wasn't could enter that space. No explanation as to the purpose of the group was given at the time, and in fact never has been, leaving me with considerable room (35+years) to idly speculate. (See, next chapter.)

The lady was not someone who I knew extremely well – I might have met her two or three times previously – and, if I remember correctly, she was from somewhere in South America, and actually went back there shortly afterwards. I do remember being with her before the exhibition at a barbecue arranged by Hiroshi [4.7], where we were offered (apart from a limited supply of beef) a range of guts and entrails – anything from the carcass that is normally discarded – served up as delicacies, and that, being a polite guest, I ate what I was given.

If I remember correctly, it was the second day when, noting that I was looking tired, she took me outside the gallery and sat me down on a chair to "give my shoulders a massage," which she then proceeded to do in front of the passing crowd, all the time explaining the basics as above, and naturally the sign by which I was to recognise others. It being late in the afternoon, when a little tiredness was coming through, and not knowing quite how one should react otherwise in these circumstances, I just sort of said "Oh!" to myself a couple of times and went along with the ride.

Back in the gallery, one of the first examples I was shown of the sign being formed was a young girl of twelve or so pointing at one of my paintings. I let this go at the time (I was not in any position to argue), but simply following the tremor of her hand, she could have been making any the countless similar signs that are regularly introduced in movies and novels related to societies of this nature, giving me my first whiff of "Excuse me!!!" And from this point on, although the woman kept leading me, she did not actually verbally tell me to do anything. Neither was there a voice in my head instructing me in any particular manner, but rather I simply understood that this was what was expected of me. I understood, also, that I was not to make it obvious what I was doing.

At a previous event in a large store in Osaka, I had appeared with a number of other foreigners each selling their own wares, both painting and selling my work, and at this time, we had had cartoon portraits sketched for us and hung in our own booth, and I had brought this to the present exhibition for fun. (The portrait wasn't exactly me, but it *was* fun.) However, at this point, I was required to bow to my own likeness and at the same time thank my parents for giving birth to me, which I duly did. I do know that the latter is a very established custom in Japan, expected when young people graduate from school or university, or otherwise are recognised as adults. However, at this point, and coming from a separate culture, it not being anything I could truly relate to, I merely went through the motions. That said, observing form over content, as always, being the better part of social intercourse here, presumably it satisfied. (It was only a number of years later, on deck, returning from a visit to the coral reefs off the Australian coastline, and after experiencing two hours of uninterrupted beauty observing and photographing reflections on the surface of the sea and cloud formations – vague puffs of white, clustering and re-clustering against the open sky – that I was moved enough, from my heart, to thank them for their part in bringing me into this world.) As to why I should be required to pay homage to an image of myself, other than it being a possible reference to some counterpart/counterparts who may exist out in the world (or universe) somewhere, I will leave to the reader.

[6.9] Visitors (a.k.a. 'society members'):

Naturally, this included just about everybody I already knew (foreign and Japanese), including a large number of associates and students from the company; my sumi-e teacher and family and a whole group of students that I knew through him, just about every member of Koji's family, who all came to stay for the occasion; a number of friends from the gay community; customers from Koji's bar, and etc., etc. Also, thanks to media exposure, we had a very large number of people who I had never met before, who in the end could perhaps best be described as a representative cross-section of the world as it exists: the good, the bad and the indifferent. (Some examples are given below.) Also, as the one person who truly knocked me, my 'worst-student-ever' from the company – who had managed to intake nothing in over ten years of classes and (although there was nothing actually wrong with him in his own way as a person) could perhaps generously be described as "thick" – made an appearance, really making me question what was going on. Quite what were we supposed to be?

***

[6.10]

The phone rang precisely at nine. I hadn't been expecting any calls as the gallery wasn't due to open for another hour. Perhaps it was for the owner.

"Is there anyone there?"

"No."

"I'm at the station. Will it be all right if we come now?"

"Yes."

Even as I put down the phone, I realised an oddness in this conversation. First off, I was there. But more than that, my own voice had sounded very strange, not normal (close that of a lost child) which stuck a little uneasily in my mind.

And ten minutes later, they came. The man, tall and slim and I would guess somewhere in his late fifties, was dressed very smartly in a greyish suit, and walked with the same air of confidence that I had recognised in his voice. Bowing at the door as I welcomed him, but with no effort to make anything that could be considered small talk – he did not actually speak to me other than to say "Thank you" as they left – he then put all his attention into viewing the paintings on display. However, he was imbued both with a natural sense of authority and quiet politeness that I appreciated. He also was, quite apparently, a senior member of one of our local yakuza (underworld syndicate) organisations.

"If someone from abroad can come to Japan and produce something like this, exactly what kind of shit does that make you?" (This is a free translation, but the tone is most definitely presented as intended.)

This was addressed to a man of indeterminate age who had been following him step by step around the room. Possibly around half his boss' height – from the moment they had entered the gallery, he had remained hunched over in a frozen cringe, hardly raising his head enough to recognise his surroundings – and even now, he stayed still; no response attempted, locked inwards, and his boss appeared no longer to notice him until, prior to leaving, he was somewhat curtly required to sign the visitor book on the reception desk at the entrance. This, as checked shortly afterwards, amounted to a spider's scrawl – certainly, nothing that I could read.

And they left. And that was it.

FF: Two days later, we had three local 'chinpira' (low-ranking yakuza hoodlums) who came in and made a great show of lounging about (legs fully outstretched) on the stools in the centre of the room, which under the circumstances I could only smile at. And fairly quickly perceiving that they were not having quite the intended effect, they stood up and swaggered out.

(Not by any particular choice, but both of my homes here have been positioned quite close to the offices/headquarters of (at least, what at the time was) one of the largest groups of Japanese gangsters in the country. There since has been a very strong effort to wipe them out, but at this time they still had a strong presence in the community.)

***

[6.11] 'And then he kissed me':

Seated among a small group around a low table in the centre of the gallery, I was introduced to an older gentleman, a very pleasant man I would reckon was in his early eighties. After we had talked a little while, and I was about to get up and circulate (the room was quite crowded), for no apparent reason he suddenly leaned across and kissed me lightly on the lips. Again, not quite knowing how to respond (no one else in the group had reacted in the slightest), I leaned across to return the favour, upon which he quickly raised his hand indicating that that was not to be done. Throughout the conversation, there had been no indication, and even now I do not believe that he was gay or even that he was attracted to me. This had to be something different – at the time, I took it as some sign of recognition or possibly respect – and in my life since, it has happened only two or three times (once I do remember in particular with a gay person I actually liked) but in each case there was always that quick indication that it was not an action to be returned from my side.

***

[6.12] Three months earlier:

(The reader may interpret the following short story as they wish. Nothing is claimed here other than the fact that all events stated are recorded as they happened: This is not a story that one easily forgets. At a minimum, it should offer some indication as to the state of my mind at the time.)

He stood, his arms on the fence, looking down across the city. The hospital complex was clearly identifiable, and he knew the room; its position and number, the shikishi, with its painting of a single narcissus,[8] perched on the window ledge, that had been given at the time of his visit; and the man in his bed, his face wan from repeated medications. At this distance, he should be close enough to be known, and the same time far enough away not to be recognisable. And remaining still, he concentrated on that image, his full attention on making some kind of contact, until, released (but still not knowing), he moved away from the edge to continue his walk.

John and Mark:

John (an American in his sixties) and Mark (his Japanese partner of more than twenty years, and in his late forties) had appeared some two years earlier, with no particular reason given other than Mark was there to see his family (he was from a good family in the area, and John also was well-off), and moving in the same circles, we became friends. It was only very much towards the end, after he was hospitalised with cancer of both the brain and his 'internal organs'[9], that we came to understand that he had come back to Japan to die.

They had their own agreement to play around, and I actually fell, rather heavily, for Mark, but his taste in men (as is commonly the case) was apparently quite different. Still, right through, I cared for him very much as a person, which would presumably explain subsequent events, and when Koji told me – this I

---

[8] Flowers can have very different associations in varying cultures, but for me personally the narcissus (being very common here and also matching my painting style) was essentially a substitute for all the very early spring flowers that I cared for in England.

[9] The medical classification here in Japanese includes the intestines but otherwise covers a considerable area and is extremely vague.

guess would be after my visit to the hospital – that he had said he wanted to 'hug' me (the Japanese word, 'daku', here also having sexual connotations), momentarily it gave me quite a jolt. And then some two weeks after the above walk in the mountains, I was with Koji on the way to our plot of land in the countryside, driving up a long, straight incline on the expressway (I still know the exact spot, and even now with Kensuke re-live the event each time we go in that direction), and in the quiet (other than for the bare necessities, we tended not to talk in the car) I felt a 'buzz' – best described as a fine ticker-tape or microfilm being stamped into place one small square at a time as it extended there and back across one small inner section of my brain. And then completed, it was now in the lower cavity below my chest, again moving right and left in exactly the same manner. And I sat quietly, letting it move of its own accord, until Koji suddenly boomed out something into my ear, and the chain (/connection?), or whatever it was, was broken.

And, shortly after this, the doctors told Mark that, while his inner organs were still affected, the section of his brain that had been cancerous had cleared. And when the two of them walked into the gallery, big smiles on their faces (I hadn't been told they were coming), I hugged him very hard and long in front of the whole world.

(A month or so later, after his death, John told me that, although most of his works had been 'troubled' – he had been an artist all his life – his last painting before they came to Japan had been that of an open blue sky, which I chose to read as a suitable requiem. And I still keep him close in my heart.)

***

[6.13] "I have been waiting so long to meet you."

From the first day, people brought flowers: the large decorative potted orchids that are common at this type of event, together with lilies, chrysanthemums and just about everything that was available on the market at the time. With corners quickly taken up, by the third or fourth day, the whole central area of the gallery had become a riot of colours and contrasts, just awaiting a suitable centrepiece. And then I had my roses.

Although I had not met her before – it was only in recognising her husband, Mr Ohta, smiling behind her that I worked out who she actually was – she entered the room with such an expression of total joy on her face, it was as if we had known each other forever. And without a moment of hesitation she gave me the largest bunch (50 stems) of the most beautiful deep-red roses. Although I had known her husband from our work together in the company, we hadn't been close, but from that point on they and their children became the closest of friends, her husband actually managing to visit my last exhibition two years ago.

And then there was a woman who brought a small vase of wild flowers, which she insisted on placing next to my manga portrait, and which would've been quite reasonable if she had not kept on insisting upon how much effort it had taken her find them, particularly one flower she emphasised as extremely rare and difficult to find, which for me, knowing the mountains and knowing that flower in particular as reasonably common, did not particularly impress. (I instinctively didn't like her; the sense that she was exaggerating her importance and at the same time that she represented an uncomfortably fawning presence.) Even today, the only possible connection that I can make here is with the 'wild flowers in a jam-jar' for which I won prizes as a child, the flower that she emphasised being very similar to the one that had been singled out as (for a child of eight) 'rare' by the judge when awarding me first prize, which may be, but at the same time seems rather too far out.

***

[6.14] 'Queens':

For six to eight years, from my late twenties into my early thirties, Koji and I took to weight training at a local gym where there were two coaches, one of whom took his body building very seriously (and even now, at close to eighty, enters contests), and at one point we were invited to his home to meet his wife and daughter (around 14 at the time). Both of them were the loveliest of people, but nature had been shockingly unkind to the mother (her jaw and cheekbones were strongly distorted), and for whatever reason she had been fated to pass her genes along to her daughter. (Facially, they were almost identical.)

I had sent an invitation card to the husband, not really expecting anything as I hadn't seen any of them for quite a while, and in fact he did not make an entrance (leaving me wondering at the time if I was to ever count him as a 'member'). However, his wife and daughter did come – the mother much as I remembered her, but the daughter now towering over her (she was well over six feet, taller than any Japanese woman I have ever otherwise met), and most wonderfully (at a time when people who had even the smallest deformity were seldom seen in the streets) in the way that they held themselves and walked in the most natural, and at the same time refined manner possible, they exuded 'presence' – their own very personal magic: And, assuming the existence of some other realm out there, either of them would have been a queen.

***

[6.15] The girl and the rabbit:

Very early on in my studies, my teacher had given me a rather old, small clay-ware rabbit with a narrow hole in its back and one at the mouth, which, it was explained to me, I could use when I wished to replenish the water on my ink-stone while I was painting. (I did actually use it for short while, but very soon found it much easier to scoop in water from my brush-wash bowl – not very elegant but far less fuss, and in fact what my teacher did in class.) That said, it did come useful placed together with the ink-stone at the entrance to exhibitions so that visitors could sign the guestbook using brush and ink – this still being quite common at the time.

And someone brought a young girl of around 10 or 11 to see me, introducing her as having recently started studying sumi-e painting, and also that she liked rabbits. This being in the afternoon of the final day, I only had two shikishi left on the table in front of me, but I stood them up in front of her and told her that she could have the one she liked. This was not exactly a test, but she quite naturally (and correctly) took the one a child would, rather than the one I, as an adult, would have chosen, and she was very happy with it, and I wrapped it for her to take home. However, this all done, the lady who had brought her stood there and once again said, "And she likes rabbits very much." And then a third time, looking over towards the entrance desk, something to the effect of, "All her life she has loved rabbits." And all that I could come out with was, "Oh that's lovely. You should paint rabbits," until eventually they left. And it was only much later that it dawned on me that I was supposed to have responded with an "Oh, I have the perfect thing for you."

[6.16] Tiredness:

Quite to what extent the whole of the above event (/events) had been stage-managed, I cannot say (I went over the matter so many times in my mind after the fact – see next chapter), but in retrospect I do know that, at best, I was taking part in some very peculiar form of 'theatre', and that in the end, I (or rather my emotional base in terms of extreme highs and lows) was being (at certain points, quite nastily) manipulated. But now, getting towards the end, and the above being no more than a very small sample of the type of encounter I was being repeatedly exposed to, it became apparent that someone (presuming that they had even considered the matter, which may not be so – the intention from the start had been to send me over the top?) had made some heavy miscalculations as to quite how tired the whole situation might actually make me.

For the record, apart from everything described above (the preparation in terms of painting, planning, and interviews, etc. and the intense excitement and success of the event itself), at that time I had been subject to a heavier-than-normal workload for quite some number of years at the company, and for the past five or more years had been spending two days each weekend involved in very heavy physical work cleaning up our plot of land in the countryside. However, at this stage, I was in a state of extended tension, experiencing moments of both pure exhilaration and overwhelming tiredness, and clearly fine-wired for a breakdown. And coming towards the evening on the final day, having gone into the toilet at the back of the gallery, I flipped. Unable to take any more, I allowed myself to succumb to the exhaustion and started suffering from extremely severe delusions.

And from this point on, I was working along what I described in [4.6] as my 'fine line'. At certain points, I was out of control. At others (indicated as necessary) I was reacting to others' instructions; very much 'doing what I was told'. And again, at others, although to the onlooker my acts would naturally appear extremely strange, I was acting of my own volition: I knew exactly what I was doing. And finally, there were points which will have in the end to remain unclear. As I came to recognise later, there is a lot of deceit – even to the point of fooling oneself (in order to fool others?) – in this new world I was entering.

[6.17] A black hole:

He sat, cut off from the outside world by the small and now empty back office. The owner, after informing him that the main light bulb in the toilet had gone, had taken herself back into the gallery. And the absence of any noise, together with the cool darkness, was totally pleasing. And he sat...his mind empty... Until, knowing that that same outside world would not leave him there forever, he stood and moved over to the small sink, which did have its own very small, somewhat reddish light bulb above it, just enough for him, as he worked at his hands, to be able to see the weariness in his face. And then looking beyond into the empty mirror space, he recognised a dark absence – a black hole, way out in space, waiting there to draw him in and on to someplace far, far away – to whatever was out there on the other side. (There had to be somewhere on the other side.) And understanding that this was the right thing to do (it being what he always did when he was desperately lonely; back in the 'buttery' bar in college, blind drunk from a rugby binge; and then later twice as he worked his mind around to ending things, yet again, 'once and for all', he stripped off all his clothes, flushing each one down the toilet to emphasise the finality of the situation.)

And there was a knock on the door.

(They couldn't have left me just that little bit longer?)

***

And they found me a new, light grey tracksuit to wear (I still have the top.) And the ambulance came and (together with Koji and Mrs Oka [4.2]) took me away.

[6.18] Getting out of a tight squeeze:

Driven directly into the hospital basement, a totally bare space (cement walls and exposed pipes), I was laid out on what I can only describe as a central slab, where a young doctor came to examine me. My head was clear enough to answer his questions (my mind had been perfectly lucid right the way through to this point), but before I could even begin to speak, I found myself experiencing a tickle low down in the back of my throat that, after forcing itself down into my chest, quickly developed into a paroxysm of deep coughing that was way out of my control. And suddenly without any warning, my whole body was erupting in spasmodic jerks, and the reverberations were deafening. And I could do nothing. The young doctor did spend quite a while attempting to calm me, but then, after leaving the room, he came back to say that the hospital could not admit me in that condition and left. Koji and Mrs Oka helped me stand, the coughing ceased, and we walked back up the short distance to the entrance and I was out. And here it became apparent that Koji had had the good sense to have us taken to the hospital closest to our home, a simple 10- to 15-minute walk up the hill. And the sun was shining, and for the first time in a long time I felt I could relax.

And, as they say, all would've been well again, except for the fact that coming up to the local railway line just below our apartment building, we found the narrow road on the opposite side of the crossing blocked by a group of boars.

Boars are common up in the mountains here, and fully grown males, which are really large and powerful (I had met one previously, and taken a very roundabout detour through the woods in order to keep well out of its way), and females with their young when they are still small, are not to be tangled with, but this group – seven or eight females and their half-grown young – which had presumably come down to rummage for food, did not seem particularly aggressive and, presumably with the ulterior motive of it allowing me to leave the other two, as neither of them would come with me (actually, I was teasing them), I decided that they would do me no harm and went forward on my own.

If the walker is not threatening, and if they are approached carefully, boars tend to be the ones to shy, but in this case, they did not have the space to easily get around me, and at the same time clearly not wanting to go backwards, they formed into a somewhat disturbed huddle on the narrow slope. Whereupon, partly as a result of my still being in a lightheaded state but more because it seemed a common-sense approach, I lay down on the tarmac and allowed them to approach and sniff me. Which they immediately did, and presumably having decided that I was nothing to be afraid of, they trotted off down across the line to continue their search, and I got to walk up home in peace.

[6.19] The induction ceremony:

(Reader warning: The following couple of sections are not for the overly squeamish, and not recommended to be read over dinner.)

It was much later in the evening (I would have no idea of the time here but it was completely dark outside) when I walked out of the house and again up the hill as far as a small side path, somewhat overgrown with weeds and uncut branches, which I had seen many times previously but never been along, and for no reason other than it seemed worth the inquiry ("Curiosity killed the cat!"), I went in, soon finding myself at the foot of a rough flight of stairs leading up to a small shrine. The shrine building (since destroyed in the earthquake) was not in view, but I knew it to be there because I had glimpsed it previously from a separate entrance. And from this point, I recognised that I was being told what to do.

First, I had to take off my clothes (which I did, folding them neatly and placing them at the side of the path), and then I was instructed take up a yoga pose and hold it for a specific period of time. I cannot remember exactly how long for now, but it was nothing that would normally be especially difficult if I had been at home. However, here I was in my bare feet on a rough slope, and I found that I could not hold the Vrksasana tree posture – standing on one leg with the other leg bent upwards, foot across inside of opposite thigh, and arms held aloft with palms together – for the required amount of time, leaving me a little frustrated, until I realised that the answer would be a Savasana posture. (This latter merely requires lying flat on the back and relaxing each one of the body's main pressure points before letting the mind enter the heart – whereupon the heart itself becomes a 'sun', radiating its energy throughout the whole body.)

And now we get to the unpleasant bit, where first I was ordered to defecate and, that completed, to take a bite out of what had just come out. At the time, I allowed this to go by – observing to myself that it was my own turd that I was eating and it was clean – but, considered much later, as an initiation ceremony, which is presumably what it was supposed to be, if this was the frat-boy culture level of intelligence we were working at (I was well over 40 at the time), it wasn't anything to be impressed about. And then to 'leave my mark', everything had to be smeared on the rocks by the side of the path (plus the grass, to clean off my hand as best as I could), and this was followed by a short (and for me, hurried) walk around the block, leaving at the top end of the steps and entering back into the grounds the way I had come in originally, after which I was allowed to get dressed again and go home. All one really needed, you might think, for a pleasant night out.

However, reaching our building, it occurred to me to wonder whether the boars might not still be around, and with nothing else really to do (there was no one home), I kept on down as far as the railway line (naturally, the boars weren't there) and then right on down as far as the main road just above the hospital, where, instead of crossing, I crouched down (modern dance style) outside the door of a small corner shop (a lonely sort of place that very few people visited even in the daytime) and proceeded to stretch and circulate my arms and legs in a somewhat exaggerated and highly pretentious manner for what must have been a number of minutes, before it clicked with me that there was nobody there (not even any cars passing at that time of night) to watch me making a fool of myself. However, it was also midway through this 'performance' (my arm raised elegantly to the sky) that it came to me that it was exactly that.

(Exercising at home with CDs, and utilising a combination of rhythmical motion, deep breathing, yoga positions and the little I have learned of tai chi, there are times, as with the bamboo painting described above, when I recognise that I have been taken to a point beyond myself – my whole body reacting solely to the music. Equally, there are points when I recognise that the moves, although they would almost certainly appear identical to any onlooker, are in fact subject to a certain (if only slight) exaggeration that has been directed by my conscious self.)

And now, viewed from my present position, I suspect that the whole of the above involved a certain element of 'payback': I had done as was required, and for a short while, I would do as I pleased.

And then, tired again, I wandered up the back streets until, close to home, again for no reason except perhaps that I was after some quiet, I entered the garden of a rather large house, where moving up to the entrance, a woman (in a novel, she would no doubt be represented as a 'hag') appeared at the bay window. The room was dark behind her, but pulling the lower corner of the curtain aside and waving her hand at me vigorously, she indicated that I should leave. She also appeared to be shouting at me, her mouth forming words, but it was nothing that I could hear, and in the end I came to assume that what I had seen was an apparition (she wasn't the first and most certainly not the last of the visions that I was subject to – see 'Ghosts' [8.9]), and I suspect that the first thing that any real owner of a house like that might have done in such circumstances would be to call the police. However, at the time, I simply nodded my acquiescence and left.

And back home (the following being me plus a couple of beers at work): Having started a small fire on the top of our 'kotatsu' (low table) – and for all my being over the top, I was careful to keep it small and, in the end, poured beer over it, so some part of my brain was definitely at work here – I made an attempt to masturbate using the empty beer can. (This was not really successful and not recommended, although, with something of an effort, I did visualise myself melting the metal around the opening in the top of the can to get myself in.) And then really having had enough, I blanked.

And the next day they came home.

***

[6.20] The first thing that I noticed when I got up off the couch (where I had spent the night), was that they had taken my 'envelope opener' – a small, slim dagger with a highly decorated metal handle, of the type a ninja might have hidden about his or her body (it was an antique), and although I do understand why they might have taken it, I certainly wasn't in the mood for stabbing anyone. And more importantly, I have never been given it back, which does annoy me even now.

And then there was the empty metal box on the table (which had been received during the exhibition – the cookies now gone) that for no reason I picked up and started examining, only to discover that my eyes were functioning in a way that I had never experienced before. What had been merely a rather pleasant but somewhat flat (/insipid) floral design on its exterior – something that my brain had up to that point dismissed as nothing more than common (/mediocre) – had become vividly alive, and I was suddenly appreciating the colours and detailing in a very special light. I did quite easily recognise this as a form of heightened awareness, but even so I found it very difficult to replace the box on the table and let the moment go.

Years later in Australia, I found a very elegant and inexpensive antique dish, apparently originating in Germany, which utilised traditional Japanese (birds, grasses, insects) motifs on a shocking-pink background (certainly not Japanese, but the combination worked) and that at first viewing appeared in the above light: It was brilliantly beautiful. Also, fortunately, it kept much of whatever it possessed even after I brought back to Japan. Up to now, I had always assumed that finding it in the way I did, made it something special. However, juxtaposed here with the above story, its existence might almost be interpreted as a warning to the many people who collect antiques (commonly – at least here in Japan – at incredibly high prices), and until disabused of the fact on some local version of the "Antiques Road Show," remain convinced of the value of their 'finds'. Without care, it must be extremely easy to end up with some old tin box (or its equivalent).

[6.21] A visit to the quack:

They claimed that he was a psychiatrist, but after a 15-minute interview in which I answered everything he asked me as politely as I could, he claimed that I had been repeatedly screaming at him. This could not have been possible because Koji and Mrs Oka had been sitting in the next room and they would have heard anything that I had let out in more than a normal speaking voice. I subsequently agreed to drink the medicine that he had provided, but otherwise just refused outright to have anything to do with him. (Psychiatry at the time was not yet a developed profession here, but in this case, he was operating out of a very narrow, back-alley joint, making me wonder how they had actually found the place.) At any rate, as a result, from this point on I decided I would have to act as my own physician, analysing in the best manner I could whatever was thrown up at me, which has been the case.

[6.22] Practicalities:

The clearing-up process:

Advice from one of my teacher's students given during the exhibition: "If you get over-tired, make a list." And it worked; my first involving some 50 to 60 items (paintings to be completed, backed, framed and delivered; letters and cards to be written (in formal Japanese) and an endless number of people to be met and thanked for their contribution to the exhibition's success – vital here on a social level), each crossed off as completed and then replaced by a second list of some 40 items, and then a third, slightly shorter, and so on, until eight or nine months later, I had a clear slate.

Work:

Roughly a week after the above events, I went back to the office to see if I could get back into my work routine, only to find that, faced with my students, I was totally incapacitated: My brain blanked, and my mouth literally would not open. This was exhaustion. Also, for quite some time after this, I found myself incapable of picking up the telephone. And then again two weeks later, we had a repeat, which naturally the company could not accept, and I had no choice other than to resign. However, one step at a time, and with a lot of floundering around (being hired and fired) in the process, I found work here and there, and also a lot of people offered their help, which I gratefully accepted. Actual details are limited to the following, which are listed here mainly as important for understanding subsequent chapters.

Mr Shimizu:

This was the man who had purchased the Chinese peony painting on the night before the opening. Worried as to what had happened, shortly after the above events he visited me at home, and I received a considerable amount of help from him including introductions that allowed me to work in two (one in the countryside and one in the city) of his company's facilities, and also to translate a book on local business practices.

Hiroshi:

I spent a certain period teaching him at his office [7.35], and also, he introduced me to the Tani family, where I ended up teaching both children and the mother privately over quite a long period of time.

The Emperor Hotel:

This was a large hotel in Osaka where I worked for two years teaching hotel staff.

And now, for a minimum of three and a half to four years, life became a matter of 'survival', not so much on a financial level, but rather, in the same manner that I had had to take time out to find myself during my three years at university, I suddenly had a new self to fathom and a completely new – and up to that point unimaginable – world within which I was required to locate that same self.

Chapter 7
Finding a Way Out

[7.1]

And so what to make of it all, or any of them? Or more precisely, how and why had I been landed in this situation? Without the modicum of a forewarning, I had been left floating around in the equivalent of a gelatinous soup; carried along by both unlimited and unchartered cross-currents; unable to do anything other than concentrate on staying afloat, and all the while searching for some means to determine the whys and wherefores without being dragged under – only at some point awakening to the fact that the only way to progress was to go with the flow; to let things be as others would have them and presume that, this being the way things are, I would eventually find my way – in essence, everything that comes naturally to a child, (although, on the plus side, here I did have the advantage of having an educated, adult mind and all the experience that comes with it.)

[7.2] Identifying the problem:

Observation: Living abroad (observing cultural differences), being gay (recognising who's who in town), teaching the spoken English language (in which the tone of voice and facial expression are essential ingredients for any communication), and through my studies of traditional arts, yoga, etc. (with their emphasis on precision in positioning and concentration), I had already developed a considerable consciousness of others; their actions, reactions, choice of words, body and hand movements, etc., and now I became ultra-conscious, taking in every possible detail of my surroundings. (See below, [7.3].)

Analysis: The Dali Llama, who I would describe even today as a person I admire regardless of his religious affiliation, in reply to a question as to how to achieve enlightenment, simply suggested that the young man "Think." And that was the sum total of his advice. Irrespective of the matter of enlightenment, which was not at the time a matter that I was even close to considering, reading this at the time did give me considerable encouragement, thinking being something that I had been trained to do from a very young age, and in fact I did find much of what was happening could be tackled as a puzzle: Place the pieces as they should be, and a whole picture will fall into place. But with much else, I had no choice but to first simply accept whatever stimuli my brain was being subject to and subsequently try find some reasonable (if not provable) explanation for anything (and there was a lot) that I could not understand – all this without going into denial or rejection, and equally importantly not allowing myself to go completely off the rails.

Placing the facts in context: Practically, this required a re-evaluation of all the assumptions that I had based my life on up to that point: There was nothing that couldn't be considered possible. It also required taking each unexplainable event as it occurred (many such incidents were in fact repeated, allowing me to extend my initial interpretations) and one by one eliminating as much as could be explained by known science or through logical explanation, while at all times questioning and keeping a determined dose of scepticism, this requiring an inordinate amount of experimentation that in the end would cover weeks, months and even many years. Right from the start, having no idea where this might take me, at worst I did understand that I was educating myself as to the possibilities of the human brain, which, as they say, 'on paper', couldn't be bad.

And the truth? Even today, I do not know. At a certain point, I found myself settling on certain storylines or themes – the ones that seemed to make most sense, or at least the ones I could feel comfortable with – but these can only be possibilities as to what is/might be or isn't/might not be, and (if you like, the primary objective in writing this section of the book) any further inquiry will have to be left to others who might show an interest.

[7.3] A note on observation and the promotion of patience:

A "Shaolin Temple" movie (a personal favourite):

The hero applies for entry at the temple, only to be told that first he must build a bamboo scaffolding right away around the outer wall. This naturally takes him a number of months. And then upon completion, it must be dismantled – with each strut returned to its correct storage space. Again, a further number of months pass; all the while the monks within the temple grounds are involved with the most intricate of hand and foot movements as they advance their training. And finally, applying again but refused entry for the third time, he returns home, where he engages with his enemy, and they fight – in this case, using their arms only, at full speed but with neither actually physically touching the other – this being strictly mental combat. The hero prevails. His enemy, having met his match, bows, and retires. And the hero's village is left in peace.

***

When I first started my studies here, I was introduced to the word 'nusumu', the direct translation of which would be "to steal," but here it is used to mean the stealing of specific techniques from one's teacher through direct observation – the ones he would never directly teach you, for the simple reason that they take years of personal effort to acquire. The teacher will naturally offer certain basics to any new student/apprentice, but beyond that the student is expected to use all his or her senses (/wits) to pick up what is not (and in many cases cannot be) directly taught, and in fact, in the one area I truly got into (ink-painting), this is the way I was taught.

Students received two lessons a month, when we would gather and watch our teacher individually evaluate our work and then paint another piece for each of us to attempt to copy during the following two weeks, which required hours of work on our part at home. However, I very quickly came to understand that a large part of the real study was done during the class itself, where, particularly during the first so many years, I would kneel or sit cross-legged on the tatami mats for up to eight to ten hours, just watching the way the teacher applied ink to the brush and then manipulated it so as to obtain various effects on the surface of the paper. (As one example here, he always nipped the tip of the brush between his lips prior to applying it to the paper – which very few of the other students would do, as it meant you ended up with permanently blackened lips – but which, from the start, I copied. That said, it took a period of many years before I worked out that this was not only a means of confirming the amount of liquid in the brush, which has to be carefully controlled, but also a way to apply a thin layer of saliva to the tip, which helps to control the flow of ink out of the brush.)

And then, as one progresses, one tries out different types of brushes and papers and different inks, all of which in a variety of combinations produce different effects, more (or less) suitable for the various subjects you are required to tackle. And finally there are the 'mistakes': moments of forgetfulness; selecting the wrong paper or brush; tea stains; the points where you really 'mess everything up,' only to realise that you have created some quite original effect. And those points, suitably developed, become your own, very personal techniques – equally protected.

Also, luckily, our teacher, understanding that we were living in a modern age, encouraged us to experiment on our own, which, being from the West, I took up on right from the start. Even so, it took a period of over fifteen years of the above, plus hours and hours of both painting and sketching, etc., before I decided that I had developed enough to stop lessons and strictly begin to work on my own.

[7.4] Recognising quite how much we don't see:

There is one very important caveat to the above (also noted below in [7.14] related to telepathic communication) directly related to the fact that, if you are not interested in any particular matter, its existence is unlikely to enter your consciousness, at least to a strong enough degree to truly register, and this fact I have found has tripped me up (even up to relatively recently) on numerous occasions, with each case where it has happened having to be factored out sometime later in the thinking process – this commonly involving discounting a whole series of events or retracting a complete hypothesis dependent on one misinterpreted 'fact'.

As examples, I could give Koji's wood carving leading to my own personal interest in carvings and sculpture generally, up to that point never even considered. And now, just being with my present partner, Kensuke, who works with older people in a day-care centre, has made me strongly aware of a whole different segment of public activity. And, in particular, walking around on the streets in town – places I have been hundreds or even thousands of times – it can still shock to find a building I have never seen before in my life: simply because I have never really looked, or at least if I have, the fact that there was a church or hotel or whatever there has simply gone past me.

Taking photographs has also made me very conscious of the above. So many times, surrounded by crowds of sightseers or passers-by, when searching for a subject to engage my camera with, I have found moments of quiet beauty and solitude in very public spaces: From the resultant photograph itself, you would imagine I was completely alone. And in the end, this itself has contributed to the – rather sneaky – pleasure of the act.

[7.5] Initial thoughts:

All the considerations listed below passed through my head, and in many cases were returned to repeatedly, over a period of five to ten years – five to get myself reasonably adjusted, and then at least another five to get myself working on the finer points. However, most importantly, following the considerable initial meanderings, and the truth regardless, I aimed to get by as much as possible on the easier-to-grasp hypotheses – and in the main, other than the few points that up to the present time I still have not really been able to account for, this worked.

Also, although I do understand that my brain was overtired for a long period here, I was not acting under the influence of any drugs, at least nothing more than beer, which, having managed with it all my life up to the present time, I chose not to count.

- This was me? That is to say my own brain, for some purpose of its own – to give some kind of interest to my own life – was having me on? These were just people with their own lives, with me (for whatever reason) imposing my twisted form of 'reality' upon them?
- Even now, I would accept this as a possibility, but if so, I have an (out of this world) incredibly fertile imagination and should certainly have attempted more than three books in my life.
- Or, in the same vein, I had created a world so that I could have the pleasure of destroying it?
- Again possible, but to what end?
- Other people were in some manner trying to make a fool of me? Or, as something that might be closer to the truth: I was being used?
- In terms of attitude, in the way everything has been presented to me right the way through, from the Japanese side, it has always been and remains a 'we are special' society – with a few conveniently placed (and pliant) foreigners to give it a certain respectability – which is the way the Japanese in general do like to present their version of the world. And they do love it when foreigners go along.
- I have an unstable mind.
- In all honesty, despite (or perhaps because of) all the experiences I have had in my life, I cannot understand what this means: I have a mind that works as it works; and, taking into account an assumed 'step-by-step, stage-by-stage' development, has done so in a very consistent (/stable)

- manner throughout my whole life. I do know that in this area, as human beings, we are extremely limited in our knowledge as to how our own brains work.
- I was pushing myself toward self-knowledge? – for my own and/or the education of others?
- Always, from the time I was a child, having wanted to be a teacher, ultimately this above everything else does make sense. However, at the time (and even now) it did seem a very strange way to go about things. (And otherwise, why have I had to waste all this time and energy – a good half of my whole life – on what in the end still seems to be a rather inconsequential matter?)

All the above considerations were made on the assumption that, although we were 'a society', presumably we were also a society of human beings. However, quite naturally, a whole range of other considerations passed through my mind.

- We were aliens? (This together with all the related SF concepts: Time travel? Black holes? Time warps? If light waves bend in magnetic fields, what else might? ...)
  I do not deny the possibility here, but if I am an alien, there is nothing really more that can be said: Any reader's idea of what an alien might look or act like is going to be as good as anything my mind could dream up. Naturally the simplest of answers here would be that all living things on earth (human beings and every variety of flora and fauna included) can be described as 'creatures resident in space', and all we need to make ourselves aliens is to imagine ourselves as viewed from any point outside our own solar system, which should not in and of itself require any great flights of the imagination.

**

Years earlier, Koji came back home after closing his bar well after midnight and woke me up to tell me that there was a UFO in the sky above our apartment building. Only half inclined to believe him (he was very drunk), I went up the stairs with him on to the flat roof space we used at the time for hanging out our laundry, and he was correct. At least, we clearly had what was an 'unidentified flying object' – circular in shape, silvery in colour, hovering in full sight to the south of the building and emitting a steady, low whirring sound. And I stood with him for some 30 minutes at least, watching it repeatedly move right to left and back again until, feeling a little cold and finding the scene rather boring (nothing was happening!), I went back into the apartment and waited until Koji came down some ten minutes later to tell me that it had stopped its movements and then suddenly (as in standard UFO practice) "moved off rapidly back up into the distance." (This last part I did not personally see.) So what had we been observing?

The night sky was quite heavily clouded over (no stars) and (following a mathematical approach), considering the angle from which we were viewing it, to follow that flight path, whatever it was would've had to be fairly low down, and it had seemed somehow too small to be 'large enough' (how big are UFOs?), and at the same too large to be anything small enough to be controlled from the ground, which left me stuck. (As the only possible 'rational' conclusion that I could come up with at the time: it could possibly have been a very large circular kite, made from some metallic material with a highly reflective surface, that had floated away from its owner and somehow caught its string somewhere on a local piece of infrastructure (the sound I had heard being the whirring of a very long kite tail, which I do know exist in Japan). But this, even now, seems completely wrong. (Although there was a wind, it was not that strong, and the flight path at that height was too steady. Seen today, I would've assumed it to be some kind of fairly large drone.) However, considering all the far stranger things that I have seen in my life, this is one event that, all things apart, seems remarkably 'normal'. At least here I have the comfort of knowing that I am not in particular the 'odd man out'.

As a point of caution: During the period I was growing up, in any serious discussions in this area, the concept of 'human beings as central to life in the universe' was still the core belief, and the subject of 'aliens' was in large part confined to their appearance in science fiction and comic books. As a child, the possibility of UFOs was something to be played around with in the mind, in much the same way as zombies have taken up the imaginations of younger generations today, it being more a matter of, "They may be there, but probably aren't." And this, over a very short period of time, has been turned on its head and replaced by something very close to; "Of course they are there. All we have to do is find them," commonly with the nuance of, "and then everything will be all right." (Or, as in "Men in Black", they are already here.) And this, together with "Once we have established our colony on Mars (/the moon)…" (Note, not; "If we ever…"), etc., etc., seems to be developing into something of a sop, with far too many people inclined to the concept that, "It doesn't really matter what we do here. After all, there's a whole universe out there to welcome us." (Or at least the ones with the money.)

Circling around this matter at one point in my discussions with Hiroshi [7.35] (I was actually suggesting that human beings might really have gone too far and were heading for extinction), he broke into something close to a panic, coming out with: "We can't wait around for another heaven knows how many millenniums for cockroaches to develop their brains!" Again, the reader is entitled to their own interpretation here.

Therefore, on the assumption that I am a bona-fide alien (and if I am, once gone, I assure you I won't be coming back), I would suggest that all governments around the world (strictly in terms of preservation of the species, a.k.a. mankind) very seriously start considering priorities; precisely where (in terms of investment of time, energies and money) you should be heading. Understanding that space exploration and the dream of AI may provide a certain amount of entertainment for the young mind (and equally that proving the existence of the Higgs boson or the chemical properties of neighbouring planets must have some value in terms of understanding the universe), perhaps a proportion of your energies (and, more importantly, government money) might be better employed directed it to your own (truly precious, and fast going-to-the-dogs) natural world.

I am not in a position to argue the origins or effects of global warming. (I do understand that the world climate patterns that I took for granted as a child no longer exist.) However, fully understanding the degree to which present-day culture has become dependent on such materials, there has to be some serious consideration of the elimination of all forms of (or, at a minimum, non-degradable) plastics. "Mad Max" and "Sea World" may provide some appeal on the screen, but I doubt the experience in real life would be particularly agreeable. And quite honestly, I would suspect that if the world actually gets that far, the reality of the situation will be far beyond any of even the best of today's directors' imaginations. The money being where the money is, some of the larger petrochemical companies and/or oil- (/coal-) producing nations could perhaps start considering investing a part of the very substantial profits they have made so far into cleaning up the mess they have created (and presumably quite feasibly make some further profit in the process).

***

And in another realm:

- I was in some manner spiritually (or otherwise) 'possessed'?
- FF: "Big, Big Bamboo! Bamboo!" This was a rhythmical phrase set to a rather nondescript tune (presumably selected for its phallic connections) that for no reason got stuck in my head and just went around and around without a single moment's break for at least three full days, sending me nearly crazy. For those who may have seen the scene in "Ghost" where Whoopi Goldberg is suffering from a similar fate (which I did enjoy), this is NOT fun!
- I was a fallen angel? The latest (gay!) Jesus?
- (Why not? Some people are still looking.) Brought up in the Christian tradition, neither of these particularly appealed. And in particular, the idea of becoming yet another prophet to have his life and words banded around piecemeal, grated badly.
- I was something out of the Buddhist pantheon? A Bodhisattva – an enlightened being who out of compassion doesn't go into Nirvana, but instead stays back and helps others to find salvation? (See [7.20] below.) Alternatively, I was some form of Buddhist warrior god? Or I was an assistant to Enma, the King of Hell, a wrathful god said to judge the dead and preside over the "Hells" or "Purgatories" and the cycle of afterlife?
- Passing through, I actually rather fancied both of these. And, in the latter case, if I were to be judging others, it did become important that I be able to judge myself, and equally to rid myself of any potential prejudices, which I also felt was not a bad aim.
- I was connecting (in some shamanic fashion) with the afterlife and/or spirits of the dead? And if not a spiritual world, then 'the unseen', whatever that might be?
- A year and a half after Koji died, during the summer 'Obon' festival period, which is when spirits of the dead are considered to return to communicate with their loved ones, he spoke to me. Or at least (and

understanding that this need not have been so), I heard a voice which, for a number of reasons, I assumed to be his. [18.18])

[7.6] Why would this be, in any sense of the word, a group?

As can easily be inferred from an overall reading of this book, I have an extremely strong aversion to the basic idea of cliques, particularly those that seek to exclude, and equally to people who tend to overestimate their influence in the scheme of things, both of which very much seemed to be the reality in this case. Foremost in my mind, because I personally have always tried to apply my brain to any situation, I have always taken this as one point of reference when I have met people socially or been asked to interview others, and it is a trait that (rightly or wrongly) I still admire. (Neither Koji nor Kensuke received a particularly high-level education, but both have (/had) minds that are quite capable of appreciating carefully presented reasoning.) Also, from a logical point of view, if the group had so much access to my mind (/thoughts), how was it that they appeared to know so little about me? And again, knowing so little, why did they assume that I might agree with any objectives they might have? And taking the above in total, my first instinct, therefore, had to be rejection, with the question to myself here being: "To what degree this was a matter of false pride?"

- I or we as a group were something special?
  Assuming 'secret' includes the concept of being 'something special,' (and otherwise, why bother?), to me this would immediately imply 'having certain abilities,' but taking an overall view of the people who entered that gallery, I found it very difficult to find any kind of common denominator.
- As a group, only we were capable of communicating with our minds?
  This I almost immediately discarded. Human beings have incredible capabilities covering a whole range of physical and mental activities, and to what extent any particular potential is actually developed is going to vary considerably depending upon circumstances. So my choice was, until proven otherwise (and it never has been to my satisfaction), to include all. (That group members might be limited to those who are aware of this potential did occur as a possibility, but even this I am very queasy upon.)

And above all, if we were truly some form of group, to what end did we exist?

- We were here to help each other?
- Coming from my own tradition, this had to be met with, "Why can't you be a bit more generous and help anyone who you sense is in need?" And even if this was so, how?
- We were here to help others?
- Again how?
- Or taking another Buddhist concept and twisting the matter around somewhat: Our purpose was to create suffering through which others could realise their compassion?
- This was a thought that right through has held me in considerably. If I was in a position to bring about such suffering, there had to be a need to exercise considerable caution.
- Or we were creating (or, working to correct) some imbalance in the system?
- We existed to exert control; a power clique hiding in broad daylight?
- This also brought up the possibility of others; some superior power at a level way above our comprehension – controlling us as we like to think of ourselves controlling nature? And perhaps others, controlling them? And here as a personal conclusion: "Maybe there are. But so what!!!" Either way, there was nothing I could do about it. Given a little thought, this is actually no more than a repeat of the Greeks and Romans creating their respective gods and/or (if you wish to refer to computers or AI), the movie "2001."

[7.7] New areas requiring examination:

The following explanations include brief excerpts taken from what was an extremely long and complicated process. However, in total, they should give a sense of the kind of things that were happening around me during this period. With each consideration given, I have included at least one example. Numerous similar examples are included as they appear within the various events described in later chapters.

Telepathy: For ease of understanding, I will start with what for me was a definitive episode in that the message was received both directly and in the individual's own voice.

While I had so many indications – incidents, comments, etc. – of the possibility of what was happening, it was only after a period of some eight to ten years, when I received a highly detailed message from a very panicked ex-student, then in the US, that I finally gave up trying to convince myself that what I was experiencing could not be. The story was that, leaving a building with some other students, they had been held up by a man with a gun, and that he had taken it upon himself to wrest it out the gunman's hand. (This was entirely in character, acting on the spur of the moment being his forte.) At the time of receiving the message I was on my way to see his mother, and some twenty minutes later when I arrived at her home, she told me that she had just received a phone call from him, and then repeated the story that I had just relayed to me in the train. (An alternative reading here could be that I had, for whatever reason, picked up (/tuned into) a private telephone conversation.)

***

I first read about telepathy when I was in my early teens in the book, "Day of the Triffids," with the young hero, as he moves from England to Asia then down to Australia, gradually becoming aware that he is communicating in this manner. (For the record, this element of the story is ignored in the movie.) Also, I did pick up some time ago from a newspaper article that, for Australian Aborigines, with their need traditionally to cover very large areas of open territory when hunting for food, in the past it was very natural to use this ability, but that nowadays it was not really necessary any longer as; "We all have cell phones."

However, faced with the possibility that others might be communicating with me in this manner, again scepticism had to be the order of the day.

- I was well aware that I had heard voices, but this was telepathy. Or what?
- And then in a more complex vein, if telepathy was to be understood as "receiving others' thoughts," how was I to know that a 'thought' that occurred to me was in fact mine? And how was I to discriminate between such an 'original thought' and an idea that had been planted, or even myself answering some voice in the back of my mind?

And, as with everything, the same questions went back and forth repeatedly in my brain until, in the end, I simply stopped thinking and allowed things to work as they presumably should.

[7.8] Unlooked for comments, incongruent remarks:

Right through from the beginning and even today, I find people trying to indicate to me that they have some kind of access to my thoughts; to something I have said, or more commonly, a thought that has recently passed through my mind.

"I didn't know…"
Shortly after the events described in the last chapter, Hiroshi (who to my mind, had to have been a key organiser of the whole affair) for no apparent reason came out with, "I didn't know that you had studied yoga!" which in the manner in which it was presented (outside the context of what had happened at the shrine that night) made no sense, there being absolutely no reason whatsoever why that particular matter should have been brought up at that particular time. (Other than recently with Kensuke, I have never mentioned any of the events that occurred that night to anyone. Also, with respect to my above comment on people seemingly having so little knowledge of who or what I was: This was someone who at the time I had known for over twenty years, and even with the supposed advantage of having access to my thoughts, wasn't even aware that I had been practicing yoga for a considerable part of that very long period?)

"You have a lot of friends in Osaka."
The phrase: "You have a lot of friends" has been thrown out at me a number of times when there was no apparent reason why the person speaking should be (or how they could be) aware of the fact, why it should be of any importance to the conversation at hand, or quite exactly what 'friends' were being referred to. However, the above comment came from Mr Ohta (the husband of the lady who brought me the roses [6.13]), who up to the time (our only contact being in the office) would not have had any idea of the amount of time I had been spending in that city. (At the time, it had been a regular drinking and play spot for many years.)

"You don't like my friends, do you?"

This came from an Australian friend, Jeff, who we had originally met many years earlier on a ferry boat returning to Kobe from Kyushu. He had visited us in Japan a couple of times after that and we had exchanged Christmas letters regularly, in which he invariably mentioned "picnics at the races" and "parties on his friends' private yachts," which as anyone who has been reading this book will understand is not my world. However, when we in turn visited him in Sydney for four days, he produced a very pleasant schedule for our visit, which we totally enjoyed, with the only touch of dissonance coming as we passed through a clearly very expensive yacht harbour, when he came out with the above question. He had not made any previous comment about his friends, and coming out of the blue as it did, I did not quite know how to respond. More than the question itself, it was the insistence of the 'do you?' tag that struck me – at that moment, his voice was projecting overt antagonism. And I could only presume that there was something going on in the background.

'Bong!'

My first Apple computer at one point developed a very bad habit of making a strong booming sound to indicate that it had fully warmed up and was now ready for use. (My present machine also does this on certain occasions.) Unfortunately, there was nothing I could do about this, and I just let it go, until one day in class, one of my cheekier young lady students suddenly came out with a perfect imitation; a long, drawn out 'Bo…oong!' (We were online!) – upon which the whole class fell apart. And from that time on, she made a point of inserting the sound at certain key moments (something akin to the precisely timed calls from long-term audience members, made during periods of high tension in Kabuki performances[10]) until it became something of a class joke.

And as a final afterthought in this area, going back to the 'alien' theme: At university, at the same time the American man from my postgraduate group was suggesting that I visit New York, he also came out with the rather unusual statement: "You arrived rather later than we did." Passed over at the time, perhaps now I might ask, "From where?"

---

[10] Warning: This is not for the inexperienced. Such calls are considered part of the performance – timing and presentation (/pitch of voice) must be flawless – and, very seriously, any offender is likely to be thrown out of the theatre.

[7.9] Hearing my own voice:

It was also at this time that I for the first time in my life became aware of myself thinking, every single thought – even the briefest of thoughts that passed through my mind – recited within my brain as it occurred. And very quickly I discovered quite how active (and offensive) my mind could be. I would be looking at something or someone and my brain would go, "God! That (/He/ She) is ugly!" or, "That is not the kind of person I would ever like to have to deal with." And then the person would look at me and I would think, "Oh, no! They didn't pick that up?" And also, at the other end of the scale, there was, "Ooh! I rather fancy him." Here, particularly, I do remember one very good-looking guy I really would have gone for (it was summer, and he was beautifully muscular and tanned), looking across at me – directly into my eyes – and, to my great embarrassment, laughing repeatedly.

'Mu' (nothingness) is described in many ways: as being sensitive to or involved in the moment, an acceptance of what is, an opening of your mind to the present state or simply 'being'. Words can be interpreted in a million ways, but if anything, I had the odd feeling that what I had experienced up to that time – a continuation of childhood innocence, if you like – could just as well have been some state of 'mu', and (through all this silliness) someone was attempting to drag me back into the morass.

[7.10] Hardware:

Any reader who did not have the opportunity (or lacked sufficient interest) at school to study basic science texts related to radio waves or the human body might take a little time out with the Internet at some point to extend their knowledge of (/question/ confirm) any of the points noted below.

It has become extremely fashionable to debunk science and scientific 'facts', which is in some senses fair, in that (apart from the reality of too many people cherry-picking their statistics for profit) at present levels of investigation, much of what is occurring has to depend to some degree on open speculation. However, certain basics that we do have the opportunity to learn at school can be of use. If I had been aware of the following earlier (I was never keen on biology and we did not have the Internet available at the time), it would have saved me a lot of headaches. However, as an established scientific fact, crystals are known to absorb, store, amplify, transduce, and transmit a variety of vibrational (electromagnetic and electric) energies. Or more directly: "Skeletal bone structure, <u>which is known to be formed of solid crystal</u>, has the ability to convert vibrational energy, such as sound or light waves, into energy." There is also the related matter of synapses; the points on individual brain cells where electrical pulses carrying messages leap across the gaps between the cells.

Therefore, if you choose to take any human being (you yourself), and (for easy reference) turn them upside down holding the head in your hand, with the extended spine and limbs as a form of highly flexible aerial – one that may be positioned at will (think, complex yoga poses) – you will be in possession of an extremely sophisticated (and electrically activated) transmitter and receiver, which is also (most conveniently) connected directly to the ultimate software; the human brain (a supercomputer, the practical usage of 80% of which is at present unknown). And subsequently, if we choose (that is, train ourselves) to do so – or equally probably, as a natural function, operating without any choice on our part (certainly very much within reason) – we have the potential to obtain the direct input of anything that is out there anywhere (including, quite possibly, ultra-high or -low wavelength frequencies that would be outside our normal physical range).

And stepping out a little into the world of Dr Doolittle: Regardless of whether human beings can truly communicate with animals, all vertebrates, in that they are known to have brains and spines, will meet the above conditions, and there is no reason to believe that they are not also capable of using this particular gift of nature to their advantage. At any rate, considered in this manner, it would seem that we are living within a far greater state of complexity than (at least at present) we are truly capable of grasping.

[7.11] One step further:

The following can be understood as indicating quite how far my considerations were ranging at the time. Also, I do know that, while not too long after this event I did start using similar situations to my own advantage, here I actually was a little taken aback by the incident as it happened. (See "Learning or Teaching?" [7.26])

Sketching a pair of lion dogs ("A-Un". [13.12]) in the grounds of a temple in Osaka, and with my thoughts idly wandering over a variety of matters, I found myself making a series of somewhat derogatory remarks in my brain about the Buddhist priest(s) who I presumed were running the temple complex. This was being done with deliberate intent on the assumption that somebody was actually listening – I sensed someone somewhere was wrongly criticising me and I was not in a good mood. However, at this point, a very large wasp swooped down and began circling close into my head, presumably not with the best of intentions (it showed no sign of moving away), and I had to change my line of thought very quickly. And the moment I did, it left me.

***

And into paranoia. Flies as spies:
Shortly following the above incident with the wasp, I became extremely sensitive towards any insect that I noticed around me, and particularly at home (for quite a long period), even the tiny flies that would get into the house in summer and hover around the kitchen waste, or for some reason scurry around on the surface of my morning paper – they liked the smell of the ink, or they were there to analyse the sweat from my hands? – became suspect. (Essentially, I was viewing insects as drones – long before the latter appeared on the scene.)

Viewed from the present, there was actually a reason for this, or at least it involved a natural progression: Washi (Japanese handmade paper) used for painting or calligraphy, provided it is stored correctly, ages well (allowing the creation of certain effects that would not be possible on a freshly produced sheet of paper), but it is also easily damaged by certain insects which take to its natural fibres. As a result, right from the time I started painting, I have always been very careful (/paranoid?) about keeping insects out of the house. And today (Sept. 2018), coming to the end of one more long summer, I still find myself talking to them (even as I attempt to swat them out of existence), and thinking back to that time (when I was subject to a very solitary existence), it is equally likely that I simply needed something or someone to address my thoughts to – as you would to a pet dog or cat.

[7.12] Voice streaming (Think, tuning in to your preferred wavelength):

Sitting on the train lost in thought, and then when you stand to get off, you notice someone walk halfway down the carriage and deliberately take the seat you have just vacated. (Until that time, although there were plenty of other seats available – the carriage at times being close to empty – they had apparently been quite happy standing.) And when this happens not once or twice, but rather becomes a regular occurrence (including people starting to change seats), you begin to wonder just why that might be happening.

And then years later in a 'Maori village' in New Zealand, when I go to replenish my plate from the buffet, a young man comes along and takes my seat (again, for no reason – I was with Koji; everyone was midway through their meal and there were dozens of other spaces available). And then when I come back, he stands and moves away (giving me a somewhat odd look in the process) and Koji comes out with: "That man. He was Korean, and he just asked me whether you speak the language." (I had studied a certain amount at the time. My brain had been tuned in to Korean?) Note: The level of my Korean still being considerably lower than that of my Japanese or English, even now I tend to notice it more when Korean words appear in my brain, these including a "Chuuka hamnida!" (Congratulations!) – delivered shortly after I had started living with Kensuke.

[7.13] Forms of interference:

Rain:

In the same manner that bad weather can block radio or television waves, over time I developed a sense that (in particular, heavy) rain will also prevent any brain-to-brain connection – making typhoons a perfect time, if you wish to do so, to think privately.

A ringing in the ears:

The Frey effect: It is known that short radio waves (used to relay messages from cell phones to antenna towers) can be directed at an individual's brain receptor site, known as the auditory cortex, to create the perception of loud noises, including ringing, buzzing, and grinding, that may cause brain damage. It has also been confirmed that an intelligible signal can be transferred in this manner.

Although over the past few years the problem seems to have disappeared almost completely, throughout a very long period after the exhibition, particularly when I was working on my word processor (and later, my computer), I would suddenly get a fine ringing in either one of my ears which, depending on the day, could get intense enough to considerably disturb me. At the time, and quite the reverse of the above, I took this to be too many people trying to probe (/listen in to?) whatever thoughts were passing through my mind at the time. (I did also understand that, from a medical viewpoint, it could have been stress related.) However, regardless of the cause, I very quickly found that to rid myself of the problem (almost instantaneously), a mentally projected "Piss off!" worked wonders. (There was never one time when it didn't.)

And crowds:

Hasedera, a temple in Nara prefecture, is extremely famous for its Chinese peonies, and naturally in late April when they are in full bloom, it attracts a large number of visitors. Arriving early, and walking up into the temple with Koji, we had no problem at all. However, on our return, we were obliged to literally fight our way through a packed crowd (not an inch of space), all pushing their way up the village street towards the temple entrance, and within a very short time we both found ourselves fighting back nausea (my brain was in a hyper-active state and under an enormous amount of pressure) and we could do nothing other than move out into a small park beside the road, and then after resting, find our way down the back streets towards the station. And ever since (and particularly as I have aged), I have learned to be very careful about getting trapped in crowds.

[7.14] Finding the right connection:

All of the following has to be after-the-fact speculation, and in reality, I know no more now than I could have come up with right at the start so many years ago.

- If you are meeting someone you know well on a fairly regular basis, the chances are that (provided both sides recognise the intention) you are going to be able to establish some kind of personal system without too much difficulty. Even so, this will naturally be that much easier if the other person is in their home or office, as against walking around a busy department store, alone in the mountains, traveling along a crowded expressway or on vacation halfway around the world: that is, establishing a correct location must presumably at some point enter the equation.
  Considering subsequent events, this determination of position more than anything appears to be a key element in the whole matter, and possibly this is one reason why working within a group was considered important. At least, a considerable amount of my own training, and my own later involvement in the training of others was very much directed at this point. (See "Games," below [7.22].)

- And beyond that, there are, as they say; "People who know people who know people," which (assuming that one can take for granted an element of trust) cannot be rejected out of hand.

I did, in fact, discover rather late in life that I actually had, for many years, a 'one-step' connection to the Imperial family here. So, who knows?

***

And then, on the assumption that as a group we were trying to hide something: How can you be sure that you are actually talking to the person you think you are talking to (cf. present-day Facebook fraud) or prevent eavesdropping (hacking)?

There are naturally many considerations in this area, available on the market if you wish to read any "Book for Dummies: How to be a Spy." However, initially (in actuality, for many years) not being in a state to let my thoughts go in any other way than they would at the moment they occurred, I do understand that, at least in the early stages, my conscious thoughts (which, being able to clearly hear them myself, I had to presume were open to anyone who might have such capabilities) were an open book. And later, as I became more comfortable with myself, knowing that in large part people who do not know you are not really going to be understanding anything that they are hearing, I came to regard the point as irrelevant.

As with the above comments on "observation," every point that will promote or prevent communication in daily life – cultural background, interests, individual experience, overall range of knowledge, linguistic abilities, etc. etc. – will presumably help with (or, alternatively, prevent unwanted) connections. And presumably, one can also work on personal conceits. My Japanese is naturally limited but, in my own language, I sense that I was at a distinct advantage here, simply due to the fact that English language instruction (particularly related to spoken English) in Japan is *so* bad, and at the same time Japanese people are *so* over-confident as to how much they understand, that if anyone was actually trying anything of complexity, they didn't stand a chance. (I also suspect that Koji deliberately played into this by limiting his study to sitting in a separate room reading a Japanese-English dictionary and refusing to allow me to teach him anything. At one level, we needed a contrast?)

FF: A year after I arrived in Japan, I became close friends with an Oxford graduate, Robert [4.6], who arrived here one year after I did, and before he found his partner and moved off to Tokyo, we spent a lot of time together at the local bars simply enjoying each other's company. (At the time, he was the only person who I could let my hair down with in my own language.) And when we were enjoying a discussion, we did not appreciate being interrupted, particularly by Japanese men who neither of us were interested in, even if they spoke English reasonably well. Normally people could take a hint, but in this case the guy couldn't (/wouldn't). Therefore, to keep him out while keeping him in, I slipped an overly-carefully presented, "I suppose..." into the conversation – untranslatable into Japanese for the simple reason that there are too many possible interpretations of actual intent (AI): In this case I was indicating that we might play around a little bit and move out, as it were, onto a limb. Which is in fact what we did, leaving him so far behind in his comprehension that in the end he got totally bored and turned away, which was our intention. I am fully aware that socially this is not the nicest of habits, but he also was being extremely rude. And it did work.

[7.15] "You are telling the truth?"

At some point, there was a question put forward, which came up repeatedly both in my mind and in somewhat pointed conversations with others, as to whether I was telling the truth.

And here, perhaps, I again found myself at a certain advantage, in that as a result of the experiences in my youth (See "The power of a lie," [2.8]), I did have a strong aversion in this regard, that is, I had a bad habit of telling the truth (at least as I saw it), and for people who might find acceptance of this point difficult (a lot of people do), if lying reflexively may be understood as reasonable, then surely telling the truth reflexively may also be considered a possibility.

And related to 'polite comments' or 'white lies': Although I fully follow the concepts of 'tatemae' [5.3] as in the offering of exaggerated praise ("That is absolutely beautiful!") together with the 'honne', on occasion unbelievably nasty (/snide) remarks that follow once the artist is out of sight ("She thinks *that* is a flower arrangement!") – these both comments by my teacher about another senior teacher in the same ikebana school – as being standard in all the traditional worlds of art that I have been involved in here, this is one facet of the culture that I have not at all taken to, and unless I am viewing something that I really like, I tend to stick to suitably neutral "Um's" and "Ah's."

FF: Quite early on after the exhibition, I was at a party (See [5.14]) where, as a getting-to-know-you diversion, all the guests contributed a small gift, which were collected and then 'pulled out of the hat', providing a certain amount of laughter and a simple means of starting up a conversation without the requirement of a (what normally would be the essential) business card. And, as might be expected under the circumstances, I received a children's book (in English, no less – all the other guests being Japanese) introducing the story of Pinocchio, with the (pointedly referenced) implication that I, as with the chief character in the book, had finally been granted my wish of becoming human. (And that presumably after all the years of lying that I had been involved in!) Understanding that I might not need it, one of the older guests, who possibly had a grandchild, was polite enough to change it with his own gift…but, again, quite what does one say here?

Other 'hints' thrown out around this time included 'the shedding of one's chrysalis' – from grub to elegant butterfly – and far more practical in terms of its presumed connection with telepathy (again, if you turn the picture upside down), the underlying mass of spores connecting fungal colonies.

[7.16] Under other's control? Controlling others?

(During my early recovery period.) Sitting by myself watching the television, my back against the sofa, for no reason at all my vision darkened and continued to do so almost to the point that I could see nothing in front of me. And then as I sat, not really understanding how I should react, gradually my eyesight returned, and I was back to normal. The whole thing would have been a matter of three or four minutes, and it was all gone. This was me? My imagination? Simply a result of tiredness? 'Others' playing with my mind. Something or someone taking total physical control of my body movements? Or what? And, once more, taken together with all the events surrounding the exhibition, this left me with more questions than answers.

All societies accept the concept of control over children, necessary for both an imbuing of the culture and a means of giving the child a sense of being or belonging, the security blanket that we all need at this early stage, and responsibility for this is given to parents, family, teachers and/or that society's spiritual leaders. Rather than control, which can easily imply 'of a forced nature', influence or tutelage might be considered a better overall description here. However, working with adults – and certainly not in this manner – was not something I felt at all comfortable with. Then again, it became a matter of learning to go with (and then at times, and possibly more importantly, against) one's instincts.

Hypnotism:

I have never liked the idea of hypnotism, or more specifically of being hypnotised, and even writing this today, although I do understand that it is very likely that at certain points in my life, I have used the technique, I would not claim any knowledge as to how it might work. Also, it is certainly not anything that I would attempt to perform in a public setting.

That said, as one very clear example of 'something going on', which occurred shortly after the exhibition when I was teaching (this being with the same student who later sent me the above panicked message from America):

As far as I was concerned, we were having a regular class, when suddenly, for no reason I could have put a finger on, he fell into a trancelike state, and he was no longer with me. There was a scrap of paper on the table in front of him, and putting all his concentration into that blank space, he moved his pencil – I'm not sure whether it was according to or against his will – but watching him, I could see that he was writing in hieroglyphs, or something very close – up and down, from left to right. I said nothing until a noise from the other room caught his attention and looking up the spell was broken. Seeing what he had done, and clearly rather embarrassed, he quickly drew the paper below the table, and screwing it up, threw it into the basket at his side. And nothing else was said. (At the time, I assumed this was some ancient Egyptian or Persian script, but very recently on television I have seen an example of the written Mongolian language, which was remarkably similar in style, so we could very easily have been working in a present-day context.)

And one case where I will never be sure: A young girl of twelve or thirteen who came for private lessons together with her mother and an older student who I had been teaching for a number of years. The older student was planning to take her to England to take part in summer course of dance lessons (she actually went and enjoyed them). Initially, no problem to teach at all (she was a very sweet girl), after a couple of months or so of lessons, for no apparent reason at all, she suddenly started breaking down in class – crying her eyes out and incapable of stopping the tears flowing – this getting so bad that it was decided that it might be best if she stopped classes. (After she returned from England, she tried again but with exactly the same results.) And having had the above and other similar experiences, it has always worried me that I might somehow have caused the problem.

Sleep:
Japanese people will sleep just about anywhere; on a park bench, in trains or buses (this being irrespective of whether they are seated or are hanging from an overhead strap), and equally they have perfected the five-minute nap – something I still cannot do. This is presumably related to the fact that (at least in the families I have seen) they have no particular time schedule for being put to bed when they are young (they are allowed to go to bed at whatever time they wish), and also very much due to the fact that, as adults, they are over-worked. A senior computer programmer at the company, who I knew to be only getting three or four hours sleep a night, would regularly walk into class and, each time first giving me a quick apologetic nod, would place his head on the desk and sleep for the full one-hour lesson. It was the only way he could manage his existence, lack of sleep here still featuring regularly in cases of 'karoushi' (death due to overwork).

However, from very early on, I have been very conscious of myself, or others being suddenly overtaken by bouts of sleepiness. With certain private students, who would be 'out' for periods as short as a minute or less, I have been very tempted to associate such events with hypnosis. Rather separately, with Koji (and today, occasionally, Kensuke), when the two of us have fallen into this state at the same time (both of us suddenly feeling exceptionally tired), there has always seemed to be competitive element involved: For whatever reason, one of us wants the other asleep. In particular, with Koji, viewed in a straightforward manner, it could be considered that we were working against each other. (In Australia, when he was extremely insistent that I go back to bed in the early morning and I didn't, I managed to photograph an extraordinary sequence of the morning sun rising behind a heavy squall over the bay, which I later used to great effect in an exhibition of my paintings.) However, from early on, I also sensed that this was in fact one of us helping (/covering for?) the other. And much later on, on the premise that two brains are better than one, it occurred to me that we might actually be connecting with or even possibly utilising the other's brain in some manner.

[7.17] A 'magic' world:

(All the following occurred in the very early years after the exhibition.)

An empty water glass on the desk, suddenly full; walking down towards the station and a neighbour mysteriously appears at my side; drawing into the station platform, with the number of people waiting to board the train suddenly multiplying – all sudden changes that, at the time they occurred, I could in no way grasp. It was actually this last event (which was too much of a jump to explain otherwise) that eventually got me to realise where the problem might lay. Basically, I was having mini blackouts (of the type that you can have when you have been drinking excessively). At the time, I assumed that this came from excessive tiredness. However, considering the above situation where my students clearly were losing their sense of presence for brief periods, it could just as easily have been some other person in the vicinity sending me to sleep (/blanking my mind). Either way, this can be taken as an example of how easy it is to misinterpret events, and this was one of a number of occasions when I had to reconsider a whole series of incidents that I had grouped under a certain theme.

[7.18] Prescience. Knowing what is in store for you:

(This is just one of a number of similar stories. Others have been placed in context in their respective chapters.)

I had known it was going to happen from early on that morning. I had sensed (/ 'seen') it – a car coming from behind me so fast that I would not be aware of it until it was onto me – but it was not until I was almost at the point that I recognised the spot. (I was walking down a narrow side street very close to the point where it intersected with the main road, and not on a route I would normally take.) And before I could think to take any action, my ears caught the sound of an engine revving as it might on a racetrack, and it was there, cutting across my path and taking the corner at full speed. Not harmed in any way other than for a very strong sense of shock (without any consideration for myself, to cut out onto a main thoroughfare at that speed was reckless in the extreme), I turned the corner myself only to find the same car parked some 20 yards along the road in front of a set of traffic lights, allowing me to get close enough to take a swipe at its rear end with the bag I was carrying. But this apparently not being enough catch the woman's attention (she would be in her late thirties?), she was off the moment the lights turned green, and I was left with yet one more phenomenon to ponder upon.

[7.19] With Koji. Learning the ropes:

Right from the start, all communications (with very few exceptions) were silent. We had been together over twenty years at this stage, and we were already very sensitive to each other's body expressions and movements, and now we had to get our brains that much more in sync. From quite early on, I did pick up that in certain areas, while it was important that we understood each other, it was equally important that others should not automatically be following our conversations, that is, the aim was to obtain a certain amount of privacy in our relationship. This could be done through slight variations in our natural speech, an unnecessary nod, or even the way one of us yawned very early on in the morning. Presumably not everyone could be listening in all the time.

***

Being nudged into form:
Watching the television one evening, I sensed that I was required to answer what seemed a rather simple (1+1=3?) question that had popped up in my brain, but before I could do so, I got a warning nudge and quick look from Koji, who was beside me on the couch: I wasn't supposed to appear to understand too much. That is, I wasn't to show my hand so easily. There was also the matter of me 'voting my approval' – presumably for consideration for (possible?) inclusion in the group. In one case, we were watching a music programme where the latest pop idol was being introduced (and as is the case with pop idols, being promoted to the hilt), and I picked up that I was supposed to give my approval (this presumably being what one did with young pop idols being promoted to the hilt). Quite honestly, she was attractive and could sing the basics (which many can't), but even so (on the understanding that I wasn't in any sense aware of what I was really looking for) I could not see any specific potential that might have made her different from any other 17-year-old on the screen. However, again a nudge, and she was approved. (She actually lasted 25 years, which in the business these days is quite a good record, but even so, how special she is (/was) I still could not really say.) Exactly what are you looking for?

And there was also the time when the Japanese song I had just finished singing at a bar we commonly frequented in Osaka was met with by silence from a group of well over thirty customers (most of whom I knew reasonably well). This was not a matter of (the quite common) people not paying attention (in which case, there would have been a continuation of the general buzz of conversation), but rather a total, absolute, shocked silence. (There had been nothing special about the song itself or the way I had sung it, and the only thing I could assume was that something had been communicated; that, or something had, as I came to refer to it, 'clicked' – some 'association' had been made.) However, this apart, returning to my seat, the first thing that Koji said to me was, "Don't ever talk about this to Mrs Oka!" The occurrence here being in a gay bar and she is being my official legal sponsor at the time, I could not imagine any reason why I might have considered even mentioning the matter to her, but it was said with such urgency that again it made me wonder. What exactly where we hiding?

And as a little bit of me having my own way:
Right the way through, there were only very few times when Koji did not stay in character, with the only time that I really got to him (in the end, he hit the roof – he actually screamed at me to stop) being when I spent a full morning singing "When the red, red robin comes bob, bob, bobbin' along," at first quietly to myself, and then simply following the refrain in my brain; my response to this outburst (again, in my brain) being, "Look, I didn't start this!"

For those who might not know the song, it includes the lines: "Wake up, wake up you sleepyheads / Get up, get out of bed / Cheer up, cheer up the sun is red / Live, love, laugh and be happy!" To what degree this was serious I would not care to say, but the idea that occurred to me in my mind was that I "was calling on my 'sleeper spies' to awaken and fulfil their duties!"

[7.20] "And feed them on your dreams. The ones they pick, the ones you'll know by." ("Melody Fair."):

During this early period, of the many possibilities that I considered, two somewhat contrasting tales found their way into my thinking processes. These were not ideas that my mind had in any way set on as 'a truth'. They were merely considerations put out there as possibilities, both for me and (presuming others were listening in) for public consumption – the type of stories that, given the free rein of countless imaginations, tend to expand exponentially. (And although it didn't actually occur to me at the time, if I was to have to think my way out of the confusion, surely it was reasonable to ask that others also take up their share of the burden.)

1) I was the equivalent of a Bodhisattva [7.5], that is I had 'full knowledge' and had returned in human form to help others in their quest for the same.
2) I was at the other extreme, experiencing life as a human being for the first time; strictly a child in the learning process – this being the origin of the poem, "Child." (Or, naturally, I could be somewhere in-between.)

This latter tale, I suspect, in the end got milked rather too thoroughly: Sometime later, a man (a mutual pick up in Osaka), whispered in my ear wanting to confirm whether I was in fact the "Golden Child" (referring to the child – a Buddhist acolyte with magical powers – in the 1986 movie starring Eddie Murphy), which had been on at the movie theatres here around that time, leading my present self to wonder quite what level of tragi-comedy (/farce) I might have been participating in over the past 30+ years. The final comment of the gallery owner at the time of my last exhibition two years ago was, "And so the child will die?" If it is necessary to state the obvious here, at least to my knowledge, all children (for whatever reason) at some point die! And why might that be my responsibility? Whatever! Someone somewhere here has a story to tell.

Finding a partner:
Developing theme (2), as a 'child' it would be natural (why not?) for me to select a partner with whom I could stay through presumably countless rebirths (taking up in turn all forms in the universe), and each of us helping the other in whatever manner possible so that both of us might attain enlightenment or its equivalent – a true understanding of the universe. Or, assuming I had been here much longer, I was looking for a new partner (this latter idea being developed fully on my visit to Korea described in Cpt 10). The reader here will follow that the above was intended as no more than a riff on a very basic (/close to zero) layman's understanding of Buddhist theory. However, it did provide a very attractive storyline, and was actually used as a key theme in the novel I wrote prior to this book.

As to how the above matter was to be achieved; initially, being at home most of the time, it amounted to me lying on the couch in front of the television selecting faces and types that appealed – a pleasant enough pastime, particularly in my state at the time. Naturally, from force of habit, here I was concentrating on the men.[11] And (on the understanding that this was, at least in part, a pastime) if nothing else, over time I did come to understand that I actually had a considerably wider range than I would have imagined.

[7.21] Developing connections (a start):

When I was not in the mood for television, which was quite common at this time, I would take a book to bed and read myself to sleep, leaving the bedroom light for Koji to turn off when he came in himself. Which is what he did, until from a certain point onwards, I noticed that his timing had begun to match my own, and each time – shortly after I placed the book away from me and just as a fine drowsiness was taking me – he would walk in quietly and turn off the light, before returning to watch whatever programme was on at the time. That is, we had established some form of recognition of the other's thoughts at a certain distance, and from thereon, all we had to do was expand our range.

Rejection: Sitting by myself one evening, waiting to receive a live report (breaking news) from Australia, I was quite comfortable until they started wiring up the Japanese reporter to start his presentation, and then my brain just came out with a very emphatic "NO! Not him, NO!"

I subsequently came to understand that live broadcasts (where both ends are subject to a very straight connection) can be very tricky, but here there was something that, for whatever reason, I could not accept (I was laying down the law). And the poor guy (he was only young), without any notice, got hustled back from the camera and replaced. To the present, I do not know why my brain reacted in this way: I was indicating to whoever was in charge on the other side that I did not wish to be recognised as present? And/or I did not need this particular connection? Or I was simply testing the waters? (This last point I actually doubt very much. I was vehement in my tone of rejection.) However, what happened, happened – and as always was taken as a lesson for me.

---

[11] This may seem a little unfair to the other half of our species but, in my defence, and perhaps odd as it may seem, I already had – and still do have – a very clear idea of the kind of woman that I like.

[7.22] Fun and games:

Switching identities. "She thought it was me."

He walked down the narrow path between the gravestones, wondering whether the woman would be there. It was a very small graveyard, one of a number in the area, most of the others private – associated with some shrine or temple – but this one run by the municipality and making for a simple shortcut through to the railway line, was used by everyone in the neighbourhood. With previous caretakers, there had never been any problem, but she hadn't been in any manner friendly from the beginning, and now that she had been 'in residence' for about a year (she had a small room in a prefabricated unit into which she would retire when not performing her duties), she was treating the place as if it were her own property, glaring at him every time he walked past. (Koji had told him that this was not a favour applied exclusively to him, but on a personal level that didn't help. Understanding that as a foreigner he stood out, he was always particularly polite and did not disturb the owners of the graves when they came to clean up their plots and/or pay their respects.)

A week or so previously, she had put up a 'No entry. No passage!' notice on the gate at the bottom end of the path that had quickly disappeared, and now he could see she had taped up three more on the side of the hut. This was getting a bit too much. He listened carefully for a moment, but there was no sound from the inside and without thinking any further he reached up and ripped all three down. And then two more from the other side, and a final one from the gate, and screwed the whole lot up in his hands as he walked off down the hill...

And then telling the tale to Koji that evening: "Yes, I know. And she thought it was me." Upon which they both burst out laughing.

Two days later, as he was passing the hut, he experienced a full run of pain through his body. But this was not the first time and, as he had previously, he let it pass. And shortly after, she was gone – given up and left for good.

A set of dinner plates:

Mr Shimizu (purchaser of the Chinese peony painting) and his wife were coming to dinner. Koji had decided on having a curry as the main dish, but not having a suitable set of dishes in the house (he had decided they had to be 'that much larger' than the plates we had at home), I had been sent into town to see what I could find. Having gone around all the main department stores and specialist shops that I knew of without finding anything that might do (I wanted something nice, but I didn't want to overspend on anything that might be used only for the one meal), I was now approaching my limits.

This was a store that, seemingly having everything but at the same time nothing in particular (they sold a wide assortment of items including both kitchen and tableware), I had walked past many times previously without ever having had the inclination to go inside and look around. However, I had now run out of both options and time, and I had to find something, which in the end, hidden away at the back of a final, bottom row of shelves, I did – not anything excessive, but with a pleasant floral and fruit (of the sort that you can find anywhere, except that it wasn't) design that made it quite presentable for guests, and most importantly meeting that 'that much larger in size' requirement. (Koji, at this time, was being excessively fussy about this kind of thing, and unless I was sufficiently mentally prepared to put up with another argument, I had no choice but to go with the flow.)

And at home, our guests arrived, dinner was served, and with the appearance of the curry, Mrs Shimizu immediately came out with: "Oh, these are the exact same plates we have at home!"

And a vase:
Mrs Kawano was the owner of a residential hotel along the coast (and also one of my first students in Japan) who had originally come to me to learn the basics when her husband had suddenly passed away. Being in her fifties at the time, and me very new in Japan, she was exceedingly (almost excessively) kind to me (See 'first ghost', [8.9]), and although she only studied with me for a short while, she used what she learned well, traveling around over 40 different countries, in large part on business and apparently very successfully, and we kept up our relationship right the way through until she died. As to why I chose to buy the vase for her (we were in Kyushu at the time at a very small pottery close to Koji's home), I am not quite sure, but I imagine that having been on the receiving end of her generosity for so long, I considered it an opportunity to give something back.

The package was opened in the main dining room of the hotel, a large, brightly sunlit room overlooking the seafront, and although admiring it as a 'nice' piece (which was as intended – I didn't have the money for anything more), she very quickly remarked that, "It wasn't quite the colour that she had had in mind." And fully understanding her intent in the matter (this being considerably after the above affair with the curry plates), I picked it up and took it into the entrance hall, a considerably less well-lit area, placing it on the table there next to a much larger (and far more expensive – it would be in the hundreds of thousands of yen) piece that was permanently displayed there. (Having been involved in the hotel business for a very large part of her life, she knew what good pottery was, and she had told me more than once that this was one from one of the top potters in Kyoto – a number of them who are the elite of the elite in their field.) And the colouring was identical. And I said no more.

The fence:

It was night-time; there were two or three of us on the outside and one man approaching us speaking rather excitedly (/angrily?) from within the compound. I do not recall having ever met him before, but I assumed it was his house. And then at one point he paused, and there was some form of understanding among us (that 'click'). He was 'trapped' on the inside, and we were on the outside 'free to walk away'. And we (for whatever reason – I still have no idea what series of events led to this particular denouement) had 'won the day'. However, here, for the first time, I understood that this was something beyond just Koji and myself, and that in some manner we (again, the questions of who or why?) had been working in a group. And also, from this point on, I began to recognise sequences of 'challenges' or 'games', some quite simple (on-the-spot) and others far more complex (extending over periods of months or even years).

And as with all games, there were penalties for the losers and rewards for the winner. In the above case at the hotel, Mrs Kawano, forever generous, actually commissioned a painting, which she (also forever the businesswoman – cash in hand beating out a credit card any day) then cut the promised payment by 20% at the time it was handed it over. This, in its turn, was settled sometime later in a manner satisfactory to both sides when she insisted on buying me a set of dishes at an antique fair, at which time I accepted on the condition that whatever she bought cost no more than that 20% difference. And overall (considering how many others seemed to turn sour at the end), we had a very solid and equally 'good-fun' relationship. At least personally, I couldn't have wanted better.

[7.23] And a lemon for the loser:

Resting in an open space at the top of the mountain before starting my descent on the far side, a man approached me from somewhere out of the crowd.

(It was a busy weekend, with two or three large groups of walkers gathered in the same area.) Considerably taller than myself and good looking (I would accept "mountain-climbing hunk" as reasonable description), no word was spoken from beginning to end, but right from the start he made it very clear what he wanted: I was expected to unzip his trousers and get down on my knees in front of him. Although in other circumstances I would have loved to (this actually was in line with a fantasy I had dreamed up some years previously when I was much younger and when the mountain paths had been relatively unoccupied), no way was I going to follow this type of instruction at this particular time. (I will admit that, as he kept standing there, strong legs firmly apart – he refused to move and was totally insistent as to what I was supposed to do – I did come very close to putting out a hand.) However, we were, in the end, out in full view of every person around us, and presumably recognising that nothing was going to happen, he indicated (again no words spoken) that, as a penalty game, he would race me down the mountain. Nothing was said as to what might happen if I lost (which I did – he actually just smiled and left me to complete the last section on my own), but, as a game, it taught me a lot about descending straight down a thickly wooded mountainside at full speed: There was no attempt to turn left or right even once, and the somewhat meandering path, which I would normally have followed, was totally ignored.

In terms of what you can learn from the way other people treat you, in many ways this proved to be an excellent lesson. (I suspect that part of what I was being taught here included the matter of being careful what I was wishing for – which seemed a fair point.) Also, it gave me a clear reading of his nature: without any hesitation, he was a person who, in other circumstances, I would have appreciated as a friend. (This in comparison with other cases of penalty games that I was subject to, some of which, to my mind, came close to malicious, and certainly were not appreciated.)

[7.24] Developing a system. Setting the rules:

This was essentially me in the very early stages trying to put a little order into my world in an effort to keep myself in a positive frame of mind. Although the idea for such rules came from actual experience, they in fact were set in an extremely arbitrary manner on the understanding that presumably others (depending on their predilections) would choose as necessary to break them. (Essentially, tell a dog to "Wait!" and then turn away to see what happens.)

However, once established, on the assumption that some others might, I did personally follow them.

- Chess or 'Shogi' (Japanese chess)?
- One key difference between the chess game as it is played in the West and Japanese chess is that, in the Japanese version, a piece taken from the board may then be reused against one's opponent, and shortly after clicking on to the concept that we were working in teams, I did get into an argument with a voice in my brain telling me that we were playing according to Japanese rules – that is someone who had been exposed as belonging to my side could now be used against me. My argument back was that they were dealing with a foreigner and that was it! A player who was out, was out! (This was actually at the very early stages, and as my understanding of what I was dealing with rapidly expanded, the point very quickly became redundant.)
- Washrooms as 'time-out' spaces.
- The idea that, with a washroom implying privacy, others would not listen into your thoughts while you were in there. (Note that this was very much a "Wait!" rule.)
- The V-sign.
- Even today, that a reversed two-finger peace sign (so that you are showing the back of your hand to the person you are addressing), gives you the English version of the American one-finger 'Up-yours!' (/ 'F…off!') gesture is a fact that is still not generally known in Japan, and for my own pleasure – my reasoning being that some understanding of this fact would, at a minimum, indicate a slightly wider outlook on life, I made it a personal rule to accept such signs at face value.

FF: Some forty years ago, Mr and Mrs Hamada's (school receptionist) daughter, Yukiko [4.2], early on in her stay at my parent's home in England, when attempting to purchase two stamps at the post office in town, and raising her fingers to ensure that the number was clearly communicated (she was having a problem getting her message through), was surprised to find the counter clerk's face at first reddening considerably and then turning to anger as, (not understanding why he could not understand), she emphasised the number by repeatedly shaking her outstretched fingers in his face. And although she asked, neither my mother (who, belonging to her generation, would probably not have any idea of the sign's existence, let alone its meaning) nor myself (at least, I was not prepared to go into any detail on the matter) could explain exactly where she had been wrong.

- The 'ehen mushi'.
  The powerful coughing fit that I experienced in the hospital basement after the exhibition was repeated only once, some months later in the centre of Motomachi, one of Kobe's largest shopping arcades. Exiting a shop, where I had been talking with the owner's wife, who I knew quite well, I suddenly felt that same throat tickle welling up to the point that I was once again hacking my lungs out and totally out of control – my body being thrown from side to side across the main thoroughfare, this continuing for at least five and possibly up to eight or ten minutes. And it was from this time that I began to associate the feeling, together with the associated short clearing of one's throat, as a form of recognition or a new point suddenly appreciated by the inner consciousness.
  And later in a dream: Attending a prayer meeting in what I assumed was a mosque; first one, then a second and third low cough (echoing my own) coming from among the rows of bent heads.

FF: The cave tour at the Waitomo Caves in New Zealand includes a standard stalactite-stalagmite section, followed by a boat trip through to the cave's entrance – the boat pulled along an overhead rope – when above you, you get to view a whole colony of glow-worms, in absolute stillness and shedding a deep blue light throughout. (Koji described the scene as "the Cosmos.") Before we entered, we were informed that, as any a loud noise would frighten the insects enough for them to extinguish their glow-lights and thus negate the whole experience, it was essential that the boat section of the trip be completed in complete silence. And naturally, this being the case, the moment I had settled my body low into the boat frame as instructed (an awkward position at the best of times), I started to feel that same fine scraping sensation strengthening at the back of my throat.

[7.25] Timing/Coincidences:

I have read detailed explanations of 'coincidences' as being exactly that; occurrences that happen quite by chance, and at one level I can fully appreciate this as a totally reasonable explanation. However, to illustrate a case that actually happened, if I was involved in training someone as to the importance of position and timing, while meeting in town would be relatively easy, to have them drive some 10 to 15 km from their home and 'happen to meet me' at a junction a ten-minute walk from mine (this on a red light), would seem like a reasonable advanced test – although, as the walker, I presumably would have had more leeway for adjustment here. (It was also around this time that – as a teacher – the importance of 'learning to lose' entered the equation.)

FF: In London, the day after Sally (the Canadian member of our Kobe Nook group [4.7], long back in her country and married) came running out of a restaurant that Koji and I were passing in Earl's Court, the three of us came across Andy (the eldest son in the Maltese family that I stayed with in New York [1.11]) slurping shellfish along the South Bank, and later that evening I found Koji and Andy kissing each other in our hotel room – making me wonder (presumably not a coincidence) how the American friend at Oxford had come to choose that particular family for me.

[7.26] Hide and seek:

"Sir, apparently someone saw you riding along ~ Avenue (the main road from the hotel to the station) on a bicycle." This followed by some considerable tittering from my group of young telephone operators who I was teaching English to at the Emperor Hotel in Osaka – all of whom were fully aware that I didn't ride a bicycle to work. And I, also, had to laugh. (There had been numerous references to 'Where's Wally?' ('Waldo' in the US), in the media over the previous few weeks, but this was the first indication to me that I might have been cast in that role.) And then some two weeks later, sitting in a bar in the centre of Osaka after work (it was, I think, a gay bar, but I had never been there before and I have never been there since), a rather podgy man in his late thirties with a somewhat reddened face (he clearly had been running) rushed in and, without even a glance in my direction, seating himself at the counter came out with, "I'm from the Emperor Hotel!" And the barman, not knowing quite how he should reply to this, asked him what he would like to drink.

This type of thing happened a number of times, so often in fact that it wasn't too long before I began to question whether I was still on the learning or teaching end of the spectrum, and presumably at some point there was (particularly with my students) a switch around this time. I am not sure how this particular game (or, for that matter, any of the others) started. However, if I were to accept the fact that I was (at least at some point) the source, there must have been a certain degree of duplicity involved. None of a whole series of similar games were in any way planned consciously, but rather realised after – sometimes long after – the fact, and even then, not let on to. No doubt, if the game had been openly thought about at the time, I would've been giving everything away from square one, which would not have made sense.

The photograph:

Spring, and a Japanese man suddenly thrusting his video camera into my face while keeping up a highly unpleasant (I came very close to hitting him) background monologue about how he had encountered a 'foreigner taking photographs of cherry blossom'. Even today, I am not sure whether this was a new game that someone had dreamt up, or simply that I had happened upon an obnoxious drunk. (He clearly had been drinking heavily.) However, in time it did become an extension of (/actually a considerable step up from) the above 'Hide and Seek' – the protagonists both having cameras, and, beyond the matter of recognition, the question would be who took a photograph of the other first (these situations invariably occurring on long trips abroad).

The nicest example I have of this would be a Japanese lady who had, in her time, represented her country as an Olympic shot-putter. Met in a helicopter taking us up to view Mt Cook in New Zealand, and later on the streets of Queenstown – where she showed me her (literally) matchbox-size camera and explained that she had taken some photographs of me that she would like to send me – in her best photograph, she had caught me taking a photograph of the summit of the mountain. In contrast to my photograph, which didn't turn out too well, hers was as totally professional as she made me look. However, when we got back to Japan, I did select a few of my nicer shots and (she had won) sent them to her.

Then in Scotland with Kensuke (2014), there was a man who looked as if he might be professional popping up at my side with his camera, and very quickly, before taking a shot and then disappearing from sight, coming out with; "This is a rehearsal!"

[7.27] And as an example of a 'game' that was not at all appreciated:

One reality: The following are excerpts from a letter sent to friends around the world shortly after returning from Australia in Jan. 2001.

"Flaking out in Melbourne: Being with old (and also new) friends who all went out of their way to help me get through everything, made the visit exceptional. When people are very kind, it touches me very deeply, and I honestly don't know how to thank them… You will note that New Zealand is not included in the title. This is because (in what is tending to become an embarrassing habit) I overdid things again, exhausting myself to the point that I had to spend a night in hospital. The reasons are varied, I guess. Both of us had really done nothing but work for the previous year. Also, I was trying to translate as much as possible for both Koji and the other way round for the friends we were staying with, which in the end can get very hard. And again, we had arranged what by non-Japanese standards was a rather gruelling schedule – two and a half days at each port of call. We had planned to travel around the South Island of NZ by car (Koji driving) but in the state I was in, we decided that it would be safer to retire from the game while we were still in it and make another foray at a later date."

And another:

Waking up in mental hospital.

The cold woke me up. I was in an overly large room; four cream walls, high ceiling, and a space where you would normally expect a doorway, and with no furniture in it other than the slim bed that I was lying on with its one thin sheet. And I could only lie there feeling the cold – I couldn't understand why it should be so cold! – and wondering why this might be.

I remembered the farewell dinner and being plied with lots of wine, and then back in the house in the evening, and everyone still drinking – until I went upstairs to pack for the New Zealand section of our trip. And at this point, already being far too tired and equally seriously worried about Koji driving for the first time in a foreign country, I made the mistake of allowing the perfectionist side of my mind, with its need to question every possibility, to take over (all the what-ifs in life that no one can ever cover) and in the end going into what Henry, the friend we were planning to stay with in New Zealand (introduced in [12.4]) quite correctly labelled a tizz-wazz. And after that, nothing but an exhausted blank.

A man appeared in the doorway space wearing a simple white, slipover gown, identical to the one I was wearing. He made no attempt to approach, but the way he was staring across at me – with an inquisitive look that at the same time held a rather scary element of blankness – made me feel highly uncomfortable. And then without saying a word, he left. And for no other reason than to rid myself of the cold, I made myself sleep.

And the next morning, one of them came for me – the one I was least acquainted with. I can't remember his name. I had only met him perhaps twice. (That Koji did not come at this point did not help. The reason given was that they were all working to get us on a plane home.) But then thinking that we might leave, I was told that we had to wait for the head doctor's permission. He would not be in for an hour, and unless he cleared me, it being a mental institution, by Australian law I would not be allowed to leave, which seriously had me panicking a little. I had no desire to stay another night in that particular place. However, he did come, and I was officially recognised as 'not mentally unstable' and driven back to the house.

***

I had worked with Adam for two years or so at the head office and we had got on very well. He then went back to Australia and found his partner, who I do remember actually visited us here at home one time. However, this time, right from the start we were informed that both of them were open (and quite happy) about sleeping around, and a certain element of general seduction had been clear right from the first evening of drinks with 'friends', Andy going out of his way to impress Koji with the size of his arms and leg muscles, taking him off to view videos in private and whatever right from the moment we had arrived, with Koji an equally willing participant. However, for me, neither he nor his partner were at all sexually attractive, and as explained in [1.3], I was not psychologically set up for any kind of orgy.

Arriving back, I was told that they had cancelled all our New Zealand bookings and arranged a flight to get us home, which I could only agree with. I had had enough. And then they all had a good laugh explaining how I had told the medical assistant they had called that, "if he stuck that needle in me, I would fart," and that that was exactly what I had done. (Being extremely averse to having needles stuck in me, what I actually said was "fight," but presumably I didn't have the energy in me.)

Also, as to why I had had to be put in a mental institution; "There hadn't been room in any of the other local hospitals." I couldn't just have been put to bed. (Privately, Adam mentioned it to me that this was a penalty awarded for losing a game related to an Australian video that we had used in classes when we had worked together in Japan. This was well prior to the exhibition, and certainly at this time I had no idea that people were playing games. However, under the circumstances, there was nothing to be said and it was left at that.)

Returning to Japan, the above letter was written (in total we did have a very good time). We kept in contact for a year or so and then the relationship dried up. And in the end, whatever it was supposed to be, being locked up in a madhouse simply to allow your partner to have a night of free sex with half a dozen other men is not something easily forgiven. (Another run down the mountainside would've seemed to make more sense.)

In situations like this, it tends to be habit and social custom that carry you along, and it actually took me over two years to understand that I no longer wanted anything to do with them.

[7.28] Another disruption: "The Great Hanshin-Awaji Earthquake" (Level 7+ on the Japanese scale):

On the morning of the January 17, 1995, shortly before 6 am, we were awoken by a deep rumble and strong tremor, both of which were over before we could become in any sense aware of what was happening, but in those very few seconds, the lower half of the city together with the whole bay area were essentially destroyed, this including uprooted railway lines, bridges torn apart and whole sections of the expressway toppled. The newly built city hall somewhat mysteriously lost its middle three floors, the upper and lower sections remaining as they had been constructed. Higher up the hill, where we live, this damage was not immediately apparent (there were houses in various states of collapse right the way up the mountainside, but equally there were many others that apparently had not been touched), and although the top third of our kitchen cabinet had been dramatically dislodged, and we had a lot of breakages (with all the better glass and ceramics going first), a brief look outside did not indicate any particular serious damage in the area, and it was not until we visited a friend's apartment lower down the slope later in the morning that we began to get an idea of how serious the event had been.

***

Lessons on how not to react in a state of emergency:

The bureaucracy as it is maintained in Japan operates smoothly to the extent that events stay in line with the scenarios (this including emergencies) envisioned by its creators, and fully detailed manuals prescribe precisely how to act within the context of such scenarios. However, events such as large earthquakes (or, for that matter, meltdowns of nuclear reactors) will not automatically go by the book, and in such cases, overly rigid manuals can prove extremely limiting: In the case of the Kobe earthquake, they in effect paralysed the whole system.

Early in the morning, upon receiving the televised news of the earthquake, the members of the fire-brigade in a small town in the north of prefecture, understanding with almost full certainty that (earthquakes and fires being inseparable) their services would be required, set off towards in the city in the south. And other than for this one small group (later, until some slightly saner voices got into the mix, publicly criticised for their 'insubordination') nobody but nobody moved! And why not? It had been determined in the manuals that; "In case of an emergency, no (medical or other) unit under the direct control of the prefectural government was to take any action without receiving the full authority of the prefectural governor." And naturally (all communication systems being down and the city half in ruins), he was not to be found. (I am not quite certain here, but I think that at the time he might actually have been outside the city. However, regardless…)

And the fires started: I could see a number of coils of smoke from our veranda from very early on in the morning. And nobody moved. And more coils. And nobody moved. And two hours later, when the contingent from the north arrived (apparently, they were one of the first groups on the scene) the maze of narrow streets in the Nagata area of the city was a totally out-of-control, raging conflagration, eventually contributing considerably to the very high body count (in total, over 6,000 deaths) connected with the quake.

And closer to home:

At 8 am, two hours after the earthquake occurred, the electricity supply was suddenly 'restored' for a total of five or six minutes, after which we again lost all contact. This in itself would not have been important except for the fact that during this very brief period, presumably an electric spark ignited some connection in the air-conditioning system which had been installed beneath the roof of a very large and newly completed house directly to the south of our building. (They had at least six large air-conditioning units on the outside of the house, so the wiring inside would be quite complex.) However, it was not until the early afternoon when smoke started pouring out of a small hole in centre of their roof that this fact became apparent. Fortunately, this was quickly picked up by a number of our neighbours, all of whom (this being the good part of neighbourhood relations here) went into immediate action. The local fire station was contacted, but all the fire engines were now (naturally) in Nagata. (One out.) Three of us took our building fire extinguishers into the home itself, but the fire was both unapproachable and too far gone for extinguishers of that size to have any effect. (Two out.) The closest water supply valve (buried in the road) was located, and a full-size hose was obtained from a company building nearby, and this having been unrolled was found to be of sufficient length. (Sigh of relief!) Until it was found that hose and valve connections would not fit. (Even today I find this very hard to believe. The hose itself was required by official fire regulations and had been purchased directly from our local fire department. And if it would not connect with the city installations, quite to what end? However, three out.) And yet still other minds had been at work, and we 'went traditional' – the whole neighbourhood (close to two hundred people) gathering to take part in a 'bucket-relay', with water taken from a small stream that ran by the roadside up the hill.

Naturally, there were also the to-be-expected few onlookers who, perching themselves on the closest wall, took it of themselves to partake in the entertainment in full measure – a selection of the local elite including the house owner herself, who I can understand not participating (she would be in a state of complete shock), but also one younger couple who I happened to know personally (the husband coming from one of the richest property owners in the neighbourhood) whose house, directly adjacent to the burning building, would, without the efforts of the lesser members of the neighbourhood, have been completely destroyed. People's sense of entitlement at times can be quite overwhelming.

The rear of the burning house had been built with one straight wall which came up rather too close against a section of our property, but this did enable one group on our rooftop to focus on what was still a hole in the roof, while two other lines working from our third and fourth apartment levels concentrated on keeping the wall cool. And we were holding our own. Until…

The line suddenly stopped. And calling down from the rooftop, I was informed that "the police had arrived and that we had been ordered to cease operations because 'someone might get hurt.'" I could appreciate the point – we had already had one or two scary moments when the wind had blown the flames that little too close over our heads – but not wishing to lose my home (or, for that matter, our neighbourhood) – spotting the man, now at the foot of the stairs, I shouted down in my best (and loudest) Japanese, telling him that he was "an idiot" and to "get out." And this being the type of occasion where having a foreign face and temperament can work to your advantage, he followed my advice.

And we won out. The house itself was burned to the ground except for the one back wall, which held right to the end. The upper section of our building wall closest to the house was badly scorched, but we had prevented the flames from jumping the gap. A fire engine did arrive right at the end in time to put out the embers, and no one was harmed. Our neighbours, not by any means being short of money (and presumably with insurance), rebuilt. (For the record, we were not offered any direct compensation, but the city did help, and we came out of it none the worse.) And congratulations were offered all round. (This is just one of many similar stories that circulated after the event, and in no case did officialdom come out well.)

And if there has to be some good that comes out of it all:
My most vivid memory of after-events here was a scene on television of a local school which was being used as an emergency centre. And seated at the entrance, in charge of all the comings and goings (people requesting admission, receiving supplies of blankets, food and clothing, etc.), was a young schoolgirl who could not have been more than thirteen or fourteen. And she was in full control, projecting a sense of efficiency that was far beyond anything you would normally expect of someone her age, far better than a lot of older people I have had the chance to observe. Also, for the first time in its modern existence, Japan discovered 'volunteers': Hundreds and thousands of people from all over the country came to help – for months and months at a time. And ever since, each time there has been a disaster anywhere in the country, people have volunteered. Also, in each case, Kobe City has made a point of immediately sending out an official team including a group of 'locally bred' experts – all average citizens who one way or another took control at the time and subsequently gained

practical experience in crisis handling and counselling services and really know how to organise.

And early this year (2018), the government made an official announcement that "in the case of any emergency such as an earthquake or flooding, the average citizen was expected to 'look after themselves.'" (Up to the present time, in such cases "always follow the direction of the relevant authorities" has been the officially promoted position.) That is, they have realised their limits, which to me seems sensible. And people will step up. They always do.

***

And while we were fire-fighting, Koji had taken the other tack, and on the assumption that the building actually might go down, he had collected all our valuables and packed the car ready for flight, and although it was not necessary for us to leave immediately, for a number of reasons (including the fact that I had just started translating the 350-page book mentioned in [6.22], which had a time limit for completion), we decided to move down to the southern island of Kyushu to be with his family – at least until the electricity and water supplies were restored.

The day after the quake, we both left the house, me walking east and Koji walking west. Three stations along our local line, I knew that there was a road that crossed directly over to the far side of the mountains, but the question was whether it still might be open – rockslides (sometimes the whole side of a mountain) being common enough here without any particular encouragement. And some three hours later, I returned home with a carton of milk for my troubles (I had met a man at the roadside, selling what was left of his wares), but Koji had better news: the road to our immediate west was still open – which it (presumably) was – until we arrived there the next morning in the car, only to find a large road sign flashing the reality of both blocked roads and tunnel. And here, Koji also hit a roadblock; this in his mind: "The road was open! He had seen the same sign yesterday and that was what it had said! The road was open!" And all we had to do was to keep driving forwards and we would be up and over and out of this unreal existence – this that could not be!

And the only way I could get him to take his foot off the accelerator was to repeatedly scream at him, and then again, until I could force him to take in this new truth: There was no road over the mountains, and we had to find another way out. And the moment he finally applied the brakes, his head cleared, and without even looking at the sign to verify whether or not what I had been saying was correct, he turned back down the hill and then again to the west. There would be another road (there was), and somehow – despite having to somewhat gingerly negotiate our way past a certain number of half-toppled buildings – we would get out (we did).

And again, that hidden trauma:
More than any memory of the earthquake itself (which had, in effect, passed in our sleep), it was with the after-effects that we truly got to understand how deeply it had disturbed us: In Kyushu, given Koji's nephew's room to sleep in, we were laughed at by the whole family for immediately taking down every object off the top of his chest of drawers, but we refused to sleep otherwise (both of us terrified that in the case of another quake something might fall on our heads – and I still keep nothing above our sleeping positions in our bedroom at home). Also, the slightest banging of a door would have me literally jumping out of my chair. And for a long time after the event, my mind refused to consider the purchase of any expensive breakable items, there being no point if they were only to be destroyed in the same manner.

And then eight years later, in the Maori museum in the centre of Rotorua, placed together with an older Japanese couple from Tokyo (four of us in the small theatre) watching a film on the history of New Zealand, we got to 'experience' a giant earthquake (including the benches we were sitting on starting to move), in what was for me a rather too perfect simulation of the experience, at which time I found one section of my brain reduced to a state of complete panic – I was aware of myself clinging on to the bench with both hands, fingers tightly clenched, but could do nothing about it. (Koji was also in a similar position, totally incapable of any movement.) At the same time, a separate section of my mind was registering the Japanese couple sitting there one row in front of us, quite calmly as if nothing was happening: They were on a Disney ride.

[7.29] Side-trips:

Our car registration number, indicating that we were from Hyogo Prefecture, immediately identified us as fleeing from the earthquake, and repeatedly, when we took a drive out to take a break from my work, we had people approach us with drinks or snacks and very commonly offers of money, the latter of which we repeatedly refused, it not seeming right under the circumstances; we still had a home to go back to. Even so, these were all kindnesses that were very much appreciated.

cf. Officialdom: Three years after the earthquake occurred, it came out that the Kyoto Prefecture authorities, which had organised a campaign to collect donations for survivors, had 'omitted' – if I am correct, 'forgotten' was also used here as an explanation – to remit those funds (a considerably large amount) to the city, although I do believe we did receive them eventually.

[7.30] Selecting a world of my own:

Japan has whole range of potteries and potters ranging from porcelain to heavy ceramics, many locally developed and equally many with roots in Korea or China, and in the majority of cases heavily dependent upon local clays, which (together with locally developed glazes) tend to define the 'look' of a particular style, and from very early on I had decided that it might be nice to collect one piece each time I visited a new area, initially as a souvenir, and then later, when I could find an interestingly shaped vase, something different in which I could arrange flowers. And as pieces can become considerably expensive, from very early on I decided I would have to limit myself to one representative piece from any particular kiln or (particularly with the famous) groups of kilns.

Within driving distance of Koji's hometown, there is a pottery (its roots in Korea) which produces 'Agano-yaki,' utilising a very distinctive whitish-green glaze, a colour that, not being anything like the greens that may be found naturally in England, I initially found some difficulty relating to: It was only after I started climbing regularly that I found it exists here as a spring green – the leaves of one particular tree in the mountains taking on that identical shade in their early growth stages. (The colour changes completely as its leaves open.) And after this discovery, I did come round enough to purchase a full-size vase, and quickly found that it was perfect for any kind of arrangement – from traditional Japanese to the most modern. And invariably the colour enhanced, never once clashing with, or detracting from the natural colours of the flowers themselves, which I had assumed it would. (If my memory is correct, the small piece of pottery that I gave to Mrs Kawano [7.22] came from these potteries.)

And directly south from here, in the Hikosan mountain range, there is another grouping of (originally) younger sons who, with only the eldest of the family allowed to remain in Agano to take over the family business, were obliged to start anew with their own kilns. And of the two, this is the area that I have always tended to find more enjoyable, partly because it is very spread out, and perhaps more so because, not being in any manner restricted by tradition, each kiln tends to be far more unique in its style of produce. However, it was on one of our trips here that Koji pulled up by the side of a roadside stall and indicated to me that I was to "choose my own world"; that this was very important, and that I was to be very careful in my selection.

And in front of me, to select from, I had a tableful of well over two hundred ceramic globes – small spheres, each with a finger-sized aperture at the top, just large enough to hold one or two small flowers. Of equal size (less than 10 cm in height) and covered with a standard glaze, each only distinguishable by a delicate shading created by fine flecks of a slightly darker brown apparent beneath the surface, they were in effect all the same, and at the same time all different. And given time (you aren't always), I took it; lifting, turning and sorting until I found one I decided I liked, and in fact still now have displayed at home, and although it only cost me a very reasonable ¥500, it does have its own 'presence' and (at least to my mind) will stand up to comparison with any of the much larger (and far more expensive) pieces on my shelves.

And, again, "the game": At home we already had a (purchased on our first trip to the UK and far more expensive) Irish crystal rose bowl, which turned on its side and its base ignored could be taken at a reasonable representation of the globe, and this is the one that some months later (drawn in precise detail), someone did chose to represent as the world in a cartoon in our nationwide English language newspaper. (I do admit that the small piece that I purchased in Kyushu would not have created quite the intended dramatic effect, but it was and has remained a world that, given the choice, I would stay with.)

[7.31] A visit to a Home:

During the short break of six or so minutes when we had our electricity restored, early on the day of the quake, we received a telephone call from a paraplegic friend in Kyushu. A neighbourhood friend of Koji's from the time he was quite young (Koji knew the man's older sister well), we had visited Tomonobu at least two or three times on earlier trips, and he had developed a habit of telephoning us once or twice a year, when he would get a member of the staff in his nursing home to dial our number for him. Naturally, he wanted to know how we were, but his first words to me when I answered the phone were that "the moment he had heard of the earthquake, he had had a moment of 'enlightenment,'" (he used the word, 'satorimashita'), which I understood as him reaching some level of understanding (/acceptance) of the reality of having been born into that particular body – his whole existence since birth.

And he was the only person who was able to contact us in our home: With all the members of Koji's family, we had to queue to use our local public telephone. This, for some reason, did not sit well with Koji's eldest sister, Sachiko, who did not seem to be able to understand why someone who was not in any manner (at least in her eyes) closely related, had been able to make immediate contact with us, whilst she as 'head of the family' had not been able to do so; her attitude – she was seriously offended – here being such that it really made me wonder why that might be. (See [18.14])

And now being based in Kyushu, we were able to go and see him personally, the visit itself (including the very roundabout route, which was required to get to his Home, which was way out in the middle of nowhere) being very much as it always had been. He was never informed that we were on our way as, apparently, if he knew someone was coming, it would make him inordinately excited, bringing him in some cases close to having a fit. But he was, as usual, very happy to see us and that we were well.

Then on our way back, Koji missed a key fork in the road, and not being in the mood to do a U-turn, decided that (all roads presumably leading to Rome) we would take another route back into the centre of the town, a feat which he did find not impossibly difficult. However, arriving back at his middle sister, Narumi's [18.14] home, where we were staying at the time, we found his brother-in-law, again in a seemingly highly offended mood, demanding to know "where we had got to?" This was not in any sense because we were late (the missed turning could not have involved more than a ten-minute detour, and it would only be about four in the afternoon, far too early for us to be late for a meal), and looking him directly in the eye, my mind came out with: "If you can't follow us around here in your neighbourhood, how on earth do you expect to know where we are when we are in Kobe?" which proved to be a direct hit, bringing him up dead in his tracks. And nothing else was said. The point had been made.

[7.32] A note on keeping others on/throwing others off your trail:

In the following situations, it is very likely that both of the above was occurring at the same time. Particularly if this was to be a matter of training, it would be essential to have at least some people aware of your movements.

Shortly after we started driving out to the plot, Koji was introduced to some shortcuts, which were very often quicker routes but also helped us avoid the rather high payments required on the toll-roads and expressways. However, from the beginning, there were certain sections on these backroads that for some reason made him uncomfortable – he didn't like the 'atmosphere' or the people we saw along the way – and even though it was only relatively a short drive, he would insist on stopping at certain points, particularly at a parking area on the expressway which was no more than a kilometre from our exit, sometimes for fifteen to twenty minutes, which got to be highly frustrating. (As far as I was concerned, we had work to do!) However, in the end, my interpretation had to be that in some manner he was 'organising' (/settling) his mind. And after a year and a half or so, the whole thing did clear, and he was able to make a straight run of it.

And then (this with both Koji, and more recently, Kensuke), every time we have been setting out on a longer journey (going away for a number of days), we have invariably ended up taking some roundabout route to get out of town, commonly finding ourselves way away from where we should be. And again this frustrated, until, after a certain point, I began to take it as the norm.

[7.33] And when the mind doesn't clear:

Part of the reason that I finally decided to get this whole story down on paper is that the daughter of one of our close friends, Shino, who I have known since she was a baby, and then a very sweet (if light-headed) child/young woman, was clearly exposed to the same influences that I was, but at a much younger – early twenties – age, and at that time she was drawn in so deeply that she in many senses became incapacitated. (I do not know this for a fact, but I suspect that she was told about the society by her father at too young an age. I do know that he told her about the personal relationship between Koji and myself very early on.) And even as she approached her forties, she clearly was still getting drawn inwards, incapable of controlling whatever impulses existed in her brain. On one such occasion, when she was visiting our home with her parents, she drove the first so many hundred kilometres in roughly two hours before taking something like six hours to drive the last four, arriving well after midnight. During this time, she refused to listen to her father's directions (he pretty much knew where they were), and although I could easily have given her a place to return to or even gone to find them – they were very close – she would not park the car or make a telephone call, and she just kept driving around, and around and around.

And on another occasion, out in the countryside planting seeds and weeding vegetable beds, she suddenly couldn't do anything – she was disturbing more plants than weeds – and she stood up, got into the car and drove off for something like three hours, until her father got really worried and went off to find her, which he in fact very quickly did. Again, she had apparently been driving around in circles, out of sight but just a short way from where we were working. Then on the way home, about fifteen minutes after starting our drive and just after getting on the expressway, she suddenly pulled into the parking area and insisted that she had to buy something – I can't remember quite what, but it certainly wasn't anything of great importance. Then having opened the car door to get out, she for the first time seemed to notice another car parked beside us with at least two passengers seated in the front that I could see, and quickly closing the door again, came out with: "I can't park here. They are 'teki' (enemies/ foes/ adversaries) and they might be listening in." That said, she quickly moved the car up about six spaces before re-parking and getting out to do her shopping. Neither her father nor I said anything, but we did keep a very close eye on her for the rest of the trip.

Re-reading the above, I can understand that an average person would take this as "There is something badly wrong inside that head," which I can agree with, except that I can only see echoes of what went through my own brain in the early stages – ideas (/possibilities) that I have managed to work through, at least to the point that none of it worries me any longer – and somehow she seemingly got blindsided by those same possibilities.

[7.34] The journey home:
Clear of Koji's hometown but still in the countryside, we were driving along an open stretch of road and facing, for whatever reason, a seemingly never-ending flow of cars passing in the other direction, when it occurred to me that they were there for us (/for me?): Word had got out that we were leaving, and they had assembled at this spot to bid us farewell. And as the line continued, it

seemed natural that I should raise my hand (papal-like) in recognition; which I did, carefully at first, and then – as it became clear that with the road now winding considerably Koji's mind was concentrating on more practical matters – more openly, with a truly regal sweep of the forearm (rehearsing for some future life?). And this went on for quite some time until Koji, waking up to the fact that things had gone a little too far, came out with a very brief, "Cut that out!" Which I did. If you recognise the extent of the arrogance expressed in the above (I was being totally serious here), you will see how far in terms of self-importance (/self-aggrandisement) my mind was ranging at this stage.

And then we were on the highway, and I was in pain – in this case in the lower half of my body – at first whimpering and then crying out loud; it was so bad. And again Koji told me to "Stop it," but this is not something that one can do at one's will – with both legs frozen, the pain was far too intense. And for the next 10 or 15 to 20 minutes, I remained in a total, excruciating agony until, just as swiftly as it had come, it cleared. And it was as if it had never been.

A parking area on the expressway:
There are much larger, more popular stops on the highway, but here there was nothing much more than a few vending machines and basic toilet facilities, and also one cleaning lady, who apparently had the place to herself. And Koji indicated that she had to be greeted; not spoken (or even nodded) to, but 'acknowledged'. In consideration of the range of people who had visited during the exhibition, this was not any particular surprise, but it did lead to a reconsideration (some three and a half years on) of the whole situation; that is, why would that extreme range of characters be beneficial to whatever aims the group presumably had? And in time, I came to take this concept that we had to be everywhere as a necessary (even essential) condition if we were to have any practical effect.

That much later, walking through a group of homeless people parked by the Okura (Kobe's most expensive and exclusive hotel), it shocked me a little to see two men – one totally drunk and violently aggressive, and the other someone who had a mien of refinement that seemed totally at odds with his condition – quite clearly operating in full harmony. And again later, happening to see a photograph in the paper of a seemingly perfectly pleasant Korean man who had been arrested for murder, it occurred to me to wonder whether that might not be the price one had to pay in order to be in a position where you could 'be of use'.

And if so, what was the position of the person who had presumably died at his hand? And then there were all those people I instinctively disliked: We were all merely, as Shakespeare would have it, 'playing our parts', and I had been given one of the better (/easier) roles to play?

Conclusions apart, considerations in this area – including the possibility of being born paraplegic, or with some other limiting condition – did result in a considerable amount of introspection on my part, and as such presumably had its own value, but in the end, not wishing to send to myself crazy, I had to stick with the fact that, until proven otherwise, we all are as we are, and of necessity can only be accepted in the manner presented.

And here also, there was one more 'first time' experience for me. For whatever reason, the shutter on my camera suddenly would not operate. The scene itself wasn't anything particularly dramatic – simple outlines of trees and vegetation – but the sky was heavily overcast, creating what was a rather unusual atmosphere and making me wonder whether I might not be able to produce something a little more distinctive than the usual. However, having lined up the whole shot, nothing would work. However much I pushed down the shutter release, it would not move. Changing my position slightly and resetting everything, I tried again. And again, nothing. Turning around a hundred and eighty degrees, everything was in working order (this resulting in one very much unneeded shot of a desolate parking area). And then back again, where again the mechanics were out of sync. The photograph was not to be taken.

I would note that this was way before digital cameras came into use and therefore (although I did have exactly the same problems occurring after I changed to digital) the problem could not have been (as with certain cases described in the next chapter) one of electronics [8.10].

[7.35] Hiroshi:

A storm over a teacup:

This was a rather elegant English bone-china cup, given to me by Hiroshi shortly after the exhibition – for whatever reason I would not know: It was intended as some form of apology for 'inconveniences caused'? Admired, and then quickly stored away, that would have been the end of the matter except for the fact that Koji, having been informed of the gift, erupted in what I could only interpret as an exceedingly complex paroxysm of jealousy. "Why had he bought it for me? Why hadn't he bought a pair of cups; one for me and one for him?"

This not just once, but on and on until, getting on the phone to Hiroshi, he insisted (/shouted down the line) that "he also be bought a cup." And at this point, if Hiroshi had told him to go and take a walk, I would have understood. But Hiroshi obliged, and an identical cup was purchased and handed over. (In time, both cups disappeared, I presume to one of Koji's family, for whom he commonly appropriated nicer items not in use. In other cases, this being done without any consultation, it actually did annoy, but in this case perhaps they were better gone.)

Sometime after this particular incident, I did have sex twice with Hiroshi, once (a touchie-feelie) in his office and once in his apartment, neither time very impressive. A nice enough person in his own right, in this area he wasn't at all exceptional, with sex a physical act and nothing more, and twice was quite sufficient.

***

Hiroshi was a fan of 'things mystical', this including a trip to Egypt to take part in a ceremony conducted in one of the pyramid tombs to "release the energy from his lowest 'chakra,'" (he explained the ceremony to me, but was not very clear as to what or if any energy had been released), and then to India "to have his fortune 'read in leaves,'" the fortune-tellers here apparently being quite famous. On his return, he told me how every fact he had been given about his past had been completely correct (this long before Facebook, et al), except for the fact that the reader had mixed up his mother's and father's names. He was also given certain pointers to his future (presumably about how successful he was going to be with his various businesses), which he did choose to believe until Kobe had its earthquake and most of what he had built was destroyed, at which point ("If they hadn't been able to predict an earthquake of that magnitude, how good could they be?") they fell off in his esteem. He also became fascinated with the power of crystals and New Wave philosophy: I worked through two books related to the latter with him as a part of his lessons – one a rather simplistic novel, and one (apparently written by an 'expert') explaining the basic philosophy, which, regardless of any realities, as there was a contradiction in the basic arguments being presented on every other page, did not especially impress.

FF: Returning home from an evening out in town, I did one time work up the courage to place my future in the hands of a street fortune-teller, only to find the following morning that, as the alcohol had worked its way out of my system, so too had those (if I remember correctly, considerably expensive) chosen words of wisdom, whatever they might have been.

***

And in the meantime:

The following are two unusual one-time-only experiences that occurred around this time. (I have no understanding at all of what they were or might mean. The reason they are included here is that I do remember describing at least the first to Hiroshi.)

(At home) A soft stream of energy emitting from my forehead (from a spot directly between and slightly above the eyebrows – where Hindu women wear the decorative vermillion 'bindi' dot after marriage) and returning sullied some ten days later. (Sullied is the only word I can bring to mind here. If I were talking about air, I would use 'pure' when going out vs. 'polluted' on its return.)

Returning home with Koji after an evening out in Osaka, following him into the apartment, I distinctly felt what I could only describe as a 'spirit' entering the upper area of my body, whilst a second, no longer required, left through the door.

[7.36] Sign language:

Being alone at home quite a considerable part of the time after the exhibition, I had started tuning into the occasional 'shuwa' (sign language) programme, both basic lessons and the short news programme that goes with them, this leading very quickly to (1) being approached by a man in a shop wanting me to help him find a particular book – if this was a test, I was not up to the level, (2) encounters in gay bars – knowing the basic greetings, this I could handle, at least for very brief 'conversations' and (3) a very intriguing moment with Mr Kondo.

Mr Kondo worked directly under Hiroshi, and each time I went to give lessons, he would be in the next-door office working with the two secretaries/assistants there. I had known him for a long time, and we got on very easily with each other. And then one afternoon, when I had arrived a little early and was waiting in the outer entrance hall, he came out to talk to me for a brief moment (no more than two or three short sentences), but it was immediately apparent to me that, while his arms were moving in a very natural manner (nothing like they would be used if you were actually taking part in a conversation with a deaf person), his hands and fingers were (apparently quite unwittingly) forming the signs that corresponded to his verbal message. (The sign for 'Osaka', which I had remembered because it had stuck out as somewhat unusual, came through very clearly.)

[7.37] Contemplating a way out:

There were two points coming through, both in the relatively early stages, when I did actually approach the possibility of taking my life. If the second could be described as more dramatic, of the two, the first was probably the more serious. Even now, I could not really say how much true intention was in there. It was not that I particularly wanted to die, but rather it was an attempt to rid myself of (the encumbrances of?) life.

When days shorten:

Early autumn, very badly drunk, alone and lonely; having fallen into a deep sleep on the last train, I was way along the coast, resting on a set of breakwaters in a section where I knew the undercurrents to be extremely dangerous, well after midnight, and all I had to do was slip into the dark waters and swim out a short distance to where, not being at all a powerful swimmer (and certainly not in the sea), I had a reasonably good chance of being carried away. And then there was a man who had passed me (naked on the rocks), on the way out with his angling rod and equipment to try some night fishing, and now some twenty minutes later I could see returning, his light hanging at his side. Scarcely pausing to note my presence (as I knew he had on the way out), he made his way back along the sea wall, and any resolve still with me left with that light. And finding a taxi, I went home.

On the wrong side of the fence (2):

(With Koji.) We had been to Uji (the green-tea area) on the outskirts of Kyoto, where I had (with the intention of developing them into sketches) taken a number of photographs of the lotus flowers at the Mimurotoji temple, after which we had visited the Zen temple, Mampukuji with its (heavily Chinese-influenced) images of the Buddha and his eighteen disciples. As wood carvings, these are exceptional, and totally different to anything I had seen up to that point in Japan. At the same time, I found a number of them frighteningly overwhelming in their power to intimidate, and ultimately, with my mind in the confused state that it was at the time, even after we moved into other quieter areas in the town, highly disquieting. However, rounding off the day, we were now back in the centre of Osaka having what was intended as a 'quiet drink'. Right from the start, there had been a tension in the air (we had actually argued about whether we shouldn't go directly home, as it had been a long day), and somewhere along the line, something (I will never know what it was) set him off. Suddenly jumping up from his chair, "he was leaving," and he was out of the door and into the elevator before I could even try to stop him. Following as quickly as I could and deciding that the staircase had to be the better bet if I wanted to catch him, I ran the full way down, only to find myself on the inner side of a thick-wire netting that blocked the main entrance. And he was gone, and at some point, shortly afterwards (I remember getting out of the building), I blanked…

And I was in a large park by the river. (I presume this would be on one of the islands in the centre of the city.) Searching out the toilet, both to relieve myself and at the same time find some sense of privacy, I took a moment to think how I might proceed, but in reality I had too much weighing me down; too much that I didn't understand, and too much that I was not privy to. The park along this section was open grass down to the river, but I had noticed that at its far end, there was a thick clump of bushes, which my (now much older) mind says that if I had been serious, I would have simply walked across to and got on with the business at hand. But perhaps, returning to my exhibitionist streak, there was a desire to go out in style. Removing all my clothes (and ignoring the man who happened to come in at the final stages – that was not the reason I was there), I set out towards my goal with a firm step, shortly to be met by a stream of wolf whistles from the array of couples seated on the benches by the river. And straightening up to my fullest height (I have always had a deep chest and at this time I still had a good part of my yoga-trained body remaining) I made my most of the moment and paraded off into the darkness.

The river appeared (as the sea had been) black. First in, and as a measure of my true intent, bought with my first salary (actually, an advance from the school) went my camera. At least, I could eliminate the day. Next, my bag, with all the rest of my possessions, including the clothes I had had on my back. And following it with my eyes, and as it moved out into the flow, fully recognising the despondency in my heart for what it was, I turned and went back the way I had come. The police, as they should have, had been called. I was covered with a thick blanket, and with the media cameras waved away, hurried into their van and off to their precinct for the night, only to be collected the next morning by Hiroshi, Koji having "been too embarrassed" to come for me.[12]

***

Selling oneself on one's own myths:

Naturally, the church's teachings would (/should?) have been perfectly sufficient here. However, at some point, my mind being occupied with both the concepts of rebirth and/or being caught in a time loop and forever having to relive the same life until you 'get it right', (an extended version of "Groundhog Day"), I did eventually manage to convince myself that whatever might happen, I must not commit suicide, and, since the above, each time I have had even the faintest of urgings to move in that direction, I have used that reasoning to draw myself back from the edge.

---

[12] I did visit Mimurotoji and Mampukuji temples again recently with Kensuke, and this time was pleased to be able to enjoy both of them to the full.

Chapter 8
"You Only Live Twice"

The following considerations should be understood as an attempt to make sense of a whole range of dreams and hallucinatory phenomena as I have experienced them.

[8.1]

I began to dream, or rather to remember my dreams, in my mid-thirties. I have given this period as a rough guestimate, because I know that this was the time my father died and I distinctly remember a dream shortly before his death, where he appeared with the flesh on his face shrivelling and wasting away as he stood in front of me. I don't actually know what the medical cause of his death was, but I am presuming it was some form of cancer. (I know he smoked all his life, right to the end, and that he was badly sick, my middle brother looking after him before he died.)

As a small child, I must've had my share of dreams, but as I grew older, I guess I was so involved with living that my mind had no time or need to occupy itself with what might be happening in that other world. But from this time, I found my recall of certain segments (in many cases extremely long sequences), remaining in my brain with a degree of clarity equal to, if not surpassing my daylight experiences. (My brain had determined that every aspect of my existence required my examination?)

Naturally, there were the standard, 'everyone-has-them' dreams – expressions of regret or imaginations of what could have been. I cannot count how many times I have gone back to university to study or (after losing my job at the company) returned to work (the same elevators, in different stages of repair, invariably stopping at the wrong floors) or forgetting to fill in my work hours for my monthly salary claim (which naturally didn't exist). I also had one very long dream of happily being back at Oxford, and then suddenly realising that I had left Koji back in Japan, being torn as to how I should proceed. And this time, it not being possible to have everything in life, I was grateful to wake up.

Also, I very quickly became aware that the dreams I was having, to a large extent were deriving to some degree from newly registered points or others' comments; actions taken, or stray thoughts that had passed through my mind during my waking hours, and not invariably, but very commonly, I could see a direct connection.

In Stage 1 of what I now refer to as "my self-improvement phases" – when I was working on the idea that "to be good, I would have rid myself of what was 'bad'" – I decided I needed to eliminate some of my more egregious bad habits, such as not having, for what seemed at the time an eternity, washed behind my ears, etc. And three or four nights later – this directed to any young person who believes they can get away with such things forever – I found myself vomiting up (/half choking-to-death on) a thick stream of torn fingernails – presumably, my whole lifetime's work in this area being disgorged in the instant.

And much more recently, as my body has weakened with age, I have had dreams where I have found myself unable to take even one step forward, or more than once collapsing from a minor heart attack – real or imagined, in the end I couldn't say – but still at the time disturbing. (The good thing about such dreams is that, with the passage of time, you do get used to them.)

I also found that I could, in a very rough sense, classify my dreams essentially into three types:

(1) Somewhat nondescript, neither-one-thing-nor-the-other dreams – when I was at all troubled, or when my mind was in a searching (/problem-solving) state.
(2) Wake-you-up nightmares – which in time, perhaps surprisingly, I learned to understand as myself in a fighting mode. And
(3) When I was excessively tired from those same fights, something beautiful or funny just to keep me going.

And as an example of (3):
I had turned down an invitation from Mrs Oka [4.2] to go to a sumo tournament two or three days earlier. It was not something that I would have had

the opportunity to do normally (they were exclusive ringside-seats), but I knew that I did not have the energy for the overly formal socialising that would have been required if I had taken up the offer, and it had been left at that.

And the dream:

I am with a young (from the lower rankings?), rather sweet-looking sumo wrestler, dressed as he would be in the ring – naked other than for a thick cream-coloured 'mawashi' loincloth wrapped around his waist – the two of us seated in a full-size toy train, done out in all the colours a six-year-old child would appreciate, with its narrow rails running high in the air ahead of us above a deep green valley sprinkled with patches of flower-filled gardens – a half-natural, half-Toyland world. And the wrestler; young as he was and clearly fascinated with the experience, making no effort to even notice his companion. (I might just as well not have been there.) There was nothing erotic here. Rather, to the contrary, it was the innocence of the whole scene that appealed, and it has stayed with me as a to-be-used-as-and-when-necessary, pick-me-up experience right the way through.

[8.2] Dreams as a place to allow personal fears or constraints a certain rein:

Returning from our plot in the countryside, the road passes through a long tunnel before descending rapidly down the mountainside into the city, and for many years we had a one-lane-going-up, two-lanes-coming-down system, which allowed for a considerable amount of racing-car style jostling (something which Koji took to quite naturally) right the way down to the lowest set of traffic lights, where the road suddenly divides into three main strands and a number of rather oddly inserted cut-offs, and (with priority given to bus routes and the invariable car illegally parked by the roadside) this was a run that terrified me for years; until one night I took to a skateboard (something I have never done in real life – I had been watching "Back to the Future"?) and completed its longest unbroken section (about three km.), in one long, exhilarating sweep. This never removed the fear completely, but at least I learned to release the whites from my knuckles, and fortunately we never actually hit anything or anyone right up to the time the city finally got clever and switched to a two-up/one-down system – that much more efficient and far safer.

[8.3] Snakes:

In England, as a child, I was taught about adders being poisonous, but being recognisable, they did not particularly instil any fear. I also knew that they were relatively small snakes. However, here in Japan, snakes come in a range of sizes, and not having been educated as to how to distinguish between the numerous different species, whenever I have come across them in the mountains, commonly baking themselves in the sun on some convenient rock on the pathway, or occasionally falling out from a high bank way above my head, I have invariably erred on the side of caution.

At some point leading up to the exhibition, I was with a group of friends, spearfishing just off the east coast of Awaji Island, south of the city. The man who had arranged the trip had mentioned that snakes commonly came out from the undergrowth in the area (apparently to feed on the local rats), but that they weren't particularly harmful, and beyond the comment being made, the matter had been left that.

This being a first experience, I was not getting any results (I had no trouble holding my breath underwater, but I had a lot of problems keeping my aim), and pulling myself out of the water, I decided I would wait around until the others came out. Then wondering whether I might not find something of interest for my camera, I started to work my way towards a small promontory which was blocking my view towards the mainland. We had based ourselves on a narrow strip of rocks, volcanic in origin (now with surfaces smoothed but riddled with cracks and orifices), which made walking a little awkward, but I did progress until, looking down into one of the recesses, I found myself confronted with a thick head poking out from the darkness. Straightening (I had nothing to ward it off with), I quickly became aware of a second and then a third – this one in full view, a good three metres in length – all of them close to motionless but apparently highly conscious of my presence and waiting for me to make my move. Quite how long we held our positions, I couldn't say, but I must admit to relief when a loud voice called out from across the water asking if I was all right, startling them enough to retreat to wherever they had come from. That was the reality.

And then there were the dreams; initially, just the single, thick, protruding head, but then serpents in every shape and form, one after another over a period of a number of years.

Symbolism:

Early on, when I told the English teacher I was working with at the time that I was having 'snake dreams', all I got in return was a rather knowing, "And you know what that means (Hah! Hah! Hah!)." Not actually 'knowing', I assumed he was referring to some erotic or phallic connection, but even at the time I was very aware that East and West can have very different interpretations in this area and that this didn't have to be the immediate answer.

There actually was a background of eroticism here: Although nothing came of it, I know that both Koji and I were rather taken by the man who had suggested the trip to the beach, and I can understand an association with my fear of the snakes themselves and my dislike of the idea of Koji's personal attraction to him (or later, to others?). However, the dreams themselves became so complex that I sense there also must have been quite a lot more behind the matter. (For an introduction to Eastern thought, any reader interested can look up Buddhist or Hindu references to snakes (/'naga') and/or dragons, all of which are integrated in a highly complex manner in the various cultures in the region. However, to cover one aspect briefly:

Naga is the Sanskrit word for cobra. In ancient Indian art, nagas are depicted as human from the waist up and snakes from the waist down. They also sometimes appear as giant cobras, and in some Hindu and Buddhist literature they can change appearance from human to snake. Originally depicted as creatures bent on harming others, in time they became understood to be guardians of Buddha – pictures exist of the Buddha or other sages sitting under the canopy of a giant cobra's hood.[13]

And the dreams themselves:

Originally frightening enough to have me regularly wakening up with a sharp scream, I did in time learn to exhibit a certain level of control. Taken from this latter period:

- Fast walking against a strong wind across a field of flattened grasses, only to recognise that in part my weight was being supported by a tightly

---

[13] Related to cobras, I do have a very clear memory of a scene from a TV documentary of a full-grown, excessively large king cobra approaching at full speed a tethered goat that had been set out as bait. In this case, I admit to being very glad to be on this side of the screen.

packed raft of snakes underfoot – all fully aligned and heading towards some (/the same?) as yet undisclosed goal.

- Heading up the road from the hospital where I had been taken after collapsing at the exhibition, instinctively sensing danger, and turning to find an oversized albino snake approaching fast – plainly with myself in its sights – I duck low; only to have it rear high above me and catch at a small bird in full flight.

And awake: Relieved that it was not me, but still wondering why that bird had had to have its life taken in my place. (A short time earlier, we had visited the white snake museum in Iwakuni, an attractive city in Yamaguchi prefecture at the western end of Honshu. In this area, this snake is traditionally considered a guardian deity of the home.)

- Snakes eating snakes.

Initially quite small in size and then, with each dream, growing larger until (observing the whole scene from high up on a stone bridge) I watched two of the most gigantic serpents sluggishly approaching each other along the riverbed, one finally engorging the other, only to then itself – its innards fully bloated – expire from the effort.

- Night-time: Enveloped in a strong, protective glow of light and moving with a firm stride down through the temple/shrine compound, totally unheeding of the ranged cobras (poised at their finest), striking out at me from all sides.

Whatever it was they represented, I was no longer afraid of them.

[8.4] Practicalities:

"The pons area in the brainstem is both responsible for basic biological functions like breathing and sensory perception and also the area in which we dream."

As hypotheses:

If we may take the above quote as representing present, generally accepted, scientific understanding, then it would seem to make sense to speculate that the pons area (which adjoins and is structurally continuous with the spinal cord) would be a natural choice as a place for any intake of telepathic communication (itself, by nature, sensory).

Dreams are commonly understood as being of value in that they help us organise (/intake/ absorb/ analyse) our daytime learning experiences. And on the understanding that that such experiences can include telepathic intake, it would not be unnatural at all for that intake also to be included in some form in one's dreams.

And in addition, the mere fact that we can if we choose both observe and remember our dreams, implies that dreams could also be a place where we can be in direct contact with any telepathic intake as it takes place during the night-time period.

[8.5] People:

Far, far too many – all the people you have yet to meet and never will.

***

- Particularly when I was concentrating on my English-Japanese grammar text, I would commonly find myself teaching classes, if in a somewhat irregular manner – with students wandering in and out at will. (A few, who actually returned on and off, did seem to be making an effort.) Once (very recently) I taught an art class, so it is possible I did at the end make some progress in that area, also.
- And naturally there were engagements with the erotic, particularly (presumably in compensation) as I aged and was no longer capable of performing quite as I would have wished in the daytime hours. In these cases, the trick, if anything, would be in avoiding those I did not wish to meet.

And of the people I know and recognised (Only one or two are listed here. Others are spread throughout the later chapters taking their respective places in their own stories.):

- Carl, my friend from university introduced in [1.1], has regularly made appearances right the way through, although it is very difficult for me to recall any point at which we actually talked together (he has a very distinctive voice), at least in any detail. And beyond that, there was one time when the whole of my mathematics group (all six of us) and our professor were together moving around a somewhat nondescript room,

making me for the first time consider whether we might actually have meant anything together as a group.
- **Childhood friends:** During the writing of this book, just about all of my childhood friends have one by one returned to make their own form of farewell, but these, much as I would wish them to have been true connections – which at least some may have been – I am equally prepared to accept them as mere 'apparitions' dragged up out of the depths of memory.
- **Kazu:** Kazu was one of the 'local characters' described in Cpt 4. Initially coming into Sono as a customer, we quickly became friends enough to go out drinking together after he had finished work. Owning his own restaurant and being that much older, he took it upon himself to pay, which considering the number of bars we could go through in an evening, was as well. (I could never have contributed in any sense meaningfully to that amount.) Both at work and after hours, he lived his part (that act that you put on to entertain the world) unremittingly. And we enjoyed each other's company. He loved joking around and singing karaoke and flirting with all the women behind the bars. Although married (his wife worked beside him in the restaurant) and with a son, he was not in the Western sense a family man – home being more of a place to sleep off the effects of the night's excesses, this at the time a common pattern here. He did come into the exhibition, but only to sign the book and leave. And here he was not anyone I knew: Shrunken, stooped, diminished even, and in many respects identical to the man who had been dragged through by his Yakuza boss on that earlier morning, he had skulked in and out before I could even begin to approach him. (In the chaotics of the aftermath, this never got explained.) And then he died, falling down the steep staircase at the back of his restaurant, and he was gone; although I did keep up with his family, eating at the restaurant (now run by his wife) whenever I was in the vicinity and eventually attending his son's wedding.

And then I had the dream:
Dressed in a deep-sky-blue costume, seated jauntily (very much in character) on top of a large rectangular wallposter (the background colour fully matching his clothing) and grinning widely, he could have been a pixie or sprite. He did

not speak (the message I took to be in the smile), but merely indicated to me the words written below him, which at the time I could not comprehend.

However, a few days later, going into the restaurant, his wife explained to me that, getting older as she was, although the basics would remain the same, they had decided to contract the restaurant out to a larger company, which is exactly ("Under new management!") what was being advertised in the dream. And why the scene in blue? 'Little Boy Blue' (from the children's rhyme) had been my very personal (never told to anyone, including Kazu himself) nickname for him throughout the time I knew him, and with an appearance in this form (and whatever the reality), the perpetrator most certainly had his sense of humour.

[8.6] A dream that could have been otherwise: (Jan. 2001) At the entrance to the incline-railway at the Blue Mountains Scenic World, Katoomba, New South Wales:

It was exactly as I had seen it in my dream – the open space; the large, somewhat cumbrous entrance gate area leading to the railway (I also had an image retained in my brain of being inside what I had assumed to be a large elevator/lift – presumably, the railway – going down into the valley. However, this was not to be.) We were with Jeff [7.8], our friend from Sydney, who had brought us on a day-tour to the Blue Mountains. He had, as usual, prepared a very detailed plan for the day, and being somewhat behind schedule at this point, something had to be cut. However, he had taken us that far and explained what we would be missing, and we returned to the car. At this time, he was very late on in his life and got tired easily, and we fully respected his decisions.

I can only assume that both scenes in the dream came from some form of telepathic input (from Jeff or whoever being quite irrelevant). However, that apart, and here risking the possibility of a certain confusion, I would note that if I had been in a similar situation but with no memory of that dream, I could have reported the whole scene as a classic case of déjà vu – which I have experienced numerous cases of at regular intervals, particularly during the latter half my life. As with the 'coincidences' mentioned in the previous chapter, I can fully understand the concept of déjà vu explained as "moments confused with previously experienced moments," but the above explanation, within context, also holds.

[8.7] And the dream that got away:

Two years after my second trip to Korea (described in Cpt 10) and shortly before the age of 60, the doctors having found a number of major blockages in my arteries, it became urgently necessary for me to undergo by-pass surgery on my heart. Informed that there was no more than a 5% chance of things not going smoothly, unfortunately I was destined to join the less fortunate, ending up first with an elongated cavity running down behind the centre of my ribs, which had to be flushed (/sterilised) every day for a couple of months until healed, and then the wires in my chest pulled one by one until they finally located a separate infection closer to the surface, resulting in the standard one month hospitalisation extended to close on six months for final clearance. (With all gratitude to those who worked to save me, I do still find watching any scenes of open-heart surgery extremely distressing, invariably finding myself turning my eyes away from the screen.) However, kept under heavy sedation during the first week after the operation, I had one recurring dream that remained scored into my brain: Centred within a tangled cluster of medical tubes and wires, first a rotation of two or three different faces, and then one emerged.

And some four months later, on my first official foray out of the hospital – a walk that, rejoicing in my freedom, took me a good three hours as against (as I was informed when I returned) the customarily authorised ten-minute stroll – I met the man in person, or rather he found me. And here I do find myself admitting to perhaps one serious regret in my life, or at least an 'it would've been something beyond nice' moment.

Nearing the end of the day, finding myself in an open space beside one of the main rivers and pausing to settle on which might be the most suitable route back to the hospital building, he came out from behind me, walking on a full eight to ten yards before abruptly turning and, clearly recognising me but unsure as to quite how he should act in response to the realisation, stood staring at me in what I could only interpret as some form of intent wonder. And I, too, was held. Not Japanese, but again then not from any country I could place, he was for me, in that moment and at that time, 'perfection' – everything I had ever wanted in a man, both physically and in his quiet demeanour. And I, likewise, was left at a loss. More than anything, I was drawn to go with him, which is clearly what was also in his mind, but much as I could so easily imagine holding him, I still had bandages strapped to my chest, the wound not as yet fully healed. And we stood and stared at each other; that gap (which in other circumstances – those few days later, on a separate walk – would not for one moment have held) remaining frozen in time until, acknowledging my pragmatic side, I indicated that whatever dream it was we might have conceived together could not be. And understanding, or perhaps not, he turned away across the bridge to follow his own road home, and I followed the river back up to my reality.

[8.8] Dreams and creativity:

Dreams are extremely convenient vehicles for the imagination, in that shapes and colours can be changed, and images magnified or shrunk to create to form a pastiche of images, and some the most dramatic scenes that I included in the novel that I attempted prior to this book came directly from my dreams. These included a run through a series of caves (this coming from a real daytime experience when Koji and I were in Kyushu), the collapsing of a huge ravine and a full modern-ballet scene – all seen and recorded in my brain in the fullest detail. And then, as I imagined the book sold and successful and perfect for adaptation, the music appeared – small phrases which, upon wakening, I extended first into a soliloquy for the disheartened hero and then a finale for the full cast.

And then there were scenes (huge water-buffalo dragging a laden cart through the raging waters of a flood) that truly made me wish I had had the artistic training to reproduce them as paintings in their own right, and others perfect for the camera (which I invariably had forgotten); and modern sumi-e, one of which I still have listed in my brain as 'to be worked on'. And time passes.

[8.9] Apparitions:

All you need is a screen:

The first 'ghost' I saw (in my mid-thirties) was that of a large and extremely beautiful plate, deep within the rather shabby washroom mirror in the small corner bar run by Isamu, who had started the place after Carl's death [4.11]. Naturally, seeing it in that position momentarily shocked, but then recognising it for what it was, I let it go and went back to the counter to continue my drink.

And the plate itself? A deep wine-red in colour and with the raised design of a chrysanthemum flower half-hidden beneath the full glaze, it had been purchased very shortly after my arrival here on a trip to Kyoto with Mrs Kawano [7.22], with me paying what for me was a considerable amount for it. (Mrs Kawano, being my student at that time, had a habit of buying everything for me, but here, deep down wanting it to be truly mine, I had insisted the purchase would be made with my own money. (However, it coming from the showroom of one of the top potters in Kyoto, I would not be surprised if that much extra had not been handed over behind the scenes.)

And why a 'ghost'? A couple of weeks earlier, in the heat of a very bad argument with Koji, I had picked it up from its display stand and, it being my most valued possession, had smashed it to the ground to express the degree of my anger (/pain), though whether this ever got through to him, I will never know. I destroyed other beautiful (/expensive) things in the course of fights during this period (often under the influence of alcohol), but this was the one that hurt me. It was both exceptionally beautiful and something I truly cared about. And naturally, it had remained with me – or, as they say, "come back to haunt."

And (considerably later, sometime after the exhibition) in ghostly form:

A young man and woman peering into a bush, the man, for whatever reason, holding a camera, looking for an appropriate angle.

Lost at night in Osaka (Osaka being a very large city that is remarkably easy to get lost in), I knew that I was drunk, with all that implied, but this was different. It was as if I had slipped on Gollum's ring; the figures being real enough to touch, but with the full understanding that they weren't. They could almost have been a 3-D imprint on the mist, except that I wasn't truly confident that there was a mist there at all, the evening having been clear up to that point. And they stayed with me, clearly talking quietly between themselves, until, losing interest, I moved to walk away, and they were gone.

[8.10] 'Poltergeists':

I have named them poltergeists understanding that they would not normally be classified as such but not knowing how else to describe them. The first appeared on my home television set: the face of a/the devil (this again being the Japanese version, Enma, commonly seen carved into Noh masks or in the Kabuki theatre). I had been watching my regular television programme when suddenly the screen went blank, and I had the face staring out at me. And nothing happened, except that he stared. And I stared back. And forth... And then he winked at me – a very smart, knowing wink. And then, just as quickly, the frame had changed and I was back to my regular programming, wondering quite what it was that I had seen. (This was quite early on in the learning process.)

The second case occurred a considerable time later when I was setting up a small television set I had in the classroom to watch a video with my students.

Rummaging around in my drawers a few days earlier, I had found a magazine purchased when I was just seventeen in a small backstreet shop in Manchester, containing photographs of nude bodybuilders – naturally, that being the time, no frontal shots, but the nearest thing to pornography available, at least to someone of my age – and taking a final look before it got thrown, I found the one pull-out photograph that I had always liked; that of a rather pleasant man in his thirties, arm muscles flexed and head turned just enough so that you could see that he was smiling, and with a pair of extra-large, well-rounded buttocks – not something you would perhaps normally go for, but in this case I did.

And now, switching on the TV so that I could set the video, I suddenly had three sets of large, well-rounded buttocks, all packed into a tiny screen – the perfect 'mooning' shot. And you could see the faces of the men behind, clearly taking full enjoyment in their presentation. And as they kept wiggling their butts, it became an exceptionally funny scene. But then all I could think of was my students (a group of ladies in their sixties who were due very shortly) walking into the classroom with that on the screen, and I had to cut it. And then, even with the television off, I was half-terrified that they might still be there when I turned it on again or, worse still, suddenly appear in the middle of a scene of "Breakfast at Tiffany's." However, whoever they were, and a joke presumably being a joke, they were kind (/sensible) enough to leave it at that.

[8.11] Placing the inner world on the surface of the eye:

The following, in the end, I would judge as no more than a technique, but even as a technique it does have its relevant insights, and therefore...

Lying on my mattress attempting to get to sleep, which very often took a little time when I was at my most tired, I would find myself examining the small patterns of dust on the surface of my eyes as I blinked (a fast upwards pull followed by a slow settling downwards as they fell), and occasionally (as you see with clouds) I would find patterns of birds or trees or oddly shaped faces, which I could then re-form or destroy with yet another blink. And one step on from this, I would find the greyish mass of dust particles opening up into a screen (I would guess formed by the heavier layer of liquid on the outer surface of the eyeball) and I would suddenly find myself viewing a full-coloured image as you would in the cinema. This could be anything; general scenery, children playing with a ball, a person's face, whatever. (This could also be done lying on the couch in the daytime or, I later found, lying back in a dentist's chair waiting for a filling to harden sufficiently. Yet another version would be to look at an open window or other brighter light source for a certain amount of time, and then closing the eyelids concentrate on the image of light that remained.) And once discovered, this became something of a game which I would play with each night before I went to sleep, or in the morning if I didn't feel I wanted to get up immediately. As to what I was seeing (it varied every time), I came to the conclusion that I was projecting an image formed at some unconscious level in the inner recesses of my brain on to my own personal cinema screen. And it worked. I did it for years, and then after stopping for a long period, tried again, and found that it was still there. (Explaining this to one or two of my students in their mid-thirties, all I got from them was a rather bland, 'Oh, I see! And…?' reaction, which did make me wonder whether it was at all special. However…)

And as examples of what I saw:

At the conclusion of one series, I very clearly remember the face of a man wearing a knitted balaclava helmet – I could only see his eyes staring out at me and thinking (for whatever reason and reality apart) that I was staring at the face of 'my enemy'. (Think, "Lord of the Rings" – Pippin viewing the eye in the crystal ball.) My mind at that time had been occupied with the north-south problem in Ireland, which I assume is where I got the connection from.

And shortly after I had visited a what would have to be described as 'specialist' gay bar in Nagoya, where there was set of prison bars placed between the customers and the bartenders, I got a view from the back of the bar with what was clearly a silhouette of the back of my moving head, that is the bar as it would be seen by someone standing directly behind me. (As to how I received, or possibly composed, this image in my brain, I can only leave open. However, it is very much what I saw. The scene was held for a number of seconds.)

And then there was the spider that I nearly let escape. By this time, I had learned to project the scene on my eye that much further onto the white of my pillowcase, and relaxing my attention for a moment, I watched as it climbed up the side of the pillow and tentatively put one leg and then a second over the top fold, wondering whether it should make a run into the darkness behind. And at this point, unsure myself as to what was happening, I quickly retrieved it into my brain.

(Hiroshi's take on not letting the spider go to was that "I had done the right thing." And he was completely serious.)

[8.12] Practicalities: Using the mind to fill in the gaps:

I have a small ink-painting of a boy riding a bull (a standard subject in Asian art), painted (presuming it is genuine) by one of the top twentieth century sumi-e artists in Japan and purchased in a flea market in Tokyo for essentially nothing. At first glance, which was all I needed to make the purchase, I immediately took in what I recognised as the strength and sturdiness of the animal, its overall presence, and the underlying strength in its gait. And then later, extracted from its cracked frame and examining the stroke-work in detail (it was in part purchased for my own studies), for the first time I saw that its foremost front leg, the one that gives it its sense of purpose (/its forward movement), was in fact represented by nothing other than open space – the upper section of the leg together with the hoof and heel are clearly apparent, but there is no effort (or, in fact, necessity) for the artist to actually depict the positioning of the central section. And then, even after fully registering this fact, and viewing the whole again, you find the overall effect in no sense diminished. I understand that, for any reader not accustomed to this style of art, my above descriptions may not be immediately apparent. However, quite irrespective of any attractiveness of the painting itself, the point I would like to make here is the degree to which our brain can compensate for what actually isn't there – a point which is fully relevant to the following explanations.

[8.13] Projection mapping (faces on faces):

"If you have the ability to project an image that you have in your mind (onto and then) beyond the surface of one's eye (the above spider and pillow), where exactly do the boundaries between one's perceived vision and 'reality' lie?"

I recognised the face, but I couldn't quite make the association – exactly who he was or when I might have met him – but then he had passed me and was lost in the crowds. Another second or so of wondering, but then there had been no apparent sign of recognition on his side and I let it be. And now out in the Motomachi shopping arcade, he was there again, turning into a side street. (He had cut back up from Chinatown?) But again, the connection would not come up, and I kept on walking. And then a full kilometre along the arcade, and there was a man walking with his wife or girlfriend (or someone) – and again the same face. Somewhat frustrated now, but with very little I could do about it, I turned into the side street where I knew the gallery to be, and entering, he (the real person – my artist friend, Mr Kuromaru, who I hadn't seen for at least two or three years, but who I did now recognise) was there to greet me.

As I came to interpret this: Very simply, I had had him 'on my mind' and I had projected that face onto the passing faces in the crowd. Presumably, this had required certain similarities in the basic features of the persons selected (facial shape, eyebrows, distinctive hairstyle, etc. – height and overall build could also be considered here) as a point from which to extend the fuller portrait. (There was also the possibility that we might have been in some state of telepathic (or other) communication, but this was secondary to the matter at hand.)

[8.14] Seeing 'yourself' in the moment:

In the same sense that a spare depiction of facial expression on an illustration or cartoon character (Think, the original sketches of Winnie the Pooh) will allow the viewer (particularly if it is a child) to better project their own feelings onto (/into) that character, there is a certain type of face, commonly found in Buddhist statues, that, depending on the sensitivity of the person involved, will reflect that viewer's prevailing mood. And if this is so, provided that you are viewing a suitably 'neutral' face, there would be no reason not to have a similar experience with a living person.

As a proposition:

If you have something (/someone? / some part of you?) that is visually expressing (self-sourced or some other person's) anger inside your brain – some image picked up from memories or whatever – and you find yourself casting that image onto another person's face, they will (for those moments) appear angry.

This actually occurred to me in class with one of my older, long-term students, who at one point suddenly and for no reason appeared excessively irritated, so much so that I had to ask how I might have offended her, to which (perfectly in character – she was an extremely calm person) she replied, "Nothing. Why?" And presumably this may also be applicable to any other feelings or reactions that you sense you are observing in others.

[8.15] Growing up:

A man of Korean origin who I had taught privately for six months asked me to teach his junior high school daughter [10.2], and later, when he found that she had settled in well, told me that he would "put her in my care until the time she left Kobe."

And a few nights later, I had a dream, which again in its way was an echo, during which an African man put his children in my charge "until the time they were fully grown." The whole family, including his wife, were present in the room. And waking up, I accepted it for whatever it might or might not be, and as always let it pass.

Fast forward some twenty-odd years to a small gathering with Makiko and her husband, where the main guests were three ladies from Tanzania – a social event that had been arranged for them as part of a six-month JICA (Japan International Cooperation Agency) training course. None of them knew each other well and all three were of different ranks in their own country's bureaucratic system, and the lady concerned here happened to be lowest in rank and, more importantly, this was the first time she had ever been outside her country (both of the others had been to Japan previously), making her very much out of the loop in terms of conversational topics and general amiability. However, in the afternoon, and after I had given each of them a small painting I had done for them, she warmed to me somewhat, telling me that I should most definitely come to Africa and paint lions. (It being a little too late on in my life, I demurred.)

And the time went on and, as we were leaving, I turned to make some comment to her. (The others were already outside the apartment.) And there was a man's face, almost certainly someone of her tribe, floating slightly in front of hers. Allowing myself a certain flight of fancy as to who it might be, my first guess took me to some future reincarnation of myself getting ready to paint lions. Or, assuming that the image had come from her, it could have been her husband, that or a future husband or son. And then (me, as always, being very slow on the uptake), as a thought that came to me as I was in the course of writing this particular section, perhaps it was her father, who could have been the man who had introduced his children to me in that dream? Whatever, she was very happy when I told her what I had seen, and particularly the fact that, to my mind, he was an exceptionally handsome man.

[8.16] Filling a frame:

Very early on with my computer, before videos became the norm, if I found a photograph of someone I liked, on the understanding that physically, all the models were extremely similar, I would invariably bring it in, so I had a full view of the face, and this is where I let my imagination work. And then on the train one day, I found myself in a carriage with a whole series of advertisement flyers hanging from the ceiling, each one with a full-length photograph of a rather attractive body builder. Approaching my station, I looked down for a moment, and then up again to take a last look – to find the one flyer immediately above me (the only one in the whole carriage) now had a close up of the same man's smiling face.

Japanese handmade paper as it ages can, in the wrong conditions, attract mould, leading to surface damage (darkened patches), and two or three years after the exhibition, this happened to a woodblock print that we had purchased years previously when Koji and I had first met. The transformation had been quite sudden, making me wonder why it might have happened, but otherwise, there being nothing we could do about the matter, it was left hanging in its position in the 'tokonoma' alcove in my work room. And then a number of months later (quite some time), looking across at it – something I did regularly as it is very attractive print – I noticed that the overall tones (the print itself is in large part done in creams) appeared much lighter. And viewed up close, I found it returned to its original pristine condition – not a single spot of damage – which is how it has remained since.

- (Travelling into the centre of Kobe.) When I have nothing to occupy my mind on the train, I tend to alternate between people-watching and viewing the passing scenery, and this day, there being very few passengers standing, from my position up against the door, I could take in the full carriage as freely as I wished. Everything was perfectly normal: The train was accelerating as we left the station and, across the aisle, two women were conversing animatedly – until there was a moment (briefly registered) when they no longer were, and the world was still. And, without warning, I was standing inside what amounted to a three-dimensional print. That, except for the fact that outside the windows, the world was as it had always been – houses that I recognised (it was a trip that I had taken thousands of times) rushing past at full speed. Personally, I was fully free to move I could turn my head and swing my body from left to right (I looked up and down the carriage more than once. I could feel my hand holding onto the rail at the side the door, and I also lifted my foot), but otherwise the whole interior – everyone and everything in there – was frozen into place.

And then as we reached the next station, the world returned to normal: People stood and exited the doors, and others entered to take their place. And I continued into town.

(Fortunately, not having any means within my reach to even begin explaining quite how this might have happened, this latter example remained a one-time experience.)

[8.17] Dreams as a 24-hour phenomenon:
The following may be considered a proposition.

Whatever is on your mind:
During the lead-up to the exhibition and under severe pressure to produce that 'one painting' [6.5], I began to see Chinese peonies everywhere; on the cream wallpaper in the living room, in the concrete on the station platform waiting for a train to go into town – anywhere that presented enough open space for my mind to expand: full flowers, leaves and buds, in just about every combination you could imagine. I also had a very similar experience when I was doing a whole series of sketches of clusters of cherry blossoms, in which case the outlines of the flowers were appearing among the cracks and smudges in the still rather thick pile of our living room carpet. Both cases here could easily be described as "the mind working overtime." However, in terms of what actually was happening, it would seem to make more sense to simply say that the inner processes of my mind were at some level being allowed to take priority over my daytime vision.

Scientists in the West apparently approach dreams and apparitions as quite separate entities. However, as illustrated above:

(1) I know that during my REM periods of sleep, my mind is capable of consciously observing and remembering the dreams that are passing through my mind. And equally:

(2) I know that my brain is capable of consciously (and very likely unconsciously) projecting both still and moving, black and white and full colour images taken from my subconscious onto my surroundings – what we would normally refer to as apparitions or hallucinations.

Which, taken together, would indicate that, if a dream may be described as "a succession of images, ideas, emotions, and sensations that occur involuntarily in the mind," apparitions become nothing more than dreams intruding into one's daytime experiences. At least, I would submit a possible relationship.

As to why we do not normally hallucinate: In the same sense that in the daytime, a time when your mind is fully occupied in thought and when the full attention of your sensory system (eyes, ears, etc.) is concentrating on the present reality of daily activities, it will not register (/turns off/ rejects) any pain in your limbs, those fleeting images that we tend to observe in our semi-conscious or subconscious during the dream process would not in normal circumstances be noted.

And as aiding the process: Certain drugs will by their nature (/are designed to) take our attention away from our daytime environment, and presumably thus free the mind up to observe (for better or worse) what we otherwise might not. Excessive tiredness would naturally work in the same way. And equally, it would seem quite reasonable to assume that repeated serious meditation [13.13] might also be working towards that necessary 'removed state', and that in the end it would not be unusual if it produced a similar effect.

[8.18] And in areas other than the visual:

Working on my painting at home, I found myself suddenly subject to a clinging (/cloying) sensation in the inner nostrils and throat that I also immediately recognised as the smell of narcissus blossoms, and using the moment, I allowed my brush to work on a somewhat abstract presentation of the flowers. Only a small painting, unfortunately it did not survive the backing process and now no longer exists, but the experience itself (the only one that I have had in this area, at least that I can be fully confident about) was illuminating. As to the mechanics, I would have no idea how this operates, but it does indicate that our brains can be equally effective in this area, also.

Group phenomena:

With five or six students some five years after the exhibition, the tables and blackboard placed in the centre of a large, open office-cum-storage space (they all worked for the same company), and suddenly we could all hear the very loud ticking of a clock. We all had watches, but they clearly were not the source, and as far as we could see there was no clock on any of the walls. The sound continued for what must've been anything from up to ten minutes, whereupon it suddenly stopped, and we were free to continue the lesson. I can understand that to label this as a group hallucination may have some value, but beyond the mere definition, the words themselves do not seem to make any sense. None of us, as far as I could judge, were under the influence of any drugs and what was happening clearly had no religious association. Tiredness may be considered (everyone in Japan always is) but all my students were in their early twenties, and I was well out of my own personal stage of exhaustion by this time.

I will say that, after the lesson finished, we carefully searched the room and did find a small bedside clock (one that you would set at home with a morning alarm), which I assume must have been the source (it did tick), but how that sound was magnified and carried to the centre of the room where we were gathered, is not an area I would care to tackle. (The immediate term that comes to mind is 'atmospheric conditions'. Otherwise, if pushed, I could only perhaps group this with the enhanced vision I experienced with the metal box in the aftermath of the exhibition [6.20], but this was myself only and I do recognise myself as very tired at the time.)

And related to the matter of how I knew I had seen a guardian lion in my dream before the exhibition, I would note that while Christians will invariably have dreams or (group) visions related to Christ or Mary, those whose minds find associations with Buddhism will inevitably relate tales of seeing a Kannon or dragons. And if that doesn't seem somehow odd, or at least something that might be questioned, perhaps someone else might care to explain why?

***

[8.19] And then finally, as you do with everything in life (and not really being in any position to do otherwise), you learn to accept:

I was singing, but not in any kind of voice that I had ever heard before – certainly not from any human being, so much so that I almost stopped in mid-phrase. My brain was following the lyrics as they appeared on the screen but otherwise, I was not in control. The voice itself was disconnected, disassociated; a formulated dissonance, a strain of verbal percussion gone wild – as if someone was trying to tune a guitar with unaligned strings; atonal; releasing what could have been six notes in the same breath. And there was equally nothing that could be recognised in any sense or form as 'melody'. But even as it was completely wrong, it totally matched the karaoke background coming from the speakers (it was a Japanese song that I had sung many times previously). And giving it a moment, I relaxed, and just let it go on through to the end – the oddest of choral fantasies – exactly as whoever or whatever had released it into my mind intended it to be. And everyone smiled and applauded. And no one commented as to the irregularity of the event, as you would think someone might have. And the evening went on.

The whole of the above was a highly creative exercise, with the only point in question being exactly who was doing the creating. Even now, I could only describe it as 'something working through me', but it was an experience that, in the final analysis, I actually very much enjoyed.

Chapter 9
Tales from the Mountains (Japan)

(Details of the more famous places mentioned can easily be obtained on the Internet.)

[9.1] Mt Rokko and the Rokko mountain range:

The Rokko mountain range, with Mt Rokko as its highest point (931 m.) runs behind the city here and is accessible from a number of points, making it the perfect place to get away, particularly during the week when fewer people are out and about. Starting to walk regularly in my mid-thirties, by the time of the exhibition, I had familiarised myself with so many of its interwoven trails that in my mind I had come to adopt it as my 'back garden'. Walking through the seasons, at least once a week, each day would bring some new aspect or sense of discovery. Also, as I was practicing yoga during this same period, I quickly learned how to pace myself – a wider stride on the flat stretches and slower, shorter steps as the path rose – so that, in the main, I had no need to pause due to loss of breath. And after the exhibition, it provided me with a place where I could free up my mind and work to accommodate the disorders in my life.

[9.2] Mrs Osaka from Osaka:

Mrs Osaka had come in late at the exhibition and purchased the one painting that I would perhaps have preferred not to sell. This was not because it was a particularly bad painting, but rather that its attraction was in its colouring, and although I was using colours at this time, as a personal challenge I had already set my mind on producing paintings that were done only in ink. However, she clearly did like it, and was very happy to take it home. There was also the fact that her surname and the name of the city she lived in happened to be the same, making it easy to commit to memory.

And two or three years on, walking along my usual trails, for some reason her name kept coming up in my mind. (On one side or the other, or possibly both of us were trying to communicate?) However, as I walked, my brain repeatedly came out with, "No," "No," and then again, "No," (this for well over 30 minutes) until at one spot, it suddenly came out with, "*That* is Mrs Osaka from Osaka!" And at that moment, my whole body was flooded with pain.

[9.3] On pain:

Pain is extremely difficult to describe: the type and particularly the degree to which it is felt.

Early on after the exhibition, I was asked by my 'inner voice' whether I wanted to "feel the (associated) pain," and I answered "Yes." This was not intended as any form of masochism. Essentially, entering what was for me a completely new world, I wanted to have a full understanding of what was happening to my body, and if pain was to be a part and parcel of the whole experience, I wanted to know.

I find no difficulty, as per Western medical theory, relating a wide range of pains that I have felt during my life to straightforward physical or mental (/stress related) problems. As a high school student, I do know that, playing around on the trampoline, I very likely damaged my spine enough to require a slipped-disc operation in my early thirties (this leading to my taking up of Hatha yoga, which at the time cleared all the pain), and I can easily understand how this might have continued to affect my overall nervous system, particularly in terms of pain in the lower half of the body (the most extreme case of which was described in [7.34] in the car with Koji in Kyushu). This particular incident was introduced because of the timing (previously, in our whole trip of three months, I had experienced no sign of any pain at all) and the very long period it continued before quite suddenly vanishing completely. Also, from my forties, I have had a problem with diabetes and my related heart problem, which I can also easily understand as being a connected to a variety of physical pains.

However, by far the most common type of pain I have experienced, and at the same time the least easy for me to try to explain away, has been the 'cloud effect', where my whole body is enveloped – I have commonly used the word 'flooded' – in a thick, uniform cloud of pain moving from the air above me down through the whole system, which can continue for anything from a few seconds (as described in the above Mrs Osaka example) up to a number of (7–8?) minutes (see the next chapter on my trip to Korea). The sense is that I an acting as a conduit for some form of electromagnetic cloud or 'thick mist' that exists in the atmosphere above/around me. (This can be compared with the similar, but quite different 'one-off experience' given below.)

Also, noting that I was given the choice not to feel the related pain, taken that the brain in normal circumstances is fully capable of blocking feelings of pain triggered by external sources (e.g. a needle prick[14]), it would seem perfectly reasonable to surmise lower-level flows of electrical or electromagnetic energy passing through my body which my brain elects not to register. And thus, if I had chosen to be free of pain, a switch of some form could have been applied, presumably that would not have affected any of the other experiences described.

[9.4] What? Why?

As ideas that have passed through my mind (all or none of which may have any relevance to the reality), I am (or presumably we as a group could be) involved in:

- A clearing of the air waves; stray thoughts or misdirected messages, excessive concentrations of manmade (radio, television, computer, satellite) communications – anything that might 'interfere' with our own personal communications?
- Helping others (team members only or on a much wider scale) removing excessive stress (pain/frictions) from their systems (/ 'the larger system')? Helping in some manner to protect others in my team? Taking responsibility as a teacher to clear up students' foul-ups?
- The purging of spiritual existences; the souls of dead or those who have lost their way? (See the next chapter in the Korean mountains.)

---

[14] As a small child, I stepped on a thick darning needle that broke off as it entered my foot just above the large toe (a centimetre off and the toe would have had to be amputated). My mother found the top half on the floor, but then the other half having seemingly disappeared, the matter was forgotten until a number of months later, when I complained about an awkward stiffness in that area, and taken to the hospital, the problem was identified and removed.

- Others are controlling (/attacking) me? I do understand that I can be physically controlled (see Kumanokodo, [9.13] below), which means that others could similarly work to damage me by creating unnecessary stress and/or physically debilitating symptoms.

Related to bad memories and trauma, I can easily follow the (western medical) concept of these repeatedly bringing up associated pains. At the same time, I do know that by far the largest number of associations that I regularly bring up in my brain are of a positive nature – if anything these are related to the healing of other's hurts). And beyond that, in relationship to the games being played, I can only say that I strongly associate the pain with 'winning', and here the question becomes whether we are really working with or against the other groups in the game? (The longer I continue, the more I tend to feel that we are competing to see which team can pick up the largest volume of waste on the beach.)

Also, as a one-off experience:
Out in the countryside, giving a short speech to a group of Japanese, a number of whom I was meeting for the first time, partly as a joke and partly to show off a new phrase that I had just discovered somewhere ('chinamini' – used to introduce 'an aside' – "This is not particularly of any importance, but for the record…"), I concluded by pointing my finger back over my shoulder in a very general direction and came out with a; "Oh, and by the way, that is where I come from." And, for my trouble, and as they say, "to great applause and laughter," I received what felt like a very strong electric shock directed into the tip of my index finger – the closest equivalent I could think of would perhaps be static from a doorknob, except for the fact that I was nowhere near any wall or object in the room, and the pain was far stronger than any static that I have ever experienced. If an air pocket of this type is a scientifically understood process, I fully accept it as such, and I would note that it has only happened to me the one time.

[9.5] Mt Rokko at night:

"When you walk through a storm, hold your head up high, and don't be afraid of the dark./ At the end of the storm, there's a golden sky and the sweet silver sound of a lark./ Walk on through the wind, walk on through the rain, though your dreams be tossed and blown./ Walk on, walk on, with hope in your heart and you'll never walk alone./ You'll never walk alone." From the musical, "Carousel."

Carousel is the story of a young, somewhat rough and ready barker at the fairground, hanged for an accidental killing and then allowed to return to the earth for one day to tell his former girlfriend that he actually loved her, something that he had never been able to do in real life, and "You'll Never Walk Alone" is sung close to the end of the play by the full ensemble as he is being taken away by the police to be sentenced to death. When I first saw it as quite a small child, a large part of it went over my head. The first scene, in particular, which started out with a man – the barker after his death – hanging out large cardboard cut-out stars on a washing line (presumably in punishment for his crime) was completely unfathomable to me at the time. However, much later when I saw the movie, I empathised with the barker's position (the truth being that I fell a little both for the actor and the part). Over time, the song entered my 'repertoire', to be called up as and when needed, and the following is one time (actually, *the* one time) when it fully served its purpose.

***

[9.6]

He had stopped trying to understand why he was doing this; the silliness, the senselessness of the whole thing was beginning to wear – the necessity for the fight; the banging, throwing, breaking and screaming that was required each time (and this must have been the third or fourth time that it had happened) just to get him out of the apartment, and then the trudge up the mountain in the dark (it was always late at night), and always ending up nowhere.

Tonight, as usual, he had crossed over from the city side with the intent of walking; just to keep walking, the urge to return to that moment as it had been, even now redolent in his brain. But he was worn, much more than he would've cared to admit. And this being so, the first few specks of rain as he had walked down the final slopes to the village road had weakened his resolve, leading him to backtrack all the way up to his present spot; where the path narrowed into a thin neck, and where the drag of the mist on his hood had finally brought him to a halt.

The tiredness in his mind did not come from any lack of knowledge of his position: He knew exactly where he was; every corner of the winding path, every mal-placed stone; where to place the sole of his shoe to obtain the strongest (/safest) leverage – right up to the top road and then over and down into his own valley. Rather, it was the inner workings, the endless questioning of his brain that weakened: forever probing, striking out wildly in all directions; not knowing who or what it was up against. The thought of moving off the path for a while passed through his mind. People did get lost up here – so close to the city you wouldn't credit it, but they did – occasionally with only their bodies reclaimed. And to be totally apart might bring him some peace for a while. (Being alone in the mountains always brought him peace of mind.) But then a brief glance at the steep drop into the blackness to his left brought him back to the reality of his position, and he turned his eyes upwards once again and forced the movement; two, three, and then four long-drawn steps up the steep embankment until he was back to where the path widened into its course. And again he stopped.

Here out on the bluff, the drizzle had returned strong, and he was exposed directly to a gathering wind, together with a thickening darkness that threatened, and, for the first time in all his sallies into the mountains, brought fear. Tired as he was, in normal circumstances his eyes would stay low on the ground, but now they were free only to register whatever was intended for them – an orchestrated obfuscation: "Do as the blind chorus dictates!" And with no notice given, the path that he had known so well was no longer his, the surety of his course lost to the stunted trees and bushes that narrowed the trail, gathering it in at the edges – dark entities, black silhouettes that, as they swayed, blocked his way forward. And the sky itself withered away…

And now his brain touched on the murmurings of a melody, long held deep inside for precisely this moment in time, and with no real consideration – it only being the callings of childhood, what one did when one was afraid – he set the melody free, at first no more than a low hum and then a simple formation of lips around lyrics, setting the strength of his voice against the force of the wind. And again with the trust of a child; that there had to be some voices out there somewhere that were with him, he brought his body forward, step by step, as it should; his brain recognising a corner turned and then one more until – just as quickly as it had come upon him – the wind was gone, the rain had softened to a patter and he was free to walk as he would.

There are moments under severe stress when the brain can be thrown into disarray, and for me this was one of them. At the point described, I was genuinely afraid. Of what, I am not even now truly sure, but having walked that path repeatedly over a large number of years, and knowing it so well, a place where I was by definition 'safe', to suddenly have it ripped away from under me was something more than terrifying.

FF: My final attempt to get myself away came on the last day of the year, and it being the start of the official New Year holiday period with its attendant traditional food and drink and must-watch TV programmes, it took Koji throwing the television set at me to get me out of the house. And by this time, I was truly tired of the whole situation, and even before I got to the top pass, I had decided I had had enough. But then walking back down, I began to encounter small groups of climbers making their way up the valley. This, in my tiredness, I half-registered as somehow irregular, and, in my turn, I was getting one or two odd looks. However, as is done in the mountains, I exchanged greetings and at least two people asked me for (and were duly given) directions. And then a little way further on, it clicked with me that they would be heading to the summit to greet the New Year (we were still on the Eve side of midnight). And it must've occurred to them to wonder why some crazy foreigner was coming down the mountain just at the time he clearly should have been going up.

[9.7] And as to quite what demon had driven me repeatedly back onto that course:

Earlier in the year, we had visited Shimane prefecture, considerably west of Kansai and on the Japan Sea coast, most famously known for being the least-populated prefecture in Japan (this, with my dislike of crowds, making it – along with Ehime prefecture in Shikoku – a must-go destination).

Making our way through a temple complex, Koji had wandered ahead slightly, and in his absence, I was drawn to a crowd clustering around the gate of one of the smaller temples. The main gate had been left open to allow a view of the interior, but then a metal gate had been lowered across the opening to disallow any entrance by the general public. Inside, a group of worshipers were seated on low stools facing the main altar in front of which the priest was reciting a sutra reading from the Buddhist scriptures. And there was a power (/allurement) in that voice; some combination of depth, strength, timbre, resonance that both drew and mesmerised; a demanding quality that required that I approach and 'be close'. And working my way through the crowd until my full body was pressed against the mesh, if I could have passed through its horizontal struts, at that moment, without any hesitation, I would.

And then there was Koji's arm pulling me away.

(In total I tried four or possibly five times, the first two or three in all seriousness. I was intent on walking the 250+ kilometres back to that temple to find that voice, the first time falling into a roadside ditch in the dark and injuring my ankle enough to know not to continue, at least at that moment. And in the end, presumably the voice lost its hold.)

[9.8] And some who stay:

Shortly before the exhibition, walking up my regular paths, I fell in step with a Japanese man, Mr Morino, who happened to be walking in the same direction and roughly at the same speed, and over the years, although we met only infrequently, we became very good friends. Certain people quite naturally demonstrate a particular disposition that allows them to operate within contrasting frames of reference, and Mr Morino was one of these. Both well versed in all the key Western philosophies, which he would discuss quite energetically as we drove along in his car, he would then slip in (and devote the same amount of attention to) his cassette tape of traditional Japanese children's songs. Born the eldest son in a very influential family in a neighbouring prefecture, he chose to give up his rightful inheritance (apparently including a large factory) to his younger brother, and then compounded the crime in his wife's eyes by refusing other than the most basic of promotions in a local bank, leading to a rather messy divorce in which he lost both his house and his sons, who (in all senses, fairly) took up their mother's side of the argument. He then married a lady who shared his love of the mountains with him (she belonged to a large group of keen hikers of which he was one of the leaders), only to die shortly afterwards from cancer. However, on a visit to his hometown, he told me how as a young man of seventeen or so brought up in the Buddhist tradition, he had been passing by a church in his city (he showed me the building) when he was 'summoned'. And without any particular thought to the contrary, he simply got off his bicycle and walked in. And he remained with the same church right through to the time he died.

Apparently, he had planned his own funeral down to the last detail. However, with close to 500 attendees, the minister offering the eulogy was in the unfortunate position of having to address a group of attendants who were not only not Christian but also were fully conversant with and shared a love of the one area that was key to his life – the mountains – a place the minister himself admitted he had never stepped ("Apparently, it is very beautiful up there" – this repeated two or three times), and in offering a summary of his life, he was reduced to reciting a list of the branch offices Mr M had been rotated through each time his immediate superiors had not known what to do with him. And it was only when the representative of his mountaineering group spoke (and then sang) that the service came alive, the congregation united in their celebration of their common cause and attesting to the true meaning of his life – everything that had created his power and appeal as a human being. In the end, I sense that the mountains are where he worshipped. At least, that was where his heart was, together with those close to 500 people gathered in that church.

And in the sense that I also am happiest in nature or anywhere natural beauty can be found, Koji had to be right in pulling me away.

[9.9] And as a final note on "Carousel":

With every man with whom I have slept over a very long period, all those who I have cared for even a little, I have told them (not untruthfully) that I love them. This has probably caused me more trouble than it was worth in that a lot of them believed me, though I would also note that in Japan, also as a truth but more as a practicality, each one of them was also told that I had a partner to go back to. And, noting that I was commonly drunk in these cases; even if it wasn't the full truth, the worst it could do is leave them with something to forget.

Children believe. Give them a Santa Claus and they will vehemently defend his existence right up to the point where some adult unthinkingly cuts him away from them. And here, right from a very young age and unknown to anyone except myself (so he could never be taken away from me), I had the story of a man who was given a day to return to earth and tell the person he had hurt that he truly loved her – romanticism at its finest – and at one level, I do admit to being a romanticist. (My excuse for the numbers involved here would be that, not knowing who to tell, I told everyone.)

And then you get to a certain age and ask yourself what (beyond the romantic) I was trying to communicate with all those declarations – what, if anything, I might actually have meant. And the best answer on a personal level that I could come up would be: "I care. I am there for you – in some manner, even if only for the moment or (if you choose) as a memory."

And now that I am with Kensuke, knowing that we do not have a lifetime (at least, in any normal interpretation of the phrase) to feel free to do so, this has become a way of life – both of us letting the thought out as it comes to us – either verbalised or through a carefully placed touch. (This was one promise that was made at the time we started out that has worked very well for the both of us.) And again, that much older, sometimes when he isn't physically close – in the hope (/belief?) that I am making some connection somewhere – I find myself repeating the phrase in my brain, almost like a mantra.

[9.10]

And perhaps as a not unrelated comment – that it is not a bad habit to keep a phrase or memory from which you can take strength in times of need – there were two black Americans:

One was a young woman in New York (I would guess in her mid-thirties) who I worked under for one day at a rather large restaurant to which I had been sent after arriving for work at my regular pancake house in the morning two minutes late. (If you were one minute late, a replacement was called in and you were reassigned.) It was only one day, and we had very little chance to speak other than for her to instruct me about my work. However, two or three days later, when I was back at my regular workplace, she walked in and ordered a coffee at the counter, and in the five or so minutes she took to drink it, we talked about where I was from and odd bits of nothing. And then she noted how impressed she had been by the way I had handled the aftermath of a full plate of food that I had managed to throw (/smash) all over the floor during the busiest lunchtime period. (At the time, I had simply cleaned it up and re-ordered, and nothing else was said about it. As an admission, I had to struggle through a few seconds of panic before I managed this as it was a rather high-class restaurant.) However, she then stood up, thanked me for the coffee, placed a 50-cent tip on the counter and left. The whole thing was done in a very business-like and efficient manner (she was a very attractive woman, but she didn't really smile, at least not to be noticed, right the way through), so much so that it made me wonder. And then thinking afterwards; that she had presumably taken part of her day off to come and find me out simply to compliment me seemed something special. I was twenty at the time, and to her, a nobody. And a 50-cent tip was what you might get, if you were lucky, for serving a full meal to a family at a table (with lots of polite chatting-up) – certainly not for a coffee at the counter. And in the end, I chose to read it as an indication of (a mutual) respect, and it stayed with me.

And some fifteen years later, at a gay nightclub in San Francisco (I was there with Koji), there was a tall, very handsome black man who called me out onto the floor, and for one dance we lost ourselves to ourselves – somewhere deep within, circling in our own world. And as the music stopped, I looked across at Koji, somewhere far away in the distance, leaning against a long empty wall and seemingly totally unaware of where he might be, and utterly forlorn (/rejected). And the man, noticing my glance, fully understood. And as the music started again, we danced, but this time with a certain care; step by step pulling away from what we had created between us. And when the music stopped again, he was a very handsome black man in a gay nightclub in San Francisco, and I was someone from somewhere going back to his partner. And then as we separated, he spoke to me: quite seriously, with just three words; "You are good." (And he was not referring to my dancing.)

Both of these encounters were intensely brief, but right through my life I have held the pride (and resultant courage) that I gained from them in my heart, and every time I have been tired and close to losing trust in myself or whatever it is that I am in this strange life that I am living, I have held the gift they gave to me close in my mind, and they have, in their own way, protected me.

[9.11] The Kumanokodo. The power of other minds:

The Nakahechi section of the Kumanokodo pilgrimage route runs from Tanabe (Wakayama prefecture) on the western coast of the Kii Peninsula and moves eastward into the mountains towards the Kumano grand shrines. There are a variety of paths available, but my objective being the Kumano Nachi Taisha Shrine and its famous waterfall, I chose to take two days, spending one night at a small but very friendly hot spring inn at the halfway point.

A brief rest along the way:

Finding the entrance, I purchased a map and also a staff – de rigueur, but equally extremely sturdy and subsequently used for many years of hiking. The walk itself alternates between stretches of mountainside and paths through small villages and hamlets, and passing through one of these, an older lady and gentleman who were sitting out in their garden invited me to join them for a cup of Japanese tea, which I was very pleased to accept. After the exhibition, when traveling, I had started to take with me a small pack of photographs of my paintings and flower arrangements, which I used as a self-introduction, and here I brought them out as a means to pass the time, this leading to the wife bringing out photographs they had taken of the area, which in the late autumn, when the early morning mists lay over the valleys, can be very beautiful, and she gave me a set of three, which I felt (aligned) might make the background for a nice painting. And with thanks all round, we said goodbye.

[9.12] "Bugger the temples." (I will take the fall.)

The approach to the waterfall at the Nachi Taisha Shrine is down a very steep flight of steps, and the waterfall itself can be seen from the top of the steps bordered on either side by rows of thick cedars, making for an extremely unexpectedly beautiful first viewing and resulting in the above quite unplanned reaction in my mind. At the same time, the moment the words came into my head, although 'bugger' would hardly rate as more than the softest of expletives in England, and I had in fact been referring to the beauty of the waterfall (the reason why the shrine had been built in the first place), I did (as a gay person) realise the potential for mistranslation. However, that which had been said having been said, I was not in any mood to send my brain silly with explanations, and the shrine complex being set at a much higher level behind me, I decided that I would first go down to the base of the fall to take photographs, which I did. And now returning to the same spot, I could see a flight of steps zigzagging up the mountainside towards the shine, and although there was a bus available, I decided that having come that far (I had walked two days to get there), I could walk the rest. And then as I crossed the road, my initial overly casual reaction to the fall came back into my mind, and I took to wondering.

At my first attempt, I must have managed six or seven steps before I felt the resistance. Retreating slightly, I tried again with exactly the same results. There was a heaviness in the air laid across my path which I could do nothing to remove. I was not in any sense tired, and my legs were in perfect condition, but I was facing an invisible barrier and, regardless of how I made my approach, there was no way in which I could move forward beyond that point. Apparently, I was not going to be allowed to see the temples. And having made three or four efforts, each time rebuffed, my mind finally came out with; "OK, if you don't want me to come up, I won't." Temples and shrines are not in any sense rare in Japan, and I was sufficiently tired not to be prepared to make the effort. I have seen the shrine itself on television many times both before and since, and it is beautiful and very much recommended for a visit, but that said, the truth being that I had come to see the waterfall, the walk down the steps proved perfectly sufficient.

[9.13] "You could have asked."

Initially, my taking of photographs was intended as a means to supplement my sketching. However, the first photograph that I recognised as good enough to be framed as a picture was taken walking along the Kumanokodo trail. At the time I took it, I had had no particular expectations – it had started raining and there was a light mist clinging against the hills across the valley – but, taken through row of stunted pine trees, the result was actually very calming, and enlarged, framed, and hung on my classroom wall at home, I found it perfect as a place to retreat into when I was at all pressured by my younger or more energetic students.

And with the one having come out so well, I had had two more from the same series enlarged. And back home, finding both to be borderline, I was arguing with myself as to which one might be worth framing when I was suddenly interrupted by a voice in my head (immediately recognised as the lady who had offered me tea on my walk) coming out with a highly overbearing, "We wanted a painting!" (Returning to Kobe, I had sent them a thank-you letter together with two or three of the photographs I had taken on my walk, but apparently that had not been sufficient.) And then before I could get over the rather rough (almost aggressive) tone in her voice, I found that I had lost control of my arm movements and, quite against my will, I was pulling at the edges of the photograph that I had in my hands until it was completely torn in half. Momentarily stunned, and a little unsure as to how I should proceed but not wishing to be outdone (at this point, I could sense the strength in my arms returning to me), I decided that the easiest thing to do would be to pick up the second picture and treat it in the same manner. It wasn't anything special and it would save me the cost of having it framed. (And it was my choice.)

[9.14] Ohsugidani. The Valley of the Giant Cedars. (Prescience.)

It was an elegant fall – a simple, straight drop; perfected understatement – and enclosed within the surrounding arc of trees and the shallow spread of water at its foot, with the addition of a slight mist lifting from the lake to carry the eye away from the not particularly attractive clusters of rocks at its foot, he could imagine himself attempting a picture of it without too much of an effort when he got home. Certainly, it would make for an easier subject than one or two of the other, far more dramatic waterfalls he had viewed coming up the valley.

A glance at his watch indicated that he would have to limit his stay here to one or two quick photographs of the place: He had spent rather more time than he intended on sketching the last (far grander) waterfall, and he was not really sure how long it would take him to get back to the hut in the valley. He had told them he would be staying a second night, but he was unsure of the distance he had come to get to this point, and with the path losing itself along the riverbed in parts, he did not want to be walking in the dark. Leaving his rucksack by the side of the path and slinging his camera around his neck for safety – it would not do to have it damaged at this point – he clambered down the rocky slope to lake level and took the three or four photographs he felt would cover what he needed. And he was done.

It had taken him a full two days to get to this point – an early morning bus and boat trip followed by the long trek up the valley to the hut, and then today – with a total of seven waterfalls photographed and/or sketched. And now he could return. Mission completed! And with that came a brief but overwhelming wave of tiredness, making the slope that he had so casually found his way down now look considerably steeper than it had from the path. He paused for a moment to see whether there might not be an easier way – there was no clear route visible from the spot where he was standing – but it was not more than a thirty-metre stretch at the most, and gripping his camera lens to prevent any swing, he stepped up onto the first ledge. From this angle (the light had changed?), it was apparent that the rock face was damp in sections, and edges were more rounded that he had previously noticed, but as he climbed, it occurred to him that this was a path that he knew, and as with the car in town, he recognised that something was about to happen; in this case not quite what, but 'something'. And with each step he took, the feeling strengthened – until he was there, and now fully aware, he laughed out loud. And thrown backwards, he rolled, twisted and turned, and rolled yet again back down the slope, his body instinctively forming into a curl as it relaxed against the curves of the rock, allowing it to carry it him where it would – exactly as it had been trained to do. And all the while his camera held triumphantly high above him in the sky.

[9.15]

Other than being a little difficult to approach, Ohsugidani is an extremely attractive valley to walk along. It can also be, in parts, extremely dangerous; particularly one very narrow ravine, where hikers are obliged to pass along an uneven ledge that is the only path along the side of the cliff and where apparently a number of hikers have lost their lives. (I was informed that the majority of these were in fact experienced walkers who died as a result of being overconfident in their athletic skills.) I was also warned about not attempting the walk in the rain, which at the time, lacking any real experience in the matter, I took quite lightly. However, some months later, I did see a scene on television taken after heavy rain (close to the hut where I had stayed the night), where the whole valley was totally overrun with raging waters, and I did take the point.

(For those who do enjoy hiking, as a general comment here, when it does rain in Japan, river waters tend to build up <u>very rapidly</u> and in the shortest of times can become deadly, carrying away everything in their path.)

[9.16] **First snowfall on Mt Fuji:**

To appreciate the beauty of Mt Fuji, one has to be at a certain distance from the mountain itself, and the following is a brief record of my walk up to the top of Mt Kobushigatake (2,470 m.), which, being directly north of Mt Fuji, allows (although at some distance) a full view of the mountain from the north side. The walk itself was suggested to me by a student, then in his sixties, who had fond memories as a student of working in the mountain hut at its summit, and more particularly of the (at the time, young, but still slightly older) woman who ran the Japanese inn ('ryokan') at its foot. (And she was indeed lovely, even in her early eighties when I actually met her.)

A book guide to the mountain indicated that there were two routes to the top, and following some last-minute advice, I decided that I would take the easier valley route up (following the Chikuma River up to its source) and the next day come back along the eastern ridge and take the sharp drop back down into the valley at the end. Actually walking, I discovered that the valley route could be done there and back in one day (a small group with light rucksacks passed me twice; once going up, and again when they were coming down), but in terms of the overall experience, having the extra time at the top made it very much worth the stay.

[9.17] Sensing the light:

Very early on when walking Mt Rokko, my mind would deliberately search out subjects that I might possibly use for my paintings. However, as the paths grew more familiar and I was more comfortable turning my attention inwards, I began to find spots where my legs (sometimes in midstride) would of their own accord stop moving, and provided I then took the trouble to look around me, I would have a 'picture' of some form placed before my eyes. This would invariably be only on that day and at that time – the same valley or turn in the path cast in a different light suddenly recognisable as something that would make for a perfectly-composed sketch or quick photo. And as this happened more frequently, I came to take it as my mind primed (without any particularly conscious effort) to recognise certain patterns of light and/or contrasts in the scenery. And now, walking up the valley towards Mt Fuji, I found myself stopping; here for a bamboo grove and there for a view of the stream – and at one point turning three times on the same one spot to get three perfect views. The whole of the lower valley, cross-lit in the sunlight, was filled with silver birch, spruce, and smatterings of the larger palm-sized maple, all in their autumn trappings, and higher up, there were all the signs of the coming winter; patches of snow and even one or two small icicles forming. And then exiting the valley at the top of the path onto the upper ridge, the world opened up and I was rewarded by the most beautiful view of a snow-capped Mt Fuji, with the intervening lower-level ridges cast in a blue haze extending both left and right as far as the eye could see. (Photo 3.) (Picture-wise, Mt Fuji without snow making for a somewhat sad proposition, luckily there had been a first fall the previous night, some of which had clearly caught my mountain also.)

And then as evening approached, gathering with other hikers at the peak, in front of us we had Mt Fuji; to the right (into the sunset), the Southern Alps; and directly behind us, Mt Yarigatake and the valley. And then from the left, a whole sea of clouds moving in. My last two shots as we came down to dinner at the hut were of the clouds being swept over the mountains directly below us, the closest image I could think of being the Niagara Falls – which, on a personal level, completed a quite remarkable day.[15]

---

[15] Note: There are photographers (of fashion, portraiture) who create the moment, and others who search it out, spending hours/days at a particular spot to catch that one moment. Not having that time available, I have had to settle for taking moments as they

Snow on Mt Fuji

[9.18] Day two:

Setting off from the hut in the mist at about 6:30, I had just started climbing the steep incline back up to the peak when it started to snow, and by the time I reached the top, the wind was blowing strongly, and I was very glad to find my return path and cut away down into shelter.

The section of 'genseirin' (primeval forest) just below the peak, with its heavy, rotting trunks and large areas covered in various species of mosses, has a reputation as an area of great beauty. And in the half-light and covered with a light smattering of snow, it was ethereal – a silent cathedral created in its own name.

And then it was gone, and it was raining – gradually getting heavier throughout the day and culminating in a heavy storm with lightening (this fortunately after I had got back to the safety of the inn), and from here, following the ridge above the 2,000-metre line, I was walking again in a different world.

On one of the three peaks along this course, there is a huge smoothly rounded

---

have been given to me, and this day I was particularly lucky.

rock, named in the guidebook for its size, which at the best of times would require careful negotiation. However, now almost across, and on a narrow ledge at its side, directly below me I found the wind had created a deep well in the mist, which as it swelled and receded, allowed me to catch glimpses of the autumnal foliage on the cliff face below. Mist, even without a wind, is an inconstant, making any attempt to capture that particular moment something closer to a happenstance or fortuity than any skill. And here I was dealing with repeated strong down-rushes of air, making any chances of success minimal. However, mist also fascinates, and having seen (at least in my mind's eye) what could be that moment, I was in no way able to resist.

Prior to starting this trip, I had purchased a full-sized rucksack and other equipment for walking in the higher mountains, and this had to be placed somewhere to allow me to take out my camera. There was space enough at my feet, but I sensed – knew – that it should not be put down here. (This was not at all prescience, but rather a matter of common sense. My brain was tired, and I was acting stupidly.) I also knew that if I moved another couple or so of yards further along the track, I would no longer be on the ledge, but then I sensed that if I moved that far, I would not come back. The rock was to a certain degree sheltering me from the rain at this point, and if it had to be anywhere, it had to be here. The decision made, the bag was placed at my feet and the camera extracted and focused, and I waited.

And the wind played me – teasing at the sides of the bowl, but never quite disposed to reach down to that distance required to bring out those colours as I had seen them. And finally, accepting what was not to be, I could do nothing but repack my camera and swing my backpack up and across my shoulders, at which point, the reality of its weight taking hold, the upper half of my body was being dragged outwards over the edge and…this was me blind drunk on my bicycle in Oxford at midnight, swerving to miss a car that had suddenly, inexplicably appeared in my path; that or with Koji in the car on the expressway when, without notice, we found ourselves driving directly into, and totally blinded by, the early morning sun – two other times when I have recognised myself as coming rather too close to that line for comfort…until the muscles in the lower half of my body worked to take on the strain, and I had pulled myself around into safety.

I have been warned on a number of occasions about walking by myself in the mountains, but this was the one time that I really understood that I would have been on my own up there. I did not meet anyone on that walk that day, and presumably, the weather being as it was, anyone with any sense going in that direction would have taken the valley route back down. However, it was one more case where I could be truly thankful for the work I had put in with my yoga training.

And now, finally, I was descending, only managing twice to slip off onto side trails – the first of which led me to a couple of rocky overhangs above the valley and the second to one of those paths that 'are but aren't' – each time returning until I finally hit the sign for the route down, and the rest was a matter of careful plodding down the zigzag course, across the river and down the main valley to the inn, where I arrived thoroughly soaked and quite willing to be welcomed back.

And then when I was leaving the inn on the following morning and the owner came outside, as is traditional, to see me off, as her final comment to me, she suddenly referred to her past ('that which had made her as she was') as being a "mass of tangled cobwebs." Even today, I am unsure as to whether this was intended as a warning or a plea, but I do very much understand how my student had to come to fall quite so deeply under her spell.

[9.19] Mt Rokko:

A leaf on the path:

A tiny maple, uncommon in this section of the mountains, it was the only leaf remaining – the last to retain any of its colouring on the pile (the last to fall?) – all the other leaves now tightly curled into a grey mass as nature had taken its course. But it was the colour that caught his eye, bringing him to a halt. 'Shu' is the Japanese for cinnabar, and by extension for the colour of that material (vermilion), most recognisable as the colour of shrines and their distinctive 'torii' gates. The ink pads that are required when authenticating documents or paintings also use cinnabar ink, and while such pads come in many qualities, the colour of the leaf here was of the finer variety – a slightly darker, more intense version; drawing the eye, but not to the point of being excessive or crude (which can be the case), and if it had been at all possible, he would have taken it home for his own personal use.

And again it struck him that, in all likelihood, only he would ever see this leaf, certainly as it was, others not being attuned to picking out (or much more likely lacking any interest in) any detail of that sort. Either that, or the wind catching at its underside would take it – which as he stood there contemplating its existence, it did, the moment of beauty gone, and the path dead (/uninteresting) as it had been.

A jet-black spider came out from under the leaves carrying a large cream-coloured egg (it had found some urgent need to search for a new home?), and was now crossing the path towards him until, sensing his shadow, it stopped momentarily, before scurrying off into the overhanging grass on the bank.
And before he could move, a solid-looking man passed – with a broad gait and brief nod, but otherwise keeping his own pace, until, having gone so far, he turned and called out to him; startling him somewhat by asking in a fully serious manner – seemingly with the expectation that he should know the answer; "How much longer will I be able to walk up here in the mountains?" And him, not knowing what to come out with otherwise; "I don't think that is something I could tell you." And the man, with no more than a nod, went on ahead and out of sight.

And so many (three, four, five?) years on, on a fine spring day, it was I who no longer could. A walk to the summit and back that in my earlier days would have taken me no more than two hours, for no reason that I could account for, suddenly took me seven. And recognising that I had had my time, other than the one outing when I took Kensuke up to the head of the ropeway and walked down the far side to the hot springs there, simply to introduce him to that which I had had – that part of my life – I have let it be.

Chapter 10
Tales from the Mountains (Korea)

[10.1] Mt Rokko:
He came up from behind me on the trail, which along this section was wide enough for us to walk side by side without any particular effort, and with not more than the standard, brief greeting, started to tell me about his childhood here in the city.[16] His father, like many others at the time, had been brought over from Korea during the war to work in a munitions factory here and stayed on after the war had ended and Korea had become independent. Whether or not his father had taken on a Japanese name or not (some did, some didn't), I don't recall. (A lot of the detail remains vague in my mind here.) However, after he started school, the other children very quickly picked up on his origins, and from that time on, right up to the time he left junior high school, he was both verbally and physically bullied – in some cases, very badly. The whole story was told in a quiet voice and in a very matter-of-fact manner, but at the time he finished speaking, when I looked across at him, his eyes had dampened considerably. And then, as quietly as he had come, he went on ahead of me and over the ridge.

The man described here would be in his late fifties or early sixties, which is around where I also was at the time. He didn't make it clear whether his family was from North or South Korea (we have a lot of both groups in this area), but I doubt that being one or the other would have made much difference at the time. Today, politically, the groups originally from the north get a lot of criticism because of their continuing allegiance to Kim Jong-un, but hate speech, which

---

[16] Why he knew to speak to me, a foreigner out on an afternoon walk (he showed no hesitation in speaking to me in Japanese and he clearly understood where my sympathies lay) I will leave to the reader to deduce. However, the fact is that he did. And on my side, I was sympathetic.

has become resurgent under the present prime minister (Abe), and recently has been getting very nasty, is not reserved particularly for either group.

[10.2] As historical background:

When the Japanese refer to the UK, they use the word 'igirisu', which (before soccer and rugby world cups became popular here) was also commonly translated as 'England', making the relationships between England, Scotland, Ireland, and Wales; together with the present existence of Ireland and Northern Ireland somewhat difficult for them to comprehend. As part of my explanation to anyone who asked, as to the matter of Ireland, I would tell them that perhaps the best comparison is with Japan's relationship with Korea. The British were in Ireland for some 800 years, while, in contrast – although historically the very often mutually antagonistic relationship between the two countries goes back hundreds of years – the Japanese actually only controlled Korea as a colony for a mere 35 years (1910–1945), but essentially the relationship was very similar. During this short period, Koreans were determined to be 'citizens of Japan', the Japanese language was enforced, and during World War II, they were drafted into the Japanese army or taken to Japan to work, commonly (as were a large number of prisoners of war) under extremely difficult conditions. (A number also, as Japanese citizens, did choose to move to Japan of their own choice.) And naturally, after the war, when they were returned to independence, there was a very strong swing back to their own language and culture. In 1965, a post-war compensation framework (including compensation for forced labour and intended to cover all future possible future claims against Japan) was formed under the initiative of a pro-Japan, conservative group of lawmakers in South Korea – they might be best understood as the portions of the French government that sided with the Nazis during WWII – and a large proportion of the Korean population even now cannot accept this or later settlements, particularly related to, as the Japanese government describes them, 'comfort women', or on the Korean side, 'sex slaves', who were recruited to satisfy the Japanese military's needs. (See [15.38]) (No settlement has, even at this time – at least, as far as I understand it – been made with North Korea.)

(August 28, 2018) Giving the above explanation about 'igirisu' to a 50-year-old man in a local bar (presumably educated in a rightist philosophy: "Everything the Koreans say is a lie"/ "We couldn't possibly have killed women and children"), he then went on to question me as to why the IRA might be considered terrorists. He clearly felt a strong attraction to Ireland and the Irish people. However, if this support for the Irish position is also part of the rightest philosophy here, considering my equating the positions of the Irish and Korean peoples – which makes absolutely full sense historically – it would be very natural that his mind was indicating a strong sense of confusion.

And as for the Koreans who remained here in Japan (or those who chose to come here later) – collectively known as 'Zainichi'; now with no status as Japanese, they essentially became second-class citizens, with all that that entails; a loss of health insurance, leaving them with no recourse if they became sick; an absence of willing landlords to provide housing or employers to give them work, which required a movement into slums; enforced fingerprinting (until 1993, they were grouped with other foreign workers like myself), making their origins easily recognisable when they registered in the local Ward Offices, etc., etc., and even today they suffer a lot of discrimination.

At present, roughly 450,000 ethnic Koreans live in Japan. However, it was not until the 1988 Summer Olympics in Seoul that I recall ever seeing or hearing a single comment about (South or North) Korea in the Japanese media. They were completely ignored. And in Korea the situation was apparently exactly the same. No cultural exchanges of any kind were allowed. However, from this time, with really no choice in the matter and the ice broken, there was a considerable period of rapprochement, and with the introduction on television of the first successful Korean drama, "Winter Sonata", in 2004, there was something of a 'Korean craze', with a lot of Japanese visiting Korea for the first time, quite a number actually studying Korean, and at the same time, Koreans beginning to visit Japan. (I also watched "Winter Sonata", and I guess it must be about this time that I found my first Korean bar in the city.)

Many Koreans who had lived in Japan up to this time had adopted Japanese names to allow them a little cover, but during this period, in this area also, things began to change. One of my older students, who was of Korean origin but came to me with a Japanese name, subsequently had his daughter study with me, at which time she registered with me using her original Korean family name, that she herself had chosen to revert to, and she was quite open with this in class, even finding an (older) Japanese student in class to fall for. (And he was very kind with her, insisting on walking her down to the station – using the excuse that the back lanes in our neighbourhood were rather dark. And all was quite sweet until it was decided that that he would be going off to a Canadian university to study after he graduated from high school here, and we had a few tears.)

[10.3] Another friend:

Going way back in time, my first real close relationship with a Korean person in Japan was shortly after Koji and I moved to our first apartment, and we found a small 'yakiniku' (Korean grill) restaurant under the railway line run by a Korean lady who had moved here to be with her partner. (He had left his wife in Korea and, much later, when he went back to her, she also went back to Korea.) The food was very good and served in a Korean manner – completely different from the food you find served in (Japanese) Korean restaurants in town, and also it wasn't expensive, so we very quickly became regulars and also friends, to the point that when I had to go into hospital the first time with my back, she sent up a bowl of 'bibimbap' (a rice bowl with cooked minced meat and vegetables and spices, all of which you mix up together before you dig into it) for me, just to let me know that I hadn't been forgotten. She also taught me to find wild 'ginseng' roots in the mountains, which I used to take to her to prepare and grill with our meat every year when the season came around, and overall it was a very nice relationship.

And then, shortly before the exhibition (Cpt 6), we were sitting at the counter and, pointing to the television, which was on at the time, she suddenly told me that she would "introduce me to her Korean friends," which she then proceeded to do, explaining how she had to come to meet me and adding a few general comments. Koji said nothing, and although not really understanding at the time, enough odd things had happened up to this point for me not to question what she was about, and we all smiled, and I let it go. And it was only much later that I came to assume that it actually had meant something.

[10.4] Korean bars:

Walking along the corridor towards a pick-up bar that I had recently discovered, the door on the opposite side opened and a man of about my age with a rather nice smile indicated I might like to go in. And always weak on a nice smile, I did as requested.

"Oh, you have come for me!"

This was from a pleasant enough, but for me not particularly interesting, young man serving behind the bar, and although the greeting was a little unconventional, I nodded politely, murmured something like "Not really," under my breath, and sat down. And, although personally still to be enlightened on the matter, I had taken my first steps towards Korea.

That night, the bar's clientele was mainly Japanese, but the owner, Mr Lee, who had invited me in and his partner (Mr Kan – who had welcomed me) and the other young man behind the bar (who shortly after opened a separate bar close by and who in the end became a good friend) were all Korean, and later I discovered that quite a number of people of Korean origin or from Korea itself visited. Also, a lot of the Japanese there were studying Korean and/or quite regularly came and went between Seoul, so it was quite hub and, everyone being friendly, I quickly became a regular.

Sleeping with James Bond:
Mr Lee liked to be in charge, and more importantly, he liked other people to recognise that he was in charge, and this actually, until at the end when it got a little too onerous, accounted for a large part of his appeal. (Perhaps put more strongly, he could not bear the idea that he might not be in control, which I personally recognise as a sign of a weakness at some level. However, it did take me quite some time to come to this conclusion.) This latter fact actually first came to the fore quite early on when he introduced me to one of his Japanese customers, whom he was clearly also involved with.

Shinji was in his mid- to late-thirties and physically very attractive, and he was also to a great degree an opportunist, which quickly became apparent when, having stood for a moment, he leaned over Mr Lee's shoulder and slipped his name-card into my pocket. And not having any reason not to do otherwise (I was not involved with Mr Lee at this time), I took up the invitation and slept with him at his apartment (we managed well enough together), but it was after everything was over and he was walking half naked around his apartment, that I recognised a certain animal grace (/sensuality) that I had seen (and fallen for) many, many years earlier watching Sean Connery striding along on the beach in "Dr No", and for that alone I would have been quite happy to continue the relationship. However, this proving not to be, we walked back to the station and said our goodbyes, and that was it.

Shortly after at the bar, I mentioned what had happened to Mr Lee, who was not overly pleased, particularly with the detail of the name-card being slipped to me almost immediately after he had introduced Shinji to me, and walking over to Shinji, who had come in earlier and was sitting up along the bar, he led him outside, and from that time on he was no longer persona grata. Such is authority.

[10.5] Searching for a new partner:

This was the rather odd tale which had been developed in my mind over time, woven very lightly around the Buddhist idea of rebirth [7.20], and at this point, the supposition was that I had said (/was saying) goodbye to my long-time partner and was starting on a search for someone with whom I could spend my next few hundred lives.

A tea bowl and some tea:

Liking and collecting Japanese pottery, I have seen a number of pieces used in the tea ceremony that I have understood as extremely beautiful, but the ceremony itself is not anything I have ever been particularly attracted by. (To my ikebana teacher, tea ceremony enthusiasts were always excessively polite in the ceremony itself, but then the moment they got out, reverted to their everyday, somewhat crass selves. I wouldn't go so far to say that myself, one of my nicest students being a tea ceremony teacher, but I never really got past the basics on the two or three times I was invited.) However, this time was rather special. I was to be introduced to my future partner. Nothing, naturally, had been said out loud, but the man who was seated next to me in the ceremony I knew to be of Korean origin, and the situation being as it was, we were seated in the positions of honour – him to my right and closest to the master of ceremonies who prepared the tea. He received his bowl first, and then watching as mine was being prepared, I could see that, for some reason, the bowl the tea ceremony master had selected for me was quite different, not just from the one that was already in use, but from anything I had ever seen before. (Under the circumstances, and knowing they do produce tea bowls, I presumed it was Korean.)

Every culture has its own spectrum of colours that in many ways both sustain and define it, and these were not any colours that I was familiar with – oranges, greens and yellows, all daubed in broad strokes on the inner surface of the cup – "somewhat dirty modern art" would probably be my best attempt at any description – and being much more used to the darker, more restrained subtleties of the Japanese variety, I couldn't really say I liked it. However, duly received, I performed (to the best of my understanding) the correct motions prior to and after drinking it and then, following etiquette, proceeded to 'admire' the bowl itself. And here I had what might be best described as a moment of insight related to what the ceremony itself may be all about – this, in large part, being why this particular paragraph has been included here.

As noted above, I did not find the bowl itself attractive. However, green tea itself has its own very distinctive colouring, and overall it matched. And now circling the bowl in my hands (ostensibly to allow me to examine the interior in more detail), the little liquid that was left caught against the sides and slurred (the cusp of a comet's tail drawn out against the night sky), and everything came together, with all those what only a moment ago had seemed ill-placed, highly discordant marks becoming one with the motion of my hands. And for the briefest of moments, the time it took for the tea to fall back into the base, what I had in front of me was perfection.

[10.6] A tea ceremony bowl is not an object to be placed and admired. To be truly appreciated it must be held, with in many senses the key to its beauty (its, very often deliberately distorted, shape and texture) coming through the sensory perceptions of the palms and fingers of the hands as it is turned and tilted during the ceremony. The colour, smell, and taste (and particularly the consistency) of the tea also are naturally important, and with each bowl being of a different size, considerable experience is required to balance the amount of tea powder and the quantity of hot water used in its preparation. All this I had fully grasped (at least, theoretically) some time before the above experience. However, the above slurring could not have happened if the tea itself had not been of a perfect, matching consistency with the curved surface of the bowl – just rough enough to form what was an extremely elegant spread. And in the final analysis, the overall effect was actually produced by (at least) three pairs of hands; those of the potter (his glazes and subsequent firing of the bowl in the kiln); the tea ceremony master (with his choice of tea, handling of the fine bamboo ladle used to scoop it from its container and whisk), and my own turning of the dregs.

And as a brief detour:

If you mention the words 'tea ceremony' to any (these days, probably any older) Japanese person, they will immediately come up with 'wabi' and 'sabi' – concepts that are again, to their minds. unique to the Japanese disposition and thus impossible for any person of foreign origin to grasp. Not to detract from any value of the ceremony itself, but on the understanding that it was originally introduced as a pastime for the 'daimyo' class (in England, the highest levels of aristocracy), whose tastes at the time ran to the gilded and/or ultra-gaudy, both can be understood, in one sense, as affectations (/or possibly an 'indulgence' for those who have everything), this being particularly true for wabi, perhaps best described as "an appreciation of 'calm' and the simple in life" – essentially, something any farmer working his land at this time would have easily related to. Also, even today, anyone who appreciates the cyclical rhythms of nature would have no problem at all with sabi: a tranquility which comes with an understanding of the aging of both things and the landscape, all things that carry an echo of the past or the passing of time – a sensibility towards the inherent value in well-used antique furniture, the gnarled trunks of ancient bonsai; rustic scenery, weathered rocks; the colourings of dead leaves and grasses or, for me, personally, in England; late autumn as it draws into winter on the Pennines and the long-gone world of "Wuthering Heights".

[10.7] A first visit:

The original suggestion had come from Mr Lee. I had mentioned that I liked walking in the mountains, "so why not try the mountains in Korea and then visit the capital, Seoul?" Also he had recommended I go in September, when the autumn leaves were at their best, and I had spent the previous six months or so studying the very basics of the language. Shortly before I left, he noted that he wouldn't be able to come with me, but he gave me the phone numbers of two friends who lived in Seoul and who would be able to help me if needed.

And two or three nights later, I had a dream.

I was at a road crossing, and as the lights turned green and I began to move out, two men approached me, one from my right and one from the far side of the road. Both came into clear focus before the changing lights forced me back, but as the features blurred, I had what felt like a brief heart attack, which quickly brought me awake.

And as it is with dreams of this nature, one of the two I actually met, the second was kept from me, and the heart attack, although survived, unfortunately came at the worst of moments, high up in the mountains.

***

A puff at a cigarette:

(The following is introduced here only in relationship to an incident that occurred while I was in Korea.)

Not too long before I left Japan, Mr Lee at the bar offered me a cigarette that he had just lit, and which I accepted. Finding it a not-unpleasant flavour, I actually took a second, deeper drag before he quickly stopped me. Presumably, I was not intended to smoke it. And it was returned and, as usual, no explanation was given.

[10.8] Getting there:

It is a relatively short flight from Osaka airport to Seoul, but once safe in the air I ordered a beer (and then a second) for the pleasure, and when we started crossing the Korean mountains in the south (again, cast in that delicate shade of blue), with the alcohol taking its effect, but also with the realisation that I was actually there – and more than anything (for no reason that I understood, but even so) that I was doing something that mattered to me, my eyes flooded with tears.

Inchon airport (Seoul): As the only person waiting to board the transfer bus to go to the domestic terminal, I was feeling somewhat panicky: This was the first time for a very long time that I had been in a foreign country where I hadn't been able to use English, and also I was by myself. However, when the bus arrived, the baggage handler, who had been standing aside having a quiet smoke, approached. And after placing my bag inside the luggage compartment under the bus, he turned, and clearly seeing how nervous I was, he spoke to me in Korean – which I had no way of understanding, but at the same time could: I knew what he was saying – telling me not to worry and that I would be all right, that everything was taken care of. And he took my hand and squeezed it, and there was a kindness in his eyes: He was encouraging me – not to worry, not to give up.

And then the moment was over, and letting go of my hand he indicated that I should get on the bus.

Having some time to spare at the domestic terminal and feeling thirsty, but not really having the nerve to try and order anything fancy (I was still below the most basic level in the language), I came out with the one word in Korean that I had a certain confidence with; "Mul," and the young lady at the kiosk very kindly me pointed me to the water dispenser, which is what I had been after. (Later in the trip, this one word actually came very close to saving my life, so it was worth the rehearsal.)

[10.9] Yangyang airport:

Following the line out of the plane and noticing a toilet off to the side, I decided I needed to go in and relieve myself – which I did, taking my time about it, so much so that when I came out into the lobby, it was empty – all the other passengers being outside climbing into two buses clearly marked as bound for the only two destinations of any importance in the area: Seorak-Dong and Osaek-Ri.

Seoraksan (the mountain I was planning to climb) is on the east coast of the peninsula, a little south of the border between South and North Korea, and I had worked out two possible routes, one from Seorak-Dong, north of the mountain to Osaek-Ri in the south, or alternatively from Osaek-Ri to Seorak-Dong. Both had certain advantages, but both being new terrain, I was not really sure which way I should take. At the time I was planning the trip in Japan, I had argued myself back and forth and then back again without reaching any conclusion. And now I stood between them still not being able to make up my mind. And consequently (not really believing I was doing this, but) I watched as the one bus left and then the other, and I was left to myself, with apparently no staff at all remaining in the building. (Yangyang is a very small airport that had been opened up only recently in the hope that they would be able to attract Japanese tourists directly from the Kansai and Tokyo areas, and initially, with much of the series filmed in that area, it had attracted "Winter Sonata" fans, but at this time it was only handling two or a maximum of three flights a day.)

Coming back outside to the car park area again, I noticed one man sitting off to the side on a low bench having a smoke, and having no other alternative, I walked across and spoke to him. I can't remember which language I used but he spoke back to me in Japanese. Now somewhere in his seventies, as a child his education had been in Japanese, and we had no problem at all communicating, and he suggested that if I would wait for him to have a second cigarette, he would take me into town so that I could get a regular bus to Osaek, an offer that I very gladly accepted.

Showing him my pack of photographs, my bamboo ink-painting particularly impressed (they also do a lot of ink-painting in Korea), and from this point on our conversation became totally enlivened. In the car on our trip into town, having himself climbed Seoraksan many times, he gave me all the details I would need to help me get up the mountain, including what time to start (to be up by four and be off, at the latest, by five in the morning) what to carry with me (plenty of cucumbers – cucumbers in the mountains in Korea being carried as liquid refreshment[17]), etc., etc., before finally, reaching the bus station, he found my bus for me, and after giving detailed instructions to the driver as to exactly where he should put me off, bid me farewell. I wouldn't recommend indecision as a way to get through life, but in this case, it worked remarkably well, and it did make for a very warm memory.

Arriving in Osaek, two university students with a little English (from here, I found a number of people who could speak English, some very well) guided me to a small hotel where, with the help of my basic grammar book, I managed to get past the rather gruff owner in his cubbyhole at the entrance, and to be shown my room by his much more friendly son. And then after finding a restaurant for what turned out to be a very satisfying meal in the evening (here also, I was recommended to buy cucumbers), understanding that I had to be up early in the morning, I got back to my room for some sleep.

[10.10] Seoraksan (1,770 metres):

Tackling the mountain from the south side turned out to be a very steep climb, with only two-level sections where one could really stop for a break, and carrying a full rucksack (I was to be there for ten days in total, and also had my sketchbook and camera equipment with me) I had to proceed fairly slowly. The rucksack actually caused a number of comments and quite a few smiles, particularly from a mixed group of young hikers at the entrance gate. With no language ability I was stuck for any reply, but it did give me a chance to smile back, which as it turned out came in handy later in the day.

The Confucian element in Korean culture has led to very high degree of respect for seniors in society (even with a difference of only one year), and on this walk, twice I was given an opportunity to see quite how strict such relationships are.

About to take a break about a third of the way up the mountain (I hadn't yet lowered my rucksack), a young man (in his thirties?) approached me, again in Korean but clearly with the gist being that I must be having a hard time carrying that sort of weight up the steep mountainside, finally he patted me on my

---

[17] At the time, I did not really understand this point, but upon reaching the hut at the summit, I did learn that water at that height is not commonly available and was suitably ticked off for my lack of consideration.

shoulder with his open palm, after which he went back to join his companions, where he was suddenly strongly berated by a man who I presumed to be the leader of his group. And almost before I could get my rucksack on the ground, he was back in front of me, bowing and apologising profusely for what must have been, at least in Korea, a very serious offense: He was clearly very embarrassed. Whether it was some mountain climbers' breach of etiquette, or simply the fact that I was older and he was treating me rather too casually, I do not know, but I sensed it may have been connected with the pat on the shoulder, which possibly could have been considered condescending, but he had been speaking in such a friendly manner that I would never have interpreted it that way, and I just smiled and let it go. However, he actually retreated bowing, so it must have been something serious…

[10.11] Another kind of beard:

The next opportunity to stop was at a 'waterfall', or at least that is how it was described on the map – actually, it turned out to be a point where a very narrow stream cut across the mountain side – but as all the other walkers were leaving the path, I went with them, and it was here that I caught my first glimpse of the creature I have since referred to as my 'mountain man' (Korean style mountain ascetic, hermit or whatever). 'Creature' may be a little unfair here, but I could not describe him other than to say that – deeply tanned, lank, approaching or in his early forties, and with an untended, objectionably thin, long, and straggly beard (for lack of any other expression, perhaps best described as 'unkempt facial growth') – he disquieted. Cupping water to drink from the stream, clearly none of the other hikers, particularly the women, felt comfortable near him, and I, also, kept my distance. And then, as people left, he lifted himself up, and moving very speedily, cut his way between them back up to the path and around the corner out of sight. The group I had met one level down (with the young man who had patted me on my shoulder) had now caught up with me – I had left them eating a late breakfast – and deciding that I should be reasonably safe following them, I made my way back up to the path and restarted my walk. However, rounding the corner, they were all gone, and he was there, sitting and resting his lean body against the slope at the side of the path. And now it was his eyes, which came at me direct and challenging, daring me to walk up past him – and unsure as to how to proceed, I stopped and waited. And for what seemed a long moment, we both stayed as we were.

The slope we were on was relatively short and straight, with yet another corner at the top, and quite suddenly, the man who had been bringing up the rear of the group, presumably concerned that I had not stayed with them, reappeared at the top and stood looking down at me. There was no attempt to speak, but the message came through clearly: "If you wish to do so, you may go back down, with no discredit to you." And understanding that I understood, he turned and disappeared. And that being enough to break the spell (no way was I going back down), I started walking again, and now seemingly losing all interest in me, the man stood, and before I could take ten steps, he was away and out of my sight. And I kept plodding...

A little higher on the path, I started meeting people who were coming down – either they had started well ahead of me, or possibly had been walking a different trail, or even better I was approaching the summit, but I was now comfortable enough to exchange a "Good day!" in Korean with them as required, and when a couple of Japanese women came down towards me chatting most volubly in the Kansai dialect, I quite naturally greeted them as I would walking in the mountains around Osaka. They hardly blinked as they passed me, but then ten yards down the path, the one did a double take and suddenly came out with:

"That man! He just spoke to us in Kansai-ben (dialect)."

"He couldn't have. He's a gaijin!"

I gave them a brief smile, but then continued on my way, not having the strength to go back down and explain. Older women in the Kansai area have a well-deserved reputation for their love of gossip (/gossiping) and I still had a long way to go, the walk down on the other side of the peak, although apparently with gentler gradations, being far longer than the section I was on.

And again that much higher, looking across to my right, I could see what appeared to be two concrete shelters, which with a little thought I recognised as bunkers or foxholes, both facing south, presumably built to shelter the North Korean army when they were in retreat. And with this recognition there came a strong rasp of tobacco – the singular pungency of an unfiltered Gitanes or Gauloises – coalescing against the back of my throat, impregnating the membranes; its strength and/or the thought of those who had died there, bringing tears to the eyes. And there being nothing more that I could do, I prayed ("In and of") that they be at rest. And the slope eased. Until 50 yards on, when I was again faced with my 'mountain man', now running at full stride down the slope towards me. But before I could even begin to react, his face broke into a broad, welcoming smile – and without any sign of dropping speed, he passed me by, his arm outstretched as he flashed me a broad thumbs-up, and he was gone.

[10.12] Life's reprises:

"You can only be had so many times before you learn to see it coming."

Up another 100 yards on the path and around one more corner, on the left side of the trail, I had a tall Korean man who I shall refer to as Big Boy (BB), and on the right his much smaller sidekick, Chib (an abbreviation of the Japanese for a small child or runt), and very clearly they had been biding their time with the intention of intercepting some innocent backpacking foreigner, who had now arrived in their view. Big Boy greeted me in Korean. Chib, who spoke a little English, and right the way through worked as Big Boy's translator, asked me where I was heading (for Seorak-Dong – followed by an exchange of knowing glances) and then if I had been to Korea before ("No." – again, those glances), and then without any further exchanges, we were walking together up the path. This being far from the first time that I had been waylaid in life – in England, or Japan – I would most likely have come out with an "Excuse me, I wasn't born yesterday." But then with linguistic restrictions (and perhaps here a certain tiredness), as one does in these cases, you learn to go with the flow.

And they stayed with me; at the mountain hut – where a young man did fortunately half fill my water flask for me; and then on to the next trail, where, as it narrowed, BB (moving at a fast pace) led and Chib followed up behind, with me neatly ensconced between. (I could only assume that this was the path to Seorak-Dong, but with the sky being overcast, I had no means of knowing in what direction we were actually walking.) And it was at this point that I had my heart attack – a strong pull at the chest, reverberating through to the brain and forcing me to stop in my tracks. Recognising that something had gone seriously wrong (the blood had been drawn from my head), Chib, for the first time showing his nature as the more considerate of the two, seriously asked me if I wanted to go back to the hut, but then BB was shouting back down the trail at both of us, and the moment gone, I waved it away…

High up on the ridge path, BB, after taking a quick look up and down the trail, moved left onto a somewhat overgrown side-path and indicated that I should follow. This involved crossing over a coiled mass of barbed wire, but they were leading and by this time I was far beyond questioning any motives. It clearly was a path and would take us somewhere. It was only when we had moved considerably down the slope that I remembered reading that (in order to protect the natural environment), when any one path is found to have been overused, walkers are barred from entry for a minimum of six months, and presumably this was one such path. (As I was getting over the wire, a passing group had given us some rather strange looks.) That is, we were now on our own and likely to stay that way for quite some time.

[10.13] Examining the 'spoils':

We had stopped for lunch at the foot of a tall rock that we had just descended, and my pack, once opened, naturally became an object of inquiry. If they were going to take something, presumably they would want to know what it was or whether it might have any value. In fact, other than my camera, which I kept close to me while I was eating, and although I would not have liked to lose my sketchbooks, there was very little of anything of value in there. (As a habit, I kept my money and passport on me at all times.) However, after a brief rummaging around, it was my Korean textbook that took BB's attention. Initially, this might have been the fact that it was a Japanese-Korean version, and clearly I was not Japanese. (The Japanese and Korean languages, both originally using the Chinese ideographs, come very close structurally – a Japanese student working seriously can be fluent in Korean within six months or so – and I had decided to work from Japanese rather than struggle again with the huge differences that exist between English and either language.) However, very quickly, he became fascinated with the basic word list at the back of the book, where I had highlighted every piece of vocabulary that might be related to an engagement or marriage. (I had come prepared.) And here it was as well that Chib's translation abilities were not quite up to the required level, and quite a bit of any explanation that I might have given got glossed over.

A second nod to seniority:

At some point (almost certainly after the meal), with whatever excuse, BB had taken hold of my rucksack and set off down the hill, and now he was really forcing the pace, with the clear intention of leaving me behind, but I also had had practice moving my way down steep slopes, and the pack now containing my camera, I had every reason not to hold back. Even so, with his much longer legs, it was not at all easy keeping up with him. (Chib was way behind us.)

And then there was an older woman in her sixties or so at the side of the path who, with one sharp command, brought him to a halt. (And it was here that it really came through to me that I was in a very different society.) Turning to face the woman, without any hesitation, he bowed. Then came the lecture: "What was he doing treating a foreigner, a guest in their land, in such an undignified way?" "Couldn't he see that I was struggling hard to keep up with his pace?" "Didn't he know to treat older people with respect?" And on and on – all the time with BB silent, his head down to the ground until, suitably remonstrated, with one final bow, we set off again at a much more refined pace down the slope.

"Nice to know you!":

And we were with people again, the numbers growing the further down we walked, until, at a confluence in the paths, a large group of younger people standing to our left were suddenly laughing and giggling and pointing in our direction: I was back with the group I had met in the very early stages of my walk in the morning, and taking advantage of the situation to indicate to BB that I would like to have my backpack returned to me, he had no choice other than to go along with my request – and a few hundred yards on, we were standing in an open space by the roadside. Wherever we were, clearly, we had completed our walk.

[10.14] A final gambit:

(The following conversation, as usual, was translated by Chib in somewhat broken English.)

BB: "We have our car, and we can take you to Seoul. And you can come and stay with us."

Me: "I have fixed a hotel, thank you."

(This was not exactly true. Not certain when I would be arriving in Seoul, I had not yet made a booking, but I had selected the place and fully intended staying there.)

BB: "What is the name of the hotel?" (The name was given.) "OK (determination at its finest), we can cancel it for you."

Which, there being a public telephone close at hand, he proceeded to do until, the conversation clearly not going the way he had imagined and apparently somewhat frustrated, he turned to me and insisted that I take the receiver. The man in the hotel spoke excellent English and was extremely polite. However, when asked whether it would be possible to book a room with them, he came out with a very direct; "No, Mr Olton. You will not be staying here." This being so far from any standard, "I'm sorry, Mr Olton, but the hotel is fully booked tonight," or "We could hold a reservation for you from tomorrow evening," it stayed with me very clearly in my mind. And when I thought about it later, I really had to wonder who exactly had decided that this should be so. However, with BB at my back clearly getting more and more agitated by the moment, this did not seem a time to quibble, and I thanked him and replaced the receiver.

There being nothing else that I could think to do, we walked down the road, the man fuming at my side – angry at me, equally angry at his sidekick and quite possibly a little annoyed with himself. But more than anything, he was clearly furious that I had lied to him about booking a room in the hotel. (In contrast, all he had attempted to do was to steal a stranger's belongings and leave him stranded in the mountains, possibly to have a second heart attack, but why should one be concerned about that!!!) However, by now the tiredness was really taking hold and I was in no way capable of getting into any further arguments.

And we were at the end, standing in the middle of a wide divide in a carpark, with BB still pushing for me to go with them in his car, and myself close to collapsing: I need a lot of water at the best of times, and not having drunk for a considerable time, I could feel my mouth going dry. And then Chib, seeing my condition and understanding quite how serious the situation might be (they really had gone too far), took my arm and pushed me towards a small entrance at the end of the divide, which upon careful viewing I recognised as the front of the hotel I had left that morning. We were back in Osaek.

And staggering back into the hotel and faced with a group of unbelieving faces (quite what had this crazy guest been up to?) it was here that that word, rehearsed so carefully at Incheon airport (now so far back in memory) came into full use. It took three efforts from my dried lips: "Mul," "Mul," "Mul" – but then the son moved, and I got my water, and drank every glass he gave me.

Early the next morning, the restaurant not yet being open, for no reason other than I sensed the path had to be re-walked, I set off back up the hill. It was only 400 yards or so up through the village to the start of the mountain path and today I had no pack, but the hill was quite steep, and I took it slowly. And as my mind turned to the previous day, on cue, whatever it is or was returned, and very quickly, with each step I took, my whole body was enclosed – drenched in a thick cloud of pain – relief only coming when I finally turned back at the entrance gate to the mountain trail, which I decided was as far as I could manage. Then walking back down the hill, a small truck momentarily pulled up at my side, and I was treated to what I assumed was a Korean "Oss!" – "Oss!" being a shortened form of "Ohaiyou gozaimasu!" (Good morning.) which is used in a rather rough but friendly manner as a greeting between Japanese men. But here the man at the wheel was the owner of the hotel, the man who had been so curt with me on my arrival two days previously. And lending me a spirited smile, he drove off down the hill.

[10.15] A phone call:

"Mr Lee said that if you called, I was to tell you that he would be arriving in Seoul tomorrow, and that if you telephone him when you get to Seoul, he will meet you. Apparently, he has arranged for somewhere for you to stay."

(My reaction here was, "Oh, that is why I 'will not be staying' at the hotel I had planned to stay at.")

This was Mr Koh – the man who had been walking across the street towards me in my dream before I collapsed. Now back at the hotel, and the reactionary shock from the events of the previous day having finally set in, making me in the need for some reassurance, I had called him, hoping to be able to hear my own (that is, English) voice. Mr Lee had noted that he spoke both English and Japanese, while Mr Kang (the other man from the dream, who I later got to meet) only spoke Japanese. Unfortunately, for whatever reason, he insisted that we speak in Japanese, but just the knowledge that I would not be on my own when I arrived in Seoul was enough to settle my mind, and I thanked him very much for the information. Mr Koh had a very pleasant and caring voice and given the choice I would have been very happy to match it with the attractive face that had appeared in my dream, but upon arriving in Seoul, I was told by Mr Lee that he had decided that "I would not now be meeting him." No explanation was given for the change of heart (Mr Koh was not someone he could assume would follow his wishes? Something had 'clicked', suddenly making him want to become more involved?), but as I was now there under his charge, I was not in a position to object. However, I do, even today, admit to being a little disappointed.

[10.16] A Day to myself:

Osaek is a very small village. However, there was a short but very attractive valley, its sides consisting of a series of huge rock pinnacles, running to its west, and in the morning, before the tourist buses from Seoul arrived to view the autumn foliage (when it became impossible walk against the crowds), it provided a very pleasant place to take photographs and generally relax. And at lunchtime, a very sympathetic lady who was eating there with her family, seeing me by myself with only rice balls to consume, walked across to me to give me a cucumber. I also managed a little sketching on the eastern side of the village, and at the end of the day, I had time to purchase a few small souvenirs and then a full meal at one of the local restaurants. And the next day, considerably refreshed, I took the bus to Seoul.

Leaving the hotel in the morning, one of the staff introduced me an older couple who were travelling on the same bus. Neither of them spokes any English or Japanese, but they would help make sure that I got there safely, which they actually did – helping me change buses along the way and explaining exactly where I was in the bus station to Mr Lee when I called him after we arrived in Seoul. Also, the husband kept trying out short phrases in Korean on me, the final (textbook) sentence as we arrived in Seoul being "The River Han is the longest (/widest?) river in South Korea," which, even though neither apparently are strictly true, being able to hear what he was saying straight off, gave me something of a lift. And then along the way, there was the very smart (and a little frightening) Korean soldier – rifle slung across his shoulder – who stepped up to check the passengers and the interior of the bus in general, this being one time when it did really get through to me that I was in a country that was, if not strictly at war, certainly not in a state of peace. (Later, there was a huge, solid sculpture in the Olympic Park in Seoul entitled "Peace", that I could only interpret as representing a giant tank – its barrel facing north – this presumably reflecting the reality of the time.)

[10.17] Seoul:

The small hotel that the master had selected for me was in the centre of the gay district. It was also close to a flower shop, which was very carefully pointed out to me, supposedly referring to some hint that I should have received prior to arriving, but which in reality made no sense to me at all. (Understanding that this does not reflect well on the efficiency of the system as a whole, I did have a similar case when I received my first student at home, where I was walking her through a whole series of explanations that she should presumably have already fully understood but clearly didn't.)

And from this time on, we spent every day doing everything every tourist does; visiting palaces and museums, the changing of the guard, shopping for gifts and bargains, circling parks and driving or walking up one or the other of the many hills that – un-noted initially among all the high-rise buildings of a modern metropolis – can appear at times to have infiltrated the city overnight, and the existence of these hills, together with the broad sweep of the River Han, its breadth alone making it highly imposing, eventually came to define the city for me.

And in the evening, there were the bars, the larger ones with stages and mirror-balls for Karaoke performances, my only trouble here being that I found myself limited to English (which at the time I very rarely sang in) and Japanese (which, considering the historical relationship between the two countries, I couldn't overdo). To solve this, I ended up buying a number of Korean CDs to be studied for my second visit. I actually did this so successfully that the following year I had over 20 Korean songs I could approach with full confidence (but still had not really mastered any of the standard phrases required for basic conversation).

[10.18] Food:

I enjoyed everything I ate in Korea on the two times I visited – this with the possible exception of the 'gimbap' rice rolls, the Korean version of which (we have the similar 'makizushi' in Japan) I invariably found somewhat dry. However, on this first trip, I did have the benefit of the master's knowledge of the area, and some of the food – from the 'samgyetang' (a full chicken in a spicy broth), which we ate the first night, right through to the single raw pepper that I was offered by the owner of one of the top restaurants in Seoul (a friend of Mr Lee) – was truly exceptional. I knew from experience that peppers can be very hot, and when I first received it (about 10 cm in length and presumably taken straight from the plant), I was a little unsure as to how it should be tackled, but the owner indicated that I should simply break it in half and put the lower half in my mouth, which I did. And as the best description I can attempt; as I bit into it, I had the equivalent of a fifty-year whiskey of the plant world spreading its gossamer-like vapour – a blending of the most subtle (both sweet and bitter) flavours imaginable – lapping endlessly across my palate, this lasting a considerable time until quite suddenly (unavoidable in that it was a pepper), it was hot! However, that said, I would still list it among the finest of the varied culinary experiences that I have had in my life. The rest of meal, delicious as it was, fades in comparison.

In the bars, there were the large and generously piled fresh fruit plates, presumably providing a certain balance for the amounts of alcohol consumed. And there was garlic, garlic and more garlic, which I quickly learned to eat platefuls of, without even the slightest remaining stay on the breath – in Japan, an assumed automatic. There clearly are preparation methods and preparation methods.

[10.19] People:

Other than the owners of the bars we visited, I was only introduced to two men; the first, Mr Cho, who within three minutes of being introduced, walking along a suitably dark alley, squeezed my hand in a very friendly way. This unfortunately was noticed immediately by my guide, who very quickly indicated to his friend that I was 'off limits', and the hand was removed. (Presumably, Mr Lee wanted me for his own pleasure – or at least, if there were to be any playing around, it was to be at his will. Right the way through, I got the impression that Mr Cho, in more ways than one, was in some way very special to him. And he was a nice person.) And then there was Mr Kang, the second man from my dream, who (again unfortunately) I did not relate to at all – everything about him putting me on my guard – but here it seemed that Mr Lee was determined that I sleep with him, and on the last day of my visit, unable to refuse an invitation to his home "for lunch," it became apparent that this was intended to be a threesome (which naturally was not going to happen), although it did take a certain degree of determination to keep them off: "Do go and look at Mr Kang's bedroom. It is really beautiful."

With its huge double bed, it was, but I didn't go in.

[10.20] Just quite whose marriage are we talking about?

An hour-or-so drive outside Seoul, there was a 'tourist village' of houses gathered from around the country, representative of the historical changes in lifestyle and architecture on the Korean peninsula. The place itself was suitably interesting, but beyond that, it is mentioned here simply because it provided the background for two rather different events.

We had been walking separately, spreading our area of interest for a short while, when Mr Lee came walking across to me with a panicked look on his face, and a very obvious erection beneath his trousers. (If he was wearing underwear, it was of the looser variety.) This was not in reaction to anyone he had seen: We were in a family-oriented park, and he had merely been looking at one of the old buildings, when for no reason whatever he had had an arousal which just refused to go away. And it didn't. And it wouldn't. Not for a good ten minutes, during which we had to walk around very carefully trying to make ourselves (and the offending organ) as inconspicuous as possible. (As to quite why it happened, presumably these things do. But it did, at least on my side, amuse.)

There is a certain type of person who cannot resist – they always have to let you know that they know, that they are 'in on things' – and this time, it came when we were at the foot of a rather low, grassy knoll, looking at a winding path that curved its way up to the top point, when Mr Lee suddenly came out with: "This is the marriage path." (Nothing in this area had ever been mentioned openly up to this point.) However, wandering our way up to the top (it was a walk that in all likelihood had been made to entertain small children), it did occur to me to wonder whether any life path (never mind a series of lives over a period of hundreds of years that I had originally conceived) could be quite so easily navigated.

A reprise of sorts:
The only other time that the marriage concept was at all mentioned, was in a rather out-of-the-way basement bar late at night, when Mr Lee asked me what I might think of the bartender as a partner, and I told him, quite honestly, that "he would be a nice person to live with." More than anything, he was 'normal' – a very pleasant-faced sort of person who you could probably meet anywhere – which is actually very much what I was in need of at the time.

And shortly afterwards, starting a song on the stage, I sensed someone encouraging me to 'perform'. And not wanting to disappoint, I set off into a series of coughs, hacks, squeaks and groans (plus the odd stamp of the foot), basically inspired by the manner in which I sang the song described at the end of Cpt 8 [8.19], but while at that time the whole event had been totally beyond my control (it was nothing that I could have even attempted to repeat), here everything was a heightened artificiality; a late-night show put on for the final coachload of tourists in town – except that even they (if they had ever been) were now long gone, and the bar was empty other than for ourselves and the (to me) somewhat unimpressive owner. (The barman, perhaps fortunately – I would have been embarrassed to have him watch me – had retreated into the kitchen at this point.) That said, I can only presume that it satisfied. At the time, my take on the situation was that if they didn't recognise what they were seeing for what it wasn't, they weren't really up to much. (It was late, and I was getting very tired of the continuing insistence that I jump to his master's voice – whoever the master might be.) ...

And then, in our final moments, preparing to leave to the airport, we both found ourselves emulating dreamy-eyed lovers. (After all, I was to return the following year.) And once again (with shades of Oxford and the IOW), as to who was fooling who, I would not know.

[10.21] And a year later. A second visit:

Setting the tone:

On my arrival, met by Mr Lee and his partner from Japan (they were planning to return to Korea and open a new bar in Seoul, which is eventually what they did), I was very quickly informed that he would have relatively little time to see me as he was also receiving a visit from business acquaintances from Taiwan, and that also he would have to spend some time with his family (he had a wife and grown son in Seoul, who had been ignored on the previous visit). If this was intended as a put off, it was accepted. However, at the same time, he also made it clear that I was expected to be available on demand – initially no particular problem as I had been seeing him on and off in Japan. However, the first time we actually managed to get together in the hotel, noting that he was spending the largest proportion of his time viewing himself in action in the mirror, it did come to me that we were approaching a pivotal point in our relationship.

That said, the situation did leave me with time to explore the city on my own, something I had not been able to do during my first visit, and this I came to really enjoy. Seoul, much of which must have been destroyed during the Korean War, at first sight does not have the impact of any of the older cities in Europe, but very quickly I grew to like it, its openness making it very comfortable just walking the streets. Also there were the families – on the underground and in the parks; this particularly at the weekend – and everyone smiling. (In Japan at the time, it was relatively rare to see fathers out with their children, the standard scenario being just the mother and child, possibly together with a grandmother or friend.) And in the evening, I now knew enough bars to find my way around on my own, and when we did meet up, I was just one of a crowd, which resulted in me meeting a considerably wider range of people (both in age and background) than I had on my first visit.

[10.22] Views of history:

Half by accident, I found a monument (a series of carved scenes, each of which I photographed to show my Japanese students) commemorating the first uprising of the Koreans against the Japanese colonial government on March 1, 1919. Unfortunately, entering at the wrong end, it took me some time to work out exactly what it was. However, it did get me a wedge of persimmon and a greeting from one of the old men seated around the side of the small park, and it also got me interested enough to purchase a book on Korean history to take home. And then:

"Why have I been brought here?"
(At the North-South border between the two Koreas.) Why we had spent two hours driving up here I was not quite sure. All I really remember from the place now was a long run of barbed-wire fence and some rather empty green fields, what appeared to be a bridge to nowhere, an odd stall for souvenirs and cold drinks, and small groups of people meandering to and fro. (What is one supposed to do in such places?) Understanding that it will have a strong meaning for Korean people, there was nothing here that I could personally relate to. Almost certainly I had had a better view from, and certainly more sense of the true reality of the war at the top of Seoraksan.[18]

Four of us had taken the journey; Mr Lee driving, his partner by his side, and myself and a Mr Kim, a university professor who had spent at least a couple of years in America and who made an interesting person to talk with on our trip. And all was well until we arrived back at my hotel and Mr Lee came out with, "And now you two can enjoy yourselves." That is, we were apparently expected to go together into my hotel and have sex. How serious he was about the matter here, I cannot say, but he was clearly deliberately using both myself and the other man for his own purposes, and equally he was in full deceit mode with his partner. (His partner was actually fully aware of what was going on and, more than

---

[18] This was close to my parents' reaction to the old "foreign merchants' enclave" in Kobe, which for Japanese people, it being a somewhat exotic part of their history, will naturally attract, but for an English visitor, it not amounting to more than an extremely dry tour around a group of minimally furnished and somewhat decrepit diplomats' houses, it is not anything that enthrals. My mother's comment on the furniture was, "We have better than this at home," which, although I understood the statement as perhaps a little harsh, I actually had to agree to.

anything, the above comment seemed a matter of keeping his jealousy factor under control. On my side, I had no sympathy at all for the partner, having noted him back in Japan playing around in plain sight with other customers when Mr Lee was out of the bar. He liked to make this very obvious.) Mr Kim himself, was extremely pleasant, but he did not come over as anyone I would of my own choice go to bed with. And beyond that, the proposal had come from so far out in the blue that I had no time to make any required adjustment. Although we had conversed considerably throughout the trip, there had been no sign at all from him that he might be interested in me in that area. And getting out of the car, and making it very clear to all three of them that I would be going into the hotel by myself, I left them to sort things out among themselves.

[10.23] Goodbyes:

On the last night, I arrived rather late at the bar where I knew everyone was going to be: I had not felt well earlier in the evening and had almost considered giving it a pass. However, just about everyone I had met being there made for a pleasant gathering, and when Mr Lee and his partner left, I stayed on with a group of the partner's younger friends and Mr Cho, the man who had squeezed my hand so nicely on my first evening in the Seoul one year previously. And as things go, we ended up back in the hotel, both of us drunk but equally alive enough to make the best of our short time together. And the next morning, when Mr Lee arrived and asked me what had happened, I told him (these are times when honesty does make a certain sense). Naturally not approving, and having sat on the bed and thought a little about the matter, he came out with a very brief "Goodbye," and left the room. This actually did sting for roughly two seconds, before receding into a lightness of spirit that I carried with me out through the narrow backstreets to the bus stop – being fully familiarised with the area at this point, there was no further need to go by the flower shop – and then the airport and back to Japan, where I admit to collapsing in total exhaustion. (I had to call Koji to pick me up from the station, a distance I would normally walk easily.)

And perhaps now re-evaluating all the events in and leading up my visit, I sense that, for whatever the reason, I was openly involving myself in something that could never be. Right from the moment he opened the door of his bar on that first night welcoming me with such a brilliant smile, I was fully aware that the whole thing was some form of fabrication: We were playing to a field, expanding on a storyline from nowhere. And right the way through, while it was quite apparent that he was (he assumed, successfully) stringing me along, I on my side was giving him enough soft talk for him to believe that there might be something there (which at certain points, he did seem to believe, as perhaps I did also). And at the end, by sleeping with the one man I knew that, for whatever reason, in his mind was not to be permitted (this after refusing every man he had tried to push onto me), I do know that, conclusion foregone, I was hitting back at what I read as a highly ingrained (and totally unrecognised on his part) level of arrogance.

Stories of this nature do not end in any tidy manner, and as I continued going to the Korean bars in Osaka over a number of years, I was subject to a series of events – deceit, evasion, attempted theft and deliberate fraud – each one shading the next and perhaps creating a worse image than would have been normal. However, together with all the attendant experiences, I did get two trips to Korea, somewhere I would never have taken it upon myself to go without the original encouragement. And there were also a number of people who I met only briefly (/momentarily even) along the way, but whose kindnesses brought with them a very natural affinity, and collectively they did help to balance my overall impression of the country.

And today, although I doubt I will be going to Korea again, for my own pleasure, I continue to watch Korean television dramas, quite a considerable percentage of which (on a good day) I can now both hear and understand reasonably easily.

"Chowa yo!"

Chapter 11

The Way We Are
Identity

[11.1]

"Every child born, for better or worse, is dealt a hand, and each individual, together with the help or hindrance of those they are obliged to (or in time choose to) inter-react, has to learn to handle this in the best way he or she is able."

Formative influences:

(Note: To avoid any unnecessary clutter, the following is simply a statement of what, at the present time, we know, as opposed to what we as individuals coming from disparate cultures or backgrounds choose to believe.)

Conceived as blank slates, with only our genetic imprints to define us, and beyond that, for better or worse, what the world, i.e., the family (/local environment/ society/ culture/ religion) in which we are placed, has to offer us, we grow up, at least in our initial years, accepting (/having no choice but to accept) this 'reality' as the norm. A child born in a palace, slum, or war zone; treated strictly or indulged; starved, beaten or sexually abused; with only one or no knowledge of parents, or with restricted physical or mental abilities, is naturally going to assume that "This is what life is!" and this will only be modified when and if they are exposed to and are able to gain some understanding of other viewpoints.

(From the newspaper a number of years ago: A considerable number of young children – brought up in Russian orphanages, where they had not been subject to any strong demonstrations of affection – after being adopted by American families, were found unable to accept typical American-style hugs and kisses, which the adoptive parents showered upon them to try to show them that they were both loved and accepted. Never having been treated in this manner, they had no means of making what to the new parents was a natural connection between the intention and the physical action, and many of them actually screamed violently if they were held in this way.)

[11.2]

In all societies, I would guess that a large proportion of people who grow up within what is understood as 'the majority opinion' or are placed in some manner as 'above' in the hierarchy of things – men in patriarchal societies, those who have a sense of racial superiority, having parents with money or position, or members of that particular group's 'elites' – are never truly required to think or question. Far more likely, they will simply assume that they are experiencing 'the world as it is (/and should be)', and with that confidence they are free to get on with whatever path they may choose to pursue, spared the effort of ever really having to wonder why. And in the case of 'born-and-bred' elites, I suspect that for a large number of them, to get beyond that initial intake, or even that it might occur to them that there are cases where they could be called upon to compromise that position in some manner, might be that one bridge too far.

When Matt [4.2] visited two summers ago (with both of us now in our seventies), shortly after his arrival, he told me how coming along on the train to our station and passing the hospital where his first two children (lost to him following his divorce with Gail) had been born, he had found himself shedding tears, and then the following day got somewhat annoyed to hear that I had told Kensuke about the matter. Presumably, this was not in line with the overall impression of the type of person that he was that he had been trying to establish in Kensuke's mind. I had told him that it was our rule to share everything, and on his part, Kensuke, who had met Gail twice earlier and was fully aware of the background, took the fact that he had cried as totally understandable. I have included this here simply because it was the one time when I have been with Matt that I have seen him directly express his feelings in any manner that I would consider open. Every other time I have been with him or had the opportunity to observe him interacting with others, his manner has always appeared at a certain level to be simulated; forever enveloped in an overlay of precisely calibrated bonhomie that he presumably was trained to inhabit as a child.

And then back in full form: Here mainly to visit friends from his younger days before moving up to Tokyo to drum up more business with certain Japanese companies he works with, he was out of the house most of the time, but on his final day, we spent the morning with him in town, whereupon after a request to 'borrow' (as in what used be referred to as 'cadging') small change for his luggage locker at the station, he then came out in his best Japanese insisting that "he wouldn't be offended if I paid for" the lunch that we were having together before he got his train – this before I had even offered. Considered de-rigueur in Japan, Kensuke was quite ready that I do this, but having paid for everything when Matt had spent a day taking us around in England, this for me was going that one step too far, and I in my turn 'insisted'.

In contrast to the above, if you recognise yourself to be maligned in any manner, that is 'treated unfairly' or openly discriminated against, or possibly subject to some debilitating condition or accident which brings up the question of "Why me?", from quite early on, you are required to do some serious thinking about life – which although it may be hard at the time, viewed as a toughening-up process, in the long term will not automatically be a bad thing.

[11.3] Pride and Prejudice:

"For any individual in any society or of any background, the creation, projection and protection of a personal identity, which inevitably includes an element of self-righteousness or pride, is essential for the degree of self-respect or mental stability required to face living."

My first experience as a child with what might be described as overt discrimination was, whenever someone referred to Irish people working in England, the word invariably would be paired with "navvy." This was from when I was very young, and in the early stages I didn't have any understanding of the real meaning of the words, only later understanding somewhat vaguely that they were 'road workers', but right from the start I could easily get the sense that they were a people to be looked down upon. I was only cleared of this misunderstanding – that is, that all Irishmen were navvies – when, working in Saudi Arabia, I found out that one of the other English teachers, who was a graduate of Cambridge, also happened to be Irish, this providing my brain with a highly abrupt shock, far more than might be thought possible, but it was not anything that I had ever had a chance to think about, and things that you are taught as a child do tend to get embedded. It is very easy to imagine that, with some very different (/unpleasant) first experience here, or merely if I had been more susceptible to my parents' lines of guidance, I could have been left with a lifelong prejudice in this area. And then also very early on, we had gypsies (Roma), one group of whom came into our entrance road with their horses and wagons presumably with the intention of setting up camp there, when I do remember they were very quickly sent packing by my father together with two or three of our other neighbours. And, more personally, when I insisted on visiting an elementary school friend whose family lived on a municipal housing estate, that is his family was clearly viewed as not very well off and thus not really 'respectable', I clearly remember being told by my mother that "I shouldn't bother with him," and that "I wouldn't be associating with him when I got older," which, even as a child, did offend. At the time, (and this remains true even now), all the friends I made at my elementary school were special to me, and to have one referred to in this manner was not pleasant.

We also had a large community of Pakistanis who lived "in that other part of town," and much later, when Yukiko [4.2] was staying with my parents for six months, a young Pakistani man, who she was studying with in town and brought home to introduce to my parents, was also quickly sent on his way. (After a little thought, I did understand here that my father was in fact correct, as she was a young woman from abroad and fully under my parents' care, and that naturally he was not prepared to take any risks in that area. And many years later, when there were scandals reported of younger Pakistani men sharing their white girlfriends with older friends and relatives, the point did truly come home.)

The intention here is not in any way to imply that my parents were educating me to demean others (although this is in actuality what they were doing): In their minds, they were merely guiding me as to the reality of the society I was growing up into – their society as they understood it – and indicating in their own manner, as all parents do, their hopes for my future. And very probably, if I had remained in my hometown, in all likelihood I would have held those prejudices myself, at least for a far longer period than I actually did, and quite possibly all my life. And presumably we can understand that this is what happens in all countries, at all levels of society. The children of both owners and servants in a moneyed household will be taught their position in life from very early on. (As an exception to the rule here, I did once read of an English aristocrat who directed that his son, from a very young age, be placed under the charge of each member of his staff, starting with the servant responsible for cleaning the family shoes, and presumably he grew up fully conscious of their contributions to the household.)

My experiences at Oxford also did give me some first-hand experience of 'being looked down upon', which although at the time unpleasant, as my world opened up, did allow me, one step at a time, at least to try to not automatically look down on others – in practice, not something easily achieved. (I would also note that my experiences at this point were balanced considerably by my interactions with my postgraduate group, allowing me the understanding that there were extremely intelligent people out there all around the world who presumably were not quite so restricted by their upbringings.)

[11.4] "There but for Fortune." Joan Baez:

I initially took this song – entreating the audience to imagine themselves as a young man cast into jail for no other reason than his bad fortune – as a plea for empathy, only later coming to understand it far more as a simple proclamation of the vagaries in life that we all in one manner or another are subject to. Life can be remarkably capricious in its seemingly arbitrary hidden maze of twists and turns, and if you personally find yourself subject to some degree of misfortune along the way, you could perhaps look to these lyrics for guidance. At least, they have always worked for me.

[11.5] The hole:

"If you dig yourself deep enough into a hole, you will eventually lose sight of whatever else there might have been out there. And for those born deep in that hole (that 'frog in a well') or are cast in there by forces beyond your control, it will require more than a strong arm to draw you to the air."

And in this respect, as a child I was extremely lucky; the more restricting aspects of the education my parents bestowed on me leaving me in no more than a shallow hollow or depression, which, thanks to my early schooling experience, I was halfway up the sides of before the real game even started. At the same time, it is easy to understand that with a different temperament and exposed to a slightly different run of experiences, I could so easily have moved in some quite different direction. And perhaps as an illustration of a minor blemish on the surface:

"Knowing what you are missing."

A recent television programme introducing a day-care centre for elderly people, where the whole group were involved in growing vegetables – each individual (including some in wheelchairs) helping at their own pace and as they could, one snip at a time – brought into focus a man in his nineties, who was clearly quite active and involved in the whole process, to the point of pulling and taking a bite out of a carrot they had grown; there being nothing unusual in this, except that, as was noted, being turned off carrots for some reason as a small child, it had taken this amount of time (90 years) and this particular experience of actually growing vegetables, to free his mind up enough to try once again, and actually find them delicious.

[11.6] The limitations of the brain (AI):

Referencing the determination of a personally programmed interface, which over time will come to dictate how each one of us, as the in-every-respect unique individuals that we are, come to relate to the world.

As an odd (and highly imperfect) analogy that still may be of some use.

The hermit crab: A small crab that, to protect its shell-less hinder parts, makes temporary use of whatever vacant shells it can find available on the beach, upgrading in size and shape as it grows and develops, and withdrawing into that shell when threatened in any manner, only to emerge when it senses that it is safe to do so.

Externally, the above noted 'shell' can easily be understood as a human child's cot or playpen, room, home, garden, local community, school, etc., but alternatively it could perhaps be more profitably viewed as the innumerable connections and associations within the brain that create the areas wherein the child feels more (or less) safe or can express themselves with fuller (or less) confidence; and that, in turn, will define how they move on to the next stage in their development – the people they choose to associate with, interests, personal habits, 'values', the manner in which they establish their own habits of attention, etc. – and eventually, the way they identify, communicate with or react to the world as a whole; an inner shell (/set of guiding principles or constraints) that can provide the temporary shelter essential to the formational process and, in time, as lifetime habits are formed and there is no perceived requirement for any further expansion, we settle on as a basic framework for our relationships as adults.

And in all cases, this configuration – upon which we rely so heavily to make both the simplest of everyday decisions and equally far more serious judgments as to what our minds will accept or reject – sets the tone for (or again, viewed in a negative manner, will restrict) all practical decision-making and inter-reactions with others that we experience throughout our lives.

And that said, for any person who at any stage in their life comes to regret past actions or choices, the answer here is "Don't!" In reality, with almost 100% certainty, you could not <u>at that stage</u> have followed any other path than the one you chose to take. If the point must be deliberated, take that time to intake whatever lesson from it that it might hold for you, and then move on.

Chapter 12

The Way We Are
Venturing out Into the World
Coming up Against Different Cultures

If you meet a man with orange eyes,
    And you pause to think and ask him why,
    Do not be surprised if he replies:
    "It's just my disguise.
    But incidentally;
    Why are your eyes so blue?"
(With an acknowledgement to whoever penned the original version of "Going to St. Ives.")

***

[12.1] Losing control of the storyline:

Human beings, both as individuals and as a representative of any social grouping, like to place themselves central to the text. Invariably, they are the norm, and it is always 'the other' who is described as different (/strange/ abnormal). When you come up against someone you find 'different', you have to be aware that in the same manner that you cannot understand (/accept) them, they are just as likely to be rejecting you. And understanding that in many ways this is no more than a defensive posture, you could equally say that to the degree you are afraid of them disturbing you in your comfortably set ways, they also fear the coming of you and yours.

Living in any society will require the determination of a balance between what is required to give a person peace of mind (/a sense of security) and the ability as necessary to intake concepts that are, by degree; different, foreign, alien, offensive, etc. Not so many generations ago, most adults could carry on with their lives without any real need to understand anything beyond their own personal horizon – what they had been taught to accept as a child. However, if you wish to go out into in this hyper-connected modern world, a minimal understanding of the fact that other lifestyles and approaches exist, and are in their respective societies considered equally valid, becomes essential. To question one's identity requires a considerable degree self-examination and careful consideration of 'what is' – or perhaps more importantly 'what isn't', i.e., all the things that you did not grow up accepting as normal.

For most people, this is going to require a drawn-out process very possibly over a period of a number of years, and also it is easy to recognise that almost inevitably, the world being too big of place, too full of variety for any one person to intake as a whole, this process is going to have its limits. That said, I suspect some basic grasp of the concept at as early an age as possible would do no harm.

[12.2] "I have the right to dress (/speak) as I wish."

"Of course. But do not assume that is going to be automatically appreciated, or accepted, in every neighbourhood you choose to walk."

Public displays of any strong (particularly, religious) affiliation; wearing an oversized cross or any religious habit; Jewish men wearing yarmulke skullcaps or Muslim women wearing the burka; turbans and long beards, etc., all of which stand out and misinterpreted can stand out in a highly aggressive manner – the wearer very easily appearing to be challenging that society's (religious or other) standards – for that reason alone do require some consideration.

Having lived in Saudi Arabia, I have no personal problem with women wearing a burka, although I can easily understand the average Westerner feeling extremely uncomfortable with such a person's presence in their society. The unknown is invariably threatening, and not having a person's face or hand movements in easy view – both areas in which we are trained to read and react to – will inevitably be highly disconcerting. And in fairness to both sides, to any man or woman who insists on the right of Muslim women to wear a burka in Western society: "Why should that be acceptable while it is considered wrong (/totally unacceptable) in any majority Muslim society to have women at the beach in bikinis?" (WGFTG!)

Strongly religious people, who will commonly assume that their religion bestows the right to dress as they choose, may find it difficult to appreciate the following, but any of the above in the wrong country or social setting can be perceived in exactly the same manner as large proportions of many societies will view bicycle gangs in leather and chains, gays in drag, overly obvious prostitutes, those who flaunt their wealth, drug addicts; nose rings and tattoos, blacks, Asians, coloured people or whites; the excessively tall, short, overweight; loud Americans! loud Japanese! loud Chinese! loud Australians! or the 'foreign' of any stripe, etc. etc.

(People from any country, when they are traveling in groups, excited to be abroad for the first time and equally knowing that they are not going to be understood, will not take any particular trouble to lower their voices. At the same time, when you are listening to a language which is completely foreign to your ears, a hundred voices at the breakfast buffet repeating simple statements such as. "That looks delicious!" "I had that yesterday," and "What time are we leaving this morning?" can, in its unrestrained volume, easily register as an encroachment into one's personal space. And every large group, from whatever country – including your own – will be perceived in precisely this manner.)

Understanding that many people do have no choice in the above matters, (you cannot change your nationality, colour or height, and you are not going to shave a beard or remove a turban merely to meet the other's convenience), it is equally true that, whenever you find yourself in another country or entering a community with which you are not familiar, the chances of you finding yourself unwelcomed – stared at, physically avoided, or possibly in the worst cases, placed at the end of verbal abuse or even attacked – simply based on your appearance, are going to be far higher than might initially be imagined.

(Cairns, Australia, 2001.) Returning to our hotel room after breakfast, an older Australian lady walking ahead of me, without any warning, turned to greet me with a somewhat agitated; "Aren't Japanese groups incredibly noisy?" (I don't think she had noticed Koji behind me. It was a Japanese-owned hotel, but there were no other Asians on our floor. Also, there was the fact that the groups in the dining room had been Chinese and Korean, but they were, I admit, Asian and noisy.) However, taken aback both by the suddenness of the situation and the seemingly undue aggressiveness in her voice, the only reply that I could come up with was, "I live in Japan," this resulting in an abrupt disconnect (/shocked silence / 'mujun' [5.11]), requiring me to make a quick follow up with, "I have been there since I was young," (hopefully read on her side as, "I was born there,") as an attempt to mollify, which in fact it did apparently do to some degree, bringing on a facial expression which I could only read as something close to ("Presumably, in that case, it cannot be helped!") commiseration, upon which, as we reached our room, she left us to be.

[12.3] Cues and Miscues. Crossed signals:

Flying from Japan to England with Koji, shortly before our plane was due to land, the British stewardess who was handing out disembarkation cards politely asked Koji whether he had a British passport, to which he answered "No." She then, after the briefest of glances in my direction and with no further comment, gave him, and then me, cards to be filled in. This being a little too much (I, too, having a certain pride), I returned mine with a polite (Excuse me, but!) "I am British," to which she appeared quite startled. And it was only after landing safely, when we were in line at customs, standing behind a rather stiff-looking Englishman in tweeds, that it came to me that I was wearing a pair of bright canary-yellow trousers (in fashion that summer in Japan) and that that might perhaps have been the reason for the misunderstanding.

Many years ago, acting as a (rather nervous, first-time) interpreter for a Japanese magazine interview with a famous French ballet company, which involved the Italian male lead speaking in French to another member of the group, who then spoke to me in English, which I translated into Japanese, things were not going very well. Basically, the other side didn't trust me: They clearly didn't think I was getting things through, and as we had relatively little time to complete the interview – we were at an official farewell party being given by the city authorities – the Japanese reporter was getting increasingly frustrated. And then suddenly, without giving any particular thought to the matter, I began to imitate the Italian French pair and wave my hands and arms around in the closest I could get to a 'Continental manner'. And it worked. (They were instantly at ease.) Both of them broke into big smiles, and everyone relaxed, and we got a very nice interview. And if any conclusion is required here, you are what you appear to be would seem a fair comment.

My present partner, Kensuke, walking around in town, blends in completely as the Japanese person he is. However, particularly in the summer, when his slightly darker-textured skin develops into a full tan, he could easily be misrecognised as anything from Southeast Asian to Mediterranean in origin. (At one point, I actually found a photograph in the newspaper of man in Bangladesh who, at that angle, appeared identical.) And together in town, simply the fact that he is with me identifies him in the average Japanese eye as 'foreign' (this even on our visit to his home-island way down in the south, where a vendor at a local stall actually complimented him on the "good level of his Japanese!"), this initially providing a certain amount of amusement for the both of us. However, after seven years, it has also had the somewhat unexpected result of providing a real, in-time, 'foreigner-in-Japan' experience for him, this developing to the point that he has actually come close to blowing up in anger at the manner (as described in Cpt 5) he was being treated by his compatriots.

Everyone claims to be able to, but exactly how does one decide on another person's nationality or background?

[12.4] Recognising your limitations:

Mindset:

Reactions to unforeseen or unwelcome events will very often be determined by the mood you happen to be in at the time: On a good day they can be passed off with a short laugh or a mild shrug, while on a bad day they might result in a burst of anger. In contrast, a 'mindset' could perhaps best be taken as a mood that has hardened into a set habit, and in this sense, can very commonly predict outcomes.

Henry:

From northern New Zealand and coming to Japan for the first time in his early fifties, he discovered the world of men. (He had had girlfriends but never married.) Within a year, he had found a Japanese partner, and shortly after, moving in that same world, we met and became friends, on the whole getting on very well together, his younger partner (we are still friends) also being good fun. However, six years later, really having no choice in the matter, he left. And if I were to make one claim as to why, I would have to say it was 'mindset'.

There was, in fact, nothing that was wrong here at all, nothing that could have been changed; The odds against him succeeding were just too high. Being very intelligent, he tried exceptionally hard with the language, the local customs, and his partner, but he had come here (at least, what proved for him to be) too late in life. A trained lawyer with good social connections in his own country, he had naturally grown to expect things being done in a certain manner, and if there were problems, he knew how to overcome them without any particular effort or stress on his part. He was 'nicely settled'. Put with a slightly negative nuance, this would be 'set in his ways'. (It may actually be that he came to Japan to get out of this settled existence.) And now, in a new environment and faced with a completely new set of rules and configurations, he was lost. If he had a limited himself to the idea of one or two (even three) years in the country, I don't think that there would've been the same problem, but he was serious about his relationship, which, for every reason, could not be taken back with him to his home country, and he had decided to give it a go, even though from quite early on it was apparent that he was in many ways simply out of his depth. And the frustrations built; one at a time, small things, seemingly unimportant at first, but then developing that overly rapid exponential growth that they will when they never cease to cease; until, at some point, for whatever final reason, it became too much.

And that was it. And from that point onwards his brain became determined to find fault with all those 'facts of life' that he could no longer control, everything that didn't match what he had come throughout his life to understand as 'the order of things'. Going into a bank, he would blow up at the teller – for the simple reason that they didn't handle checks in the same way that they would've been handled in New Zealand. Or he would pick on the way food was served in a restaurant. Or, on another day, it would be a complaint about how long it took for his students to begin to understand 'the basics' of the English language. And each of these (in themselves seemingly minor) incidents, together with countless other perceived slights (including all the disagreements he had with his partner), were, over the months and years, cultivated into what became a 'narrative of grievances', proving to his mind (/his trained web of established thought/ his 'shell') quite how uncivilised (and eventually unliveable in) the whole society here was. On one day in particular, walking up into the mountains, and pausing and looking out over the city, he remarked on quite how drab and dirty it all was, the factory chimneys spewing their never-ending filth high up into the air. He was, in fact, quite correct (it wasn't a nice view), but at that particular time I was musing in my mind as to quite how beautiful the sea in the bay looked reflected in the morning sunlight, both of us, in effect, feeding our own personal narratives; that, I would guess, being why I am still here and why he left.

To give a pleasant ending to the story, although he did leave his Japanese partner here in Japan, when Saburo visited him in both Australia and New

Zealand, they had absolutely no problem together – none of the constant fights they had had while he was here, and in the best way they could – with regular letters and telephone calls in his steadily worsening Japanese and Saburo's bravest efforts at English – they stayed together right to the end.

[12.5] Range:

Everyone has a certain range in which they will feel comfortable interacting with others. Over the years, I have cut a number of people out of my life for the simple reason that our understandings of the world have been so far apart that there no longer has seemed any reason to continue the relationship. That is, the efforts involved did not seem worth the meagre satisfactions that might have been gained if I could, in any way, have communicated in at least some part.

Donald:

Having come to Japan very early on (quite some time before I did) and quickly finding himself a position at a local university (which became his whole career) he took it for granted that every single person he knew or any entity he had any kind of relationship with; colleagues, friends, acquaintances, Japanese society as a whole, and particularly his Japanese partner (originally a student who he had started an affair with) were there to serve his better interests. This in itself would not have mattered, apart from the fact that he also took the greatest pleasure from the denigration of others; colleagues, friends, acquaintances, Japanese society, and again his partner, who took the brunt of a large part of his constant ill-humours. (His partner was also remarkably faithful – actually very loving – to him, even going back to Scotland with him close to the end. This was something that at the time I could not understand, and I actually spoke to the partner a few times about it. However, again, in its own way and as things will, their relationship worked.)

Donald also painted, in watercolours, and visiting one of his later exhibitions where I happened to be the only one there, he took me to a small open bar outside the gallery, where I was made subject to a full hour of his fault-finding and general gripes. (The drinks here did not help.) With Henry (above) in a similar mood, the overall rhythm of the exchange would generally allow me certain points where I could intercede and move our conversation towards lighter subjects and we could enjoy an evening, but here there was no such opening. (This wasn't the first time that I had noticed the matter, but when we were at parties, I could be 'polite' and circulate, but this time this wasn't possible.) And now really understanding quite how far I was outside my comfort zone, I had to say "Enough!" And this became the last time that I really ever bothered to speak with him: It was far too much like hard work. In contrast, Henry could spend any amount of time with him with no problem at all. They had a whole world that overlapped, Henry also being of Scottish origin probably helping a lot. Simply put, Henry's 'range' allowed him to be with both myself and Donald, while my own precluded any meaningful relationship with Donald at all. And again, in the world as it exists, this needs to be accepted as a fact of life. That is:

"That there are people out there that you do not (/will never) like (/agree with/ understand) is to be expected, and that there are people who do not (/will never) like (/agree with/ understand) you is equally normal and to be fully expected."

And, forgetting for the moment that rather inane concept of 'peace' – as in "I want peace in the world," or "Give peace a chance!" – which invariably is couched in one's own terms, that is "Peace as I see it (/from my angle/ on my terms)", if you wish at some point to get together with those 'others' in at least a reasonably civilised manner, perhaps the last phrase in the above sentence should be "to be fully respected."

And as a possible humbling factor, it does need to be understood that one's 'range' as described here is not only your area of comfort but is also a measure of your limitations.

[12.6] Cultural appropriation, interpretations, and cross-cultural references:

"Cultural products move from place to place, from country to country, and morph (/adapt/ are adapted) as they move, this particularly true in the present modern era where imagery is collected and freely dispersed across continents, commonly, if not always, for commercial gain. Words and forms are appropriated and then re-appropriated. No culture ever has (or ever will) remain frozen in time, and no individual, however much they may wish otherwise, is going to prevent this most natural of progressions."

"A rugby anthem's unlikely origins in slavery." (NYT. March 10, 2017)

Commenting on the current usage of the song "Swing Low, Sweet Chariot" (apparently first sung in this manner in response to a hat trick of tries by Chris

Oti, an Englishman of Nigerian descent, in an international match against Ireland in 1988) by supporters of the English international rugby team, the gist of this article was that:

While, in the United States, "Swing Low, Sweet Chariot" enjoys the status of a 19th-century African American spiritual with lyrics invoking the dark past of slavery and oppression, the song in England has been developed as a boisterous drinking song turned sports anthem. Josephine Wright, a professor of music and black studies, who sang it with her family at her mother's burial service, expressed regret that such usage indicated a total lack of understanding of the historical context of the black slave. Also, another professor at the University of Michigan found the "historical amnesia" to be troubling and felt that more education about the song would be of use.

The following response is for the most part addressing any Black-Americans who might be reading the book, but the point is valid for anyone, in any country, anywhere.

This is not in any manner a problem of "historical amnesia," at least certainly not in the sense of loss of memory. Almost without any doubt, the very few English people who have any deep understanding of the history of black slavery in America are going to be highly trained specialists, and thus very few and far between.

I do not know what an equivalent curriculum would be for an average American student, but studying at grammar school so many years ago (my middle brother with his secondary education would not come anywhere near this in what he was expected to cover), we first had to memorise 1,500 years plus of our own (UK) history (kings and queens, et al), followed by 'British' history (our own colonies and their interactions with those of all the other European powers) right around the world – the US actually appearing as a relatively minor actor in this area (if I remember correctly, you did throw us out at one point!) – and then European history (all its wars and constantly changing boundaries) to master. This was all before I was seventeen. And this being our system at the time, and not studying any history at university, my education in this area stopped at 1914, essentially resulting in me being given no information on anything related to either of the two World Wars. I ended up reading about World War II, both on the European front and (living in Japan) in Asia after I came to Japan. Also, having a direct interest in both countries, I have read books on both Japanese and Korean history. However, my knowledge of the black experience in America, with which I have complete sympathy, has on the whole (of necessity – everyone is limited as to what we can do in the short time we are here) come from general reading and movies. The world is a very large place, and things being as they are, you cannot expect (in the end what amounts to) your very small voices to carry that far.

And quite separately, as an English rugby player's side of the story:

My one memory of singing "Swing Low" – together with the requisite hand gestures, devised by who or when I do not know, but most certainly including one or two of which were very deliberately vulgar – was in 1964-65 (?), as a member of my college rugby team returning by coach from Twickenham Stadium after watching an England-New Zealand All Blacks game. I would note here that even fifty years ago, the song had a long history, and we were very clearly taking part in what we understood as 'a tradition'. However, that apart, my guess as to why a clearly spiritual song should have inspired this treatment is most importantly, 'that being a spiritual song, it was understood as religious', and therefore – in the men's world tradition of sailors and pub-drinkers, it was (again, rightly or wrongly) considered open game for this type of adaptation. As related examples, all Americans use "Oh, my God!" (Originally used as a curse word) without a blink of an eyelid, and "Bloody", as in "Bloody this!" and "Bloody that!" (Used in England to express anger or frustration – basically in the same manner as "f…king" is used in America) is a contraction of "By my lady!" – the lady here being Mary, the mother of Jesus.

And for the record, "f…k" (with its very nasty, aggressive sexual contexts, and when I was young considered to be a 'No, no!' word, particularly in front of ladies – my mother was unaware of the word [7.24]) – is now used as common currency worldwide, fully popularised initially as I understand it by black Americans. (Thank you for your trouble.) Then again, for some reason I cannot understand, the word is not permitted in print, although the word 'shag', which is identical in meaning (presumably because it is British, that is, in this case 'foreign') is considered quite acceptable. If you really wish to insist on keeping your own, in this case most certainly I would agree. Unfortunately, this is not how the world works.

However, to come back to the song, I do remember it at the time as having a very beautiful, uplifting melody and lyric, and that it was also great fun to sing – perfect, as far as I can see, for its present use (without the sign language) as a sports anthem. I actually saw the scene which was presumably responsible for producing this article on a news programme here in Japan, and it being a part of *my* history, and more particularly my youth – which at seventy, is very precious to *me* – it quite truly moved me. But regardless of whatever I may say, more than anything, in England, it is understood as a fully integrated part of English rugby culture, which I doubt, even if you could get them to follow its historical background, you are going to stop a crowd of that size from using. And, as to the last time I personally heard it sung, this was by a young <u>black</u> Scottish man who was teaching it (hand gestures and all) via Skype to a young Chinese man in Hong Kong (both laughing their heads off, as young people are apt to do with this kind of material). This was, I admit, a scene from a movie ("I'm Daniel Blake." 2016. Director, Ken Loach), but it was expressing a reality that, much as I understand you wish it might not be so, I doubt any 'education' is going to change. (As a general observation here, I have noted that when young people from any country are learning a foreign language, almost invariably they very quickly pick up on curse words, which they then love to sling around quite freely, in most cases because they do not understand the true strength of the words or gestures they are using and therefore cannot understand quite how offensive they are being.)

And to the lady who sang the song at her mother's funeral, while fully sympathising, I can only suggest that if you ever actually do get to hear again the song as rendered by a group of rugby supporters, embrace it for what it is, a beautiful and enduring gift from your culture to the rest of the world.

[12.7] Language:

Esperanto, that dream for a world language that all will speak, could never be. The moment it spread beyond certain limits, it would be adapted, transformed, twisted, and torn apart to meet the needs of whatever social group it had been adopted by. This is notably apparent today in the repeated mutations of the English language (not just in the official, English-language nations) as it has spread around the globe. Nowadays, everyone has their own version of 'English', and perhaps, much as it goes against the grain as the English language teacher that I have been all my life, this also has to be understood as unavoidable. People (/peoples) will always want (/need) 'their own'. We are, in the end, comfortable in smaller groups, and part of our self-definition here will involve linguistic mechanisms – either the newly coined fads of young people, the carefully presented scientific/economic jargon of the elite and/or the familiar dialects of one's youth. That is, if there ever was 'one common language', (presumably as spoken by Adam and Eve) the fragmentation process described in the Tower of Babel is in fact nothing more than a foregone conclusion. The French are still not happy with this idea, but you can't have things all ways. If you wish to have your language used internationally, you have to accept that it is to go to be subject to a certain (/considerable) degree of transformation.

[12.8] Sports and food:

The Japanese were delighted when judo became an Olympic sport, that is until competitors from other countries started to take the medals and the International Judo Association took it upon themselves to adjust the rules. And now we get (sometimes quite snide) comments in the media to the effect that the original sport is losing/has lost its 'spirit' – that it is no longer 'Japanese'. (These comments, quite naturally, tend to disappear when the home team is winning.) And the only thing one can say to all this is:

"You send your child out there into the big wide world, and naturally he or she will develop and grow. Judo is no longer Japanese. It is an international sport."

(If the UK ever started complaining about what had been done to the rules of the innumerable sports that had their roots in their respective countries, we would be nowhere. And the world would be far worse off for it.)

And the same thing applies for sushi. That sushi is now internationally recognised is of great pride to all here, but then again, they hate the idea of California Rolls, and a recent comment by an Australian on a television broadcast noting that in Australia they have five basic sauces (not just soy) which they apply to the dish, was met in the studio with expressions of amazement – "This cannot be!" – all round. But this happens in any country. In England, Indian, Pakistani, and Chinese foods have all been adapted very successfully to the local taste, and Japan itself has its own versions of 'curry rice' and 'roast beef' and, to note one of many, the Italian pasta 'Carbonara', none of which have any relationship to the originals, but which they are very happy to consume. In the local shops here, we also have 'English Muffins' – to me an American confection that I first encountered in New York and have never seen in England. And, miracle of miracles, being fully aware of the reputation of white sliced bread in England when I was young, 'English Bread' is actually sold here in town at premium prices. And you can go on and on.

[12.9] Music and songs:

When I first sang the Japanese karaoke version of "My Way", I got what can only be described as a very tepid response, nothing like I normally received when I sang it in English. When I became more familiar with the Japanese, it did eventually come to me that this was directly related to the negation of any strong individuality that exists in Japanese culture, resulting in much milder lyrics. Singing the Japanese version in the manner that I did, with all the bravado and assertiveness that I associated with the Sinatra rendering, would be far beyond the comprehension of any average Japanese person at the time.

The singer, Fubiki Koshiki [4.11], was shown in a recent TV documentary going to France to research what 'real' chanson was about and discovering absolutely nothing that she could empathise with. (She was in a different world.) However, she was an extremely striking performer with a very strong stage presence and, while certainly not Edith Piaf, the (naturally almost exclusively Japanese) audience loved her.

[12.10] Symbolism:

"With symbols (/marks) being used by mankind over thousands of years, it is to be expected that over the ages very similar (even identical) signs, have been used by different cultures in different manners."

What is known as the 'swastika form' has existed for thousands of years in Hinduism, Buddhism, Jainism, Judaism, Christianity, and Islam, and can be found throughout Asia and in many other areas of the world, predating by centuries Hitler's Nazi propagation of the symbol. (Ref: "The Buddhist Swastika (manji) and Hitler's Cross." by the Rev. Kenjitsu Nakagaki, republished with Stone Bridge Press in September 2018.) In other words, if you choose to travel anywhere throughout Asia, at some point you can expect to see the sign. And to anyone considering visiting Japan, you should be aware that it can be found on temple buildings (and as a standard marker on Japanese maps indicating their position), and also on clothing and household items.

Understanding that the symbol as used by Hitler is to be fully condemned, and equally that it is still being used by neo-Nazis and white supremacists to promote hatred, the reality being as it is, perhaps the easiest approach to be taken here is that (in the same manner that the triangles $\triangle$ and $\triangledown$ can be understood as completely different signs), Hitler's cross and all pre-existing symbols actually are quite separate entities – the Buddhist standard version standing square on its facade with left-turning arms, and Hitler's version being right-turning on a 45-degree angle.

To those who strongly object to the swastika mark, I cannot tell you not to hate. That is your (in this case, perfectly understandable) prerogative. But equally, you do not have the right to assume hatred coming from others simply because they own a green frog or have a sign on their wall that appears similar to the one that stirs hatred in you. First learn the difference! And then if you note a white supremacist displaying what is in fact a Buddhist symbol, they should be congratulated on their peaceful ways and let be. And to those who might still object, get practical. You cannot simply eliminate over 2,000 years of history overnight, just at your convenience.

[12.11] Discrimination, real and perceived:

Taking your prejudices with you into a foreign society. Seeing insult or slight where it isn't intended:

A very small (/petite) Japanese lady, probably in her eighties, got seated on the subway here between two average-size foreigners on her right and a very sweet looking, young American man on her left (who also happened to be very tall, large, and black), and as we approached the next station, she suddenly moved off and stood beside the door in the adjoining carriage, apparently waiting to get off. However, she didn't, and noticing this, the black man got rather upset. The way he saw it (he was clearly new in Japan, and he was judging her as he would someone in the US) she was acting in a racist manner. She was, however, as was quite clear to the other four of us, not simply avoiding him because of his colour, although that would be part of the problem. Almost certainly, she had never in her life been in proximity to anyone of his size and blackness and being overpowered (/probably terrified) and unable to cope with the situation, she had been unable to do anything except move away. Also, being Japanese, she had probably deliberately moved into the next car so as not cause offense to anyone, but unfortunately this had had the opposite effect to that intended, and as he got more and more indignant, none of us (I was with Kensuke directly across from them) could do anything except try to laugh the situation away until, very fortunately, she did get off at the following stop.

There are two points to be considered here. First, you have the young man's immediate assumption (presumably coming from his experiences growing up in

America) that he was being discriminated against because (and only because) he was black. And secondly, there was his total inability, as is common to any foreigner, to conceive that there might be reasons other than the ones he was assuming for what had happened, which unfortunately would directly reinforce the initial belief. (It can be noted here that, as a cultural trait, Japanese people among themselves do, whenever possible, prefer to sit with a gap between themselves and the next person. Also, there was the possibility that, not easily being able to see outside the carriage easily, she had mistaken how far the train had got on the line, something which, at my age, I do commonly.) Regardless, this kind of reaction, if not grounded quickly, can easily develop into an obsession, or at its worst something close to paranoia – the self-dug hole in the ground noted in the previous chapter.

All foreigners regularly complain about how they are stared at or made to feel unwelcome, particularly on public transport. I also had numerous similar incidents occur to me (including, early on, walking into a specialist medical clinic shortly along the coast, with the whole waiting room reacting to my presence with a total silence, which then continued through to the moment I left), which over time I did learn to come to terms with. And once you do, you don't notice that invariably empty seat beside you, and one step on, when you relax enough to stop sending out those excessively self-conscious vibes, you find that empty place filling naturally.

In my mid-thirties in an underground station in Kobe: An old Japanese lady in her late seventies or eighties, who was clearly confused, looked up and down the somewhat sparsely populated platform before walking a hundred yards or so to where I was standing, and avoiding three or four Japanese on the way, to ask me (the only foreigner present) what train she should take. Naturally, I told her, and she thanked me.

[12.12]

Baye McNeil, a Black-American who has been writing columns for the Japan Times Community Page over the past few years, started off attempting to record the 'black experience' in Japan, including the both good and bad experiences of the large number of Africans who now live here. This being perfectly reasonable (actually highly commendable, and equally interesting in the sense that he has picked up a number of success stories in the black community), the only comment that I can make here is that every single discriminatory event that he has noted as part of that 'black experience', (including being repeatedly stopped in town – literally every hundred yards or so – by overly zealous police officers to have one's identity checked), I also personally experienced learning to live here as a young, white Englishman. That is, in the end, I find it very difficult to see quite what is 'black' in there.

In one of his earlier columns – "Bring back that Kobe feeling, 'cause it's gone, gone, gone." – Mr McNeil noted that on a visit to Kobe to attend a foreign writer's conference, he was pleasantly surprised to find that, on the trains in town, nobody was looking at him – no one recognising (even, considering) his 'blackness' as of any importance in their lives. Considering the above story, it may have been that he was lucky in his encounters here, or perhaps it is that we are just that much more laid back in this area generally. However, in the same article, he also did note being upset about the need to argue with a Scottish man (in his words, "an arrogant European") about the (theoretical) usage of the 'n' word by white people – the idea that if black people can use it, why not him?

Fully understanding his reactions here, I can only say that, as with the above case of "Swing Low", the matter of 'colour' (/slavery) for Americans (Black or White) naturally is a highly emotional issue. However, such is not the case for any average person with a European background (or for that matter, although they may face prejudices of their own, any black person who has come to Japan directly from Africa), and that in this respect, such a person cannot be expected to approach that subject in other than what will appear to an American to be a cool, cerebral (/arrogant?) fashion. And beyond that, I can only assume that either (it being firmly embedded in every Scotsman's blood), the man was having someone on, or – equally possible – he was merely expressing himself as any serious adult person (and there are many in life) attending a serious writer's conference might be likely to assume automatic.

[12.13] Names and associations: Japs, Gaijin, and "The tale of a golliwog" (with a suitably happy ending):

During World War II, the word Japs came to be used in a highly derogatory manner by the American and allied troops fighting in the Far East, and at the time I came to Japan it was a word that was carefully avoided on all sides. However, shortly after I arrived, a group of young Japanese chose to create their own brand, "Japs," even opening a shop on one of the main streets in town. I would imagine that this was done in the same spirit as with the 'n' word above or gays choosing to refer to themselves as 'queer', the principle being to remove the sting. The brand itself never really took off, the shop lasting possibly five or six years, but it was a stand being made, which I could follow. It was also around this time that my parents visited for the first time, and my father, for whatever reason, took it upon himself to tease all my Japanese friends and acquaintances by using "simple English" – which to him meant Northern English dialect (which, naturally, none of them could understand), and also – just for the fun of it – the word Japs. This latter point of insistence became a little tricky for me, but my father being my father would have nothing of it: "'Japs' being nothing more than an abbreviation of 'Japanese', what was the problem?" And, actually, having been stationed in northern Scotland during the war, that is not directly involved in any direct confrontations with Japanese troops, he was, on the one side, being truthful. He, of course, knew that there could be other interpretations, but he was having fun, and in the end, I gave up and just let him have his way with them. Either way, most of what he was saying was to them unintelligible, and they on their side, if they had picked it up, hopefully would have had no problem understanding that there was no ill-intention involved.

Gaijin:
Gaikokujin is the formal word in Japanese for 'foreigner', with the abbreviation gaijin also very commonly used throughout the society, and for at least the first fifteen years I was here, in the foreign community it was generally taken that they were interchangeable. At least, I never heard anyone say otherwise.

Koji's niece, Kaori, when she was very young and beginning to understand differences, at one point worked it out that I was a 'gaijin', only to have her parents correct her and explain that I was an 'igirisujin' (Englishman) [10.2]. Consequently, the next day walking around in town (at that time, they were living in a port city), every foreigner we met was pointed out very proudly as an 'igirisujin', and nothing could be said to persuade her otherwise. If her uncle was an igirisujin, then naturally the others must also be so. And as adults, we all took it with the serious wink that it fully deserved.

And then fifteen or so years on, we had a new, somewhat aggressive American columnist (See "Law," [15.13]) on our community page in the English newspaper, and suddenly all the little children running around shouting "Gaijin!" at foreigners were said to be doing it with the full intention of being rude, the logic appearing to be that, as gaijin is an abbreviation of the more formal (to his mind, 'correct') gaikokujin, it must be insulting in the same manner that Japs is a derogatory version of Japanese. And, with no other notice given, we had people writing to the newspaper horrified about how rudely they were being treated walking around in town. And as far as I know, this particular interpretation has never been corrected, but even now I still refer to myself personally as a gaijin, and nobody (at least, in this neck of the woods) seems to find it in any sense irregular.

The tale of a golliwog:

My fascination with golliwogs began when, as a child of seven or eight, I started collecting the full series of stamps that were offered on the Robertson jam jars sold in my father's shop (It wasn't until I was at university that I came to understand the word Wog as used in a derogatory manner – as in "Wogs begin at Calais," the title of a highly-attended university-society debate.) And then shortly after we moved to our new home away from the shop, I remember coming home to find my mother and grandmother seated on the living room couch hard at work sewing for me what became a true and steady friend: my own, cotton-wool stuffed, black satin golliwog, complete with blue shorts, a red jacket, buttons for eyes and strip of fur for hair, with a nose and mouth embroidered in to complete the effect. And taken into bed at night (my brothers both had teddy bears), I hugged it tight – right the way through until it was no longer in any condition to be used – and even then, for a long time, I refused to let my mother throw it out. And all my life, from Oxford to London and Saudi Arabia, and right through, I have never had any problem at all in relating to any black person I have ever met.

[12.14] Storytelling:

"All people live, making choices and expressing themselves, in accordance with the age they live in and to criticise them for that is to misunderstand the inadequacies of your own."[19]

In consequence, any film, book, stage play, musical or other work of art produced in the past has to be understood as created specifically for the audience of its day, and, regardless of whatever reason you might think otherwise, judged

---

[19] Or perhaps put more directly: "So confident that others in their time were wrong, what makes you feel that you, in your age, are right?"

as such. (This equally applies to all criticisms of historical figures and their likenesses.)

"Nobody likes to be viewed other than they like to think of themselves, particularly if the opinion can be construed in any manner as demeaning or critical. That said, young people everywhere need to understand that you are not only the person you consider yourself to be, but also a person as observed through other (not necessarily generous) people's eyes, and there is, never has been and never will be any way of avoiding this."

"Mockingbird reconsidered." Book review by Roxane Gay (black author) (NYT. 19. 6. 2018)

The review itself here is irrelevant, but I would like to pick up two points, common to a large number of reviews and recent newspaper articles. The reviewer naturally notes her personal dislike of the original story and film and describes them as "outright racist," this together with the claim that the black characters are no more than "narrative devices" and not fully realised as human beings. (I have noted similar criticisms regularly occurring in reviews about books written by men but including only "shallow descriptions" of the women in the story.)

To take the two points separately:

"If the racism had not been explicit, the story would have lost a large part of its meaning."

(You cannot dress up violence (/violation) to be anything other than it is, not if you wish to have the truth out.) And equally, this is why the story is of value today, not to black Americans, but there are an incredible number of people around the world who need to develop some sense of what racism in America means, if only to give them a necessary opening to the reality of similarities in their own societies.

Secondly (fully understanding the concept of "characters merely being 'narrative devices'" as a criticism):

Considering the reality of black-white relationships at the time, does Ms Gay think that a <u>black woman</u> in the same period and situation would have had sufficient knowledge to write about white people as "fully realised human beings," not merely, (to paraphrase), "figures onto which the black people around them can project various thoughts and feelings"? As a gay man, if I were to include a lesbian character in any fiction I wrote today, with my very minimal background in the area, I would not even attempt to include other than a light sketch of the character. (If I had a close lesbian friend who would agree to being interviewed to allow me enough background to introduce her as a (fictionalised) central character, and presumably if she vetted the results before any publication, I might get something closer to reality, but presumably such a person would not have been automatically available at the time Mockingbird was written.)

I cannot understand modern reviewers' apparent inability to understand the impossibility of not writing as the person you are. No single human being, and this includes any person who puts words to paper, can view the world in any other way than they know it. Any male author can only write about women as he has been exposed to them (through his education and personal experience), and this is exactly the same for any woman who wishes to write about men, and in all cases, they will be "projecting their own thoughts and feelings" (and writing from a highly limited perspective – the true "World according to Garp!"). This is what any and every author (good or bad) does and is in fact the whole purpose (admitted or otherwise) of writing the book in the first place.

And if, as a young writer, you believe you have any understanding at all of how a person's views on 'life' change as their age changes, sincerely, hang around a little. At the ages of 40, 50 and then 60, I was told to my face (and as you might understand, did not appreciate) that I was "still young," but as each decade passed, I did come to recognise my way of thinking changing – not in the matter of knowledge accumulated, but rather the manner in which (/the angle from which) my mind was approaching that same knowledge. At the same time, I have had the experience of being young, to which you might say, "but not as I (/we) do," and that is exactly the point. As with the above example of lesbians, I am incapable of imagining growing up not understanding life before social media, certainly not with any reality. Presumably, if I studied the matter, I could work the idea into some form of fantasy, but that would most definitely be my limit. Go ahead and write your own!

And in the end, the real point to all of the above becomes:

"Why do Black Americans keep insisting on the understanding of others, which by definition is impossible?" I do not have a Black American's background, and for that simple reason could never ever understand 'racism' as a black American does. (As a gay person, I do understand hurt.)

***

"Don't push others away, identifying with your own group to the extent that you are rejecting all who might otherwise have some sympathy for your position."

"Hallelujah Baby" [1.13], seen so long ago in New York, was a tale of American Blacks coming into their own, and beyond that, in the finale, where the heroine finally comes into a realisation of her own (black, white or whatever!) humanity, it became for me also, a young white, English, gay man, out of my country for the first time, a celebration of life, instilling in me a total joy of being. And having based my whole life on that, I have come to find the repeated negativity that I see reported today, particularly in the black community, something more than disheartening.

[12.15] And for all:

The ease of modern travel and tourism has worked remarkably to reduce the sense that we are in reality living on a planet both of considerable size and with a population of (as of May 2018) 7.6 billion people, each one of us with very distinctive approaches to life as we experience it. And in light of this fact, there would seem no reason at all that you personally should expect anyone to like, respect, or even consider your existence of importance merely due to the fact that you are religious or, for that matter, gay, heterosexual, American, Japanese or whatever. In the end, you stand by yourself, and presumably will be judged by the people you meet in accordance with the way you interact with them. And if you go out of your way to offend, or alternatively do not make any effort not to be perceived as offending, naturally troubles will ensue.

That you may protest that this is "not as it should be" is easily understood, but that it is so is something that cannot be avoided, and – this addressing every one of the 7.6 billion persons concerned – merely professing that you personally are "being wronged" is not going to get you anywhere.

In all fairness, if you expect to be treated in a certain manner, surely it is incumbent that you consider how others might wish to be treated, the commensurate phrase here being "consideration for others." And if you are not prepared to go that way, you are perfectly entitled to your choice.

"What is good for the goose is good for the gander!"

Chapter 13

The Way We Are
Understanding Formative Influences:
Religion and Religious Principles

As a statement of intent: "Every single person around the world, wherever they live, is entitled to his or her own spiritual beliefs; their personal interpretation of God, Allah, gods, Buddha, afterlife, ghosts and spirits, otherworldly elements, etc., and equally all persons are free to exercise their right to doubt or deny the existence of any such God, gods, etc."

The following is not in any manner intended to deny anyone of their beliefs, i.e. enter into any arguments as to the reality of God or Buddha or…but rather to list certain points that I have occurred to me on such matters. Also, it must be understood that all comments are limited to personal experience and observation rather than any reading of religious texts. I only recently attempted to read anything of any detail on Buddhism, Taoism, Hinduism, the Jewish diaspora, the Egyptian pantheon of gods, etc., and this only briefly.

[13.1] Where I feel I personally benefited from my exposure to church teachings:

My parents were not – other than on the occasional Christmas, when we attended as a family – regular churchgoers, but as a small child, I was sent to Sunday School at our local Methodist church, where I learned what you might call the basics: caring for (/trying not to hurt) others, not to steal or tell lies. (These, I would submit, are fundamental requirements for any society that wishes to promote its own stability.) I also attended the same church with my Boy Scouts group once a month, after which we paraded through the local neighbourhood, thus contributing to the sense of a local community. However, it was only on my recent forays onto the Internet, reading that Methodism in the UK gives special emphasis to actions which bring justice to the poor and disadvantaged, that I realised quite how much must have been instilled in terms of certain basics that have followed me through my life. I also admit to being intrigued by the fact that the church was given its name due to the fact that John Wesley, the founder, chose a 'methodical' approach in his analysis of the workings of the Church of England, to which at that time he belonged. (cf. The Dalai Lama's comment on the need to think [7.2].)

At the same time, there was nothing that held me in any spiritual sense. There was no sense at all of awe or reverence, and even very recently, re-visiting the UK after a long period of absence, I found a number of churches and chapels where I could very easily understand people being at peace and praying, but personally I felt no sense that I needed such a place. I am very fond of churches, shrines, and temples for their innate quiet and beauty, but I can be at peace in a garden, park or on a mountain trail, and people generally, if they really care to, can surely pray anywhere.

As noted in earlier chapters, I have stolen (once) and deliberately lied (twice), and I am fully aware that I have hurt (hopefully, a limited number of) other people at various times during my life, but, that said, I do very much value those teachings that were imbued at that early age.

I can also understand that belonging to a religious group, as with any grouping of similarly minded people, can very easily provide a sense of companionship (/belonging) and a stable base from which to view this somewhat erratic world, with the proviso that any excessive emphasis on inclusion will, of necessity, produce exclusion. (See next chapter.) But, on balance, I feel that this could also be said for any reasonably closely knit group, and of itself cannot truly be criticised.

Love: I have commented on love in the personal sphere in [9.9], but in a religious context, and if it is to have any meaning, it is perhaps – as difficult as it might be – showing respect for others; their thoughts and beliefs, and I cannot go beyond this.

[13.2] Gripes:

I can easily follow that 'a truth' in a religious sense may be considered 'something that is believed', (and here again, I will emphasise that every individual is fully entitled to their beliefs), but if, as many strongly religious people claim, such truths should be considered 'inarguable facts', I am sorry but this I do not accept, certainly not in the sense that "I can see the sea from my window," or "Iron sinks in water," are 'facts'.

From Wikipedia: As percentages of the world's population; Christianity 31.5%, Islam 23.2%, Irreligious 16.3%, Hinduism 15%, Buddhism 7.1%, Folk religions 5.9%, Others (1%).

Religious leaders around the world invariably like to represent themselves as "of the true faith," which may be stated as quite reasonable, on the understanding that there are thousands (and possibly tens of thousands) of other claimants to that same title, who all would seemingly, by virtue of the strength of their beliefs and/or representation, have the right to make that same call.

[13.3] Interpretations of "God's will":

I cannot understand how Catholic priests, who in reality can have no understanding at all of what a marriage really involves, and certainly not in the modern sense, can consider themselves in any manner qualified to determine what might be considered "God's will" in this area.

A number of years ago, the head of the Catholic Church (or possibly a group of Cardinals), referring to the Church's ban on use of condoms, issued an edict about "sex used other than for procreation," stating essentially (I don't have the exact quote) that utilising sex for pleasure was only for (/done by) animals. My partner Koji's immediate reaction here was to note that, if anything, the opposite is true, i.e., that animals on the whole, at least as far as our present knowledge goes, with few exceptions, use sex essentially as a means of procreation. It is only human beings that have developed the intellectual capacity to use sex, among other things, to demean (as in rape or molestation, and perhaps where you would consider a condom might come in useful), as a means of obtaining erotic satisfaction or, in many cases, to demonstrate a sense of caring. (That, the hierarchy disapproves of!)

And ranking along with the "You can be heterosexual, but you mustn't have sex (other than how and when we tell you)" of the Catholics, from the Mormon church, we have: "You can be gay, but you can't act on it!" Particularly when one considers the original acceptance of polygamy in this sect, this has to amount to something close to a joke. (Who or what exactly do you think we are?)

"Religion offers a path from self-reflection and confession to atonement and absolution." (Quoted from article in the NYT.)

Also regarding the Catholic/High Church: I can understand forgiveness as a means of easing a person's worries or distress. However, if, as a believer, you accept confessions as a priest's assurances of exoneration from sin at face value, and you choose to think about it a little carefully, provided you make sure you confess everything you have done before you die, essentially you are free to commit any sin you care to name and still get to go to heaven. And what exactly, in terms of creating a 'good' society, which I would assume is one of the aims of the church, is the point in that?

[13.4] Heaven and Hell:

When speaking to a child who is meeting the concept of death for the first time, it is easy to understand the usage of the word 'heaven' (a beautiful, safe place, where nothing can harm you) as a means of providing comfort. Also, the threat of hell is easily understandable. All societies, regardless of any religious affiliation, with almost complete certainty, have similar expressions. However, it is when these words are used as absolutes (as they are by many religious entities with the aim of exercising control over believers) that my mind starts to query.

There is an old Irish song, "Fiddler's Green," where a fisherman is contemplating his death and imagining his own version of a heaven of "clear skies – far away from the cold coast of Greenland, with dolphins playing in the surf and fish jumping on board at will." And when he returns home; "with no work to do, he can just go to the pub and meet up with the lasses and drink all the beer and rum he wishes for free." (Note that at the time this was written, we are based in a strongly Catholic society,)

The above, naturally, has to be understood as irony (the song is extremely amusing), but equally the words are totally sincere, and essentially, in talking of such a heaven, the writer is doing no more than express a wish to be rid of what he finds cumbersome in life and have at his fingertips everything he takes pleasure from. All of which I find quite reasonable. But I can easily imagine lots of other persons who would not really accept getting rolling drunk (or free rolls in the hay) – everything that the Church officially looks down upon – which are clearly implied here, as their concept of heaven. And if you are really open on this, it would surely all boil down to everyone having what they want and none of the travails of our present existence. And hurrah for that!

And in such a case, what would your personal take on heaven be? Or hell? –

if you choose to list up the things you find cumbersome; talking to people you disagree with, don't find interesting, don't like or, more particularly, don't approve of? Or things you are simply afraid of: spiders ("Lord of the Rings"), rats (George Orwell's "1984"), fire (hell itself), pain (/sickness/ torture), the uncertainties of life and death? I am assuming here that an admission to an 'eternal' heaven will remove the need for consideration of this final point. And as a separate point, how is it explained as possible for an un-embodied spirit to feel pain?

And if I may, as a personal take:

This world as heaven or hell:
How unwise the parent who, in threatening hell, condemns their child to just such a fate, as they find themselves entrapped in that same web.

How wise the child who, falling into hell, in doing so unfolds his or her mind to the possibilities of another, more encompassing – and possibly more generous world.

And in this sense, I would posit that (at least while you are alive) you are where you choose to put yourself.

[13.5] Judaism:

From "Child": On the wherewithal of war. "Why should you hate me, who you do not know? First learn who I am, and then if you have reason, let hate come to the fore."

(Early July 2017) Two or three nights ago, two men (stern faces, up close – both, if I am correct, correspondents at the New York Times) burst into my dreams demanding to know if I disliked Jews. And, without any consideration, I replied: "No, I do not dislike Jews." Upon which, they disappeared, and I woke up, and reconsidering for what must be the umpteenth time (I have thought about this a lot!), again I came to the conclusion that: "No, I do not dislike Jews," for the simple reason that I do not know any Jews to dislike. Other than the young Jewish man with whom I visited the Catskills [1.14], the section on which I had just completed and guess would be why the men in the dream appeared in the first place, to my knowledge, I have only met one other person who I would know to have been Jewish – a very pleasant (very polite and at the same time very easy-going) Israeli lady who I met when I was interpreting for a television show introducing different countries' Christmas/New Year dishes and spoke to probably for a total of two or three minutes.

I only read about "Christians holding the Jews responsible for Christ's death" when I was an adult (it was nothing I had ever been introduced to as a child), and the Church itself being of no real consequence to me at this point (either way, I was bound for hell), naturally, this did not register as a reason to dislike Jews.

The Jews as bankers: Some time ago, I read that "historically, in their wanderings, land not being easily accessible, the Jews had no choice but to turn to financing as a means of making a living," which seemed a very reasonable accounting for this situation. However, at the same time, moneylenders, as they used to be referred to, for every reason, are never going to be the most popular of people. (For comments on Israel as a political entity, see [14.5] / [14.6])

At the same time, being resented for controlling wealth is not in any manner a mark of censure limited to the Jewish peoples, another example that comes to mind easily being the Chinese minorities in Indonesia or Malaysia, which are both politically and religiously discriminated against by their respective Muslim majority populations.

[13.6] Islam:

Again, having no real knowledge at all of the Islamic religion, I'm not in any position to make any specific comments here. However, while I was in Saudi Arabia, I was once able to view Islamic law (as I understand it) in action at a public whipping. First, a man in his thirties or early forties was prostrated and his sentence read, whereupon he received a total of fifty lashes, which were clearly intended to be painful. A boy of possibly eleven or twelve years, was then laid in the same position, where he received some twenty hits – the first nineteen of which were delivered with the lightest of hands (he barely winced), and the last with enough intent to let him know what it really felt like, just in case he wished to continue along his present path. Including the public shaming, it seemed a very reasonable dispensation of justice, although I must admit that I would not personally wish to witness a thief having his hand chopped off, or a beheading. One other facet of the law is the opportunity in a serious case for the injured party or their family to forgive the guilty party, right up to the moment of execution, and if you accept forgiveness as a virtue, this seems quite reasonable. However, I have also read of at least a couple of cases where this amounted to allowing the perpetrator(s) to get away with so-called 'honour killings' (invariably of women), which becomes far more questionable. (For Islam as a political entity, see [14.8].)

[13.7] Buddhism:

Zen on the run:

I have in fact met three Buddhist priests in Japan. Two are described below. The third, being the young priest who officiated at Koji's funeral, is included in that section [18.15].

Although there have been recent efforts to change this, over the largest part of my stay here, there has always been a general image promoted here of Buddhist priests as highly solemn and remote. However, in my fifties, I did have the good fortune to have as a private student one priest of about my own age who was remarkably good fun, joking freely about the world in general and with an ever-present smile on his face. Unfortunately, always at death's beck and call (his main job as a priest being to officiate at funerals) and regularly having to cancel or cut off lessons in the middle to bike off to yet again another ceremony, after six months or so, much as we were enjoying ourselves, we had to call it a day.

The second man I briefly met in a gay sauna, recognising him more than anything else by the (immense) size of his legs. We have a Buddhist sect in the Kansai area where, as part of their very strict physical and mental training, acolytes are, with only a thick wooden staff for balance, obliged to rapidly trek up and down around a fixed course on the high mountain side repeatedly without any break for considerable periods of time and in all seasons and weathers – a fixed number of circuits are required every 24 hours – and this particular man had at the time just completed the most difficult version this training, remaining in motion, if my memory serves me correctly (other than for the three hours of sleep allowed each night), for a period of six months, a record which had not been met at the time for some decades. Early on in his challenge, he was shown descending through the woods on a very narrow rocky path on the mountainside at full speed. (The television cameras had to be placed at separate points along the trail to catch brief shots of him as he passed, there being no way they could've followed him at that speed.)

And it can only have been a short time after this was announced that, in the circumstances as described above, I actually met him. He had taken a private room, but with the door left unlocked, people were taking interest and I couldn't help but wait my turn. Best described as a calm presence and clearly physically at his peak, he was lying on his mattress – quite naked apart from a small towel draped across his private parts (standard in all bathhouses in Japan). Neither of us spoke, but he allowed me to touch his legs, before indicating politely that I should not go any further, at which point I left, with presumably the whole process repeated until he found someone who personally met his needs. (Either that or, quite possibly, he slept alone.)

And perhaps to stay on the theme, Ikkyu-san, a Buddhist acolyte who was renowned for having a brilliant mind from a very young age, and who is taught in elementary school textbooks here as an example for young students (he is also a subject of a television manga series), upon reaching the state of 'satori' (enlightenment) [7.31], his purpose in life accomplished, he left his temple to wander, very quickly finding a young woman whose blindness prevented her from recognising the considerable difference in their ages. However, here, for the first time acknowledging the sensuality of his nature, he took her to an inn, and from that time stayed with her right through to the moment of his of death. (This is part of his life is not covered in the standard school curriculum.) From an orthodox Christian outlook, and in the parlance of my youth, he perhaps could be described as a "dirty old man," but it is a fact that both were providing for the other's needs, and I would imagine they would be a very well-balanced pair.

At the time I was considering my life after Koji, I met a similar coupling where a much older man was living with a (from my viewpoint, very attractive) blind man who would be in his early fifties, and the older man, having reached a certain age where he understood that he was no longer capable of carrying out his duties, and this being the way life works here, was looking for a replacement for himself. At this point, I actually indicated an interest, but was politely told that the candidate had to be in his seventies (I would be around sixty at this point), and that was that.

I do understand the deliberate restraint of one's sexual urges as a means of ascetic training. Certain poses in my book on yoga were recommended as suitable for this purpose in particular. However, I do know that (in terms of self-development) there are many other areas in life where control of the impulses can, as necessary, be applied equally effectively.

The afterlife:
And again, Hell: On television here recently, a man who had spent his life assembling a collection of Japanese (Buddhist based) artworks related to hell –

sculptures, paintings, etc. – going back over the past few centuries, showed his favourite print. In it, as one small detail in a whole panorama, a man is shown held upside down, with molten lead being poured into his backside by the most fearsome of devils. And more to the point, he is clearly enjoying it. Personally, although this would not be my choice as a form of relaxation, it does again point to the fact that one man's hell may be another's vacation. And it was very funny!

Buddhism today:
With the present aging of/decline in the population here, particularly in the countryside, a lot of (particularly the less well-known) temples and shrines are finding it difficult to continue, there being no one to take over the day-to-day activities or basic upkeep of the buildings. Also, on a recent visit to a very large temple complex in Kyoto – only slightly off the beaten (that today meaning 'tourist') track, Kensuke, who is Buddhist, was shocked to see the lack of care being given to even the very basics around the grounds: I noted only four people, all older and who I guessed would be local volunteers.

[13.8] Religious practices in Japan:

Buddhism (with its variety of sects – Japanese often registered as believers in more than one), Christianity and Shinto all exist in Japan. All are utilised in some form for weddings, with Buddhist or Christian funerals being the norm. For non-Christian Japanese (the large proportion), Christian-style weddings – either in a church or wedding-hall (where an 'officiating priest', suitably attired, may be hired by the hour) – were originally introduced as a fashionable alternative, which is, in large part, what they remain today.

In the same category of 'imports', you could also include; Christmas – decorations in the streets, trees and cake for the children, and for those who have a partner, a trip to a love hotel on Christmas Eve (apparently, relatively few young men being interested in sex these days [17.2], now going out of fashion) ; Valentine's Day – women originally gave chocolate to the men (including company bosses and English teachers, who were supposed to return the favour on "White (chocolate) Day"), but these days, having got rather fed-up of the whole matter, they tend to use the opportunity to purchase the best quality chocolates for themselves to gorge on; Easter – Easter eggs; and Halloween – dressing up and invading the streets of Shinjuku (Trick or Treat has actually been adopted by some families with children). Note that the easily recognisable common denominator here is 'commercial opportunity'.

[13.9] Shinto:

The one religion here that is native to Japan, goes back in time to include details of the mythological creation of the islands themselves. However, in the present day, at least to the general public, it is far more connected with the processing (including seasonal festivals) of day-to-day living; prayers at shrines invariably being for oneself or family – asking for good health, success in life, help in passing examinations, finding a partner for marriage, etc. And foreigners who are familiar with any of the monotheistic religions (including myself when I first arrived) do find considerable difficulty in identifying it as a 'religion'. On the other side of the coin, Japanese people in general find it very difficult to comprehend the intensity of those who strongly believe in one God. (If I chose to attempt this today, it would have to be some abbreviated form of my presentation on 'joushiki' in [5.4], but I doubt that even that would be truly understandable for any Japanese person who has not lived for a considerably long time outside their own culture.)

The word 'kami' is used in reference to an energy (spirit, essences, or 'god') central to any phenomena that inspires a sense of wonder and awe in the beholder and testifying to the divinity of such a phenomenon. It is considered quite irrelevant as to whether they represent good or evil. Kami and people are not separate; they exist within the same world and share its interrelated complexity. Kami also refers to the singular divinity or sacred essence, that manifests itself in multiple forms such as rocks, trees, rivers, animals, or specific places. (Shinto and worship of Emperor as a kami (a deity in human form) are as commented on in [5.13].)

A Shinto shrine is a building in which a kami is enshrined or housed and is considered a sacred space inside which the kami spirit actually dwells and is accordingly treated with the utmost respect.

On a personal level, and as an example perhaps of how the religions in Japan are intertwined, my greatest problem in terms of comprehension (or more particularly practice) here was at the time of Koji's death [18.15]. The funeral rites, following his family's beliefs (Koji himself was not in any sense religious) were Buddhist, and following those traditions, I kept an altar in the home for the requisite 49 days – at which I prayed every day and, on the assumption that his spirit was still present, I talked with him about things that had happened, or my feelings or whatever – in practice, very much of a healing process. A number of friends who hadn't been able to attend the funeral also came to pay their respects. "Rest in peace!" has a direct equivalent in Japanese. However, also part of the prayers given in a regular Japanese household (following Shinto ritual and including a separate family shrine) include asking the deceased to, "Look over me (and/or our family)," and even a request from the partner to "Let me stay here a little longer," the reason being that, once dead, every person becomes a kami, this idea at the time (particularly as I was translating the word in my mind as "god") very foreign to my thinking. However, put back into its original meaning as "a spirit (/essence) belonging to a world that we do not understand," it does make full sense.

[13.10] Beliefs clashing with modern medicine:

There is a prevalent view in Japanese society (originating in Buddhism) that a dead body should not be violated in any manner, that is, no part should be removed from the body prior to its cremation. Also, although the problem has been around for well over 30 years since heart transplants became technically viable, there is as yet no social consensus on the condition of brain death as against the actual stopping of the heart. A law permitting the donation of organs (including the heart) was passed some 20 years ago, but in the latest figures (2016), only 64 donations were recorded, and there are still regular news reports of parents having to take their young children to America for a heart transplant, even though the cost (invariably the parents have to collect contributions – commonly in the streets) and the unfairness of the situation when viewed from the position of similar parents in the States also waiting in line for organs, have regularly been reported on in the media here. (The figure for donations in Japan is 0.7 per million persons, as against 8.4 for Korea and 26 for America, which amounts to a considerable difference.) I can sympathise with the sentiments, but again they seem to be wanting things both ways, which does not seem a way to go.

And beyond that, on a social level (as with Koji's funeral), you have the deference to family wishes as against those of the individual. If I belonged to a Japanese family, I personally could agree to donate an organ, and then have that wish revoked on my deathbed by one of my parents or another member of my family based on their personal wishes. This is one more area in which I find my basic upbringing clashes directly with local cultural expectations. Quite apart from the practical benefits involved, for an individual to make such a decision is not in any sense easy, and to have that decision open to a second reading by another person (regardless of the relationship) does not seem correct.

[13.11] Using religion (/other religions/other customs) as a vehicle for self-reflection:

At my last exhibition (shortly before I started writing this book), observing that I had photographic images taken in an English cathedral, Japanese temples and a Japanese shrine, a Japanese visitor, seemingly a little confused, asked me why I would have all three in the same room. Considering the fact that all three do co-exist in Japan, this does now appear to be a rather odd question. However, my answer at a time was that they were all in one sense (as with all religious/spiritual beliefs) representing the same truth – at least as representations of a certain aspect of our nature as human beings, all being attempts to make some sense of what we are or where we come from; the nature of the world, disorder and inevitably the nature of the universe.

If you consider a situation where nature was the only teacher available to man (which until very recently was the norm in many places on the earth, and may still be in a few untouched spots), it is easy to imagine both a reverence for and simultaneous fear of the unknown, and at the same time a sense of a life-giving power that envelops all, and these concepts still exist in many societies' philosophies and religious beliefs today. To feel awe in the presence of an ancient tree or rock is even today within reach of many, regardless of their religion. And in the same manner, life being nothing more than a blending of creative and destructive forces (enabling the philosophical realisation that for life to exist, so must death), that Hindus in India should worship Ganesh: The Lord of Beginnings and Remover of Obstacles, and Lord Shiwa: Destroyer of the Universe, as a precondition for its renewal, makes complete sense.

[13.12] A guide to living in the moment – "A-Un":

Throughout my time in Japan, I have received various explanations of the significance of the Chinese guardian lions seen in pairs in front of temples and (in Japan) shrines [6.5], one of the earliest and simplest being that the male lion, on the right with its mouth open, and the female, on the left, its mouth closed, represented the inhaling ("A") and exhaling ("Un") of a single breath, which over time I came to regard as an expression of 'the moment' – that constant state of renewal resulting from the simultaneous creative and destructive processes that exist within all living forms – an ever-present gateway in time that all things that exist must pass through, and what may actually be a truer representation of life and death than our somewhat self-centred notion of birth as 'entering this world' and death as a 'final expiration'. At the same time, walking up through those gates, you are passing through one of those many moments that, regardless of all else, make us unique in our point of reference, that is in our personal relationship with the world – and by extension, the universe. (Photos 4. /5.)

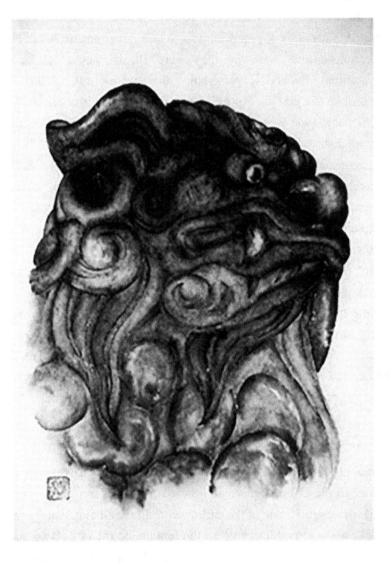

Chinese guardian lions: "A-Un" – "Un" 60 cm X 90 cm

Chinese guardian lions: "A-Un" – "A" 60 cm X 90 cm

[13.13] Hatha Yoga. (Zen):

Disregarding the matter of enlightenment for the moment (the average person does not really have this luxury [13.15]), the following is a brief explanation of the eight to ten years I spent studying Hatha Yoga, which stresses appreciation of how the body functions, meditation being of secondary importance. This was done by myself, using a series of books I happened upon in one our small bookshops in town. (See ref. list. If still in print, highly recommended.) Also, at one point, I did a small amount of the Chinese 'Tai chi', which also requires slow movements and controlled breathing, and which I can understand will easily have the same effect.)

From the beginning, I found it almost impossible just to sit and meditate, but after much study, I did learn that by concentrating on the state of your body – recognising which limbs, muscles, internal organs are being stretched or massaged, the effect of controlled intake and expelling of the breath, deep breathing, etc. – you do eventually reach a stage where the mind is emptied (this perhaps best explained by describing it, as with all sufficiently repeated motions, as the point at which concentration is no longer necessary), which is presumably a similar state to that which meditation alone will induce. I would emphasise that nothing here was learned – each successive realisation coming quite freely during the process of simple repetition, and each leading to yet one more refinement of some particular element within the pose. Also, in time, I found that I was internalising certain events or experiences, or more particularly, my reactions to those events or experiences: In my mid-fifties, even though I had long stopped any serious practice, I would on occasion be suddenly aware of my abdominal muscular system working quite naturally to massage my inner organs in the manner it had been trained so many years earlier. (Thinking now, this was perhaps a warning that I ignored, eventually resulting in my requirement for heart-surgery.) And throughout all the above studies, I sensed it was keeping a calm concentration that was the key. I have noted that in the US recently, Yoga and Zen meditation are being touted as a "road to happiness," but perhaps the aim should more be understood as searching for an inner calm that will then lead to better (/more solid/ happier?) relationships with the people around you.

Breathing:

Beyond the actual poses, learning to breathe well – expanding the lungs to their full extent, holding the breath for long periods with still enough control remaining to then completely expel all air at your chosen speed – required considerable practice, and after a certain time, taking instructions from my text, I took up what I refer to as 'yoga swimming', which I would highly recommend to anyone who, for any reason, is interested in improving their breathing skills. (This can or need not be combined with any standard yoga training. All you need is a pool.) Basically, this amounts to swimming breaststroke with your head immersed at all times in the water. (Speed here is totally irrelevant – you are concentrating on the breathing process.) Initially, one or two strokes is quite sufficient, at which point you forcefully expel all the breath from your lungs into the water, and then raising your head slightly (so that your nose is just above water-level), you allow the vacuum formed in your lungs to work freely to intake a new batch of fresh air through the nose. You do not make any effort to breathe in. Your lungs will do the work for you. And as you continue swimming, you simply repeat the whole process.

Starting this, I found I could quite easily swim 50 to 100 metres, and then as I progressed, the same distances without raising my head from the water. (That is, I was holding my breath for that full length of time.) And at the same time, I managed to continue swimming eventually for distances of up to three to four km without taking a break. (In fact, I found that taking a break would disturb my concentration to the point that I had to leave the pool.) The most important thing here is keeping to your own pace. You cannot force your condition. If initially you can only manage one stroke and then one stroke, stopping in between, that is perfectly satisfactory. And then, taking as long a break as you require, you try again.

FF. The power of the mind (/coordinated movement):

In a lunch break in the sixth form at school, with nothing in particular to do, one of our class friends taught us how to lift a body with nothing more than our little fingers – described below because it actually is considerable fun and does not particularly require any great strength. The person to be lifted is seated on an upright (in our case, a classroom) chair, and the four persons doing the lifting stand two to the left and two to the right, placing their little fingers only under the knee joints and armpits of the sitting person. (At this point, it is a good idea to test how far the body can be lifted upwards from this position. In our case, with each one of us in turn in the seat, we found any movement at all impossible.) The standing persons' hands are now stacked up one at a time (/one over another) in order on top of the seated person's head and the seated person is told to relax fully. The persons standing now breathe in deeply and then fully expel the air from their lungs three times, all the while pushing their hands down firmly onto the seated person's head. Then on a count of three, the little fingers are placed under the respective body joints and the body is lifted into the air. This can be done outdoors, but probably in the sense of understanding quite how high you have gone, it is not a bad idea to do it in a room with a fairly high ceiling, which is what our classroom at the time was. The biggest boy in our group, who was over six feet and considerably overweight with it, went up like a feather and almost hit the ceiling, and when my turn came, I equally went up with no effort at all, and it was only as the ceiling came down on me and I panicked that the spell was broken – the sense of weightlessness was suddenly gone – and I fell.

The same boy also introduced us to the Mayurasana or Peacock Posture yoga position, essentially balancing your body (stretched-out parallel to the floor) on your forearms. This is normally done with palms on the floor, fingers extended toward your feet and elbows tucked in under the abdomen, however he taught us to do it resting our palms on the windowsill of our classroom with our heads poked out into the school yard. Where he got it from – there was no mention at all of yoga – I do not know, but I do remember managing it without any particular trouble, although it is listed in my yoga book as one of the more difficult asanas.

[13.14] What all religions (/beliefs) offer:

All beliefs can be understood as both having a calming influence and providing a sense of stability; of being in control of your life. But then again, this can also be said of the familiarity of everyday routines or habits; watching the sun go down or a child grow.

Also, I have noted that much of what I learned through my yoga exercises (physical exertion, concentration, repetition, balance, controlled breathing, spatial reference) is provided in some manner or other in all the world's religious rituals (strenuous pilgrimages including repeated prostration, kneeling, bowing low, singing, prayer, chants, the Maori extension of the tongue (which is also a yoga exercise), the "Wasshoi" cries used when carrying portable shrines in festivals, etc., etc.) But again, all these also do appear repeatedly in the arts and sports worlds; ballet, opera, folk dances, the playing of musical instruments; in Japan, all the traditional art forms – and, if you wish, Charlie Chaplin-style factory-line work or even pachinko (although the accumulated smoke in the pachinko parlours in Japan, would certainly not help with the breathing processes). Perhaps if there is a difference in any of these, it would be the degree of input (/study/ training) together with what might be considered the ultimate aim of the process.

Also, referring to Voodoo or Shamanism, it could be noted that: in the same sense that placebos used in medical tests are commonly sufficient to cure a disease, what people believe does tend to work.

[13.15] "Come out of your temples":

This was my reaction to what I sensed was an 'inner conversation' with whoever, when they were telling me how I should "control my feelings" and "keep calm at all times," etc. I only have a layman's knowledge, gained mainly from observing (in real life and from TV documentaries) the training monks undergo here but somehow I sensed (and still do) that for all the lectures they may receive and books they study (with no one to disagree with – they are merely following the directions of their superiors), if they really wish to test what they believe, there can be no substitute for a direct involvement with life.

On religious tracts:
Although I can understand the matter as fascinating for certain minds, I have a strong sense that it must be overly easy to get caught up in all the finer nuances of the ancient texts – the 'how many levels of hell there truly are' – all the details that form the fault lines for disagreement, and this in particular when the aim is prove what amounts to a particular sect's 'selling points'.

There are a considerable number of religious speakers on television in Japan who, regardless of any practical understanding, are content to quote excerpts from the scripts – this I suspect intended to create a certain gap that will set them apart as 'knowledgeable beyond' (and therefore not to be questioned). And, on the whole, this type of person, dependent as they are on book-learning, tend to stand out for that fact alone and on the whole do not move. In one particular case, with a priest who did nothing but quote the Buddhist scriptures, I had to conclude that this represented the limits of his world.

And then there are certain people who take their beliefs to a higher level. They have learned to encompass truths based on and at the same time beyond the confines of the teachings of their particular religion – truths related to their existence as human beings.

The son of a top priest at a large temple, determined to be a writer, was given until the age of thirty to pursue his dream, and he used the time wisely – learning about life working in bars and clubs in Tokyo, until, not having managed to produce anything, he returned to the temple as promised to follow in his father's footsteps. And once installed, and reaching the age of forty, he wrote his book, introducing Buddhism to the masses, and it proved a bestseller. And both he and his wife, who was introduced in the same programme, were magnetic.

And, in comparison, there was a lady (very popular on the television circuits) who became a priest rather later in life (that is she did have considerable experience with everyday activities). However, on one programme that I watched (she could be interesting), after a long discussion on 'the ways of the world', she expressed strong surprise – closer perhaps to shock – that the man she had been partnered with (a businessman who had no background at all in religion) should have at least the same – or possibly even deeper understanding of the areas they had been discussing than she did. (I suspect that to her mind, she felt she had studied hard to reach that position, and that it was difficult for her to appreciate that he might have obtained the same understanding quite naturally through his everyday activities.)

[13.16] Different people wearing the same robes:

Years ago, when I was applying for a permanent residence visa from the Japanese government, I was required to obtain a certificate to indicate that I was free from any venereal disease. Even after it is fully cured, it is normal for traces of syphilis to remain in the blood, which in my case (having contracted the virus at university) invariably necessitates a second test to show that I am in fact not a present carrier. The hospital to which I had been sent for the test was operated by a Christian organisation with a large number of nuns involved in the daily handling of patients, and at the time the results of my second test came through, as one of them handed me my official document, she told me that "I was very lucky that they had been able to clear me, or otherwise I would not have been able to receive my visa." Although I did not say anything at the time, this strongly offended. It was not what she said as much as the way she said it, the supercilious tone she employed. Essentially, in her eyes, I did not deserve to receive a visa. She was, of course, entitled to that viewpoint, but on my side, it was none of her business; certainly nothing she should be commenting on, and not in that tone or with that look. At any rate, for a number of years after this, each time I came upon a similarly dressed nun in town – on a bus or train or just passing in the street – I reacted as if it were her. (In some cases, I would deliberately move my position so that the person was not in my sight.)

Fast forward to a TV programme I happened to cut in upon recently, where a nun of the same order was being interviewed about someone (the subject of the programme) she had helped, and in explaining why, she noted that when she was young, in her early twenties, her mother had told her that far more important than her receiving the love of others was that she should offer love unconditionally to others, and at the same time that it had taken her well over 30 years to really understand this. I am not a Christian, and it is strictly of no consequence to me whether an entity that Christian people refer to as "God" exists or otherwise. However, I could understand precisely the feelings that she was expressing. (I have, in my better moments, actually used the identical words myself.) And more particularly, it was fully apparent that she was both speaking from her heart and noting realities that had come directly from her personal experience. And she, also, glowed.

And finally, as suggested reading, particularly for Americans who cringe at the word 'socialist':

From an obituary in the NYT ("Lessons from a 103-year-old Jewish East London Socialist." Daniel Trilling. Nov. 16, 2018.), you have Max Levitas, a Jewish man who was also a full-blooded communist, but used those beliefs throughout his life to protect the groups (Eastern European Jews, Irish, and most recently Muslim) of all the 'ordinary working people' who lived in his neighbourhood in the East End of London.

[13.17] Positioning yourself below the other:

(April 2018.) Talking with a man who was about to start training to become a Buddhist priest, his intention being to replace his father, something that had not attracted when he had been younger, I found the best advice that I could give him was that regardless of how much he studied or the position he attained, he should always understand himself as below those who he was teaching. In his early forties, he seemed to find this somewhat difficult to follow, and thinking now, perhaps an easier explanation might have been "to at all times consider himself in a position to support rather than preach down (/dictate) to" – which I have noted many leaders, regardless of the nation or religion that they are representing, so easily come to assume as their right.

Towards the end of a Korean drama that I watched a few years back, an older, considerably wealthy woman, understanding that she was getting older and that the world she had known as her own was passing beyond her, took herself for possibly a final visit to the family temple. I do not know whether this was peculiar to her sect or rather a manifestation of her state of mind at that time, but when she kneeled and bowed in prayer before the main statue of Buddha in the temple, she did so with her hands fully opened and palms raised upwards to the sky, which is the first time that I had seen an example of this in any religious situation anywhere. (It may be common, but it is not something I had previously met or noted.) However, it did appear to my mind as a perfect representation of opening oneself to the universe, and at the same time a gesture that came very close to expressing what I was trying to say to the young man in the above paragraph. And shortly after this, out drinking with Kensuke, to illustrate what was essentially the same matter, I took up that same position in front of him, and then asked him whether he would (/could) do the same in front of me. (I was at one level being quite serious here. At a minimum, I was putting myself in his hands.) And naturally (this being before we were actually living together), he didn't (/couldn't). I don't know how he would feel about it now we are in a far more stable relationship, but at the time, the idea clearly frightened him.

Chapter 14
The Way We Are Understanding Formative Influences: The Fine Line Between Influencing and Controlling Others' Thoughts and/or Actions Philosophies and Religions as Power Centres

[14.1] Philosophies:

Going back into history as far as you wish, people who question in order to develop new theories (religious or otherwise): philosophers, scientists, sociologists, anthropologists; Darwin, Marx, Freud, Einstein, Descartes, etc., will inevitably be building on and/or breaking away from what they see available to them as represented in their culture and at that particular time in history, and when you move outside of that time frame or into a separate culture, much of what may be accepted at the time as 'correct' (in Japan, 'joushiki') may not automatically be accepted as so in a completely foreign culture and/or a modern setting. (Mathematics, in the sense that once proven, its relevance is not lost regardless of where you happen to be, would seem to be the exception here.)

As comparisons:

Freud, who I first read about when I was quite young and although clearly a pioneer in his field, merely seemed to be imposing his own very narrowly determined views onto what had to be a far more wide-ranging set of possibilities. Then in my fifties, a university student counsellor of some twenty years asked me to work through the English version of a book on the life of the philosopher Jung, which she herself had studied at university in Japanese and unfortunately found almost impossible to understand, and working through it (a year-and a half project) – with me attempting to interpret the meaning of each paragraph on each page, became an education for the both of us. Jung, to the extent that he was prepared to fall in with his basic philosophies, was initially both supported and promoted by Freud, this followed by a very public falling-out that, reading the book, which described Yung's travels through Africa and India and his reactions to various aspects of their considerably different cultures, was very easy to understand. Freud both built and promoted his reputation on what eventually amounted to a very limited range of personal experience, while Jung, however correct or incorrect he was in his final observations, clearly was making an effort to expand his outlook over as wide a range as he possibly could.

Recently, watching a television debate centred on a group of both male and female European graduate students with White, Asian, Hispanic, Arab, and Black African heritage, and monitored by a white American male Harvard professor, at each point when there was any strong sense of disagreement between the participants, he invariably drew them back into the conversation using Western Philosophy as point of entry; this on the face of it not a problem (and with his background, I doubt he could have done otherwise), but considering the range of the participants' backgrounds including the fact that a number of them were female, I found this to be an extremely narrow approach in terms of solving the world's differences. Rather than someone imposing his own personal framework of reference, to have had a moderator (/panel of moderators) who could have brought out the philosophical or any other background that led students to making their original, considerably diverse statements of opinion, although not necessarily resulting in any agreement, might in the end have been more educational for both participants and viewers.

For some years now, NHK, the equivalent of the BBC in the UK, has run a series of programmes under the title of "Cool Japan," this initially being directly related to government efforts to promote a more modern image of Japan in foreign countries. Each week a group of foreigners from a very wide range of countries around the world (itself a great improvement from the original token 'Americans' employed in this manner), are encouraged to argue and express their opinions (in English) on some particular (Japan-centred) theme. Initially, there was a very clear emphasis on proving that Japan was in fact "Cool!", and even when the large majority of the foreign panel went totally against this concept in certain areas, there was always a 'senior Japanese expert' to wrap up the programme (here, naturally, in Japanese) in such a manner as to reassure the (presumably, mainly Japanese) audience that despite what they had just heard from a few foreigners, everything was well with the world, and that they were living in the best country ever. (In effect, you had a direct equivalent of the above Harvard professor's usage of, to his mind, the 'not to be questioned' arguments based on his chosen philosophy.) How much of this final presentation the foreigners really understood I do not know (none had been in Japan for more than a few years), but either way, they had no way of objecting to the content, and I am fairly sure that, much as they enjoyed being on television, they would have a sense that they were at one level being used, this leading to a very confrontational atmosphere in the studio, not just with the Japanese moderators, but also between Chinese and Indians, Americans and Russians, etc., each trying to promote both themselves and their ideas according to the world pecking order. (In the end, everyone in the studio was looking down on – laughing, very often in a highly supercilious manner, at – everyone else, and after watching a few of the broadcasts and understanding that this was merely another representation of Japan as I knew it, I let it be.)

And now, thirteen years on and tuning in on the odd one or two occasions, I have found a similar but rather different programme. The format is identical, but the tense atmosphere that existed has in large part gone, the main reason being that the three members of the Japanese team involved have over the years learned to approach whatever subject is up for discussion in a far lighter manner, using the programme more as a means to promote the quite correct understanding that "different countries around the world all have different ways of doing things" (and naturally Japan has its (superior?) way), and this in turn has affected panel members, allowing a more free exchange of information ("In Russia, Nigeria, Brazil, etc. we (/don't) do…"). And everybody still laughs, but the superior attitudes on all sides are in the main gone. There is still the point here that, when a young woman from China comes out with, "In China, we (don't) do…" and this is translated by the host in Japanese as, "Oh, in China, you (don't) do…" in effect you have a nation of some 1.411 billion people being represented (/defined?) by the knowledge/experience of a single woman in her late twenties or early thirties, but presumably the main point of "people being different" is getting through.

[14.2] Working from incorrect 'facts' or 'understandings':

A number of years ago, a professor in Okinawa, to great fanfare, produced a treatise proving that the existence of the future tense (will do) in English was the key to understanding the difference between English-speaking people and Japanese (essentially, to his mind, proving the uniqueness of the Japanese race). Without going into any detail, although WILL, (regardless of its official, and totally misplaced, grammatical title) has a number of uses, in this case he was referring to situations where the speaker is merely speculating about future possibilities, and in this case it does have direct equivalents in Japanese, in other words, his whole argument, presumably developed over a number of years, was based on a complete fallacy and subsequently would not be worth the paper it was written on.

And, in another, slightly different case, a rather distinguished (again Japanese) art (/history?) 'expert' dismissed an old print of a 'street scene' in London as "clearly a forgery," describing as "impossible to contemplate" the fact that a pub was clearly depicted adjacent to a church. Presumably, he had never been to England (at least the one that I grew up in), the pub being the time-honoured place to repair to after a Sunday morning service.

Naturally, many books of learning are still of great importance, and all will give some insight into the world as it is or once was thought to be, but particularly today, with its emphasis on grand theories and instant glory, it may be as well to approach them (this one included) as no more than the (well-researched, considered or otherwise?) opinions that they actually are.

[14.3] When religious and worldly authorities overlap:

Beyond their roles as promoters of faith, religious groupings are simultaneously organisations through which political power can be expressed, and therefore, to the degree that they choose to affect political decisions, I feel can quite fairly be judged on two quite different levels.

Two quotations:

"Real Buddhism is about mercy, wisdom and dissolving confrontation."

This would seem perfectly reasonable except for the fact that it came from a Buddhist priest from Taiwan who has recently set up a large temple complex in the Republic of China with the full approval of President Xi, a man who (in line with all previous Chinese administrations) has apparently set out on a worldwide mission to politically destroy any authority of the (Tibetan) Dalai Lama, and who is also, incidentally, concerned with taking over political power in the aforementioned Taiwan.

"Faith gives you a minimum moral standard."

This from a recent convert to the above priest's sect, which I was fully responsive to and respect: She was clearly presenting her feelings in a completely genuine manner and joining the sect had helped her and her husband considerably. However, understanding her actual position, I would be tempted to stress "minimum" here.

And here you have the problem in a nutshell.

Political advantage: The priest was offering his services (at a minimum, a veneer of respectability) to the Chinese government, while at the same time expanding the number of believers in his sect and presumably his influence on both sides of the straits in the event of any future political convergence of the two sides (selling yourself to whoever/whatever[20] vs a certain advance in an individual's sense of morals or ethics), perhaps offset by what could be referred to as acceptance of yet another level of 'conditioning'.

However, if we are to work from the initial quotation by the head priest, perhaps this could be considered a start.

The spreading of doctrine:

The above is not a particularly rare example of how beliefs are propagated. The various sects of Buddhism imported from China were initially promoted in Japan in precisely the same manner – that is, by finding someone in power who was prepared to take up their respective cause. The Portuguese Jesuits also made an attempt in this area, converting certain 'daimyo' (local warlords) to their faith, but, unfortunately, at the start of the Tokugawa era when the country was unified for the first time and its leadership determined that all outside influences should be banned, they found themselves on the losing side and banned from any further practices. (Ref: 2016 film version of Shusaku Endo's novel "Silence", directed by Martin Scorsese.) Also, one could note the Catholic church's recent overtures in China. And naturally, to people educated in the West, the concepts of 'riding on the coattails of the conqueror' and/or 'evangelism' would easily come to mind as other common means of spreading beliefs. And also, today in Japan, we have what might be described as the 'telephone campaign'.

---

[20] It is no coincidence that, in the same manner that Putin has chosen to reinstate the position of the Orthodox Church in Russia, President Xi has also reintroduced Confucianism into his political support system.

Soukagakkai is a large Buddhist lay organisation politically represented in the Japanese Diet by the Koumeito party, with which I have had the oddest relationship (if it even may be called such) for something approaching forty years, starting with the owner and her partner of the lesbian bar in town (See "Crabs", [2.17]). I do not really know how close Koji was with them at the time, but shortly after he closed Sono and they moved out of the city, I do know that the only time they contacted us was at election time, essentially to be assured that "he would 'most definitely' vote for their party." (The first few times, Koji did spend a certain amount of time arguing with them, but then very quickly learned to say "Of course," and then take his choices from elsewhere, upon which (and presumably having a long list of 'friends' to contact) they would immediately hang up on him. And eventually, prior to every election, it got so that we could almost time the arrival of that single ring. I can understand the principle of 'getting out the vote', but in the end, the whole process for the both of us became highly offensive.) And then when Koji passed away and they sent me a kilogram bag of mouldy (black spots throughout) rice as a final farewell gift, I reckoned that was as far as we could go.

And then after Kensuke actually moved in with me (some two years after Koji's death), and I started getting odd telephone calls from some local representative, I discovered he had been an active member of the same group for a large part of his life. And here I had to put my foot down. Regardless of his feelings, I was not prepared to accept that extent of intrusion into my private life on anyone's account. He does now get regular official notifications by mail, but on the whole, they get put aside.

Koumeito (officially a left-wing party) is now aligned with the Liberal Democratic party (LDP), which under Prime Minister Abe is decidedly placed to the right. Initially, Komeito claimed that this partnership would help keep Abe in check to a certain degree, but naturally this has not happened. However, on the personal level, this has in fact helped, as Kensuke has got to the point that regardless of any past connections, he now makes his political choices as he chooses. At the same time, he has had the good sense to keep all the basic teachings (in particular, the requirement to help others) that he received from the organisation as a young man.

And as a note to all religious or political entities that like to use their youth corps to spread their message, there was a period here in Japan when we had visit after visit of young Mormons knocking at the door repeating verbatim everything that they had had installed in their young (and clearly highly impressionable) brains, and over a relatively short time they did develop a well-deserved reputation for being nothing more than a group of airheads. (Sending people abroad makes sense, but surely some respect could be afforded to the intelligence of the local populace.) I would suspect that any Russian or Chinese communist 'true believers' of the same age would receive short shrift (particularly in America) if they took it upon themselves to come knocking on your door in this manner. I have noted that China, with its Communist Youth League and Confucius Institutes being set up around the world, is (quite correctly) beginning to get a certain amount of criticism in this regard in the Western media.

It is not difficult to recognise why certain religious groups – American evangelists again come to mind here, also a number of Islamic factions – and political leaders – Xi in China and Kim in North Korea, etc. – go all out to get at young minds at the earliest possible moment. However, although any individual brought up in this manner in the West might choose to laugh at how those cute little red scarves tied around the neck in that far away country represent "indoctrination at its finest," in terms of inculcation, there isn't really much difference between the one and the other. All fervid believers rely on the indoctrination of their young. And on a slightly less-elevated plane, you could easily include Boy Scouts (swearing allegiance to God and the Queen), national anthems and saluting the flag; the constant glorification of a nation's deeds and the equally important avoidance or, as necessary, denial of misdeeds [15.5].

[14.4] A problem of modern government. A plea for separation:

In a recent article on the political situation in Argentina, it was pointed out that, related to the prevention of interference in the ongoing election process at the time, "the laws of the country, passed 30 or 40 years ago, had, in the face of modern communication systems and the Internet, lost all relevance."

Any non-religiously-based philosophy (and here I would include all 'platforms' of political parties) can relatively easily, providing there is a political will to do so, be adjusted or disregarded at will. However, when you are you referring to laws officially promulgated by a single God, or any strongly religiously orthodox sect, it becomes very difficult, if not impossible, regardless of how the needs of that society change, to move away from the original strictures, and practically you end up with the rules created for a society which existed hundreds or thousands of year ago being used to enforce present-day decision-making – this equally "in the face of modern communication systems and the Internet." Hard-wired dogmatism that insists on across-the-board acquiescence to certain sets of values will at no point help in the promotion of flexibility, a high degree of which I suspect is going to be required for governments around the world to keep any semblance of authority in the near future. To take one very obvious example of women around the world rapidly coming to understand their (what up to now has been a very deliberately controlled) position in society, anyone who wishes to continue in this manner is, to put it mildly, going to be facing a challenge of major proportions.

(It could be noted here that, in terms of a political need for flexibility, the ancient Egyptians actually had it right; their rulers promoting a continuous death and regeneration of a whole range of gods; with myth, tales and narration at all times being nuanced to match the central requirement of "protecting the state against outsiders.")

However, perhaps regardless of all the above, observing how a wide range of religions have exercised their political power throughout history right up to the present time, if no more than to give equal protection to those of different beliefs, it might seem sensible to aim as much as possible for a clear separation between the powers of all religious organisations and governments.

[14.5] Israel:

The following comments are essentially my reactions to a very careful reading of all (supportive or otherwise) articles on present-day Israel's situation in the NYT over the past two and a half years while I have been writing this book, and the presentation overall is intended as an extension of the above argument related to excessive religious influences.

My first real introduction to Israel came some fifty odd years ago at university, through the reading of numerous newspaper reports, at which time the reality of WWII (including the Holocaust) was far more immediate in the social consciousness, and at this time there was a strong undercurrent of support for the Jewish position, and it was relatively easy to understand and accept the idea of a group of people who had been treated so badly wishing to return to a 'homeland'. Equally, that the Palestinians were not happy with this made perfect sense. If I was to understand British colonialism to be, in large respect, a thing of the past (and as of the mood at the time, something not entirely reputable –

which has been a point repeatedly brought up to me throughout my life and which I do understand), it did not seem entirely correct that Palestine had been handed over by Britain without any real discussion with or apparent consideration for the wishes of the local populace. However, over the many following years, there was always the prospect of a peace treaty left dangling and, as an observer, at all times one was left to hope.

[14.6]

And today: Israel is a modern, fully-developed military and economic power, with both nuclear and cyberweapons available in its arsenal; the peace process is a thing of the past, and considering America's totally one-sided approach in the matter, extremely unlikely to be revived; Orthodox religious thinking is quite apparently in control – notably in determining the process of which persons get accepted to be 'authentically Jewish' and also in Israel's claims related to Jerusalem as a capital, where 300,000 Palestinians still live in the eastern section of the city, and a place, at least as I understand it from recent reading, the original Zionist founders of the state were not interested in; a protective wall has been built with, as again was noted, all natural water sources kept within for any time when a serious drought might occur (others, apparently, may be damned); settlements proliferate forever with the evident support of the Israeli government; and synagogues are under attack in Europe, where one gets the sense that the juries are out.

And viewed from afar, present-day Israel would seem to be no more than an extremely fortuitous (coming off and taking full advantage of the Holocaust[21]) land/power grab. Or perhaps, put more accurately, the Jews were merely replacing the previous colonial power; the British, who were replacing the Ottoman Turks, who were replacing…ad infinitum. But then again, you still have to come back to the rights of the people (including many Arab Christians) who actually lived in these lands over the centuries. And if one is to argue acceptance

---

[21] The Holocaust: I fully understand that a very large number of Jewish people died in a very horrible manner in the Holocaust, but, in at least as far as my knowledge extends, equally targeted were numerous Polish citizens, homosexuals and members of the Roma (gypsies), none of whom have used the fact to represent themselves as martyrs to the cause, and to acknowledge that others did die would not be undermining your claim, and in terms of a little sympathetic understanding, might even help.

of ancient rights or beliefs as a guide as to who gets to rule, you have the Native Americans in the US and Canada, the Aborigines in Australia, and Maori in New Zealand as a start. At least, I cannot see why one claim should be respected any less than the other.

Jewish people cannot suddenly, merely to serve their convenience, treat so many hundreds or thousands of years of history as if it had never existed. Or, at least, if they do, they might expect a certain level of resistance. (And if the 12 million members of the Palestinian diaspora do choose to come back to claim *their* land some hundreds or thousands of years from now, presumably you will understand and hand it over without any complaints.)

Jewish critics in the newspaper regularly complain that for Europeans to be anti-Israel is to be anti-Semitic, but this is totally incorrect.

For most people, any foreign nation can only be judged by the manner in which it is presented through the media, and particularly when the country is not personally well-known, it is common that the actions of that country's government (which are the facts most commonly recorded) become the face of the nation. In the same manner that I would not blame an Englishman living in Japan for decisions made by the British government (although I do understand that some Japanese might), I would not hold any Jewish person living in America or any other country in the world (and, for that matter, Israel) automatically accountable for decisions made by the Israeli government. I do understand that the world is not so simple. And with regards to present-day Israel, people outside are naturally going to make personal judgments based on what is happening politically both inside the country and in the 'settlements', etc. All are all actions taken by the representatives of Israel, quite regardless of the fact that they are Jewish, and I would think quite rightfully being judged as such.

And regarding the settlements, to return to the Old Testament and the tenth commandment, "Thou shalt not covet thy neighbour's property", which Jewish people presumably take with a certain seriousness: Are we to understand that God was referring here only to Jewish property? That is, if your neighbour happens not to be Jewish, you are open to plunder as freely as you wish?

I can understand the concern that Jewish synagogues are being attacked by Muslim jihadists in other countries around the world, but this is a political situation in which both sides believe they are right, and even understanding that they are acting wrongfully, I can equally understand that they might see their actions as the only possible alternative. And, most definitely, in this case they are equating Jewish people around the world with Israel's Jews. That is, that a person who is anti-Semitic will be anti-Israel is natural, but the reverse is not going to be an automatic truth.

And as one more point: How does the Orthodox clergy come to believe that they have the right to determine the political future of their state, and equally feel that they have right for their young not to be called up to practically defend that same state? – the situation here appearing identical to that in America where many top level politicians like to think that they can assume control of the movements of their military forces while having, in one manner or another, avoided serving in those same forces when they were young men. ("I have the right to control. Others may die.") And directly related, referring to the situations in both Saudi Arabia and Iran; In the absence of a Messiah, the need for a jurist cleric to determine what is 'correct' has to be somewhat questionable.

And perhaps, as two final comments which could be applied in a far more general context in too many societies around the world:

On the understanding that a number of the remarks I have referenced above were carefully crafted by Jewish writers for political reasons:

"If you use a public forum to preach politics, you can expect politics and nothing more in return."

Or to be very direct:

"When you make it clear that you don't give a damn about what people think about your actions, don't expect them to care much about your self-perceived 'problems.'"

Having lived my life in relative tranquillity. I can afford to stand on the sidelines, but people who step-by-step are being deprived of their land and homes (and this is certainly not a situation limited to the Israel-Palestinian problem) cannot. And as always, faced with the basic choices, that there are some who choose to fight back should not be beyond the average person's comprehension, wherever they may live or whatever society they may belong to.

And finally, speaking as a complete outsider, Jewish people (at least a certain section of them) seem to make a lot – almost a selling-point – of how they are looked down upon, how only they have suffered as they have. Seriously, they should truly consider (or at least make some effort to study, even if only lightly) other nations' and/or religious groups' histories. And this goes for any group that feels they have been unfairly treated in life. There is – and historically always has been – a lot of suffering out there! There would seem to be far too many people who go through life using their personal (and/or group) history as a crutch or a defence mechanism – attacking the other for "not liking them." And in the end, an audience can only take so much of; "You don't like me," "I am (/my religion/nationality/sex/colour makes me) a victim," as an excuse for personal weaknesses (this particularly when it results in aggressive tendencies) before it gets very boring.

I do understand that Jews have been pushed into this position by history, but this is also a number of Japanese persons' excuse for their rejection of and by the world, and the result is the same. At the same time, I would fully support any Jewish person who could find it in themselves to make even the smallest of efforts to recognise what has happened and what is happening in Israel today in the name of your religion.

[14.7] An echo through time:

From a recent Japanese TV news programme: A young Orthodox Israeli Jew (in his early twenties?), questioned as to where he might be interested in traveling abroad, answered that he had "no interest at all" in traveling anywhere outside his community. For the only slightly older the Japanese news reporter who was interviewing him (and very probably on his first assignment abroad), the young man's reply came as a somewhat startling revelation (he was visibly shocked), and he actually repeated the question to make sure that he had heard the answer correctly, only again to receive a very abrupt (approaching the curt) response – apparently the question itself was in some sense offensive ("Why would I need to travel abroad?") – upon which he turned his back (this, ironically, for me, a very 'Japanese' response) and strode back off down the hill from where he had come.

There was an immense gap here; a gulf, a broad crevasse that neither side (each with their own upbringings/backgrounds) had even the remotest chance of envisaging where it might come from, let alone crossing. For the young Jewish man, back in his community, I doubt he would consider the matter twice. But for the reporter, and I imagine a number of Japanese viewers of the programme, there might have been a questioning in the mind. (In a real sense, this was me back in the Catskills [1.14]. I, also, at seventy, was quite honestly shocked.) And there is very much of a chicken-and-egg relationship here – withdrawal creating a coldness of reputation, leading to rejection, and subsequent further withdrawal. At one level, it does not matter how one person or group chooses to present themselves to the world (to each their own), but equally there are consequences.

[14.8] The inevitable ripples:

It was noted that when the present administration in the United States made open its unmitigated disregard for any consideration of 'human rights' in its dealings with other countries, this had considerably increased the likelihood of other nations openly taking up that exact same call towards their own ends. (In reality here, in terms of which countries it finds, temporarily or otherwise, to its advantage to associate with – President Sissi and his predecessors in Egypt coming up here as an obvious example – America has been using the concept of 'human rights' as a fig-leaf for quite a number of years now, but it is true that your present president has made the matter impossible to ignore, which in one respect may be something to be commended.)

And now Israel, also, has clearly set its own example, bringing us:

– In India, Modi's Bharatiya Janata Party's recent demands that "Hindus be recognised as the only true claimants to one thousand years of 'Indian' history" – another ancient culture to be reborn as a modern-nation postcolonial state?

– The desire for a caliphate.

(NYT: "The lingering dream of an Islamic state." By Azadez Moaveni. Jan 16. 2018.)

The writer is noting that, regardless of the present situation of ISIS (who it is admitted, "went about it the wrong way" – in that they were claiming the existence of a 'state' when in fact there were none of the basic requisites for government yet in place), there is still lingering dream for "an Islamic homeland" among many young Arabs, and he is pondering quite seriously as to what form any such state should take. For anyone who is interested in this article at all, it will presumably still be available on the Internet. However, as points which immediately came to my mind:

And then why should an Islamic state (as the author seems to assume) be Arab-centred?

Indonesia, Malaysia, Pakistan, Afghanistan, Bangladesh, Nigeria, Albania, and on and on, all have majority or at least large proportions of their populations who are Muslim. They would be eligible for citizenship? And those who chose to fight for ISIS who did not have Arab blood would not be welcomed?

A quick glance at the Internet gives me 73 sects of Islam (I am presuming Sunni). These would all be allowed an equal position in the state, or (as in present-day Israel) would one or a certain number be placed as superior, of greater importance in the official hierarchy? And again, who would you be kicking out this time? And then, they too, would be classified as terrorists?

Whites in the alt-right movement in America openly claiming their need for their own homeland.

Amusingly, Trump has made this possible by supporting both them and the Jews that they disparage, but the reality in terms of a state to be imitated is Israel. And as queries here: DNA tests would be mandatory? (Reading in various newspaper articles how this is working out, and with human beings sharing 99% of their DNA, I would suspect a number of the one-hundred-percenters might find themselves out before they start.) Also, any children (LGBT or otherwise – they will arrive!) who choose to associate in any manner outside your community will be automatically evicted?

Christians who wish to form (/retreat into) their own communities.

This immediately brings to mind the Amish church in Pennsylvania, who for hundreds of years rejected modernity only to have their young finally succumb (who could resist?) to smartphones.

And ultimately, no one can isolate themselves from the realities of what is in the process of becoming a very small world.

[14.9] Putting the cart before the horse:

As a statement that I have seen or heard numerous times in different arguments:

"You have to accept that God exists, and then you will understand."

If you believe in God, this will be the most natural of statements. However, you could equally say:

"You have to accept that Allah (as understood by Muslims) exists, and then you will understand."

"You have to accept that the Buddha exists, and then you will understand."

Or alternatively:

"You have to accept that 'God (/all gods) are merely figments of the human imagination introduced some few thousands (/mere hundreds) of years ago by those who found it convenient to do so and passed down through the generations into your truly innocent minds,' and then you will understand."

And as noted in Cpt 5, the Japanese also use this technique as in, "You are not Japanese and therefore you can never understand this (/us)." which is used for no other reason than to emphasise the uniqueness and inevitable superiority of their own culture and/or to reject any argument against their manner of thinking – which I submit to be the aim of all of the above statements. And having lived with the latter for a full fifty years, you will forgive me, but I can only say that you are perfectly welcome.

And as they would once greet all and sundry at any fairground of repute: "Roll up, roll up, whoever you are. You 'pays' your money and you 'takes' your choice."

***

"Far more than what you choose to believe, it is how you live and act within that framework, how you choose to craft those beliefs to the benefit or otherwise of those around you that matters."

Living in a new world order, and as a plea for community: I do understand the desire for a closer, more spiritual order. However, perhaps if certain churches could put a little less emphasis on absolute control and a little more on generosity in their treatment of others, they might find more people open to their message.

"Before you agonise over details of the afterlife, first concentrate on the now – taking one existence at a time."

The world I am in line to vacate is in a very bad state, and perhaps it might make more sense to concern oneself with one's present existence rather than any speculation about the afterlife. It is of no consequence whether the realms of God or the Buddha or any other deity exist or not. Presumably, if they do, they will find you (or you them) all in good time – that or whatever hell you belong in. (And considering the way they act, why so many people assume they are fit for some kind of heaven is way beyond me.)

Chapter 15

The Way We Are
Understanding Formative Influences:
Social Constructs and the Internal and External Promotion of Authority

Note: All points made below are applicable over a very wide range of individuals, groups or nations, far beyond those detailed in the examples.

[15.1] Nations and their myths; what is, in general, referred to as 'history':

One unexpected product of reaching my present time in life has been the discovery that I now find myself capable of viewing the past in units of 'lifetimes' (today, anything up a hundred years), which as a younger person was only comprehensible to me, if really at all, as a matter of 'generations', which with young people at the time commonly marrying and having children in their teens or early twenties, amounted to a considerably shorter, and at the same time unsatisfactorily vague, period. (Quite what was 'a generation'?) As a result, I now find that events that as a child (or even in my twenties and thirties) were understood as from the 'far distant past', can now be taken on (/in) in passing (a mere 25 lifetimes ago!) and an odd sense of equanimity.

[15.2] A very brief overview of history:

What we know:
The large majority of, if not all societies in today's world have been produced as a product of repeated aggressions. Tribal groups on all continents were fighting each other long before the white man ever appeared on the scene. This

is not intended as any excuse for colonialism (which is one more example of such aggressions), but rather a statement of fact. Also, it can be noted that while such aggressions have included numerous cases where widespread empires continued in some cases for hundreds of years, or in the briefest of cases no more than the odd decade or so (Genghis Khan, the Persian, Greek and Roman Empires, Hitler), inevitably each one has in the end suffered from a loss of influence (/collapse) resulting in the main from overconfidence (/overreach) leading to uprisings in appropriated territories; this and/or inner dissension.

It being human nature, even the smallest of groups will never agree about everything. While in sufficiently small units, the need to protect the group's existence will very likely prevail as a unifying force, as the group expands in size, and with the need for a detailed political platform leading to more restrictions that everyone is required to adhere to, naturally there will be dissenters who, if they fall away at the edges, will not likely be noticed. However, when they are vying for top positions, splits can easily become inevitable.

And as intimately related, referring to killing, torture, the taking of slaves and rape, etc.: There is nothing particularly original about a people killing or enslaving others in the name of their own 'superior' cultural ways. This is the way that things always have been done and such violations still remain common today. And again, on a historical level, presumably this did not start with, nor is it limited to any specific race.

That said, considering how long this has been going on, and the present amount of human and financial resources being devoted to nothing more than the physical and economic destruction of other societies – this to no apparent end – and equally, with the potential for the total destruction of the other (/all) having grown exponentially on all sides, might it not be time for those in charge to consider trying another style – presenting an inclusive (as opposed to dominating or divisive) theme? For the record. I am not proposing any 'revolution' here, but rather a change in attitudes that may at some point tilt the scales towards somewhat more peaceful resolutions of conflict.

[15.3] History as it affects the world today: Dealing with the detritus from the past:

The real problem with history is not particularly the details of what happened, although for the sake of future generations these do need to be aired as much as possible, but rather all the leftovers – vast areas of land taken with no recompense; deposed royal/imperial households (/autocrats) left standing in the wings; countless cultural artifacts removed (/stolen) only to decorate the original victor's museums; long trails of arbitrarily imposed boundaries and/or sets of rules quite unrelated to the original customs and beliefs of their inhabitants; and, possibly most important of all, certain assumptions (based on those long-past conquests) as to the natural superiority of one's race, nation, philosophy, etc. over 'the other' – all of which remain as irritants to be constantly scratched or recycled at will by any authoritarian-minded leader or group intent on establishing their pre-eminence and/or expanding their power, allowing them to prop up whatever vision they might wish to sell to their peoples of some "fore-ordained future," and as necessary become (yet again) one more excuse for (naked) aggression.

One can also include here all those alternative interpretations; Which side was the original aggressor? How well or badly the defeated nation was treated? How many were killed in any particular battle or massacre? – with disagreements here as to whether any event should be even classified as a 'massacre' or 'genocide.' And all the unsettled disputes and grievances related to historical rights of possession, the bits that got left over: the status of Northern Ireland; British/Argentinian claims to The Falkland Islands (Malvinas); the dispute with Spain over Gibraltar; Japan's disputed (by Taiwan and China) possession of what they refer to as the Senkaku (Diaoyu/Taioyu) islands: Japan's claims to the Korean-possessed Dokdo islands (Takeshima); and the Chinese claiming just about anything and everything in the neighbourhood, Taiwan included, that they can put a name to, etc. etc. (Possession being nine tenths of the law, names in brackets are those given by other claimants.)

And if we are to again refer to religious groupings here, we have; the Sri Lanka Buddhists treatment of their Tamil population and Myanmar's treatment of the Muslim Rohingya, and all the internecine quarrels between the various Sunni and Shiite factions. The Russians would very much prefer it if they could return to their Soviet status, and the Americans seem determined to attack anyone who might care to blink an eyelid in their direction: "Any excuse for a good old war!" – a statement which when young I very much associated with the (to me at the time long-gone) "British Empire," but as with everything can be practically updated.

All the above in fact represent no more than the cherry picking of events from the past – and there are many more – to promote what amount to some highly blinkered vision of the future, which in by far the largest number of cases represent no more than a simplistic and one-sided desire to "return to the glories of yore," presumably to pick up things just as they were left off. And if this is the case, exactly who is proving what to whom?

(A direct corollary here would be that groups in any society determined as 'minority' or of lower status, and/or nations that – at any time, going back as far as you wish – can be considered at some point to have been 'defeated' can inevitably expect short shrift.)

[15.4] Education and the Media. Putting yourself into perspective:

Under the concept of 'media' here, I include all political pronouncements, news or entertainment sources and all attendant commercial images. A large number of people will be more susceptible to a well-crafted movie, video series or commercial, that is to commercial interests (in the US, the superhero; these days, male, female, black or white, who will invariably conquer any enemy singlehanded) than they would be influenced by any education they might have received in school. And as a quick quiz for any American reader here: Who won WWII? Certainly not Private Ryan! (You could check out the Russian contribution.)

"On a personal level, and regardless of any 'truths', any information that is input into an individual's brain is of importance only to the degree that it influences (/informs/ warps) that person's worldview."

Tasuku Honjo, the Japanese 2018 Nobel laureate for Physiology or Medicine, when asked what advice he would give to young students here in Japan, immediately came out with, "Understand that what you are being taught at school is wrong, or at best highly limited in scope, and work from there to obtain your own truths."

Here, naturally, he would be referring to the world of medical research and its attitudes towards cancer (the area of his life's work) when he was young, but I could say exactly the same thing about the English language education system as it exists at schools in Japan today. And in a far wider sense, he could have been talking to any child in any country about the input that they are made subject to during their formational years, which inevitably, in terms of areas taught and information covered (and regardless of any political slant) can only be extremely limited.

"In the large majority of cases, it is not what you are but rather <u>what you are</u>

perceived to be that will affect other's judgments about you. And more importantly, and much more than is generally understood, what you perceive yourself to be (in large part, what your society, or rather the limited segment of society that you personally are exposed to, teaches you to be) is in fact going to be far more influential on your judgment of others than any of the (again, extremely limited and commonly stereotypical) information that you are likely to have received about them."

Or put more simply, "If, without considerable contact (/personal inter-reaction), you assume that you have any true understanding of what other societies (or other segments of your own society) are about, or that they might have any other than a highly superficial understanding of you, forget it!" ([5.5]/[5.6])

[15.5] Controlling the media narrative:

The Chinese artist and dissident, Wei Wei, now apparently living in Berlin, who was the architect responsible for the central "Bird's Nest" design of the main stadium at the Beijing Olympics in 2008, has written considerably on the restrictions placed on its citizens by the Communist regime there, and the effect that they have on those citizen's minds – wearing away their willpower and distorting their sense of reality. Accepting this as a completely reasonable description of the situation in China, I would add the following.

"The leaders of all countries (/their 'establishments'), making full use of that nation's educational systems, news and recreational media (and utilising all means of subtle distraction and/or misplaced emphasis, together with the glossing over, ridicule or out-of-hand dismissal of any inconsistencies), both select and interpret – write, rewrite or, at a minimum, nuance – historical facts to their advantage, with each nation and/or political grouping asserting its superiority and/or victimhood, and to the largest extent possible denying any guilt or particular intent regarding any of the more untoward affairs in its the past (cf. Korean and Japanese descriptions of the Japanese occupation of Korea)"

And, rightly or wrongly, you cannot expect otherwise, this being nothing more than a requirement for a stable society.

If you take up a position (as almost any society or social grouping is required to do at some point in order to further its existence), you have to be prepared to defend it. And if 'facts' are not at hand (or can be in any way disputed), an 'official' (that is, politically approved by the leaders of the day) version of reality becomes the norm. And in large part, populations, or at least a sufficient number of them to permit a continuation of that particular ruling segment, will acquiesce. (This actually remains true right down to that smallest of groupings; the family, each with their own appropriate 'skeleton in the closet' – all the things that you don't ("for their own good") tell the children – and presumably also including everything that the children, on their part, don't tell their parents.)

And further, on the understanding that yesterday's 'events' are today's 'history', and that today's 'breaking news' (at modern turnover rates) is likely to be long forgotten by the weekend, the manner in which that everyday news is presented (keeping the viewer hooked at whatever cost) becomes vital to the protection of that same image.

And in the final analysis, there is nothing particularly remarkable about any of the above. People on the whole do require a certain solidity of base that comes with belonging to their 'own culture'. And many, if they cannot be satisfied with the everyday humdrum (/tedium) of what they have at hand, will require that 'little extra' to help carry them along and provide the sense that they are in some manner special in the order of things; the natural sense of importance that comes with even the mildest association with the pomp and solemnity of whatever (royalist/ nationalist/ elitist/ communist/ religious, etc.) tradition or, conversely, revolutionary aim that they happen to find appealing.

Corollary: "Just because the media don't talk about a subject, it doesn't mean it doesn't exist." And equally: "Any report you read about anything can be assumed to be to some extent biased."

That is, if you want any reliable news about anything, you are going to have to search it out yourself, and simply finding reports that you agree with on social media, or any cable TV channel is not going to get you anywhere.

And as the simplest of advice here for any younger person who might be interested: Read widely. Make an effort to search out opposing opinions, or preferably look for commentators/authors who are prepared to examine both (/as many as possible) sides of any argument. And more than anything, note what is *not* stated:

"The easiest way to influence (/take control of) any argument is to deliberately omit inconvenient facts."

[15.6] Freedom:

Submitting to the call of the crowd.

An English-born expatriate member (top-level manager) of the multinational company that I worked for in Japan, who in his earlier years had been sent to work in South Africa when it was still under Apartheid, explained to me how very quickly he had found his moral compass compromised and had truly looked down on, that is applied racial discrimination at its worst, against the black population there. (At the time, we were discussing the degree to which we had been affected by the society here in Japan.) I do not really know whether this could be classified as 'survival instinct', but he also said that after he came to Japan, he quite naturally reverted to his former manner of thinking, and all discrimination in that area completely disappeared.

Commenting on the Falklands War, my mother's cousin, a grammar school headmaster who had taught history all his life and who normally was the calmest of individuals, admitted to me how, even though he was fully aware of the need for a balanced approach, he had found himself caught up in the total feverishness of the moment as "our valiant British troops moved south to take back our islands." And here it was the BBC who kept their heads and, much to Prime Minister Thatcher's chagrin, chose to report the news from both sides.

Both of the above stories are related to the difficulty (or even impossibility) of fighting against a prevailing or dominant mood, and from this perspective it is very easy to understand how such a large proportion of German society fell under Hitler's spell, and equally why present-day Germans, presuming they continue to fight hard not to have that history repeated – as they have been doing very successfully up to the present – should not feel overly bound by and certainly should not be overwhelmed with any particular shame about the facts of the matter. The recent claims by certain right-wing groups in Germany that to have a monument commemorating the Holocaust is somehow an expression of guilt or humiliation is completely incorrect. As a monument, it represents a sincere apology to all those who suffered, and for that reason alone is to be fully admired. Germany today is fully accepted as a valid member of the world community, and Hitler is, quite correctly, understood as part of history, and if left that way, this should present no problems with regards to Germany's (or Europe's) future.

The same concept can also easily be extended to the senior management (the only requirement of whom is to make money for that company's shareholders), and even lower-level workers (imbued with the concept of loyalty and also in strong need of their job) in any large-scale tobacco, fossil fuel, agricultural chemicals, tech industry, pharmaceutical or weapons ("We aren't pulling the trigger!") corporation, making it, other than in very rare cases, totally impossible for them to even conceive that their company's position might be ethically or morally incorrect. And the few voices which are not muffled will inevitably come up with the (perfectly correct but) very tired, "if we don't, others will" argument.

And then working down the scale a little, in any group where being permitted into the inner circle requires a strict quid quo pro – a high level of or total submission to the leader(s) set of rules – any local gang, mobster syndicate, religious cult, college-level or other 'secret society', etc. – the chances are that very quickly you are going to learn to fall in with that particular vibe, and without any particular consideration, start thinking and acting according to the wishes of that group.

And perhaps even taken one step further, I sense that this could also easily account for the Stockholm Syndrome; the psychological alliance that some kidnapped hostages develop with their captors as a survival strategy during captivity, which on the face of it does appear irrational, but depending on the character of the individual concerned, would seem quite reasonable. Almost all the groups listed above commonly include some element of coercion, and there are many types of people who, for a variety of reasons – being unhappy with their daily lives, loneliness, the psychological need to have others (/someone/anyone) in control, that or simply being accustomed to having others (including a dominant parent) tell them what to do – would easily find themselves submitting to and associating themselves with such treatment.

And when Princess Diana chose to take her young sons along the banks of the Thames to visit the homeless, no doubt she was fully aware of what this would mean in terms of opening up their minds to a far wider world than they would ever have been privy to brought up within the (by all accounts) somewhat claustrophobic atmosphere of the Royal household in which their grandmother, Queen Elizabeth, and father, Prince Charles, received their education. At least, in terms of their freedom, they are the first generation of Royals who have had the good fortune (/privilege?) of being made aware of the actual position of a large number of their countrymen before they were required to take up their public positions as representatives of their country.

In contrast, Queen Elizabeth, with her far more closeted upbringing (being educated privately at home), and whose first real encounter with the wider world would only come when she was obliged to take on her official duties, particularly as Queen after her father's (King George VI) sudden death – from which moment, in her position as "Head of the Realm and Commonwealth," she would be required at all times to maintain that level of aloofness required to set her apart from "all beneath her position," the gap between herself and her subjects would be well established before she could even have the slightest opportunity to view the light beyond, and as a result she would have had no occasion to develop what might be termed a human touch (something that her mother, coming from a very different background, had in spades), that is a period in her life where she might have been exposed to the true reality of human frailty. And the time being the time, and circumstances, there was no way in which it could have been otherwise – and that she wouldn't get along with Princess Diana is a foregone conclusion.

FF: Walking along a cliff-top path on the IOW, I popped my head up over the hedge to find the Queen walking by. If I had wished, I could almost have touched her. I am not in any sense a royalist, but I do admire her for what she has done within the narrow confines of her life.

[15.7] There is always going to be a price:

All forms of power (both political and commercial interests – as presented through your media of choice) involve the manipulating of others' perceptions of their needs – for the nation's or your own personal 'security', 'a meaningful life', 'happiness', 'hygiene', 'health', 'presentation' (fashion, make-up, creams and cleansers, cosmetic surgery, et al [15.10]) – all competing for your attention and money. And if this can be taken as the highly limiting construct that it is, what might 'freedom' be?

Naturally, there is the commonly acknowledged "freedom to see things in different ways."

In my mid-fifties, traveling around New Zealand by coach – each day with a different driver and each driver with a different take on life, pointing out the world around us as they saw it – over the course of eight or nine days, I received five or six completely different lectures on (and resultant impressions of) the country and its people in the most natural of manners: On the one day, we were treated to a description of the beauty of a whole range of natural features (in particular the lupin plants – originally brought over from English gardens but now gone wild – which happened to be in full bloom when we were visiting):

and then on the next, a full-blooded excoriation of those exact same plants as an alien species (those "disgusting weeds that proliferate eternally") together with a detailed exposition of all the damage that they (together with a whole list other plants and animals) had caused to the local flora and fauna, right down to the destruction of the natural course of rivers, and on and on. And in both presentation and content, both drivers were completely correct.

(And with the equal surety – having seen them do it so many times – I could surmise that a considerable number of the group of Japanese tourists who were in the same bus on that first day would not have seen or heard, or even had a chance to appreciate any of the beauty that I was having so carefully pointed out to me, for the simple reason that they would all be fast asleep.) To the average Japanese mind – that is in accordance with their upbringing – tourism tends to be reduced to food, accommodation, and the satisfaction of "having been there," 'there' being whatever was listed up as a 'must-see' point in the agency's brochure – and anything else that happens to fall in between can be disregarded.

Traveling in my parents' car through the Trossachs in Scotland in the mid-seventies with Koji and Kerry [4.7], one of our American teacher friends from the early days in Japan – and having been taught from my early childhood to be constantly on the outlook for "whatever might be out there" beyond the car (/train/ coach) window – it shocked me to see both of them repeatedly fall asleep in the back of the car until we reached some particular destination, at which point both woke up, took a look around, and then in perfect tune with my father as he restarted the car engine, once more closed their eyes.

And then, viewed in the converse, as an individual you could perhaps be said to lack freedom to the degree that you are (as in the above case of the expatriate manager in South Africa) subsumed in any particular culture to the degree that you are no longer strictly in full control of your actions. All military cultures are quite naturally (and presumably of necessity) designed to subsume, as are all strongly nationalist or religious cultures.

Also one can consider any form of addiction: alcohol; gambling; drugs; collections of shoes, brand goods, antiques of debatable value (/plastic toys) etc. that somehow get out of hand – purchases made for no other reason than you feel an urge to make that purchase: "I have money, and therefore I spend."

[15.8]

Whenever my student, Mrs Tani [6.22], found a particular piece of kitchen equipment that she liked, she would invariably purchase six of a kind, her reasoning being that she might never be able to find something exactly like that again. She actually showed me her collection – a wide basement with whole rows of shelves packed full of glasses, dishes, full dinner services, cutlery, rice cookers, juice mixers, etc. that she would never ever use; most of the electronic equipment was already out of date. And it was only later, when she moved out of that house into a much smaller building in the centre of the city and she actually started a working career, that she figured it out that they might be better disposed of.

I also came something close to this type of situation in my late thirties when, purchasing for the third or fourth year yet another expensive sweater for myself at Christmas, it dawned on me that I was doing it more than anything to give myself some vague form of assurance that I was "participating in the Christmas spirit," (I had quite sufficient clothes in my wardrobe), and at this point I decided that this was a way that I did not really want to go. As a replacement of sorts (everyone needing certain pleasures), I started concentrating more on collecting small items on sale at flea markets or the junkier antique stores, where the pleasure came in finding attractive pieces of reasonable quality at the lowest prices available.

FF: Mrs Tani, who with her husband ran both a jewellery store and pawnshop, at one point introduced me to one of their customers, a 70-something-year-old man who, having reached an age when for the first time he felt free enough to spend all the money he had toiled through his life to accumulate, had suddenly discovered the allure of precious gemstones, in particular as set in highly ornate, 18-carat gold dress-rings, each costing hundreds of thousands of yen, this together with at least three or four heavy gold bracelets on each wrist. There was nothing at all vulgar here (I never saw him make any attempt to show them off to others), neither was there any motive for financial gain. He was simply someone who in his late years had discovered the pleasure of possession, and each ring (three or four on each finger) was being worn purely for his own appreciation, which, at his age, had to be better than hoarding them in the back of a cupboard or safe. And what do you spend your money on?

And then the third or fourth time I met him (he had to come to purchase yet one more ring), he was complaining of pains in his knuckles and wrists and asked me whether I might know what could be done about the matter. Naturally, in my position (my student was running a business), I could not say anything, but I suspect that if they had been made of lead, they would no doubt have been interpreted as some perverse form of self-torture. And as to how safe this was (my rough guess would be that at any one time he would be wearing over 15 million yen's worth of jewellery), he was a well-known character in his neighbourhood, but it did occur to me to wonder what might happen to his collection if he suddenly collapsed in the street. (When Carl died in hospital, this so many years ago [4.11], he had two gold rings taken off his fingers before his body had had time to cool.) Even so, presumably they would have served their purpose and, as with all such things, have in their own manner 'been passed along'.

And then, at an even more elementary level, 'being caught up in the crowd at a concert – juvenile screaming contests'; or as you get a little older, 'joining in standing ovations for what are no more than average performances' could be added to the list, the Japanese doing this latter regularly, particularly if they are at a performance that involves foreign artists.

FF: Years back with Koji, when entering a rather small theatre to watch a performance by a famous European ballet troupe, each member of the audience was handed a single red rose, which we were instructed to throw onto the stage at the final curtain call to show our 'appreciation' (this for a performance which we had yet to see). The stage itself being rather small resulted in a somewhat cramped overall atmosphere (and for me personally, not a very pleasant experience), but this being Japan, we all dutifully held on to our roses right through to the end, at which point every member of the audience stood and queued patiently in the aisles, each one of us tossing our rose at the feet of a somewhat bemused ensemble. Today, with Kensuke, who happens to have similar feelings on the matter, we tend to just sit in our seats and wait the whole thing out; or whenever given the opportunity, opt for slipping away from aisle seats.

For younger people, any choices related to any of the above can easily be understood as a simple learning curve, which every person in the world is subject to. Also, if one is considering the overall concept of freedom, clearly the point at which any (at least on paper) 'free choice' can be said to have become a burden for any one individual has got to be very much a matter of personal choice, but in the sense of consideration of one's development; as one grows older, at times when it becomes natural to consider the possibility of certain changes in one's basic mindset, to keep some consciousness of the above duality of the concept cannot harm.

[15.9] American freedom: Freedom as a social construct. Confrontation as a way of life:

(The following is written with the full understanding that, as with everything, the American system is one more way to do things, and that in fact the US at present is going through a very bad patch.)

A large part of American society, in its own way, has become highly addicted (with every comment on addictions as made above valid) to their own very unique concept of freedom – a freedom that exists without any of the normal controlling or balancing forces that are widely accepted in more moderate societies. "I am American, and therefore I have 'the right to be free,' 'the right to be or become anything I like.'" This being a natural extension of the ever-promoted "American Dream," there would seem to be no particular problem here, but when 'right to be' becomes 'right to do'; the right to offend, regardless of how much discomfort (/pain) it might cause the other person involved, the right as a minority (however small) to dictate; the right to be as 'in your face' as I choose to, the right to demand everything I want exactly in the way I want it and reject anything that does not suit me, it would seem that as a society somehow you are on the wrong track. (And if you choose to take this attitude outside your own country – wherein I will allow, you are entitled – you cannot be expected to be welcomed by all with open arms.)

[15.10] A note on setting up stall in Vanity Fair:

A (questionable) need vs an equally questionable (corporate) greed.

– Take a fact: Some men go bald when they are young. Forget a fact: Baldness is the natural result of having an excess of masculine hormones. Add a twist of the truth (set a trend): Women don't find young men who are bald attractive. And expand as required: No one likes to be bald. And, Presto! You have the recipe for never-ending sales of men's hairpieces, wigs, and lotions. And in this morning's newspaper, as front-page news: "Japanese scientists regrow hair at record rate."

"And we all look just the same": Start with a snapshot of what appears to be a woman in her mid-forties – this until, when interviewed, she suddenly sounds like the 72-year-old woman that she in fact is. Slowly and steadily expand (in both directions) the age-range of the models until (in the latest commercial) you are featuring a woman in her mid-thirties. And again, Presto! You have established a market for an 'anti-aging' cream that, in distending the skin and fashioning a certain shine – which together remove all traces of wrinkles – makes every older woman suddenly believe they are 30 years younger, and at the same time ropes in a large number of younger women who presumably haven't yet figured out that they are paying a considerable amount to look like someone who is 80. (It does take certain careful level of observation to appreciate the differences.)

"Tits and Arse." (As in "A Chorus Line.") Creating the unreal: The first time I really questioned the (now seemingly very casually approached) concept of cosmetic surgery was watching a report on a singer in Japan who, having had her mouth operated on to make it "smaller" and "more cute" found that suddenly, not being able to open her mouth up wide enough, she could no longer sing as she previously had, resulting in the abrupt ending of her career. This only came out considerably later: At the time, she had, to all appearances, vanished. Also in a separate TV programme on the subject, an American woman in her sixties who, to my mind, could only be described as totally unattractive, repulsive even, coming out of surgery for the umpteenth time, exclaiming "how much better she looked now," perhaps unable to comprehend (or her brain unable to accept) that when she went in, she had looked far worse than she had after the previous session, or the one before that. And I cannot think of any one singer or TV personality here who has at any time had such surgery (and again, quite apparently more than once), where you could say it has not over the long term severely detracted from their looks. I know that, for young people, "20 years on" is a long time in the future, but if you do choose to have (particularly facial) surgery, understand that this is around the time when you are going to see the real consequences of your choice.

– And from the virtual world, you have young Chinese women regularly changing their faces (/facial expressions) – particularly the shape of their eyes, to make them rather rounder – before they post any selfies on the web. Not any problem, you would think, until you find a similar tale of a young American woman who lost her boyfriend simply because the overall image she had created on Facebook was far too far away from her real self, and in the end she had been unable to satisfy the expectations her web fantasy had engendered.

[15.11] Dealing with the laws of the land:

"There will always be rules or circumstances in life that will not automatically benefit you, and at any point, you may choose to fight, accommodate, walk away from, possibly think a little about, or simply live with the matter as you wish."

That said, faced with those in positions of authority, particularly in other countries, I would warn any younger people that assumptions as to how you might be treated in any particular situation are not necessarily going to pan out when you are abroad.

"All legal systems exist to serve the 'interests of that society' as conceived by those in power. And equally, it is the nature of things that all countries have different concepts of what might be 'in their interests.'"

At the same time, as noted in [5.3], while in English, as is the case with many European languages, the aim of speech is commonly one of precision or distinction in argument, the Japanese language, to allow the expression of one's opinion in the most acceptable manner possible, is deliberately phrased ambiguously, using both vocabulary and presentation that allow for the broadest possible interpretation of whatever subject is under consideration. And naturally, both these points are echoed in their respective country's legal systems.

All Japanese laws, legal procedures and legalistic terminology (reflecting their socially-promoted need for a 'harmonious solution', with no loss of face on either side – which can actually be understood as firmly biased towards those in a position of authority) are purposely left vague to allow a large margin in interpretation, this in effect allowing those in charge (as in the recent Carlos Ghosn case) to exert their authority with as much leeway as possible, and in many cases governmental 'guidance' (essentially, a simple statement to the effect that "perhaps this way might be better") has long been considered a perfectly sufficient means to promote change. To the Western mind, the aims here can appear to be approaching a deliberate obfuscation, resulting in distraction or detraction from the clarity of any particular argument, and this is in fact the case. However, obfuscation being essential for the orderly regimentation of the society here, there is no other way that it could be.

And then, in America, the need to accommodate the fundamental concept in US society of "the right of free speech" has resulted in the need for the legality of just about everything to be defined in the clearest manner possible, with all disputed incidents to be read strictly in accordance with stated laws. All appeals are apparently to be accepted and may be argued in court and solving problems through litigation has become the essence of what is conceived of as 'social justice'. (A large number of companies in the US are at present getting around this by insisting that employees sign contracts limiting their rights to making such claims in court, but that would be another story.) In contrast, in Japan, 'appealing' as a legal process, in the sense that the individual then becomes a disruptive element in the face of society, is not generally considered good form. (Also see, "You do not make a fuss!" [16.6].)

In everyday matters, this deliberate lack of clarity of rules and regulations actually allows them to be interpreted very much according to the requirements of the moment; to be applied as strictly or leniently as the situation demands or seems fit to the investigating officer. To anyone caught up at all in the law here in Japan, this naturally has its potential advantages and disadvantages, but in each case when I have been, I have found resulting judgments to be completely fair. When I have been in the wrong, I have been treated accordingly – instructed to make suitable apologies (absolutely essential at all levels in society) and when I have actually caused damage (as a result of my occasionally excessive imbibing of alcohol), make the necessary monetary reparations. And otherwise, all treatment has been very much to my advantage. Early on, called to the central tax office in Osaka to be questioned about how I was filling in my returns, the officer in charge actually worked out that I had been considerably overpaying up to that time, and helped me with all the paperwork to make amends. Also later, when I was working on my own, I found the local tax office to be equally helpful. (That said, in the very earliest stages when none of us spoke Japanese, I do remember a considerably hostile Immigration Office official whose window everyone, but everyone desperately tried to avoid, but at least he was reliable in his unfriendliness, and we quickly learned to be suitably obsequious in our approach.)

[15.12] Cases where you may choose to fight:

Japanese law clearly states that: "Banks are not permitted to make a copy of a foreigner's resident card." However, from my own experience (in that it has happened multiple times in my own bank here), I do know that, if a resident does wish to complete any transaction within a bank, established practice – here as determined by the respective bank authorities – dictates that you hand over your card to be copied. Naturally, you may, if you wish, choose to argue your point (and the bank will argue back), but in the end, I prefer to save my time.

[15.13] A case of forbidden entry (to a public bathing facility):

(Full details and criticism of the following can be googled at: Japan Times, Debito Arudou > Strange story of Debito > Clark, Gregory. More supportive descriptions of his actions are also available in this section.)

In the early nineties, the Japan Times took on David Aldwinkle as a columnist for their "Community" page. His often contentious columns, under his Japanese name of Debito Arudou (and considering his totally antagonistic attitude towards the society here, I can only presume that his taking on of Japanese nationality was done for publicity purposes), did actually take up a number of problems that the foreign community face here, but in terms of attitude; "I am Japanese but/and I insist on being treated as I would be in America!" he was, at least to my mind, completely and utterly off target.

Traditionally, that is before the large majority of families started bathing at home, in terms of their social function, public baths in Japan (and this would include hot springs in their respective areas) were a gathering place for both men and women in any particular neighbourhood to relax at the end of the day surrounded by familiar faces, this being essentially the same function that an English pub performed in its day. (While it is easily possible to find a drinking establishment within walking distance of most homes in England, in Japan, residential areas are on the whole kept quite separate from drinking (/ 'entertainment') districts, and thus not available for this type of gathering.)

However, in the above case, apparently the public baths involved did not appreciate the large number of rather rowdy Russian sailors (a large number of whom were not familiar with Japanese bathing customs and who naturally would not be welcomed by local patrons) taking over their facilities, and as a result, all foreigners were banned, including Mr Arudou (who, although he was legally Japanese, did not have the right looks), a case that he chose to taken up in court as a case of "racial discrimination" and win. As to whether this practically aided anything, I am not sure, but I know he did write a book on the subject and eventually returned to America, from where he occasionally contributes columns to the JT, basically making the same points he has been doing for the past twenty years or so.

That said, over the years, even after my Japanese reached a reasonable level,

I have not been admitted to (or if I have, very quickly have had it communicated to me that I am not welcome in) a number of bars, the occasional eating establishment, and in one case already noted (after the appearance of AIDS) our local gay saunas. And with the exception of the sauna (where one time, very drunk, I slipped in the back entrance/exit without paying, just to make my point), I have in all cases acceded. All over the world, people go to bars, restaurants, or hot springs to enjoy themselves, and regardless of principles, I on my side also do not wish to waste an evening in the presence of others who clearly do not enjoy my company. It is as simple as that, and the law regardless, if you choose to force yourself on or act in any manner aggressively towards other customers, be it in a Welsh or Irish pub, a Texas saloon, or an exclusive bar in Upper Manhattan, it will not be appreciated.

[15.14]

Also, as a separate but very important point, a considerable proportion of Japanese drinking establishments, those commonly known as 'snack bars', are in reality extremely small (20–15 or even 10 seats), making it essential that they do not offend their carefully cultivated regular customers. They represent, in and of themselves, tightly knit communities, and in this type of establishment any exceptionally unruly customer, foreigner or Japanese, will be asked to leave and very commonly turned away if they choose to come again another night.

Gay bars in particular tend to cater to a specific type of clientele (age- or interest-wise), and particularly in the smaller bars, they can be very discriminating in who they admit. In this type of situation, the owner will normally simply say sorry or indicate that it is a 'private club'. Even for first-time gay customers (Keisuke does this automatically when we go into a new bar), it is considered polite to inquire whether it is OK to enter, and I also do this naturally, if only by bowing my head, when I enter a small shop in the countryside. This is no more than a matter of etiquette, which has (the law regardless) evolved very naturally to meet local conditions over a considerably long period and as such, I feel, should be respected.

Regardless of the above, these days there are a considerable number of establishments (covered on the Internet) that do accept foreigners readily, and most certainly for any short-term visitor to Japan, these are to be recommended. Once Japanese people have taken it into their minds to open up to any foreign presence, they are highly welcoming. And if you are uncertain as to where you might move on from that spot, you can ask the owner (or other customers) for suggestions.

(In the above context, the present ban on tattoos in the majority of public baths and hot springs in Japan, these still commonly being associated in the Japanese mind with anti-social groups (yakuza), makes full sense. However, if Japan really wishes to open up to foreign tourism, this is another area in which they are going to have to do some serious thinking.)

[15.15] International Law:

The above also will naturally extend to local interpretations of International Law, e.g.:

Human rights: "Naturally we accept them, provided you follow the basic rules of our society." – a statement which could be made equally truthfully by Russia or China – or, if we wish to be perfectly honest, in America, where successive administrations do seem very carefree in their interpretation of and application or otherwise of the concept. (Not to overstress a point here, but this is precisely how the Americans choose to view all "International Agreements." That is, "We insist on having all other countries (including China and Russia) abide by 'International Law,' even though we refuse to sign such agreements (the International Court of Justice (ICJ), the Law of the High Seas) on the understanding that 'they may be used politically against us.'" To paraphrase: "We can arrest you for war crimes or whatever, but don't think about touching us." (WGFTG!))

Racism: the Japanised version of which, until recently, the average Japanese has tended to associate with the United States treatment of Black Americans.

The degree of flexibility of 'reasonable doubt' etc., where the English version is (for all the reasons given) aiming at as precise a definition as possible, while any translation into Japanese (naturally expressed in the unavoidably opaque terminology of the Japanese language) prohibits that same precision.

As a result, however clearly worded an English legal document might be, it can only be translated into a far more ambiguously presented Japanese script, and to expect otherwise is inviting a true breakdown in communications – a 'mujun', or impossibility as introduced in [5.11]. That is, there being no real equivalent here, to demand what are understood as "clearly defined legal rights," American style, will naturally not be automatically accepted (or, depending on the case, even understood), and everything that appears clearly stated in the English version will inevitably become open to consideration according to local interpretation in the Japanese version.

Even today, although Japan has signed the relevant United Nations accord on the matter, any foreign person (particularly a man) who upon divorce wishes to reclaim a child according to the laws of their land is still going to face a hard fight in the local courts here, which almost invariably (as a matter of tradition) will support the mother's position.

***

In the above public baths case, Arudou was challenging the system as it exists according to his very American interpretation of "upholding the law as stated." Also, to the Japanese mind, which is in the end far more important than any legal utterance, to be accepted as Japanese (which he was also claiming to be), more than anything involves the outsider accepting the status quo (joushiki) of the land, and therefore in both respects, even though he won his case, he was demanding the impossible.

[15.16] The vocabulary of officialdom. A need for some reappraisal of the usage of vocabulary related the projection of power:

As has already been illustrated in the case of Japan in Cpt 5, a very large part of taking control of any discussion involves the promotion of one's own interpretation of key vocabulary – defining the terms (in this case, strictly the language used) of the argument (/disagreement/ conflict).

(All the following words italicised in {} brackets are listed on the principle that if you are to attempt to understand other societies, you need to understand your own.)

[15.17] Propaganda:

Propaganda is one of numerous words commonly used to simultaneously demean the other and elevate the self, as in: "We represent the truth; our enemies deal in propaganda," used most recently, and notably, by US Vice President Pence referring to North Korea's determined efforts to stand out at the opening of the recent winter Olympic Games in Pyeongyang. Unfortunately, with the whole world of politics being nothing more than a vehicle for propaganda; the promotion of that group's official version of itself to the world (and all governments lying, or at least 'bending the truth' to benefit their own cause of self-promotion), the above statement has in the present day become little more than an absurdity.

"Propaganda requires a captive and/or assumedly submissive (/susceptible/ gullible) audience."

A number of years ago, as the speed of worldwide communications increased, I noticed a seeming total lack of understanding among politicians as to how words and expressions that were clearly being addressed towards a local audience could be interpreted as they spread around the globe – their inability to appreciate the effect that their overly blunt statements might be having on audiences in other countries – and the situation in this regard, with every word spoken now immediately subject to the finest of analyses around the globe, actually seems far worse today.

The following is a Japan Times newspaper article originally published on Nov. 8, 1942, and reprinted as part of a historical series after seventy-five years. (Rather than the realities involved, this has been included here as an illustration of the true exercise of propaganda. All italics are my own.)

"American and British soldiers who surrendered to the Imperial forces on the Hong Kong, Malaya, Philippine and other southern fronts *are enjoying life* at the various war prisoners' camps in the Japanese mainland, Chosen (Korea) and Taiwan, at which *accommodation* has since been found for them. *Their treatment is just, in keeping with the moral principle upheld by the Imperial forces. Their lives are perfectly safe, while they have a guarantee of their subsistence.* The prisoners at the camp in Taiwan *are feeling grateful to* the Commander of the Imperial Army in Taiwan, for the books, foodstuffs, cigarettes other things which he gave them when he visited the town some time ago. Some of them have written to Lieutenant-General Ando, expressing their appreciation of his generosity. The military authorities have decided to employ these war prisoners, of whom there are a great many, in various undertakings for the extension of the nation's productive power. Many of these prisoners are already engaged in various fields, *receiving proper rates of wages for their work*.

Vigorous activity is seen in the unloading of cargo at Tokyo Port, the front gate to the capital and the supply route for the Tokyo citizens who united as one mass of fire hard at work in their wartime tasks with the ultimate objective of annihilating America and Britain. Men wearing beret-like Scotch caps and others wearing British Navy caps are silently and orderly at work. Some of them, tucking up their sleeves, make a boastful show of their arms tattooed with the names or faces of their sweethearts. Work is done in an orderly manner here every day. Efficiency in war work has increased since the war prisoners came."

***

And anyone who does not know the alternative versions (plenty exist) could do a little reading on the matter.

And as an off-the-cuff: Why does an American columnist feel the need to say, "our great democracy" (the ultimate myth – See, [15.22]) rather than use a more commonplace expression such as "our country"? Recently, I have been getting the strong feeling that the phrase is being put in there with no other aim than to convince the writer himself of its supposed truth.

[15.18] Honour and Integrity:

(Recently presented by the former American Secretary of Defence, James Mattis as central to his beliefs in the mission of the US Armed Forces in their military actions in the Middle East and Afghanistan.)

Fully respecting Mr Mattis' background, and equally that, in an age that lacks any moral certainty, people who are involved on the field of battle would require such words as a means of providing a certain psychological balance in their activities, considering the amount of killing (particularly on the American side) that is now being conducted from a distance utilising bombs and missiles, I cannot see how words that originally defined rules of conduct in hand-to-hand combat can have any true relevance in the world of modern warfare. And in particular here, fully understanding that you can take out your enemies with a great deal of accuracy (and each time you get it slightly wrong, large numbers of innocent people) in this manner, I fail to see how sitting in front of a computer screen and pressing buttons in order to direct military drones (essentially, playing video games with living targets) could in any way be associated with either of the words quoted.

And equally appreciating that Mr Mattis is not of this ilk, the above consideration does again bring to mind certain politicians who have never even come close to facing a loaded rifle or the edge of a sword proudly referencing their own 'warriors' and 'samurai'.

[15.19] A view from the bottom end of the pile. Preserving social custom. The ultimate conceit: Lineage:

Shortly before Diana married Prince Charles, it was noted in the English newspapers that her lineage (that is her relationship to previous British Royal Houses) went back hundreds of years, far longer than the present House of Windsor and that in that sense she had more claim to English 'royal blood' than Charles himself. Having all respect for Diana herself, I can only note that every family has a history that intakes from its past and every man woman and child alive has what is known as an ancestry. That said, why exactly should any ancestor that I have who might have made a wrong step at some point be potentially dismissed as 'a common criminal', while certain classes seem to consider that their own ancestors (who presumably, to get in the position they have, have repeatedly committed far worse acts) should collectively be elevated to the position of having {*lineage*} or the benefit of {*coming from good stock*}. And other than being the descendants of people who have taken power at some point in large part through deceit and/or mass exterminations, what exactly are {*sultans*}, {*emirs*}, {*shahs*}, {*royalty*}, {*kings*}, {*queens*}, {*aristocrats*}, {*imperial lines*}, {*supreme leaders*}, etc. etc.?

[15.20] Selling yourself as a (/the) superpower:

As a common theme in my media intake on 'Americans' in college and early on in life, I repeatedly found comments related to their "ignorance about outsiders," "their resistance to the learning of foreign languages," (foreign movies with subtitles being the ultimate "No, no!") and the underlying assumption that "everyone will (or at least should) think the way they do," (the "we want everyone to see the world as we see it" syndrome) as defining traits. Letting alone the first two points:

To see yourself at the centre of the world (/the universe?), that is as a great many of Americans appear to view themselves today, must be a heady experience. Born immediately after the war, and subsequently educated to understand my country of origin as England (or the UK); that is after Great Britain and its Empire had ceased to exist, and where its 'failures' (excesses no longer paraded as virtues), could be (if not by all) acknowledged as not anything to be particularly admired, did allow me to develop a somewhat more distanced approach when I was introduced to the concept of the so-called 'superpowers'. And today, living outside the country, it has been highly amusing (even fascinating) to watch various American media representatives in the NYT as they have, according to mood, elevated or demoted the same small patch of land I happened to be born in, ranging from the highly patronising "Little England" to the more neutral UK and Britain (with even, when the British government's policies of the moment have fallen in line with those of their own, a "Great" thrown in there for extra effect).

(The Japanese have taken another tack here: Through the promotion of the concept that they are "misunderstood," or rather that they "cannot be understood," even those in the lowest of social rankings can still (and commonly do) indulge themselves in the belief they are in some sense "superior to all.")

America as a "young country."

In the Japanese media, whenever they feel the need to exhibit a little one-upmanship, the US is invariably described as "a young country," this in contrast to "the long history and established culture of Japan." However, in terms of importance upon the world stage, here defined as "interference, aggression and/or promotion of raw power," both are relatively recent entries, and neither, in their own ways, (at least, at present count) has exhibited any particular success – other than causing an immense amount of destruction and the subsequent intense hostility of the populations of those other 'lesser' countries involved in their ventures.

[15.21] Regression:

Throughout the 20th century, enormous progress was made in the elevation of working (/poor) people, largely through the hard-fought-for development of labour unions, the promotion of human rights, protection of the environment, prevention of disease, the elimination of poverty, etc., all generously encouraged and promoted by the United States.

And now, having reached the 21st, centred on that same United States, we seem to be witnessing the wilful destruction of close to just about every element of that system.

I doubt whether there was any particular identifiable point at which the pendulum started to reverse its course here, but most certainly the end of the

Cold War when, as the storyline goes, "Capitalism won and Communism lost," must have had a strong influence on trends. This victory in itself would not have mattered except for the fact that, in the strange reading of the American political psyche, where capitalism is perceived of in its rawest of forms – "The Market (that is, as the possession of money determines it) is invariably right." – has seemingly reduced all economic theories that ever were to, "The stock market is up, and all is well with the world."

In contrast, Communism (with a brush painted large during the McCarthy Era) has come to be interpreted as "anything with even the slightest whiff of socialism," which, in its sweeping prognosis, damns not only left-leaning governments but also any society that provides government support (social or medical) for those who haven't already 'made it'.

Understanding that systems in Europe, including the UK, are not by any means perfect, and that, as is also true here in Japan, a number of people do work to cheat the system – moneyed people don't!!! – it still astounds me to so regularly read just about all American correspondents' – political affiliations irrespective – (at times, highly) demeaning descriptions of how others have chosen to operate their societies: "There are a thousand and one ways to cook a stew."

The end of the Cold War was also clearly important, in the sense that the military-industrial establishment now found themselves short of an adversary to practice their ever-expensive charms on, resulting in the necessity for Bush's "Axis of Evil" (See below); the removal of Hussein in Iraq resulting in a total upheaval of the Middle East; and after 9/11, that ever-tantalising prospect of wars against as-yet-to-be-determined 'terrorists' – read; "those we resolve to be in opposition to whatever our latest 'security concerns' dictate" – who, if one wishes to take a more romanticised approach to the matter; in the manner of Angelina commenting on the Laws of the West in "Romancing the Stone": "However many you manage to clobber (and presuming that you look hard enough), there will always be others begging for the same treatment." (Even today, a considerable number of Americans are still identifying themselves with the 'frontier spirit', not apparently as yet having clicked to the fact that the world as a whole is running out of open plains to conquer.)

(JT: 11.11.2018): "All countries should avoid addressing disputes through coercion or intimidation."

Reported as a US official statement to China on removing their missile systems from the South China Sea, much as I can agree with the sentiment (possibly with the 'all' expressed in italics and underlined), considering the way the US government regularly conducts its "official overseas business," this has got to amount to the most fatuous statement I have ever encountered, and presumably the Chinese told you so.

America, as the principle troublemaker in the world over at least the past 30 years (and allowing that the UK political establishment, with its "special relationship" and yearning to retrieve its title as "British" has for the most supported them in their very many misadventures), if it is not careful and regardless of Presidents Xi and Putin (who naturally want an in on the picture), is within a whisker of establishing itself in most of the world's eyes as the nastiest of small-minded bullies.

And as one final point related to the Cold War: It did not occur to those up in the heights that in the end they might have won out, not merely due to any military superiority, but rather because of all that generous support that they had provided, not just financial but what used to be described as "soft power." Good will requires a considerable effort to build up and maintain, and can just as easily be destroyed overnight, and right at this moment, you seem to be making a good job of it.

[15.22] The moment democracy died:

Another key event (when a tiny little voice in the back of my brain really went, "Uh, oh!") would be when the American Supreme Court chose to equate money with free speech, from which point any attempt to obfuscate the truth as to who was calling the shots went screaming out of the window. From recent reports, it would seem that just about every representative of either party in the House or Senate is a millionaire or billionaire, or if not quite up to that level, sponsored (heavily) by some millionaire or billionaires. And moving rapidly on from there, where once "rules created by the rich for the rich" used to be the meme, we now appear to have graduated to, "the best (/indisputable) rule is no rules" or put more directly, "the fewer restrictions, the more money you have at your fingertips, and damn the rest" – a concept that Silicon Valley has also clearly picked up on – that or perhaps, with Google and Facebook in the lead, they were the true originators of.

On paper, the claims of companies such as Amazon, Airbnb or Uber that they are providing convenience (/matching up the market and the consumer) would seem reasonable, but at the same time, considering their effect on established social practice (at least in the more developed countries) – hard-fought-for legal restrictions related to worker rights (Uber, Amazon) or safety regulations that must be met by any hotel or similar establishment's ownership (Airbnb) – they are proving to be highly destructive forces.

"Different societies have different sensibilities, which are not there just to be walked over."

In Osaka, we initially had individual unoccupied apartments (presumably purchased cheaply) and now extended to numerous whole buildings, registered under the Airbnb system, all with ownership unclear – that is there is no one neighbours can complain to if any problem occurs – where endless trails of Chinese tourists come and go, picking up the key at some other point in the city in the evening and returning it the next day; all very well for those making their bit out of the system, but again all (waste disposal, noise, fire, etc.) regulations thrown out the window. And presumably none of them are paying any taxation. (The local media here have tried to identify actual owners on a number of occasions, but as yet have not been able to do so.) The central and local governments on their side, and in their usual hodgepodge fashion, are adding rule upon rule further complicating the situation and satisfying no one in the process. And reflecting the lack of any passport registration at such places, a matter legally enforced at all regular hotels, Osaka recently had the case of an American man murdering and dismembering the corpse of a young Japanese woman at one such 'minpaku', before transferring the whole package to a second to allow him to dispose of the parts at his own convenience. (He was, fortunately, caught.) Airbnb may claim as much as they wish that this is not what they intended, but this is the reality on the ground.

Uber, on the other hand, is offering nothing other than a very basic and clearly easily replicable computerised system that any established taxi company (or group of companies) who are already fully in compliance with local regulations, given the right local government support, could easily introduce (and hopefully will do so). And other than that, in terms of management practices, in their manipulation of their manual force (who they conveniently refuse to even recognise as employees), they are no better than any of the nastiest mill owners that existed in the late 19th and early 20th centuries. And, as we have all been made fully aware: "This is the future." "This is progress." "And to hell with any of you who might not think so." And, as they say in Chicago, "All that jazz!"

FF(?): **The trickle-down theory:**

The Republican Party (/the rich in general) like to claim this as an excuse each time they legislate yet one more tax cut or loophole in the law which acts to their financial advantage.

In a recent news programme, repeated in prime-time at least two or three times (the Japanese loving to knock their closest neighbours as hard as they can at every opportunity), employees at a large hotel in one of the major cities in China (Beijing or Shanghai?) were shown on film cleaning both the washbasin unit (including the cups and glasses to be used by the next five-star guest) and the toilet bowl using the same towels and cloths. (Hopefully, they were doing this in the right order, but there was apparently no guarantee.) A hotel management representative, explaining the reason for the problem, noted that although they were allocated up to 45 minutes to perform their tasks in each room, the generally accepted target among employees was to get in and out in a maximum 15 minutes. And more importantly, the extremely low wages that such cleaners received made it impossible for the hotel to obtain other than the lowest level of workers for such jobs. This explanation was presented in the most matter of fact of manners, and there was no indication at all that the situation might be expected to improve in the future.

Whether the really rich ever use five-star hotels, I wouldn't know – it may be that they own enough real estate around the world not to have to suffer the inconvenience – but perhaps at some point (and if they happen to stay at the above hotel) some people are going to get the service they deserve.

And as an update from the local news, the largest newly opened hotels in Osaka are now finding themselves unable to utilise a large percentage of their rooms, simply due to the fact that they are unable to find staff to make the beds. At the present moment, they are relying on students new out of China, who do not as yet have the Japanese ability to handle anything other than the most rudimentary of jobs, and as with the above case in China, they are being paid accordingly. If you are expecting anything in the order of 'Omotenashi' (traditional Japanese hospitality) in these places, I would suggest that you consider other alternatives.

[15.23] A note on hatred:

"If you wish to deepen your understanding of the world, at some point you have to attempt to observe what is beyond."

In a recent news article about Steven Spielberg, he noted that he has been expanding his work collecting video records of Holocaust survivors for his personal museum to include recordings of people who have suffered in other conflicts around the globe. He also expressed a personal desire to "attempt to understand why people hate."

As noted in the introductory sections of this chapter, there will always be the totally predictable, historically determined and politically motivated "All the usual suspects," "Once a minority to be hated, always a minority to be hated," "The eternal enemy" factor, which can be observed in numerous societies around the world, each with their own self-cultivated prejudices. It is also easy to see hatred arising among those who (repeatedly) see their beliefs (/base identity) rejected. However, perhaps as to why some persons are more susceptible in this respect:

"To be outward-looking in your approach to life requires a certain degree of confidence in yourself as an entity existing beyond the narrow confines that 'society' has demarcated for you. Conversely, the more an individual's experiences in life have led them to exaggerate to the point of total identification with one facet of their identity (be that Orthodox Jew or Palestinian resistance fighter) – their 'range' as described in [12.5] – the more likely they are to react aggressively if they find that defining element open to censure or disparagement."

A natural extension here would be the so-designated 'self-hatred' – expressed commonly in the form of an outright hatred for others who are not limited in that same manner – commonly noted for closet gays who, solely because of their position in some (CIA, military, religious) hierarchy that rejects the gay condition, find themselves simultaneously obliged to both live out and condemn their own condition. (In today's Japan, the 'hikikomori' – people of all ages who have chosen at some point to remove themselves from society, can also easily find themselves in this position, with similar results. See, [16.13].)

Certain types of people – again those who, for whatever reason, are incapable of concerning themselves with whatever might be beyond their very narrow and established viewpoints – require 'those of a lower status' in order to preserve (/protect at all costs) the 'decency' or 'propriety' that they relate to their self-perceived position as "upright and right-thinking members of their society or religion." And in cases where the other refuses to accept that 'determined' position in the order of things, and particularly in cases where they choose to fight (/laugh back at) that definition, it is very easy to see frustration welling up into something approaching hatred.

[15.24] The consequences of awareness:

Regardless of economic level, human beings are remarkably compliant provided that they understand themselves to be part of an established environment, in large part because, within that environment, they know the rules, the way things are done, and subsequently can get along with the business of living without being constantly on their guard against the unexpected, and even in groups with a lower status or at poverty level, provided that they can establish a certain routine in their daily lives that will allow them to get on with their business, however lowly that might be, they will find a way to exist. And some 50 to 60 years ago, this was suitably sufficient. However, in today's interconnected world, with its ever-pervasive social media opening up new avenues for recognition of both social disparities and possibilities – the claims of LGBT groups and feminism; the drop in respect for (/total lack of trust in) the traditional political, scientific, and academic establishments; whole communities suddenly finding themselves without their key industries and discarded due to forces beyond of their control; the lure of foreign soil, etc. – you are suddenly in a situation where all sides now feel free to consider themselves an 'injured party', this naturally resulting in a great deal of incivility, and at its most unpleasant, the overt articulation of direct expressions of aggression and hatred.

And in this situation, the chances of being heard over the clamour for any direct calls for {*politeness*}, {*respect*} and/or {*general decency*} (here, strictly the concepts as determined by those who those who consider themselves deserving of such treatment) – and all of which do have direct associations with those same previously incontestable elites – would seem to be fairly limited.

[15.25] And evil:

Of the countless words that dehumanise – {*savage*}, {*barbarian*}, {*uncivilised*}, {*the uneducated masses*} – that are used to disparage and or demean, to place others too far below in the order of things to prohibit any legitimate response, one that seems never to fail to hit the target is 'evil'.

In a lighter incarnation (taken from a BBC documentary), there is a ritual Hindu dance on the island Bali where good and evil fight for predominance, and where, at one point, evil is banished, but where it is noted during the final sequence (when evil returns) that this can only be a temporary defeat in that good (essentially, what is determined by society as 'correct') cannot exist without evil (what is determined by society as incorrect) and vice versa.

"Wailer":

Not too long ago, I watched a Korean film with the odd name of "Wailer" (the Korean title being "Kokuson"), which at first viewing appears to be the ultimate mishmash of drugs (magic mushrooms), zombies, a female spectral form/ghost, the Christian Devil and devils in general (naturally including, it being Korea, a somewhat odd Japanese man living in retreat in the mountains) – all representations of 'evil' – who together (quite untraditionally) conquer. Combatants include a very weakly represented church, a traditional Korean shaman – actually an apparent jack-of-all-trades who, in addition to all his flags and drums, also keeps a statue of the Buddha conveniently packed into the boot of his car, presumably to be used as and when requested (and paid sufficiently?), and the local police, one of whom at the film's start commits the sin of sleeping with a local barwoman repeatedly, if unknowingly, in full view of his (10- to 12-year-old) daughter.

Enough was left vague enough to allow for countless interpretations.

Kensuke, being Japanese, simply noted that overall he didn't find the film really enjoyable and otherwise refused to comment. However, he did admit that he did not appreciate the idea of the automatic association the Korean characters in the film make between the Japanese man and evil, although from a historical angle it very much makes sense. Also, himself belonging to a Buddhist sect, I'm sure that he would not react well to a statue of Buddha shown slung into the back of a truck.

On my part, however, other than being a suspense shocker of sorts, foremost it was clearly a tongue-in-cheek presentation about getting our (both good and evil) belief systems cross-wired in this modern world: At the end, the village policeman central to the story loses everything, in large part because his brain is in overload and he is no longer sure as to what – God, invading spirits, zombies, ghosts, the infallibility of the police investigation that he represents – he truly believes or should believe in. Very clearly here, you can have too much of a good (or bad) thing.

Also, another point that came through was that, closely viewed, it was the protagonists themselves who were, in essence, creating the evil that eventually destroys them: Close to the end, after repeated and relentless goading ultimately triggers what amounts to a state of raw anger and aggression in the Japanese man, he essentially obliges the young Christian priest, who has finally worked up the courage to confront him, by appearing in the form of the Devil.

***

As one conclusion here, one could suggest that evil only exists for those who wish to see it as such. Or possibly, the admonition "Not to see, hear nor speak evil," with its implication of "Be pure of heart," might be better replaced by the more specific: "Seek not to overly admonish (/provoke/ despise), and thus create evil in other's hearts." (I have noted in [14.6] that being anti-Israel – in the sense of disagreeing with the present Israeli government's policies – does not, to my mind, equate with being anti-Semitic. However, I would suggest that if the Jewish newspaper correspondents who seem convinced that this is the case, keep repeatedly pushing the matter in this way, as in the case of the Japanese man above, you will end up getting exactly what you are wishing for. Why should I, or anyone else for that matter, not let you have your way? Ditto for American blacks in their seeming distrust (/disregard) of all whites and white people's thinking.)

Or, then again, if evil truly does exist, it perhaps lies within those who apparently require the word to vindicate their exaggerated sense of superiority (again, their 'position').

"It is perfectly reasonable to like something that others do not. However, when 'I like that,' slips into 'That is good,' and then more specifically 'That is right,' or 'I am right,' (which, when a person becomes even more entrenched in their views, can easily strengthen into a definitive sense of righteousness or zealotry – what amounts to a wilful ignorance of others' right to differ), that is where you will find evil. And evil here is not with the other; the despised, the damned, but rather in the heart of the one who, for whatever reasons of avarice or inflated pride, will not accept the other as equal in their humanity."

Particularly as it is used in a political context, evil is nothing more than a convenience, created by those in power to perpetuate that power, and subsequently comes to include the right to ignore (those beatings, those awkward deaths of the innocent on the battlefield), demean (all those who do not match your criteria), and ultimately, without compunction, take the life of the other (/the infidel) at your whim. In any event, on a practical level, it being one of those words commonly used by those who wish to draw the listener's attention away from their own actions (usually unpleasant in intent), each time you hear the word, the reader could consider what the speaker might be attempting to hide.

[15.26] Dreaming up yet one more 'enemy of convenience'. George W Bush's "Axis of Evil":

(On the understanding that I do not in any way support the existence – and certainly not the usage – of nuclear weapons.)

The present leader of North Korea is not, by any standard international comparisons, particularly evil. He merely, like a large proportion of our world leaders (/prime ministers/ presidents/ dictators) of the free world or otherwise, both wants and seems determined to get his room to strut. I understand that he doesn't, by all accounts, take any excessive care of (and, in fact, treats very badly) a considerable proportion of his population, but he has managed, rightly or wrongly, to convince a sufficient number of them that he has certain aims and is in control – which, taken in its entirety, in this modern world does not make him particularly unique. That one of those aims has been to obtain what amounts to a small number of nuclear weapons (as opposed to already having and fully deploying a very a large number of the same) does not, upon consideration, seem particularly reprehensible, especially as it appears fully evident that none of those who do have them – regardless of so-called "International Treaties" – are giving even the slightest consideration to giving them up. Small countries, surely, have as much right as others to protect themselves. And why depend on overbearing neighbours such as Russia and China when you don't have to?

(2.20.2019) JT headline: "Sanctions will stay until North eases threat."

As a personal comment: Any so-called "threat" has always been and always will be on the US side. North Korea is not going to attack America for the simple reason that it does not wish to be annihilated. (If anything, North Korea requires support for its economy first, and then a settling of the matter of its weaponry – strictly in that order.) In the present situation, it cannot be expected to do anything other than retreat further into its shell.

The smaller nations in the UN got themselves together quite justifiably in 2017 to pass the Treaty on the Prohibition of Nuclear Weapons. In the same vein, would it not be possible to consider a treaty totally rejecting the concepts of 'hegemony' or 'spheres of influence', (in effect, the right to indefinitely hold military bases in foreign lands and/or invade those lands at will) and at the same time 'sanctions' of any nature (the right to freely destroy another nation's economic base), which seem totally unsuited to solving any of the complications of this modern world? When any leader, merely to satisfy their own (internal) political agenda, feels free to put an area that includes the whole Korean peninsula, Japan, and for that matter China and Russia under the threat of a devastating war and possibly the spread of a nuclear fallout (and I say that as a person who lives here), it has to be clear that the present system, however much the powers that be might care to claim otherwise, is not working. To this end, there would also have to be an understanding that individual nations, as much as possible, need to work out their own problems without forever depending on their respective 'big brothers'. Certainly, if Japan could not automatically be assured of America's protection, it would very quickly have to learn to be far more civil-mannered in its approach to some of its Asian neighbours.

Naturally any such agreement would not be accepted by all, but at least it would be clarifying the debate.

[15.27] Japan:

Hiroshima. Tears:
1972. Signing the visitor's book as we were leaving the memorial museum in Hiroshima, I found a note in the message column written by an American woman, which said very simply, "So what!" Coming only two years after my arrival in Japan, and the visit having affected me very strongly, this shocked. However, just three years later, I found myself fully agreeing with the sentiment. So what changed?

[15.28] The creation of a fiction:

The World War II years have always presented an extremely delicate subject to broach in Japan, and particularly with the present Liberal Democratic Party (LDP) government under Prime Minister Abe promoting an even more extreme than normal exculpatory narrative of war memory (backed by the right-wing Nippon Kaigi (Japan Conference) – which has a considerable number of both local and central government elected officials as members, together with the 'uyoku' (right-wingers who thrive off hate speech), it is a subject that these days I tend to avoid unless I know the person I am speaking to very well.)

The LDP has been in control of the country for the largest part of the last seventy years and might appear something of a monolith, but in practice, as it has always been composed of a number of distinct factions, it has been able to provide a certain range of distinctive policies that at least provided some semblance of democracy. However, considered as part of the full political spectrum here, it runs from right-of-centre to hard right-wing, and from the start, as a party, it has always chafed at what it considers to be the unfair criticisms of Japan's actions during World War II; the victor's definition of war criminals (including Prime Minister Tojo being equated with Hitler); the imposition of a constitution (still being fought over at the present time); the restrictions on their Emperor system; and particularly that they should not have been allowed to muscle in and have colonies in the way that all the Western powers were accustomed to doing at the time. That is (if you ignore the fact that they lost the war) the actually perfectly valid supposition: "What were we doing that was different to what everyone else had been up to for the past few hundred years?"

But more than anything, they wanted (and still do) to be seen as "the 'beautiful nation' (as invoked by Abe) of their pre-war imaginations," and anything that might stand in the way of that must of necessity be repudiated.

In Germany, it took them two wars to get to the understanding that there had to be some other way, which led to the European Union as it exists today, but throughout the time I have lived here, I have wondered whether the Japanese needed a second chance (that is, to lose another war), before they could convince themselves that it perhaps wasn't the right way to go. The present Abe administration is doing everything it can to keep up pressure on North (and South) Korea, in large part because he so desperately needs the threat of a war (if not a war) to help promote his desired change in Article 9 of the Japanese Constitution, the so called "Peace Clause," and he is fully aware – and equally it is of no consequence to him – that if America does decide to go over-the-top and attack the North, almost without any doubt, it will be the South Koreans who will be hit hardest. (Japan already has fully viable Self Defence Forces, and here I suspect that Abe is actually more interested in getting a broader foothold in the international weapons business. [17.6])

Article 9: "Aspiring sincerely to an international peace based on justice and order, the Japanese people forever renounce war as a sovereign right of the nation and the threat or use of force as means of settling international disputes. In order to accomplish the aim of the preceding paragraph, land, sea, and air forces, as well as other war potential, will never be maintained. The right of belligerency of the state will never be realised." (Note that this, as was all of the present Japanese Constitution, imposed on Japan by the American victors in the war. It could also be noted that it is that same America that – once again, presumably for their own gain – is pushing Japan to revoke this article.)

[15.29]

Abe's personal interest in all this is that he wishes to both clear the name and carry out the personal wishes of his maternal grandfather, Nobusuke Kishi, the 'Economic Manager' for the Manchukuo Army during the Japanese occupation, imprisoned for three years as a Class A war-crime suspect and then released by the US government so that he could "lead post-war Japan in a pro-American direction," and eventually Japanese prime minister from January, 1957 to July, 1960. For anyone who is even mildly interested in the present-day impasse between Japan and the Korean peninsula and on to China; and more importantly, as an indictment of racism, the debasement of women and the manipulation of politics for personal gain (/unmitigated corruption), and perhaps to allow a certain understanding of what Japan's present-day prime minister represents, a brief reading of Kishi's Wikipedia (English) entry is highly recommended.

And so, one step at a time – one step forward, two back, two steps forward, one back – or whatever it has required, they have steadily pushed to have to their version of events accepted, first within Japan and then by the world. Unfortunately for them, there are still a considerable amount people both in the country here and on the outside who have direct personal memories of exactly what happened during that period, and they do know the difference between fact and fable.

The tale as the central government would prefer to have it understood – which is also the story that for most young Japanese nowadays would come close to the limits of their knowledge: "World War II was essentially a series of battles – starting with Pearl Harbor and ending with Hiroshima and Nagasaki – fought between America and Japan. We fought hard. The Americans won, and now we are the best of friends." (Overall, the Japanese, when they come to studying history, take things very lightly – this including not wishing to emphasise that a large proportion of their culture originates in Korea and China – and a considerable amount does tend to get glossed over.)

And when Asia is mentioned, there are invariably two tales:

"We were there to help!" "We were there to free the natives from their colonial oppressors. That or, "Look at all the good we did." "The Taiwanese appreciated all our help with development of infrastructure and education. Why can't the Koreans also be grateful?" (Or even, "It is impossible that the Koreans could not have been happy to have been occupied by the Japanese" – from a JT article by a Japanese correspondent in New York.)

The statement about Taiwan is actually completely true, and for a number of years I found it highly odd, until I read a report noting that after the Japanese left and Chiang Kai-Shek together with his Kuomintang nationalist forces arrived from the mainland in 1949, the Taiwanese nationals were treated considerably more harshly than they had been under the Japanese, which, if true, presumably would make for the difference. Also, there are a few of the Pacific islands (Borneo, if I remember correctly, is one) – where what the occupying forces did was appreciated in some form – which are regularly visited by Japanese television crews to record their more favourable memories, together with the little Japanese they remember.

(However, as freedom fighters?: I fully understand the alliance with Subhas Chandra Bose to fight against the British in India but, considering how they had already treated the peoples of Korea and the Chinese in Manchuria, to even imagine that, if they had won the war, the Japanese would have stood back and said, "We have evicted your oppressors, and now in our great magnanimity, we give you back your lands to govern freely as you wish," is so far beyond belief that it can only inspire ridicule.)

[15.30] And then, in contrast: "We didn't."

"The Rape of Nanjing (the Nanjing Massacre) did not happen. Or if it did, it was only a minor occurrence, with nothing like the number of civilians claimed to have been affected." "The Japanese Army had nothing to do with the recruitment of sex slaves/ 'comfort women.'" (For something, a little closer to the reality, see the Nobusuke Kishi Wikipedia article)

And closer to home: "Okinawa was 'unfortunate,' but all the things the Okinawans claim happened there – the Japanese army using Okinawan civilians as human shields, killing them, and forcing them to commit mass suicide during the American invasion of the islands, etc. – didn't." (The Japanese government had to be taken to court to prevent them eliminating the above facts from modern school textbooks.) The Okinawans also have a very complicated relationship with Japan, which continues today with the emphasis on the never-ending presence of American forces on their island.[22]

And as much as possible ignored; the Philippines, Singapore, the Bataan death march, prison camps, Burma, Guam, Malaysia, Hong Kong, Thailand, Java, Bali, etc. do not rate a mention.

And otherwise, the emphasis is on all the sufferings Japanese citizens had to endure in their retreat from Manchuria, or in the Russian prison camps, and how hard life was in Japan during and after the war.

Backpedalling from contrition:

Japanese government administrations claim to have repeatedly apologised for their actions in Asia, and in fact they actually have, but then every time they do, someone in the political establishment comes out with that same "But": "But we didn't…" "But it was nothing like as bad as it is claimed to be." "But we were only trying to help," etc., etc. – that is, in effect, doing everything they can to refute the original stance. And as might be expected, those who were directly affected take full political advantage of the situation to scream foul, and we are back to square one.

If Japan truly wants peace:

'History' can be argued, but during the fifty years I have been here, there has been absolutely no attempt at self-appraisal (/reappraisal) here – nothing like I have seen in Europe, or even in America with Vietnam or the Korean War. All we ever get to hear is: "Everything we did was good, or at the very least done in good faith. And anyone who might claim otherwise; all those Chinese, Koreans, British, Australians, New Zealanders, Filipinos, Dutch, etc. (even though they were actually there) are to be ignored, because we say so." And fifty years on, this can get a bit hard on the ears.

---

[22] At the time Okinawa was handed back to the Japanese government in 1971, the official agreement determined that the US could indefinitely occupy Okinawa militarily. The Okinawans have repeatedly protested that they are tired of this presence, but it remains highly convenient for both the US government – who are strategically positioned perfectly to protect their 'interests', and the Japanese – who don't have to worry about protests on the mainland. And if anyone is actually bombed, presumably "it will only be the Okinawans," who being racially of different stock are not rated overly highly on the mainland in the hierarchy of "matters to be considered."

The one ray of light in all this has been the attitude and actions of the newly abdicated Emperor Akihito (/Now, Emeritus) and his wife, Michiko (see below [15.38]).

[15.31] And viewed from closer up:

From, "Child": On the wherewithal of war. "And should you care to heal the scars of war and hatred, consider history's long convoluted paths of slaughter and retaliation, and go to greet thy neighbour with a bowed head."

Parents not talking to their children about their past (/youth) is common the world over (I imagine in many cases – and regardless of any skeletons in the closet – finding the right time, or just the time, would amount to an easy explanation), but in Japan, war histories (/experiences/ memories) have, almost without exception, been hidden from view, and it was only very recently that I learned that Mr Hamada [4.8], who I have known right through my life here, was one of the few people to experience the bombings of both Hiroshima and Nagasaki. (Immediately after Hiroshima, his 'tokkotai' kamikaze unit was ordered south.) Nothing else was said about the matter, but I do know that fortunately he did live to a good age.

Sayori Yoshinaga is a very famous actress here, and she also is known for her annual readings of poetry (some written by children) about the atomic bombings, and on one occasion she actually went to Seattle and gave a reading to a group of Americans in a church there that was later presented as a television documentary: The reading itself was well-received (attendees' applause and a number of their comments were recorded and suitably translated). However, coming out of the church, the American man who had organised the whole affair (the minister at the church?), repeating comments about how touching the poems were and how well the feeling had come through in her voice, also quietly mentioned to her (this being presented both politely and very sincerely) that, "It would perhaps be nice if she could also occasionally read some poems written by Chinese or Korean people, who had also suffered at Japanese hands in the war." And, naturally, the Japanese media being as it is, the latter part of the comment did not get into the programme. (There is that which can be said and that which cannot, and there is to be no muddying of the waters.)

At my last exhibition in 2016, where, along with paintings and photographs, the poem "Child" (including the section on war) was presented, among the many visitors, there was a lady who was fifteen when she lost use of her lower arm and had her hand crippled (to a shell?) – at the time, this would automatically exclude the possibility of any future marriage or children. This she showed to me when I asked her to sign the visitor's book (and cried when I took it). Also there was a man who, after telling me he was four years old and in Hiroshima at the time of the bombing, and then talking with me a little (he also cried) noted that "all he wanted was 'peace.'" And in my heart, understanding that I could never do this, (I don't think his brain in that state could have comprehended the fact, and more importantly I think his lack of comprehension would've actually hurt him), I wanted to tell him that if he really wanted peace, or perhaps more than anything peace of mind, he should go to China and find some of those who were hurt in a similar manner and sit and talk with them. (Japan actually has a 'Peace Boat', which every year takes the young volunteers on board to places such as Auschwitz and Chernobyl. Perhaps they might consider concentrating more on their Asian neighbours?)

I actually told both of the above stories to a man I had worked with years previously at the company. He is a very pleasant man, well-educated and in his sixties, and having worked with foreigners all his life, fully familiar with how we speak. Nonetheless, although he did understand that the media was not correct in not translating the minister's comment, when I told him my last thought about how about the man from Hiroshima, he shook his head, very briefly but very hard: It was not a subject to be even contemplated.

Waxworks:
Shortly before I came to Japan. I visited Madam Tussauds in London where they were holding a special exhibition of "Japanese atrocities during World War II," with scenes depicting the Siege of Nanjing, with all the raping, looting and murder involved; the Bataan death march – fallen prisoners at the end of Japanese soldiers' bayonets; the atrocious conditions and torture in the Japanese prisoner-of-war camps, and the infamous Unit 731, where live human subjects were used for research on various diseases including bubonic plague, typhoid and tuberculosis, etc. and also where biological weapons were in production. And then six to eight years later, one of the Japanese managers at the company came to tell me that he had seen the same exhibition on a recent visit to London, and, while noting that he had felt a little offended, asked me why that type of exhibition was being promoted "so many years after the war had ended." And I

told him that "Japan had Hiroshima," – which incidentally I still think to be a fair comment.

I have the fullest sympathy for all those who were killed, maimed, or suffered the long-term effects of the nuclear bombings, and I am, as already noted, totally against the usage of nuclear weapons, particularly in this modern age where one bomb can clearly do far more damage than the ones that were dropped here in Japan. And I equally understand that publicising their effects has been a very important factor in spreading the worldwide opposition to nuclear weapons. However, that said, considering the full arc of the war, the bombs were, in the end, of relative insignificance. To die from the explosion of a hand grenade, the lunge of a bayonet, torture, repeated beatings, sickness or starvation, fire bombings (as occurred in Tokyo and the Kansai area – as was the case with the above lady with the mangled hand), or even having to live a full life after being repeatedly raped, as the 'comfort women' (regardless of who recruited them) were – none of these were pleasant. The Japanese government have always supported Hiroshima and Nagasaki as a card; an official grudge that could be wielded politically against the Americans when debating the rights and wrongs of the war, and it was only this last year or so with the UN vote against the nuclear weapons states and the Nobel prize for ICAN, that they found themselves with no choice other than to admit publicly the truth that Japan was under the protection of the American nuclear umbrella, and Hiroshima and Nagasaki, et al were being left out to dry. And as is always the case in these matters, those who suffered.

Note: (Wikipedia) From 1937 to 1945, an estimated 26,000,000+ civilians (the large majority of whom must have been in the Asian theatre) died as the result of the Japanese invasion of their countries. (This as against the estimated 1,000,000+ Japanese civilians who died during the same period.) And for the Japanese government to believe that that reality can be just swept under the table as if it had never existed is an insult not only to all those who died, but also the intelligence of anyone who has even the most basic of facts available to them, which, with the Internet in full swing, an awful lot of people do these days.

Odds and ends:

[15.32] Responsibility:

When I have on occasion been asked to what degree I consider myself responsible for my country's colonial history (notably once from a man in Australia who, having been born in Mauritius while it was still under British rule (1810–1969), rather pushed the point), to the degree that I do understand the British were responsible for a great amount of pain and suffering in the world, I am suitably contrite, but in the end, having neither family nor political connections that I know of that would even remotely connect to me to my country's colonial past, I'm sorry but I personally do not (/cannot) feel any responsibility in this regard at all. (In the case of Mauritius, I had in fact no knowledge of historical details or even a clear map in my mind as to its geographical position that might have allowed me to even begin a conversation here.)

However, considering the matter today, my position would be that; "No other person is any more responsible for their nation's history than you are for yours." They are responsible for how they choose to present that history and may (/should) quite rightfully (as is being done in many recent novels and alternative accounts) be taken up on that point. Otherwise, as a member of one nation that has subjected others repeatedly to their will, perhaps if any individual can be said to be capable of taking responsibility (/expressing contrition) for the past actions of their nation, organisation or 'tribe', it is to the extent that they choose to take that common past as a humbling (rather than self-elevating) factor as it relates to the manner in which they proceed with their own life.

[15.33] "Retreat is the greater part of valour." Brexit:

Not having had the privilege of voting on the matter in the first place, and fully understanding it as the total catastrophe that it has become, other than to note that this is perhaps an example of how history does inevitably catch up on the present, I will refrain from any comment. And whatever one's position on this matter, in this case history has most definitely yet to be made.

[15.34] "Divide and conquer":

Taught the concept in school history classes (particularly in relationship to India,) and already with the understanding that my own society was controlled in precisely this same manner, this did then (and even today), make considerable sense. The taxi driver who drove us around in India for a full week in my mid-thirties, was in fact very polite (/tactful?) when I asked him about this matter, his main complaint being that while the British were there, they "could have perhaps helped a little with the education of the local population." Also, a Tanzanian man who I had the fortune to meet recently explained that individual tribes in his country had been restricted to certain crafts (/jobs/ skills/ trades/ duties), and that this process had ultimately left them divided and simultaneously (in terms of taking the reins of power) impotent.

However, the Hindu caste system as it existed (and still exists) far before the British arrived in India, with its 'dalit' untouchables, does not seem that much different, and Japan also had its own caste system – daimyo, samurai, farmers, merchants, 'burakumin' (again, untouchables) [5.13] – remnants of which (with its family registration system), still exist today, and therefore the principle in itself does not seem in any sense particularly rare.

(The British in India were apparently careful to see that usage of the English language was in large part restricted to the Indian elite. This can be compared with the Japanese elimination of the native culture through the enforcement of their language. But even in this latter case, while the Japanese may claim that, in the enforced usage on their language at all levels of colonial society, they were stressing integration and harmony, in reality they were doing nothing more than add one more bottom layer to their very carefully defined hierarchical system.)

[15.35] "We would never act like this!"

"Pointing out the weaknesses in other societies or traditions can only promote complacency. An occasional, 'We're not as good as they are in that area,' or even 'We are equally bad in that respect,' might stir some progress towards self-improvement."

Understanding that it goes against the grain to have one's own society criticised, particularly when it has become standard media fare to proclaim otherwise, and even more so to be forced to place oneself on precisely the same block as your loathed neighbour, it invariably amazes me how commentators who find themselves so easily condemning actions or events in a foreign country can seemingly pass over (/completely ignore) identical or even worse events from their own recent history.

ISIS and other terrorists who blow themselves up for their beliefs:

Invariably condemned as 'unthinkable' and 'inhuman' by the same Japanese government and media who in their next breath choose to deify the actions of the Japanese Army and Navy 'Tokkotai' – Special (suicide) Attack Units (Ref: Wikipedia) who performed precisely the same acts (utilising planes, speedboats and mini-submarines equipped with explosives) "for the glory of the homeland." "Ah, but they are terrorists!"

The present Chinese government's efforts to secularise the Moslem Uighur population through the usage of 'indoctrination camps':

This as against the Canadian Indian children forcibly taken from their homes to be educated in 'residential boarding schools' ("plagued by under-funding, disease, and abuse") and the mandatory removal from their aboriginal homes of mixed-descent children in Australia "in order that they might be cultivated into becoming white-citizens." (Wikipedia: Stolen Generations.)

Opinions might differ as to quite which is worse here but given all as efforts by those in control to eliminate the other's culture, in the fact that they are apparently not as yet stealing (this would no doubt be described as 'separating' in America) children from their parents, the Chinese here would seem to come out as the more humane. Otherwise, the main difference would perhaps be the lack of any expectation that the Chinese government might at some point in the future apologise for their actions. (Even there, it did it take the US 43 years to apologise for the internment of American Japanese during WWII, so it is always to be seen what the future might hold.)

American complaints of "Russian interference in elections":

The CIA has been interfering repeatedly in foreign election processes for decades now (and ditto for inserting viruses (/cyberweapons) into enemy's computer systems) so, other than the possible involvement of your present president, what exactly is the problem here? WGFTG!

And not to push a point; "The enemy invariably lies. Naturally, we do not."

(Wikipedia) Prior to the invasion of Iraq in 2003, President George W Bush announced that he would possibly take action to topple the Iraqi government, because of the threat of its weapons of mass destruction, stating that: "The Iraqi regime (under Saddam Hussein) has plotted to develop anthrax, nerve gas and nuclear weapons for over a decade… Iraq continues to flaunt its hostility toward America and to support terror."

Iraq was invaded, Hussein was overthrown and executed. No weapons of mass destruction were ever found. (Prime Minister Blair in the UK, who fully supported Bush, did not come out well on this matter either, but still cares to proclaim his innocence.)

And then, never mentioned at the time of the above invasion or in its aftermath, you look back a little to the Iran–Iraq war of 1980–1988 where (Wikipedia): "According to Iraqi documents, <u>assistance in developing chemical weapons</u> was obtained from firms in many countries, including the United States, West Germany, the Netherlands, the United Kingdom, and France. Also, a report stated that Dutch, Australian, Italian, French and both West and East German companies were involved in <u>the export of raw materials to Iraqi chemical weapons factories</u>." Also, declassified CIA documents show that "the United States was providing reconnaissance intelligence to Iraq around 1987–88 (the time of the war) which was then used <u>to launch chemical weapon attacks on Iranian troops</u> and that the CIA fully knew that chemical weapons would be deployed. The 'international community' remained silent as Iraq used weapons of mass destruction against Iranian[s] as well as Iraqi Kurds."

(I was actually made aware of this last particular fact in the newspapers of the time where it was commented on once or possibly twice, but I do know that as with all such problematic details, it was very quickly set aside.)

And even today, opinion leaders in the New York Times are still claiming the US as the true champion of "freedom, democracy, decency and the rule of law." The American establishment, as it has existed for quite some time now, only shows any real interest in "freedom, democracy, decency and the rule of law," as an excuse to attack others who to their mind don't. And otherwise, according to their convenience, they will cuddle up to any freewheeling dictator they choose.

For any younger person who is at all interested in any of the above as it is related to current events, an easy starting point might be the joint British and American coup against Iran in 1953, basically manufactured to protect their oil interests, which even today, and regardless of all the present emphasis on Israel's woes, is still fundamental to all Western (and other outside) interference in the Middle East. (Conceivably, if levels of destruction continue in this manner for much longer, there might be some slender hope that even the producing nations in the area will come to the conclusion that, despite their present economic dependence, the more quickly the world is weaned off the usage of oil for its energy uses (thus ridding them of American interference for once and for all), the better – in all senses – their chances of survival.)

And then taking the matter that one level further. Three newspaper articles in the one day:

NYT. (14.3.2019) "Who to elect for a 3 am global crisis." By Thomas L Friedman.

The article, in fact doing no more than presenting a list of all the problems the world faces at present, is in and of itself no problem. However, referring to "power relationships," there are the predictable denunciations of "three big regional powers": Russia, China, and Iran, all basically out to dominate their regions and fully prepared to use force with that aim in mind (America isn't?), together with the claims that only the US has the resources and the experience to help other countries cope with state failure. (I had always assumed that America's specialty – at least in the Middle East – was spawning state failure.) In the article, Friedman is in large part quoting from a new book, "The Rise and Fall of Peace on Earth", by Michael Mandelbaum (Johns Hopkins emeritus professor of US foreign policy). However, shortly after this (and I am assuming here that the comment is his), you get the (again, considering every point made throughout this chapter) totally absurd and utterly unbelievable assertion that "democracies are less prone to starting wars." (This is a direct quote.)

On the understanding that you cannot have wars without weapons:
(JT: 14.3.2019) "Trump is winning, and Putin is losing in global arms sales." By Leonid Bershidsky, Berlin.

The gist of the article is as stated, but a quick read will ascertain the following facts.

Of the world's five top arms exporters – America, Russia, France, Germany, and the United Kingdom (which together account for 75% of the market) – four are democracies. (A quick glance at Wikipedia indicates that Israel, yet one more democracy, as of writing is holding sixth position.)

The US closed $55.6 billion worth of arms deals in 2018, 33% more than in 2017. In contrast, Russia claims a steady $15 billion in sales. US exports were 75% higher than Russia's in 2014 through 2018.

The flow of armaments to the Middle East rocketed by 87% in the last five years. (Only 16% of Russia's exports went to the Middle East.)

Global arms sales showed a 7.8% increase from 2014 to 2018 compared with the previous five-year period. And between 2011 and 2017, the average annual death toll from conflict neared 97,000, three times more than in the previous seven-year period.

All of the above bringing me to be unavoidable conclusion that, even if democracies (with the US way ahead of the pack here) "aren't prone to making war," they certainly know how to make a lot of money from them.

And finally, in "To blunt sanctions, Iran turns to Iraq." By Alissa J Rubin. NYT. (14.3.2019), you get a statement from a former Sunni speaker of the Iraqi Parliament to the effect that if one can consider Iran as a small body with a big brain, the United States can presumably only be described as a big body with a small brain.

And there you have it in a nutshell – and straight from the horse's mouth.

[15.36] Learning the true costs:

"Future generations need to be taught history for exactly what it is."

Working my way through the above presentation, it has come to me that I have never ever been quite so conscious of the pointlessness of war. As a younger person at school, and even reading the various books on the subject that I have as an adult, I was never really fully aware of wars or the conquering of other nations as other than a somewhat abstract 'series of battles or skirmishes' each with their heroes, distinguished leaders, strategies, expansions and retreats. And all subsequent pictures on the screen (large and small) in their rendering of such wars, can very quickly desensitise one to any realities: "What exactly is one watching?" "And why (having no control over the matter), should that be of any importance to me?"

And if I have to come to any conclusion here, it must be that if children around the globe are to receive any common education that might help them as they grow, as is the case with worldwide pollution and climate change, this is one more area where some special attention needs to be brought to bear.

[15.37] Monuments and memorials:

Ref: NYT: (31.10.2018.) "Slave trading past no longer in the shadows." By Alissa J Rubin.

In this article, Jean-Marc Ayrault, the mayor of the French port of Nantes at the time of the 2012 opening of the 'Memorial to the Abolition of Slavery', notes that he does not want to see people set against one another or blaming one another, but rather examining their shared history. (France was the third largest of the European nations dealing in the slave trade after Portugal and England. An estimated 12 million slaves, traded for cloth and other goods from African tribal chiefs were taken to the Americas by European traders, about 10.7 million of whom survived the trans-Atlantic passage.)

And in Britain, they are still fighting for a simple memorial ('Memorial 2007') in a rose garden in London's Hyde Park.

I would understand such a memorial as a form of acknowledgment of the true situation by the political establishment in Britain, unfortunately a recognition that they are clearly not at present willing to give, or presumably the money would have been provided some time ago. However, considering the fact that a similar memorial in Nantes was desecrated and broken beyond repair shortly after being placed in position, that is, was totally ineffective, for children in their early teens, who should be the target for any real education in this area – still at the stage of processing facts and as yet far too young for anything that requires serious deliberation or reflection, and rather requiring some more intuitive, emotionally based experience, something they can physically react to without any consideration – a permanent exhibition in any of Britain's main museums, including well-presented facts together with some 'attraction' – an enclosed space where they could be given the opportunity to sit shackled and squeezed tightly between rows of black slaves as they worked the oars in as close as possible rendering of the conditions slaves at the time faced, and possibly including a final 'overturning/flooding of the galleys', could be considered. There are lots of artists around who specialise in work with sound and light to considerable effect, who I am sure could be persuaded to contribute ideas. Certainly, Liverpool, which is apparently considering a memorial, should take a close look at Nantes' final solution.

[15.38] "We can have ours, but you can't have yours."

The Meiji Jingu shrine in Tokyo acts as the equivalent of a national war memorial for some 2.46 million war dead. However, since Japanese Class-A war criminals were enshrined there in 1978, its position and particularly the strong support of the politician members of the above right-wing Nippon Kaigi [15.28] has made it highly controversial, particularly in China and Korea. Also, since this time, no Japanese emperor has visited the shrine, creating a somewhat odd impasse, stemming from the fact that the shrine and many of its supporters consider it central to promoting the Imperial system as it existed in its pre-war form, with the emperor worshipped as a 'kami'. Most recently (12.10.2018, JT), the head priest at the shrine was exposed on Twitter and forced to resign for criticising the now Emperor Naruhito and Empress for trying to "crush the shrine" by not visiting it. (Over the years, it has been suggested that a more neutral site might be considered for such a monument, but each time, in large part on political grounds, this has been rejected.)

The Emperor Hirohito (/Emperor Showa) who was reigning at the time I arrived in Japan until his death in January 1989, shadowed at all times by the question of the degree of his involvement in WWII, other than for his official duties, was obliged to keep a relatively low profile. In contrast, the now newly abdicated Emperor Akihito (/Emeritus) and his wife, Michiko, have striven very hard and in large part successfully to counter that image; on an international level, by traveling abroad to pray for the souls of both Japanese and the enemy soldiers who died at various battle-sites throughout Asia, and within Japan, by making it clear that they were relating very closely to the people who had suffered in the various natural (earthquakes, typhoons and tsunami) and manmade tragedies during their reign, together making repeated visits to the temporary evacuation shelters set up for those who had lost families and homes, and deliberately kneeling (something previously inconceivable for a member of the Imperial family) in order make their exchanges more intimate. And in terms of how past events can be used to determine the future, they have in fact managed to set a fully recorded precedent supported by more than 80% of their countrymen that will be hard to argue with as their sons take up the mantle. (Their son, the present Emperor Naruhito and his brother seem equally of this bent.)

A matter of equivalence:

Some time ago in the Japan Times, a Western correspondent writing about the above shrine noted in particular the problem of the museum maintained within its grounds, which is in effect there to present a series of displays on WWII designed to corroborate the above-described right-wing's positions on the war. This was actually a number of years ago and I cannot find a record of the particular article for reference. However, as much as my memory allows me and in line with the general gist of his presentation: Following complaints from certain foreign visitors to the shrine about certain highly-biased descriptions placed in front of the displays, they had recently created a brand-new set of 'English translations', which in and of itself would seem to be of no matter, except for the fact that they had left the original Japanese explanations precisely as they had previously been, making it totally respectable for the foreign visitor while keeping its intended "We are beautiful!" message for its Japanese audience – essentially duplicity in the extreme. With the average Japanese (even after years of study) being so poor at English, the government here seems incapable of understanding quite how fluent in both the reading and speaking of Japanese so many foreigners living in Japan are today.

One example provided in the article that, in particular with my English background, stuck out somewhat conspicuously, was the Japanese description given in front of one of the original steam trains used on the Burma-to-Thailand railway, boasting of the fact that the full length of the line had been completed in 15 months, "something that the British army engineers, with all their efforts, had been unable to accomplish," at the same time skipping over the fact of the between 180,000 and 250,000 Southeast Asian civilian laborers and about 61,000 Allied prisoners of war subjected to (in many cases brutal levels of) forced labour during its construction.

And now, with Thailand considering an application for their end of the line to become a UNESCO Cultural Heritage site, the name to be placed on the application – "Death Railway", its locally accepted name as "the source of the over 100,000 deaths of those who were forced to labour on its construction," or the far more benign, "Historical Railway – World War II," presumably to be perceived more as the splendid feat of engineering that the Japanese would wish it to be seen, has become a matter of contention.

At a recent meeting on the matter, Borvornvate Rungrujee, president of the Thai chapter of the International Council on Monuments and Sites, or ICOMOS, Thailand, who, while admitting certain political pressure (noting that Japanese officials have expressed concerns about the use of the name to him), advised Thailand not to use "Death Railway" for official heritage designation on the grounds that doing so would seem like pointing the blame in Japan. (Quite who else might there be to blame?) And in contrast, from "one of the local participants", there was the perfectly generous: "I insist on using the same well-known name. I do not want to point out Japan's past conduct, nor do I blame them, but it is a fact." (Essentially, a reiteration of the above French mayor's statement.) A decision is to be made later in the year. However, as an example of the outcome of a similar case:

Having discovered the potential for increased tourism predicated by designation as a UNESCO World Heritage Site, of late, both central and local governments in Japan seem to have taken to the concept with a passion, one of their more recent successes being the registration of a group of sites as "symbols of the rapid industrialisation of Japan," these including Hashima Island ('gunkanjima') in southern Kyushu, originally a site for coal mining now essentially deserted. Unfortunately, as pointed out by the Korean government during the initial stages of the application, it also has a history as a site of forced labour prior to and during WWII, and prior to any recognition, they insisted that this point be made clear in all related descriptions, and this was eventually agreed on by both sides. However, on the day of final approval, immediately after the UNESCO WHC meeting, Japanese Foreign Minister Fumio Kishida publicly announced that "the remarks 'forced to work under harsh conditions' by the Japanese government representative did not mean 'forced labour'." UNESCO rightly complained and demanded that the agreed-upon description be inserted in all descriptions on the site. However, as of the present moment, nothing has been done about the matter.

Lee Yong-Soo (comfort woman and activist), interviewed at 89 by a JT reporter: "What right does Japan have to tell us what to do with statues placed here? It's absurd."

The 2015 'Final and Irreversible' settlement on the comfort women issue between Japan and South Korea, recently revoked by the present Korean administration to the great annoyance of the Japanese side, was made between the (ultra-right) Abe administration and Park Geun-hye – the now-imprisoned (25 years for abuse of power, bribery, coercion, and leaking government secrets), ex-president daughter of General Park Chung-hee, both a military dictator and Japanese wartime collaborator who, while in power, signed the original war-reparations settlement between the two countries in 1965. Basically, by making a cosy agreement with his former rulers (which he presumably also profited from – again see Wikipedia article on Kishi), he forfeited his citizens' right to demand any restitution for their own personal maltreatment.

In a recent (Feb. 2019) letter to the NYT, a Japanese government official made the points that the comfort women agreement (including apologies and financial reparations) had been totally fair, and again stressed the 'Final and Irreversible' clause as Japan's case against Korea's invalidation of the agreement. However, one point that he did not note was that the agreement also included "the removal of certain memorials to the women involved" – one placed strategically in front of the Japanese embassy in Seoul – and also a clause stipulating the need to "refrain from raising the comfort women issue in the international arena." He also did not note that prior to the signing of the agreement, Abe made no attempt (as a personal opinion, "did not have the decency of character") to actually meet or personally apologise to any of the very few surviving women involved.

And as an indication of quite how important the Japanese political establishment in general feels this to be, the city of Osaka recently broke off its 60-year sister-city relationship with San Francisco because the mayor there refused to remove a similar statue. They clearly very much do not wish to be perceived in a bad light.

Ref: NYT: (20.2.2019.) "Plans for war memorial bring accusations of whitewashing." By Jamie Tarabay.

And today, in Australia, you have the American warplane manufacturer, Boeing, sponsoring a war memorial in Canberra centred on losses of Australian soldiers in Afghanistan, the project (funding arranged behind closed doors) negotiated with the present War Memorial director, Brendan Nelson, who was Australia's Defence Minister from 2006 to 2007 (peak years of the fighting in Iraq and Afghanistan). And as noted in the article, the museum display is set to include an F-111 strike jet, an aircraft that has never played a role in any Australian combat operations.

Presumably, as is the case with any social media commercial, you get what you are paying for.

[15.39] National heroes. Perpetuating the ultimate myth:

Taking a 'national hero' to be an 'outstanding leader', it is very easy to understand that they should, in their time, have had monuments created in their honour, both in their own lands and others that were conquered in their name. However, equally understanding such persons to have actually been (no more than) 'outstanding leaders to the people their actions benefited', it becomes natural that those monuments be no longer welcome once those same lands retrieve their independence.

However, in cases where those 'heroes' were responsible for countless deaths and inordinate levels of suffering (including the deaths of those they commanded) and understanding that a large proportion of younger people today are going to come up against such stories very quickly as they interact with the whole range of information available on today's Internet, might it not make sense to have these facts (simply presented as: "This is the reality." "This is war.")

made open to younger generations in the course of their basic education? And possibly if you wish to promote a little empathy in the process, students could be asked whether they would accept their neighbourhood today being totally destroyed, and family or friends being killed and maimed in such a manner, to allow someone on the other side of the world the pleasure of celebrating yet one more such 'hero'?

For aggressor nations, and in this group I would include all former colonisers (and if you wish to bring this into the modern context, 'world policemen'), if you are going to record (/have a memorial) for all those who died in a war (which I fully understand and respect), perhaps you could consider including those on the other side (in the majority of cases, a far larger number than your own) who are only dead because you or your compatriots chose to interfere with their lives for nothing more than your own profit, power games and/or personal aggrandisement. Far more than you can begin to understand it, "The king is stark naked," and has been for quite some time now.

[15.40] That said, as a final suggestion (and for lack of a better word): "Peace monuments."

If the world is ever going to make even the slightest of dents in today's political cultures of silence and secrecy (/avoidance of responsibility) there is clearly a strong need for testaments (in the form of public spaces and monuments) to both war and slavery.

Germany has already moved a considerable way in this direction. And also, I have noted above the recently retired Japanese emperor's understanding of the need to include all those who suffered as a result of the Japanese military's actions in Asia prior to and throughout WWII in his visits and prayers.

For any two or more countries (/sides) that have been in a state of occupation or war, would it not be possible to agree to identical (simple stone) monuments detailing the number of deaths and injured on both sides (and with *total body counts* stressed) during the overall period concerned (and/or in the main battles) to be placed openly in both countries for the benefits of both populations. In the case of any remaining strong disagreement, approximated figures as given by both sides could be included together with a consensus figure taken from accounts provided by more neutral parties, but to preclude any future arguments, there would have to be an agreement that precisely the same accounts appear on both monuments.

This would, if only one step at a time, be eliminating those points of irritation (the "detritus" introduced at the beginning of this chapter) that invariably come up each time there are disagreements between any two parties in their everyday relationships. Equally, it would allow the citizens of (particularly) the original aggressor nation to have a much fuller appreciation of quite what their leaders were involved with, and, as with the above Nantes memorial, allow opportunities to open the eyes of younger people to the realities of the world. And with the present computerisation of educational materials, there would be no reason not to have such figures (simplified to total deaths/injuries on both sides) detailed in all educational materials that refer to the subject. (Any educator in any country could, in fact, contribute here by simply regularly pointing out such basic facts (starting with internal wars) to their classes.)

When my brain originally came up with this idea, I was thinking specifically of the very highly politicised disagreement between Japan and China on details of the Nanjing massacre. Figures for actual deaths range from over 200,000 as the figure estimated by the International Military Tribunal for the Far East in Tokyo, to more than 300,000 on the Chinese side. Much lower figures, including total denials of the event, are at present being given by right-wing revisionists in Japan (the equivalent of Holocaust deniers in Germany). However, apparently most scholars (including those in Japan) accept figures from 50,000 to 300,000 dead as an approximate total. (Wikipedia)

I cannot see today's administration, with its overall attitudes towards the war as recorded above, accepting anything in line with my above proposal at the present time, but at some time in the future, if they do wish to make any progress in their relationships with the Chinese government, it could be a point from which to start discussions. And in a similar manner, might something like this not be a way for the British government to approach (/soften the burden of) such problems as the remaining existence of Cecil Rhodes (of Rhodesia – present day Zimbabwe) monuments in Oxford, and other outstanding disagreements with previous colonies.

And perhaps extended: An electronic noticeboard in any of the world's main cities (New York's Times Square, London's Piccadilly – possibly sponsored by one or more of the main independent news organisations in that country) regularly updating the total number of deaths and injuries resulting from any ongoing wars that that particular nation is (even mildly) involved in?

I can see this as a very uphill trip, but unquestionably some form of effort needs to be made on all sides.

Chapter 16
The Peculiarities of Confucianism in the Modern Age
(1) Personal Relationships

The following is a series of observations on Japanese society as it has evolved over the close on 50 years I have been here, with a particular emphasis on how Confucianism, a philosophical system created some 2,500 years ago for a very different (/closed) world, is holding up to the advent of (far more open) modern communication systems.

I can understand Confucianism, in its historical context and as a subject of investigation for academics, as a highly fascinating discipline from which a great deal of knowledge can be acquired. However, in the manner in which I have observed it applied in Japan today, and on the understanding that it has provided a great number of benefits to the population here, it equally does have a number of serious problems, which, unless approached with great care, are going to provide serious constraints on any future development. Also, although I admit my knowledge of the true situation in other countries as relatively limited, much of what is noted below will equally apply at least to South Korea, and presumably to some degree in any other country (present-day China?) where Confucianism is recognised as a guiding principle.[23]

---

[23] (On the understanding that all societies, regardless of the name they choose to go by, are run to benefit their elites.) On the political spectrum, in terms of freedoms offered, Confucianism (with its insistence on all subjects being subservient to the state) has the potential to be (and in reality, almost certainly is) far more restrictive than Communism – which at least takes the 'working class people's voice and their right to rise up against their oppressors' as its raison d'être – ever could be.

[16.1]

As noted in earlier chapters, over the centuries, Japan has introduced elements of Buddhism and Confucianism (through/from China) and Christianity (from Europe), all of which, together with the indigenous religion of Shinto, have competed to greater or lesser extents for influence with successive governments. However, during the Edo period (1603–1867), following the unification of Japan and during the time Japan closed its doors to all external influences, in order to balance the rivalry between these groups, the government decreed that in matters of morality, Confucianism would be regarded as having first place. Buddhism was to take precedence in matters of religion, and Shinto in matters of state. (Christianity was officially banned.) Taoism, the religion that was originally coupled with Confucianism in China, as far as my understanding goes, has never featured very strongly in Japan's history, although I have come across it occasionally in modern Japanese society with groups that apparently associate themselves with pre-war military tendencies.

Although much has changed since, even in post-war society, Confucianism – although never described as such – is still clearly relevant, with key points stressed as social order/harmony and the responsibilities of the population towards the nation/government (in contrast to the government's responsibilities to the populace, the norm for descriptions of democracies in the West). Obedience to authority in general (/one's superiors, 'seniors'), self-control, restraint, conforming and 'preserving face' (the understanding that others should not be embarrassed publicly) are also all understood as important elements[24], and all are perfectly valid components for a well-organised society. However, it can be noted that independence, curiosity, self-reliance, and consideration for others regardless of their position, all of which can be considered balancing factors when determining an individual's tendency towards authoritarianism, are totally absent from the mix here.

---

[24] For anyone interested in what has been left out, a quick view on the Internet will give you other elements such as "leaders exercising mercy," "familial responsibilities" (dealt with below), "love," "humanity" and "Do not do to others what you do not want done to yourself," which are all commonly found in other societies around the world, and if these concepts are addressed correctly, you are clearly open to the possibility of a much kinder (/gentler) interpretation of the overall concept. However, I very much sense that at least in Japan, responsibility to the group has been emphasised far beyond any concepts of love or compassion – which can be interpreted in far wider terms.

[16.2] Confucianism as propagated through educational practices:

The purpose of all education systems is to produce young citizens who (1) will fit in with and (2) be of practical use to the societies they have the fortune to be born into, and perhaps should be critiqued accordingly.

That China, at this particular point in time, is reintroducing a number of 'selected' elementary schools that are, as their main charge, required to produce children who are well drilled in the teachings of the Communist Party (or rather, the more recent "Rules according to President Xi," which as I understand also include certain elements of Confucianism), considering the type of country he wishes to lead, is a perfectly natural and to-be-expected progression. In the England I was brought up in (and here I can only reference personal experience, and I do know that much has changed in the way the education system is organised) discipline-wise, the grammar school I attended had a simple and essentially well-organised system: There were rules as to what was and wasn't allowed, together with an established line of progressively more serious punishments – from standing outside the classroom, staying behind after school and writing lines ("I must do my homework." 300 times / "I must not smoke in the toilets." 500 times), to a strapping in the headmaster's office or, in the most serious of cases, suspension or expulsion. Children, as all do (self-included), broke the rules but, when caught, accepted whatever was coming to us, if not necessarily as fair, then at least as having an order to it, and ultimately as representative of a certain accountability to society. That is, we were being taught what to expect as adults in our social system. (In a recent conversation with Japanese acquaintances in the same age group, this was apparently the same system that was employed in their schools at the time. But if so, I can only note that much has changed since.)

FF: Both prefects in our last year at school, one of my cheerier classmates, who was also a chemistry buff, took the liberty in the school lunch-break of walking into the playground and gagging a group of first-year kids with a rag he had soaked in some chemical taken from the school labs, and coming back into the classroom, he proudly pointed out to me the results of his work – six to eight dazed, somewhat sad and lonely twirling figures, lost out in the concrete ocean of the school yard. And we both had a good laugh. (And he was punished.)

[16.3] Nursery and elementary schooling:

"Everyone gets on well with each other. And if they don't, we make them."

This is a quote from a Japanese elementary school teacher interviewed by a local newspaper in America (to her mind) promoting the 'caring qualities' of the education system in her country. (I suspect that, in England, the above statement would be laughed out of the corridors.)

I fully understand the concept here of teaching children to work together as a group; cleaning classrooms and generally helping with the upkeep of the school being identical to what is expected in terms of being a 'good neighbour' when working in the countryside, where even today, as I experienced, one is expected to contribute to the general upkeep of the narrow paths and waterways running between individual properties. However, that said: When a new student joins a class in Japan, while in England I sense it was assumed that we would automatically do so, the class teacher here invariably makes a point of stressing (almost to the level of admonishing) the need for class members to "get on well with" the new member. And regardless of the above-stated intention, there is clearly a principle of control at work here, the implication of a need to accept the other and "become friends" in itself being a form of constraint. In a recent newspaper article, an American boy who had been put through the system by his parents picked up on this immediately. As he described it, his experience throughout was (an extremely unpleasant) one of "regimentation."

Encouraging the sense of 'all being equal' when it is clearly not true:

This is to a certain degree echoing the grammar school/comprehensive school debate that existed when I was young in England. However, in Japan, the debate becomes more related to the suppression of individuality, and, in practice, a denial of those who are more academically and/or physically gifted, are naturally slim or overweight, or are more socially adept or inward-looking etc., all of which, with suitable encouragement and guidance, can be harnessed to a society's benefit.

[16.4] Elements that run through the system:

Rote learning:

The whole education system here (including all testing) is premised on the student's ability to intake and subsequently repeat facts, with seemingly very little emphasis on how those facts might relate to each other. And for adults, television quiz shows (with very few exceptions) put the emphasis on the memorisation of those same names, faces and facts.

Helping one of my high school students work through a short descriptive passage in his English textbook, an excerpt from a short story that he had been given for his homework, it quickly became evident that while his whole attention was concentrating on memorising word-for-word, phrase-for-phrase translations of sentences (as was expected of him at school), he actually had no appreciation at all of the somewhat subtle relationships between the characters portrayed or any of the emotional reactions that immediately came to me as a native reader.

Rules for rules' sake:

This is, more than anything, the one factor that grounds the whole system: "Rules exist to be followed. You do things not because they make any logical (or otherwise) sense. You do things because that is what you are told to do – or more specifically, and in no manner open to question; 'That is the way things are done.'"

Foreign parents, (and these days, commonly a number of Japanese), often note the insistence upon a wide range of largely or totally irrelevant school rules, and in the worst cases the existence of two or more such rules that directly conflict. The best example of this latter recently was of a girl who was a natural brunette ordered to have her hair dyed – the rule here being that "All students' hair must be black." Her foreign father, who naturally was concerned about the matter for a number of reasons, did point out that the school also had a rule that stated, "Students must not dye their hair," but apparently this had no effect: The school insisted that her hair be black, that is, they selected the rule that was more convenient for their purpose. Quite how the matter was finally settled, I do not know, but it was picked up as an anomaly in the local media. And children not being quite as slow on these matters as the authorities might imagine, the (still young) girl herself had the common sense to note that, "It was the school's insistence that 'everyone must act in the same manner' that presumably was one of the reasons she was being bullied for being different."

(And when you grow old enough to make purchases through online mailing services, the above makes it quite feasible to state in a contractual agreement presented on the television screen that: "All products which fail to satisfy may be returned," directly followed by a second sentence which states; "There are some products which may not be returned." Quite whatever that might mean!)

"Too many cooks"

I cannot remember my parents appearing in either of my schools except for the relatively rare (once a year, when I was at elementary school?) "Parents Day", during which they would observe possibly one or two classes. Other than that, we had reports detailing our academic progress to be taken home at the end of each school year, and that was it. All disciplinary problems within the school (except for the most extreme), were handled by the school with no parental or otherwise outside interference. At the same time, once outside the school's framework of authority, parents were considered responsible for any problem that their child might create. Also, headmasters at all schools were promoted from within the system, that is, all were fully experienced teachers.

And in comparison, in Japan:

As in America, there are PTA (Parent Teacher Associations), which involve a considerable amount of interaction among the parties concerned, including teacher visits to the child's home, arrangements for sports days and the like, resulting in the potential for considerable parental interference. I am not really sure just quite how bad the situation was when I first arrived, but I do know that over the years, the burden in terms of responsibility for the child's (both moral and academic) upbringing, has been shifted more and more onto the teachers, to the point that, at present, any and all problems (particularly in the cases of bullying or suicides) are now taken up by the media quite automatically as being the result of 'poor educators' at schools, and the parents, almost without exception, are being given a free pass.

The person imbued with the highest authority in a school in Japan (the equivalent of a headmaster in England), is invariably promoted from the outside. None are or ever have been teachers, and subsequently, other than their experiences at school as students, none know anything about teaching – a specialist task which requires years of direct experience working with children. This is also true for local boards of education, who directly report to the Ministry of Education in Tokyo, making them at the best administrators and commonly ex-bureaucrats. Historically, this comes from the fact that, since the end of WWII, in direct reaction to the excessive government control in the pre-war situation, on a political spectrum, schoolteachers have invariably taken a strong leftward (anti-war) bias, and presumably this is the closest the government could come to bringing them under their control. However, this (commonly excessive) interference does not aid in any smooth running of the system.

'Senpai-kouhai' relationships:

If elementary schools involve everyone being kind to everyone, high-schools exist solely for the purpose of cramming your way into the highest grade of university possible (the key to one's future), this together with exposure to a very swift change to disciplinary ('Spartan') methods of training aimed at the development of senior-junior, 'senpai-kouhai' relationships – the junior in the relationship inevitably deferring to the senior (initially centred on club activities, extending right up through the adult sports and business cultures, and, in the end, the whole society). And once in, university may be regarded as 'time off' – that you got into that particular university being the only requirement for graduation – this traditionally followed by a full ten years of training as 'new employees' to become 'company men'. At least this was the system until relatively recently when, following the bursting of the bubble economy together with the advent of the alternative world now provided on social media, young people seem to have gone into complete revolt. (See [17.1])

[16.5] The (questionable) benefits of a college education:

Fully understanding the irony in the following as related to my own progress at university; "If you are not going to study, why bother?" Then again, if the only requirements stipulated in your selected curricula be that your brain retain yet further quite evidently superfluous data, and you know that regardless of any efforts made, you will be receiving that graduation certificate, again; "Why bother?"

I did teach for a very short two years at a local women's college, which if nothing else gave me the opportunity to experience the true reality of the above, the worst case being a young woman who attended only one class and did not even bother to turn up for her 'final examinations', who I refused to graduate – this not accepted by the college authorities, fundamentally the argument being that her parents had paid for the course and she was entitled to her certificate. And still I refused, and subsequently lost the job; something which I very quickly came to appreciate: Essentially, they were wasting their time and mine.

And as an alternative route: A young woman who joined the company as a receptionist at the front desk signed up for evening English classes (open to all employees), at which time I very quickly discovered that she spoke extremely well. Her father had refused to "waste his money on a third-rate women's college education," but had agreed to send her to one of our more well-established

English schools in town, which he knew had a reputation for making their students study hard. And it had worked – within months, she had been picked up by one of our foreign managers to work as his personal secretary.

[16.6] The exercise of personal control over others. The social conditions underlying bullying:

There clearly are a considerable number of people (both male and female) who, for whatever reason, have a predilection for bullying – that is taking pleasure from the exercising of their personal power over (/demeaning) others – and here I am using the word in the widest possible manner to include both verbal and physical violence together with and/or sexual predation, etc.

As conditions that can foster such bullying, or the circumstances under which it could be expected to flourish, in the West one can easily point to the misuse of authority in families, educational facilities, the military, religious organisations (priests in the catholic church, nuns in charge of children's homes), the police, businessmen, politicians, 'elites' of all types including the super-rich, etc. – all of which are regularly reported in the media – the easy read here being that the position of the individual in that social unit, organisation or hierarchy, together with the degree of authority attributed (/assumed) is creating the excuse in the individual's mind for misuse of that position. Also, there are also those who operate and/or take advantage of situations where they are outside the range of any authority, in situations where physical and/or psychological advantages commonly apply/are applied; stalkers, molesters, etc., schoolchildren out of the teacher's sight; posts on social media, where chaos can so easily reign in the form of blogs, bots, trolls or whatever, and pure, unadulterated maliciousness seems the order of the day.

And then there is Japan.

Stressing that the following could be referring to *any person*, regardless of their actual position (/level) in society:

"All the elements of Confucianism described at the beginning of this chapter could equally be interpreted as conditions for supporting a socially approved (/institutionalised) exercise of control of any one member over any other individual in that particular grouping."

That is, any person who, for whatever reason, chooses to assume the role of 'senior' and exercise their authority over another, also knows that the other person involved, as a direct result of their social conditioning, (1) is expected to conform (/show self-control) and (2) far more importantly, (presuming the presence of others) in order to 'protect social harmony' and 'preserve face' (and, as this is commonly understood as including the 'face' of the person who is doing the bullying), is expected *not to make a fuss*.

That is, the same system that is creating opportunities for the demeaning of others can also be understood as providing the requisite conditioning for the required targets.

As a result, you have a situation where, while in America you seemingly have an exaggeration of individuality that encourages children to pick on others, here it is almost certainly the suppression of that same individuality (the proverbial hammering down of that protruding nail) that produces exactly that same result or possibly worse.

[16.7] Reacting to bad cases:

England: He apparently had been put through three or four schools by his parents in the hopes that he might settle somewhere, but it wasn't working. I only saw him here and there around the grounds a couple of times in the few days he stayed with us, and then the one time when he approached me in the playground at lunchtime, where I was standing by myself on the strip of sand we used to crack marbles. There was nothing particularly wrong with him except that he was downtrodden, mentally beaten, in some manner empty – his school uniform drowning him out of existence. If he had been born a baby bird in a crowded nest, he would have been dead by the second or third day, pushed out or buried under by his greedy siblings. Not capable of more than a neutral stare, eyes empty – he was contemplating whether he should or shouldn't take another step forward. He wasn't really expecting help; he was far beyond the stage where he might have considered pleading. And he stood there three or four yards from me, with no lead up, nothing to give him an excuse to approach, and I had nothing, nothing I could give: I had no desire to hurt him, but then again absolutely no way of relating to him or knowing how to react to him. For me at that age (16 or 17), he was a first, an alien species, which nothing in my upbringing that far had led me to understand existed. And he left, and that was the last I saw of him, although a rumour did circulate to the effect that he had settled in at his next school.

[16.8] Japan: "One does not stand out." "One does not create a fuss."

(Travelling on the train to Osaka in the late evening.)

A tallish woman in her mid- to late-thirties and a far-shorter-than-average, rather grubby Japanese man of around the same age, sitting directly across from me in an otherwise empty carriage, the woman pulling herself up tight into the corner of her seat as far away as she possibly could from him, her gaze held firmly downwards at her feet, and he in his turn inching in towards her with each lurch of the train, his intent totally clear and his eyes repeatedly shifting across the aisle, challenging me to do something about the situation. And fascinated that this type of scene should be unfolding before my eyes (this not being a world I could ever enter or, in reality, even begin to comprehend), I sat and watched as, having moved as close to her as he possibly could, he then lightly lifted his coat allowing it to fall in part in across her knees, this followed by clear movement of his hand up against her thigh (again checking my reaction; I had noticed?). And she, on her part, eyes still on the carriage floor before her, stayed frozen in position until the train stopped at the next station, where she pulled herself up and out of the door. And he was out behind her, and I was left to reflect on the consequences of my inaction. (I can imagine a lot of younger women today doing some silent screaming here. However, if you would bear with me a moment.)

The initial embarrassment here actually stayed with me for many years; the event occurring in my late forties, it was not until I was in my mid-sixties that I told the story to Kensuke (who, this being Japan, barely reacted at all – quite what was the problem?). At the same time, even while the scene was unfolding before my eyes, this feeling of inadequacy was tempered by certain thoughts, which as I have aged have become more forward in the brain.

The man was actually of little importance, doing no more than following his basest of instincts, and if he represented a mean existence, both of them were sad (in the Buddhist sense, deserving of compassion – 'aware no mono' – characters you might find at the lowest of lowest levels in "Les Misérables"), with the outside world seemingly holding very little for either of them. And equally, if he had made his actions any more direct, I am confident in myself that I would have moved. But more than anything, it was the woman's passivity.

From the moment she entered the carriage right through to their exit, she made no effort whatsoever to indicate with her eyes or body language that she required my help, some motion which would have appealed to the English side of my brain and drawn me in. (Quite possibly, there was bit of Margaret Thatcher's 'standing up for yourself' way of thinking in there. However, I very quickly made the mental decision that if she was not prepared to challenge him in some manner, I could not move.) And going back to the event today, almost certainly the real deciding factor limiting both her and my own responses: We were in Japan, and in Japan, in public, one does not create a fuss. (Ref: [15.6] on 'the power of the pack'.)

None of the above is to excuse, but it is a reality. Today, both station workers and the police are highly responsive to 'chikan', men of all ages who molest or grope passengers in crowded trains or take snapshots beneath schoolgirls skirts as they ride the upward escalator, and we also have women-only carriages to protect those who feel the need. At the same time, as a result of there having been a number of cases where women have deliberately lied about being touched – in the most infamous case, made into a film, the man losing both his job and family as he refused to accede to her claims and pay the minimal ¥50,000 fine – it is now possible to take out insurance to cover the possibility of being falsely accused. (There is money to be made anywhere in life.)

And perhaps to clarify my above reaction a little (and possibly put the whole of the above in a slightly better light): The following may appear quite unrelated, but they are in fact similar examples of my own and other's reactions to the same social constraints.

(Again, in my mid-thirties, in a calligraphy class.)

Looking back across the room, I notice a student in his seventies, face pale and head slumped back against his seat. Clearly something is wrong, and as the teacher is dealing with another student, I walk around and, opening his mouth, find his tongue caught back against his windpipe and preventing him from breathing. Inserting my finger, I release the tongue and then recognising that he is recovering, return to my seat. Another student, noticing that he is not well, brings the matter to the teacher's attention, resulting in general commotion across the room, until it is clear that he is back to normal, while I sit alone looking away, terrified that if I attempt to explain the full reality of the situation, someone might have noticed that after inserting my finger in his mouth, I *had not washed my hands*. Even now I do not fully comprehend my reaction here, but I do know that shortly afterwards I left the group.

(On a crowded train, pulling into a station.)

A woman carrying a heavily laden baby stroller and with a very small child in her arms stands and, after leaving the carriage, looks back to see her second, three- or four-year-old boy, settling in to fall asleep on the seat she has just vacated. And not wishing to get back on the train – an express that would take them considerably further along the line – she calls out repeatedly for him to come to her, a call which he is too far gone to fully register. And here, I reacted; swiftly picking him up in my arms and, before he knew what was happening to him, placing him outside on the platform beside her, after which I returned to my position besides the opposite door and, as the train pulled out, as was requisite, carefully positioned my eyes on the view outside – the most important thing at that moment being to accentuate that nothing out of the ordinary had occurred. Shortly after which, a Westerner, who I assumed to be of a similar age, walked towards me and, tapping my elbow to attract my attention, came out with (a surprisingly sincere), "That was fantastic! I could never have done that," before returning to his position along the aisle. And otherwise, the whole carriage, self-included, kept their eyes carefully averted right through to the Osaka terminal, where we all disembarked.

[16.9] The dominant, the dominated:

During the course of its integration into the language here, although the reality exists if you choose to search it out, the concept of SM has to a great extent lost the direct hard-sex references it has in the West – both male and female television personalities here are quite happy openly positioning themselves as one or the other – to the point that it could perhaps be better replaced in English by the initials DS, the D standing for "the dominant half of a relationship" and the S for "the more mentally submissive." At the same time, in whole sections of society here, there tends to be the assumption that if you are not recognised as a person to be respected (and by that I would stress as meaning; *respected according to the rules of Japanese society*) and thus to be looked up to, as a matter of course you become subordinate and there to be looked down upon, which extended becomes, more directly, if you are not in a position where you are controlling (i.e., the dominant half), you are there to be controlled (to submit). And in large part, with a commonality that could not envisioned in the West, this is accepted by both sides as completely normal, standard practice. This is the way things are.

[16.10] Humour:

(More specifically, what the audience is expected – or in the case of young people, taught – to laugh at.)

As with all countries, Japan has a broad range of styles of humour; some quite soft, gentle, and some quite clever, even self-effacing, but at the same time a good proportion of what is seen on television here invariably amounts to positioning the (/some) other party as no more than a subject (/object) to be made a fool of. If you wish to be accepted as a 'talent' (/personality) on variety shows in Japan – a group which includes a large number of so-called (at least people who started out in life as) comedians – to give everyone else on the set (and presumably the audience) the opportunity to laugh hilariously, you have to be prepared to look and/or be made to look stupid. That is, being repeatedly subject to ridicule is de rigueur, together with (on the principle that if you've laughed at it once, you're not going to laugh at it a second time) what amounts to a forever-escalating mental and physical degradation: What used to be slapstick, pie-in-the-face, slapping over the head with a rolled newspaper, now involves having someone fall (/pushing someone) into a pit or a tank of slime or boiling hot (/ice cold) water, the sole function of the 'talent' being then to suitably over-react – express surprise or shock, grimace or scream as is called for, the degree to which they manage to do so determining their value to the programme and presumably viewer ratings. A group of comedians known as "The Drifters" could be noted the originators of this style in its softest form, but almost certainly the one individual most responsible for this development was the film director and comedian, Beat Takeshi, who, with his 'gang' of younger comedians, whom he personally trained in his own style, created a series of such programmes, where the central theme became the demeaning of others for the viewer's (/his own?) pleasure. And invariably it is the 'strong' (those who are accepted/have made it) mocking the 'weak'; which will include the overweight, skinny, big-breasted, 'busu' (ugly-faced – an epithet almost invariably thrown at women only, and almost invariably by men who would most certainly not rate very highly on any ranking for 'most handsome male in town'), gays (lots of hand-waving and preferably in drag), those not so quick on the uptake/slow witted (often, this type of personality is required to exaggerate that angle to appear "even more funny"), children of mixed parentage (See "Joy" below), and anyone and everyone who is prepared to grovel at the chance to appear, even once, on television. And together with these, you have those who are in no position to answer back

(/anyone perceived to be in a position of weakness); those who due to some (drugs-, sex-, yakuza-related) scandal (at least until they call a press conference to 'apologise' for their misdeeds) have been relegated to the waste-bin of TV history – and they are hit hard, the principle throughout being that all are out there to be made fun of, props to be manipulated at the director's (/management's/ sponsor's/ advertising agency's) will and accepted only as much and as long as they are willing to follow the script, there being no end of half-baked nobodies waiting in the wings to be picked up in their place. And even those who have officially 'made it' cannot be overconfident, waiting for that slightest of missteps that will topple, according to the standard process, apparently common around the world, of digging out the dirt and then holding onto it until it can be applied to maximum effect. (So you got paid for your trouble, and so what?)

It was somewhere in the 1990s that my brain came up with the phrase, "heta o uru jidai," literally "selling yourself as someone who can't"; an "untalented 'talent'" – this resulting in studios packed with those who are there expressly to draw a laugh based on the premise that they are '<u>not</u>': not funny, can't sing, have no real knowledge about any particular subject (this on faux news-analysis programmes), are not in any way interesting, can't speak or read Japanese correctly (these often actually far more interesting as people than a large number of the so-called 'highly educated', who have dutifully memorised all the words but come over as totally cold in character and in large part exceedingly dull).

Viewed from the present moment, a large part of the above can in fact be attributed to the ever-expanding number of competing channels available; first on television and then in the modern social media, with nowhere near enough new or original information or talent to spread between them, this leading to the seemingly endless watering down of what is no more than minimal content; virtually identical programmes with equally boring announcers, stories that have all been told countless times, 'experts' who can do nothing more than parrot the official line (if not that of the government, then that of the individual channel or its sponsors). In comparison, as a child in England, we had three channels; BBC1 and 2 (for lighter and more serious entertainment), and ITV (with its commercials), which together seemed perfectly sufficient to meet society's general needs.

A 'talent' named Joy (by his Japanese mother or English father, I am not sure which) who was popular over a certain period and still does appear on certain programmes, was sent to England at least twice to report, first on the colleges in Cambridge, where I was pleased to see the students he interviewed sized him up very quickly (he was being rather too open with his conceits) and very politely but determinedly put him in his place, thoroughly taking the Mickey out of him. But then the second time was a trip around the centre of London to "investigate fish and chips," the only English food they really know to comment on here, which having purchased four or five samples of, he then one by one declared "Cold!" (he'd been carrying them around town for heaven knows how long, so what would he expect), and then, after one half-bite, "Completely horrible!" before – this presumably at the request of the programme director – with a true look of disgust on his face, violently flinging each package down onto the pavement at his feet. And everybody in the studio, perfectly on cue, screamed with laughter.

This was also true for a recent programme on the Princess Diana tapes regarding Charles' infidelity, where the whole studio repeatedly erupted at every jibe cast by the host. I do not particularly admire Prince Charles and certainly not his treatment of Diana, but I am sure that not one of the studio 'panel' here would ever conceive of treating any member of the Imperial family in that same manner.

Children learn by example, and this type of programme being on at all times of the day every day of the week, I cannot believe that they are not influenced. (The recent wave of videos taken from the Internet of strange accidents and/or young people from around the world acting not so cleverly has to a certain extent put a damper on the worst types of the above type of programme, but they are still around.)

[16.11] And further muddying the waters: Conflicting schools of thought:

There are many ways to educate young people as to their position within their group or society overall, ranging from the 'strict discipline', 'uncompromising', 'learning to take it', 'push yourself until you break' methodologies, which in the West we tend to associate with military training, but which in Japan are commonly introduced at a much younger age through club activities at the start of junior high school, right across the spectrum to the 'never raise your voice or hand' option, and of late, opinions in society have split so dramatically on this matter that we now have these two extreme and highly conflicting principles battling it out in public, with seemingly very little possibility of some form of consensus anywhere on the horizon.

'Boryoku', with its dictionary definition of "(usage of) force or violence," was a word originally associated with yakuza groups, and its first real exposure in the world of education came from what was described at the time as the Totsuka Yacht School scandal (1980–1982). Initially founded as a reform school for problematic students, the solution here involved the most aggressive forms of Spartan training including heavy corporal punishment, this eventually resulting in two students at the school dying and two going missing at sea, for which the head of the school was eventually imprisoned. (Since his release in 2006, two other students at his reopened school have apparently committed suicide, with as yet no clarification of circumstances, but the fact that I did not register these latter deaths in my daily input may be testament to the comparative regularity of such events throughout society at the present time.) However, the above incident did lead to a wider recognition of the problem, leading to the emergence of an 'anti-boryoku' movement aiming to eliminate corporal punishment of any kind in the classroom; a suitably proper objective in that there are still many educators who believe in a show of strong force to emphasise their position of authority, with cases regularly exposed nationwide, except for the fact that there has been seemingly nothing (in the manner of the rules-based system that I experienced as a child) introduced to replace it, leaving teachers in the classroom with a strong need to promote discipline without any practical means to do so.

And thus we have a recent news item showing a video of a 15-year-old boy viciously kicking his teacher, who had no means to resist (at all times he kept his hands in the air making it clear that he had no intention of hitting the boy). The video was taken by one of the other students, presumably at the beginning or ending of a class, with no one moving in any way to protect the teacher.

And, of need, at the other end of the scale, we now have university lecturer, Professor Ogi – in the media in general known as "Ogi mama" – whose basic precepts include:

"A child must never, ever, at any time be hit by their parents or schoolteachers (this covering even a light slapping on the legs of toddlers)."

"They must never be made to feel embarrassment in front of others."

"Consideration of their feelings must be prime at all times."

"All signs of disobedience must be met with a carefully reasoned approach, to which the child will naturally respond."

And this will rid the world of all its present problems.

And with mothers – still considered socially responsible for the upbringing of their children – taking these admonitions to heart in droves, it is now considered 'unfair' to award places in races at elementary school sports days – the contention here being that "losing may cause the child unnecessary embarrassment." And most recently (Jan. 2019), we have had reports of at least one restaurant that has had so much trouble caused by small children running amok, with neither parent making any effort to bring them under their control, that the owner has been forced to introduce a total ban on all children in that age range. That is, in terms of a system, they have managed to land themselves with two extremes, neither of which would seem in even the slightest manner satisfactory. And that this might lead to a strong element of bafflement and/or distress on the child's part, as to where they might stand in the scheme of things, would seem a foregone conclusion.

Bullying at elementary schools has now become frequent enough to receive considerable attention in the media. In 2017, a total of 414,000 school children of all ages were reported bullied, double the figure of two years ago, this despite an "Ijime (Bullying) Prevention Methods Promotion Law," passed in 2013, which requires schools to take specific steps to both prevent bullying and enable its early discovery. Student suicides are still commonly reported in the media, but with both school administrations and local education committees feeling they have a reputation to protect, refusing to accept responsibility for even the most manifest cases has become commonplace. And even with so-called "independent investigating committees" that are created to investigate such suicides, "We say they weren't bullied, and you had better believe us!" has become a shockingly common attitude.

And if the above in total can be taken from the teacher's perspective, beyond their regular teaching and club activity responsibilities, they are now being held fully responsible for their student's moral development while having to deal with direct aggressions from those same students, their parents, school authorities, and to a large extent, the media.

[16.12] And in society at large:

– A few years ago, young children used to die quite frequently as a result of their parents' negligence – being left in a hot car in midsummer while the mother went to play pachinko – but more recently we have had a number of cases where the child has been fatally mistreated in the name of 'discipline' (in reality, domestic violence gone overboard) – in the latest case with a 40-year-old father, as he was being arrested, stating in the calmest of manners that he had been doing nothing more than "correcting his child's bad habits" as any father would, that is, he had been acting both correctly and perfectly within his rights.

(As of 20.3.2019) The government plans shortly to introduce an 'amendment', details as yet to be determined, as a form of administrative guidance [15.11] with no stated penalties, assumedly for any parents who might be "tempted to cross this line." How this is supposed to help with the reality that clearly a number of parents are already well over that line is not noted. The requirement here seems to be that those in charge <u>are seen to be doing something</u>, and provided that rudimentary element is satisfied, presumably others will be, too.)

All the martial arts (and, by extension, competitive sports) have traditionally relied on strict disciplinary training methods ("If you want to win, you have to suffer."), and even today there is a deep-seated opposition to any sense of any tampering with the established system.

In the world of sumo: Tashi Saito, a 17-year-old wrestler was beaten to death in 2007. And during the course of the past twelve months, we have had two top-tier wrestlers obliged to retire for violently assaulting their 'juniors'. Lots of suitable murmurings by the Sumo Association were duly noted by the media and subsequently the matter, yet again, forgotten.

A Nihon University American football defensive player (the top team in Japan) committed an extremely late and vicious hit from behind against the quarterback of Kwansei Gakuin University on the first play of the game on May 6, 2018. Recorded on tape, the player was initially lambasted in the media, until he eventually spoke up, claiming that he was following his coach's instructions and under the threat that "if he did not do so, he would not be selected to play for the team again." The head coach repeatedly refused to accept any responsibility, eventually conceding that he might have said "something to that effect – something that the student had taken to mean that he must act in that manner, but 'at no time was an order given'." (See "sontaku" in [17.6].) The association suspended the team from official games until 2019.

(2013) In the world of judo, a top coach in the All-Japan Judo Federation was forced to retire as punishment for his abusive training of female judokas. Here, with Japan at the time still vying for the Olympics, action did have to be taken, with the Japanese Olympic Committee cutting funding for the All-Japan Judo Federation and ordered it to take preventive measures. It has also established an anonymous reporting system for any violence, harassment, or misconduct in sports.

And as a fully serious comment on this final matter from a middle-aged woman in the street interviewed for a television news programme: "If the coaches are too kind to them, I wonder whether we will be able to win any medals in the next Olympics?"

FF(?): Learning a lesson (or two): (TV documentary.) A martial arts national coach in his fifties is taught how to ride a bicycle (something he had never previously got round to learning) in a period of roughly two hours by Japan's top professional cyclist at the time. And his final comment at the end of the programme (voiced with sheer incredulity – based on a lifetime experience, he had no way of understanding how such a feat could be achieved without it): "He didn't even raise his voice at me once!"

And then, just to prove that nothing has changed: (A cut from a recent news programme.) A three-year-old child in a pool pulling back on his tears as he is shaken strongly back and forth by his swimming instructor and given the admonition to "swim, drown or give-up," the implication being that to take that third choice would be the ultimate admission of his failure as a human being.

[16.13] And when the system does not work:

"You can drag a horse to water (but you can't make it drink)":
Official numbers of students refusing to attend school over long periods remain at over 100,000 annually, with bullying, anxiety and other emotional problems, psychological exhaustion, and troubles with friends and teachers all cited as reasons. At the same time, there have been various reports of such students, after being directed towards a freer educational environment – putting a greater stress on relationship building than academic results – having become fully successful in their development, and therefore it is not a matter that seems insolvable.

Runaway children: Applications for missing person searches were submitted for nearly 20,000 runaways aged between ten and nineteen in 2008, a related problem here being that, in order to exist on the street, girls are engaging in what is known as 'enjo kosai', (entering a relationship with older men for money), yet another convenient euphemism in that the government does not wish to call it the prostitution that it is.

However, the real quandary that Japan has been facing for a number of years now is that in far too many cases, the horse is refusing to even approach the trough.

Total withdrawal:

The existence of 'hikikomori' (children who retreat into and refuse to emerge from their rooms – or at best find themselves not able to reintegrate in any true manner into society due to some combination of low self-esteem and/or depression – in many cases for decades) has become a serious and apparently unsolvable social problem here. As to why they exist in such numbers (at present estimated to be around half a million, with over 400,000 over forty) has even now not been determined. All the problems mentioned above no doubt play a part. However, I sense that what is occurring is that the young person is suddenly coming up against an overload of expectations – originally instilled by parents, teachers, society and/or an over-confident self – what for them at that particular moment is a non-negotiable gap between what they have come to understand as "'the brilliant future' awaiting them in life" and the somewhat different (/much sterner) realities of the adult world – forcing them into an, at times panicked, retreat back into the world as they have known it up to that point (their own personal shell or safety zone), whereby they get left so far behind that any further development is prohibited.

In the cases that I personally have come upon here, all have come from fairly well-off households, indicating that at one level, they very likely have been spoiled; led to believe that they deserve society's attention while at the same time sensing (almost certainly, correctly) that at some level things are not working out as they should. However, for whatever reason, in the book of life they are stuck on page twelve or thirteen. (Perhaps not directly connected, but relatively fewer young Japanese people – down from a peak of 80,000 in 2004 to around 50,000 today –seem willing to study abroad these days. Also, I should note that this kind of problem started a long time before young people ever got their hands on smartphones or video games.)

And from a recent (March 2019) JT report, in addition to the above cases, we now have another half million between the ages of 40 to 64 (76.6% men) who have seemingly withdrawn much later in life, leading me to the following reconsideration. In Chapter 5, I noted the considerable number of times that, when considered to be in some manner inferior, I have been the subject of other's open disregard (/derision), which as a younger man I tended to brush off without any particular thought given to the matter. (I, too, have my shell.) However, in the same manner that I have more recently given up on certain of my neighbours [5,18], I can understand that people in this older group, who presumably, in that they are in no way socially able to fight back, have had to repeatedly deal with far worse than I have, might at some point have taken it upon themselves to withdraw from their never-ending lives as underdogs. And if this is the case, here we are dealing with a specifically Japanese (/Korean?) Confucian culture-related crisis to which there can be no real answer unless the society as a whole chooses to change its attitudes, something that would seem almost impossible in the present situation.

The teacher as enemy:

In my fifties, a young woman in her early twenties came to my home, asking me to teach her privately. She explained that she found it difficult to communicate with anyone outside her close family, and that to come to see me had required considerable effort, but that she felt that if she could get into English, that would provide her with a way out, possibly leading to a situation where she might be able to go abroad, or at least to develop enough confidence to move forward in some manner. Recognising that she was desperate (and to a certain degree personally interested in the challenge) I agreed to give it a go. (Japanese women who move abroad, clearly having a degree of autonomy which they do not have in their own country, on the whole tend to do very well in their new surroundings, and viewed from this angle also, the idea seemed to make sense.)

However, from the start, it was extremely difficult. Essentially, her condition made her incapable of accepting criticism, and unfortunately, she could only take my correcting of her very limited abilities in the language to heart as 'criticism', and the degree of care I had to take to try to teach her and at the same time not to offend in the slightest was inordinate. In the end, she stayed with me for approximately six months, by which time she was repeatedly blowing up at me in class and I had to tell her that we could not continue. She was asking the impossible: I was an English teacher and I had not taken her on (/had no qualification to do so) as a patient. I also had a considerable number of other students to take care of.

The description of a passive-aggressive person (Wikipedia) does include "an intense conflict between dependence on others and the desire for self-assertion," which I would certainly consider to be a part of the configuration here, but reading the overall description, which does make it seem that the individual involved is actually still interacting with the outside world, I sensed that I was dealing with something rather stronger (the term defensive-aggressive immediately came to mind), the utterly disproportionate defensive posture that she kept up at all times seemingly essential for her sense of control over her own world. At the same time, it clearly was essential for her to show herself as strong enough to stand up to me – in the end, I represented 'authority' – to exert her prerogative or impose her will. Or possibly it could be understood as a (somewhat misplaced) expression of power; a straight-out rejection: Essentially, "I don't need you!"

And perhaps the same woman forty years on:
"No one has ever spoken to me like that before. Even my parents would never speak to me like that."

This pronouncement, coming from a very well-to-do lady in her sixties, was directed at a short (and somewhat misinterpreted) review that I had given of a presentation that she had just made.

Having accompanied a friend in the same class on a full month's trip to the US, visiting (and being fully accommodated by) the other student's family members and friends, she had just spent a full twenty minutes criticising both them and each and every moment of her stay in a highly rude manner. She had not had one word of gratitude for any of them. (I actually had experienced a similar situation years earlier when my Japanese teacher visited my parents' home and came back finding fault with and/or making rather snide comments about all she had seen there – actually laughing at my uncle for being proud of the Japanese gingko tree in his garden (common here, but not normally found in England) and his "old-fashioned, outdated" Japanese stereo set, which naturally didn't sit well with me, so this was something of a repeat.) However, the above was all said in front of the friend, who, being the mirror opposite in character – generous to a fault – had not openly shown any affront, and not thinking to say anything quite so directly, I chose to concentrate strictly on problems with the English aspects of the presentation. I cannot remember exactly what I said now, but I do know that I expressed myself very carefully. (Having noticed a similar attitude on her part with the other students previously, I was well aware of what I was up against.) However, at some point – I guess sensing there was a hint of criticism in the air – she took affront: I was being "discourteous," which on no terms could be accepted.

The other students in the class, who I had been teaching for well over ten years at the time and were at a considerably higher level (she had been with me no more than six months), repeatedly attempted to explain to her exactly what I had been trying to say. However, she had determined her position (the barriers were up) and the whole thing escalated to the point where, having repeated the above quote some five or six times, she flounced out of the apartment in a huff, her final words (in Japanese) being something to the effect of, "My shadow will never darken this threshold again," in the end, a suitably dramatic exit, and presumably all to the well.

To me, the same defensive-aggressive posture as with the younger woman above was at work here, only hardwired. Totally self-centred, compounded by a deeply ingrained sense of entitlement, she was not to be questioned. She clearly had always done with people as she chose to, regardless, and presumably there never had been anyone close enough who was willing to take her to task or put her in her place. And, as she was leaving, with one more: "Even my parents would never speak to me like that," my brain could only come back with, "And perhaps it would have been better if they had."

[16.14] The parents' role:

The following could be read perhaps as a form of guidance to younger people anywhere who, even as adults, cannot understand why their parents treated them as they did, and at the same time a note to any parents whose children do not seem to be progressing in life quite as it had been assumed they would.

(Note that while I have used 'parent' in all the following descriptions, in Japan, even today, in the large part responsibility for the upbringing of children falls almost exclusively on the mother.)

The following is a quote from the university student counsellor who studied Jung with me [14.1].

"In every case when a student has come to me with adjustment problems, invariably it has been the fault of the parents, and equally no progress with the child has been possible until I can get the parents to change their attitudes, which, in reality, in a number of cases where they have been basically incapable of even contemplating themselves as the problem, has been impossible."

Simple cases.
– Holding your child in:
An older student in Osaka, who over the years I have stayed friends with, at an earlier point in her life (in her thirties) as an only daughter, was prevented from fulfilling her dream of living in England by her mother, who, each time she was preparing to depart, fell sick. (The mother invariably recovered immediately after the plans were cancelled.) This would perhaps be the equivalent of my mother not wanting me to come to Japan, except that I had the advantage of being a younger son and no education (/cultural background) that pressed on me at all times to be subservient to my parent's wishes.

– And pushing her out:
Years ago at the company, an older friend/student came to me to ask what he could do about his daughter. At a very young age and at her grandparent's request ("They were lonely"), he had sent her to New York to live with them, and now, some fifteen or sixteen years later, he wanted her to come back to Japan and be a "good daughter" (his description), and she was refusing to do so. And what could he do? And I had to tell him in the politest manner that I could, that he had made the wrong choice in giving in to his parents, and that if he wished to be angry with anyone it should be with them. On her side, with almost all certainty, in terms of her value systems, she would be as close to being American as anyone possibly could be, and he could only be present in her mind as the parent who had rejected her.

A never-ending cycle. When the child becomes a parent:
A father brought up so strictly by his father that he swore he would never treat any child of his that way, matched with a mother whose own mother had been absent from her childhood (and in large part brought up by her grandmother) resulting in the ultimate spoiled brat; A man who was careless enough to have his precious dog's leg (which, I will allow him, he did care for) crushed under the tire of a passing car, and then generous enough (bragging about it openly) to have his parents pay the ¥1 million fee to have it sent to be fixed – naturally by (as checked on the Internet) "the best veterinary surgeon available in the country"; that he also happened to be situated half way across the country

being of no consequence. It was only after he was fully grown that his mother (who was my student for a considerable amount of time) came to recognise quite how badly things had gone wrong. (She had brushed his teeth for him until he was fourteen.) But even so, neither parent had any apparent qualms about purchasing a brand-new apartment for him when he married. And now he has a daughter, and I sometimes wonder how she will fare.

[16.15] "Pleased to meet you."

No one answered my first call, but I had promised that I would leave a message, so leaving it fifteen minutes or so, I tried again, this time getting what appeared to be the sound of the receiver being removed, followed by silence. Unsure as to whether I had actually made a connection, I waited until I could hear a faint noise (the television?) in the background. Presumably, someone was there, and I tried a "Hello" ("Moshimoshi"), which after some moments was returned by a somewhat tentative "Hai" ("Yes/I hear you"). And here, more than the brevity of the reply, it was the absolute lack of any emotion expressed in the voice that pulled me up short. However, I continued.

"This is Geoff. I want to confirm what time we will be arriving this evening for dinner."

"Hai."

"I'm speaking to J?"

"Hai."

"You know we will be coming this evening?"

"Hai."

"Could you tell your father...?"

"Hai."

And so it went on until I reckoned, I had got the message through and finished the call. However, I can only say that the whole exchange left me nothing short of astounded. This was a young man of eighteen, apparently a very good student (shortly leaving for university to study Russian and Chinese), and who, as I heard that evening (very proudly, though possibly a little defensively) from his mother, "could fly a glider," but then again was incapable of answering the phone. (A four-year-old child could have done better than the above, and he told me during our conversation that he had heard – but not answered – my first call.)

And that evening, when we arrived, the best he could do was to come to the door of his room, way across the very large apartment, and nod somewhat abruptly before retreating into the shadows. (That both parents – and his grandfather who was also present – accepted this, should perhaps have surprised, but by now didn't.) His sister of fourteen came out and politely greeted us, but neither were seated with us at dinner – officially a family gathering. I had known the father since he was a boy and I had been invited specifically because he "wished to introduce his son to the man who had taught him English."

And then walking with the father down to the main road to get a taxi, I told him about the morning call, to which in response, other than a (like father, like son?) nod to indicate that he followed what I was saying, he came out with, "Please get angry with him," – although quite how I was supposed to do this with someone who would not even exchange the most basic of greetings with me was not clarified.

– And then six weeks later:

"Please get angry with him." This from a second father, and this time in front of the son, who, fortunately, I have known for some time. (Although my connection with the father is only a relatively recent development, I have known his mother well since she was a young girl.) A good ten years older than the boy above, and certainly lightyears away from him in his ability to communicate – if anything, "mildly introvert" might be a reasonable description – we have, over time, developed a relatively easy relationship. However, following his parents as a fully trained artist (/industrial designer), he is at a point in his life where he is finding it difficult to settle on a way forward, and much as I understand his parents wanting to help him to get out into the wider world – they seemingly would like him to try the European market – with my own knowledge of the art world very much restricted to my experience in Japan, there is in fact little I can do for him other than to tell him to "get out there and see what happens," advice which, with his character, he naturally finds difficult to follow. And ultimately, this is an obstacle that he has to learn to negotiate by himself. Neither they nor I can do anything about it other than stand aside. His parents are, by always 'being there' for him – literally, and in many cases physically, hemming him in – are still impelling him to act <u>as they see fit</u>, and in doing so are not allowing him to develop his own decision-making processes, thus stifling his natural development (in the West what would simply be understood as over-protection impeding growth). The son himself is not by any means unintelligent and, given breathing space, would seem quite capable of finding his own way. Explaining the above to the father some weeks later, he actually finally managed to communicate to me the impossibility of what I was asking – to me, even after all these years, in fact a revelation: Essentially, in the same manner that Confucianism, with its determination of 'filial piety', requires the child to follow the will of the parent, to be considered a 'good parent', he equally had social obligations towards his child which could not be refuted; that is if he stood away as I was suggesting, he would be withdrawing from what he understood as his socially defined responsibilities as a parent to his child. That is, his justification for his actions was that his social conditioning prevented him from being anything other than a protective parent. And considering the number of similar cases I have observed over time, this would seem to make sense. However, interpreted at this level, and clearly depending on the combination of types of people involved (the other son has no problems in this respect), you consequently have both parent(s) and child effectively ensnared in an extremely uncomfortable (suffocating, even) embrace.

***

And taking the above as a whole, it is very easy to see how, in the worst cases, the presumed guarantee of 'support' that parents offer can in reality become a very nastily devised leash. I also suspect that there must be (as with the above cases of hikikomori,) a large number of cases where the child is altogether aware of and taking full advantage of the fact that their parents, regardless of how they might choose to act, are obliged in this manner to remain at their bidding. Whatever, and this I would presume true for any society, it would seem that overdependence on either side does not make for a healthy relationship.

[16.16] The establishment of trust:

Children everywhere easily understand and strongly react to parental neglect. In the most distancing of such relationships, in accepting the love of a nanny or some other guardian, the growing child must simultaneously concede the reality of (at least some degree of) rejection by their own parent(s), and this is painful. Naturally, the parents will not choose to understand it this way, but the child has every opportunity to quickly learn that the method of upbringing to which they have been subjected is not the only approach available.

"You cannot force people to do anything. You can do nothing other than make yourself available."

– **From a television documentary:** Finally responding to a daughter's worsening (/near-death) anorexic condition – which, personally, I would read as an ultimate plea for help – a Japanese father decided he would leave his (very well-paid) job and just be with her. It took many, many months of just walking and talking quietly, but she (at least at the time the documentary ended) completely recovered.

– **From a newspaper report:** A woman who had suffered immensely as a child and who, over a long period, had not responded in any manner to treatment, as a last resort, took it upon herself to adopt a child suffering in the same manner she had. Apparently, the child screamed at her repeatedly over a period of years before finally accepting her as the person she was. She then took on a second and a third, until all (including herself) were, to the best they ever could be, settled.

– **And as a (contrasting) example from real life:** I met both children, both very pleasant boys, some 30 years ago when they were in their teens, at one of the first parties I attended at their mother's house, where I very clearly remember one going out to meet friends and the other going back to his room. However, after this particular time I cannot recollect meeting the younger boy again, and it is only at a very recent party (with both parents aging and the mother presumably having finally decided that something had to done about the matter) that I was informed that; "He was now being taken to help at day-care centres for elderly people (apparently with the aid of a number of her friends), and would I care to volunteer to help in that area?" This I declined for two reasons: (1) I did not have the time or the physical energy to engage in that type of activity, and (2) I could not believe that she might expect me to take on a responsibility that all her life she had so clearly neglected, and apparently was quite happy continuing to do so: She still holds her 'gatherings' regularly (even now, to which he is not invited), and there was no mention of her being actively involved in his rehabilitation. Presumably, she is doing something, although personally I have never seen her (or talked with her about being) together with him, in or outside the house, ever.

Chapter 17

The Peculiarities of Confucianism in the Modern Age

(2) The Workings of an Economy

[17.1]

"Provided everything is seen as 'going well,' in that a country is in a period of economic growth or has reached a certain level of stability where it is understood as providing a reasonable standard of living (even in the form of handouts) for the majority, the actual form of government – capitalist, socialist, communist, democratic or dictatorial – is going to be of little concern to its citizens. It is only when things take a turn for the worse that any system is going to be (severely) tested."

At the time I arrived and for a considerable period afterwards, the general understanding was that Japanese companies existed to respect (1) the needs of the customer, (2) their employees, (3) the community and then (4) shareholders in that order, the reasoning being that provided a company could satisfy the needs of the first three, presumably it would be earning enough to provide a suitable level of dividends for its shareholders. Most large- and medium-sized companies offered lifelong employment, which included a very long and drawn-out but equally thorough training process aimed at producing 'company workers', all of whom received a reasonable level of remuneration upgraded across the board annually through generally harmonious (if noisy) management-union negotiations each spring, and designed to satisfy the requirement that, as employees grew older, married and had families, they would have the requisite higher incomes to put their children through the education system. Employees, notably in factories, were encouraged to practice 'kaizen' – finding (even the smallest of) ways to improve their practices in the workplace [2.3], which, if found to be practicable, could then be extended to other areas to improve overall productivity.

Each company's distinctive culture was instilled in new recruits through strict discipline during office hours together with regular drinking sessions with the boss (paid for by the boss himself or more commonly through company subsidies), and these evening sessions were considered an essential part of the assimilation process: The daytime was strictly for work and the night-time for socialising (a getting-to-know-you process that essentially provided the oil that kept the cogs in the wheels turning during the day). Overtime was standard, with the common understanding that, if you were interested in promotion, you did not leave the office before your boss.

All employees were strongly encouraged (/expected) to marry, with weddings among company employees common, and at this time it was assumed that around the age of 25, women would retire in order to produce children (and also be there to look after their husbands when they came home fully inebriated) and those who didn't were in the large part side-lined. On the plus side, married women were understood as being in full control of the family budget and all household-related decisions; from the purchasing of large items including house or car down to their husband's monthly allowance. Companies aimed to ensure protection from unwanted external takeovers through the cross-sharing of stocks and bonds. The concept that Japan was bereft of all-natural resources was stressed regularly in the media; the people were its only true asset, and exports "the lifeblood of the nation."

There was, to the Western eye, considerable overemployment – neatly uniformed elevator girls in department stores bowing customers in and out at each floor – but essentially no one who wished to work was left without a job, thus meeting the expectations of both sides: the reverse side of the coin of "contributing to society" being "society's responsibility to provide that opportunity to contribute." (In contrast, I do remember going into a department store in Washington the first time I visited the US with Koji and being totally shocked at the absence of floor personnel when we wanted to make a purchase.) And overall, it was a stable system and it worked.

From a Western viewpoint, particularly in terms of efficient usage of time, there is much to be criticised here. The multinational company I worked for actually unwisely introduced the Japanese system of staying over late, resulting in an unimaginable amount of wasted time – to the point that during one union strike, when senior staff with zero auditing experience were required to finish off the book-balancing for the spring tax audit, in addition to handling their own regular jobs, they managed to finish the work a good two to three weeks faster than was normally the case. However, there was money for all, exports soared, and all was more than well with the world.

And then, little by little, throughout the 1980s, with increasing numbers of young people moving into the large cities to work, all the established customs and behaviours that had anchored society to its traditional roots began to lose their hold, creating a whole new array of consequences.

The 'omiai' arranged marriage system, which had still been quite common when I arrived, essentially collapsed to make way for 'love matches', but while in England, where there was a fully established system of support that ran throughout the society and enabled young people to meet and date from very young on and, in effect, provide the learning experience that was required for them to have a chance to discover the type of person who might work for them as a partner, here there was nothing of any real equivalence, meaning that young people were left to their own devices, this resulting in considerably more divorces and children having to be brought up by one parent – in most cases the mother, very often in difficult circumstances. (Today, 54.6% of single mothers are officially recognised as living under the poverty line.) And when they did marry successfully, two- (rather than the previous three-) generation families became the norm, leaving young parents with no one to turn to for advice or practical help when they began to rear their own children, resulting in yet more serious consequences for the subsequent generation. (Visiting my eldest brother early on, it was visibly apparent that he was attempting to instil as many as possible of the lessons of his own childhood experience into his children's training, and presumably, they in their respective ways have adapted part of that in bringing up theirs, but at least here in Japan, what once were solid links in the chain have been badly compromised.) And out in the countryside, the older generation was left to fend for itself – where it still remains today.

Even so, the economy continued its growth and, initially centred on the capital, Tokyo, money, and greed took the upper hand, spawning what came to be known as Japan's "bubble generation." And with their endless, 24-hour, every-moment-to-be-lived-to-the-fullest clock, they (and particularly the women, for the first time experiencing a total lack of social constraints) created the habits of a lifetime, not only for themselves, but also, to disastrous effect, for the next generation and onwards, right up to the present, living through what the foreign media cares to call our "thirty lost years."

A note on bubbles:

When you have had a serious bubble economy burst on you, some (/a considerable) measure of deflation – the dropping of those ridiculously exaggerated prices – should surely be expected as normal. I can understand that the simultaneous fall in share prices will not be appreciated by those who like to make money out of the market, but as it was nothing more than their greed that created the bubble in the first place, more than anyone, perhaps it is right that they should be the first to pay. The average man-in-the-street has no choice in these matters, but then if they do choose to pull back on their spending a little (/considerably), I would not consider it an unnatural reaction.

And referring to Japan today: "Consumers throughout have retained their deflationary mindset simply because there has been no real reason (/evidence of any strong upturn) that might make them change that outlook. That is, considered from their point of view and whatever other 'experts' might think or wish, they are acting in a thoroughly reasonable and rational manner."

Real estate is a perfect vehicle for speculation. And with 70% of Japan's total land mass being mountainous, leaving only the remaining 30% available for agricultural or urban development, it was natural that this is where the bubble itself was initially concentrated – spreading outwards from Tokyo, first throughout the main islands and then abroad to the United States, where the larger corporations indulged themselves in a range of vanity projects fronted by the 1989 takeover of the Rockefeller Centre. (This was the time we purchased our plot in the countryside.) And then without even the slightest notice given, it was gone, and the whole nation, and in particular large corporations, found themselves thrust into existence mode, with foreign investments the first to go. And very quickly, wherever possible, full-time workers were replaced by temporary or part-time workers, these now representing 40% of the total. (Agencies for securing temporary workers have now become big business, to the extent that large Japanese and foreign corporations, including the one I worked for, now commonly operate using their own outside agencies to guide non-regular workers into their fold, subsequently profiting at both ends of the equation. And workers are being taken for a double ride.)

However, as a seemingly unanticipated outcome, at least on the management side, all large corporations are now left with two quite distinct groups of employees who, while subject to completely different conditions and pay scales, are together at all times and expected to cooperate on (/contribute equally to) all ongoing projects. And in every respect, this is not working, with a large proportion of what used to be a very loyal and malleable workforce now no longer prepared to accept company strictures that were previously assumed close to sacrosanct. In particular, complaints to local labour bureaus related to workplace harassment by older bosses (who are finding it hard to adjust to the new realities) soared from 22,153 in 2006 to 70,917 in 2016. After-hours drinking with the boss, which did in its time help to smooth out the personal side of relationships, has to a great extent disappeared. And although this in part has resulted from budget cuts on the company's side, every recent televised report on the subject seems to be hammering in the point that, as far as the younger generations are concerned, the practice is for all practical purposes to be regarded as obsolete. And to complete the equation, we now have the social-media generation coming online.

Naturally, internationally, there are going to be more commonalities than differences here. However, that said:

1) With young people spending a far greater proportion of their time on their smartphones (and thus relatively free from the influences of television described in Cpt 5), you have a whole generation who have come to assume that they are free to pick and choose their 'fact sources' as they wish, making them far more open in their questioning of a system that older generations have up to now accepted at face value.

2) Some ten years ago, one of my students, a senior high school teacher of the Japanese language (this backed up by a university professor in the same class), noted that her students were now incapable of writing even the most basic essay in Japanese without inserting an emoji smiling face or frown. (Essentially, this was their understanding of what writing involved.) However, and far more importantly, it was noted that they were becoming completely incapable of using 'keigo', the polite terms of reference that are essential to indicating one's position in the hierarchical rankings and an essential part of promulgating the Confucian ethic.

And taken in total, it would seem that much of the previously assumed automatic respect for people in more senior positions seems to be vanishing fast. (A well-established comedian on television, when turning down an invitation to this year's prime minister's cherry-blossom viewing party – no problem in and of itself – commented that he had no interest at all in meeting with that 'ossan' ('old guy' expressed in its crudest form), an expression that I could not possibly have imagined being used openly in the media referring to a prime minister during my earlier years here.)

Apparently hoping somehow to turn back the clock, Prime Minister Abe has expressed an intention to reintroduce the teaching of 'doutoku': the patriotic education programme stressing the morality centred on obligations to family and state as was taught to prior to the war – including the Imperial Rescript on Education (1890), that provided the foundation for worship of the emperor and equally promoted the concept that; "The nation is everything, the individual nothing." [25] However, with the future so unpredictable, I suspect that it is today's younger generations who are really going to have to make the difficult decisions as to how their children are educated.

'Jibun katte':

This expression (acting in a selfish manner /insisting on having one's own way /acting without consideration for others), was one more phrase that was stressed repeatedly to me in my very early years of learning here. The problem, at least as I would recognise it today, is that the phrase is invariably used by the person in the superior position, who naturally would not accept this being used in criticism of their own equally selfish (/arrogant?) positions. And today, observing the attitudes of young people in their late teens and early twenties, and

---

[25] At the time of the recent Morimoto Gakuen elementary school scandal, a right-wing school built on land obtained at a steep discount from the Finance Ministry and that was initially promoted with Abe's wife, Akie Abe (now resigned), as 'honorary principal', the local media obtained a tape a group of students (presumably at a morning assembly) chanting in unison something to the effect of, "Thank you, Prime Minister Abe, for protecting us from China." In the next day's news, together with certain comments that teachers were also indoctrinating their students with a hatred of all things Korean, there were reports of some parents taking their children out of the school, but although the purchase scandal developed into an extended court case (now running through the system), this was the last we heard of actual teaching practices. Presumably, some points are better left not overly stressed!

particularly the confidence of those who have established themselves with considerably successful careers on the alternative media, has led me to wonder whether they might not actually be capable of creating of their own accord a "jibun katte ni dekiru shakai" – "a society in which they are free to act as they see fit." (Considering the situation in America and Europe at present, whether this actually will work in practice or not remains to be seen but, in the end, it has to be their future.)

[17.2] Attempting to deal with an aging society:

"You are only of value to society as long as you are fulfilling society's needs." And society has only two requirements; that you work – and then even harder – and/or you produce babies.

As of 2015, roughly 26% of Japanese citizens were classified as elderly, prompting a recent rather nastily phrased comment by Finance Minister Aso about the need for older people to "hurry up and die!" He later apologised, but the point was made.

When I first came to Japan, 'muri shinju' or 'enforced suicide' – where a parent (usually the mother), not wishing to leave her child at the mercy of society, killed that child before taking her own life – was a quite common occurrence and fully accepted as part of her natural responsibilities to that child. (Even now, parentless children are placed at a great disadvantage within the society, and adoption is still in the majority of cases not considered a seemly practice.) However, this today has been in large part replaced by children suffocating their elderly and enfeebled parents whom they are no longer able to care for, the principal in essence being the same, except that in today's world, such children do find themselves facing charges of murder.

And as other recent statements from the top echelons of our present government: "Having children is the fulfilment of each citizen's duty towards the nation!" – this together with, at one point, a (fully serious) suggestion from the Abe administration that both young men and women who do not marry (/and presumably produce children) be taxed at higher rates and/or have their social security benefits reduced.

(July 2018) A lady member in the Japanese Diet maintains that "gays, due to the fact that they cannot produce babies, are 'unproductive' and thus not deserving of any help from the government authorities." (It was later noted that she did not mention the fact that her mentor, Prime Minister Abe, and his wife would, being childless, presumably come under the same definition, but perhaps her thinking would not extend that far.) And a week later, again in the Diet, to quieten what had become something of an uproar in the media, a male representative (presumably from the same subset) took the floor to opine that "homosexuality being no more than a hobby," any further criticism of her remarks should cease.

And as an indication of the realities Japan is facing, the following figures have been taken from recent television and newspaper reports. (This being "up-to-date" news, figures are being regularly revised, but the overall picture is as presented.)

25% of heterosexual males and females in their twenties and thirties have no sexual experience. 40% of young unmarried people have stated that they have no interest in obtaining a partner in life. Younger women are on the whole quite happy about having sex, but not particularly interested in marriage. In contrast, men who do want to get married express relatively little interest in (and with the work environment worsening every day, almost certainly do not have time for) any romantic or other side of the courting process.

The upper echelons of the government have yet to realise this, but their totally remorseless emphasis on trying to recreate an unobtainable past is boomeranging badly: They are pushing their populace far too hard and clearly in all the wrong directions.

[17.3] A highly chauvinistic culture:

Presented under the title of "Womenomics," one of Prime Minister Abe's initial promises was to "create a society in which women can shine."
The reality: Since Abe became Prime Minister, Japan's WEF (World Economic Forum) ranking in gender equality has moved from 98th to 110th (2018). In political empowerment of women, Japan comes in 123rd out of the 149 world's nations, with political representation overall standing at 10%. (Opposition parties in general do much better in this regard: As of Feb. 2019, representing the Communist Party, 32% of local assembly members (vs. 5.4% for the LDP), 54.1% of prefectural representatives, and 13 out of 18 Tokyo Metropolitan Assembly members are women. Despite any criticisms that might be associated with its name, the Communist Party does at least practice what it preaches.)

And in society at large, women have been relegated to non-regular work with less pay, fewer benefits and zero bargaining power. While the number of women working has increased considerably, over 70% of them are employed in irregular jobs and 44% of these make less than ¥1 million annually (2018). In the gender-based division of labour at home, it is still the woman's role to raise their children, and very commonly these days without the father's assistance. Men's salaries in the upper bracket remain double the payments that women in that same bracket receive.

As a reality check: Leaders in any community do not just appear, and in particular (a point which any foreigner considering taking up a long-term career here might consider), even today in any major Japanese corporation, a minimum of 20 years of meticulous training is still considered essential before any individual (male or female) can be even considered as top or other management material (this regardless of whether they actually do in the end actually 'make it'), and for Abe (regardless of any percentage that he might choose to quote as his goal) to present himself as capable of simply conjuring women leaders (political or otherwise) out of thin air is in itself ridiculous in the extreme.

There are occasional improvements: A recent investigation found that admissions for training to become a doctor at the Tokyo Medical University (and subsequently at a number of other similar institutions) had been tweaked in favour of male applicants, this continuing for at least over a decade. Even if women answered every question correctly on the initial written test, they were only allowed an 80% mark as against the 100 that a male applicant would receive, putting them at a considerable disadvantage in the following interview stage. The standard reasoning of "women tending to resign or take leave of absence after getting married or giving birth" behind the original decision in this case was subject to considerable criticism in the media, and the system has apparently been changed – 'apparently' to be emphasised here because, as noted above, any real change is only going to become evident (again) 20 or 30 years from now.

One of the greatest problems facing women with children who wish to work is the lack of nursery schools and welfare facilities in their area. This problem has been brought up repeatedly in the media, with the government invariably promising to improve the situation without any real apparent change, and the workers themselves at such facilities are both overworked and underpaid.

There is also the problem of NIMBY: Everyone recognises the need for nurseries or kindergartens, but just not in their immediate neighbourhood: "Young children are far too noisy." Or, for that matter, old people's homes: "When they get senile, you never know what might happen?" And this is now seemingly being extended to the placing of training institutions for 'foreign interns' coming into the country (see below [17.5]), with whole neighbourhoods getting up in arms against such "low-level institutions" being established in their area.

And the birth rate still remains well below the figure required to keep present population figures even steady.

[17.4] Finding people to do the work:

Unpaid overtime and working excessive hours, leading to "karoushi" deaths from overwork [7.16], still remain as blights on the overall system.

Statistics: As of March 2019, the job availability rate stood at 1.63, that is, 163 job openings for every 100 applicants. Unemployment stood at 2.3%. Among the 66.64 million workers aged 15 or older last year, 13% were 65 or older. Japan is forecast to face of shortage of 6.44 million workers in 2030. (Chuo University and Persol Research and Consulting.), and with its present declining birth rate, Japan's population is set to slump by almost one third by 2060 (World Bank). Even today, wages are showing no signs of increasing. And now in May, we have: "Government urges firms to abolish retirement ages and/or employ staff at least until age 70."

A retreat from 'convenience':

House-moving companies, the post office and similar private delivery services, supermarkets, and e-commerce companies such as Amazon, all of which require high speed and stipulated-time home deliveries, are competing desperately to recruit new employees, this at a time when, as more and more people (women, in particular), having been drawn into the workforce, are coming to depend on these services.

The high turnover of staff at restaurants is resulting in a notable inconsistency in the quality of food and service rendered. When convenience stores and certain chain restaurants started offering a 24-hour service, it was considered something of revolution. However, with it now becoming impossible to find staff to work at such stores at the offered hourly rates, following direct complaints from store owners and government 'advice', a number of such franchises are being forced to reconsider arrangements, including a reduction in the number of hours any store is required to stay open. There are also a considerable number of criticisms appearing in the media related to the unwarranted waste of cardboard used in the delivery of (notably, Amazon) goods. This, in Japan, where excessive wrapping has always been considered the norm, together with the above matter of delivery staff availability, might be taken as a serious warning as to future constraints on such systems.

Finding time for leisure:

With the ever-present emphasis on 'teamwork', if one has been serious at all about obtaining promotion at some point, taking time off from the company without 'reasonable excuse' has always been a highly questionable practice in Japan. (One can only conceive of so many relatives whose sudden demise requires one's attendance at their funeral before superiors do begin to question the matter, and Koji was in effect obliged to change jobs each time he travelled abroad with me to England or other countries.) At the same time, there does appear to be something unseemly about a nation where there is a need to create government legislation to ensure that corporations force their employees (whether they personally wish to or not) to actually take a minimum of half of their legally guaranteed holidays, something which the present government (shortly facing important elections) has finally seen fit to do. (Medium- and small-scale companies will also be obliged to introduce the same system from next year, this to include part-time employees, with threats of real fines and other punishments if they are found not doing so. And foreigners can note that once a rule is introduced, there is an effective way to make direct claims through the Labour Standards Office – 'Roudoukijunkyoku'.)

Japan also has what amounts to an overprovision of national holidays, that the government has chosen to add to as they have seen fit, notably each time that there has been a rise in media complaints about 'overwork'. (The standard per year at present is now 16, with an additional 6 awarded this year to allow extra time off to celebrate the enthronement of the new emperor.) This year, in particular, the media did regularly stress the fact that such holidays nowadays only cover 50% of the workforce (presumably another reason for the above legislation), but as a quite separate problem that has existed since I first arrived:

As with bank holidays in England, 'saijitsu' in Japan involve gatherings of huge crowds at all popular sites, together with high prices for both plane flights and hotels, excessively over-crowded trains and traffic jams extending for miles as families first flood out of and then back into the main cities, commonly leaving workers far more stressed out at the end of their 'holiday' than they were going in.

I do understand that, as an established system, this will be extremely difficult to change, but taken as a matter of common sense, workers would be far better served by a minimum of public holidays together with insistence on a standard number of days off from the company to be taken as and when that individual requires them, thus spreading out the burden throughout the year.

[17.5] The consequences of getting what you want:

Generations of stressing the need to keep the population and culture pure has led to a point where the present society as a whole is in the process of losing its one possible means of regeneration, the intake of foreigners. Even today, the government cannot feel free to use the word 'immigration'. (A similar situation exists with the question of the Imperial succession, where the right-wing still insists on protecting the continuity of the male line, and they are now down to a grand total of three male heirs, one of whom 83 years is old.) In effect, they have become trapped in their own web of conceits.

Again, from the media:

Utilising foreign labour.
"In the 2017 IMD World Talent Ranking, Japan ranks last among 11 Asian nations for its appeal to highly skilled workers. Barriers include both the language and rigid business practices. There is a clearly felt shortage of doctors, nurses, and care-workers. Also, it comes out near bottom for its use of big data and analytics in business decision making and does not have anywhere near the number of workers required for development of big data, artificial intelligence, and the internet of things, and more importantly faces a shortfall of 200,000 security workers."

Some years ago, the government introduced what they described as a "foreign technical internship programme," with workers from the Philippines, Vietnam and China accepted for the lowest level of jobs as 'trainees', in what, in many cases, has proven to amount to modern-day slavery. A recent news report noted cases recorded in one year at over four thousand farms and factories where trainees were being forced to work high levels of overtime for no pay, holidays were not being given as per contract, or where even regular work was not being compensated. Passports are regularly confiscated, and to add insult to injury, in a large number of cases, no new skills, ostensibly the whole point the exercise, are being taught at all. As of April 2019, investigations have uncovered 759 suspected cases of intern abuse, with over 9,000 interns going missing in 2018 alone, and 171 deaths between 2012 and 2017. (Close to 400 companies refused to cooperate with the government enquiry or were unreachable, so what the true figures might be here is still open.) There have been reports of foreign workers sent to the site of the nuclear plant clean-up in the north being exposed to radiation, and both Panasonic and Mitsubishi, the types of company where you would expect reasonable treatment, have been eliminated from the programme for the "incorrect usage of such trainees." And there are repeated reports of workers heavily burdened by debts owed to brokers in their own country – whom they were obliged to pay to get them here in the first place. And then after the pre-determined period, they are sent back to wherever they came from.

The most recent effort (26.12.2018), essentially introduced to put a fresh face on the matter, was a new visa system (345,000 blue-collar workers in five years) for the construction, farming, and nursing care segments (most recently re-hashed to cover "14 labour-hungry sectors," including hotels and the cleaning-up process at the Fukushima nuclear-plant). The first reaction to this on the news at the time was: "When we no longer need them, how do we get rid of them?" (The Japanese, "shobun suru" at its politest can be translated as "deal with," but the tone of voice and overall line of questioning clearly indicated something much closer to the first translation.) That is, the worker is in all respects being viewed as a commodity, to be used and then disposed of. And again, "You are there to serve of the will of the state."

For foreigners who are at the top end of the scale and well paid for their services, this will amount to no more than I did in going to Saudi Arabia as a young man, making my money and (as you wish) staying on further or leaving. However, those coming from poorer countries might question expending all the efforts required to reach the required level in the Japanese language, just to work for a guaranteed maximum five years before being thrown out on their heels. (And if at any time during that period it is decided that their services are no longer required, naturally they will be required, as was the case with numerous second- and third-generation Japanese workers originally taken in from South America over 20 years ago, to leave early.) Whichever way you think about it, there have to be better choices.

[17.6] Politics on the home-front:

"Japanese society throughout, and particularly in the conduct of its politics, is both patriarchal and conservative, and change does not come easily."

When Abe came to power during his first one-year stint as prime minister in 2006, having observed the previous Junichiro Koizumi administration do its best (to little real effect) to shake up the LDP – this completing a grand total of 9 prime ministers in 12 years, most gone before even registered – I assumed that we were close to approaching the bottom of the barrel. However, after a short period under opposition governments – the second of which, under Naoto Kan, did have the bad luck of having to deal with the aftermath of the earthquake and tsunami disaster in the north before it could get in any real manner started on trying to reduce ministry perks (/lavish overspending and general wastefulness), which it actually did make a serious attempt at – now, again under Abe for the past 6½ years, with even remotely qualified replacements no longer available for promotion, the inevitable charade of musical chairs that we have lived with for so long would truly seem to be no longer viable.

Since he came to power, Abe has had to repeatedly dismiss ministers he has selected for his administration due to both incorrect statements and actions (/cover-ups) and, more commonly, verbal blunders. His most recent selection included a Minister of Cybersecurity who, at the time of his first grilling in the Diet, came out with the fact (which he did not seem particularly concerned about) that he has neither ever used a computer nor was he aware of what a USB might be. (See comment on security workers in [17.5] above.) He also regularly mispronounced (/couldn't be bothered to learn?) the names of communities in the north who had directly suffered from the nuclear disaster, but his final downfall came from a later off-the-cuff statement that "reconstruction efforts in these communities were of relative unimportance when compared with the matter of raising money for a local politician," which did not go down well in the media.

Retaining control:

"Do you see someone who refuses to admit to a clear blunder as a bully, fool or 'someone who sticks to their guns'?"

Relations with the media:

Coming into power for the second time, Abe immediately put his own man in charge of the national broadcaster, NHK. Also, presumably assuming he would benefit from the exposure, he insisted on all broadcasters giving equal voice to all positions. However, after close on seven years, finding that this is not working (a recent positioning on the popularity charts had his personal approval rating down at 18%), he recently brought forward a suggestion (not yet taken up) that the law be changed to allow (as in the US) any media outlet to be as biased as they wish in support of any (presumably his own) party or administration.

Controlling the bureaucracy:
The Prime Minister's Office has the power to promote or dismiss senior members in any of the government ministries, and Abe above all has used this to exert his full control over all ministries. As a result, today it is generally understood that all senior officials are to act and react in accordance with his stated or assumed ('sontaku') wishes. Practically this has had two results:

In the case of scandals, of which there have been a number (the most recent to date being the exposure of faulty jobs statistics at the Health, Labour and Welfare Ministry, indicating that they had failed to pay work-related benefits to some 20 million people over a period of ten years), ministries have found themselves obliged to 'cook the books' to correspond to whatever cover story Abe or one of his selected ministers have determined as 'the truth', which, as matters have been investigated and more details leaked, has in fact merely worsened the situation. Also, there is the reality that while previous administrations had been able to put the responsibility for any particular problem directly on the ministry concerned, Abe himself is now being subject to far greater direct criticism, which, in turn, he has learned to deal with by consistently refusing to be held to account; "I didn't!" "I haven't!" "There is no proof!" "Nothing was said or implied!" "There is no reason whatever for my wife to appear before the Diet!" (This latter in the case of the above Moritomo Elementary School affair [17.1]). And when proof is presented (even a second or third time.): "I am Prime Minister. I have said 'No,' and I am not to be questioned."

Quite apart from Abe's personal desire to stay in power, the real point here is that, without what would likely be a highly disruptive generational change, the LDP has no one else of any real ability to put forward. And the opposition parties (some of which have themselves broken away from the LDP at some point) have reached a point where very few of them have anything in common, making it very difficult to present either a united face or cohesive platform. (One of the most common reasons for re-electing the LDP, and totally regardless of Abe's personal popularity, is invariably; "Under the circumstances, they are the best choice we have.")

Travel:

I have seen few politicians who both travelled the world so regularly and extensively and talked so much to so little effect as Japan's present prime minister.

Much of his time has been spent on repeated discussions with President Putin in the hope of making some kind of final settlement with Russia on the Southern Kurils (the string of islands above Hokkaido known in Japan as the Northern Territories), lost to Russia at the end of WWII. The aim has long been to have at least two of the islands returned to Japan, but Russia, understanding that if they are, this could lead to the positioning of US troops on the island, are naturally not enthusiastic about the possibility, and it would seem that at least at the present point in time, Abe has little to leverage his position with.

Abe as a salesman (and not a very good one at that):

Although he has spent considerable time attempting to promote sales of nuclear plants (this after our still-to-be-cleaned-up disaster in the north), and submarines (to Australia) and most recently was noted as plugging Fukushima's sake on his trip Davos – presumably, he did say something else of importance – he has as yet to produce anything in the way of actual results.

He does, however, keep pushing farmers to export 'high-quality' food products. Irrespective of actual taste, and as a warning to those who might wish to make any purchases, it can be noted that 2019 OECD statistics determine Japan as only second to South Korea in the amount of agricultural chemicals used per square kilometre of farmland: 1.16 tons, vs an OECD average of 0.07 tons. (And as to why Japanese people who live in the countryside are so healthy? They grow rice and vegetables for their own consumption quite separately from their professional produce. At least, that is what my neighbours did.)

Laws passed:

On the 'security' front, Abe has succeeded with forcing through a "Conspiracy Law" – specific actions to be taken in the cases of 277 different crimes against the nation, which was at the time strongly criticised by the United Nations. Also, in 2016, he managed to legalise the concept of "collective self-defence" – again whittling away at constitutional limits until they can openly say; "This is now the reality, so we might as well make it official and change the Constitution." And recently, there being an election (/possibly two) in the wind, there has been an effort to push through laws/ 'guidances' that they hope might help to reduce the numerous social problems that keep erupting.

The one real success that Abe can perhaps take pride in would be in rescuing the Trans-Pacific Partnership (TPP) after America's withdrawal from the treaty. However, although he cannot in any sense be considered to blame for the matter, he still has to find some acceptable trade agreement with US before the matter can be truly settled.

[17.7] Abenomics:

Abenomics (initially introduced as Japan's answer to Reaganomics and the UK Thatcher's Big Bang) was intended more than anything as a means of getting the country out of its deflationary mindset. And for every reason illustrated above, it has not worked. Abe himself, who appointed the governor of the Central Bank to carry out his wishes, holds full responsibility here.

Although it initially had certain high-minded aims, the policy itself has basically involved keeping interest rates down to zero or (now) minus levels, and at the same time supplying money onto the market by issuing government bonds (of uncertain value), which then have been immediately repurchased by the Central Bank, that is, essentially creating additional government debt to what have proved to be uncertain ends.

For a number of years now, I have been highly conscious of the manipulation of economic theories to meet the (government or other) requirements of the moment. However, the following is based on one of three similar presentations that I have noted recently, two in the NYT, and one on Japanese television, which I selected principally because the principle offered aims to intake all today's advanced economies (including China), and that at the same time it is fully compatible with everything that I have sensed was wrong about the situation here in Japan today.

It is a well understood fact that excessive debt will weigh down an economy, and if not controlled successfully (/kept within reasonable limits) will result in (unnecessary/runaway) inflation and formulating adjustments to an economy with this in mind (including, where necessary, providing fiscal stimulus) is understood as a key function of any government. At the same time, at least from a political standpoint ("We need your votes!"), a certain growth in the economy is considered advantageous. To this end, economic experts produce "annual growth forecasts" as a guide for both governmental and business interests, which, in turn, lead to certain expectations among the general public that whatever administration is in control at that time is expected to meet. And naturally much rests on quite how accurate these original forecasts are.

NYT (2. 4. 2019) "Time to fret about the global economics." Ruchir Sharma. (A full reading recommended.)

The author's argument: Real growth in an economy can only be driven by a growth in the working population and/or in output per worker, i.e. productivity. And from this premise, you get:

1) The 'baby boom' that materialised around the world after WWII, with its unique combination of more workers and more output per worker, created the perfect opportunity for a sustained high-level of economic growth – a circumstance that is not easily replicated in today's world.
2) In all the advanced economies today, annual economic growth forecasts are still being calculated based on the actual growth rates during this high-growth period – what was, in fact, an exceptional period in recent history – and as a result, today's estimates of how fast an economy should be growing are, for the most, overly high.
3) Politicians, who are using these targets to justify reductions in tax rates or loosening of the money supply through reduction of central bank interest rates (as is the case with Japan's Abenomics), are in reality introducing a totally unneeded financial stimulus that in a normal situation would be used to pay back previously accumulated (/inherited) debts or invested in socially or environmentally desirable projects. That is, in their attempt to reach what is in fact an impossible target, a very large number of present-day leaders (regardless of their political affiliations) are in fact doing nothing more than adding unnecessarily to government debt. (In the present economic environment, both companies and individuals benefiting from these (what effectively are)

handouts are simply acting as they might be expected to do after suffering outsize losses and using them to protect their own interests.)

In the above article, it is noted that Japan's real growth "slowed from 1.2% in the early 2000s to a mere 0.2% last year," a period that could easily be correlated with the interval from the Lehman shock to the present, but which equally gives a very clear indication of the realities of the past six years of Abenomics, where central bank calculations are being premised on a (supposedly 'to be expected') requirement of a 2% annual growth. That is, on every front, Abenomics has been (or, perhaps to approach the matter more impartially, from the beginning there was no way in which it could not have been) a squandering of both time and government assets.

And the one thing that the government should have been doing all this time, i.e. developing policies to promote a society where young people can feel secure enough to marry and start families – producing the next generation of workers who will be needed to keep Japan going through the coming century – has been left totally unheeded.

[17.8] "We do everything we like. You do everything we say." America as subject to booms and busts:

American economists make a great point of insisting that other countries' industries and businesses that are in danger of collapse should be restructured (and if necessary open to liquidation proceedings), the principle (perfectly reasonable in itself) being those bankruptcies, while not pleasant, do make way for new growth. (Unsurprisingly, American hedge funds are always fully ready to step in as necessary to assist with this process – and naturally take their percentage of the proceeds. And, equally naturally, Japanese corporations do not take great joy in these overtures.)

However, in America, at the time of the 2007–2008 subprime mortgage crisis (referred to in Japan as the Lehman crisis), which was created entirely by the American system as it existed and still exists (ref: The book and movie, "The Big Short", which makes crystal clear Wall Street's responsibility in this matter), thanks to the Obama administration of the time, all the main American banks that were in danger of collapsing were rescued, and although laws to prevent a similar occurrence were apparently enacted, they were then effectively ignored, resulting in a second and (one imagines as very possible in the not too distant future) a third (serious?) recession. (Goldman Sachs et al will get paid off again?)

And one wonders which of the weaker nations (Think, Greece) is going to be hit hardest this next time. (WGFTG!)

It can be pointed out here that what saved Japan at the time of the Lehman shock was the deep-seated conservative streak present throughout its banking system, together with the strong personal savings of the population at large, neither of which America either has or encourages. However, today, as a direct result of the Bank of Japan's (again, Abenomics) continuing insistence on zero or minus central bank loan rates (this having all but destroyed any possibilities for smaller or local banks to make even the smallest of profits), the overall banking system in itself has been severely weakened, and the Japanese government now only has the power of the stock market to offer its populace as proof of the success of its policies. And, in consequence, Abe can now only – supported in the English newspapers by just about every American economic columnist-cum-'advisor' he has been able to drum up from wherever – keep pushing strongly for the general population (and particularly the more elderly population, who are known to have considerable savings) to invest in the market (or more specifically, the unnecessary and unwanted government bonds being held at present by the Central Bank as a result of its own inane policies), which apparently some have done. However, by far the largest proportion, not confident at their age in any ability to start playing the market and, thanks in large to American pressures on the system, now no longer able to receive even the smallest return on their investments in the banks – the final straw being the elimination of all interest on their Postal Savings at the time of the Koizumi administration (2001–2006) – understanding that they still have long lives ahead of them and a very unclear idea as to what the future might hold (and, it can be noted, in precisely the same manner as all the large corporations and mega-rich, with their art collections and money placed in offshore accounts), <u>have simply chosen to take their money out of the system</u>.

(As a further downside to this matter, with it being common knowledge that many older people keep their savings at home, this has left them open to a whole range of scams, the most recent involving home thefts where the con artist actually makes an appointment for a "convenient time to visit" – the most recent case ending up with the death of the 80-year-old lady concerned. And as to making more physical purchases, also a common plea from government economists, why should older people be expected to waste their money on things they understand that they no longer have any need for?)

[17.9] A changing of the guard:

The 30 years since the bubble burst have in fact roughly coincided with the recently concluded 'Heisei' period (1989–2019), which, in an end-of-era survey, the general public associated with the Chinese ideographs 'sai' (disaster, destruction – earthquakes, flooding, volcanic eruptions, tsunami and nuclear disaster, 21%), 'hen' (change – the spread of mobile phones the advancement of information technologies, 7.1%), and 'ran' (disorder, confusion, chaos in the world at large, 6.9%) in the first three places; all, under the circumstances, very understandable. The central tenet of the system as it was promoted to me when I first arrived, 'wa' (harmony) came in ninth, with no percentage quoted. However, we now have a brand-new era, 'Reiwa', to look forward to with the Foreign Ministry's suggested translation as "beautiful harmony" or as given in a direct translation of Prime Minister Abe's address to the nation at the time of the announcement; "A culture born and nurtured as people's hearts are beautifully drawn together."

In reaction to this particular speech, the following day the approval rate for the Abe administration went up by 9.5%. And even the Japan Times, reacting to the mood of the moment, found itself obliged to come out with "a strong improvement in the labour market", as against the recently far more common – and truthful – "(debilitating) shortage of labour."

[17.10] In conclusion:

Japan:

I do know that there is still a great deal of beauty and caring in this society, together with a wide range of creative forces (there is far more to life than AI) that, if nurtured correctly, could be of great benefit to the world. That said:

As a sovereign nation, Japan is entitled to aim for whatever it wishes with its future, this including protecting its 'bloodline' (although how this is to be practically achieved without any babies being born, I cannot comprehend), safeguarding its business practices (quite how, without a sufficient number of compliant staff?), changing its constitution to allow its Self-Defence Forces to fight freely overseas (again, with recruits coming from where?), or whatever. However, limiting the argument to the immediate future, for any of this to become reality, someone is going to have to start taking into account (/practically attending to) the population's real needs, this involving some serious examination of all the realities of a situation that they have been determinedly ignoring for far too long now. And, equally, with these realities changing as rapidly as they are, and submitting that this is the true Achilles heel of Confucianism as a philosophy applicable to the modern age (a matter which at some point China will also have to face up to), some effort at encouraging flexible thinking (/a willingness to at least try other approaches) has to be the order of the day.

(As a related practical matter, it can be pointed out here that countries that do not feel they have any particular need to become embroiled in external affairs do seem to have far more time to consider the well-being of their own citizens – including the, what is rapidly coming to be seen as essential, protection (/retrieval) of the natural environment.)

The world in general:
There is clearly an urgent necessity for politicians all over the globe to start imparting some serious home truths to their populations, most particularly that there are limitations as to what can be expected in terms of economic growth in their lives or in the lives of their offspring. More than anything, there has to be an understanding that, for every reason, ever-expanding economic growth as perceived by the so-called advanced societies of today has to be understood (at least for the present) as something approaching fantasy. Even now, the world is suffering excessively from just about every conceivable ill-effect of overpopulation, and although it is nice to presume that things will go on as they always have, I seriously doubt that this is going to be the case.

Too much money in too few hands:
On the understanding that this is a fully recognised problem and certainly not one which is easily solvable or in which I have any particular expertise:

All multinational companies, regardless of where they choose to keep their headquarters, have to pay a direct tax in the countries where they are making their profits. If this requires new internationally recognised regulations, by all means.

In connection with comments following the recent fire at Notre Dames in Paris, all tax deductions for those who choose to engage in philanthropy should be done away with completely. If the obnoxiously rich cannot find it in themselves, as everyone else does, to donate their earnings freely, they should be left with the matter to hang heavy on their respective consciences. (In the end, what is money there for?)

Whatever arrangements a country has in terms of tax rates and deductions, surely it should be possible to make some minimum percentage payment compulsory. For multimillionaires (or those who have the pleasure of playing with that type of money), to have a system where, at the end of the day, they can eternally get away with paying essentially nothing, seems ridiculous in the extreme.

And as a final comment from an apparently successful leader in the elderly care industry in Japan, which, at present, being both ill-paid and extremely stressful work, has an exceptionally high turnover rate: "If you do your utmost to support your employees, they will both do the work they have to and stay with you." This is certainly not a cure-for-all, but at least it could be considered a start; if not a way back, at least an effort to move forward. A considerable number of people in this world do understand that money is not the be-all and end-all of everything, but if they are to continue to sustain the vanities of those who do, they could at least be afforded a minimum of regard.

Chapter 18
Family Affairs

[18.1]

As the third son, I presume that by the time I came around for any consideration (we were born one after another over a period of 2½ years), I was old hat to both my parents. They had been through it all before: All the first-time experiences and all the effort (tears and disciplining) would naturally come with the eldest, who right the way through remains in that position. My middle brother, Will, according to his nature, required none of that. And I, as the youngest son and it being immediately after the end of the war, got the 'hand-me-downs'. However, I also did get the pleasure of being left to my own devices. Neither of my parents ever laid down the law with me, as I was strongly aware at times that my father did with my eldest brother, but that was the only way it could be. He was the eldest and I was the youngest. And being set apart as I was from the beginning allowed me to view them all somewhat objectively, and as I learned to observe, I also learned to go with the flow, to figuratively shrug my shoulders and let whatever it was be.

As a teenager, I never needed to rebel. I only said no to my father once, at the age of 18 or so. I can't even recall what it was about, but that was it, at least until I was much older and put my foot down about the importance of my partner in my life, and (I suspect) got cut out of his will for the trouble. Whether it actually was this, I will never know – living my life out here on the other side of the world, there were many details of everyday family life that never reached my ears, but it is a fact that I was cut out of the will, with only my mother's decision to tear it up immediately after his death preventing any further complications. At the same time, they did give me all the essential tools I needed to survive in life (from my mother, I learned the basics of cooking, gardening, and decorating the house – painting and wallpapering, etc.), every single one of which has been useful in my life.

In terms of their background, other than the fact that both married in their late thirties, apparently meeting through a local 'rambling society', I was told very little. However, I did learn that my father had spent a number of years prior to the war traveling around Europe on his motorbike, a point which resonated with my own upbringing, and did give him a lift up in my appreciation of who he was.

FF: My father always had his own ideas about how things should be done, what I referred to as his stubborn side; "He knew what he knew!" For years, as a child, I remember him repeatedly praising the curative effects of a "red-hot mustard bath" to relieve a cold, and at one point he actually made one for me, mixing in a full (one kilo?) can of Colman's mustard powder into the hottest bath he could pour and had me breathing in mustard fumes for a good thirty minutes, not letting me get out until I had "taken in its full effect." I'm not sure whether others may wish to try this but, at least in my case, the cold remained. And then in my late teens, when he started bragging about "how he could do things so much faster than my mother could," I made quite a bit of money off him, betting against how much time it would take him to "run up an apple pie" or "iron half a dozen shirts" (10p for every five minutes it took him over his declared time limit), etc., the grand finale to this whole sequence coming when he insisted on showing us how to make crab-apple jelly, the apple's coming from my grandmother's garden, at which time, having boiled up the cherry-sized apples with sugar for two or three hours, and pouring the thick dross into a large muslin bag with the aim of squeezing out the liquid (which was to become the jelly), he managed to exert too much pressure and explode the whole mix over himself, my mother and brothers and a large part of the kitchen floor and ceiling, the whole sticky mess taking us well over two hours to clear up. However, this did do the trick, and for quite some time he left domestic arrangements in my mother's hands. (Much later, after he retired, he did actually become very helpful in and around the house, growing a whole range of vegetables and fruits in the garden, and producing homemade bread, etc.)

On giving:

Now that I am older and I have a lot of things I no longer need, I have developed a principle of, if I am giving something, that it should be something that, at least in my own judgement, is of reasonable quality. On one of our later visits home, my mother gave me two dinner plates that she had hand-painted (it was a long-time hobby of hers, and she was very good at it), one to be given to Koji's woodcarving teacher, Mr Honjo [4.12], who was visiting with his wife at the time, and taking them both into the living room, following the above principle (and also as a sign of respect to him as Koji's 'sensei'), I offered him a choice and naturally he took the nicer plate, which at the time annoyed my mother. I do understand why: She wanted me to have something special from her to remember her by, while in reality I didn't need anything and never have. She has always been here in my mind whenever I needed her. However, viewed from the above perspective, I would've thought the action could have stirred a little parental pride within. At least, if I had a child who acted in way, it is certainly not a matter I would condemn.

[18.2] Fighting my mother's influence:

Throughout my life here in Japan I have been extremely aware of older (and commonly overbearing) women who have a bad habit of wanting to take me under their wing, which in Japan becomes their assumption of my need for their (to me, totally intrusive) presence to guide me (even at my present age) in my life's (/everyday) decisions, when in truth they can have no real knowledge at all about my background or lifestyle upon which to base such advice. Almost certainly, this is connected to my relationship with my mother, who (as detailed in Cpt 2) on a number of key occasions interjected her presence rather forcefully into my life. Also, being the third son, and fed on the (true or otherwise) narrative that a mother likes a daughter who she can feel close to, from quite early on I became very sensitive the idea of growing up as a mother's boy.

On my parents' second trip to Japan, when saying farewell to Koji's family, my mother asked his eldest sister, Sachiko, to "look after me," which unfortunately she came to take to heart rather more seriously than I would have preferred. (I had come to Japan specifically to be away from that kind of thing.) However, his total family being very welcoming to the both of us and our relationship, as long as Koji was alive, this was (if, at times, reluctantly) accepted. In particular, each time she visited, she had a very bad habit of taking it upon herself to 'clean up' our home according to her preferences, this at times down to changing the position of various objects in our cupboards, where, to my mind, she had no business to be in the first place. Equally, presumably taking the position that her younger brother's home was hers to act as she liked in, she had a bad habit of padding around in her underwear to cool down after taking a shower, on one occasion shortly before I was expecting my students to arrive for their morning lesson, at which point I had to lay down the law.

But then, when visiting sometime after Koji had died and she started acting in the same manner – this together with an assumption that I was now an official member of the Ishida family – neither of which I took lightly to, I had to tell her that this was my home in which she was expected to act as any other guest would. Her eldest daughter, who was with her at the time, fully understood this, but then when I found her repeatedly acting in the same manner, I had to tell her she was no longer welcome. This, ultimately, I do understand as a matter of cultural differences, which cannot be avoided, but it resulted in the fact that I later had to tell Kensuke that, much as I like his family (they are very nice people), I need to keep a clear distance in our relationships. And particularly as I move into old age, I find the need to live, if not in the manner I was brought up to, at least according to my preferences.

[18.3] William (Will):

He was loving. More than anything, he was loving. Kind and loving, far more than anything I could ever understand myself to be, I never saw him a raise his voice in anger to anyone. And never demanding, not in even the mildest way. Ben, the Christian who came up home from college the one time after my coming out [1.1], who was of a similar nature, got on well with him. They were a natural pairing; smiling, and chatting together as if they had been friends all their lives.

I sense he got a very bad rap in life, although not having lived it, I couldn't really know. After a minimal secondary school education, he was trained in my father's butcher's shop, which he eventually took over, until, for whatever reason, it was no longer his and he was unemployed. He never married, I would guess partly related to the fact he had an overweight body that would do nothing other than get larger and larger (the doctors eventually decided that it was a problem inherited at birth that neither he nor they could do anything about) – this right though until, with diabetes, he lost a big toe and then a second to the surgeon's knife; and then both feet, followed by the bottom halves of both legs, all severed to prevent the spreading of an infection that could not be prevented from spreading. And beyond that they could do nothing, and he died.

At one point (again, I wasn't told about it at the time), he was found fondling a child. How bad it was, I do not know, but, as far as I know, he was not arrested (or, at least, it did not come down to serving any prison time). Still, he kept going. Particularly after our parents died, he loved getting my letters, and wrote to me regularly – every other word misspelled and grammar close to non-existent – but far more real and loving than anything my eldest brother, Ted, ever managed to put into his once a year, maximum five-line greeting.

He has appeared in my dreams a few times recently, presumably because I have been trying to remember the odd bits of life we had together; nothing special – the only exception being when he introduced me (as I chose to read it at the time) to his (new?) Hispanic family – all gathered in our old dining room at home. Or it could have been something else, it being shortly before Hurricane Maria hit Puerto Rico (Sept. 20, 2017).

FF. (Nov. 2017): There was a man, framed as he might have been in a television set, a shiny bald on top but with neatly trimmed sides, and he was smiling at me – such a warm, friendly smile that I had to smile back. And then there was a second, a little younger but also with a broad smile on his face and equally attractive, and I kept smiling. And then a third, and fourth, and fifth…for a total of seven or possibly eight; all in the same age range – middle thirties to early forties; all I would guess South American (possibly Puerto Rican – I had had the earlier dream) but certainly Hispanic, and all smiling. And as they all came into view, I could see they were seated on rows of benches in what appeared to be some kind of lecture hall.

The scene blanked, and then I was sitting on the front bench, with the whole group to my right, and one by one they leaned forward so that they could see me, and I could see them. And we were still all smiling. Then, again, a scene change, and I was out in the corridor and one of them was asking me to come and join them in the next class, but I said I had to go the other way and we parted. And then, in the dark, I could only hear their voices:

"You saw him, too?"

"Yes. He was in front of us, and then suddenly he was sitting next to us all there on the bench."

This followed by lots of laughter. And I was left there alone. But then waking up, it occurred to me to wonder whether the situation might not actually have been real, and that they had been seeing me as some form of joint apparition. Just in the hopes, if you are out there, you may contact my publishers! (And now I am smiling!)

[18.4] My personal bogeyman:

Cases of alleged molestation or rape are extremely common in today's media, and invariably the most common challenges to these claims are, "Why now?" "Why not twenty or thirty years ago when it happened?" and/or, "How can you remember something from so far back?" The following story has only ever been told to Kensuke, for the simple reason that I did not want to have secrets between us. (It is not a tale you bring up lightly with anyone.) It was also around this time that the idea for writing this book came to me and I decided some accounting was in order. I could not give any details of the timing of the incident other than very vaguely, but as to the manner in which it occurred, I have every touch and movement burned into my brain, and it still hurts – the pain and the shame of not (even now) knowing what I could have done otherwise, rippling through my life, where there should have been none.

Alone at home. A reprise:

(At 12 or 13.) I was in the cellar when he called out to say he was back home and thinking I would go up and join him (whatever I had been doing was finished with), I started climbing up the steps only to suddenly become conscious of his black silhouette leaning out heavily above me in the darkened stairwell. We had a light at that point, but it had – presumably, deliberately – not been turned on. And he was the snake – still in its motion, poised to strike; and I, the petrified mouse – trapped and aware, and incapable of flight. And as he beckoned me to follow him (nothing was said throughout the whole proceedings), I knew that this had happened before – the details blanked from memory, but this was not the first time. And following him up to his room, I undressed and lay with him on his bed. There was no thrill of expectation here, just a somewhat dulled understanding of my position – together with a profound sense of the unreal. At every point, he led; touching my body, 'caressing', and then placing his lips across mine (not a kiss), and I followed as best I imagined a lover should act – aware of the artificiality of every movement, even as my body re-positioned itself to 'react' appropriately. And him above me. Always above me. And as I got older, this scene, the origin of much of the play acting of the lover that ensued throughout my life, came to cling to my brain like some form of slime.

And then my mother's voice calling up from the hallway: "Ted? Geoff? You are home?" This followed by some very panicked dressing and hurried explanations as to why I happened to be in my brother's room; somewhere I would normally never be welcome. But at least this intervention assured that there would be no repeat of its kind.

Until it happens:

Six months or so after the above, I was in the fields below our home with our next-door neighbour's daughter, two years younger than myself. I do not recollect any 'intentions' here (I had taken her to show her the horses kept in the one of the fields), but that done and now understanding that we were well out of sight of our homes, I extended my hand – and in doing so recognised that I had become the snake and she, seated on the grass a short way from me, her back up against the wall, the timid prey.

I can never know the extent to which the experience(s) with my brother dictated the events here, but in terms of why it happened at this particular time (I was not yet at an age to find a girl – any girl – attractive or 'sexy'), it would be the horses: On the two or three occasions when I had visited them earlier, I remember the feel on my palms as I stroked them; the fine hairs, and sitting astride their bare backs in an attempt to ride them (they belonged to the local riding stables and subsequently knew enough to ignore me) as somehow mildly erotic, and I can imagine that this might have worked in on my mind. However, in the same manner that I had not been free to retreat back down into the basement, here also I was not in control.

And then just as suddenly – something I have ever remained thankful for – we could hear her mother's voice calling for her to come back into the house. And nothing had happened, and the moment had disappeared, and even today I can only hope that her mind had not registered the situation as it had existed in mine. (Nothing was ever said by anyone, and we remained neighbours for a considerable time after the fact.)

***

At a much older age, contemplating what might be the worst type of crime an adult could commit, with no particular thought, my mind settled on the defilement of a young mind – from which the reader will easily be able to ascertain the limits of my personal experience. (I can easily imagine a parent who has lost a child or experienced war at its worst coming up with a very different answer.)

And as to where the responsibility lies:

Barry was an older man (mid-forties) in our teachers' group in Saudi Arabia who was only attracted to boys within the very limited age range of 12 to 14 – why, I never asked him and he never attempted to explain – and then as they outgrew him, any attraction that they might have had died, and it was as if they might never have been. From my angle, just the idea of attempting to find a 12-year-old in that setting rather terrified me, but apparently, he wandered off base a lot and had subsequently "run into someone," as you do. The fact that at the time of meeting, the boy was already 13, set an unfortunate time limit on the relationship, but he was very happy to live with what he had.

And viewed from the opposite end of the spectrum, years ago I had a close friend who told me that he started "wanting men" when he was around eight years old. I have forgotten the exact age he first found someone, but I do remember that he was considerably younger than legal statutes would normally permit.

***

Even today I find it hard to come up with memories where Ted affected me in a positive manner; actions that invoked respect or left me with a smile. As very small children, we must have shared something, but those memories are not intended to remain, and other than in the odd photograph, I have none. Working in the shop, he was always two steps ahead with the jobs he was entrusted with, but this was taken as natural. In the basement under the front of the shop, we had a gas-fired coffee-bean roaster which required the metal cylinder containing the beans to be rotated constantly by hand for a period of up to an hour, and watching him at this work is probably the one time that I sensed something to be looked up to, something 'manly' in his actions, a point at which I actually envied him as 'older', and this in part because I never got to do this myself, packaged coffee coming in before I grew enough to wield the handle. Other than that, at around the age of seven or eight, I remember him, as a leader of our local gang, ordering me to guard ("with your life") a set of long planks being collected for our local Guy Fawkes night bonfire. And that was it, for a lifetime. And otherwise, every memory – although in truth, having lived separate lives, I have very few – is bad, or at least badly tainted.

In my earlier memories in my teens, he was always above me, this partly because of his height (he was a good six inches taller than myself), together with the fact that (it being his nature), when the occasion arose, he took it upon himself to physically position himself at a higher level, just to emphasise the point being made. He was older than I was! He was my senior! And that is how things were to remain, at least in his mind, right through to the end. (As a note to any older siblings: There is an immense gap between a ten-year-old and eight-year-old child that ceases to exist when one is thirty and the other thirty-two, or fifty even, and this he apparently never came to grasp.)

At grammar school, students in the first year were subject to a 'getting-to-know-you' hazing in the school yard, which invariably lasted about a week. Made to bend over in lines against the wall, the second-year students then leapfrogged over us, coming down onto our backs as hard as they could. (It being 'tradition', the teachers deliberately kept themselves at a distance, only cutting in if any senior students started acting a bit too roughly.) However, I do remember one day when, looking up, I could see the top half of Ted's body framed in the corridor window staring down at me with a curious measure of intensity in his eyes. At the same time, it was a totally disinterested look, allowing no sense of recognition – certainly, no sense that he was looking down on a younger brother. And looking back at him, my reaction had to be: "What on earth are you standing there for?" Thinking now, never having had the opportunity to observe me as a student before, this had to be a completely new experience for him also. On his side, at least, he was very much observing an unknown.

[18.5] Small things that add up:

A recent article on estrangement from family (NYT. "Myths about estrangement." Catherine Saint Louis), this apparently at 8% in a recent survey in the UK, explained that this was not a phenomenon that happened overnight, but did not touch why this might be so. However, if you consider the Western social emphasis on the family unit; family gatherings, parental love and love of child for parent and sibling – although not packing any of the strength of Confucianism, still one important component in our version of promoting social unity – together with the ever-present "blood is thicker than water" quotation, which Ted threw at me regularly, that it might take some time for the actual breakoff to occur could be considered natural. However, in the end, with me also, it did happen.

There are givers and takers in all areas of life, and most people represent some balance of the two, giving or accepting help as the occasion arises. However, Ted, at least in his relationship to myself and Will, only understood how to take, and right the way through in this matter he was clearly fully supported by his wife. In fairness, he was the eldest child, and he had his children, but Will, who asked for nothing, essentially got precisely that.

Early on, after graduating from technical college, I do know that with my father's help, Ted started his own small company producing ball-bearings, at one point with from 20 to 30 employees, and that later he was put out of business by foreign competition. After that, I'm not quite sure how things developed, but I do remember being told by my mother that my father had continued giving him considerable help. And then after my father had died in the spring (I had visited earlier that winter to see him but could not afford a second visit for his funeral), Ted had persuaded my mother to sell their bungalow and move everything (including some very beautiful antique furniture) down to his home in the countryside, where he had prepared a one-room annex for her. This in itself was not bad, but in the summer when I visited, she did tell me that she was not really happy there. She had been very settled in her bungalow and got on well with all her neighbours, and now she had nothing except her grandchildren, who naturally she loved, but the fact that they were still in the boisterous stages of their lives could make life tiring for her.

At the time of his 21st birthday, Ted insisted Will and I purchase for him what for us at the time was a very expensive cigarette lighter, this together with an (un-kept) promise that when we each reached our respective birthdays, he would naturally be able to afford much nicer presents for the two of us.

When I pointed this matter out to him at the time of my mother's funeral, he actually purchased a crystal beer glass for me, which I did bring back home but, it having too many associated memories, I could never find in myself to actually use. I did, however, allow it to be handled by some of my more unruly student friends from the company at a home party, at which time, together with a number of my best Waterford Crystal glasses, it was very quickly damaged. And a chipped crystal mug being of no value to anyone, it was suitably disposed of.

And then again, at the funeral, after coming out with the fact that he, too, was gay, and that he had had five children in one sense to try to prove otherwise, a revelation that I did not particularly appreciate, he actually brought up the suggestion that our inheritance might be divided nine ways – by his reckoning it would be right for his wife and children to take equal shares. The proceeds from the sale of the bungalow were never mentioned at this time or later. However, without giving it even a second thought, I told him to forget it. Legally, we had our rights, and that was the way it would be. On my side, I understood it could not actually be a large inheritance, and in truth it did not matter (at the time, I had a good job), but that Will should end up with nothing did not seem correct. Visiting him earlier that month, his house had been bare down to the floorboards and he did not have one piece of furniture (or in fact a single thing) on view from our parents' home. Nonetheless, he did at this time give me a pair of small peanut goldfish, each with waving tails and balanced on small shells, of the kind you would buy at the seaside, and these I still have on display together at home in their own modest little bowl.

My father had had his own dream of building a supermarket on the land around the shops, and to this end he had purchased three adjacent houses (subsequently rented out) and land at the back on which he had built a row of garages (also for rent), which now had to be disposed of. And eventually Will took full responsibility for all the settling of this remaining estate with the family solicitor, a full two-years work. I got my share, used to purchase our plot of land in the countryside [4.14], and presumably he took his. However, after he died, there was never any mention of where any money he might have had left went to, and the matter was left at that. Presumably, Ted needed it, and at that time I was too far gone to care.

My mother's death came on the final night before Koji and I were due to fly back to Japan. Sitting around in Ted's living room for a small farewell party, I had noticed that she was very quiet, hardly contributing anything to the conversation and seemingly quite happy within her own thoughts. It being an animated gathering, it was hardly noticed when she left us for her room. However, a little later, hearing an odd noise and checking in to see how she was, Ted found her lying on the floor where she had fallen unconscious, and an hour after that, with no sign of any change in condition, she took her last breath at the hospital. In the weeks before she died, she had talked to me a lot about the pain she was having in her legs. And correct or not, to my mind, with my father gone, she had decided that she had had enough and had simply checked out on life, which is not in any manner a bad way to end things. In the final analysis, both of them were very good parents to me. And life went on.

Every year, at the Christmas season, I would send off a typed newsletter to all my friends around the globe, giving an account of the year's activities and adding a short-handwritten note at the end of each to add a personal touch. However, for Ted, this was not enough: He was not to be treated in this manner, and I was to send him "handwritten letters" or nothing. However, having well over 60 letters and New Year cards to send off each season, I was not prepared to handwrite a listing of the same events just for his benefit, and the letter went ignored. And then a year or so later, I found myself commiserated with for not having had the pleasure of seeing my nieces and nephews grow fully into adults. For some reason, he could not appreciate the fact that I had six of Koji's nieces and nephews whose lives I was fully involved with from the time they were small children right through to the present. And on and on, until, as a final straw, I received a highly florid invitation to the wedding of his youngest child, someone I had never known other than as a toddler. By this time, all other four of his children, who both Koji and I knew well, had at various times wed (and, in some cases, divorced) without any notification of the same to me, and now he expected me to fly back to England for quite what I could not understand. And I wrote to tell him that I had had enough of his absurdities and not to contact me any further. And that was it.

Thinking now, right to the end, he was insisting on his centrality to the meaning of my life: Presumably, he had some need to rely on his identity as eldest brother – "the one who was always there to reassure and guide," while in reality, for me, apart from the hurts he had caused me, he had no part in my life. He did not exist. For many years afterwards, I actually kept a photograph of the two of us taken standing in front of the house around the time I was 15 or so, until, truly fed up with him and his conceits (and equally tired of the sight of his arm pressing down on my shoulder), I decided it was no longer needed and it got ripped up and thrown into the waste.

[18.6] Dreams:

Whenever Ted has appeared in my dreams, he has almost invariably been overbearing, always in some manner trying to mentally or physically hurt me. However, as a somewhat disturbing dream that occurred shortly after the sequence of snake dreams described in [8.3]:

With Ted, both of us still young, bouncing up and down excitedly on an extra-large mattress; suddenly presented with a scene of total exuberance – a squirming, writhing mass of newly born snakes, beside themselves with joy upon receiving the gift of life.

Upon hearing this description, Hiroshi (I had recounted the whole series up to that time to him), pronounced it to his satisfaction. To him, it was 'good'. (I presumed that, in his mind, we were recreating what I had destroyed – with the snakes gorging on each other.) However, to me, I was returning to a past that I needed nothing of, or more worryingly, we had been setting off yet another cycle of the same pain and fear that I had spent so much time and energy trying to eliminate from my mind. Either way, it was not something I welcomed. Even the best interpretation that I could bring up in my mind was that they were from the real eggs that had never hatched when I was a child [2.5], but this of itself was not of any comfort. (At this same time, telling him about Will fondling the child, Hiroshi did comment that, "If Ted had acted in that manner with me, he might have also taken the same liberties with his other brother," but this I can never know.)

And waking up thirty years on (10.4.2018.):

I had just spent a rather extended period of time, together with an old friend, wandering around an area of ruins observing a never-ending array of snakes of just about every size and variety available. Understanding that they were not to be disturbed, I had, as in the past, taken each step carefully, but none of them had taken even the slightest sign of interest in either of us. Thick, sluggish, ugly even; lacking any sense of life or energy and certainly with none of the liveliness of previous dreams, not one seemed even close to being directly threatening. If they were representative of sexual urges or some other mystical powers, it was nothing that I could recognise any longer. And whatever, even though there was still life there (one pair were copulating), I sensed it would not be too long before they started turning on each other. Or possibly they had reached the stage where they no longer had the energy for even that. In all likelihood, we had all, in our turn, simply aged beyond our time.

And in actuality, this was not the last, and I still have some time to live, but as far as the reader is concerned it will have to do. And ultimately, snakes are snakes, and (as is also the case with dragons [19.6]) a perfect place play out your fantasies.

"Win one, lose one":

This time, I stood up to him; physically went straight at him, hitting as hard as I could until he vanished from my view. Perhaps oddly, the thought that also came with this last (I hoped) dream, was that what I was seeing was not my brother, or, at worst, it was only a small part of his make-up. Rather, it was something that he had connected with (or had connected with him) as a child and also that much later connected with both me and Will – a deeply hidden need evidencing itself through his actions – and that, at least initially when he was young, he was not in control of those actions.

(10.6.2018):

Woke screaming at the top of my lungs, having had a pleasant dream broken into abruptly with a full-length view of Ted reflected in a mirror, smiling down at me – as he had in that photograph (ripped up so many years ago), his hand pressing firmly down on my shoulder.

I can understand that a more generous mind might wonder why I should react in such manner to a smile but considering that I cannot today recall a smile on his face that did not employ some form of arrogance or condescension in his attitude towards me, perhaps I may be forgiven for my interpretation.

[18.7] Koji at the end:

In the early September of the year before he died, Koji was diagnosed as having cancer of the liver, apparently related to a Herpes B virus which he carried that also strongly affected his mind.

After my two trips to Korea, during which periods he chose to spend his time in Hawaii, and then following my own hospitalisation for the operation on my heart [8.7], for a wide range of reasons, there had been a certain mutual recognition of a distance between us, which, having no direct means to contend with, I could only leave to time. After the fact, I learned that he had at one point given up on me, deciding that I no longer cared for him, which was not in any way true. However, during this period there were a series of 'difficult' incidents that built up, in effect widening that gap and perhaps creating more of a problem than should have been. And with my brain operating through this somewhat ill-focused lens, it had only come to me very slowly over a period of three or four years that something was actually seriously wrong.

First, it was the small accidents while driving – referred to and then dismissed – which eventually developed into repeated shouting matches – him not wanting me to be in the car with him and me afraid to let him drive alone. And then there was the progressively worsening drinking – discoveries of piles of empty beer cans hidden deep in the overgrown grass behind the hut in the countryside, to which he had in large part retreated and from where I frequently had to go to collect him. (Much later, I learned from Mr Hosoda from the other side of the stream [4.14] that he had been regularly drinking himself into a stupor, at one point so badly that, found on his back in the garden, he had to be taken into the hospital to be resuscitated.) And then back at home, repeatedly and seemingly desperately trying to spray-paint one wall in our back room, each time buying a different colour – none of which to his mind was ever 'right' (this being an on-and-off project for well over six to eight months). And then, with the situation worsening even further and forced to focus all my attention on him alone, I found myself no longer in any state to handle classes, and one by one had to let all my students go. Taken in during the summer at a nearby hospital, he was very quickly requested to leave when he repeatedly disappeared from his bed at night, but beyond that, not having (and not given) any medical details, I had no knowledge at any time of how far the disease had progressed, or really in any sense what we were facing.

[18.8] An operation, in the hope:

In my experience of hospitals in England, in order to allow the medical staff to get on with their work without interference, it is a general policy to keep relatives of patients out of the ward, but in Japan quite the opposite being the case, I was informed from the beginning I would be expected to stay in the hospital overnight to help care for him. Placed in a group ward, from the start I recognised that the atmosphere was somewhat different from the norm. However, it was not until I was woken up in the middle of the night by one of the men across the aisle screaming repeatedly that the ward was on fire (he was "enveloped in flames") that I realised why we were positioned directly across from the central nurse unit. Even so, I reckoned that of the six of them, Koji was by far the best behaved. Which he was. Until that was no longer the case.

Quite at what point he actually turned, I cannot exactly recall, but when he did, it was with a meticulous degree of vengeance. (At points, I found myself having to apologise to the other patients in the ward for all the noise and general disruption that he was causing.) The younger nurses on the whole were very good with him, but they were (as everywhere these days) very much overstretched, and shortly after his operation I was asked to come in in the daytime to help keep him under control – a 12-hour stint every day, each time with my heart pulling badly on the return walk from the station up to home. At this point, his arms and legs were being tied to the bed frame every night (again, common practice here), and at one point they put him into a restraining outfit (arms crossed) as used in mental hospitals, from which (Houdini style), he unfailingly managed to escape, until he would eventually be found wandering the corridors completely naked and once again restrained.

Possibly the greatest problem here was the head nurse in the ward. A lady who could easily have auditioned (and almost certainly been accepted) for a starring role in some Japanese version of "One Flew over the Cuckoo's Nest," I can understand that Koji in any condition would have had difficulty with her, but in the end the relationship developed into one of a very deep, personal antagonism on both sides. Walking in one morning to start my shift, I found him seated in his wheelchair across from her desk – the only place where she could keep her eye on him – whereupon, after exchanging greetings, she uncut both his arms and legs. (By this time, unless I was in attendance, he was at all times constrained.) But then before I could move to wheel him out, taking advantage of the moment to bend forward, he retrieved the scissors she had just used from her desk, and before either of us could do anything to stop him, he had one of his slippers in his hand, which he very casually, determinedly, and precisely, proceeded to cut into two neat halves. And again not allowing either of us time to react, and giving one of his more brilliantly vindictive smiles – he was, at one level, fully in control here and he was very clearly enjoying the situation – he took his second slipper and treated it in exactly the same manner. And not quite knowing how to take the matter any further, I bowed my apologies and wheeled him out of her sight.

Later, back at home and towards the end, for one moment, he came out of his reveries to ask me quite seriously "whether it would be right for him to 'harbor resentment' against her." The Japanese phrase 'uramubeki' is very commonly used related to spirits returning to haunt someone who has harmed them, and I had to tell him that as the problem was in large part his fault, perhaps he shouldn't, which, having apparently absorbed, he quietly slipped back to wherever he was resting.

Walking your way home. A devious mind at work:
After the operation, I had taken to first wheeling – and then, as much as possible, walking – him around the ward's corridors, initially to tire him, and then as he strengthened, with the aim of getting him back home as quickly as we could, an aim which, although never stated, was clearly on his mind also. And

during these walks, there would be (as required) a suggestion that we could go (invariably down) a staircase; a refusal to enter a certain corridor that he knew to be a dead-end (or even worse led back to his room); a swift turn towards the elevator where, before I could stop him, he had pressed the (again downwards) button, until (twice – after which I cottoned on to the purpose of the exercise, and I in my turn learned to exercise a little craftiness in my approach) we reached the long escalator outside the front of the hospital down to the open road, where a refusal on my part to proceed any further resulted in an eruption of intense anger and hostility.

And then, for relief, there were the odd touches of humour added to the mix.

Halfway around a circuit and braking as he spotted a group of nurses at the other end of the corridor, with not even a hint of irony, he rose from his wheelchair and in the moment (cue, stage left) became that irresistible, music-hall stage dandy cum man-about-town of yore. And, raising his arm high into a relaxed wave, without any ado, he came out with: "Hi there, you guys! I'm Koji Ishida! And I've just come to check on how your work is going today!" (Cue, round of merriment) before, as he moved further forward to continue the conversation, the presence of even the best comedians not being appreciated when you are changing bedsheets, they quickly shooed him away.

A few years earlier, he had once (and only once) come out in that manner with a one-liner that had completely thrown me – quite beyond any level of wit that I had heard him express previously. At the time, I read it as one side of him that he was for some reason suppressing, and that he was momentarily letting me know that, as much as anyone, he was quite capable. And in reality, maybe it was (knowing that I have spent much of my life inhabiting certain roles, why should this not to be so for him?), but now I did wonder.

[18.9] A trip to Kamakura:

Akane was the owner of what originally was a 'seaman's bar' in the port area in Kobe – this until, as the port moved to accommodate container shipping, there were no longer any seamen in town to be served – and staying open far later than most bars in the area, at some point (presumably on quieter nights) Koji had made it a habit to have a drink there on his way home. [5.10] At the same time, of all our friends, she is the one person who was not connected with the exhibition (I hadn't yet been introduced), and right the way through I have never sensed any connection in that area, which has always made her very easy for me to be with. My favourite memory of this time was the occasional dance we had together, setting Abba's Chiquichita or Dancing Queen on the jukebox and working ourselves up into a fast jive, me twirling her around and around forever. And tiny and light as she was, she let her body go until it could no longer take any more, at which point she would retreat back up onto her ramp behind the bar, growing a good twenty centimetres in the process and instantly regaining her own commanding presence.

Shortly after Koji came out of the hospital, he kept mentioning her name, and without giving it any particular thought, and understanding that this was probably going to be the last opportunity for him to be able to see her, I decided that I would take him up to the Kanto area (/Tokyo), where she now lives – on the Shinkansen express train. (So many years later, I took the same trip with Kensuke.) The outward trip went perfectly smoothly. Koji was allowed one beer on the train, and possibly two. This was against doctor's orders but in line with our standard practice on such trips, and once in Tokyo, we found a non-alcoholic beer that he enjoyed. And otherwise everything was as normal as you might find it anywhere. Taken to Akane's home, she had prepared a meal, and we spent a pleasant evening talking together. And then the next morning, after we had had breakfast and we were waiting for her to change to go out, as if waking from a reverie, he suddenly turned to me and came out with a part-delighted and equally shocked, "We are in Tokyo!" – which I took pleasure in confirming.

Far beyond anything I had imagined, keeping him in check as we moved around in town did require the full attention of the both of us. Eating a cream crêpe, a new experience for him, all was well until he started chewing at the wrapper (which in form was identical to the crêpe that he had just consumed), at which point Akane gently took it out of his hand and suggested that it was time we move on. And each time he broke away – even in his semi-comprehending state, he had his own schedule, which at all times he insisted that we keep to – she would move to distract his attention, or when he could not be prevented from moving, stay with him, leaving me free to settle any uncompleted business.

For no apparent reason, it became essential to sample a local cider drink in a tiny shop by the roadside (half consumed and then left unattended), and that much further on he was abruptly walking out of another shop where a moment previously he had been showing an intense interest in the local style of lacquered wood carvings. (The wife of the owner, who was also the artist, having had Koji's background in the field explained to her, very kindly allowed him to handle all the best pieces in the shop.) And then when I was fiddling around with the camera rather too much taking a photograph of the two of them in front of the giant Buddha in Kamakura – this admittedly a seriously bad habit of mine – he suddenly shot across the open grounds with a "What the heck! We are not on our honeymoon here, you know!" (a comment which would have made my father proud) bringing the both of us up short. (I did stop fiddling.)

[18.10] The return:

The Shinkansen is a highly efficient mode of transport, timed to arrive and leave each station it stops at precisely at the scheduled time, and no amount of pleading can get it to do otherwise. This in large part is the reason why, when something goes seriously wrong, returning services to normal can take what appears to be an abnormally long period of time. And faced with a late typhoon, together with other considerations, we decided that it might be better to return to Kobe a day earlier than planned.

From the time Koji had been in hospital, he had had a lot of problems controlling his bladder and bowel movements and it had become standard practice for him to wear adult diapers, and acutely aware of this problem, I had made sure that all our seats on the train were immediately next to the toilet facilities. However, now waiting on the platform for our first train (on the selected route, we had to change twice), with one minute to go to its arrival, Koji decided that he could no longer wait to relieve himself. The station toilets, being a good three- or four-minute walk away down the escalator, were naturally out of consideration. And presumably here his mind moved to the practical, and suddenly breaking away and moving across to a lone vending machine placed behind us on the platform, he called me over to stand beside him, and keeping his eye firmly on the outside world, he began to talk quite seriously about "how the typhoon was moving in so quickly" and "how the rain was coming down so heavily" and "that it was good that we were dry here inside the station and not out there" – all of which I agreed with until, looking down, I suddenly noticed that, without me seeing him, he had taken himself out and was very deliberately trickling his excess water against the lower panel section of the wall. And with me on his right and the vending machine to his left, no one in the world would have noticed. And, that taken care of, the train came in and we got on and I issued a very strong sigh of relief.

And then at the next stop, we had to have a repeat of the situation – he had refused to go to the toilet in the train, but now "He could not wait!" – the problem here being that the platform was far more crowded and there was no vending machine available. However, there was one older man who, realising the delicacy of the situation and with eyes carefully averted, leaned himself casually against the wall on Koji's other side, and again we had a conversation about "how hard the rain was beating against the sides of the tall buildings placed around the station square." And again, all was well until, queueing to exit the packed train as we pulled into Kobe station (there is no way in which one can move positions in such circumstances) he again found himself, this time in desperate need. And now, there being nothing but a fence at the platform edge, with no attempt at all to hide his situation, he stood with open legs and let flow in full sight of the world. And watching the crowd as they pushed to get by to the exit gates, I doubt even one of them noticed. (And if there are any younger persons out there who ever do, I could make a request here for a certain generosity in your assessment of the situation. Life is not always as you would wish it.)

[18.11] Settling in at home:

Day care services for the elderly here are very well organised, with both possible arrangements and costs initially determined according to discussions between the patient's doctor, an officially appointed 'caregiver', the patient and his or her family (in this case me). However, the biggest problem here proved to be Koji himself. Hating the experience of actually being in the day-care centre he was assigned to (in this case, definitely not their problem), although we did try overnight stays, in the end we had to settle on one day a week, which, as was explained to him each time he had to leave the house, was for my benefit. More than anything this was a matter of practicalities: Apart from the rest, I needed the time to go out shopping.

Although he never tried leaving the house alone, after waking up in the early morning hours only to find him on the point of setting the kitchen on fire – he was about to pour oil over a net-grill covered in tea leaves, this placed directly on top of our open gas-range (He was "cooking!" and not to be disturbed.) – I was in reality unable to leave him alone for one moment. However, over time this did settle into a somewhat steady, if not entirely welcomed, routine.

Early spring: A second hospitalisation at his doctor's insistence lasted three weeks, but this time, although I went in every day, I could only manage as much as my strength would allow me to, and when I found myself too tired, I informed the nurses that I would be returning home. Friends (both his and mine) visited, but perhaps otherwise only one other noteworthy incident remains.

Sitting quietly one afternoon on his bed, with Koji propped up beside me, for a long moment, I found a pale-yellow light emanating from an area at the centre of my chest – this forming a halo around his head and otherwise bathing his upper body in a soft circle of light – and during this time he did appear (and hopefully was), if not at peace, at least without pain.

FF: Throughout his first stay in hospital, he had repeatedly asked me to pull his bed cover away from his feet, something which the nurses did not approve of (he was not to get at all cold), and something which at the time I insisted was not possible. However, during the second stay, he finally came around (in a highly indignant tone of voice) with the reasoning that, "There was no way he could possibly drive to Himeji (a castle city down the coast), unless his feet were free to press the car's accelerator and brake, which the cover was preventing him from doing." And finally understanding his point, at least during the time I was with him, I allowed him his way.

And once more at home:

In the final weeks, painkillers only being able do so much, I could recognise that he was suffering considerably. Even so, he was quiet – recognising me through to the end, and quite happy sitting watching the television, his back resting against the couch between my legs, a position we had taken for many years in the past, and only speaking up to complain in a most emphatic manner about a talking dog in a popular TV commercial series ("Dogs don't talk!"), which in the long run I could not argue with. And, then as it had to be, late one evening, hearing an odd retching sound, and returning into the living room, I was just in time to find him coughing up what I assumed in the moment to be segments of his liver (actually determined to be thick blobs of clotted blood that had settled in his windpipe). And ambulanced to the hospital, he was whisked away by his doctors, and I remained the night, waiting until it was decided that they could do nothing more for him. And then in the final two hours approaching dawn, I sat by his bed watching the blips retreat until it was all finally over. The nurse who came to prepare his body for the coffin suggested that I might like to be with him for an hour or so before she started her work, for which I thanked her. And after his family arrived, he was brought home for the last time.

[18.12] Gay partnerships (/marriage):

An argument that invariably gets thrown up when discussing this matter is 'protecting family values'. I am gay, but I also was, as every gay person born before me, born into, and brought up in a family, and it was those 'family values' that started me off in life. The chances of anyone's child or grandchild having the same preferences are pretty high, and if you can start off with the fact that this is not anything unusual (i.e., create social acceptance from square one), then the need to hide (which is also a source of bullying) disappears. This is also the case for children who are physically or mentally challenged, and they also need to be put out in the open from the start.

[18.13] Our relationship:

Recognising that I am highly possessive by nature, for many years I always used the excuse that if Koji had kept things further away from home, it wouldn't have mattered. I wouldn't have had the situation quite so much thrust in my face. But then one evening after he died, a much older man in a similar relationship pointed out to me that "perhaps he didn't have a choice." And although this did take me some time to work through, I have come around to accepting that in the large part this is probably true. And then (Jan. 2018) finally circling my brain around to what should have been apparent from the start: More than anything, it was simply a matter of Koji's brain-setting being different. He enjoyed sex, and it didn't matter to him if he was with two other people who were partners. He enjoyed the interplay. And presuming this was his mindset, I imagine that, when he introduced me to all these people that he knew, he was wanting to share them (/his pleasure) with me, while for me with my background, this was effectively impossible. With just the two of us together, we were perfect for each other – this right the way through to the end. But anything beyond that for me was impossible.

[18.14] Koji's family: The Ishidas:

Growing up in the absence of parents:

Koji was the fourth of five siblings, three girls (Sachiko, Takako and Narumi) at the top and then two boys (Koichi and Ryuta), their father, a civil engineer, lost in a mining accident when Koji was three, and his mother bedridden until he was fifteen, when she too passed away, essentially leaving the five of them to fend for themselves, with the eldest sister, Sachiko, in charge throughout (a role she has never ceded). Their father having worked for the municipality, they were guaranteed minimum housing for as long as they remained in their hometown, but otherwise they lost everything. Koji moved out upon completing high school, and at the time I arrived, Sachiko (to Shinichi) and Ryuta had just married – both 'omiai' (arranged marriages), with neither really welcomed by either of them, although Ryuta and his wife Kayo did over time settle into a much closer relationship. At the time, Koji told me that the younger siblings, understanding the burden that she had taken on with their upbringing, had all pushed hard for Sachiko to marry. They wanted her "to experience a normal life," which at one level I fully understand, but at the same time I can understand why, having just completed the equivalent of one lifetime's work in taking on the responsibility for caring for her sick mother and the upbringing of her siblings, she might have resisted. The second sister, Takako, remained single for life, initially continuing to live in the family house with Sachiko and her husband until she eventually moved out on her own.

The middle sister, Narumi, who had married into a 'burakumin' (lowest caste) family [5.13], although she lived in the same town, was not in the early years ever present (or her name even mentioned). The one true pride that the family had been taught as children to hold on to was that they were descended from a samurai clan, and for Narumi to marry into what had been the lowest group in the caste system of that time, was inconceivable, and she and her husband were strictly persona non grata. It was only later, when her two sons were reaching their teens, that a certain level of reconciliation occurred, and I met the whole family.

Although we stayed with Narumi's family for some time after the earthquake and I actually got on quite well with her husband, she and I were never close, and for the most part I would have described our relationship as 'cool'. This until, at her eldest son's wedding, when something I said must have registered (/'clicked'), she came running down the stairs from her sister's apartment (I had gone out for a breath of fresh air) and with no further ado and in a state of total joy, threw herself into my arms, where, in the best Hollywood tradition, I swung her around and around until the moment was gone. And from here, it was only a short time before she died, and in the midst of everything I did not go to her funeral. This was not for any lack of respect, but rather a combination of my work, fatigue and a whole complex skein of awkward family relationships that had developed at the time. [18.16]

In the present day, it is officially illegal to discriminate against burakumin communities, but the sons, although they both married, having suffered considerably when they were young, in their own statement of defiance of a society that had excluded (and still excludes) them, finally elected not to have any progeny, for the simple reason that they wouldn't like any children they might have to be treated that same manner. Presumably, they decided that this was the only way they knew to break the cycle.

However, whenever Koji and his other three siblings were together, and particularly after alcohol had been introduced into the arena, voices became raised, and disorder and discontent prevailed, and they returned to the group of no-holds-barred, scrapping kids that they presumably had been throughout their childhood. (This for me personally, with my own background, was an education; a total eye-opener as to life's possibilities.) Initially, faced repeatedly with their endless bickering, both Kayo, who also came from a 'normal' home, and myself could only gaze on in wonder, this in fact becoming a bonding cry for the two of us: "We are not (and never will be) Ishidas!"

The perils of being too close:
Place two or more small but powerful magnets in the correct (positive-negative) order and they will hold firmly together indefinitely, but if for any reason any one of them is reversed, the repelling force will be equally strong. And here all five children had two strictly opposing forces bred into them from a very young age on: (1) the need to stick together as the only means to protect themselves against a very cold world and (2) the practical need to become highly independent. All of them, from as early on as possible and even if only in small part-time jobs, had to be able to earn money, and to do this they had to learn to present themselves to the outside world as responsible adults. Koji was skilled enough with the abacus calculator to become a teacher (of considerably older students) by the time he was fourteen, and he kept one beside him for personal use right the way through his life. And within this extremely narrow grouping, Sachiko (with Takako as second in command) of necessity became the figure of authority. And when as adults they separated, as at some point they had to, it would be natural that these breaks result in some very wide fissures.

Narumi presumably moved into the burakumin community in full knowledge of how her older sisters would react, and there was the fact that the man she married eventually became the leader of his community, meaning that she actually lived in a far grander house than her sisters ever would in all their lives. Also when the two eldest sisters eventually broke up, the division was so bad (we never got to know the reason) that they did not speak to each other for over twenty years, and it was only the intervention of Sachiko's eldest daughter that actually brought them together again.

"The desire to demean or control is in no way any prerogative of the male ego."

Sachiko's husband, Shinichi, who was somewhat older than her, was in the main a very quiet person, but when he did speak, throughout his life, it was over his wife's repeated objections: "You are not interesting." "Nobody wants to listen to your stupid ideas." "Everybody knows that!" He was not in fact excessively interesting (most people tend to get repetitive as they age), but even so, that she would berate him in this manner so openly for a full fifty years, even after their two children were born, still begs belief. Their daughters, both of whom love their father, have, as they have got older, remonstrated repeatedly with their mother about this to no effect, and with no encouragement at all from their mother, neither have shown any real interest at all in marrying themselves. (When I discussed this matter with the eldest daughter, she concluded by saying, "not to worry, as she was certain she would manage much better 'the next time around,'" so presumably there is hope.)

[18.15] Memories of a funeral:

On the wall above Koji's 'four-nudes' cabinet [4.11], from some time back I had hung the photograph of an extremely weathered stone carving that I had found in a small temple on one of our visits to Kyushu, and this, in that it represented one of the gods in the Buddhist pantheon, being deemed suitably correct, it was decided that the two together would make a suitable, if somewhat unusual, background against which to place his coffin for the final service.

The priest who officiated at the funeral was still young and clearly inexperienced but made up for this considerably with his open personality, seemingly perfectly amenable to the fact that I should be the principal mourner. Left behind by the other family members as we returned from the crematorium, by which time my energy levels were very low and I was only able to proceed at the slowest of paces, he stayed with me talking quietly – he was quite evidently interested in me as a person, a point which I very much appreciated – and then, after first taking my weight as we walked up the stairs to the apartment, as we finally came back into the house, he turned and knelt down to help me out of my shoes – not something that would at all be expected from an older or more reserved priest. And then, as he was finally leaving, he was unable to hide an impish turn of delight as he was handed one of the thick packs of beef that Hiroshi had brought with him to be dispersed as required. Whatever, he quite apparently has a solid foundation upon which to build his future.

Upon the removal of the coffin, a small altar was immediately set up with Koji's photograph and all the appurtenances required for the first 49 days of mourning [13.9]. And on a quiet day after they had all left, sitting alone on the living room couch looking across at the altar, I "attained enlightenment." The reality here is of no importance, but this is what I told Mrs Hamada (Yukiko's mother [4.8]) when she called me a short time later to say that she would be visiting with her husband, to which she, in her usual calm manner, replied that "that was quite likely." However, I do know that I physically experienced the petals of a lotus blossom unfolding one by one across my brain, until I had the full flower spread throughout, and for that very long, quiet moment, I was at peace.

[18.16] And again, those small things:

(The following is a small sampling of a whole series of events.)

– On our first visit to England many years ago, we had searched out a man's ring, in gold with a small diamond at its centre, not overly expensive but something which Koji had very much wanted to (at least in our world) openly signify our relationship. On occasion, it was worn, eventually being put aside for others that had been purchased on our travels, which did not at all worry me. However, attending the above nephew's wedding in Kyushu, he suddenly came out with one very large and expensive (and, to my mind, vulgar) ring that I immediately recognised as coming from my student's shop [6.22], and which he explained as having "come from Hiroshi while I was away." (Hiroshi was a regular customer at the shop.) How much, or even whether he had paid anything for it, was left unclear, but he refused repeatedly to remove it, and this did upset me. And then asking him why he could not have worn his diamond, it appeared that, no longer needed, this had been given to his eldest sister, Sachiko, who, timing the moment perfectly, walked up to show me it to me proudly displayed on her hand. This having gone rather too far, I left the gathering with the full intention of returning home, something I did have the good sense to reconsider. However, at every opportunity after this, each time we met, she took great pleasure in wearing the ring and deliberately waving it under my nose, the only response that I could come out with being to tell her that it was a man's ring, a point that presumably she found to be of no relevance.

– Sachiko (again with ring) and Takako, together with Koji's eldest niece, made their first appearance three weeks prior to Koji's death. They were with us only a short time, during the course of which Sachiko was polite enough to comment that the 'services' that I was offering to Koji "would no doubt cost in the range of ¥300,000 per month if provided by a professional," while Takako, who had almost certainly not seen him more than twice at the most in the past thirty years, insisted that I had to be to blame for his very weak condition: Presumably, I was not feeding him correctly. (For me, this came over very much as my eldest brother at his most virtuous.) In reality, before her arrival she hadn't been aware quite how bad a state he was in, and I do know she had received quite a shock upon her arrival. Even so, when he didn't move to touch whatever it was she had prepared for him, she actually did seem surprised.

(The one good point that did come out of this visit was that they did agree not to have him put on any life support equipment in a near-death situation. Extremely common in Japan, this is something that Koji and I had discussed in in the past as unwanted. However, legally, as his closest relatives, it was their decision to make and, fortunately, they did agree to the suggestion.)

– In the evening following Koji's funeral, the whole family sat gathered around the table at home arguing in their usual manner while I sat apart on the couch talking with Yoshimi, the receptionist from the original English language school [4.2], who is still a good friend. They were, as it turned out, discussing how any remaining monies should be distributed. (Ryuta, to his credit, did at one point here come across to me and suggest quietly that I have Koji's will validated as soon as possible – not as it later proved actually necessary, as it had been fully drawn-up by qualified solicitors and signed and authenticated at the time by the central government authorities – this many years ago.) And then, presumably with the intention of discussing the matter with me, they actually had the nerve to insist that I send Yoshimi home ("It was getting late!" – this at nine o'clock in the evening). Yoshimi, who right the way through was very close to Koji, had spent hours and hours of her time helping me to look after him while he was in hospital on his second stay, a time when none of them had even been present. And at this point I erupted and told them if they wished to continue, they could do it in the other room. There were priorities in my life also.

– Money lenders at their grubbiest do not make for a pleasant sight:

Precisely a year after Koji's death, his second sister, Takako, primly dressed in a tweed jacket and skirt, arrived unannounced on the doorstep with the clear intent of claiming what she considered to be 'her share' of whatever money had remained at the time of his death. Unsurprisingly, she did not start off in this manner, merely informing me that she had been to one of the main temples in Kyoto to have his ashes enshrined there, taking care to inform me of the full cost, which I did offer to cover, although in all honesty I did not see why I should. In contrast to his sister, Koji was never at any time in his life religiously inclined, and prior to his death he had requested that I simply spread his ashes in the sea, which I had already done together with Kensuke (see [18.17], below). At the time of his cremation, it being Japanese custom, I had naturally deferred to his family's wishes to gather their own ashes first, and beyond that, I did not feel that it was any responsibility of mine as to what might happen to those particular remains. To me, personally, they had, and still have, no meaning whatsoever.

And then came the request to look at the will, which I said I would get out for her – we were drinking tea at that particular time. And then as we continued talking, she suddenly came out with a 'recent dream', in which Koji had appeared with tears flowing down his cheeks (presumably in consideration of her state as the abused party), to which I responded by recounting a (true) dream of my own in which I had looked down into a warehouse from which Koji, who was working happily carrying cardboard boxes with my father, called up to ask me when I would be joining them. (The dream apart, gay relationships still having no legal recognition at all in Japan, I have never at any time envisaged myself as a member of the Ishida clan, but if one of us were to have to belong to the other's family in some future life, I would very much prefer it that Koji was with my parents.)

And now fully recognising the direction in which the conversation was going, I indicated that she could leave and, reminding her that she had a Shinkansen train to catch, ushered her out of the house. And that was it, until the evening when the phone rang and she was there again, screeching at the top of her voice that "She had every right to receive her money!" She had checked this with a lawyer friend, and the matter was beyond dispute! (How she had worked it out in her mind that the money should be hers, even now I cannot comprehend.) However, having anticipated the situation, that afternoon after she had left, I had double-checked that the will could actually in no way be questioned, and I could only tell her that I had had enough, and she was not to contact me again.

This was not, unfortunately, the end to the matter, as for the next two or three years, I found myself having to fend off a variety of stories about quite how nasty and deceitful I was, these all coming to me through nieces and nephews. However, she herself has never contacted me since, and (although I still keep the original will) the matter has now hopefully been put to rest.

– And again. Hiroshi:

Returning to the apartment in the late afternoon two days before Koji had to go into hospital for his operation, I found him in a state something close to panic and mumbling on about returning a mattress he had recently purchased, it having, for no apparent reason, suddenly developed a serious layer of dirty brown mould, which would not have mattered until he also mentioned that Hiroshi had been visiting and it became very clear what had been taking place. And Hiroshi was not heard from again until the time of the funeral, when he brought his offerings of best sirloin steaks – as, in the matter of the teacups and ring, always a matter of giving (or, more specifically, taking) what you want when you want and how you want it – which in the final analysis, is how I have to sum up our relationship. I did mention the above to him some while after the funeral, and he was suitably embarrassed. However, I also introduced him to Kensuke, but then not wanting to take the risk, very quickly decided that I did not want them getting any more closely involved and have since worked to keep him out of our lives. Around this time, he also remarked to me how happy I looked and that "he hadn't seen me with such bright eyes for a very long time." And even today, I wonder whether he (and whatever his 'society' stood for) understood to what degree he was responsible for that fact.

No one is in any sense innocent here, but as with everything, I have reached an age where, at least for my own peace of mind, I have decided certain lines must be drawn.

[18.17] A trip to the north:

In the midsummer following Koji's death, I travelled with Kensuke to Fukui prefecture on the Japan Sea coast in order to spread his ashes in the sea there, a trip which proved to be an extended farewell to the one while simultaneously creating what became a footing for our own future together. Koji's niece, Kaori [12.13], had suggested finding somewhere in the Seto Inland Sea between Shikoku and the mainland, but with all of Koji's family having lived there at one time or another, the associations were not something I welcomed, and the act itself being related to a very personal promise to Koji (his family had their own place to visit), I decided that somewhere as far away from them as possible, somewhere I could keep for myself, made fullest sense. And, as things turned out, being able to share the place with Kensuke made for an added bonus.

From many years back, I had had a vague interest in visiting Eiheiji, a very famous training centre for Zen Buddhist acolytes in the north of Fukui, and while the Japan Sea coast in winter is open to intense storms and high seas – the sea rages in winter – with him having spent quite some time crisscrossing the Pacific Ocean during his youth, I sensed it was not a place he would be averse to.

– Having driven along the coastal road for some while, we turned back into a short side road that quickly brought us down to a small bay. And this seeming as good a spot as any we might find, we walked out first along the concrete jetty and then over the piled boulders that replaced it until, reaching a partial break in the barrier wall and hearing the sound of children's laughter carrying across from what must have been the elementary school that we had noted a little earlier at the side of the main road, my mind settled on a fair-sized pool that had formed within the broken rocks. Climbing down, Kensuke passed the urn to me, and with little thought other than to admire the quiet presence that all such pools have, the ashes were spread, and the job was done.

And with realisation came depletion.

Leading up to Koji's cremation, more than once I had envisaged myself repeating Isamu's collapse so many years earlier at the time Carl died [4.11], but in the general hustle and bustle as his family sought out the remains essential for their needs, the moment had passed. However here, left lightheaded and at points close to nauseous, with every ounce of energy held in reserve for this one act now drained from me and no longer with the strength to even stand upright, without the slightest of warnings we were confronted with the serious challenge of getting me back across those both slippery and very unevenly placed rock surfaces. Pulling myself out of the hollow, where I could use my arms for balance and Kensuke could push me from below, proved relatively easy, but from this point on, in order to make any progress, I had to remain upright, and the need for him to support my every move requiring both of our somewhat precariously balanced bodies to be repositioned at every step, our progress remained agonisingly slow. And even back on the jetty and then in the car, I found my body still trembling, and from here it took a full two hours or so to even reasonably recover.

But as always, you do.

– Prayer:

Considering the purpose of our trip, and at the same time visiting a range of shrines and temples of different sects, each with their own views and practices, initially I was somewhat at a loss regarding exactly what prayers I should offer, less with the formal rituals than quite what words I should bring to mind, finding myself progressing through a series of quite different versions as we moved from one place to the next. (The poem "Child" does have a prayer at its end, an abbreviated version ("In and of" – "In peace of mind and of heart") which I have used in passing on visits to places of worship all around the world, but this did not seem at all right for the occasion.)

And then as were leaving the final temple of our 'tour', Takidanji (recognised as a National Treasure), we came upon its own small treasure house set aside from the path. It coming close to the end of the day, there was no one else apparently around, and Kensuke, having cared for me for most of the day after my collapse on the rocks and now also showing his tiredness, suggested that I go in by myself, which I did, only to find myself placed directly in front of a most exquisitely carved and gilded statue of the Kannon Bodhisattva. And here, without any attempt at reflection, I entered into the silence. And my mind in the instant cleared of all the muddle and chaos it had accumulated throughout, I allowed the deepest of my inner voices to speak as they would.

[18.18] A final goodbye:

Precisely one year after the above, in the mid-August 'Obon' period [7.5], high up in the mountains on Kensuke's Island, and having stepped out for moment to relieve myself, I found myself perched between the car and an area of thick grasses, perfect (at least to my mind) for harbouring any number of the highly poisonous 'habu' vipers that are known to inhabit the semi-tropical landscape in that area. And recognising something in the position that I was holding of Koji peeing on the Shinkansen platforms when we were returning from Kamakura, I smiled. And as I did, his voice came to me: "He was leaving me. He knew that all was well, that I was happy and that I no longer needed him, and that therefore there was no reason for him to stay with me any longer." And taking this to be as much of the truth as I would ever come to know, I got back in the car, and we drove on. And although he still appears regularly in dreams, nowadays often confused in my mind with Kensuke, there is never anything that troubles.

From the start, I sensed that it was of the greatest importance that Kensuke be able to relate himself to my past, and in particular, so that his presence would not grow to be an encumbrance, my relationship with Koji. And seven years later, I can say that this has worked. Koji sang very rarely, but he did have one song that had always been close to his heart and which, this having been explained to Kensuke, I would on occasion sing in his memory. Kensuke then progressed from searching it out for me to singing the first verse or so himself before handing me the mike for completion. And today, at times, when he recognises the past is on my mind, and when I am too tired to take it on myself, he is quite content to sing it in my place. And occasionally, when we have a moment to ourselves, we also take time to celebrate our own private memories.

[18.19] Kensuke:

Even today, seated on the opposite side of a crowded train, something that happens quite frequently when we are out together; chameleon-like – blending into his surroundings – I can never ever see anything in him that would attract me if he were a stranger I was viewing for the first time. Rather, it is when he is next to me and I can't view him directly, that I feel his presence. That and when his eyes smile.

On the first (and one) time I met him after I returned from Korea, perhaps the only reason I could give for picking him up was the fact that we were the only two customers in the bar at the time and both of us were very badly drunk. At the hotel, I did find him attractive, but the next morning separating at the station, for every reason, I had to send him on his way. Quite apart from the fact that I was already becoming fully involved with the need to care for Koji, with his face pallid from a bad hangover and stiff head of hair and thick facial growth both left badly unattended – and, expressing myself at my best here – "he was not someone I could contemplate walking around town with." (At times like this, he can very easily appear 'dark' or, considering his relatively short height, intimidating even, and explaining myself today, I could only say that I had, for whatever reason, managed to encounter him at a worst moment. I do also know that I cannot have looked my best at this point, either.)

However, from this time on, although we never met, each time I went back to the bar, the master would tell me that Kensuke had been in and that he had asked about me, this is continuing for many years, and over time, that final image at the station softened into a more pleasant memory.

And then after Koji died, and coming close to the end of the mourning period described in [18.15] above and in town for a drink, the master informed me that, knowing that I was now on my own, Kensuke would like to meet me and "Would I leave him my telephone number?" Which I did.

And today: More than anything, I have moved from a partner who was five years older than myself to one who is fifteen years younger, which in itself has amounted to quite a revelation. I am, in fact, in many ways happier now, not because Kensuke is any way a better person than Koji, but simply that I am older and know how to go that little more softly into life, not striking out as often and no longer with that need to confront. As a younger man, I held my anger in until the point that it exploded. Now I can't really afford to get angry at all: if I do, it goes straight to my heart. Kensuke, on his side, is of the type who explodes and a moment later has forgotten that he ever did, and both of us knowing when we have been in the wrong has made the very few disagreements we have had easily disposed of.

[18.20] The true-life force. A note on energy:

"It is only when you note your levels slipping really badly that you come to understand energy for what it is."

Part of my job as a teacher has always involved maintaining a balanced atmosphere and carrying the conversational flow, mainly through the introduction of moments of light humour, and this is a habit that, even in the most adverse of circumstances, I have found myself unable to shed. Laughing, smiling and joking when you are in physical pain or under severe stress takes its toll, and particularly when in hospital (or even today with my doctor), there have been far too many times when I have thought that I would love the luxury of being a (not miserable, but) normal patient, 'not feeling the need to entertain'.

Restarting work at home after my heart operation, and still a little uncertain on my feet, I had a new student in for a test run, who, unfortunately for me, was unable (a problem very common in the Kansai area) to dial down her voice to a level corresponding to the size of the room, this resulting in an unguarded moment on my part when I actually found myself physically thrown against the wall of the room simply by the power of her voice. She was in fact a very pleasant woman and she very much wanted to join the class, and in normal circumstances I could have easily accepted her, but in that weakened state, I had to apologise and say that it was not possible. And from this time on, with my energy levels rising and falling seemingly at will, I found myself having to fine-tune my output according to circumstances, something still true today.

"Some people assume the right to take. Others, through no fault of their own, drain."

In the seven years since Koji died and I started my new relationship with Kensuke, apart from travelling together, I have worked on a full novel, an exhibition of my artworks and this present book, all of which have required considerable input, and the fact that I have put these (together with Kensuke himself) foremost in my mind has resulted in the necessity to withdraw from certain social obligations which, in a better state, I would quite readily have been able to handle. This has, in certain cases, resulted in certain frictions, but it is a reality that I cannot do anything about.

Shino [7.33], who still at times, for all her protestations, finds herself on edge, is a person who can only drain others she depends on. After Kensuke moved in with me, she actually visited two or three times, which I could not discourage, but in the end, as I weakened, I had to tell her that she could no longer come. I have done as much as I ever could in that area, and I am longer capable of more.

Chapter 19
Coming to Terms with Myself

[19.1] Developing a degree of respect for all. (Or at least as many as is practically feasible):

(June 2018) The following statement, and the subsequent qualification, came to mind as I was watching the recent World Soccer Cup in Russia.

"Show your respect to all inasmuch as they deserve it."

From very young on, I understood respect as something that should not be automatic; that there was a need to look beyond titles, to develop a sense of respect for the individual rather than the position that person holds – this irrespective of the group they belong to or their beliefs. However, presented here and at my present age, I would note that with the word 'all', here – beyond the more basic 'all people (/peoples)' – I am referring to 'all living things', or to take it that one step further 'everything that contributes to that life' (without which we could not be, would never have come into existence in the first place).

And then, upon giving second thoughts to the qualification and essentially addressing myself: "What gives me, with my minimal and on the whole extremely fortunate sampling of life's experiences – and thus limited means (other than through the exercising of my mind) to understand any other person's individual background or formative influences – the right or any qualification to judge whether that 'other' deserves my respect?" This matter (essentially a conundrum in that, throughout life, however much we would wish otherwise, inevitably we can only view the world from our own narrow base) has been with me from the start, and as such is a question which I have found myself repeatedly returning to throughout my life.

That said, of the two, having grown up with a love of and a very clear recognition of my place in nature, my understanding of the former point has been by far the easier to bring into focus, but even so has required a considerable amount of time and consideration. And my progress with regards to the second – in reality, a constant re-evaluation of my positions and the way I conceive of myself, is as recorded in this book.

[19.2]

In my early to mid-fifties, now settled in with my students at home, I had a brief period when I sensed all the disparate parts of my life coming together; this not just the hard work put in in so many areas, but all the less-than-clever actions taken and situations I had let myself in for; all the half-completed schemes and unfulfilled dreams, half-hearted (/occasionally serious) efforts to be what I was not meant to, together with their ever-present unintended consequences – all coalescing into the one whole, and for the first time I came to have some sense of myself as 'complete', or at least as I should be – there, at that time, with those students and those thoughts flowing through my mind. And for the first time in a long period. I found myself with the freedom to look back at and reassess certain basics that, up to that point, I had considered central in (/to) my life.

[19.3] Where you choose to anchor your identity:

In retrospect, by far the greatest number of decisions made in my early teens, when I was struggling to identify myself with the larger world and thus 'exert my independence', were based on negative premises; that is what I didn't want to be associated with, this in particular in comparison with my elder brother, and occasionally my cousins. Understanding Ted as an Elvis fan, by definition I became "of the Beatles generation," although I actually bought few of their records and I do distinctly remember at a gathering with all our relatives, sitting and watching them prancing around in a field in their first (thoroughly overhyped) "Magical Mystery Tour" special, this voted by all generations present to be the most tedious and mind-numbing full two hours any of us had ever spent at Xmas. Ted took to wearing jeans, making my choice of jacket and necktie to be painfully foreseeable. And being a "Beatles fan" naturally proscribed any association with the "Rolling Stones." And then asked to identify with either the Mods or the Rockers, these two (scooter and motorcycle respectively) gangs of youths who were staging largescale battles along the South Coast of England at the time, again my mind took the more 'proper' route, going for the Mods, although this in truth was simply a matter of all the Rockers having long, unkempt ("Rolling Stones") hair. And on and on.

And then you get into your fifties, and you discover that Mick Jagger (along with many other longer-haired rockers) is a brilliant musician, and that many of those 'fantastic' singers of my youth, weren't really anything special other than the fact that they had a strong voice or a cute lyric to sell. (They *were* fun!) And then, having devoted your life up to that point to ink-painting, recognising that you can be moved by oil paintings and water colours. And whole new worlds open up before you.

– Apart from our trip to Europe, one great pleasure with Kensuke, who would be around 51 at the time Koji died, has been introducing him to various aspects of culture; art galleries and museums, plays, musicals, opera, violin recitals, etc., that he would never have had chance as a younger person to encounter, and a large part of which he has taken to thoroughly.

Visiting an expansive exhibition created from a range of twisted and half- and fully-melted steel girders and frames rescued from the aftermaths of the Kobe earthquake, this by a local artist who had taken advantage of his part-time work in industrial-waste disposal to make the initial collection, from which he had created an incredibly powerful series of works, did open Kensuke's eyes considerably as to the possibilities around him – enough to get him sketching and generally creating with his hands.

[19.4] Dealing with the past. A mind reaching out:

It was also around this time that I seriously began to consider, or rather re-consider, all those awkward, shouldn't-have-happened-but-did moments that had been let slide by, and for the first time I started to seriously consider how I might have affected others, *their* lives, rather than how such incidents had affected me. And this, in turn, did lead me to start wondering how I might apologise to those I had hurt, particularly in cases where this had involved a betrayal of trust: This being the first time it had occurred to me to seriously consider how much it might have affected Ray to see his best friend 'go crazy' in front of his eyes [2.13], I did initially find the process considerably disturbing. And possibly, the answer has been in this book, in that it has required a considerable amount of reflection on my own part to bring it into being, and during the writing of which every single person that I have cared about throughout my life has in turn appeared and talked with me in my dreams. Whether this has any true meaning at all is in the end irrelevant, but apologising through the network would seem to make at least as much sense as confessing to a priest.

[19.5] Recognising weaknesses in oneself:

"It is by no means an easy process to see yourself other than you would prefer to be seen; to recognise in yourself other's (not so admirable) traits."

At a family gathering with some twenty of Koji's relatives, ranging in age from those in their late twenties to their early seventies, one of the older members of group asked the younger participants to talk about the kind of people they didn't like. This was done very lightly and naturally, and for the fun of it a number of the older members also participated. And listening to all the comments, it quickly became apparent to me that if I had had to describe one negative trait that stood out for each individual speaker, it would be precisely the description that they themselves had just come up with. And later, applying this to my own personal hang-ups – particularly certain affectations in others that I have learned to connect in my brain, not always fairly, with arrogance – I did find to be highly revealing.

[19.6] Questioning concepts of art:

Having been concerned with various art forms, both personally and through Koji's work with his woodcarving, I did find that it was only towards the end that I was able to rid myself of considerable biases (/excessive personal pride) in this area.

Over the years, walking down towards the station below our home necessitated passing a large open window (a place I assumed to be a cultural centre of some form) which invariably had a display of modern or abstract art, none of which I could then (or even today) begin to make any sense of. And here, over time, the question became not that I disliked the work itself (everyone has their own preferences), but rather that I couldn't understand (/accept) why whoever it was (teacher or student) was bothering with what such clearly exceedingly amateurish presentations were. (Knowing that I have displayed some incredibly ugly paintings in my time, even at the time I could understand this as arrogance in the extreme on my own part, but it was something I found I could never ever get out of my brain.) This until:

A final hurdle: Painting dragons:
(Present in Chinese culture for at least 7,000 years and viewed as having agency over bodies of water, rain, floods and storms, dragons were adopted by Chinese Buddhist artists as a symbol of enlightenment and clarity of the mind

and can be found in temples in both paintings and decorative carvings throughout Japan and beyond.)

This particular work is a rendering of two dragons seemingly fighting. I use the word 'seemingly' because it has been interpreted in a number of ways – in one case, even, that they represent lovers. Originally intended as a much larger ink painting, in the end I found my techniques were not up to it (I could manage the dragons but couldn't get the right effects for the surrounding mists), so after very much reduction in scale, the final painting was done in gold linework (the genuine article) on black. However, it was in time made the centrepiece of an exhibition. (Photo 6.) And on the morning of the first day, this time the first visitor was a Buddhist priest, who walked in, bowed to me, and then standing in front of the painting, bowed, and prayed. Correctly or not, I sensed that he was in some manner recognising (in the Christian tradition, this perhaps would be blessing) the painting. Whatever, considering his overall manner, I took this as a compliment. He then took a very brief look around the room, bowed to me again, and left. (We do not talk a lot in Japan!)

FF: During the period I was working on this painting, I must have had at least five or six dreams where I was being approached by groups of Komodo dragons, Indonesia's giant lizards. Presumably, my mind being somewhat confused by the wide range of possible images available, this was the best it could come up with. However, as they are known to attack humans on occasion, they did have me waking up very quickly.

And after the exhibition, it was hung on the wall at home. (I had decided from the start that I did not want to sell the picture at the time, in large part because I doubted I would be able to get the price I felt it deserved in terms of time spent and the cost of traditional Japanese-style mounting, etc.)

And some years later, with Kensuke:

We had just finished some light DS [16.9] in the bedroom (essentially, a trial to see how we fit with each other). This time around, I had taken the more passive part, which I could only assume would be the reason for what happened next. Returning to the living room, and pausing in front of the dragons, I suddenly felt all the strength going from my legs and, collapsing onto the floor, I was overcome with a sense of helplessness; a total impotency, divested of all power, so lacking in spirit that I was incapable of facing up to even the sense of who or what I might be. And the only thing that I could say to Kensuke was, "I did not paint that!" And this was the (/a? /the?) truth: In one small corner of my mind, I knew that I had in fact done it (the process in total had taken up 400 hours of my time), but my brain said, repeatedly and determinedly, "No! Not someone like you! You could not possibly have produced that!" And I stayed there on the floor for, I would guess, around ten minutes, until I began to feel my strength returning and I could stand and return to myself. (This actually later elicited a remark from Kensuke to the effect that "it had helped him understand the reality of my situation." And having seen me in that state, it did mean that in later similar situations, nothing of that nature that I have said or done has disturbed him.)

And two months later in Edinburgh: Coming out of the crowded castle, we deliberately (I had planned our course carefully) turned into a quiet alley that led down a sharp, steep slope, where part way down, we found three young men in their early twenties sitting across the steps, one of whom asked me if I could give him some money. This was done very politely, with no sense of it being a threat (something we did meet two or three times in other places on our trip), and I gave him a pound coin that I had in my pocket and told him that I was sorry, the apology coming more than anything from an immediate sense that (money included) there was nothing I or we could do for them. On the street, all three would easily have passed (/been passed by) as perfectly ordinary young men. However, here, isolated in the silence, there was a stillness about them, a negative presence; an unreasonable (/unreadable) void. Left behind, left out, modern-day collateral damage. And fully understanding the fact and being well past the 'beaten down' stage, with no further wish to resist, they had allowed themselves to be reduced (as I had in front of my dragons) to a state of complete abjection. The world had shut them out, and now the world would have to come to them on their terms. Except that, clearly, at least at that moment in their lives (and we do, fortunately, live in moments), they had no terms. And with nothing else to say, we left them and made our way back to the main thoroughfare, where there were people.

High Street in Edinburgh is made for tourists, and we, too, as good tourists do, mingled. Or, rather, having run out of our quota of energy for the day, we attached ourselves to the flow and let it take us down the hill; past the ice-cream stands and performance artists (the ones exhibiting some form of talent), the cathedral (but we had had enough of churches for the moment) and half a dozen other attractions that I had marked as possibilities but which we now let pass. And as the road opened up to residences, the crowds thinned down to ones and twos, until we were on our own. And in the quietest of spots, on a blind corner, the three of them – or rather whatever it was that had been with them – re-joined me, and leaning against Kensuke for strength, I cried my eyes out, and let the pain come as it would.

And returning to the statement at the head of the chapter, making one more effort, perhaps to replace "inasmuch as they deserve it" with the "inasmuch as you are able" would make more sense.

Dragon (30cm. X 45cm.)

[19.7] A final note on art:

(March, 2018) Leaving aside the commercial aspects (the consumer being free to spend their money as they choose), trying to come up with a definition of 'art' or perhaps 'art at its finest' (this in any field), the best I could come up with was the rather stiff: "A representation resulting from a bond of trust between the (professionally or otherwise) trained (/thinking/ cerebral/ cortex-directed) self and what is commonly known as the 'inner muse' range of sensory influences." That is, you have two quite functionally contrasting areas of the brain working in perfect harmony, with neither in total control. In music, jazz presents itself as an easy example, or certain singers or actors who naturally connect with their live audience – resulting in no two identical performances. For an adult, this is commonly the result of a considerable amount of training; again, with music, physical control (breathing, movement of the vocal chords and body parts, etc.) first established to the degree that it no longer needs to be consciously considered at the time of action, allowing the mind to (initially) concentrate on, and in time – as a next step – with full confidence, subject itself to the artistic elements of the process. Shakespeare (or in Japan, Noh or Kabuki) not being for everybody, audience reaction is naturally going to be to the degree that particular individual's brain is attuned to whatever it is observing. Later, visiting a small exhibition of children's art with Kensuke, notably it was the children around the age of 10 or 11 who had mastered the principle: Technically, they had reached a level where they could be totally free in their interpretation of their imaginations (both in terms of composition and colouring), resulting in some very beautiful and original pieces. And then above this age, although in many senses the technique was superior, they were once again clearly following established trends (/painting as they were being taught to do), and in the process had (at least temporarily) lost that element of freedom available to the younger mind.

And finally, my mind moving to the idea of what 'bad art' might be, again ignoring any question of how a work might be received, all attempts at personal expression being of equal validity, the answer with almost complete certainty would have to be that it does not exist.

[19.8] A last exhibition:

Thirty-five years after the original exhibition described in Cpt 6, I decided it would be interesting to try one more exhibition at the same gallery, this more than anything with the intention of removing myself from what I can only describe even now as 'all the childish intrigue' of the previous event. That is, (as in John le Carré's "The Spy Who Came in from the Cold"), I had had enough of playing stupid games. I do not know quite how successful I was in this respect, but the intention itself was clearly disseminated throughout the two-year preparatory period, and (as a direct result or otherwise) in what at the time seemed amusing in the extreme, other than a very close core of friends and associates, who could in no way be expected not to come (and with even one of these going out of his way to be as rude as he possibly could be to me as he left), none of the people who had followed my career up to that point, including a large number who had actually come to the original exhibition (that is, belonged to the club), turned out to see what I had produced this time. That is, at least in the only way I could interpret it at the time, "a line had been drawn."

[19.9] Hiroshi:

Very early on after arriving in Japan, and as one of the main reasons I actually starting ink-painting, I had the opportunity of viewing a very large screen painting of a life-sized crane nestled low in a bamboo thicket. The bamboo was painted with (to me, even at the time) a somewhat excessive (and possibly very deliberate) hardness of detail, but in contrast, the crane was represented by two long straight lines (the beak), a simple swirl (the eye) and no more than two or three curved lines (a simple outline representing the positioning of the body). And other than that, there was nothing other than an untouched expanse of open space. But, for me, the creature could have been alive: My hand involuntarily reached out to touch the softness of its feathers and down. And for this exhibition's centrepiece, I had completed a large portrait of a cockerel and hen based on a similar principle; that is as much as possible not filling in the central body detail on either bird, which had, together with a certain element of lucky brushwork, worked well. And when two or three weeks prior to the exhibition, Hiroshi telephoned me to meet him for lunch to see some of the photographs I had taken of my paintings for PR purposes, and he determined that he wanted this particular painting, in the mood that I was in the time, I objected. He already had a lot of my good paintings, and in that such purchases represented money, I naturally was grateful, but this time, with all considerations of past events and with my own particular objectives in mind, I did not particularly wish to tie down my main painting merely for his personal gratification.

And then, at home by myself a few days before the start of the exhibition, and not thinking about any matter in particular, my mind suddenly came up with the words, "First come, first served" – which it turned out were precisely the words used by Hiroshi (ever the five-year-old child parading his knowledge in front of the whole class) when he walked in very early on the first day to claim the picture, which, business being business, and regardless of any personal sensitivities, was sold. He also later remarked how much lower the price was than he had expected. (Not having had an exhibition for some time, the prices had been fixed very much on the advice of the gallery owner. However, to rectify this, I did suggest that he might like to purchase one of my photographs for his office, which he did have the decency to do.)

[19.10] The gallery owner:

She was in all respects leading up to the exhibition very helpful, but in that I was paying in full for usage of the premises, this I would assume expected. It was also at this time that she came out with the comment "And so the child will die?" something which as noted in [7.19], although it did not appeal in the sense that I might actually be held responsible for a child's death, I can even now in no way account for. She also made one quite separate prophecy.

I had produced a series of invitation cards for the event, and it was one of these that she read as indicating that "a 'famous' Chinese artist would visit." Having been exposed to a wide range of unusual events in my life, and fully aware that it is so easy to be wrong about one's initial understandings, I have learned to be doubly sceptical about the claims of others. However, on the second day in the afternoon during a quiet period, a local (famous or not, I would not know) Chinese artist who clearly knew the owner well (and I presumed from the way they were conversing had exhibited his work at the gallery at some time) did walk in. That said, he made no attempt to view the pictures or speak personally with me – although he did leave his name card prominently inserted between the pages of the visitors' book for me to find, something which the owner later came over to me to confirm. (Not taking kindly to conceit or rudeness – he hadn't even bothered to look in my direction during his conversation with the owner – I told her that it had been disposed of in the wastepaper basket.) Whether this was the visit intended, I do not know, but presumably it would have sufficed. And then the next day, I did get a visit from a (later checked up on the gallery computer) top-class artist of around my own age from the Chinese mainland, who appeared together with his wife. Having only Japanese and

English to use to communicate with him, and he himself having only mainland Chinese, we were reduced to bows and handshakes together with thumbs-up signs and lots of smiles, but he did like my work (he took home a full set of my invitation cards) and I did receive his card, upon which he had a print of a fan – mountain scenery and poem in classic Chinese style – everything that, when I was young, I would have loved to be able to paint.

And then, back at the exhibition: When the first visitor arrived, the owner actually stood behind me, nudging me and whispering in my ear that I should block his path – "He wasn't the sort of person to be allowed in." However, to me he looked a perfectly respectable gentleman, who after viewing my paintings and reading the poem ("Child"), which was interspersed among the works, carefully thanked me before leaving and commented that he had "learned a lot," my response being that that was "Good!" (and most certainly what had been intended). And, beyond that, I really could not see any problem therein. However, repeatedly throughout the exhibition, she kept making odd comments to the effect that, "I should(n't) (/must(n't)) do this or that," which in the end became extremely irritating. I knew exactly what I was doing, and I knew why. Basically, I had created an exhibition and I wanted as many people as possible to see it.

And they did come, with many of them being foreigners: a Russian mother and child, young Polish couple, two men from Switzerland, a group from Taiwan, a young Chinese man working as an 'intern' [17.5] on Shikoku Island (to keep himself going, he sketched late into the night). And then a number of others who, through our long relationships, I recognised as friends. A sufficient number of paintings were sold to cover the wide range of the expenses involved. And other than a persistent level of exhaustion, something that, particularly at the completion stage of any project, I have come to take as the norm, all was well with the world.

[19.11] FF: Art by instinct:

Allowing whatever it is that is in there to have its say.

At the end of Cpt 8. [8.19], I mentioned a rather unusual rendering of a karaoke song that I was singing, which in large part amounted to me learning to trust a little of what was within and simply setting it free. The following are two other, much more recent examples.

– Working with a dozen or so smallish pieces of bleached coral I had collected from the beach on Kensuke's island, and having selected six of them which in terms of size and attractiveness of design seemed most likely to fit together, none of them were sitting easily (they were slipping around considerably) on the small wooden base that I had taken out for the purpose, and I was finding it extremely difficult to create an attractive formation, and getting highly frustrated into the bargain. Then scooping them up into my hands with the aim of taking a fresh start, my fingers slipped, and, as you might with a suitable cluster of dice, I had six sixes and a perfect arrangement.

– The creation of a fairy tale: Printing out photographs to be displayed at the above exhibition on a brand-new copy machine I had purchased for the purpose, more than once I found myself mismatching printing papers and ink settings, resulting in considerable waste. However, with one photograph (taken in the valley in Osaek, Korea [10.16]) where I actually repeated the same mistake twice in succession, I placed the two sheets (both flooded with ink) face to face with the intention of throwing them away, and then noticing that they were not quite aligned, twisted them into place with the palms of my hand. And then curious as to what the results might be, I opened them up again to find that I had created something of a wonderland – a fantasy world of demons and sprites, including an ape-like creature, a long-tailed-vole jumping up into the air in fright and a three-headed horse, which I then conceived as three children under a spell, and around which I created the beginnings and end of a fairy story (to be filled in as and how other imaginations might take it upon themselves to do so). The original photograph I have kept at home, and the fairy tale was taken home by friends who were at the time expecting their first daughter (happily born safely some four months later). (Photos 7/8/9)

In the valley at Osaek, Korea

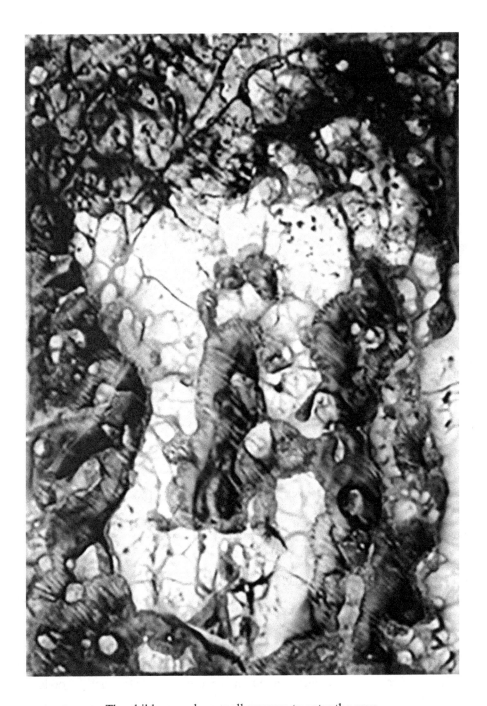

The children, under a spell, prepare to enter the cave.

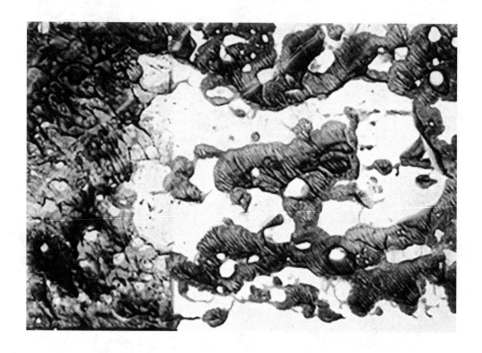

The final wall preventing the children from leaving the cave collapses and the demons flee.

[19.12] Taking yourself on:

Most people learn to live (/work within the range of) what they perceive as their needs. Each one (to the extent that they have applied any thought to the matter) has determined that what they are doing, the way they are living, what they represent is, to their minds, correct and to be upheld. And that said, it is not in any way my position to tell a young Orthodox Jew, Mormon, White Supremacist, Jihadist, strong supporter of the Chinese Communist Party, or even someone who doesn't like carrots, how to live their lives. However, having resided for so long in a society whose values are so contrary to my own upbringing and most basic of instincts, I do understand the need for as many people as possible who are capable of doing so, in some manner, to work to bridge those gaps between different cultures and beliefs. And equally, I do know that it takes considerable time and effort to be able to even to begin to approach the practical level required for this – that is, the required mindset has to be established from quite early on for it to be of any real practical use as the person gets older.

***

[19.13]

"You don't have to reject your basic beliefs to open up your eyes a little to the rest of the world."

Assuming it reasonable that respect should not automatically preclude criticism, there is presumably no reason why any individual should not take full pride in the manner in which they live and their achievements and still feel free to open themselves to similar forms of critique.

There is absolutely nothing wrong with the reality that we are all different: It is, for every reason, both natural and important that we are, in that if we all thought the same way, life would be very boring. And in line with this, it becomes perfectly natural not to agree with another individual's personal outlooks, opinions and/or choices, or to dislike (/hate/ utterly despise) them or their principles. However, at a certain point, if and when you see it in your interest to do so, it is possible to use the above statement as a learning platform in order to question your own motives; to try to pinpoint the reason why you react to certain words, situations or personalities in the way you do, why you find certain words unacceptable or offensive. And if you can start along this path, and follow it as freely as you will, step by step, in your own good time (even if you find that ultimately your opinions on the matter have not changed in the slightest), I suggest that (as in the Simon and Garfunkel song, "Bridge over troubled waters") the process will 'ease your mind'.

[19.14] Sharing moments:

As I get older, sometimes it is pleasant to find that I have 'shared a space' with some other person on my journey, with even the most tenuous of connections recognised.

(In London with Kensuke.) Returning from an evening walk in Hyde Park during which it had started to rain heavily, and no longer certain of the position of our hotel, I crossed over the road to ask the one person visible for directions, only to find that he, too, was a visitor; a man of about my own age from Saudi Arabia, who was visibly overjoyed – his face opening into a full smile and shaking my hand vigorously – to hear that I had been there in my youth. Thinking back, I would not have missed the warmth of that moment for anything. And we did find our hotel.

[19.15] A final update:

Throughout the final months of writing this book, I have repeatedly awakened in the morning to find (as with the Chinese peonies and cherry blossom described in [8.17]), a screed of print crossing my vision – an imprint of all my repeated daily efforts on the computer.

And once again trying to interpret my experiences in this area, I could only describe them as a 'range of connections'. That is, from very young on, my brain has been extremely sensitive to the fact that I was playing host to whole array of thoughts and experiences (/mindsets/ overly strong emotions) that were not directly related to what would normally be described as my own 'everyday experience'. (I admit to having experiences as a baby and young child that I cannot directly connect to, but this is no more than could be noted by any other person born here.) However, thinking again of Shino, who now as she reaches middle age is to a certain degree settling, on a personal level, I could say that in many senses the key to my survival has been attaining (/staying true to) a 'central core' as expressed in this book.

It is known that there are people with (Dr Jekyll and Mr Hyde) dissociative identity disorder (DID) who can in some cases develop within themselves a number of distinct personas, and at times it has occurred to me that they could be dealing with the same range of phenomena as myself in a rather different manner. Equally (and this is not as farfetched as it may sound), it would seem perfectly possible that a large number of (even all) those who consider themselves 'normal' in this respect could, through some combination of their own firmly embedded systems of myths and beliefs (legends, creations, illusions, delusions) – everything that allows for those passing 'brief tricks of the imagination' to be read as the product of 'a sane mind' – to be handling those same experiences within their personal definition of 'normality'. (Anyone who found themselves even half-nodding in agreement with any of the possibilities – aliens, spirits, unseen existences, zombies, etc. – that I brought up when questioning my own sanity in [7.5] is most definitely in line here.)

And then, some nights later, before I drift off to sleep, I manage to float a somewhat hazy image of a recently seen TV commercial beyond my eye, recognising it by the rather cute bodybuilder flexing his muscles in the one corner of the frame, which will give the reader some idea of where my mind is even now, causing me to really wonder what it all was about; whether it might have had any true meaning beyond the effort made?

Chapter 20

In Conclusion

[20.1] Enlightenment: "Recognition of one's place in the insignificance of being."

Living a full life only to discover that everything you have learned has already been discovered countless times before you.

Whether or not what I have experienced has any relationship to the 'Satori' described in Buddhism is of no consequence, words of this nature presumably being open to the widest possible range of interpretations, but for me personally it has been a very deep 'realisation' or 'clearing of the mind' that involves both an understanding of 'self' as a remarkably structured repository for life, and simultaneously left me in full acceptance of the fact that I am, as we all are (and as stated in the introduction), part and parcel of one long eternal moment, a continuum that we in our present existence perhaps best refer to as time. And, for the record, it has been a totally beautiful moment to be around.

Understanding that everything that I have written in this book, every thought that has passed my mind, may be completely wrong – even wildly apart from any reality – this of necessity must remain the summation that I subscribe to. Everything is only as it can be, and ultimately, with this applying to all, you can do nothing but follow your own path, to wherever it may lead you.

***

[20.2]

When I wrote "Child" in my fifties, in the section on aging and death, I presented it as a time "to renew your love – to take time to recall and be thankful for fond memories; moments of kindness and laughter, beauty and wonder…" And therefore, to take my own advice (and allow me the pleasure of including a few little bits that refused to be fit in anywhere above):

– In France for the third time, at the age of fifteen; mussel soup served in bright copper pans ('moules en gaies') on the Belgian coastline and then a bottle of rosé wine, purchased by self and downed at one go, followed by a swirl and final submission as I fell flat on my back in the park.

– A bottle of the finest champagne (costing us a fortune and therefore having to be) shared with my summer co-workers on the IOW, and then seven years later, opening a second bottle (not quite the same class but still brought back from France), almost killing my father, who was seated at the other end of the Christmas table, with the cork.

– Walking back along the clifftop road to my first hotel on the IOW at the end of a long day off; the whirring stridency of the crickets and the path overhung with summer moonlight.

– Japan: Terrifying the school receptionist (each time she crossed the room, she took an oh-so-careful detour to avoid walking under it) with a huge black spider and web (wire, wool, and newspaper stuffing) affixed to the ceiling for our first (and last) Halloween.

The surge of exhilaration felt as I experienced my first typhoon – arms wide open and body leant forward into the wind (think, "Titanic" +) – and an equal surge as we all were soaked down to the skin walking back from a "Forget the typhoon!" "Must be held!" party that evening in the slashing rain. And then, so many years later, the terror of watching repeated broadcasts of the tsunami waves following the earthquake in north Japan.

– Returning to the M hotel on the Isle of Wight some ten years later with Koji, to be met by their dog, Wagger – who had been a small puppy on my first visit there – peeing with joy on the front steps.

– Taking photographs of animals in the local zoo, where the one tethered goat reared at up at me like some crazed devil – a perfect pose that, in the end, I didn't take because I couldn't fit it all in and my 'perfectionist brain' stupidly said "No."

– In Canada; sitting out on deckchairs around a small campfire and counting the satellites as they passed above us, cutting across the night sky.

– An overcast sky and a smudge of light on the beach in Australia (a photograph that I actually sold, and one that would've been nothing without that small smudge of light).

***

[20.3]

There is a scene, common to many movies, in which an old man or woman sits lost in some reflective mood or moment, gazing out of their window at a garden, seawater lapping against the shore, or possibly just some vaguely defined empty space that represents what once was a life. I am not quite yet at this point, but outside my apartment window I do have a single, tall, straight, and very sturdy camphor tree (commonly found in the grounds of temples or shrines) which, according to its nature, only sheds its highly polished leaves in the spring when it is fully confident that its new shoots have taken firm hold. Birds nest there in spring, and young fledglings on their first flights at some point will land on my veranda to exchange morning greetings, the only times when this cannot happen being, as at present, when its branches have been severely cut back in accommodation to its latest owner's whims.[26] On overcast days, reflecting the mood, the natural darkness of the olive-green foliage can appear drab and even wilted, but on good days, when the leaves sparkle as they reflect each separate ray of sunlight, it is there to remind me of all the beauty and kindnesses (lessons both hard and generous) that I have received, and allows me to retain a certain hope for the future, if not for myself, at least for others who will in their own time perhaps come to see it as 'theirs'.

***

[20.4] Akane's story:

The following is Akane's [18.9] life story as told to me and Kensuke when she visited us here in Kobe during the writing of this book. Described in her own words as a matter of "jibun no shukumei to tukiau" – "dealing with life as it comes to you"/"acceptance of whatever life happens to bring along" – it is placed here at the end, if nothing more, as a story of courage and hope for the future.

– Akane was five when the war broke out. At this time, her father was already dead, and her older brother had left home to work, and she lived with her younger sister and initially her mother – who then found a job, so that for the large part, if they wished to see her, they had to walk three or so hours there and back. (This was her loneliest time.) She attended school as much as possible under the circumstances but was invariably described by all her teachers "as a sweet girl

---

[26] Even this year, they came, so presumably the parents must be nesting nearby.

but a bit 'slow.'" It wasn't that she didn't like studying (it was the favourite part of her day), but circumstances intervened (/proscribed). The period being as it was, during and shortly after the war, evening classes were given to those who couldn't attend during the daytime, but here also, there was a problem in that the walk home involved a well over an hour's walk back up into the mountains in the dark, and she still had her younger sister to look after. (Also, it wasn't until she was much older, when she was an adult approaching 30, that she learned she had very weak eyesight.) To earn the little she could help, she spent whatever she could scrape up on local 'dagashi' (Japanese sweetmeats/candies), and then walked to the next town where she knew they were not produced and sold them for whatever she could get for them. (Thus an entrepreneur was born.) At around 13, she was asked by a friend's mother to accompany her similarly aged daughter to Kobe where they could work in a billiard hall clearing off the tables. However, going, she quickly found the job beyond her abilities as she was too short to get her arms over onto the tables and they lasted no more than a month before returning down the coast. Although her attendance was close to zero, she was allowed to graduate from high school, and in her class photograph taken at the time, she is seated (a sun-blackened, chocolate-brown runt of 134 cm with a (Peanuts) Peppermint Patty haircut, and with, as yet no breasts – this at 17) in the centre next to her class teacher. (At the time she told us this story, she had come down to Kansai for a class reunion.) And it was apparently this teacher who believed in her and told her that, even though she wasn't exceptionally clever, she was quite capable of "becoming somebody" – a comment which held her to a course all her life. (Words of encouragement do matter!)

And coming back to Kobe, at 19 she was put in charge of an eatery (/bar?) where she had found employment. And then a second. And at 24, she was running a third which she herself had opened. Also, she had gained 16 cm. in height and her breasts had finally developed.

And then, it being a port neighbourhood, there were sailors and a yakuza gangster who threatened her first with a knife to her throat and then a bullet past her ear, and a husband (a Scot who was at times both verbally and physically abusive, but who she stayed faithful to even after he returned to his home country, right up to looking after him even as his brain wasted away in Scotland in his final days). And she made a lot of money, which she learned to invest, some to good end and some not so successfully, and at 82, fully active and in the soundest of minds, she still studies and, as she put it, "plays the market a little" to keep her hand in.

Also, there was a daughter, who I first met shortly before she was sent to Scotland for a public-school education at the age of 13, after which she graduated from university, gained good employment, and now has a loving husband and three children, who all communicate with their grandmother on Skype, and who, being in part of Scottish-Japanese blood, have in the most natural of manners taken to Irish dancing.

And, as she noted suitably proudly at the end of the telling, "she had lived."

***

Child.

Child.
You are what you see: Open your eyes and see what you are.
You are what you hear: Listen to your inner voice.
You are what you taste: Savour the moment.
You are what you smell: A rare perfume.
You are what you touch: Touch all with care.

Child.
What is the greater ignorance: to know or not to know?
What is the greater crime: to deceive others or to deceive yourself?

Child.
What is the greater trial: to learn to love through pain, or the pain of love?
What is the greater joy: to be served or to serve?
Which is the easier: to apologise for one's wrongs or to be the bearer of a forgiving heart?

Child.
You are as you speak: Speak so as to be heard.
You are as you breathe: Breathe deeply of life.
You are as you move: Move with grace.
You are as others perceive you: Bear yourself with humble pride.
You are as you create: Be as you are created.

Child.
You are as you dream.
(And if this is so, you may ponder whereupon dreams come: What influence creates, what brief encounters set one on one's path? What is it that catches the eye – catches at the heart – those others do not see?)

***

Child: On learning.

Child.
What child would not trust the teachings of his parents? And that is right. Or else how would he grow?
What child would not question the teachings of her parents? And that is right. Or else how would she grow?
And if parents, why not teachers?
Not less the words of passing strangers.

Child.
To say, "I do not like," is an opening
to self-recognition.
To say, "I do not understand," is an opening
to self-learning.
To say, "I cannot understand," is an opening
to self-denial.

Child.
Still yourself to the rhythms of the world: Learn to treasure each fleeting thought, each passing moment of knowledge, as you might a dewdrop now fallen from the early morning blade of grass or a leaf awakening to the pull of the wind. Learn to value all things living, even as you partake in their death.
Learn to celebrate the mundane.

Child.
Understand the blinding power of that which enlightens. Do not be bound by those endless trails of truth that bring with them the promise of eternal release.

Child.
Learn to understand the loss within each lesson learned, and in learning, to pass no regretful thoughts on that which has been lost. Learn to step back and let the world work its magic.

***

Child: Life as attitude.

Torn with curiosity and wonder.
Petrified with fear.
Lost in the dark
on the road to discovery.
Angry with others.
Laughing at yourself.
Filling an empty space that was loss.
Revelling or grovelling
at the bottom of the heap.
Another day to live before death,
to be celebrated or feared.

***

Child: Do not spit on people.

Child.
Do not spit on people.
Do not laugh or poke fun at others. Consider instead the fool that you are.
Do not pity people, for they will then only learn to pity themselves. Rather treat them with respect in that they will develop true pride in themselves.

Child.
Do not preach at people, thrusting your uninformed thoughts down their throats.
Do not humiliate. Rather respect the right of others to think differently so that you might also be treated in the same manner.
Do not belittle other efforts, however small or demeaning they may appear. For

it is from that first step that greatness may flow. Also know that there are some for whom it requires more effort to raise a single finger in appeal than for others more fortunate to sit astride the universe.

And for those who may have suffered in this manner:
Do not be ensnared by those who choose to hurt you. Shame is for those who occasion it in others.

***

Child: On God and other gods.

Child.
First learn, as others who came before you learned:
Of elves and fairies; those gentle spirits of the flowers and trees.
Of hammer-wielding dwarfs; guardians of rock and stone, welding steel through the fiery furnace of the earth's depths.
Of water sprites, fauns, and goblins; mischievous creatures that tease and (in bad spirits) taunt.
Child.
Learn of flame-throwing dragons; forever circling their glittering hordes of gold and jewels, fearful to emerge into the light, lest what they so treasure be usurped by others of a similar bent.
Learn of, and then trip lightly by, fiends and demons, foul-smelling ogres, powers of darkness and lost souls; all those who would prey on the evil in man's heart.

Child.
Learn the wrath of gods of wind and fire, and of the mythic gods (so human) that would have ruled, but in their grasping vanity and pride instead wrought ruin.
And when you have brought all these to mind, then consider God.

Child.
Consider, if you will, a world with God, if only to recognise the true smallness of your place in the grand scheme of things around you.
Consider, if you will, a world with God, if only to make yourself available to the goodness of His teachings.

Consider, if you will, a world with God, if only to find succour in your time of need.

Child.
And if God does not exist:
What of your morals and manners? What becomes of humility?
Where will you find a staff to support you on your way?
What becomes of man's vaunted place in this great Universe?
And what of those sins that have been so conveniently forgiven and forgotten in His name?
For if truth be known, it is not necessary to invoke the name of God (or the Devil) to do good or suffer evil.

***

Child: On character.

Child.
Learn to avoid anger, not only understanding that it stirs anger in others, but more so because it weakens, disabling the workings of the brain.
Learn to balance wants and needs. Recognise values other than those of the material.
Learn moderation in all things.
Learn inner strength.
Learn to value that which you own, and to equally respect others' property.
Do what you can, and do not fret over what you cannot.

Child.
Escape those empty nets of surety, so full of holes.
Observe carefully and with an open mind.
Learn to understand conflicting viewpoints, avoiding pedantry.
Open yourself up to others, so that they may understand you. Listen to others. Hear your own voice.
Understand that you are different so that you may learn the meaning of oneness.
Be true to yourself, questioning all actions and motives. There is no greater lesson than proving yourself wrong.

Do not to take the world too seriously.
Child
Speak well.
Learn the compelling force of reason; for without reason, words are merely an empty vessel, carrying little weight.
Learn to well express emotion: Without feeling, words are but sterile seeds, and will sway no one.

Child.
Learn to recognise influences and in doing so how to control them.
Learn to read the subtle workings of your own mind that place you on your course.

***

Child: On sloth. (You say.)

Child.
So much slips by.

Child.
You talk of hard roads
leading to nowhere.
You complain of this and that –
wasted time.
You talk of the need to progress,
thinking little of what that might mean.
You talk of eternal youth,
growing old before your age.

Child.
You mourn the passing of the earth
your hand despoils.
You feign ignorance at the state of the world
you feed on.
You talk of the world as it should be

someday.
You talk of what must be done
by others.

Child.
You cower before the future,
fearing what does not yet exist.
You talk of what cannot be,
despairing of all that could.
You babble on about being subject to the whimsy of some autocratic pedant,
casting up a litany of obstacles,
using fine words to compensate indecision.

Child
You pick on, pick at other faults,
not recognising them as your own.
You claim you seek knowledge –
parrot lame arguments buttressed by false analogy,
unwilling to question even the most inconsequential tenets of your own beliefs.
You profess your care –
willing, someday, to extend a hand.
You talk in passing of heaven and hell,
unable to envisage wherein you reside.
You stand held tight in enthral of that strange myth you call freedom, letting
dreams slip through your fingers.

Child.
You say.

***

Child: On the wherewithal of war.

"Why should you hate me, who you do not know? First learn who I am, and then if you have reason, let hate come to the fore."

To those who would away with war.
Child.
Ask
Of greed, deprivation and poverty:
What would you deem a just share of the spoils of life?
Ask
Of hard-headedness and intractability:
What art is needed to bend a stiffened pride and make it malleable?
Ask
Of the assumption of intellectual and moral superiority:
If one is to be right, how can it be but that all others are wrong? And if so, what makes that one the sole arbiter of goodness in this world?
Ask
Of those loves and loyalties; love of self, family, friend, and nation – those excluding forces that are at the root of all discord:
At what price would you sacrifice those?

Child.
Ask
Of power:
What kernel of truth lies hidden deep behind that need?
Ask
Of weakness and fear in the face of such power:
What holds down that inner voice of protest? What subjects the spirit to that which demeans?
Ask
Of victory:
What sways the mind to exultation in the face of so much bitterness and death?
And of old hurts:
What would you do with that which is blithely referred to as history – that mass of truths shaped and twisted beyond recognition to meet the needs of all and sundry?

To those who would govern well.
Child.
Search out the good in others, leaning on common understandings so that you

may leap the waters that exclude.

Learn not to stir feelings of greed, anger or envy in others. Do not flaunt power or wealth, but rather share these with an even hand.

Preach hatred and violence at your own risk.

Learn to stay euphoria.

Do not betray the trust of youth.

Tame that desire to live to acclaim that has destroyed so many before you.

To those who would exert their influence on society.
Child.
Work to be a healing force.

To those who would bend others to their will.
Child.
Examine the cracks, those fine divisions – petty strands of meanness and old hatreds that hold man from man, and understand that it is these that hold the key to power.

But also know that power built on such cracks and divisions will split and rend them to its own narrow ends, until what was the rock crumbles into an empty void of its own creation.

And if you must fight.
Child.
Know that to live is to fight.
Put behind you all fear. For you are no more competent to control your destiny than any other who lives this that we call life.

Child.
Learn that the ultimate power comes not from the subjection of others, but rather from the ordering of one's own inner world, to die at one's satisfaction. And should you care to heal the scars of war and hatred, consider history's long convoluted paths of slaughter and retaliation, and go to greet thy neighbour with a bowed head.

***

Child: On aging and death.

Exercise and nourish the mind, and more so the body to keep the mind active.
Express no regrets for wasted moments. Waste, as with all things, is a matter for contention. (Nothing can be other than it is or has been.)
Do not anger yourself with the waywardness of a body that has borne you well, regardless of any mistreatment that it may have received.
Live life knowing that death will come as it will, with no consideration of your agenda.

***

The child speaks.

And having learned all, you say: "What is it that I should do, then?"
And I would say:
"Take your knowledge and read it as you will. Do with it as you please, until it is no longer yours for the holding. Or if it be your wont, do with it as the world pleases.
"And if life is but a vehicle for dreams, and all perceived comes from within, that flash of anger, snide smirk, tender motioning, are naught but cold tears imagined in the fleeting moment, a flash of inattention as comes to us when we do dream."

***

A prayer.

To those who walk here,
To all those who have and those who will,
Peace in heart and of mind.
And wherever you may walk.

***

Newspaper, film, book references.

Introduction.

Mito Kohmon. (Tokugawa Mitsukuni: prominent feudal lord in Tokugawa period.) Featured in popular television series and manga.

Chapter 12

[12.6] "A rugby anthem's unlikely origins in slavery." (NYT. March 10, 2017.)

[12.6] Movie: "I'm Daniel Blake." 2016. Director, Ken Loach.

[12.10] "The Buddhist Swastika (manji) and Hitler's Cross." by the Rev. Kenjitsu Nakagaki, republished with Stone Bridge Press in September 2018.

[12.12] Baye McNeil. (JT.) "Bring back that Kobe feeling, 'cause it's gone, gone, gone."

[12.14] "Mockingbird reconsidered." Book review by Roxane Gay (black author) (NYT. 19. 6. 2018)

Chapter 13

[13.13] "Yoga Health." Selvarajan Yesudian. Elizabeth Haich. (Unwin paperbacks)

[13.13] "Yoga week by week", Selvarajan Yesudian. (Unwin paperbacks)

[13.16] "Lessons from a 103-year-old Jewish East London Socialist." Daniel Trilling. (NYT. Nov. 16, 2018.)

Chapter 14

[14.3] 2016 film version of Shusaku Endo's novel "Silence", directed by Martin Scorsese.

[14.8] The desire for a caliphate. (NYT: "The lingering dream of an Islamic state." By Azadez Moaveni. Jan 16, 2018.)

Chapter 15

[15.13] David Aldwinkle (/Debito Arudou). Japan Times columnist for their "Community" page.

[15.35] NYT. (14.3.2019) "Who to elect for a 3 am global crisis." By Thomas L Friedman.

[15.35] "The rise and fall of peace on earth," by Michael Mandelbaum (Johns Hopkins emeritus professor of US foreign policy).

[15.35] JT. (14.3.2019) "Trump is winning, and Putin is losing in global arms sales." By Leonid Bershidsky, Berlin.

[15.35] NYT. (14.3.2019) "To blunt sanctions, Iran turns to Iraq." By Alissa J Rubin.

[15.37] Ref: NYT: (31.10.2018.) "Slave trading past no longer in the shadows." By Alissa J Rubin

[15.38] Ref: NYT: (20.2.2019.) "Plans for war memorial bring accusations of whitewashing." By Jamie Tarabay.

Chapter 17

[17.7] NYT (2. 4. 2019) "Time to fret about global economics." Ruchir Sharma.

[17.8] "The Big Short." Movie (also book) detailing Wall Street's responsibility for the 2007–2008 subprime mortgage crisis.

Chapter 18

[18.5] NYT, "Myths about estrangement." Catherine Saint Louis.

[18.8] "One Flew over the Cuckoo's Nest." Book and movie on life in a mental ward.

Chapter 19

[19.8] "The Spy Who Came in from the Cold." John le Carré

[19.13] "Bridge over troubled waters." Simon and Garfunkel.

***

Japanese and other foreign terms.

Introduction:

Gaikokujin 外国人 (Gaijin 外人): Foreigner. (Literally, 'outsider'.)

Chapter 1.

[1.4] Herikutsu 屁理屈 : argumentative, self-opinionated to the point that they couldn't be talked to, forever quibbling

Chapter 3

[3.3] Inshallah: "If God so wills it."

[3.3] Naru mono wa naru sa なるものはなるさ: "Whatever is going to happen is going to happen"/ "Que sera, sera."

[3:11] Tataki たたき: Thick segments of bonito fish with the outer layer repeatedly flame-roasted and then basted in a traditional sauce, imbuing it with a highly distinctive flavour (the inner section remains uncooked).

[3,11] Minshuku 民宿: In England, a B&B.

Chapter 4

[4.8] Hanko はんこ/Han 判: A stamp (/seal)

[4.9] Oyakoukou 親孝行: Consideration of one's parents. Acting as a good child should.

[4.11] Deshi 弟子: Student apprentice.

[4.13] Kanroku 貫録: A 'sense of presence' or 'air that befits one's position'.

Chapter 5

[5.3] Joushiki 常識: the socially accepted norm.

[5.3] Tatemae 建前: Speaking as one is expected to by society. / [7.14]

[5.3] Honne 本音: Expressing one's real feelings. / [7.14]

[5.5] Sunao 素直: Submissive, docile, tractable.

[5.6] Ishin, denshin 以心伝心: Intrinsic understanding of the other.

[5.7] Igirisubyou イギリス病: "English sickness." Troubles with labour unions during Mrs Thatcher's period in power.

[5.8] Hai はい: Can be understood as both "Yes" and the much more neutral, "I hear you."

[5.11] Mujun 矛盾: Incompatible facts.

[5.11] Shikishi 色紙: Small square card paintings done to help cover the cost of an exhibition. / [6.4]

[5.12] Uguisu 鶯: Japanese nightingale.

[5.12] Mejiro 目白: Japanese white-eye (bird).

[5.13] Sakoku 鎖国: Period of national isolation lasting from 1633 to 1854.

[5.13] Tokugawa Shogunate 徳川家康: Japan's leading clan during the above 'sakoku' period.

[5.13] Daimyo 大名: Provincial lords.

[5.13] Burakumin 部落民: Outcasts. Those with occupations considered impure or tainted by death, including slaughterhouse workers and tanners. / [18.14]

[5.13] Kami 神: The word kami is used in reference to an energy (spirit, essences, or 'god') central to any phenomena that inspires a sense of wonder and awe in the beholder, testifying to the divinity of such a phenomenon. / [13.9]

[5.13] Utsukushii 美しい: Beautiful.

[5.13] Sugoi/Subarashii すごい/素晴らしい: Fantastic, wonderful, unbelievable…

[5.13] Nihonjin dakara koso…da. 日本人だからこそ…だ。This is an extremely strong statement, which in direct translation would amount to something like: "It is only because we are (/were born) Japanese that…we can feel like this /we have the sensitivity to appreciate… , etc., etc." // That or: "It is only Japanese who can feel… / have the sensitivity to appreciate…"

[5.13] Shin joushiki 新常識: New joushiki.

[5.14] Meishi 名刺: Business card.

[5.18] Nemawashi 根回し: Backroom consultations necessary prior to making (public) decisions on any matter.

[5.19] Kitsui desu ne! 「きついですね」: "That's being a bit hard on us, don't you think?"

Chapter 6

[6.3] Seinin 青年: Youths. (Traditionally, young Japanese up to the age of 40.)

[6.4] Happyoukai 発表会: A display of a student's progress in their respective field with much of the work displayed derivative to one's studies.

[6.5] Shikunshi 四君子: The 'four gentlemen' in traditional Chinese painting: the orchid, chrysanthemum, plum/peach blossom and bamboo.

[6.5] Washi 和紙: Japanese handmade paper. / [7.11]

[6.5] Nanga 南画: Southern Style school of Chinese painting.

[6.5] Shi (Komainu 狛犬 / Shishi 獅子): A Chinese guardian lion.

[6.7] Sumi 墨: Indian ink used for Sumi-e.

[6.9] Sumi-e 墨絵 / Suibokuga 水墨画: Ink-painting.

[6.10] Chinpira チンピラ: Low-ranking yakuza hoodlums.

[6.12] Daku 抱く: Embrace, hold, hug. The word also has sexual connotations.

[6.19] Kotatsu 炬燵: Low table with electric heater underneath, used with cover in winter for extra warmth.

Chapter 7

[7.3] Nusumu 盗む: 'Stealing' specific techniques from one's teacher through direct observation.

[7.5] Bodhisattva. Buddhist term: An enlightened being who out of compassion doesn't go into Nirvana, but instead stays back and helps others to find salvation. / [7.20]

[7.5] Enma, The King of Hell; a wrathful god said to judge the dead and preside over the 'Hells' or 'Purgatories' and the cycle of afterlife. / [8.10]

[7.5] Obon お盆: Summer festival period when the spirits of the dead are said to return to communicate with the living. / [8.18]

[7.9] Mu 無: "Nothingness." – being sensitive to or involved in the moment, an acceptance of what is, an opening of your mind to the present state, or simply "being."

[7.12] "Chuuka hamnida." Korean for "Congratulations!"

[7.16] Karoushi 過労死: Death due to overwork.

[7.24] Shogi 将棋: Japanese chess.

[7.24] Ehen mushi エヘン虫: Throat tickle.

[7.30] Agano-yaki 上野焼: Agano pottery, Northern Kyushu.

[7.31] "Satorimashita." 悟りました: "I have 'awakened' – reached a point of enlightenment." Used by Tomonobu, a paraplegic friend in Kyushu immediately after the earthquake.   / [13.7]

[7.33] Teki 敵: Enemies, foes, adversaries.

[7.35] Chakra: Main nerve centres in the spine related to an "expansion of awareness" in Yoga theory.

Chapter 8

[8.1] Mawashi 回し: Thick loincloth used by sumo wrestlers.

[8.3] Naga: The Sanskrit word for cobra.

[8.15] JICA (Japan International Cooperation Agency): Offers training and technical advice to aid human resource development around the world.

[8.16] Tokonoma 床の間: Alcove traditionally used to display scrolls and or ikebana flower arrangements, etc.

Chapter 9

[9.4] Chinamini ちなみに: Used to introduce 'an aside' – "This is not particularly of any importance, but for the record…"

[9.16] Ryokan 旅館: Japanese inn.

[9.18] Genseirin 原生林: Primeval Forest.

[9.19] Shu 朱: Cinnabar, vermilion.

[9.19] Torii 鳥居: Vermilion coloured gates placed at entrance to shrines.

Chapter 10

[10.2] Igirisu イギリス: The United Kingdom.

[10.2] Zainichi 在日: Koreans residing in Japan. Those who remained in Japan after WWII together with those who chose to come here later of their own free will.

[10.3] Yakiniku: Korean grill.

[10.3] Bibimbap: A Korean rice bowl with cooked minced meat and vegetables and spices.

[10.6] Wabi 侘び: An appreciation of 'calm' and the simple in life.

[10.6] Sabi 寂: (a tranquility which comes with an understanding of) the aging of both things and the landscape.

[10.8] Mul: (Korean) Water.

[10.11] Kansai-ben 関西弁: Kansai-dialect.

[10.14] Oss!" おっす！: A shortened form of "Ohaiyou gozaimasu." おはよう御座います: "Good morning" – Used in a rather rough but friendly manner as a greeting between Japanese men.

[10.18] gimbap: Korean rice rolls (makimono/makizushi, 巻物/巻き寿司 in Japan.)

[10.18] samgyetang: Korean dish. Full chicken in a spicy broth.

Chapter 13

[13.7] Ikkyu-san 一休さん: A Buddhist acolyte who was renowned for having a brilliant mind from a very young age.

[13.12] A-Un: Referring to the Chinese guardian lions seen in pairs in front of temples and (in Japan) shrines. Various explanations exist, including the (open-mouthed male) inhaling ('A') and (closed-mouthed female) exhaling ('Un') of a single breath.

Chapter 14

[14.3] Soukagakkai 創価学会: A large Buddhist lay organisation, politically represented in the Japanese Diet by the Koumeito party.

Chapter 15

[15.22] Minpaku 民泊: The Japanese term for Airbnb.

[15.22] Omotenashi おもてなし: Traditional Japanese hospitality.

[15.23] Hikikomori 引き篭もり: Children (and now adults) who retreat into and refuse to emerge from their rooms – or at best find themselves not able to reintegrate in any true manner into society due to some combination of low self-esteem and/or depression – in many cases for decades.

[15.28] Nippon Kaigi 日本会議: "Japan Conference" – a right-wing political organisation.

[15.31] Tokkotai 特攻隊: Kamikaze unit.

[15.38] Gunkanjima 軍艦島: Hashima Island in southern Kyushu, originally a site for coal mining, now essentially deserted. UNESCO World Heritage Site.

Chapter 16

[16.4] Senpai-kouhai 先輩、後輩: 'senior-junior' (relationships).

[16.8] Aware no mono 哀れの者: In the Buddhist sense, "deserving of compassion."

[16.8] Chikan ちかん : Men of all ages who molest or grope passengers in crowded trains or take snapshots beneath schoolgirls skirts as they ride the upward escalator

[16.10] "Heta o uru jidai" 下手を売る時代: An 'age' in which television personalities are "selling themselves as someone who can't." A world of 'untalented talents.'

[16.11] Boryoku 暴力: The usage of force or violence.

[16.13] Enjo kosai 援助交際: a euphemism for schoolgirl prostitution. (The names here keep changing, but the principle remains the same.)

[16.15] "Moshimoshi" もしもし: When answering the telephone: "Hello."

Chapter 17

[17.1] Kaizen 改善: In reality, individual workers endeavouring to find ways to improve practices in the workplace, which, when practicable, can then be extended to other areas to improve overall productivity. This is in fact no different from what I was doing when I re-organised the storage spaces above and below my father's shop with the aim of reducing the overall workload. I would note that, most importantly, in giving me full responsibility to handle this work as I wished, my father was actually encouraging a personal interest in the matter that led me to look at what I was doing as something more than simply (boring) 'work'.

[17.1] Omiai お見合い: Arranged marriage.

[17.1] Keigo 敬語: The polite terms of reference that are essential to indicating one's position in the hierarchical rankings and an essential part of promulgating the Confucian ethic.

[17.1] Ossan おっさん: A derogatory term of reference for an old man.

[17.1] Doutoku 道徳: Moral and ethical education. The patriotic education programme stressing morality as centred on obligations to the family and state as was taught prior to the war.

[17.1] Jibun katte 自分勝手: Acting in a selfish manner, insisting on having one's own way, acting without consideration for others.

[17.1] "Jibun katte ni dekiru shakai" 自分勝手にできる社会: (My phrase.) A society in which everyone (hopefully) is free to act as they see fit.

[17.2] Muri shinju 無理心中: 'Enforced suicide', commonly with a parent killing his or her child before taking their own life.

[17.4] Roudoukijunkyoku 労働基準局: Labour Standards Office.

[17.4] Saijitsu 祭日: Public holidays.

[17.5] Shobun suru 処分する: Deal with, dispose of, get rid of (commonly used when referring to waste products).

[17.6] Sontaku 忖度: guessing, surmising, acting on inference or conjecture; assuming an understanding of a senior's requirements without receiving any explicit instruction.

[17.9] Heisei 平成 period: (1989–2019) Name of the era under the recently abdicated Emperor Akihito.

[17.9] Sai 災: Chinese ideograph for disaster, destruction.

[17.9] Hen 変: Chinese ideograph for change

[17.9] Ran 乱: Chinese ideograph for disorder, confusion, chaos.

[17.9] Wa 和: Chinese ideograph for harmony.

[17.9] Reiwa 令和: Name of the new era under Emperor Naruhito.

Chapter 18

[18.1] Sensei 先生: Teacher. Literally, someone 'born before'.

[18.8] Uramu 恨む: Bear a grudge against – commonly used related to spirits returning to haunt someone who has harmed them.

[18.18] Habu: ハブ: Highly poisonous snakes of the viper family.

Chapter 20

[20.2] Moules en gaies: Mussel soup served in bright copper pans. Eaten on Belgian coastline.

[20.4] "Jibun no shukumei to tukiau": 自分の宿命と付き合う: "Dealing with life as it comes to you." / "Acceptance of whatever life brings along."

[20.4] Dagashi 駄菓子: Cheap sweetmeats/candies.

CPSIA information can be obtained
at www.ICGtesting.com
Printed in the USA
LVHW081412090322
712947LV00011B/281